Inspired Speech

Herbert Bardwell Huffmon

Inspired Speech

Prophecy in the Ancient Near East
Essays in Honor of Herbert B. Huffmon

edited by

John Kaltner and Louis Stulman

t&t clark

Published by T&T Clark
A Continuum imprint
The Tower Building, 11 York Road, London SE1 7NX
80 Maiden Lane, Suite 704, New York, NY 10038

www.continuumbooks.com

First published in hardback in 2004
Reprinted 2005
Paperback edition 2008

British Library Cataloguing-in-Publication Data
A catalogue record for this book is available from the British Library

Typeset and edited for Continuum by Forthcoming Publications Ltd
www.forthcomingpublications.com

Printed on acid-free paper in Great Britain by
CPI Antony Rowe, Chippenham, Wiltshire

ISBN 10   0-8264-6656-7 (hardback)
           0-567-04569-2 (paperback)
ISBN 13   978-0-8264-6656-3 (hardback)
           978-0-567-04569-0 (paperback)

CONTENTS

Part III
OTHER STUDIES

ABBREVIATIONS

A.	Tablet signature of texts from Mari
AB	Anchor Bible
ABD	David Noel Freedman (ed.), *The Anchor Bible Dictionary* (New York: Doubleday, 1992)
AfO	*Archiv für Orientforschung*
AGJU	Arbeiten zur Geschichte des antiken Judentums und des Urchristentums
AnBib	Analecta biblica
ANET	James B. Pritchard (ed.), *Ancient Near Eastern Texts Relating to the Old Testament* (Princeton: Princeton University Press, 1950)
AOAT	Alter Orient und Altes Testament
ArBib	Aramaic Bible
ARM	Archives royales de Mari
ARMT 26	*Archives Epistolaires de Mari, I/1* (ARM, 26/1; Paris: Editions Recherche sur les Civilisations, 1988)
ARMT 10	Dossin, G., and A. Finet, *Correspondance féminine, transcrite et traduite* (ARM, 10; Paris: Paul Guethner, 1978)
ATANT	Abhandlungen zur Theologie des Alten und Neuen Testaments
BA	*Biblical Archaeologist*
BASOR	*Bulletin of the American Schools of Oriental Research*
BDB	Francis Brown, S.R. Driver and Charles A. Briggs, *A Hebrew and English Lexicon of the Old Testament* (Oxford: Clarendon Press, 1907)
BHS	*Biblia hebraica stuttgartensia*
Bib	*Biblica*
BibInt	*Biblical Interpretation: A Journal of Contemporary Approaches*
BJS	Brown Judaic Studies
BTB	*Biblical Theology Bulletin*
BWANT	Beiträge zur Wissenschaft vom Alten und Neuen Testament
BZ	*Biblische Zeitschrift*
BZAW	Beihefte zur *ZAW*
CAD	Ignace I. Gelb *et al.* (eds.), *The Assyrian Dictionary of the Oriental Institute of the University of Chicago* (Chicago: Oriental Institute, 1964–)
CAI	W.E. Aufrecht, *A Corpus of Ammonite Inscriptions* (Lewiston: Mellen, 1989)
CANE	J. Sasson (ed.), *Civilizations of the Ancient Near East* (4 vols.; New York: Charles Schribner's Sons, 1995)
CBQ	*Catholic Biblical Quarterly*
CRB	*Cahiers de la Revue biblique*
CRRAI	Compte rendu, Rencontre Assyriologique Internationale
COS	William Hallo (ed.), *The Context of Scripture* (3 vols.; Leiden: E.J. Brill, 1997–)

CTH	E. Laroche, *Catalogue des textes hittites* (Paris: Klincksieck, 1971)
CW	C.G. Jung, *The Collected Works* (Bollingen Series XX; 20 vols.; trans. R.F.C. Hull; eds. H. Read, M. Fordham, G. Adler, McGuire; Princeton, NJ: Princeton University Press, 1953–79)
DMOA	Documenta et monumenta Orientis antiqui
DOTT	D. Winton Thomas (ed.), *Documents from Old Testament Times* (London: Thomas Nelson, 1958)
EA	El-Amarna tablets
EI	Early Iron Age
ER	M. Eliade (ed.), *The Encyclopedia of Religion* (16 vols.; New York: Macmillan, 1987)
ExpTim	*Expository Times*
FLP	Tablets in the collections of Free Library of Pennsylvania Free Library of Pennsylvania
FM 7	Durand, Jean-Marie, *Documents épistolaires du palais de Mari* (Littératures anciennes du Proche-Orient, 18; Paris: Cerf, 2000)
FM	Florilegium marianum
FOTL	The Forms of the Old Testament Literature
FRLANT	Forschungen zur Religion und Literatur des Alten und Neuen Testaments
Gesenius	*Gesenius' Hebrew Grammar* (ed. E. Kautzch; trans. A.E. Cowley; Oxford: Clarendon Press, 1910, 2nd Eng. edn)
GKC	*Gesenius' Hebrew Grammar* (ed. E. Kautzsch, revised and trans. A.E. Cowley; Oxford: Clarendon Press, 1910)
GTJ	*Grace Theological Journal*
HAE	J. Renz and W. Röllig, *Handbuch der althebräischen Epigraphik* (Darmstadt: Wissenschaftliche Buchgesellschaft, 1995)
HAT	Handbuch zum Alten Testament
HBT	*Horizons in Biblical Theology*
HSM	Harvard Semitic Monographs
HSS	Harvard Semitic studies
HTKAT	Herders theologischer Kommentar zum Alten Testament
HTR	*Harvard Theological Review*
IA	Iron Age
IBC	Interpretation, a Bible Commentary for Teaching and Preaching
ICC	International Critical Commentary
IDBSup	*IDB*, Supplementary Volume
IEJ	*Israel Exploration Journal*
Int	*Interpretation*
ITC	International Theological Commentary
JANESCU	*Journal of the Ancient Near Eastern Society of Columbia University*
JAOS	*Journal of the American Oriental Society*
JB	Jerusalem Bible
JBL	*Journal of Biblical Literature*
JCS	*Journal of Cuneiform Studies*
JEOL	*Jaarbericht…ex oriente lux*
JFSR	*Journal of Feminist Studies in Religion*
JNES	*Journal of Near Eastern Studies*
JNSL	*Journal of Northwest Semitic Languages*
JPS	Jewish Publication Society Version
JSOT	*Journal for the Study of the Old Testament*
JSOTSup	*Journal for the Study of the Old Testament*, Supplement Series

K	Tablets in the collections of the British Museum
KAI	H. Donner and W. Röllig (ed.), *Kanaanäische und aramäische Inschriften* (Weisbaden: O. Harrassowitz, 2nd edn, 1966–69).
KAR	E. Ebeling (ed.), *Keilschrifttexte aus Assur religiösen Inhalts* (Leipzig, 1919–23).
KAT	Kommentar zum Alten Testament
KHAT	Kurzer Hand-Kommentar zum Alten Testament
KTT	Tablet signature of texts from Tuttul
KTU	M. Dietrich, M. Loretz and J. Sanmartín, *The Cuneiform Alphabetic Texts from Ugarit* (Münster: Ugarit-Verlag, 1995)
LAPO 18	Jean-Marie Durand, *Documents épistolaires du palais de Mari*, 3 (Littératures anciennes du Proche-Orient, 18; Paris: Cerf, 2000)
LAPO	Littératures anciennes du Proche-Orient
LB/LBA	Late Bronze Age
LSJ	H.G. Liddell, Robert Scott and H. Stuart Jones, *Greek–English Lexicon* (Oxford: Clarendon Press, 9th edn, 1968)
LXX	Septuagint
M.	Tablet signature of texts from Mari
MARI	*Mari: Annales de recherches interdisciplinaires*
MB/MBA	Middle Bronze Age
MDP	Mémoires de la Délégation en Perse
MT	Masoretic text
NAB	*New American Bible*
NCBC	New Century Bible Commentary
NEB	New English Bible
NIB	L.E. Keck *et al.* (eds.), *The New Interpreter's Bible* (12 vols.; Nashville: Abingdon Press, 1996)
NICOT	New International Commentary on the Old Testament
NJPS	New Jewish Publication Society Version
NJV	*New Jewish Version, TANAKH* (Philadelphia: Jewish Publication Society of America, 1985)
NRSV	New Revised Standard Version
OAN	Oracles Against Nations
OBO	Orbis biblicus et orientalis
OECT	Oxford Editions of Cuneiform Texts
OTL	Old Testament Library
OTP	James Charlesworth (ed.), *Old Testament Pseudepigrapha*
OTS	Old Testament Studies
RA	*Revue d'assyriologie et d'archéologie orientale*
RAcc	F. Thureau-Dangin, *Rituels Accadiens* (Paris: Keroux, 1921).
RB	*Revue biblique*
RSR	*Recherches de science religieuse*
RSV	Revised Standard Version
SAA	State Archives of Assyria
SAAS	State Archives of Assyria Studies
SBLDS	SBL Dissertation Series
SBLMS	SBL Monograph Series
SBLSBS	SBL Sources for Biblical Study
SBLSS	SBL Semeia Studies
SBLSymS	SBL Symposium Series
SBLWAW	SBL Writing from the Ancient World

SBT	Studies in Biblical Theology
SHCANE	Studies in the History and Culture of the Ancient Near East
Sem	*Semitica*
T.	Tablet signature of texts from Mari
TCS	Texts from Cuneiform Sources
TDOT	G.J. Botterweck and H. Ringgren (eds.), *Theological Dictionary of the Old Testament*
THAT	Ernst Jenni and Claus Westermann (eds.), *Theologisches Handwörterbuch zum Alten Testament* (Munich: Chr. Kaiser Verlag, 1971–76)
TRE	*Theologische Realenzyklopädie*
TynBul	*Tyndale Bulletin*
UF	*Ugarit-Forschungen*
VS	Vorderasiatische Schriftdenkmäler
VT	*Vetus Testamentum*
VTSup	*Vetus Testamentum*, Supplements
WBC	Word Biblical Commentary
WMANT	Wissenschaftliche Monographien zum Alten und Neuen Testament
WUNT	Wissenschaftliche Untersuchungen zum Neuen Testament
WVDOG	Wissenschaftliche Veröffentlichung der Deutschen Orient-Gesellschaft
ZA	*Zeitschrift für Assyriologie*
ZAW	*Zeitschrift für die alttestamentliche Wissenschaft*
ZDPV	*Zeitschrift des deutschen Palästina-Vereins*

LIST OF CONTRIBUTORS

Lyn M. Bechtel taught at Drew University

Mary Chilton Callaway is Associate Professor of Theology at Fordham University

Frank Moore Cross is Emeritus Hancock Professor of Hebrew and Other Oriental Languages at Harvard University

Peggy L. Day is Professor of the Hebrew Bible at the University of Winnipeg

Milton Eng taught in the Department of Religion at Rutgers University

Daniel E. Fleming is Professor of Hebrew and Judaic Studies at New York University

David Noel Freedman is Professor, Endowed Chair in Hebrew Biblical Studies at the University of California, San Diego

Rebecca Frey is a doctoral candidate at the University of California, Irvine

Alberto R. Green is a Professor of Ancient Near Eastern and Biblical History in the Department of Religion at Rutgers University

Edward L. Greenstein is Professor of Bible at Tel Aviv University

William W. Hallo is the William M. Laffan Professor Emeritus of Assyriology and Babylonian Literature in the Department of Near Eastern Languages and Civilizations at Yale University

John Kaltner is Associate Professor of Religious Studies at Rhodes College

John I. Lawlor is Professor of Old Testament Grand Rapids Theological Seminary

David Leiter teaches biblical studies at the Ecumenical Institute of Theology, St Mary's Seminary and University

Baruch A. Levine is Skirball Professor Emeritus of Bible and Ancient Near Eastern Studies, New York University

Jesse C. Long, Jr, is Professor of Archaeology, Old Testament Text, and Preaching, the Lubbock Christian University

David Marcus is Professor of Bible at the Jewish Theological Seminary

George E. Mendenhall is Professor Emeritus of Ancient and Biblical Studies, Department of Near Eastern Studies, University of Michigan

Michael S. Moore is Adjunct Professor of Old Testament at the Fuller Theological Seminary

Mary-Louise Mussell is Professor of Classical Studies at the University of Ottowa

Harry P. Nasuti is Professor of Theology at Fordham University

Martti Nissinen is Professor of Bible and the Ancient Near East at the University of Helsinki

Jongsoo Park teaches in the Department of Theology at Kangnam University

Paul A. Riemann is Emeritus Professor of Old Testament at Drew University

Suzanne Richard is Associate Professor of History and Theology at Gannon University

J.J.M. Roberts is Emeritus William Henry Green Professor of Old Testament Literature at Princeton Theological Seminary

Jack M. Sasson is Mary Jane Werthan Professor of Jewish Studies and Hebrew Bible and Professor of Classics at Vanderbilt University

Eric A. Seibert is Assistant Professor of Old Testament at Messiah College

Mark Sneed is Professor of Old Testament and Hebrew at Lubbock Christian University

Louis Stulman is Professor of Religious Studies at the University of Findlay

Karel van der Toorn is Professor of Ancient Religions at the University of Amsterdam

Alex Varughese is Professor of Religion at Mount Vernon Nazarene University

Robert R. Wilson is Hoober Professor of Religious Studies at Yale University

Part I

Introductory/Background Essays

HERBERT BARDWELL HUFFMON: A REFLECTION

Suzanne Richard

It is with great enthusiasm that I accept the editors' request to write the introductory piece to this volume, which celebrates the special life and accomplishments of my good friend and former colleague at Drew University, Herbert Bardwell Huffmon. I am honored to do so.

I have known Herb for over twenty years. If memory serves, I suppose the first meeting with him was that nerve-wracking interview for a position at Drew University. I was appointed to that position despite the fact that, as I learned sometime afterward, I was the committee's first choice but Herb's second choice! Not being the favored candidate aside, I am pleased to say that Herb became a great friend, valued colleague, and enthusiastic supporter—a token of his very real loyalty and deep abiding support to colleagues, friends and students.

I am sure that the latter sentiments ring true to his students included in this volume. They will surely attest to Herb's graciousness in putting aside his precious little time for scholarly research to be available to them (his door is always open). Herb has worked tirelessly with his doctoral candidates by mentoring, advising, correcting syntax and grammar, and guiding them to a successful defense. For thirty-five years he has been the driving force behind the Biblical Studies (Old Testament) program at Drew and rightly deserves to be so recognized. The success of the program is clearly illustrated by the number of former students writing scholarly articles in his honor, on a topic near and dear to his heart: prophecy. What greater achievement could any professor desire!

This article will not assess Herbert B. Huffmon's corpus of scholarly work, for there are others within his own field of study far more competent for that task. Likewise, it will not be a comprehensive survey of his life and many accomplishments, since there are others more cognizant of both who could more adequately and knowledgeably assess them. It is my hope, rather, that through the broad brushstrokes of the picture presented here, the reader will in some small way come to know Herbert B. Huffmon in his various personae: scholar, teacher, archaeologist, pastor, and friend.

I had considered, as any archaeologist would, beginning this article with the latest, that is, the uppermost stratum of the person Herb Huffmon, and proceeding to excavate earlier levels. However, since this narrative is a reconstruction it is more appropriate to begin 'at the beginning'—that is, the beginning of my memory and my perceptions of Herb. Hopefully, the rather loose arrangement of the various loci of his life will result in a recognizable, credible, but especially genuine retrospective of the Herb we know and love.

When I arrived at Drew University in 1979 Herb was already a full professor of Old Testament. He had taken a position in the Graduate School and Seminary at the University in 1968, following a three-year teaching stint at The Johns Hopkins University (1965–68). The year before that (1964–65), he had taught Old Testament at the Chicago Theological Seminary. His very first professional appointment was at Pittsburgh Theological Seminary (1961–62), with David Noel Freedman, followed by two years as research assistant to his former teacher, William Foxwell Albright.

For most of the time that I was at Drew, the Biblical Studies Program (Old Testament/Archaeology Area) comprised Herb, Paul Riemann and myself—an amazingly likeminded group, given the fact that we were all either first or second generation Albrightians from the University of Michigan, Harvard University, and The Johns Hopkins University, respectively, and that we shared commonalities in educational background and interests. The New Testament professors in the department, Kalyan Dey, Darrell Doughty, Neill Hamilton and William Stroker, rounded out what was quite a collegial lot in Seminary Hall at the Drew University campus in Madison, New Jersey.

What were my first impressions of Herb? Like others newly arrived, whether student or colleague, it was not long before I made the connection between Herb's persona and his books (his vast personal library surely ranks as a major scholarly collection); they are somehow inseparable. Herb is a collector of books. A short excursus on his library is in order here. Herb has more books in his personal library than anyone I know, and his reputation for buying books is legendary. Entering his office can be somewhat hazardous. There are always stacks of new books on every surface, chair, or floor space, in addition to the row after row of library-like stacks from floor to ceiling in his office at Drew (as well as in his home office and garage). The standing joke among students was that, not only did Professor Huffmon own every book on the ancient Near East, but that he actually had read every one of them!

Herb's favorite pastime (some say obsession) appears to be exploring bookstores, especially rare bookstores, here and abroad. Having led tours with him, I can attest to the fact. During a five-hour flight layover in Amsterdam on one occasion we took the train into the city and, in the early morning hours, somehow found a rare bookstore. We also made the requisite visit to the museum to see Egyptian antiquities—Herb's other obsession is Egypt, but more on that later!

As it turns out, the students were right; he really has read (parts of) all those books. Herb's persona as a prodigiously well-read scholar with an amazing breadth of knowledge over a wide area is immediately apparent to all. A brief retrospective on his educational background offers an illuminating view of a young man pursuing in a programmatic fashion the tools, knowledge and experience for his life-long work and love of all things Near Eastern. He knew what he wanted to do from an early age, since he earned a BA (1954) in Near Eastern Studies at the University of Michigan after transferring from Wayne State University. It was at Michigan that he found the person who would influence the path of his career and become a lifelong friend and colleague: George Emery ('Mendy') Mendenhall. Indeed, the student was later to be the primary editor of a Festschrift in honor of his teacher (Huffmon, Spina and Green 1983).

Following his undergraduate work, Herb went on to pursue a degree at McCormick Theological Seminary (BD, 1954), working with Frank Cross and Ernest Wright (both later at Harvard). Although I assume Herb intended the BD to be a stepping-stone to future doctoral work in biblical studies rather than a terminal degree for a career as a pastor, I do not underestimate the role that religion plays in his life. Herb is an ordained Presbyterian minister, who has worked as a part-time pastor at various churches while teaching at Drew.

Herb's courses in the DMin program at the Seminary and in the Biblical Studies program at the Graduate School have drawn praise from his students and have led to awards for his teaching. His pastoral side is one more facet in the mosaic we are piecing together of the person who is Herb Huffmon. It explains to a great extent that characteristic of Herb's to be there when you need him, to give wise counsel, to be helpful and kind. He is a very sincere person and there is a real 'goodness' about him. He is a scholar/teacher who always puts students and friends first.

Returning to more biographical concerns, the next step in what appears to be a careful and purposeful preparation for a career in Near Eastern Studies led him to The Johns Hopkins University to study with one of the greats, W.F. Albright, who had also been Mendenhall's teacher and mentor. It was during this period at the Oriental Seminary, initially as a student, then as Albright's research assistant, and then again as an Assistant Professor (after a year at Chicago Theological Seminary), that Herb added to the vast store of anecdotes about Albright that he had heard from teachers and colleagues about the 'Old Man'. With these anecdotes Herb would later regale classes and colleagues.

As it turns out, Herb's interests in the study of the ancient Near East meshed more neatly with those of Mendy. Thus, following studies in language and Old Testament at Hopkins (MA, 1958) and Albright's retirement, Herb went back to Michigan (PhD, 1963) where he wrote a dissertation that would forever link his own name with those of the Amorites (Huffmon 1965). It would be the impetus for a life-long love of comparative biblical/Mesopotamian studies, particularly prophecy at Mari and in the Bible. That classic work was *de rigueur* for those of us who were attempting to understand nomadic patterns of life at the end of the Early Bronze Age, thanks to Kathleen Kenyon's and William G. Dever's perspectives on the 'Dark Age' in the Southern Levant (Kenyon 1966; Dever 1970).

It should be apparent by now that Herb's scholarly orbit revolved around a school that stressed the broad background of Near Eastern Studies in the mold of Albright's (and some of his illustrious students') encyclopedic knowledge and expertise in virtually every field. Thus, Herb is very much a person of his time and his professors (especially Mendenhall, Wright, Cross, and Albright), who, unlike the trend today to be highly specialized in a narrow field of study, were able to control a great deal of material in diverse areas. Herb and his trademark library attest to the continuation of those Albrightian ideals.

Blessed with a sharp memory, Herb is a storehouse of knowledge. Students remark on his uncanny ability to cite complete scholarly references from memory no matter what the topic, be it anthropology, philosophy, Mari, sociology, Petra or the Bible. I must confess to being as impressed as were the students. Herb's students likewise testify to his ability to hear, process data, and analyze student seminar presentations while seemingly asleep. Although such reports may appear farfetched, I can actually attest to witnessing this truly remarkable gift when, after nodding off for a short while during a seminar presentation, Herb made comments on and asked pertinent questions about the material just discussed! That he fell asleep while lecturing in class is, I am sure, a decidedly apocryphal story.

Herb is a biblical scholar who is just as well-versed in the literature, languages, and cultures of Mesopotamia and Egypt as those of Israel. My suspicion has always been that Herb's first love is Egypt—the country, its language, literature, and archaeological remains (he can never visit Egypt too many times). I remember distinctly that he could not spend more than a week one summer working at my site of Khirbet Iskander because—since he was in the area—it was absolutely essential to visit Egypt.

A particular interest of Herb's that has resonated very well with me is his deep appreciation of the importance of archaeology for study of biblical peoples, an appreciation that he held long before it became fashionable (not to say essential for a truly comprehensive understanding of the history and religion of the Israelites). Herb is not just an 'armchair' archaeologist—he has quite a nice resumé of archaeological fieldwork. As with everything he does, Herb has proved to be a perfectionist as a square supervisor. He was a very good and meticulous excavator in Area B, Square 4 in 1982, when the first outlines of the square tower and outer perimeter wall at Khirbet Iskander first came to light. His good work at excavating and discerning stratigraphy should come as no surprise since he was a Fellow at the Albright Institute in 1960–61, he worked with Ernest Wright and Larry Toombs at Shechem, Peter Parr at Petra, and Paul Lapp at 'Araq el-Emir and Ta'anach. We were fortunate also to have Herb at Iskander for a short time in 1997 and 2000.

Musings about digs and travels bring to mind yet another well-known characteristic of Herb's, and that is his indefatigable nature. Recently, Iskander staff members were reminiscing about the good old days when the political climate was more favorable for foreign excavations in the Near East. This led to recollections of a fascinating (but seemingly endless) tour of Petra by Herb in the heat of the summer that finally culminated at the urn on top of the ed-Deir Tomb and left everyone but Herb breathless. Another trip to Petra found us arriving late in the afternoon. The group decided to check in at the luxury hotel outside the city, go for a swim and get ready for cocktails; Herb, on the other hand, was quite indignant that we should want to waste precious time when there were still a few hours to visit Petra before dark. He and a faithful few successfully demanded to be driven to the site in order to get in before closing.

This reflection on Herb would not be complete without the mention of some telling remembrances from colleagues and former students, a few of which I include here. In an attempt to convey something of Herb's unique humor, sometimes subtle and dry and sometimes not so subtle, Jesse Long reminded me of his experience waiting and waiting to hear the results of his comprehensive exams. When the call finally came, Herb, in his inimitable way, tortured Jess for about ten minutes by discussing a litany of minor points concerning matters like penmanship before finally congratulating him for passing with flying colors. This is classic Herb.

I am grateful to Bernard ('Bernie') Batto for his recollections about Herb, which remind me that I would be remiss not to mention an essential aspect of Herb: he stands up for what he believes and is a person of principle, never chary about stating his opinion. Bernie recalls that it is Herb's passion for social justice and his willingness to voice his sentiments that exemplify this person of principle. That passion for social justice, witnessed by Bernie while a student at Hopkins, has had a lasting and profound effect on him to this day.

Two incidents in particular are worth mentioning. One occurred on the morning after the assassination of Dr Martin Luther King Jr. Bernie remembers Herb bristling at anyone who questioned the impact of Dr King's assassination, voicing the opinion that the whole university ought to have shut down in mourning over 'the loss of one of our greatest Americans'. Almost prophetically, that assessment of Dr King was borne out that very night when Baltimore exploded in violent rioting over the tragedy of his death. On another occasion, Herb also had the courage to take a position for a more equitable policy on the part of the United States toward the Middle East, and to draw attention to the unjust treatment of Palestinians. His comments were published in a letter to *The Baltimore Sun* shortly after the Six-Day War, not a propitious time to voice such opinions yet Herb took a public stand for what he believed to be just.

These recollections depict a man of admirable conscience and principle, one who inveighs against the inequalities in society rather like the prophets of old. His passion for social justice, so clear from the anecdotal observations above, and his passion for prophecy in the ancient Near East—the obvious choice for the theme of his Festschrift—go a long way toward explaining who Herbert Bardwell Huffmon is. His students say it best. Both Mark Sneed and Jesse Long testify that Herb's passionate and, yes, inspired teaching of the Prophets profoundly influenced their professional and personal lives, and remains today a treasured memory of their professor. What greater achievement can there be for a teacher!

I could not bring this reflection on Herb to a close without mentioning Margie Huffmon. Although it could be argued that they were fated to meet—Seminary Hall being a fairly small place—I still like to take credit for bringing them together. One day in the Fall 1987 semester when I was too ill to teach I asked Herb to cover my Hebrew class. My good friend Margie happened to be a student in that class on that fateful day and the rest, as they say, is history. They make a great couple, she now pasturing a church while he continues to teach and write, both loving all things Near Eastern and especially devoted to travel. I wish them the best always. I do not know Herb's two children from an earlier marriage, Allan and Kristin, very well, but I do know that they and all the grandchildren (plus Margie's three children and her grandchildren) surely round out the picture and provide the final brush strokes to the person, Herbert B. Huffmon.

It is with great admiration and a sense of deep friendship that I pen this slightly whimsical tribute to Herb. It was a privilege to work with such a colleague all those years, and I value our continued friendship. This reflection is just a token of my sincere appreciation for his trademark loyalty, great friendship, and strong support through the years.

BIBLIOGRAPHY

Dever, William G.
 1970 'The "Middle Bronze I" Period in Syria and Palestine', in J.S. Sanders (ed.), *Near Eastern Archaeology in the Twentieth Century: Essays in Honor of Nelson Glueck* (Garden City, NY: Doubleday): 132-63.
Huffmon, Herbert B.
 1965 *Amorite Personal Names in the Mari Texts: A Structural and Lexical Study* (Baltimore: The Johns Hopkins University Press).
Herbert B. Huffmon, A.R. Spina and A.R.W. Green (eds.)
 1983 *The Quest for the Kingdom of God: Studies in Honor of George Emery Mendenhall* (Winona Lake, IN: Eisenbrauns).
Kenyon, Kathleen
 1966 *Amorites and Canaanites* (London: Oxford University Press).

Introduction to the Study of the History of the Religion of Israel

Frank Moore Cross

If we propose to study the history of the religion of Israel today we must be governed by the same postulates which are the basis of modern historical method. Our task must be a historical not a theological enterprise. We must trace the origins and development of Israel's religion, its emergence from its West Semitic, notably Canaanite past, its continuities with the past, its innovations, individual or peculiar configurations, its new emergent whole, and its subsequent changes and evolution. This is a task and an interest that are relatively recent in Western thought. Only in the late eighteenth century—notably with Herder's *Vom Geist der hebräischen Poesie* (1782–83)—was there a serious attempt to free the study of Israelite religion from dogmatic frameworks—theological or philosophical—and to study it in purely historical terms. To be sure, Spinoza in the preceding century had raised the most serious questions of literary-criticism, arguing, for example, that it was quite impossible to accept the tradition that Moses wrote the Pentateuch. Herder proposed to examine Israel and Israelite religion as a historical phenomenon using a historical methodology in no way different in principle from the historical investigation of the history of Greece and Greek religion, searching for its place in the history of nations and in the history of religions.

The Hebrew Bible in pre-modern times had been studied as a book of divine laws, mythologically descended from heaven; or as a book of prophecies, prefiguring New Testament fufilment. Israel's history was treated as *sui generis*, without links to mundane or secular history. It was a unique, divine, even miraculous history, the history of a type folk, not an ordinary folk, a history which furnished the key to history past and future, but not a natural part of human history. While discontinuous with other national histories, it revealed the design and purpose of universal history. One perceives in these ancient frameworks and points of view theological or philosophical dogma that persists into our day and deserves examination by the theologian or philosopher.

In writing a history of Israelite religion, however, we must approach the Hebrew Bible and its religious traditions using the ordinary tools of the secular historian. I should say that it is difficult for the most conscientious and objective historian to rid him- or herself of the drag of theological or philosophical dogma. The Hebrew Bible is a primary parent of Western culture and faith. It is difficult for a child to look at a parent with objectivity. Our fundamental understanding of goodness, of justice, of truth derives from the Bible, and we look at the world with spectacles furnished by biblical tradition and its interpretation—even those moderns who despise religion.

It has been said, rightly I believe, that to understand the history of the interpretation of the Bible, one must know the entire history of Western thought. We shall skip over that long history, from Philo and the rabbis to Spinoza, and select an example or two of more recent attempts to write histories of the religion of Israel.

One of the early and still influential attempts to compose a history of the religion of Israel was the work of Wilhelm Vatke, *Die Biblische Theologie wissenschaftlich dargestellt: Die Religion des Alten Testament nach den kanonischen Büchern entwickelt* (1835). Vatke viewed the history of Israelite religion as composed of a series of stages, three in number in dialectic movement. As a devout student of Hegel, he described this dialectic in terms of thesis (*Satz*), antithesis (*Gegensatz*), and synthesis (*Vermittelung*). This is the necessary logic of history: the unfolding dialectically of an ever higher grasp of truth, or in concretely Hegelian terms, the movement of the spirit (*Geist*)—the logic of history understood as the biography of God. Vatke's categories in opposition are the familiar Hegelian ones: nature–spirit; myth–history; slavery–freedom; unconscious–conscious; exterior–interior; magic/cult–ethical.

The stages delineated by Vatke are three, the first two in opposition, the third taking up the other two in a higher resolution or synthesis:

1. Paganism: nature religion marked by slavery of nature and its timelessness, magic, cult, idolatry.
2. Prophetic religion: spiritual, ethical, historical, individual, free. Moses the liberator, initiates this stage, and the free, ethical impulse. The eighth-century prophets are the climax of this movement. They rise to a higher consciousness of God. Mechanical cultic, natural, amoral forms are overthrown in principle.
3. Legalism: in the Deuteronomistic and Priestly sources a new stage (synthesis) emerges—idolatry is defeated, and a universal consciousness gained, but also the ethical is now frozen in law, the concrete in encapsulated in the abstract. Theocratic legalism sets in, sullying ethical monotheism.

In Vatke's work, claimed to be historical, we see actually the older medieval theological framework replaced by an equally dogmatic philosophical schema. Vatke's system (I cannot call it history) is profoundly antinomian, not to say anti-Judaic or anti-Semitic. The German idealism of this period, and Christian apologetics that found objective idealism profoundly congenial, constantly plays on the oppositions, slavery vs. freedom and law vs. grace. Hegel said of Moses, 'the liberator of his nation was also its lawgiver; this could mean only that the man who had freed it from one yoke had laid on it another'. Vatke went further: the tradition, he said, that Moses was a lawgiver, formulator of covenant and theocracy is unthinkable. Law and covenant is law as is theocracy, the third movement or stage in the logic of history, the resurgence of thesis in synthesis.

Vatke sees the religion of Israel not merely as antithesis to paganism. The main thrust of his system is in the opposition of Judaism to Christianity. 'Abstract thought' (read law) opposed to 'concrete spirituality' (read gospel). Dead letter is opposed to interior spirit. In short, Judaism leads to a new and higher stage, a new thesis: Christianity in its early, creative phase, that is, New Testament Christianity. In New Testament Christianity, freedom is reborn and grace replaces law. Christianity rekindles prophetism in a higher form and is its successor. One must observe that apocalypticism, a movement of 500 years in duration, and the real forebear of Christianity, is ignored, suppressed. We note also that the ultimate synthesis perceived is the Hegelian system and the Christianity of Germany.

Vatke thus cannot view the history of the religion of Israel in itself—only as part of the emergence of Christianity, a philosophical counterpart to the medieval understanding of the history of Israel. The freeing of the history of the religion of Israel from theological forms thus, in fact, merely plunged it into philosophical schema, one dogmatic structure for another. Israel's history is understood now as a type of universal history, a stage in God's increasing self-consciousness. I have chosen to comment at length on Vatke's work for in Vatke the philosophical skeleton is laid bare and made obvious. Vatke's volume swarms with jargon and mythology of Hegel.

Vatke's synthesis and his heritage linger on. Julius Wellhausen, the most imposing figure in critical biblical studies of the nineteenth century, was Vatke's disciple. Wellhausen in his classic volume, *Prolegomena to the History of Israel* (1878), writes of Vatke: '...from whom indeed I gratefully acknowledge myself to have learnt best and most'. In Wellhausen's profoundly influential work, the Hegelian jargon of Vatke is dropped and, it has been argued, wrongly in my judgment, that Wellhausen was free of his Hegelian past. However, the essential lines of Vatke's synthesis are preserved. The anti-Judaic spirit is, if anything, stronger. Wellhausen disguises his philosophical presuppositions by arriving at his history of Israelite religion by first dating corpora of biblical literature, then arranging them in sequence and, lo and behold, coming out with Vatke's conclusions by and large. Now, however, Wellhausen can argue, no doubt sincerely, that his synthesis is based on scientific literary criticism. The difficulty is that Wellhausen's method is circular: biblical literary material, the law codes, and so on, are dated by clues that presume Vatke and Wellhausen's reconstruction of Israelite history. It is little surprising that when they are arranged in sequence they prove Wellhausen's presuppositions. Vatke had no extra-biblical controls to break the viciousness of the literary-critical circle. Wellhausen had few. The archaeological revolution was still in the future. Strangely, a nostalgic school of Neo-Wellhausenists has sprung up despite our new knowledge, and a number of leading scholars, especially in Europe, falls under this rubric. So, we are not beating a dead horse in refuting their views. The German heritage of academic idealism (compounded with Romanticism) is pervasive, and is useful in Christian apologetics and homiletics. Marvelous to say, it has even penetrated into Israeli biblical scholarship despite its antinomian and latently anti-Semitic thrust.

I do not propose to stop here to give a detailed critique of the Wellhausenist synthesis. Rather I wish immediately to turn to the constructive task of composing a history of Israelite religion. As we shall see, there has been a cascade of new, extra-biblical resources that give us new aids and insights and controls, and indeed require that we go back to the biblical sources and reexamine old work based on biblical literature alone. Out of the richness of the new data, I believe that a new, provisional synthesis can emerge—in any case extraordinary progress can be made.

The religion of Israel was born the child of ancient Near Eastern religion, and especially the religious culture of ancient Canaan. Ivan Engnell wrote in 1945, 'the first prerequisite for understanding Old Testament religion is to understand Canaanite religion correctly'. Engnell overstates, but his point is well taken. We wish first of all to understand the emergence of Israelite religion from its context, and to follow its early development. Israel does not leap full formed into history like Athena from the head of Zeus. The study of origins is always difficult but has a unique fascination. The possibility of such study in concrete detail is recent. Little more than a century ago, the Hebrew Bible was an isolated artifact of Near Eastern civilization, a monument of faith without known context or ancestry. Historical questions of 'origins' or 'emergence' could not be answered satisfactorily and indeed were rarely addressed. Today, thanks to the archaeological exploration of Israel and neighboring lands, the history of Israel has become part of the history of the ancient Near Eastern world. Israel's ancient literature can be viewed increasingly as evolving out of the genres of kindred literatures. We possess Canaanite epic literature from a century or so before Moses. The religion of Israel can now be described in its continuities with, and in its contrasts with contemporary Near Eastern, and especially West Semitic mythology and cult.

Two dynamic societies, Israel and Greece, rose from the ruins of the ancient Near Eastern world. The first societies of the ancient Near East blossomed and grew old and moribund in the course of the third and second millennia. The cataclysms that began about 1200 were symptoms of the end of essentially static and hierarchical societies. Israel as a nation was born in an era of extraordinary chaos and social turmoil. Egypt's empire had collapsed, the Hittite kingdom had fallen, the Middle Assyrian Empire was in decline, and invasions brought the destruction of the great Canaanite city-states of Syria and Palestine, most notably at the hand of Greek Sea peoples including the Philistines.

The great powers did not die overnight. Nepotistic and nostalgic successors to the old states—the Neo-Assyrian Empire, the Neo-Babylonian Empire, and its Persian successor—survived to oppress Israel and to threaten Greece. In any case, these frozen and elitist societies of the ancient world gave way to new dynamic, literate, and 'historical' societies which reached their pinnacle in Israel and Greece: Israel with its prophetic critique of state and clergy, Greece with its gift of logic and skepticism.

(For a slightly revised and expanded form of this contribution, see *BAR* 31.3 [2005]: 42-45.)

THE AMORITE HERITAGE IN THE WEST

George E. Mendenhall

Professor Huffmon's classic work on the Amorite personal names has inspired me to contribute this essay on the Amorite presence and influence in the western regions of the ancient Fertile Crescent. As usual, the evidence consists of data that fall into several categories so that specialists in one particular field of academic endeavor do not and often cannot see the entire picture.

The problem of the Amorite presence and influence in the western regions of the Near East continues to be of interest and controversy. This motivated me to disinter from the depths of the University library the old monograph of Albert Clay, *The Empire of the Amorites*. I was astonished to find that it was published already in 1919. To be sure, the academic context within which that work was produced is drastically different from the scene today, but some of his insights and information is still highly relevant, especially his statement concerning Semitic linguistic history:

> In conclusion, the writer simply wishes to ask those who continue to maintain this theory [i.e. of successive migrations out of Arabia] to satisfy themselves as to why the fair lands of Amurru and Akkad, with their attractive climates and fertile lands, a veritable 'Garden of Eden' where the oldest civilizations of which we have knowledge are to be found, should have been dependent for their inhabitants upon such a breeding place as Arabia. In short, from whatever point of view this theory is examined, it is found wanting. (pp. 48-49)

Yet even after nearly a century of discoveries, decipherments and new inscriptions, there are still scholars who maintain or assume that the Semitic languages resulted from successive waves of nomads out of the Arabian desert. It is difficult to understand why this attitude has such persistence. I would suggest that it derives from some atavistic compulsion to find a 'virgin birth' for each new culture that arrives on the historical stage—a stubborn refusal to admit that ancient societies had their own histories, their own cultural changes and adaptations. In other words, the 'unchanging Orient' and its inhabitants cannot be permitted to change—they only migrate into history, and then conveniently disappear in the face of 'fresh blood' from the desert.

The massive evidence for Amorites in the West of the Fertile Crescent exists in five distinct categories.

The first, *archaeological evidence*, is indirect, but nevertheless highly supportive. Professor Stager observed a couple years ago that the enormous changes in the archaeological levels of MB I and MB IIA certainly call for the presence of some new cultural entity that cannot be explained on the basis of the MB I assemblage—a new population group must surely have been involved. As usual, without written evidence, there is no way to determine whether that population was Malayan or Portuguese.

The second category, *evidence from linguistic history*, is more persuasive, but still controversial. Thorkild Jakobsen commented decades ago that the difference between Old Akkadian and Old Babylonian/Assyrian is the superimposition of the Amorite language upon the older dialects. We are now in precisely the same situation for the West Semitic complex known from inscriptions of various times and regions. Not until the decipherment of the syllabic texts from Byblos could the analogous process be observed in the West, for there was no way in which the pre-Amorite language could have been isolated from the new composite language that we call Ugaritic, Canaanite or West Semitic.

With the publication of my opus, *The Syllabic Texts from Byblos* (Beirut: University of Beirut, 1985), the process is now clear. The language of those texts is so clearly devoid of Amorite influence that the Ugaritic texts were entirely useless in providing analogous materials for the decipherment. Entirely contrary to initial expectation and assumptions, the gradual retrieval of vocabulary items and other linguistic phenomena revealed that the only cognates to the texts were to be found in two sources: first, of course, in the considerable corpus of Common Semitic inventory. Much more significant, however, was the fact that the mass of evidence came simply from the great inventory of Classical Arabic.

Unfortunately, a series of incompetent and/or careless reviews has tended to obscure the significance of these texts. Every review makes statements flatly contrary to the facts in the book, or ignores the evidence that is there. To add comic relief from the disaster, one review complained that computers were supposed to be used for calculating numbers, not for producing books.

It follows that the old theory of successive waves out of the desert is the exact opposite to the historical truth. Arabic has its remote ancestor in the Eastern Mediterranean, and it was taken *into* the Arabian desert at the LB–EI transition period. As the discovery of the city of Qurayya and other sites reveals, it was most likely immigration from Transjordan and the Jordan Valley that brought people and the Arabic language into the desert. It is virtually a law of linguistic history that the most archaic and original forms of any language family are to be found in the regions most remote from their place of origin. The best example is the Indo-European group, whose most archaic and original expressions are to be found at the extreme ends—in Sanskrit in the East, and in Lithuanian in the West. Another excellent example is the Celtic group, the most archaic of which is found in the latest known—the Old Irish. It is not surprising that the latest attested of the Semitic language group is found in the region furthest removed from the 'Fertile Crescent'—the Arabian peninsula.

However, the third category, *historical evidence*, is conclusive. Approximately at the transition from MB I to MB II we have Egyptian records of kings of Byblos, namely *'ab-šm* (Egyptian Ibsmw) and *yp-šm-'ab* (Egyptian Yp-smw-ib). The similarity of these names with the name of the first Amorite king of the Old Babylonian dynasty, *Sumu-abum*, is no accident; note also *Yapa—sumu-abi* from Old Babylonian Alalakh. Ugaritic records indicate that at about the same time an Amorite dynasty was established there by a certain *Atamrum*.

This historical evidence correlates perfectly with the archaeological evidence, for we know from the Execration Texts that earlier Byblian society was composed of tribes, Egyptian *wḥyt*, not chieftains or kings. It is most intriguing that in both cases, Byblos and Ugarit, there is little or no evidence of widespread violence attending this drastic shift in population. What was happening is obviously very obscure, but it certainly is relevant to observe that everywhere in the Near East societies were in the process of emerging from a dark age, the First Intermediate Period, when there were no powerful entrenched establishments to maintain their control and violently ward off any newcomers. It must be remembered and taken seriously into consideration that the Early Bronze Age in Palestine and Transjordan exhibits the highest concentration of archaeological sites of any period until the Byzantine era. The ensuing Middle Bronze I is by comparison very meager.

The fourth category, *personal names*, strangely enough, constitutes the only direct evidence we have for the Amorite language. The late I.J. Gelb and colleagues have most conveniently collected the evidence consisting of some 6000 personal names, most of them sentence names that include verbs and other parts of speech. These sentence names are very characteristic of Amorite, in contrast to the predominance of one-word names found nearly everywhere else not under Amorite influence. It is highly significant that much of the central theological vocabulary of Biblical Hebrew consists of lexical items that are of Amorite origin, such as *ṣdq*, *yṭʿ*, *ḥsd*, *ʾmn* to give a few examples. It is also important to observe that the first three kings of the Israelite monarchy have one-word names, Saul, David, Solomon, while after these three, both the Amorite sentence-names (Rehoboam, Jereboam) and one-word names (Nadab, Asa, Baasha, Omri, etc.) continue to occur in the royal lines.

I have not attempted to find what percentage of personal names in the biblical record are Amorite, but it is probable that there are perhaps even a majority of names of this origin. All this illustrates, of course, the fact that the entire population group of biblical Israel consisted of just the same amalgam of various peoples as is true in other parts of the ancient Fertile Crescent. The same fact is illustrated by the loanwords found in Biblical Hebrew that come from every language known in the ancient Near East, from Sumerian (*hekal*, 'temple') to Hittite (*qōbaʿ/kōbaʿ*, 'helmet').

In fact, it is now most tempting to find an explanation for the curious repetition of the list of 'nations' that existed in Palestine before the Hebrews—the ten nations of Gen. 15.19, the six nations of Exod. 3.8, 17; 23.23; 34.11; Josh. 11.3; Judg. 3.6. They constitute the sources of the populations that became Israel—the politico-ethnic regimes whose peoples over whom they held sway became elements in the covenant-based coalition of the ancient 'Kingdom of Yahweh'. The passage in Josh. 15.63 states this explicitly, and the same can be safely extrapolated to other regions. Judges 3.5-6 also states the same fact, but mistakenly regards the assimilation as the result of later times.

The *fifth category* consists of entirely new evidence that has only recently come to light. In 1993, Dr Ma'en Shatnawi produced a thesis for his MA degree at the Institute of Archaeology and Anthropology at Yarmouk University, Irbid, Jordan, entitled 'Amorite Elements in Thamudic Theophoric Names'. These are sentence names of the Amorite type, and the divine names are all local, native deities. However, the predicates, verbs and adjectives in the names are of Amorite origin in 34 per cent of the corpus. (I have recently learned that Ma'en has obtained his Doctorate at Mainz University, having produced a dissertation that further documents this fact from additional sources.)

This further substantiates the presence of Amorite populations in every part of the West, now including the desert fringe, and their lasting influence more than a thousand years later. Such a high percentage of Amorite names can hardly be explained on the basis of late borrowing.

There is abundant evidence that at the MB I–MB II transition period there was an explosion of Amorite peoples in every direction from northeast Syria. It is clear that in the EB period there was an unbelievably high density of population in the Syrian Jezireh. The region is dotted with ancient village tells: one traveler reported that from the top of one mound one could count 200 tells within the horizon line. This region is characterized by good soil, a rainfall that permits intensive agriculture, and a vast steppe land that permits enormous production of livestock with virtually unlimited pasturage. It is not surprising that the region produced such a surplus of population that it had to 'swarm' into other areas.

In addition, evidence from Nuzi in the east to Alalakh in the West proves beyond doubt that pressures from eastern Anatolia contributed to the migration. In both cities, the MB tablets show personal names of predominantly Amorite and Semitic origin. By the LB age the personal names are overwhelmingly Hurrian. In the eighteenth-century Mari archives there are relatively few Hurrian names, and they seem to derive primarily from the far north of the region.

The Amorite population is thus a village people of enormous productivity with its blend of agriculture and animal husbandry—which is always the case in farming economies. As such, the urban specialties of written documents and royal archives are not only unnecessary, they are highly undesirable. In contrast to some recent ideas, their social organization was not simply one based on local tribalism. As the Mari documents so amply witness, they had several large scale coalitions, such as the often mentioned Banu-Iamina and Banu-Simal. This type of confederation lived on in the Midianite confederation of five kings and, I would suggest, are the model for the confederation of tribes that constituted ancient Israel.

However, it is clear both in the East and in the West Amorite peoples did establish royal dynasties, in imitation of earlier imperial organizations—Old Akkadian in the east, and no doubt the Egyptian at Byblos in the West. Already at Mari the process can be seen to be producing tensions, when the advisor to King Zimri-Lim had to warn him to ride on a donkey, not a horse, since he was king not only of the Babylonians, but also of the Hana—native Amorites.

In view of all this evidence, it is not surprising that the Amorites never produced written archives in their own language or a writing system for the preservation of their language that is known only from the thousands of personal names that have been preserved. This does not mean, however, that they were devoid of the higher elements of culture. It has been argued for decades that the legal system in the Mesopotamian law codes is Amorite in origin—a system of 'common law' that accompanied the Amorites into the Babylonian empire, and also into the Israelite 'laws of Moses'.

In addition, it has been argued, I believe rightly so, that the famous Babylonian Creation Epic is actually an adaptation of an Amorite epic. It would thus constitute a further example of a highly cultured society that produced no written documents, but nevertheless had a rich tradition of orally transmitted poetry and folklore. From the Greek Islands to Yemen there have been recent reports of local peoples' capability to produce, without prior preparation, highly complex poetic compositions appropriate to festive occasions. The western obsession that only literacy permits higher aspects of culture is simply the result of ignorance, and sometimes invincible ignorance.

WHAT IS PROPHECY?
AN ANCIENT NEAR EASTERN PERSPECTIVE

Martti Nissinen

Why the Question?

Herbert B. Huffmon is acknowledged as an outstanding expert in matters related to prophecy. In this paper, dedicated to him with much pleasure, I attempt at answering the question of what prophecy actually is—or, to put it more humbly, how I would like to understand the word and the underlying concept as a biblical and ancient Near Eastern scholar. The word 'prophecy' is deeply rooted in the vocabulary of religious communities, but it also belongs to the academic language. However, Old and New Testament scholars may have varying nuances or even different meanings in using this word, not to speak about Classicists, Egyptologists and Assyriologists, many of whom are reluctant to mention the word 'prophecy' at all because of the theological connotations and value judgments attached to it. Hence, the question 'What is prophecy?' immediately provokes further questions.

Should the use of the word 'prophecy' be restricted to theological discourse because of its roots in religious speech? This is hardly possible, because there is no unanimous understanding of the realm of 'theology'. On the other hand, there is no reason to create an idiosyncratic language which would make theology, whatever it means, incommensurable with other disciplines.

Should the word 'prophecy', then, refer exclusively to the sources and phenomena related to religions which use it as a part of their own tradition, that is, Judaism, Christianity, and Islam? This would mean enclosing the term with a confessional wall, which would jeopardize its placement in a broader religious and socio-cultural context.

What if we take a historically or theologically influential phenomenon—in other words, Israelite or biblical prophecy—as a criterion and judge the 'prophetic' nature of other sources and phenomena by this standard? This approach has the obvious disadvantage of using one specific tradition (usually one's own) as a yardstick which represents the genuine and proper form of prophecy, and making the comparative material appear as an under- or overdeveloped distortion of the chosen paragon. Thus far, the study of prophecy has been predominantly Bible-centered. This can be explained by the fact that this field of study is occupied by biblical scholars in first place, and many of them may be interested in the history and religion of the ancient Near East as the 'context of scripture'[1] rather than in its own right. But even more importantly, an independent view of ancient Near Eastern prophecy has been impeded by the paucity of evidence. Therefore, even today, every new piece of prophecy, however small, is hailed as a welcome addition to the frustratingly incomplete picture.

Obviously, the concept of prophecy cannot be restricted to Christian, Jewish, and Islamic sources and societies. However, a broader understanding of prophecy does not make the term any simpler to cope with. What are the criteria for recognizing prophecy in sources in which this word is not inherent? Do we call a text prophecy because of its content or its religio-historical origin? Why do we call some people prophets and others not?

It is not easy to adapt a religious concept to scholarly language. The question 'What is prophecy?' has implications for the sociology of science, implying the need to neutralize the traditional theological concept in a way that makes it applicable to scholarly use. Answering the question is necessary to enable interdisciplinary communication and to remove semantic misunderstandings between scholars who should be able to recognize related phenomena in different cultures irrespective of their education and religious background.

I start my own attempt at answering the question 'What is prophecy?' with a survey of meanings of the word-family 'prophecy'. Second, I will add some viewpoints to the problem of the definition of prophecy, which is still very much under discussion. Third, I will present an overview of the sources recognizable as prophetic according to the revisited definition and, finally, I will offer some thoughts on the ideological conceptualization of prophecy in the Hebrew Bible.

The Word-Family 'Prophecy'

First of all, 'prophecy' is a word of the English language, the meaning of which is a matter of mutual agreement by the community that uses this word. The dictionary of English that I use every day, *Oxford Advanced Learners Dictionary of Current English*, doubtless reflects the semantics of current English correctly and authoritatively when it defines the noun 'prophecy' as 'a statement that sth will happen in the future, especially one made by sb with religious or magic powers', and the verb 'prophesy' as 'to say what will happen in the future (done in the past using religious or magic powers)'. A 'prophet' is 'a person who claims to know what will happen in the future'.[2] According to this dictionary, hence, the English-speaking community lays emphasis on the aspect of foretelling the future, using the word

---

1.   *The Context of Scripture* is the title of the new three-volume collection of translations of ancient Near Eastern documents (Hallo and Younger [eds.] 1997, 2000, 2002 = *COS* 1-3). The title of this collection has been criticized, all the more because many of the texts included are by no means associated with biblical texts or history (see, e.g., Loretz 1996). On the other hand, it is highly surprising that the major corpora of ancient Near Eastern prophetic texts (i.e. those of Mari and Assyria) are entirely excluded from the collection.

2.   *Oxford Advanced Learners Dictionary* 2000: 1016. The reader will note that a survey of German, French or, say, Finnish dictionaries will provide similar results.

'prophecy' of a predictive activity of any kind. The first idea that an average English speaker associates with a prophet is obviously prognostication, and even academic scholars sometimes label their sources as prophecies, if they include predictions of the future. Why, then, are the scholars who work with biblical and ancient Near Eastern sources usually not quite happy with this understanding of prophecy? Why is the future-oriented definition of prophecy, which doubtless reflects an actual development in the semantics of the English language, not as good as any other definition?

To be sure, the same dictionary gives two further explanations for the word 'prophet' in which the future plays no role at all. According to these explanations, a 'prophet', in Christian, Jewish, and Muslim religions, is 'a person sent by God to teach the people and give them messages from God'. Furthermore, a 'prophet (of sth)' is equated with 'a person who teaches and supports a new idea, theory, etc.'. These explanations insinuate that behind the future-oriented everyday meaning of 'prophecy' there is a phenomenon, the main characteristic of which is speaking to people and transmitting messages, divine messages in particular. Indeed, the very concept of prophecy is deeply rooted in the biblical tradition where it is intertwined with the notion of an alleged divine–human communication, in which a human person, the so-called 'prophet', acts as the mouthpiece of God. The same notion with respective activity is to be found also in the ancient Mediterranean environment of the writings of the Bible; in fact, different languages have inherited this word-family from Classical Greek, in which the respective word-family προφετεία denotes a comparable activity. According to Liddell and Scott's *Greek–English Lexicon*, προφητεία is equivalent to the 'gift of interpreting the will of gods' and προφητεύω to being an 'interpreter of the gods', whereas προφήτης is 'one who speaks for a God and interprets his will to man', or, generally, an 'interpreter'. This dictionary also specifies the meanings of the word-family in the New Testament, where it reflects especially the 'gift of expounding scripture, speaking and preaching', and not only that, but also predicting future events.[3]

The meanings of words in modern languages cannot be determined by their use in ancient times, of course, but on the other hand, the reading of ancient sources should not be blurred by modern semantics. It becomes evident from the Classical Greek data that the primary idea expressed by 'prophecy' was the interpretation of the divine will rather than prognostication which, nevertheless, was connected with prophecy as early as in the New Testament. The use of the word-family 'prophecy' in modern languages owes its use first and foremost to the Bible—primarily to the Septuagint, but also to the New Testament and early Christian literature. When the translators of the Septuagint needed a Greek equivalent for the Hebrew נביא, they chose a word denoting a person who speaks for God and interprets the divine will. Obviously, in their view, προφήτης rendered an idea that was close enough to what they thought a נביא was. In modern scholarship, wherever the meaning of 'prophecy' is specified, it is mostly understood along the same lines.

---

3. *LSJ*: 1539-40; cf. Bauer 1988: 1447-49, and, for the use of the word-family in Classical Greek, van der Kolf 1957 and Krämer 1959.

If the word 'prophecy', then, can be agreed to denote primarily the activity of transmitting and interpreting the divine will, it can be used as a general concept of related activities in the ancient and the modern worlds, independently of its biblical roots and religious affiliations.[4] This requires further specification regarding the concrete activities that can be adequately designated as prophecy; in other words, a definition of prophecy is needed to make the word applicable to different contexts. The definition is necessary first and foremost as an aid of communication between people who work in different fields with cognate materials. It should not be understood as a static image of truth; rather, it should be seen from the point of view of the sociology of knowledge as a methodical process that emerges from concrete needs of the scholarly community and develops along with its application.

A Definition of Prophecy and Some Qualifications

If the definition of prophecy is understood as a process rather than an entity, it is feasible to start working with an existing definition that already enjoys wide acceptance without a claim to being the final truth. Such a definition has been formulated by Manfred Weippert, according to whom prophecy is present when a person

(a)   through a cognitive experience (a vision, an auditory experience, an audio-visual appearance, a dream or the like) becomes the subject of the revelation of a deity, or several deities and, in addition,

(b)   is conscious of being commissioned by the deity or deities in question to convey the revelation in a verbal form (as a 'prophecy' or a 'prophetic speech'), or through nonverbal communicative acts ('symbolic acts'), to a third party who constitutes the actual addressee of the message.[5]

Essentially, the definition of Weippert refers to a process of divine–human communication consisting of the following four components:

1.   the divine sender of the message;
2.   the message (the 'revelation');
3.   the transmitter of the message (the prophet); and
4.   the recipient of the message.

This exposition corresponds to the prevailing views in understanding prophecy as intermediation; according to an understanding shared by an increasing number of scholars, there can be no prophecy without God (or a deity), no prophecy without a message and audience, and, finally, no prophecy without a prophet.[6] All these components are present in the definition of Weippert, which is rather broad, as it should be to avoid confining prophecy to any particular characteristics that may be

---

4.   For an anthropological, cross-cultural perspective, see Overholt 1986 and Grabbe 2000.
5.   Weippert 1997: 197 (translation mine).
6.   Prophecy is seen primarily as intermediation by the majority of scholars who have recently discussed the issue of definition; cf., e.g., Overholt 1989; Huffmon 1992; Barstad 1993: 46; Grabbe 1995: 107; Petersen 2000: 44.

common but not universally applicable, such as the spontaneity of prophecy,[7] ecstatic or charismatic qualities,[8] or the use of specific literary forms.[9] This does not mean that the definition is above criticism. David L. Petersen has recently criticized it for emphasizing too much the personal experience as a distinctive mark of prophecy (Petersen 2000: 39-41). In addition, I think the notion of 'consciousness' needs clarification in connection with allegedly divine messages, the divine origin of which cannot be controlled by anyone, not even by the prophet her- or himself. Moreover, it may be asked whether it is sufficient to describe prophecy as one-way communication from the deity to the recipient, without reference to the social environment of this communication. A few qualifications are therefore necessary.

Prophecy and Divination

My first remark concerns the relationship of prophecy and divination. In contrast to the once influential idea of a substantial qualitative difference between prophecy and divination (i.e. consulting the divine world by various means), there is a growing tendency in the present-day study of biblical and ancient Near Eastern prophecy to consider prophecy an integral part of divination, rather than being in conflict with it in general terms.[10] This does not exclude individual clashes between prophets and diviners; what matters is that the social function of prophecy by and large has not been found to be different from that of divination. In the ancient Near East, in so far as we are correctly informed by the extant documents, the primary function of all divination was the so-called *Herrschaftswissen*, that is, the conviction of the identity, capacity and legitimacy of the ruler and the justification and limitations of his (or, less frequently, her) power, based on the communication between the ruler and the god(s).[11]

I am totally in favor of seeing prophecy as one form of divination; nonetheless, I find it necessary to distinguish between different methods of becoming informed of what is believed to be the divine will.[12] If classified as a form of divination, prophecy, together with dreams and visions, clearly belongs to the non-inductive type, which does not presuppose exhaustive studies in the traditional omen literature and experience in observing material objects like celestial bodies and the entrails of animals. This is not to say that no learned techniques would have been required of a prophet, only that they were of a totally different kind than those employed by the practitioners of inductive divination, particularly by astrologers, haruspices or exorcists. The skills or aptitudes of prophets, visionaries and dreamers served the

7. This aspect has been emphasized by Malamat 1998: 61.

8. For Max Weber's concept of prophets as charismatic leaders, see Blenkinsopp 1995: 115-19 and Clements 1997.

9. This criterion is criticized by Petersen 1997.

10. See, e.g., Ellis 1989: 144-46; Overholt 1989: 140-47; Barstad 1993: 47-48; Grabbe 1995: 150-51; VanderKam 1995: 2083; Cancik-Kirschbaum 2003.

11. The concept of *Herrschaftswissen* is introduced by Pongratz-Leisten 1999, who incorporates in it all kinds of Mesopotamian divination: astrology, extispicy, prophetic oracles, dreams and the 'correspondence' between gods and kings.

12. For this distinction, see also Cancik-Kirschbaum 2003: 44-51.

purpose of reaching a state of mind in which it was believed to be possible to become directly conversant with the divine will. Usually this seems to have pre-supposed an altered state of consciousness, but the ways of attaining the required condition may have been more or less frantic.[13]

The prophets very often claim to have received the divine message in a dream or a vision. In many cases it is virtually impossible to distinguish between prophecy and other visionary or oneiromantic activity, but the difference should nonetheless be recognized; not every visionary or dreamer can be called prophet. To be quali-fied as a prophecy, the dream or vision should contain a divine message to be trans-mitted and, if need be, interpreted; however, such dreams and visions can be seen by anybody. In practical terms it is not always possible to determine whether a par-ticular dreamer is a prophet, especially if the source in question does not otherwise imply her/his prophetic role.

Prophecy and Society

Second, the designation 'prophet' not only refers to the position of a person in the process of communication but also implies a social role and function which distin-guishes the person thus designated from other members of the society, no matter what kind of vocation may be understood to lie behind this role. Polymorphous as the image of a prophet in different times and documents is, it is not advisable to presume a particular institutional background, distinctive behavior or mode of expression as a precondition of prophecy.[14] What makes a prophet different from others is that he or she is believed to have the capacity of acting as the mouthpiece of God, in whatever manner or position.

In practical terms this special faculty very often—virtually always in the ancient Near East—means that prophets are attached to the temples of the deities whose words they transmit. As members of temple communities, they were set apart from the rest of the community; some of them (especially the ones with undefinable gender role that are known from both Mari and Assyria), belong to people whose condition of 'otherness' is incompatible with the way of life of an average citizen.[15] The role of prophets also differs clearly from that of the practitioners of inductive divination, that is, scholars who were well versed in scholarly tradition and whose social esteem, at least in Mesopotamian societies, seems to have been generally higher than that of the prophets. At Mari, the messages of the prophets were trans-ferred to the king by go-betweens, which indicates that the relation of the prophets to the king was not as direct as that of the scholars with whom the king maintained intensive contact.[16] From the point of view of gender, it is worth noting that there

---

13.   For an assessment of the question of prophetic ecstasy, see Grabbe 1995: 108-12.

14.   See Petersen 1997: 27-30; 2000: 33-37; cf. also Blenkinsopp 1995: 123-29.

15.   For the socioreligious role of the Assyrian prophets, see Nissinen 2000b.

16.   This is not to say that direct contacts between prophets and the king would have been excluded; cf. Charpin 2001: 34-41 and 2002: 16-22. For the roles of the prophets *vis-à-vis* scholars at Mari, see Durand 1995: 405-408; Sasson 1998: 116-19; for the same in Assyria, see Parpola 1993: xvii-xxvii; 1997: xlvii-xlviii; Nissinen 1998: 167-69; 2000b: 107-11.

are a considerable number of women among ancient Near Eastern prophets but none among scholars, which also indicates a difference in social location.

Prophetic activity does not necessarily exclude other roles in society; the social position of the prophet may vary according to the integration of the prophetic role into the society as a whole. The often-made dichotomy between free, charismatic prophets and the so-called cultic or court prophets should no longer be upheld as a fundamental, generally applicable distinction, even though the solitary prophetic dissident, independent of human authorities and institutions, still appears as a paragon of prophecy even in scholarly literature (cf., e.g., Klein 1997). This prototype of a prophet is certainly based on a biblical model (e.g. Amos in Amos 7.14-15), but this may not quite tally with the historical facts. Moreover, the contraposition of free and institutional prophets correlates too much with ideas on 'true' and 'false' prophecy, which are confessional labels inconsistent with any general definition of prophecy.[17]

The distinction between 'true' and 'false' prophecy is nonetheless significant to the addressees of the prophetic message who ultimately decide whether or not the words of a prophet should be listened to. The social dynamic of the prophetic process of communication (cf. Overholt 1989: 17-25) is substantially characterized by the faith-based divine component. The acceptability of prophecy depends on the social acknowledgment of the speaking deity and the prophet; therefore, prophetic communication cannot be just one-way correspondence from a deity to humans but interacts perforce with the social hierarchy and belief systems of any given community. The prophets and the addressees are not the only participants in this process; it involves also other intermediaries that may be needed to transfer the prophetic message, interpreters of the prophetic words, scribes and archivists who take care of their writing and depositing, authorities who control the prophetic activity, and so on—not to forget public reactions which may substantially determine the viability of prophecies (cf. Nissinen 2000a: 268-71). All these factors, depending on the structures of the society, may stop the prophetic process or support it.

Prophecy and Prediction

Third, if intermediation is seen as the primary quality of prophecy, the eventual predictive aspect is subordinate to this quality. To be sure, the predictive meaning of the word 'prophecy' in everyday language is not without foundation in ancient sources. Prophecies are very commonly orientated toward the future in one way or another. Rather than being downright descriptions of future events, however, the predictive element grows from the position of the present situation in the divine plan, as disclosed by the prophecy.[18] Hence, a prophetic prediction, as prophecy in

---

17. See Huffmon 1976: 183-84; Coggins 1993: 93; Nissinen 1996: 193-95. I hasten to add that prophecy has never been a value-free concept and an image of a prophet can never consist of 'pure facts' alone; even a scholarly definition of a 'prophet' is inevitably a construct of the academic community in spite of the attempt at using it regardless of confessional prerequisites.

18. Grabbe 2003: 194, 'Prophets claimed to proclaim messages of God about his plans, but this inevitably included the future. Prediction was not all there was to prophecy by any means, but

general, fulfils the function of divine–human communication. In so far as this communication is about the future, as it frequently is, prophecies may include predictions, but not every prediction is a prophecy.

Consequently, the question arises whether texts which are predictive without showing any sign of the idea of divine–human communication and intermediation can be called prophecy in light of the meaning defined above. Some Akkadian[19] and Egyptian[20] predictive texts demonstrate the prophetic process only vaguely if at all, even though they sometimes have been labeled as prophecy precisely because they are predictions. As literature, these texts represent a genre clearly different from other ancient Near Eastern prophetic sources (see Weippert 1988: 291-94). This does not set them entirely apart from prophecies, though (cf. Grabbe 1995: 94). While removing the definitional and terminological confusion caused by different uses of 'prophecy', it should not be forgotten that the Akkadian literary predictive texts (also called Akkadian apocalypses) are literary offshoots of divination. Without actually being prophecy in the above defined meaning, they represent learned interpretation and application of divinatory sources in a way well comparable with literary interpretations of prophetic sources, which constitute my last qualification to the definition of prophecy.

Literary Interpretation of Prophecy
It may be discussed whether the literary reinterpretation, or *Fortschreibung*, of prophetic messages can still be called 'prophecy' at all. In strictly phenomenological terms, the subsequent literary interpretation of prophecy, liable to alter or invent prophetic words and figures, could no longer bear this designation. The questions arise mainly from the Hebrew Bible; in extrabiblical sources, the temporal distance between the prophetic performance and the written record is usually not very long, hence the literary and interpretative process behind them is nothing when compared with the formation of the biblical prophetic books that took centuries.

However, the Neo-Assyrian collections of prophetic oracles do testify to the reuse of prophecies in new historical situations, and prophetic words are also used in literary contexts, either as quotations from written sources or as freely invented paraphrases (see Nissinen 2000a: 263-68). This evidence, without being volumi-

---

it was certainly there'.

19. The so-called Akkadian prophecies or Akkadian apocalypses, including the Marduk Prophecy, the Šulgi Prophecy, the Uruk Prophecy, the Dynastic Prophecy, and the two texts that simply bear the titles Text A and Text B. For an overview of these texts, see Grayson 1975: 13-22; Ellis 1989: 146-57; VanderKam 1995: 2091-94 and cf. the translations in *COS* 1: 480-82 (by Tremper Longman) and *Prophéties et oracles* 1994: I, 98-114 (by Philippe Talon). For the definitional problem, see also Nissinen 2001b.

20. For example, the Prophecies of Neferti, the Admonitions of Ipuwer, the Demotic Chronicle, the Prophecy of the Lamb (for these and other relevant texts, see the articles collected in Blasius and Schipper [eds.] 2002); cf. the translations in Lichtheim 1973: 139-84; *COS* 1: 93-110 (by Nili Shupak) and *Prophéties et oracles* 1994: II, 6-30 (by Didier Devauchelle). For discussion of these texts as 'prophecy', see Shupak 1989–90 and Schipper 2002.

nous, is enough to demonstrate that the prophetic process of communication did not necessarily cease when the message reached its destination, but could be continued by subsequent hands. Hence, a definition of prophecy should not *a priori* exclude the literary products that emerged from the scribal interpretations of prophetic words. Rather, these should be considered secondary prolongation of the prophetic communicational process.

Prophetic Records from the Ancient Near East

Any definition of prophecy is a scholarly construct that can only be formulated in interaction with sources that are considered to represent the prophetic phenomenon in one way or another. Definitions are needed to delimit the relevant source material, but, on the other hand, the sources may compel us to rethink the definition. Therefore, answering the question 'What is prophecy?' is a process that should not be paralyzed by unyielding and over-exact definitions. On the other hand, an inventory of ancient Near Eastern prophetic sources should not be understood as the formation of an extrabiblical canon, but rather as a provisional assessment of the present state of knowledge.

There exists a wide spectrum of ancient Near Eastern sources that either reflect the prophetic process of communication sketched above or mention a prophetic designation like the Hebrew נביא, or the Akkadian *raggimu, mahhû/muhhûm* or *āpilum*.[21] At present, the updated list of documents that meet these requirements constitutes a group of some 140 individual texts, consisting basically of two kinds of sources: oracles of deities in written form, and references in documents of different kinds—letters, inscriptions, administrative records and religious texts—that mention prophets, quote their sayings, or speak of their activities.[22] This source material can be divided in six groups:

1. The largest corpus of prophetic records comes from eighteenth-century Mari, comprising fifty letters with prophetic quotations.[23] These letters, which are virtually always addressed to King Zimri-Lim (c. 1775–1761 BCE),[24] report on prophecies delivered in the city of Mari, elsewhere in

21. For the prophetic designations, see Durand 1988: 386-96; 1995: 322-34 (Mari); Parpola 1997: xlv-xlvii (Assyria).

22. For an extensive collection of translations and normalized transcriptions of the sources, see Nissinen 2003a; translations for most texts are also included in *Prophéties et oracles* 1994: I. A brief overview of the sources can be found in Weippert 1988 and 1997 and Huffmon 1992. Additional source material has been discussed, for example, in Huffmon 1997; 2000; van der Toorn 2000b; Nissinen 2000a/b; 2002a/b.

23. The relevant letters are included in the edition of Durand (1988: 377-482), except the following: A. 1968 and A. 1121+ (Durand 2002: 134-40); A. 3760 (Charpin 2002: 33-36); ARM 26 371 (Joannès 1988: 177-79); ARM 26 414 (Joannès 1988: 294-95); ARM 27 32 (Birot 1993: 88-90); M. 9451 (Ozan 1997: 303). An extensive collection of transliterations and translations of the Mari texts has been recently published in Roberts 2002: 157-253.

24. Two letters, A. 3760 and ARM 26 223, can now be dated to the time of Zimri-Lim's predecessor, Yasmah-Addu; see Charpin 2002: 33-38.

the kingdom, or even outside its borders. In addition, the Mari corpus includes a handful of documents other than letters that mention prophets (*āpilum/āpiltum, muḫḫûm/muḫḫūtum*): two ritual texts,[25] several administrative documents,[26] a report of crimes[27] and a yet unpublished literary text, the so-called 'Epic of Zimri-Lim'.[28]

2.   The prophetic activity in the Old Babylonian period was not restricted to Mari. This is demonstrated by two oracles of the goddess Kititum (Ištar) to Ibalpiel II, a contemporary of Zimri-Lim and the ruler of the Kingdom of Ešnunna that was located northeast of Babylonia.[29]

3.   The second largest corpus of ancient Near Eastern prophecy derives from seventh-century Nineveh.[30] This Neo-Assyrian corpus comprises eleven clay tablets, including 29 individual prophetic oracles addressed to Kings Esarhaddon (681–669 BCE) and Assurbanipal (668–627 BCE), who ruled the Assyrian empire during the time Manasseh and Josiah were kings of Judah in Jerusalem; hence, the Neo-Assyrian prophets roughly coincide with the 'classical' prophets of the Hebrew Bible.

      Apart from the oracles, there are more than twenty Neo-Assyrian texts—inscriptions, letters, administrative documents, cultic texts and a treaty—alluding in one way or another to prophets (*raggimu/raggintu, maḫḫû/maḫḫutu*) or their sayings, and giving an impression of how prophecy was utilized and valued in Neo-Assyrian society.[31]

4.   The Mesopotamian documentation of prophecy is supplemented by a random collection of individual texts from different ages and different geographical areas that is classified as prophecy because of reference to a human intermediary transmitting divine messages, or because the texts include prophetic designations. The temporal and geographic distribution of these odd pieces of prophecy is surprisingly wide, ranging from the twenty-first[32] to second[33] centuries BCE and covering considerable parts

---

25.   A. 3165 (Ritual of Ištar, Text 2); A. 1249b+ (Ritual of Ištar, Text 3); see Durand and Guichard 1997.

26.   ARM 9 22; ARM 21 333; ARM 22 167; 326; ARM 23 446; ARM 25 15; 142; A. 3796; A. 4676; M. 5529+; M. 9921; M. 11299; M. 11436; T. 82, quoted or referred to in Durand 1988: 380-81, 386-87, 396-99.

27.   M. 9717; see van Koppen 2002: 356-57.

28.   The relevant excerpt of this text is quoted in Durand 1988: 393.

29.   FLP 1674 and 2064; see the edition of Ellis 1987.

30.   SAA 9; see the edition of Parpola 1997; cf. Weippert 1981; 2002.

31.   Most of these (Esarhaddon Nin. A i 84–ii 11; Ass. A i 31–ii 26; Assurbanipal A ii 126–iii 26; B v 46–vi 16; T ii 7-24; SAA 2 6 § 10; SAA 7 9; SAA 10 109; 111; 284; 294; 352; SAA 13 37 [= LAS 317]; SAA 16 59; 60; 61 [= ABL 1217+; CT 53 17+; 938]) are analyzed in Nissinen 1998. For additional material, including the 'Marduk ordeal' (SAA 3 34) (dupl. SAA 3 35), a decree of expenditures from the time of Adad-nerari III (SAA 12 69), the letters SAA 13 139; 144; 148, and the Tammuz and Ištar ritual K 2001+, see Nissinen 2000 a/b; 2001 and Huffmon 2000: 57-63.

32.   The letter of the King of Ur to Ur-Lisi (TCS 1 369; see Michalowski 1993: 55) mentions a *maḫḫû*.

33.   The Late Babylonian astronomical diary concerning the year 133 BCE reports a prophetic

of the ancient Near East. The texts represent different genres, including letters,[34] administrative texts,[35] a literary text,[36] a ritual,[37] lexical lists and omens.

There are also some borderline cases in which the reference to prophecy is still to be substantiated, notably the two Hittite fourteenth-century plague prayers with a possible reference to prophets among other practitioners of divination,[38] the references to persons called *munabbi'ātu* in administrative lists from thirteenth-century Emar,[39] as well as the three texts from Nuzi and one Middle-Babylonian omen from Assur mentioning people called *āpilum*.[40]

5. A few important documents testify to the existence of prophecy even in the West Semitic milieu.[41] The oldest of them is the Egyptian Report of Wenamon referring to a prophetic appearance in Byblos in the eleventh century.[42] The later sources are written in different forms of Aramaic, namely the inscription of Zakkur, king of Hamath (c. 800 BCE), who in his distress receives an encouraging oracle from Baal-Šamayin through prophets ([b]yd ḥzyn w byd 'ddn),[43] the inscription of Deir 'Alla from c. 700 BC reporting a vision of Balaam, the 'visionary of the gods' (ḥzh 'lhn),[44] and the roughly contemporary Ammonite Citadel inscription with an oracle of the god Milkom.[45] Finally, Papyrus Amherst 63, an Aramaic text in Demotic script that still lacks an edition, probably includes a

appearance; see the edition in Sachs and Hunger 1996: 216-19; cf. Nissinen 2002a.

34.   In addition to the one mentioned in n. 38, a fourteenth-century letter of the king Tušratta of Mitanni to Amenophis III of Egypt contains a quotation of an oracle of Ištar/Šauška of Nineveh (EA 23); see Moran 1992: 61-62.

35.   That is, Old Babylonian texts from Tuttul (KTT 306.6; see Krebernik 2001; I am indebted to Professor A. Malamat for bringing these sources to my attention) and Elam (MDP 18 171); a Middle-Assyrian proviant list from the thirteenth century mentioning 'prophets and prophetesses' (*maḫḫû, maḫḫūtu*) in Kar-Tukulti-Ninurta (VS 19 1; see Freydank 1974); a Neo-Babylonian list of temple offerings (OECT 1 20-21) and some Neo-Babylonian decrees mentioning people designated as 'sons of Prophet' (YOS 6 18; 7 135).

36.   That is, the Middle Babylonian 'Righteous Sufferer' text from Ugarit (*Ugaritica* V, 162); see Nougayrol 1968: 267-69.

37.   That is, the Late Babylonian *akītu*-Ritual (*RAcc* 144-45); see Thureau-Dangin 1921.

38.   CTH 378; cf. Weippert 1988: 297-99 and the translation in COS 1: 156-60 (Gary Beckman) and in Singer 2002: 56-69.

39.   Emar 373; 379; 383; 406; cf. Fleming 1993.

40.   Nuzi: HSS 13 152.16; 14 149.6 and 14 215.16; Babylonia: KAR 460.16; cf. Lion 2000.

41.   On West Semitic prophetic texts, see Weippert 1988: 300-302; Lemaire 1997; 2001.

42.   Text: Gardiner 1932: 61-76; translation: Miriam Lichtheim in COS 1: 89-93 and Robert K. Ritner in Nissinen 2003a (no. 142).

43.   Text: KAI 202; translation: Alan Millard in COS 2: 155 and Choon-Leong Seow in Nissinen 2003 (no. 137).

44.   Text: Hoftijzer and van der Kooij 1976; translation: Baruch A. Levine in COS 2: 140-45 and Choon-Leong Seow in Nissinen 2003a (no. 138).

45.   Text: CAI 59; translation: William E. Aufrecht in COS 2: 139 and Choon-Leong Seow in Nissinen 2003a (no. 136).

prophetic passage.[46]

6.   Prophecy is even documented in Iron Age Palestine by two or three
     Lachish ostraca from the late seventh century that mention the word
     nb'[47]—and, without doubt, also by the Hebrew Bible which allegedly
     contains prophetic words and references to prophecy from the pre-exilic
     period down to late postexilic times.

In spite of the surprisingly high number of individual extra-biblical texts listed
above, it must be admitted that the evidence for prophecy in the ancient Near East
is haphazard and uneven, the share of the texts from places other than Mari or
(Neo-)Assyria being about one-eighth at best. The vast chronological and geographical distribution of the bits and pieces supplementing the source material from
Mari and Assyria is nevertheless impressive, documenting prophetic activity of
some kind in different parts of the ancient Near East through the centuries and thus
witnessing to an established tradition. Only Egypt is missing from this list; apart
from the Report of Wenamon, no Egyptian texts have thus far been identified as
prophecy (that is, according to our definition; there are a few texts that have borne
this label because they contain predictions of future events[48]). What can be learned
from the wide distribution and meager amount of the documents is that it seems
to have been a rarity that prophecy was ever written down. This is why we are
dependent on the tip of the iceberg that occasionally peeks out from the ocean of
the ancient Near Eastern source material. But even these bits and pieces are important because they show that prophecy indeed is attested all over the ancient Near
East and thus can be regarded as an established tradition and institution among
other forms of divination.

With regard to the Hebrew Bible, the question arises whether everything that is
written in the so-called prophetic books should be called prophecy, and, if not,
whether or not it is possible to separate the prophetic from the non-prophetic in
these writings. These questions are notoriously difficult to address and are open to a
methodological debate about the possibility of identifying the 'authentic' voice of
the prophets, or at least the oldest strata of the prophetic books. This inevitably
leads us to our fourth topic, the interpretation of meanings imposed on prophecy in
the Hebrew Bible.

Ancient Near Eastern Prophecy—Ancient Hebrew Prophecy— Biblical Prophecy

The ancient Near Eastern records of prophecy have turned out to be indispensable
for understanding not only the prophetic phenomenon in general, but also the
cultural and conceptual preconditions of prophecy in the Bible. Mainly because of

---

46.   Translation: Richard C. Steiner in *COS* 1: 309-27; the relevant passage (col. vi, ll. 12-18) is
treated on p. 313.

47.   That is, ostraca 3, 16, and possibly 6; text: *HAE* 412-19, 425-27, 433-34; translation:
Dennis Pardee in *COS* 3: 79-81 and Choon-Leong Seow in Nissinen 2003a (nos. 139-41).

48.   Cf. n. 20.

its long and complicated literary history, the Hebrew Bible constitutes a document very different from other ancient Near Eastern prophetic sources. Not only does the interpretative process of the prophetic books of the Hebrew Bible prevent an immediate access to the historical phenomenon of Israelite and Judaean prophecy, it has produced a great deal of fiction as well.

There is no need to contrast extra-biblical 'facts' with biblical 'fiction', though (cf. Ringgren 1988; Barstad 1993). It cannot be said that there is no ideology or theology, or even fiction, connected with prophecy in extra-biblical sources. That prophecy could be used as an effective tool for political purposes becomes extremely clear from the documents of Mari and Nineveh. The residual documents of Old Babylonian and Neo-Assyrian prophecy have likewise been preserved only to the extent that they have occasionally been written down and handed down to posterity. This was not done as a matter of routine, but for specific reasons. At Mari as well as in Nineveh, the interpretation of prophecy and the attitudes toward prophets were governed by political, social and personal needs and preferences, hence the viability of prophecy was determined by its ideological expedience.

The *ipsissima verba*, that is, the actual spoken words of individual prophets, are as impossible to find in ancient Near Eastern sources as in the Bible. A written prophecy is always scribal work, and it is ultimately beyond our knowledge to determine to what extent the scribe would, or could, transmit the exact wording of the prophecy. The development from oral performance to written record happened under material restrictions and linguistic constraints, and the path from the prophet to the recipient may have been a complicated one.[49] Moreover, the ancient Near Eastern sources include quotations that may be purely literary imitations of prophetic language rather than actually proclaimed prophecies. In this respect, the ancient Near Eastern sources for prophecy are no less enigmatic than the writings of the Hebrew Bible.

Obviously, the problem of *ipsissima verba* emerges from the need to separate the 'original' prophecy from 'secondary' additions and interpretations. However, it does not seem to have been the primary task of the scribes to conserve the words uttered by the prophets in pristine condition but, rather, to make the messages viable and communicable. A prophecy makes no sense if it does not meet with any response in the audience; hence, it must be intelligible to the addressees (cf. van der Toorn 2000a: 232-34). This brings us back to the social dynamic of prophecy, which is not just words from the mouth of the prophet but a process, all components of which are relevant. A prophecy means nothing unless it is understood, interpreted and applied in a specific socio-religious and linguistic environment, whereby interpretation is not a matter of perverting the original words but making the message significant.

What makes the Hebrew Bible a special case is the creative exegetical reinterpretation of prophecy and its application in varying social and ideological circumstances of the Second Temple (both Persian and Hellenistic) period. Admittedly,

---

49. See Sasson 1995: 607; van der Toorn 2000a; Nissinen 2000a; cf. Charpin 2001: 31-33; 2002: 14-16 who reckons with more precise transcriptions of orally delivered prophetic words.

the Neo-Assyrian sources do reveal the beginnings of a comparable development, but nowhere in the ancient Near Eastern literature are we able to find such an interpretative process lasting for centuries, during which prophecy was virtually transformed into exegesis and gradually developed into a theological concept.[50]

The biblical conceptualization of prophecy goes hand in hand with the change in the image of the prophet observable in the Hebrew Bible. As a consequence of the religio-political upheavals of the seventh and sixth centuries BCE (the Assyrian hegemony, the destruction of Jerusalem, the Babylonian exile and the rebuilding of the temple), prophecy, among other things, was assessed from a new perspective. Undoubtedly, prophecy continued to exist in the Second Temple period; however, the somewhat wild and precarious quality of prophecy, the real origin of which is beyond any human control, had to be disciplined to meet the requirements of the authoritative theology, or theologies, of that period. It is by no means exceptional as such that prophecy was supposed to conform to the ideology of prevailing religious and political authorities; in Assyria, for example, the prophets were presumed to promote the imperial royal ideology, and it was highly inappropriate to prophesy against the king or the crown prince (cf. Nissinen 1996). In the postexilic Judaean community, again, the Torah became the precept of prophecy, and Moses, the mediator of the Torah, the model for prophets (Deut. 18.15-22).[51]

As a result of the sixth-century socio-religious changes, the image of a prophet underwent a transformation from diviner into preacher. This transformation happened in a creative literary process in which the prophetic inspiration lived on in the work of the scribes.[52] As heirs of Moses and the prophets,[53] the scribes ultimately structured the image, the history and the canon of biblical prophecy and caused not only the image of the prophets, but prophecy itself to become a literary phenomenon and a part of a symbolic universe where different types of religious tradition—Torah, prophecy and wisdom—were joined together as aspects of the scholarly construct of revelation.[54] The literary prophecy also provided the principal channel of expression for the growing eschatological tendency of the Second Temple period, which caused the biblical prophetic literature to become an eschatological composition and paved the way for later apocalypticism.

Since the bloom of literary prophecy eclipses the concrete manifestations of prophecy, it is difficult to know what actually happened to prophetic activity in the Second Temple period. Even without the assumption of the total cessation of prophecy,[55] it seems that the traditional kind of transmission of divine messages declined

---

50. The conceptualization of prophecy is reflected by the word נְבוּאָה in late biblical (Neh. 6.1; 2 Chron. 9.29; 15.8; Sir. 44.3), Qumran and Mishnaic Hebrew; for this term, see Hurvitz 2000: 151-52.

51. Cf., e.g., Blenkinsopp 1995: 163-65 and Köckert 2000: 98-100.

52. In German, this phenomenon has been called 'prophetische Prophetenauslegung' (Steck 1996) or 'schriftgelehrte Prophetie' (Lau 1994).

53. For the succession of Moses, the prophets and the scribes, see Veijola 2000: 216-18.

54. For the theology of revelation as a scholarly construct in Second Temple Judaism, see van der Toorn 2002.

55. For contrasting views of whether prophecy actually ceased in the Second Temple period,

and became socially marginalized, as implied, for example, by Zech. 13.2-6 (cf. Petersen 1995: 128).

Because of the process described above, the word 'prophecy', being used of the concrete phenomenon as well as of its literary interpretation, has an ambiguous character. The pre-exilic Israelite and Judaean prophecy is represented only to the extent that the exilic and postexilic editors of the Hebrew writings have considered it worthy of reinterpreting. In their present form, the prophetic books of the Hebrew Bible document in the first place how earlier prophecy was chosen, edited, interpreted and rewritten to serve the ends of the editors and to correspond with their idea of prophecy and its significance. This inevitably distorts the picture of pre-exilic prophets and their activities, but even the nature of the postexilic prophecy remains faint in concrete terms.

To overcome the difficulties resulting from this ambiguity, it might be helpful to draw a distinction between *ancient Hebrew prophecy* on one hand and *biblical prophecy* on the other. According to this distinction presented here as a working hypothesis, ancient Hebrew prophecy (or: ancient Israelite prophecy, but this designation has the disadvantage of being connected with problems concerning the concept of 'ancient Israel') describes the concrete transmission of the divine word in the Hebrew language in ancient Palestine by persons that qualify as prophets, that is, a phenomenon belonging to the context of ancient Near Eastern prophecy. Biblical prophecy, for its part, is no longer a representative of the 'authentic' prophetic phenomenon, but a part of a literary, intertextual system, interwoven with the development of the formation of the Hebrew canon consisting of Torah, Prophets and Writings. In other words, biblical prophecy means prophecy as interpreted by those who created the writings that gradually took the shape of what we call the Hebrew Bible. Within this context, all prophecy in these writings belongs to the category of biblical prophecy, which, however, is historically and literally rooted in ancient Hebrew prophecy. Textual remnants of the latter are likely to be found, if not from deep under the Near Eastern ground, then from the bowels of the biblical text. However, the methodological problem concerning their identification in the latter remains to be solved.

BIBLIOGRAPHY

Barstad, Hans
    1993   'No Prophets? Recent Developments in Biblical Prophetic Research and
                Ancient Near Eastern Prophecy', *JSOT* 57: 39-60 (repr. in Philip R. Davies
                [ed.], *The Prophets: A Sheffield Reader* [The Biblical Seminar, 42; Sheffield:
                Sheffield Academic Press, 1996]: 106-26).
Bauer, Walter
    1988   *Griechisch-Deutsches Wörterbuch zu den Schriften des Neuen Testaments
                und der frühchristlichen Literatur* (eds. Kurt and Barbara Aland; Berlin and
                New York: W. de Gruyter, 6th edn).

see Greenspahn 1989 and Sommer 1996.

Ben Zvi, Ehud, and Michael Floyd (eds.)
2000   *Writings and Speech in Israelite and Ancient Near Eastern Prophecy*
            (SBLSymS, 10; Atlanta: Society of Biblical Literature).

Birot, Maurice
1993   *Correspondance des gouverneurs de Qaṭṭunâ* (ARM, 27; Paris: Editions
            Recherche sur les Civilisations).
Blasius, Andreas, and Bernd Ulrich Schipper
2002   *Apokalyptik und Ägypten: Eine kritische Analyse der relevanten Texteaus
            dem griechisch-römischen Ägypten* (OLA, 107; Leuven: Peeters).
Blenkinsopp, Joseph
1995   *Sage, Priest, Prophet: Religious and Intellectual Leadership in Ancient Israel*
            (Louisville, KY: Westminster/John Knox Press).
Cancik-Kirschbaum, Eva
2003   'Prophetismus und Divination: Ein Blick auf die keilschriftlichen
            Quellen', in M. Köckert and M. Nissinen (eds.), *Propheten in Mari, Assyrien
            und Israel* (FRLANT, 201; Göttingen, Vandenhoeck & Ruprecht): 33-53.
Charpin, Dominique
2001   'Prophètes et rois dans le Proche-Orient amorrite', in Lemaire (ed.) 2001:
            21-53.
2002   'Prophètes et rois dans le Proche-Orient amorrite: Nouvelles données,
            nouvelles perspectives', in Charpin and Durand (eds.) 2002: 7-38.
Charpin, Dominique, and Jean-Marie Durand (eds.)
1997   *Florilegium marianum III: Recueil d'études à la mémoire de Marie-Thérèse
            Barrelet* (Mémoires de *NABU*, 4; Paris: SEPOA).
2002   *Florilegium marianum VI: Recueil d'études à la mémoire d' André Parrot*
            (Mémoires de *NABU*, 7; Paris: SEPOA).
Clements, Ronald E.
1997   'Max Weber, Charisma and Biblical Prophecy', in Gitay (ed.) 1997: 89-108.
Coggins, R.J.
1993   'Prophecy—True and False', in H.A. McKay and D.J.A. Clines (eds.), *Of
            Prophets' Visions and the Wisdom of Sages* (FS R. Norman Whybray;
            JSOTSup, 162; Sheffield: Sheffield Academic Press): 80-94.
Durand, Jean-Marie
1988   *Archives épistolaires de Mari I/1* (ARM, 26/1; Paris: Editions Recherche sur
            les Civilisations).
1995   'La religión en Siria durante la época de los reinos amorreos según la docu-
            mentación de Mari', in P. Mander and J.-M. Durand, *Mitología y religión del
            Oriente Antiguo II/1: Semitas occidentales (Ebla, Mari)* (Estudios Orientales,
            8; Sabadell: AUSA): 125-533.
2002   *Florilegium marianum VII: Le culte d'Addu d'Alep et l'affaire d'Alahtum*
            (Mémoires de *NABU*, 8; Paris: SEPOA).
Durand, Jean-Marie, and Michaël Guichard
1997   'Les rituels de Mari', in Charpin and Durand (eds.) 1997: 19-78.
Ellis, Maria deJong
1987   'The Goddess Kititum Speaks to King Ibalpiel: Oracle Texts from
            Ishchali', *MARI* 5: 235-66.
1989   'Observations on Mesopotamian Oracles and Prophetic Texts: Literary and

Historiographic Considerations', *JCS* 41: 127-86.

Fleming, Daniel E.
1993   '*nābû* and *munabbiātu*: Two New Syrian Religious Personnel', *JAOS* 113: 175-83.

Freydank, Helmut
1974   'Zwei Verpflegungstexte aus Kār-Tukultī-Ninurta', *AOF* 1: 55-89.

Gardiner, Alan H.
1932   *Late Egyptian Stories* (Bibliotheca Aegyptiana, 1; Brussels: La fondation égyptologique reine Élisabeth).

Gitay, Yehoshua (ed.)
1997   *Prophecy and Prophets: The Diversity of Contemporary Issues in Scholarship* (SBLSS; Atlanta: Scholars Press).

Grabbe, Lester L.
1995   *Priests, Prophets, Diviners, Sages: A Socio-Historical Study of Religious Specialists in Ancient Israel* (Valley Forge, PA: Trinity Press International).
2000   'Ancient Near Eastern Prophecy from an Anthropological Perspective', in Nissinen (ed.) 2000: 13-32.
2003   'Poets, Scribes, or Preachers? The Reality of Prophecy in the Second Temple Period', in Grabbe and Haak (eds.) 2003: 192-215.

Grabbe, Lester L., and Robert D. Haak (eds.)
2003   *Knowing the End from the Beginning: The Prophetic, The Apocalyptic, and their Relationship* (JSPSup, 46; London and New York: T&T Clark International).

Grayson, A.K.
1975   *Babylonian Historical-Literary Texts* (Toronto Semitic Texts and Studies, 3; Toronto and Buffalo: University of Toronto Press).

Greenspahn, Frederick
1989   'Why Prophecy Ceased?', *JBL* 108: 37-49.

Hallo, W.W., and K. Lawson Younger (eds.)
1997   *The Context of Scripture*. I. *Canonical Compositions from the Biblical World* (Leiden: E.J. Brill).
2000   *The Context of Scripture*. II. *Monumental Inscriptions from the Biblical World* (Leiden: E.J. Brill).
2002   *The Context of Scripture*. III. *Archival Documents from the Biblical World* (Leiden: E.J. Brill).

Hoftijzer, Jacob, and Gerrit van der Kooij
1976   *Aramaic Texts from Deir 'Alla* (DMOA, 19; Leiden: E.J. Brill).

Hübner, Ulrich, and Ernst Axel Knauf (eds.)
2002   *Kein Land für sich allein: Studien zum Kulturkontakt in Kanaan, Israel/ Palästina und Ebirnâri für Manfred Weippert zum 65. Geburtstag* (OBO, 186; Freiburg: Universitätsverlag; Göttingen: Vandenhoeck & Ruprecht).

Huffmon, Herbert B.
1976   'The Origins of Prophecy', in F.M. Cross, W.E. Lemke and P.D. Miller (eds.), *Magnalia Dei: The Mighty Acts of God: Essays on the Bible and Archaeology in Memory of G. Ernest Wright* (Garden City, NY: Doubleday): 171-86.
1992   'Ancient Near Eastern Prophecy', in *ABD*, V: 477-82.
1997   'The Expansion of Prophecy in the Mari Archives: New Texts, New Read-

ings, New Information', in Gitay (ed.) 1997: 7-22.

2000 'A Company of Prophets: Mari, Assyria, Israel', in Nissinen (ed.) 2000: 47-70.

Hurvitz, Avi
2000 'Can Biblical Texts Be Dated Linguistically? Chronological Perspectives in the Historical Study of Biblical Hebrew', in A. Lemaire and M. Sæbø (eds.), *Congress Volume, Oslo 1998* (VTSup, 53; Leiden: E.J. Brill): 143-60.

Joannès, Francis
1988 'Archives épistolaires de Mari I/2: Deuxième partie', in D. Charpin, F. Joannès, S. Lackenbacher and B. Lafont, *Archives épistolaires de Mari I/2* (ARM, 26/2; Paris: Editions Recherche sur les Civilisations).

Klein, Wassilios
1997 'Propheten/Prophetie: I. Religionsgeschichtlich', *TRE* 27: 473-76.

Köckert, Matthias
2000 'Zum literargeschichtlichen Ort des Prophetengesetzes Dtn 18 zwischen dem Jeremiabuch und Dtn 13', in R.G. Kratz and H. Spieckermann (eds.), *Liebe und Gebot: Studien zum Deuteronomium* (FS Lothar Perlitt; FRLANT, 190; Göttingen: Vandenhoeck & Ruprecht): 80-100.

Kolf, Marie C. van der
1957 'Prophetes', in *PW* 45: 797-814.

Koppen, F. van
2002 'Seized by the Royal Order: The Households of Sammêtar and Other Magnates at Mari', in Charpin and Durand (eds.) 2002: 289-372.

Krämer, Helmut
1959 'προφήτης κτλ. A: Die Wortgruppe in der Profangräzität', *TWNT* 6: 783-95.

Krebernik, Manfred
2001 *Tall Bi'a/Tuttul—II, Die altorientalischen Schriftfunde* (WVDOG, 100; Saarbrücken: Saarbrücker Druckerei & Verlag).

Lafont, Bertrand
1984 'Le roi de Mari et les prophètes du dieu Adad', *RA* 78: 7-18.

Lau, Wolfgang
1994 *Schriftgelehrte Prophetie in Jes 56–66* (BZAW, 225; Berlin: W. de Gruyter).

Lemaire, André
1997 'Oracles, politique et littérature dans les royaumes araméens et transjordaniens (IXᵉ–VIIIᵉ s. av. n.è.)', in J.-G. Heintz (ed.), *Oracles et prophéties dans l'antiquité* (Paris: De Boccard): 171-93.

2001 'Prophètes et rois dans les inscriptions ouest-sémitiques (IXᵉ–VIᵉ siècle av. J.C.)', in Lemaire (ed.) 2001: 85-115.

Lemaire, André (ed.)
2001 *Prophètes et rois: Bible et Proche-Orient* (Paris: Cerf).

Lichtheim, Miriam
1973 *Ancient Egyptian Literature: A Book of Readings.* I. *The Old and Middle Kingdoms* (3 vols.; Berkeley: University of California Press).

Lion, Brigitte
2000 'Les mentions de "prophètes" dans la seconde moitié du IIᵉ millémaire av. J.-C.', *RA* 94: 21-32.

Loretz, Oswald

1996   Review of Hallo and Younger (eds.) 1997, *UF* 28: 791-93.

Malamat, Abraham

1998   *Mari and the Bible* (SHCANE, 12; Leiden: E.J. Brill).

Michalowski, Piotr

1993   *Letters from Early Mesopotamia* (SBLWAW, 3; Atlanta: Scholars Press).

Moran, William L.

1992   *The Amarna Letters* (Baltimore: The Johns Hopkins University Press).

Nissinen, Martti

1996   'Falsche Prophetie in neuassyrischer und deuteronomistischer Darstellung',
        in T. Veijola (ed.), *Das Deuteronomium und seine Querbeziehungen*
        (Schriften der Finnischen Exegetischen Gesellschaft, 62; Helsinki: Finnische
        Exegetische Gesellschaft and Göttingen: Vandenhoeck & Ruprecht): 172-95.

1998   *References to Prophecy in Neo-Assyrian Sources* (SAAS, 7; Helsinki: The
        Neo-Assyrian Text Corpus Project).

2000a   'Spoken, Written, Quoted and Invented: Orality and Writtenness in Ancient
        Near Eastern Prophecy', in Ben Zvi and Floyd (eds.) 2000: 235-71.

2000b   'The Socioreligious Role of the Neo-Assyrian Prophets', in *idem* (ed.) 2000:
        89-114.

2001   'City as Lofty as Heaven: Arbela and Other Cities in Neo-Assyrian Proph-
        ecy', in L.L. Grabbe and R.D. Haak (eds.), *'Every City Shall Be Forsaken':
        Urbanism and Prophecy in Ancient Israel and the Near East* (JSOTSup,
        330; Sheffield: Sheffield Academic Press): 172-209.

        2002a 'A Prophetic Riot in Seleucid Babylonia', in H. Irsigler (ed.), *'Wer
        darf hinaufsteigen zum Berg YHWHs?' Beiträge zu Prophetie und Poesie
        des Alten Testaments, Festschrift für Sigurdur Örn Steingrímsson zum 70.
        Geburtstag* (Arbeiten zu Text und Sprache im Alten Testament, 72; St
        Ottilien: EOS Verlag): 62-74.

2002b   'Prophets and the Divine Council', in Hübner and Knauf (eds.) 2002: 4-19.

2003a   [with contributions by Choon-Leong Seow and Robert K. Ritner] *Prophets
        and Prophecy in the Ancient Near East* (SBLWAW, 12; Atlanta: Society of
        Biblical Literature).

2003b   'Neither Prophecies nor Apocalypses: The Akkadian Literary Predictive
        Texts', in Grabbe and Haak (eds.]) 2003: 134-48.

Nissinen, Martti (ed.)

2000   *Prophecy in Its Ancient Near Eastern Context: Mesopotamian, Biblical, and
        Arabian Perspectives* (SBLSymS, 13; Atlanta: Society of Biblical Literature).

Nougayrol, Jean

1968   'Textes suméro-accadiens des archives et bibliothèques privées d'Ugarit',
        Ugaritica, V: 1-446.

Ozan, Grégoire

1997   'Les Lettres de Manatân', in Charpin and Durand (eds.) 1997: 291-305.

Overholt, Thomas W.

1986   *Prophecy in Cross-Cultural Perspective: A Sourcebook for Biblical Research*
        (SBLSBS, 17; Atlanta: Scholars Press).

1989   *Channels of Prophecy: The Social Dynamics of Prophetic Activity* (Minnea-
        polis: Fortress Press).

Oxford Advanced Learner's Dictionary

2000   *Oxford Advanced Learner's Dictionary of Current English* (ed. S. Wehmeier;

Oxford: Oxford University Press, 6th edn).

Parpola, Simo
1993   *Letters from Assyrian and Babylonian Scholars* (SAA, 10; Helsinki: Helsinki University Press).
1997   *Assyrian Prophecies* (SAA, 9; Helsinki: Helsinki University Press).

Petersen, David L.
1995   *Zechariah 9–14 and Malachi: A Commentary* (OTL; Louisville, KY: Westminster/John Knox Press).
1997   'Rethinking the Nature of Prophetic Literature', in Gitay (ed.) 1997: 23-40.
2000   'Defining Prophecy and Prophetic Literature', in Nissinen (ed.) 2000: 33-44.

Pongratz-Leisten, Beate
1999   *Herrschaftswissen in Mesopotamien: Formen der Kommunikation zwischen Gott und König im 2. und 1. Jahrtausend v. Chr.* (SAAS, 10; Helsinki: The Neo-Assyrian Text Corpus Project).

Prophéties et oracles
1994   *Prophéties et oracles. I. dans le Proche-Orient ancient; II. en Égypte et en Grèce* (Supplément au Cahier Evangile, 88-89; Paris: Cerf).

Ringgren, Helmer
1988   'Israelite Prophecy: Fact or Fiction', in J.A. Emerton (ed.), *Congress Volume, Jerusalem 1986* (VTSup, 40; Leiden: E.J. Brill): 204-10.

Roberts, J.J.M.
2002   *The Bible and the Ancient Near East: Collected Essays* (Winona Lake, IN: Eisenbrauns).

Sachs, Abraham J., and Hermann Hunger
1996   *Astronomical Diaries and Related Texts from Babylonia. III. Diaries from 164 B.C. to 61 B.C.* (Österreichische Akademie der Wissenschaften, Philologisch-historische Klasse, Denkschriften, 247; Wien: Österreichische Akademie der Wissenschaften).

Sasson, Jack M.
1995   'Water beneath Straw: Adventures of a Prophetic Phrase in the Mari Archives', in Z. Zevit, S. Gitin and M. Sokoloff (eds.), *Solving Riddles and Untying Knots: Biblical, Epigraphic, and Semitic Studies in Honor of Jonas C. Greenfield* (Winona Lake, IN: Eisenbrauns): 599-608.
1998   'About "Mari and the Bible"', *RA* 92: 97-123.

Schipper, Bernd Ulrich
2002   '"Apokalyptik", "Messianismus", "Prophetie": Eine Begriffsbestimmung', in Blasius and Schipper (eds.) 2002: 21-40.

Shupak, Nili
1989–90 'Egyptian "Prophecy" and Biblical Prophecy: Did the Phenomenon of Prophecy, in Biblical Sense, Exist in Ancient Egypt?', *JEOL* 31: 1-40.

Singer, Itamar
2002   *Hittite Prayers* (SBLWAW, 11; Atlanta: Society of Biblical Literature).

Sommer, Benjamin D.
1996   'Did Prophecy Cease? Evaluating a Reevaluation', *JBL* 115: 31-47.

Steck, Odil Hannes
1996   *Die Prophetenbücher und ihr theologisches Zeugnis* (Tübingen: J.C.B. Mohr [Paul Siebeck]).

Thureau-Dangin, F.

1921   *Rituels accadiens* (Paris: Leroux).
Toorn, Karel van der
    2000a   'From the Oral to the Written: The Case of Old Babylonian Prophecy', in
                Ben Zvi and Floyd (eds.) 2000: 219-34.

    2000b   'Mesopotamian Prophecy between Immanence and Transcendence: A Com-
                parison of Old Babylonian and Neo-Assyrian Prophecy', in Nissinen (ed.)
                2000: 70-87.
    2002   'Sources in Heaven: Revelation as a Scholarly Construct in Second Temple
                Judaism', in Hübner and Knauf (eds.) 2002: 265-77.
VanderKam, James C.
    1995   'Prophecy and Apocalyptics in the Ancient Near East', *CANE* 3: 2083-94.
Veijola, Timo
    2000   *Moses Erben: Studien zum Dekalog, zum Deuteronomismus und zum Schrift-
                gelehrtentum* (BWANT, 149; Stuttgart: Kohlhammer).
Weippert, Manfred
    1981   'Assyrische Prophetien der Zeit Asarhaddons und Assurbanipals', in F.M.
                Fales (ed.), *Assyrian Royal Inscriptions: New Horizons in Literary, Ideologi-
                cal and Historical Analysis* (Orientis Antiqui Collectio, 17; Roma: Istituto
                per l'Oriente): 71-115.
    1988   'Aspekte israelitischer Prophetie im Lichte verwandter Erscheinungen des
                Alten Orients', in G. Mauer and U. Magen (eds.), *Ad bene et fideliter semi-
                nandum* (FS Karlheinz Deller; AOAT, 220; Kevelaer: Butzon & Bercker;
                Neukirchen–Vluyn: Neukirchener Verlag): 287-319.
    1997   'Prophetie im Alten Orient', *Neues Bibel-Lexikon* 3: 196-200.
    2002   '"König, fürchte dich nicht!", Assyrische Prophetie im 7. Jahrhundert v.
                Chr.', *Or* 71: 1-54.

CURRENT ISSUES IN THE STUDY OF OLD TESTAMENT PROPHECY

Robert R. Wilson

Throughout much of his scholarly career, Herbert Huffmon has focused his attention on the subject of prophecy and prophetic literature, both in ancient Israel and in the ancient Near East. In particular he was one of the first scholars in the modern period to recognize the importance of using comparative material, ancient and modern, to understand the social setting out of which biblical prophecy came. As a tribute to his work in this field, the following essay will consider several recent trends in the study of the biblical prophets and then will suggest some fruitful avenues for future research. However, before turning to a consideration of the contemporary scene, it will be helpful to set recent research on prophecy into its broader historical context.

Throughout the past century biblical prophecy has played a central role in communities of faith, both Christian and Jewish. This situation is certainly not just a modern phenomenon, but one which has its roots deep in the Second Temple period, when Jews and Christians began to see the biblical prophets not only as accurate predictors of the future, but as advocates of high moral and theological values. For the most part, similar views were held by the nineteenth-century biblical scholars who shaped the modern field of biblical studies. Julius Wellhausen, for example, believed that the prophets were the creators of ethical monotheism, a position he inherited from his teacher Heinrich Ewald. Similar positions were held by most of his scholarly contemporaries, including Bernhard Duhm and W. Robertson Smith, and have survived deep into the twentieth century in the work of scholars such as Martin Buber, Abraham Heschel, and Yehezkel Kaufmann, among many others (Clements 1976: 51-75).

In the minds of many nineteenth-century scholars, the ethical sensitivity and theological creativity of the prophets could be traced directly to their status as inspired individuals. Under the influence of German Romanticism and the pioneering poetic studies of Robert Lowth, scholars such as Duhm and Hermann Gunkel saw a close connection between inspiration and poetry, which was taken to be a basic feature of prophetic speech, whether oral or written. Thus the traditional picture of the biblical prophet was created: the Israelite prophets were poets, but inspired poets, whose sensitivity to the divine voice created ethical monotheism, a religious perspective that was unique within the biblical world (Wilson 1998: 213-18).

Although this traditional view of the prophet lasted for most of the twentieth century, at least in some scholarly circles, it was continually challenged as biblical scholarship tried to absorb new methods and new data as the century progressed. These challenges were not all equally serious, but at least three of them are worth mentioning, since they were not decisively met in the scholarly discussion. As a result of this failure adequately to meet the challenges, unresolved issues have remained dormant and from time to time have re-emerged to trouble the modern discussion.

First, Duhm and the other early scholars who saw the prophets as divinely inspired poets possessing unique religious insights also recognized that not all of the prophetic material in the Bible was poetry. What, then, was the revelatory status of this others material? Duhm's simple answer to this question was to locate divine inspiration only in the poetry, but such a move greatly reduced the amount of prophetic material that could be considered valuable for ethical and religious purposes (Clements 1976: 54-55). Without intending to do so, Duhm thus raised the question of how the prophet's original experience of inspiration was related to the final literary form in which that inspiration was preserved. This question was soon to become more complicated when Gunkel pointed out the probable oral background of prophetic oracles and also noted their stereotypical character. His work suggested that the path from prophetic inspiration to written text was much more complex than Duhm had realized, but Gunkel never fully worked out how the literary process actually worked (Gunkel 2001).

A second challenge to the traditional picture of the prophet came from Gunkel's observation that prophetic oracles were originally delivered in a particular social setting, an observation that turned scholarly attention to the way that prophets functioned in a particular context. Beginning with the work of Gustav Hölscher on prophetic ecstasy in 1914, a number of scholars have used comparative anthropological data to try to understand Israelite prophecy and in the process have raised serious questions about the uniqueness of prophecy in Israel. While some scholars working in this area have not used sociological comparisons to challenge the validity of the original prophetic experience, others have suggested that sociological comparisons point in the direction of a social determinism that would call the uniqueness of Israelite prophecy into serious question (Blenkinsopp 1996: 35-39).

Finally, the discovery of references to prophetic figures in texts from Mari and Emar and the recent republication of prophetic materials in Neo-Assyrian texts have again raised questions about the uniqueness of prophets in Israel as those figures have traditionally been understood (Parpola 1997; Nissinen 2000; Roberts 2002). To what extent can the distinctive character and theological or ethical value of Israelite prophecy still be maintained when there is accumulating evidence to suggest that Israel's prophets were not all that different from similar figures attested in surrounding cultures?

While some scholars of biblical prophecy have simply tried to ignore these three challenges or have tried to deny their relevance, others have tried to grapple with the challenges, although to date no consensus has been reached on any of them. It should come as no surprise, then, that these same unresolved issues have re-emerged and are playing a role in some of the contemporary debates about the nature of prophecy and the prophetic writings. Although we cannot survey all of the

modern discussion in detail, it is instructive to note how these unresolved challenges have emerged in the recent work of A. Graeme Auld, Robert Carroll, and
Philip R. Davies.

A. Graeme Auld began the most recent wave of attacks against the traditional
view of the Israelite prophet about twenty years ago in an article in which he argued
that the biblical picture of the Israelite prophet was a relatively late creation and
could in fact be seen in the process of formation within the various literary layers of
the book of Jeremiah. Auld pointed out, correctly, that in the poetry of the book
Jeremiah is never given the title 'prophet'. Auld understands this fact to mean that
in the earliest literary layer, the oracle collection, Jeremiah was understood to be a
poet and not a prophet. When individuals bearing the title 'prophet' do appear in
this early material, they are always viewed negatively. On the other hand, in the
book's later prose layer which is shared by the Hebrew and Greek texts, the title
'prophet' is used more neutrally. Finally, in the still later prose found only in the
Hebrew text, the title 'prophet' is applied to Jeremiah himself. According to Auld,
this development in the use of the title reflects a gradual change in the writers'
attitudes about the figure represented by the title and suggests that the traditional
picture of the prophet is a fairly late creation in Israel. He then suggests that the
picture, once developed, was retrojected into other prophetic writings and stories,
including such crucial texts as Deuteronomy 18 (the description of Moses as
prophet) and the prophetic stories in Samuel and Kings that explicitly portray
individuals as prophets in the Mosaic line (Auld 1983).

Scholars fairly quickly responded to Auld's suggestion. Robert P. Carroll immediately reacted positively to Auld's proposal, and took it as support for the thesis
that biblical pictures of prophetic activity were unreliable. The reality of biblical
prophecy, whatever it might have been, cannot be recovered, he argued, and the
interpreter must therefore concentrate on the literary dimensions of prophetic texts.
In short, one should read Jeremiah as a poet without recourse to a misleading picture of Jeremiah as a prophet (Carroll 1983).

Recently Auld's thesis has surfaced again, this time in the context of Philip R.
Davies's book on the canonization of Hebrew Scriptures (Davies 1998). There are
many complex features in Davies's argument, but the following summary is adequate for our purposes. The great civilizations of Mesopotamia and Egypt developed something like literary canons (i.e. textually standardized works grouped
together in a comprehensible way and viewed as core collections of the civilization), but they were able to do so because of highly trained and specialized scribal
guilds that clustered abound the palace and the temple. Canonization was therefore
a government- or temple-sponsored enterprise. The situation in these countries was
very different from the one that existed in Israel, where at least in the pre-exilic
period the government(s) did not wield enough control over the country to establish
the sort of large-scale state-controlled literary activity that was possible elsewhere.
To be sure, there must have been scribes associated with royal courts and temples,
but they were relatively few in number and not necessarily in agreement with each
other religiously or politically. Literacy outside of scribal circles was minimal, and
few people would have been able to create anything like a biblical book. Therefore,

the canonical process in Israel must have begun much later than scholars have usually thought, certainly no earlier than the Persian period, and perhaps not until the Hellenistic period, when Israelite literacy rates rose under the influence of Hellenistic culture.

When these thoughts about literacy and writing are applied to the formation of the prophetic canon, the results are fairly predictable. Davies accepts Auld's argument that prophecy as it is portrayed in the biblical text is a fairly late creation, and Davies then suggests that prophecy as we think we know it from the Bible was created as the literary process leading to canon formation progressed. To put the issue more sharply, the biblical literature, when it was finally formed, *created* biblical prophecy, and did so at a relatively late stage in what we think of as the biblical period.

In a recent article, Davies develops his thinking a bit further (Davies 2000). He suggests that in the pre-exilic period there were Israelite religious figures who delivered divine messages orally to human beings, and probably most particularly to the king. He also suspects that from time to time letters reporting these oracles might have been sent to the king and that the letters would have been filed in the royal archives under the name of the sender or under the name of the intermediary. In time, Davies thinks, oracles from the same individual might have been copied onto the same scroll for the purpose of preservation and for convenience of filing, but these collections would not have resembled a biblical book. In the Persian period or later, as Israelite historians began to shape in writing the history of Israel's political life up to the exile, the stage was set for the written oracle collections to come in contact with the growing notion of a national history. This contact then moved in two directions. On the one hand, the collections of oracles began to pick up historical material that eventually supplied the prophets with a historical context. On the other hand, prophetic oracles invaded the historical narratives, eventually yielding the sorts of stories now preserved in Samuel and Kings.

It is interesting to note that in a peculiar way Auld, Carroll, and Davies all return to the original position of Duhm: the Israelite prophets were poets. However, unlike Duhm, all three of the modern scholars separate poetic creativity from divine inspiration, thus undermining the primary foundation of the traditional view of the Israelite prophet. Prophecy in Israel was primarily a literary phenomenon, at least so far as we can reconstruct it reliably. The traditional notion that the prophetic writings were rooted in the prophets' own religious experiences seems to be missing from Davies's work. Furthermore, prophecy was a relatively late literary phenomenon and must reflect the time of its creation, sometime between the Persian and Hellenistic periods. Finally, although Davies seems willing to allow that Israelite prophecy had some antecedents, he doubts the traditional picture of originally oral oracles being written down at an early stage because, in his view, very few people were capable of writing them down.

The current revisionist views of prophecy not only return the scholarly discussion to its point of origin with Duhm, but they also raise again the three major unresolved complexes of issues that I identified earlier as challenges to the traditional view of prophecy: (1) the question of the path between prophetic inspiration and the final written form of the prophetic texts; (2) the role of society in shaping biblical prophecy; and (3) the extent to which biblical prophecy was influenced by similar phenomena elsewhere in the ancient Near East. Davies in particular has views on all of these issues, and those views constitute a direct challenge to traditional notions of the uniqueness of Israelite prophecy. However, none of his views are immune from criticism, and I would suggest that the next phase of the debate should in fact reopen the issues that he has raised. There is new work to consider with respect to all three complexes of issues, and a re-examination could prove fruitful.

However, in the remainder of this paper I want to concentrate on only one complex of issues: the light which recent work on the relationship between oral and written literature might shed on Davies's arguments.

In recent years scholars of oral literature have considerably refined their notions of how traditional oral cultures make the transition from orality to writing. This new research has been helpfully mediated to the biblical guild by Susan Niditch, and her detailed discussion does not need to be repeated here (Niditch 1996). For biblical scholars, probably the most important point emerging from the new research is that traditional cultures do not in fact leave orality behind when they begin to use writing more heavily. Rather both oral and written literatures continue to exist together for a long period of time and interact with each other in various complex ways.

The implications of this new research for the study of biblical prophecy are just beginning to be explored (Ben Zvi and Floyd [eds.] 2000), but a recent article by James Crenshaw provides a concise outline of the basic issues and suggests a creative new approach to the problem of how oral prophetic oracles eventually became part of written texts (Crenshaw 2000). Crenshaw sees three basic questions that need to be answered: (1) Why were prophetic oracles preserved in the first place? (2) How and by whom were they preserved? (3) Were they preserved orally or in writing?

In order to answer these questions, Crenshaw looks at the situation of wisdom literature, where the picture of the process of preservation and transmission is somewhat clearer. In answering the first question—Why were oracles preserved?— he notes that in the case of wisdom literature there was a feeling that wisdom instruction was thought to be a universally positive force in the shaping of human lives and in the shaping of society in general. The sages thought that their teachings were intrinsically good, and for that reason alone they were worth preserving and passing on to the next generation. At this point, though, it becomes clear that prophetic oracles and wisdom teachings are not fully comparable. Perhaps a few people may have thought that prophecies were good in and of themselves, and such people might have preserved oracles simply because they thought it good to preserve oracles, but this is not highly likely. Crenshaw therefore suggests that perhaps prophetic disciples might have had a vested interest in preserving the words of their master, just as the students of the sage preserved and passed on their master's teachings. Perhaps too temples and royal courts preserved oracles because they touched on issues important to particular officials or institutions, or perhaps these official organizations were simply in the business of preserving everything that came their way.

Without denying these explanations for the preservation of prophecy, I would suggest some other factors that might have been involved. To begin with, although some wisdom writers saw their instruction as having a religious dimension to it, much wisdom was secular, sometimes militantly so. The search for wisdom was a human enterprise and dealt with human and this-worldly things. In contrast, prophecy was clearly religious, and prophets made the claim that the word they transmitted was the pure, unaltered word of the deity. I suspect that almost all of the people in ancient Israel, no matter what their social status or when they lived, early or late, would have been prepared to accept such a claim in principle, even though they might have had doubts about particular claims made by particular individuals. I can therefore imagine a king or a royal bureaucrat deciding that there was no point in taking a chance with a prophetic oracle. It might very well be from the god, so why risk angering the god by ignoring it or throwing it away? Certainly if the prophecy involved a threat or a warning, the recipient would be grateful for the opportunity to avoid disaster. Similarly, if the prophecy contained supportive divine words, they would be taken as an important endorsement for present behavior, even if that behavior were otherwise controversial.

In the society in general, other dynamics may have operated. Prophets who were judged by their societies or even by their support groups to be false (i.e. they built up a bad track record of predictions) were probably eventually forgotten. But the situation with true prophets was somewhat different. These prophets had managed to obtain and keep the support of a group of disciples, who had a vested interest in their prophet. The disciples would have had a clear motive for preserving oracles that turned out to be true, for such oracles would have enhanced the authority of the prophet. Furthermore, the fulfillment of the oracles demonstrated that they were truly of divine origin, and they were therefore thought to be an endless reservoir of revelation. They had more divine truth to reveal, so it would have been important to preserve them so that future generations could hear the divine word for their own time. Examples of this process of reinterpretation can be found within the biblical text itself. Hosea, for example, takes judgment oracles which were eventually fulfilled against the Northern Kingdom and then applies them to Judah (Hos. 6.11). Similarly, Isaiah reinterprets promise oracles that were fulfilled in the period of the Syro-Ephraimitic war and applies them to the Assyrian crisis of 701, when they were again fulfilled. Then the prophet or his disciples recast them as promises directed to the Babylonian exiles (Isa. 7–9). In the case of true prophets whose words were unfulfilled, the disciples would have had an incentive to preserve the oracles because they would not have accepted the judgment that they were in fact unfulfilled. True prophets cannot have unfulfilled oracles, so the problem must lie elsewhere. Perhaps the disciples did not understand the oracles properly, or perhaps they were to be applied to a future time. Perhaps future disciples would realize that the oracles had been fulfilled after all. In any case, the unfulfilled oracles needed to be preserved so that they could eventually be shown to be fulfilled. (Promise oracles by prophets such as Jeremiah, Isaiah, and Ezekiel would fall in this category.)

Finally, some prophetic oracles are terribly obscure, and it may not have been clear to the disciples what the oracles meant or how the disciples (or anyone else) were supposed to react to them. Examples of these sorts of oracles are particularly obvious in Isaiah's words dealing with the crisis of 701, which are a mixture of judgment and promise (Isa. 10; 18; 28–33). Obscurities of this sort would have provided a strong motive for preserving the oracle, so that there could be more time to puzzle over the interpretation.

Crenshaw's answer to the second question—How and by whom were the oracles preserved?—again appeals to an analogy with wisdom. The teachings of the sage were preserved by the disciples, so it is likely that disciples played a role in the preservation of prophetic oracles. Disciples are explicitly mentioned in Isaiah (8.16), and in Jeremiah there are narratives mentioning supporters connected with the royal court (chs. 26 and 36). The narratives in Kings also refer to prophetic groups gathered around Elijah and Elisha. Crenshaw also suspects that in some cases royal or temple archives might have preserved oracles if they involved the king or the religious establishment. It seems to me that Crenshaw has a strong point here, and I fail to understand Davies's reluctance to consider the important role of the prophetic disciples.

Finally, on the last question—Were the oracles preserved orally or in writing?—Crenshaw comes down decisively on the side of oral transmission, again on the analogy with wisdom literature. Wisdom instruction was oral, and students were expected to listen and learn. As Crenshaw accurately notes, even as late as the Persian period people are enjoined to listen to instruction and to take teachings to heart; they are not exhorted to consult a written text.

On the question of oral vs. written, then, Crenshaw takes a position diametrically opposed to that of Davies, who sees very little role for oral transmission. The truth, however, may lie somewhere in between or in some combination of oral and written transmission. Certainly Crenshaw is right that oral transmission would have been available to most members of the society. However, the possibility of the early writing down of oracles cannot be ruled out. Anyone theoretically could become a prophet, and the possibilities would have included priests and royal officials, as well as highly trained technicians such as the Levites. In fact, if the narrative texts are to be believed, there is a connection between the Levites and prophecy, and a prophet like Jeremiah had supporters among court officials, as well as access to a professional scribe. Ezekiel was a priest and presumably also could write, or at least knew people who could. In short, while oral transmission of oracles is likely in the pre-exilic period and perhaps even into the Persian period, there is no evidence to suggest that some writing of prophetic oracles could not have taken place in the pre-exilic period apart from the royal court or temple, particularly in the neighborhood of Jerusalem.

It should be noted that none of this discussion so far touches on the question of the accuracy of the prophetic narratives in Samuel and Kings, and numerous questions remain on this point. Are they in fact as late as Davies claims? In favor of Davies's position would be the observation that the picture of prophetic activity, particularly in the Elijah–Elisha stories, does not much resemble the picture derived from the prophetic books. In Samuel and Kings, prophets are often engaged in miracles and acts of power, while in the writing prophets these features seem largely absent. However, miracles play a large role in stories from the Hellenistic world.

On the other hand, stories like the Elijah and Elisha stories do not seem to fit well against the background of the Persian or Hellenistic periods. The political issues of the stories are very specific, and the religious stance of opposition to the worship of Baal would be difficult to understand against a late background, unless Baal is intended to be a stand-in for any foreign god. Furthermore, the type of Yahwism reflected in the stories is unusual and would be hard to place in the period after the exile. It just doesn't look like post-exilic Yahwism as we know it from undisputed Second Temple texts, and the growing accumulation of evidence on prophecy in Second Temple times suggests that the phenomenon in that period was quite different from what is described in the earlier biblical texts (Gray 1993).

This preliminary examination of just one of the issues raised by the current debates on prophecy also has something to contribute toward assessing the validity of the traditional scholarly view of prophets and prophecy and in particular speaks to the question of the uniqueness of Israelite prophecy. Although Israelite prophecy certainly shared much with similar phenomena in other cultures, both ancient and modern, the notion of a chain of reinterpretations of both fulfilled and unfulfilled prophecies seems to have been peculiar to ancient Israel and its successor communities. This notion has not yet been adequately studied, but it should certainly be on the agenda for future discussions of the traditional view.

BIBLIOGRAPHY

Auld, A. Graeme
    1983   'Prophets Through the Looking Glass: Between the Writings and Moses', *JSOT* 27: 3-23.

Ben Zvi, Ehud, and Michael H. Floyd (eds.)
    2000   *Writings and Speech in Israelite and Ancient Near Eastern Prophecy* (Atlanta: Society of Biblical Literature).

Blenkinsopp, Joseph
    1996   *A History of Prophecy in Israel* (Louisville, KY: Westminster/John Knox Press, rev. edn).

Carroll, Robert P.
    1983   'Poets Not Prophets', *JSOT* 27: 25-31.

Clements, Ronald E.
    1976   *One Hundred Years of Old Testament Interpretation* (Philadelphia: Westminster Press).

Crenshaw, James
    2000   'Transmitting Prophecy across Generations', in Ben Zvi and Floyd (eds.) 2000: 31-44.

Davies, Philip R.
    1998   *Scribes and Schools: The Canonization of the Hebrew Scriptures* (Louisville, KY: Westminster/John Knox Press).

2000 '"Pen of Iron, Point of Diamond" (Jer. 17.1): Prophecy as Writing', in Ben Zvi and Floyd (eds.) 2000: 65-81.

Gray, Rebecca
1993 *Prophetic Figures in Late Second Temple Jewish Palestine* (New York: Oxford University Press).

Gunkel, Hermann
2001 'The Prophets: Oral and Written', in *idem, Water for a Thirsty Land* (ed. K.C. Hanson; Minneapolis: Fortress Press): 85-133.

Niditch, Susan
1996 *Oral World and Written Word* (Louisville, KY: Westminster/John Knox Press).

Nissinen, Martti
2000 *Prophecy in Its Ancient Near Eastern Context* (Atlanta: Society of Biblical Literature).

Parpola, Simo
1997 *Assyrian Prophecies* (SAA, 9; Helsinki: Helsinki University Press).

Roberts, J.J.M.
2002 'The Mari Prophetic Texts in Transliteration and English Translation', in *idem, The Bible and the Ancient Near East* (Winona Lake, IN: Eisenbrauns): 157-253.

Wilson, Robert R.
1998 'The Prophetic Books', in John Barton (ed.), *The Cambridge Companion to Biblical Interpretation* (Cambridge: Cambridge University Press): 212-25.

Part II

PROPHECY IN THE HEBREW BIBLE
AND THE ANCIENT NEAR EAST

THE LAMENTING PROPHET AND THE MODERN SELF:
ON THE ORIGINS OF CONTEMPORARY READINGS OF JEREMIAH

Mary Chilton Callaway

> Jeremiah is the most accessible of the prophets;
> Jeremiah is the most hidden of the prophets.
> —Herbert Huffmon (1999: 261)

The Jeremiah that inhabits twentieth-century Bibles and commentaries is a man alienated from his culture, conflicted in his feelings and anguished in his prayer. Gerhard von Rad, whose *Message of the Prophets* still has a place in many college and seminary courses, writes of the Confessions, 'The intimacy of spiritual inter-course with God here revealed, the maturity of self-expression, and the freedom in admitting one's own failure and making no concealment of God's censure, is a manifestation of the human spirit at its noblest' (von Rad 1962; 1965: 173-75). More recently Walter Brueggemann (1998: 114) describes the Confessions as 'the most direct, candid and intimate prayers that we know about in the O.T. ... These passages are models for the depth of honesty that is appropriate in prayer.' Although the years between von Rad and Brueggemann have brought significant advances in Jeremiah scholarship, the portrait of the prophet as a model for the anxious life of faith in the twentieth century has remained constant. A variation on this theme suggests that conflict with the political and religious leaders of Judah was mirrored by the more important spiritual torment within the prophet's own inner depths. Von Rad writes that one reading the Confessions 'is haunted by the impression that the darkness keeps growing, and eats ever more deeply into the prophet's soul'.[1] When he concludes, 'The darkness that the prophet was powerless to overcome...constitutes a menace to very much more than the life of a single man: God's whole way with Israel hereby threatens to end in some kind of meta-physical abyss', von Rad makes Jeremiah the existential prophet *par excellence* for the twentieth century (1965: 174). The portrait of Jeremiah as a man characterized by inner struggles with himself and God is equally prevalent in both those com-mentaries that assume the biblical text presents a somewhat constructed character and those that assume the text is transparent.[2]

---

1.   See von Rad 1965: 172. In his commentary, *Jeremiah*, Jack Lundbom titles the section on Jer. 20.7-14 'The Prison Within' (Lundbom 1999: 851). The heading for these verses in the NAB is 'Jeremiah's Interior Crisis'. For a trenchant analysis of why this language does not reflect the anthropology of ancient Israel, see Di Vito (1999) and Anderson (1991).

2.   The former is seen, for example, in Brueggemann (1998) and Polk (1984), while the latter view is held by Thompson (1980) and Holladay (1986, 1989).

This reading of Jeremiah finds its immediate roots in nineteenth-century biblical scholarship, in which *Wissenschaft* is intertwined with German Romanticism. Bernhard Duhm, whose commentary remains influential in part through its echoes in von Rad's work, adds a lengthy summary statement at the end of his comments on Jer. 20.14-18. He is among the first to use the term 'confessions':

> Such a poem in the mouth of a prophet is almost alarming to us. A Christian would consider it an offense to speak in this way. We have here a man who, driven by despair, exposed his emotions without concern and exhibited shocking frankness when he let the whole world know what he had experienced and how he had felt himself to be weak... It is as if he were making a public confession (*Beichte*) or wanted to punish himself, in that he bluntly reveals his weakness... For any man of natural feeling (*natürlichem Gefühl*), Jeremiah succeeds in the highest degree precisely in these confessions (*Konfessionen*)... It would be most desirable to be able to discover the particular occasion of this lament (*Klage*). However, in spite of Baruch's biography, a great deal of the life of Jeremiah remains hidden from us. We must be thankful that Jeremiah himself has allowed us to look so deeply into his inner life, as no other Old Testament writer has done. He is the most personal (*subjektivste*) of all the prophets; he shows that here in these confessions (*Konfessionen*), in that he never betrays in them the least hint that he thinks his suffering might serve the good of his people. (Duhm 1901: 168)

It is Jeremiah's sensibility that gives him affinity with Duhm and his contemporaries of 'natural feeling'. Although the terms are by no means identical, Duhm's '*natürlich Gefühl*' and Brueggemann's 'honesty' are genetically related, and each resonates with deep-seated cultural norms of its day. There is some resistance to the dominant reading of Jeremiah but it is on the whole, in the words of Robert Carroll, 'a majority report on the book of Jeremiah which will continue to flourish wherever the Bible is read'.[3]

Has the sixth-century prophet of western Asia been transformed into a paradigm of Western culture? Since he seems to be here to stay, this Jeremiah is worthy of some investigation. An intimation of his character may well inhabit the biblical book that bears his name, but the introspective character that Western culture now calls Jeremiah came into being slowly, with the contributions of faithful readers past becoming virtually embedded in the received text through translation, liturgy, religious tradition and art. Like Ricouer's 'dead metaphor', this modern reading of Jeremiah has become so ubiquitous that it is virtually invisible as interpretation. It has come to be the 'plain sense' of the text. My purpose here is to explore its origins, not to discredit it, but to understand it as a theological rather than a historical-critical reading.[4]

---

3.   Carroll 1986: 56; see also Reventlow 1963. W. Baumgartner's 1917 form-critical study of the Confessions as laments gave nuance to the psychological interpretations. For a useful overview of scholarship, see Diamond 1987: 11-16.

4.   K. Stendahl (1963) showed the importance of this distinction when he challenged modern psychological readings of Paul in his now classic 'Paul and the Introspective Conscience of the West'. That article was reprinted in Stendahl 1976 with a response to Käsemann's critique on pp. 128-33.

Jeremiah's First Interpreters

Jeremiah has from the beginning been somewhat shaped in the image of his inter-preters. Efforts to tease apart the layers of the biblical book of Jeremiah, while by no means finished, have led to a broad consensus that the exilic redactors shaped the prophet's words in ways that supported their understanding of themselves as the true remnant of Judah. The explicit identification of the good and bad figs in Jer. 24.5-10 is but one example of redaction that shaped Jeremiah's words into an affir-mation of the exilic community. Although disagreement remains about the precise dating of these verses, it is hardly in doubt that words have been put into Jeremiah's mouth for the purpose of supporting the identity of an exilic community.[5] The com-plexity of the figure of Jeremiah in the biblical book is at least in part a result of the various groups responsible for preserving the prophet's words and vying to shape his life into a story compatible with their own. That no one succeeded fully, so that the 'historical' Jeremiah has eluded the grasp of readers from the very beginning, is a testimony to the vigorous interpretative activity that characterized the formation of the book of Jeremiah. The process of shaping the prophet into a figure who resembles his readers was already deeply inscribed on the biblical text itself.

Although the modern emphasis on Jeremiah's inner life is notably absent from the interpretations found in the luxuriant growth of Second Temple literature, interest in the *figure* of the prophet is apparent. One of the earliest stories becomes so persistently reiterated in variant forms that it might almost be called the received tradition about Jeremiah from the Second Temple era. The earliest witness appears to be 2 Macc. 2.1-8, part of a letter written to encourage the Jews in the Egyptian diaspora to observe the festival commemorating Judas Maccabeus' rededication of the temple. According to the story, Jeremiah told the exiles to take with them some of the fire from the altar of the temple. Then 'he ordered that the tent and the ark should follow with him' to a cave on Mt Sinai, where he hid them, along with the altar of incense, and sealed the cave. Rebuking followers who had tried to mark the way, he declared, 'The place shall remain unknown until God gathers his people together again and shows his mercy' (2 Macc. 2.7).[6] The story clearly gives support to the new festival of Hanukkah, called in 2 Macc. 1.18 'the festival of the fire', by demonstrating an unbroken chain of authorities who preserved the temple fire from Jeremiah to the present. The biblical prophet who bitterly attacked the false religion of the temple becomes here an authority for rededicating it; the biblical prophet who saw that the temple treasures must fall into the hands of the enemy is here transformed into one who preserves them from harm. The elaboration of these traditions in the Baruch literature, and especially the heightening of miraculous and eschatological elements, is only one indication of the way that the literary Jeremiah

---

5.   See, for example, Seitz 1989; McKane (1986: 605-17) offers a balanced summary of views.

6.   Although the origin of this story is not known, the textual stimulant on which it is based is probably Jer. 3.16; the list of Temple vessels in Jer. 27.19-20 and 52.17-23, which lack the treasures hidden by Jeremiah in the story, may also be an influence.

was, in John Barton's words, 'made in the image of the prophetic figures known in the late Second Temple period' (Barton 1999: 317).

The aspect of Jeremiah's persona that is perhaps most widely used and recognized is that of weeping prophet. Textual pegs on which to hang the tradition are easily identified (Jer. 9.1, 18; 13.17; 14.17), but the reason for the tradition's persistent influence is probably the Septuagint's title θρῆνοι ιερεμιας ('Lamentations of Jeremiah') for the Hebrew *Echa*. The figure of Jeremiah is brought into sharp focus by the Septuagint's superscription: 'And it happened after the capture of Israel and the ruin of Jerusalem that Jeremiah sat down weeping and lamented this lament over Jerusalem'. The image of the lamenting prophet is extensively elaborated in the narratives of *2 Baruch* and *4 Baruch*. The latter has Jeremiah weeping five times in the space of 24 hours. Hearing that God is about to destroy Jerusalem, Jeremiah cries to Baruch 'Avoid the rending of your garments, but rather let us rend our hearts; and let us not draw water for the troughs, but let us weep and fill them with tears. For the Lord will not have mercy on this people' (*4 Bar*. 2.5).[7] Jeremiah weeps before, during and after the fall of Jerusalem. This Jeremiah is a palimpsest on the biblical prophet, for the readers understand his tears, like their own, to be for the destruction of the temple in 70 CE. The tradition of the weeping prophet has similarly influenced Luke's distinctive portrait of Jesus (Lk. 19.41-48). Only Luke prefaces the 'cleansing of the temple' by showing Jesus outside Jerusalem speaking prophetic words of doom that echo Jer. 6.6, and weeping over the city, in a verbal echo of the LXX superscription to Lamentations. Finally, the authority of the weeping prophet tradition became secure in the West when, in 1611, the translators of the KJV rendered the title of *Echa* as 'The Lamentations of Jeremiah'. Although they generally favored the original Hebrew over church tradition, the translators in this case followed the Septuagint and Jerome's Vulgate in attributing Lamentations to Jeremiah. With this decision they inscribed the midrashic figure of the weeping Jeremiah on the text of the English Bible.

One more tradition about the figure of Jeremiah worth noting here is the insistence in the post-biblical literature that the prophet was outside the city when it fell to the Babylonians. It is a puzzling interpretive turn, because the Bible clearly places Jeremiah in Zedekiah's court of the guard during the fall of Jerusalem (Jer. 32.1-3; 39.11-14). Yet both *2* and *4 Baruch* open with scenes in which Jeremiah is ordered to leave the city before it falls to Nebuchadnezzar because 'your works are for this city like a firm pillar and your prayers like a strong wall' (*2 Bar*. 2.2). Jeremiah was to be an iron pillar and bronze wall against the people of Judah (Jer. 1.18); in the Second Temple traditions this role is turned inside out and the prophet's presence actually insulates Jerusalem from destruction. Why is this? We may find a clue in the many stories about the efficacy of good works and prayer (especially of a seer or holy person) in the religious literature of Second Temple Judaism. The Jeremiah of *2 Baruch* is a contemporized version of the biblical figure; a model of the holy seer whose very person embodies divine power. The

---

7. Text taken from *OTP*: II, 418.

tradition is enriched in rabbinic tradition, in the homily of *Pesiqta Rabbati* 26.[8] When the Holy One lures Jeremiah out of Jerusalem to buy his uncle's property (Jer. 32.6; 37.11-12), an angel breaches the city walls, saying, 'Let the enemies come and enter the House, for the Master of the House is no longer within'. Seeing the smoke rising from the burning city Jeremiah cries out, 'O Lord, you have deceived me' (Jer. 20.7). Here the biblical prophet's brief against God has been transformed in the *Pesiqta* into a prayer of anguish because Jeremiah has become the cause of his people's destruction. Like earlier stories, this one portrays Jeremiah as one who beautifully embodies the primary religious values of his interpreters, values quite different from the ones that underlie nineteenth- and twentieth-century psychological readings of Jer. 20.7.

In summary, we have seen that the Jeremiah of Jewish and Christian tradition by the third century CE was at least in part a holy seer who hid the Ark until the Endtime, and who witnessed the burning of Jerusalem from outside the city, where he sat mourning its destruction with laments and weeping. This glimpse at the early *Nachleben* of Jeremiah aims only to highlight the traditions that occurred repeatedly in different contexts across several centuries. One of these in particular will persist in its influence on how the Bible was read in the West.

Rembrandt's Jeremiah

The era of the Second Temple and the first few centuries after its fall produced a rich lode of stories and traditions about Jeremiah, but few of them appear in modern interpretations of the prophet. An exception is the tradition of the weeping prophet, inscribed on English Bibles in the title of Lamentations as well as in artistic representations of Jeremiah. It was this ancient tradition, newly interpreted in the seventeenth century, that laid the groundwork for the modern readings of Jeremiah as paradigm of the modern religious person. The Renaissance had already bequeathed a retrieval of the classical idea that 'man is the measure of all things'. Erasmus read the Bible in Greek and Hebrew, and used it as a plumb line to test the traditions and practices of the Church. This new role of the Bible, coupled with Renaissance exuberance over the power of human intellect, fueled the movement to produce English translations of the Bible in the fifteenth and especially the sixteenth centuries. To the high anthropology of the Renaissance, the Reformers on the Continent and in England added a theological dimension that forever changed the status of the Bible in Christianity. In their belief that people were capable of encountering God more or less directly through the words of Scripture, they emphasized the human heart and mind as a primary arena of divine activity. This Reformation ideal informs a gloss to the reader on the New Covenant prophecy in Jer. 31.31-34, printed in the margins of the Geneva Bible (1560): 'I will give them faith and knowledge of God for remission of their sins...so that it shall not seem to come so much by the preaching of my ministers as by the instruction of my holy Spirit' (Hill 1993: 272).

---

8.   See Braude 1968; for a fuller analysis see Callaway 1996.

Figure 1. *Rembrandt,* Jeremiah Lamenting the Destruction of Jerusalem *(1630)*
(Rijksmuseum, Amsterdam)

Rembrandt's famous painting *Jeremiah Lamenting the Destruction of Jerusalem* (1630) is a visible marker of a new understanding of the prophet, one that continues the ancient fascination with the figure of the man while changing the focus from external actions to inner life. Emphasis on the interior life of the prophet is so much a part of modern historical-critical commentaries and annotated Bibles that it is almost invisible as a development in the history of exegesis. Of course there is no straight line from the interpretations of the seventeenth century to those of the twentieth. In fact, the earliest written mention of the painting goes back only to a record of sale in 1767, which describes it as Lot outside the burning Sodom. The identification of the subject as Jeremiah lamenting the destruction of Jerusalem seems to appear first in 1897 (Bruyn 1982: 282). However, Rembrandt's *Jeremiah* provides evidence that the foundation for modern interest in the inner life of the prophet began to be laid in the seventeenth century.

The painting was done when Rembrandt was twenty-four years old, during a period of fascination with representing the faces of old men in chalk drawings as well as paintings. Simon Schama has described it as 'arguably the most haunting of all Rembrandt's solitary patriarchs of this period'.[9] Until recently, art historians believed that the model for Jeremiah might have been Rembrandt's father, Harmen Gerritszoon van Rijn, a successful miller who had gone blind. Although the identity of the model remains uncertain, the same old man clearly appears in Rembrandt's painting *The Apostle Paul at His Writing Desk*, completed just before *Jeremiah*. His is also the face portrayed in several *tronies*, facial portraits that capture the personality of the subject.[10] Like these portraits, *Jeremiah* foregrounds the distinctive features of the old man in the manner of a character study. With different props and background, this Jeremiah could indeed be a miller from Leiden. The prophet is at the center, bathed in light, and the destruction of Jerusalem is a darkened and distant background. By choosing the genre of portrait rather than the traditional narrative painting most often used to illustrate biblical scenes, Rembrandt shifted the focus from the story of Jerusalem to the person of Jeremiah. To understand how this happened, it will be helpful to identify the elements generated by biblical traditions over against those that pressed on the artist from his own culture.

Exegetical Tradition in Rembrandt's Jeremiah

The primary elements of the painting represent aspects of the Jeremiah tradition that are not found in the biblical book, but abundantly elaborated in the apocryphal and pseudepigraphal literature of early Judaism. Jeremiah is lamenting *outside* the burning city, in accordance with the Septuagint and the traditions of *2* and *4 Baruch* as well as the later rabbinic version in *Pesikta Rabbati*. The figure of the angel holding a flaming torch, barely visible above the burning city, is integral to the story in *Pesikta* and its forerunners. The treasures heaped up by the prophet's left arm are not the δῶρα ('gifts') given by the Babylonian captain of guard mentioned in LXX Jer. 40.5, but the δωρεάις πολυτελέσιν ('rich gifts') of Josephus's version (*Ant.* 10.157-58). The curious position of the prophet's right arm and foot create awkwardness so uncharacteristic of Rembrandt's poses that it must be significant. It is perhaps an image of the story in *Pesikta Rabbati* 26. The prophet's absence from Jerusalem, which allowed its destruction, mirrors the biblical trope of God withdrawing his right arm in the time of Israel's need. Throughout the Psalter God's right hand is a source of deliverance, but the poetry of Lamentations inverts the image:

> He has cut down in fierce anger
>   all the might of Israel;
> he has withdrawn his right hand from them
>   in the face of the enemy... (Lam. 2.3a)[11]

---

9.   Schama 1999: 281; Schama's analysis of Rembrandt's social and religious context in 1630 (pp. 270-83) is superb.

10.   For the standard art historical presentation, see Bruyn 1982: 278-84.

11.   Sandford Burdick of the Hebrew University of Jerusalem appears to be the first to propose this interpretation. He sees the figure of the prophet as a stand-in for the divine presence (Burdick 1988).

Most obviously, the image of the *sitting* lamenting prophet is emblematic of post-biblical interpretation. Rembrandt's painting, then, clearly portrays the *interpreted* Jeremiah of early Judaism. Could Rembrandt have known the literary form of these traditions? The University of Leiden was rich in Jewish scholars as well as bibliographic resources, and it was an important center for biblical studies.[12] Rembrandt's interest in literary sources of ancient biblical interpretation is apparent in the fact that he owned a copy of Josephus's *Antiquities*.[13]

In addition to reading the biblical Jeremiah through the lens of Jewish tradition, Rembrandt drew from a long established Christian iconographic tradition of Jeremiah lamenting the fall of Jerusalem. A brief look at two predecessors of *Jeremiah* will illustrate the ways that Rembrandt transformed the traditional iconography of Jeremiah to serve his interest in the realistic representation of the face as representative of the inner life of the person.

An early image appears in the ninth-century Greek manuscript *Sacra Parallela*.[14]

Figure 2. *Jeremiah's Lamentation over Jerusalem*, Sacra Parallela, *Fol. 258v.*
(Bibliothèque nationale de France, Paris)

12. See Perlove 1995: 168 n. 21; Perlove argues that the destruction of the Temple was cited often in contemporary Dutch Protestant literature as a warning against schism, especially the conflict between orthodox Calvinists and the more liberal Remonstrants, who rejected the idea of predestination.

13. Rembrandt's extensive reliance on the *Antiquities* is documented by Tümpel 1984: 185. See also Zell's contribution to the exhibition catalogue 'Rembrandt Creates *Rembrandt*: Art and Ambition in Leiden, 1629–1631' (Zell 2000). Josephus's use of Jeremiah is analyzed in Begg 1995.

14. Although the date is secure, there is debate over whether the provenance is Palestinian or Italian. See Weitzmann 1979.

The city and the prophet form a diagonal on the page, in a juxtaposition that is the early artistic representation of narrative. The image appears to be an almost literal interpretation of the Septuagint's superscription to Lamentations. The prophet's eyes direct the viewer's attention toward the doomed city, just as his words evoke its image in the biblical text. At the same time, the beautiful city in the picture can represent the heavenly Jerusalem, to which the prophet's uplifted eyes gaze. Jeremiah is an eschatological prophet, in keeping with traditional exegesis of his oracles of restoration and with the allusion in Mt. 16.14. The illumination therefore simultaneously represents the plain and the anagogical sense of Scripture, following the exegetical scheme of John Cassian (c. 360–440 CE)[15]

Although Rembrandt did not know this image, the continuity of its elements in artistic tradition is visible in a Dutch Bible that the Rembrandt scholar J. Bruyn suggests 'may well have been Rembrandt's point of departure' (Bruyn 1982: 282-83).

Figure 3. *Headpiece to Lamentations of Jeremiah
in Willem Vorsterman's Bibel (Antwerp, 1532)
(University Library of Amsterdam, Rare Book Department)*

Like the Greek illumination, this Dutch woodcut shows the prophet seated outside the walls of Jerusalem. The same diagonal arrangement, moving from lower left to upper right corner, organizes the picture. However, two differences are apparent. First, the prophet and the city are integrated into a single landscape; Jeremiah is clearly sitting outside the city rather than simply thinking about it. More important, though, is the way the sixteenth-century artist has reinterpreted the scene. The prophet's gesture, as well as his eyes, directs the viewer's gaze not to Jerusalem but to the book on the ground. It is the very book in the reader's hands, not the scroll of the sixth-century prophet, but the codex of a printed Bible. Even the prophet's cap, in line with the book, makes him a contemporary of his readers, a figure of the

---

15.   See du Lubac 1988: 134-38. Cassian likens Scripture to a fertile field, whose fruits can be divided into four lots.

Reformation. The truth of the prophet's words was sadly confirmed by history; their truth for the reader's own life must be discovered by meditative reading of the book.

The pose of Rembrandt's Jeremiah is clearly borrowed from iconographic tradition that visually represented the Septuagint's superscription to Lamentations. In addition to the two above, an image of the prophet sitting on a hill outside Jerusalem appears in the widely used *Speculum humanae salvationis*, a lavishly illustrated fourteenth-century history of salvation whose printed version is one of the first books printed in the Netherlands. Michelangelo's massive Jeremiah, painted just over a hundred years earlier than Rembrandt's, sits in a similar pose. Albrecht Dürer's widely known drawing of *Melancholia* was quite possibly an influence as well.[16] Although Rembrandt began with traditional iconography of Jeremiah, he dramatically changed the focus from the role of the prophet to the face of the man. A diagonal of light that is both fire consuming Jerusalem and illumination of the prophet divides the picture. The distinctive use of light and shadow, Rembrandt's signature use of *chiaroscuro*, focuses the viewer's attention on the prophet's face, bathing it in a luminous glow. The traditional pose of Jeremiah has been transformed into an individual face full of years and pain. The wisps of gray hair and the wrinkles on the brow, caught in the light, signal to the viewer the prophet's life of sorrow. Also caught in the light is his bare foot. Although it is part of the traditional iconography, Jeremiah's bare foot here is startling in the context of the formal garments, and it highlights his humanity.

In the two illustrations above, the prophet's eyes and hand direct the viewer's gaze. But if the Jeremiah in Vorsterman's Bible directs us to open the Scriptures on the ground, Rembrandt's Jeremiah draws us inward. The picture compels the viewer to focus on the human person palpably present at the center of the painting. The distancing of Jerusalem, the luminous face, and the inward gaze of the prophet all draw the viewer into Jeremiah's interior world. While the earlier pictures of Jeremiah outside Jerusalem represented the power of the divine word, Rembrandt's portrait emphasizes the humanity of the prophet who himself is the locus of the divine word. His gaze directs us not to the arena of history, the burning Jerusalem, nor to the book under his elbow, but inward, to the tormented soul of the prophet.

Seventeenth-Century Culture in Rembrandt's Jeremiah

If Rembrandt's *Jeremiah* is indebted to Jewish tradition and traditional iconography, it is equally infused with the culture of seventeenth-century Holland. Three factors in particular are pertinent to our study. The first is the artistic convention of portrait painting. Rembrandt was of course not the first to paint realistic human figures full of emotions and passions, but he lived in a time when artists were

---

16.   Bruyn (1982: 281) notes that 'the attitude of the figure is related to the usual formula for Melancholy'. Benjamin Binstock (1997: 245) creatively proposes that 'the splendors of the Temple are displaced and rendered useless, like the instruments for measuring the world at the feet of Dürer's Melancholia'.

beginning to articulate the challenge of art to make visible what is interior and unseen. The first Dutch treatise on painting, *Schilder-boeck*, written in 1604 by Karel van Mander, two or three years before Rembrandt was born, was widely read and reprinted. An unusual section of the manual was the chapter on *affecten*, the passions. Van Mander was influenced by the conventions of theater, and exhorted artists to portray a subject's passions by careful use of posture and gestures. But the face was to be the primary messenger of the passions. The area of the brow espe-cially afforded a theatre for the emotions. Van Mander describes eyes as 'mirrors of the spirit', 'windows of the soul', and 'the seat of desire, the messengers of the heart' (Schama 1999: 19). Van Mander's language reflects the growing fascination with the idea that the human person was above all an interior space in which dramas of the passions were played out.

The most significant aspect of Dutch culture for our purposes is the central place of the Bible, particularly in Leiden, Holland's second largest city. The University of Leiden was founded in 1575 as a gift from William of Orange in recognition of the citizens' tenacious defense of the city during a yearlong siege by the Spanish. The experience of oppression and subsequent freedom from the Spanish had particularly cemented the affinity of the Dutch for the 'Jews' of the Old Testament (Landsberger 1946: 105-109). Biblical studies were important from the beginning, carried out by a faculty that included Hebraists and a library holding, *inter alia*, Daniel Bomberg's first printed Hebrew Bible with rabbinic commentary (1524–25). The official Dutch translation of the Bible was produced in Leiden between 1626 and 1635. The Bible in the Netherlands in the seventeenth century was a 'dramati-cally humanized Scripture' (Schama 1999: 199), intended to help Christians read the biblical stories as their own story. Paintings of biblical characters and scenes were prominent features in the prosperous homes of Dutch merchants and magis-trates. In good Calvinist understanding, these works of art were neither adornments (that would be too worldly) nor enhancements to prayer (that would be too Catho-lic), but representations that made Scripture part of the daily life of the household. The humanistic portrayal of biblical characters made them like fellow inhabitants of the room and companions along the way. Calvin often likened Scripture to a mirror, set before God's people to show them who they are and what they should do.[17] Rembrandt's biblical paintings put this mirror onto the wall of the patron's home.

A third factor that colored Rembrandt's interpretation of Jeremiah was the theology of John Calvin. Calvinism was the religion of Leiden, which was full of tension between the dominant Calvinist Reformed Church and the more liberal Remonstrants, who sought to soften the strict election theology. Calvin wrote an extensive commentary as well as over 300 homilies on Jeremiah, of which only twenty-five are extant. The commentary blends a proto-scientific approach that places the prophet in his historical context with frequent references to the ecclesi-astical struggles with 'Papists' facing Calvin and his colleagues. Calvin's description

---

17. For example, Calvin comments on Jer. 15.20 that 'the condition of all God's servants is set before us as in a mirror' (Owen 1950).

of Jeremiah's historical context is telling: 'The first thing then to be observed is the time when he began to teach: as religion was then so corrupted, and every one invented errors to suit his own humor, the office of Jeremiah must have been hard and arduous' (Owen 1950: 1). Calvin sees an almost perfect congruence between Jeremiah's situation and his own. Not surprisingly, then, the anthropology of the seventeenth century is also read into the biblical text in Calvin's commentary. One of his constant themes is the interplay between the hidden depths of the human heart and the Word of God. For example, interpreting Jer. 11.18, Calvin paraphrases the prophet's (imaginary) response to his persecutors:

> The recesses of the heart are indeed intricate, and great darkness is within; but God sees more clearly than men. Cease then to make this objection which ye are wont to raise against me, that I am presumptuous in bringing forth to light what lies hid in darkness, for God has appointed me to bring these commands to you: as he knows the heart, and as nothing escapes him, and as he penetrates into our thoughts and feelings, so he has also designed by his word which he has put in my mouth to render public what ye think is concealed. (Owen 1950: 110)

The text of Jer. 11.18 says that God gives Jeremiah knowledge of the plots his enemies are hatching against him; in Calvin's elaboration, the divine searchlight illumines not simply plans, but whatever lies within 'the recesses of the heart'. For Calvin the historical prophetic word that 'renders public what ye think is concealed' becomes for Christians the Word of God that 'penetrates into the inmost thoughts and hidden feelings, even to the marrow and bones, so as to distinguish between thoughts and feelings' (Owen 1950: 111). Calvin's commentaries repeatedly relate the words of the prophet to his interior disposition. Two contemporary theological ideas are rather clearly read into the text of Jeremiah. The first is that God acts in the hidden depths of the heart; the second is that this encounter between God and the inner person occurs most reliably through the Scriptures and prayer.

Conclusions

In Rembrandt's Leiden, the human heart was the intimate arena in which the faithful knew God, and Scripture was the teacher that prepared the heart. True to this theological understanding, in Rembrandt's painting divine activity is not outside, in the burning city, but inside the prophet. Rembrandt's Jeremiah was a person like the viewer; consequently, his inward gaze could draw viewers to contemplate God's activity in the landscape of their own souls. Calvin and Rembrandt were part of a much larger history that would ultimately lead to the modern idea of the self and the privileging of inner experience.[18] But Rembrandt's *Jeremiah*, painted at a crucial juncture in this history, helps bring to light aspects of modern exegesis of the biblical book that are almost invisible to us because they seem so 'natural'.

---

18. See Taylor 1989: 227-30. The influence of Rembrandt's *Jeremiah* on modern art is explored in Friedman 1984, where Chagall's painting 'Loneliness' (Solitude) is an especially poignant rendering.

Krister Stendahl wrote that 'Few things are more liberating and creative in modern theology than a clear distinction between the "original" and the "translation" in any age, our own included' (Stendahl 1963: 96). It is a distinction not always easily made. Perhaps Rembrandt can help us to see it, and thereby ourselves, a little better.

BIBLIOGRAPHY

Anderson, Gary A.
    1991   *A Time to Mourn, A Time to Dance: The Expression of Grief and Joy in Israelite Religion* (University Park: Penn State University Press).
Barton, John
    1999   'Jeremiah in the Apocrypha and Pseudepigrapha', in A.R. Pete Diamond, Kathleen M. O'Connor and Louis Stulman (eds.), *Troubling Jeremiah* (JSOTSup, 260; Sheffield: Sheffield Academic Press): 306-17.
Baumgartner, W.
    1917   *Die Klagegedichte des Jeremia* (BZAW, 32; Giessen: A. Töpelmann).
Begg, Christopher T.
    1995   'The "Classical Prophets" in Josephus' *Antiquities*', in Robert P. Gordon (ed.), *'The Place is too Small for Us': The Israelite Prophets in Recent Scholarship* (Winona Lake, IN: Eisenbrauns): 557-61.
Binstock, Benjamin
    1997   'Becoming Rembrandt: National, Religious, and Sexual Identity in Rembrandt's History Paintings' (unpublished PhD dissertation, Columbia University).
Braude, William G. (trans.)
    1968   *Pesikta Rabbati: Discourses for Feasts, Fasts, and Special Sabbaths* (New Haven: Yale University Press).
Brueggemann, Walter
    1998   *A Commentary on Jeremiah* (Grand Rapids: Eerdmans).
Bruyn, J.
    1982   *A Corpus of Rembrandt Paintings* (The Hague: Martinus Nijhoff).
Burdick, Sandford
    1988   'Rembrandt's *Jeremiah*', *Journal of the Warburg and Courtauld Institutes* 101: 260-64.
Callaway, Mary C.
    1996   'Exegesis as Banquet: Reading Jeremiah with the Rabbis', in Richard D. Weis and David M. Carr (eds.), *A Gift of God in Due Season* (JSOTSup, 225; Sheffield: Sheffield Academic Press): 219-30.
Carroll, Robert P.
    1986   *Jeremiah: A Commentary* (Philadelphia: Westminster Press).
Di Vito, Robert
    1999   'Old Testament Anthropology and the Construction of Personal Identity', *CBQ* 61: 217-38.
Diamond, A.R. Pete
    1987   *The Confessions of Jeremiah in Context: Scenes of Prophetic Drama* (JSOTSup, 45; Sheffield: JSOT Press).

Duhm, Bernhard
    1901   *Das Buch Jeremia* (KHAT, 11; Tübingen: J.C.B. Mohr).
Friedman, Mira
    1984   'Marc Chagall's Portrayal of the Prophet Jeremiah', *Zeitschrift für Kunst-geschichte* 47: 374-91.
Hill, Christopher
    1993   *The English Bible and the Seventeenth-Century Revolution* (London: Allan Lane).
Holladay, William
    1986   *Jeremiah*. I. *A Commentary on the Book of the Prophet Jeremiah Chapters 1–25* (Hermeneia; Philadelphia: Fortress Press).
    1989   *Jeremiah*. II. *A Commentary on the Book of the Prophet Jeremiah Chapters 26–52* (Hermeneia; Minneapolis: Fortress Press).
Huffmon, Herbert B.
    1999   'Jeremiah of Anathoth: A Prophet for All Israel', in Robert Chazan, William W. Hallo and Lawrence H. Schiffman (eds.), *Ki Baruch Hu: Ancient Near Eastern, Biblical, and Judaic Studies in Honor of Baruch A. Levine* (Winona Lake, IN: Eisenbrauns): 261-71.
Landsberger, Franz
    1946   *Rembrandt, the Jews and the Bible* (Philadelphia: Jewish Publication Society of America).
Lubac, Henri du, SJ
    1988   *Medieval Exegesis*. I. *The Four Senses of Scripture* (trans. Mark Sebanc; Grand Rapids: Eerdmans).
Lundbom, Jack
    1999   *Jeremiah* (AB, 21A; New York: Doubleday).
McKane, William
    1986   *A Critical and Exegetical Commentary on Jeremiah* (Edinburgh: T. & T. Clark).
Owen, John (trans.)
    1950   *Commentaries on the Book of the Prophet Jeremiah* (Grand Rapids: Eerdmans).
Perlove, Shelley
    1995   '*Templum Christianum*: Rembrandt's *Jeremiah Lamenting the Destruction of Jerusalem* (1630)', *Gazette des Beaux-Arts* 6.126: 159-70.
Polk, Timothy
    1984   *The Prophetic Persona: The Language of Self Reliance in Jeremiah* (JSOTSup, 32; Sheffield: JSOT Press).
Rad, Gerhard von
    1965   *The Message of the Prophets*, II (New York: Harper & Row).
Reventlow, H.G.
    1963   *Liturgie und prophetisches Ich bei Jeremia* (Gütersloh: Gütersloher Verlagshaus Gerd Mohn).
Schama, Simon
    1999   *Rembrandt's Eyes* (New York: Knopf).
Seitz, Christopher
    1989   *Theology in Conflict: Reactions to the Exile in the Book of Jeremiah* (Berlin: W. de Gruyter).

Stendahl, Krister
    1963   'Paul and the Introspective Conscience of the West', *HTR* 56: 199-216
                (reprinted in his *Paul Among Jews and Gentiles* [Philadelphia: Fortress
                Press, 1976]: 78-96).
Taylor, Charles
    1989   *Sources of the Self: The Making of Modern Identity* (Cambridge, MA:
                Harvard University Press).
Thompson, J.A.
    1980   *The Book of Jeremiah* (Grand Rapids: Eerdmans).
Tümpel, Christian
    1984   'Die Rezeption der Jüdischen Altertümer des Flavius Josephus in den
                holländischen Historiendarstellungen des 16. und 17. Jahrhunderts', in
                Herman Vekeman and Justus M. Hofstede (eds.), *Wort und Bild in Der Nied-
                erländischen Kunst und Literature des 16. und 17. Jahrhunderts* (Erfstadt:
                Lukassen): 173-204.
Weitzmann, Kurt
    1979   *The Miniatures of the Sacra Parallela: Parisinus Graecus 923* (Princeton,
                NJ: Princeton University Press).
Zell, Michael
    2000   *Rembrandt Creates* Rembrandt*: Art and Ambition in Leiden, 1629–1631*
                (Boston: Isabella Stewart Gardner Museum): 113-15.

METAPHOR AND SOCIAL REALITY:
ISAIAH 23.17-18, EZEKIEL 16.35-37 AND HOSEA 2.4-5

Peggy L. Day

For the past several years I have been trying to puzzle out the mechanics, so to speak, of what I consider to be misapprehensions made by numerous scholars who have worked on texts in the prophetic corpus that employ extended metaphors to personify either cities or countries as women, specifically as harlots and/or adulterous women. These misapprehensions affect reconstructing alleged social reality on the basis of these metaphorical texts. For example, it is a widely held view that both prostitutes and adulteresses in ancient Israel were stripped naked as a punishment for engaging in these activities.[1] This punishment is alleged to be illustrated by texts such as the following that, respectively, personify Jerusalem as a whore and Israel as an adulteress and whore:

> Therefore whore, hear the word of Yahweh. Thus says Yahweh: Because your bounty was poured out and your nakedness revealed through your whorings with your lovers and all your abominable idols, and on account of the blood of your sons whom you gave to them, I am gathering all your lovers for whom you were a sweet delicacy, all whom you loved and all whom you hated. I will gather them against you from round about and uncover your nakedness before them, and they will see you stark naked. (Ezek. 16.35-37)

> Plead with your mother, plead, for she is not my wife and I [Yahweh] am not her husband, so that she will remove her whorings from her face, and her adulteries from between her breasts, lest I strip her naked and exhibit her as on the day she was born, and make her like the wilderness, and make her like a parched land, and kill her with thirst. (Hos. 2.4-5)

In a previous article (Day 2000: 296-301) I have demonstrated that the biblical and extra-biblical evidence scholars have rallied in support of the alleged stripping of whores and adulteresses in fact does not support reconstructing such a practice in ancient Israel. Thus the question becomes whether metaphorical texts such as Ezekiel 16 and Hosea 2 can be read in and of themselves as evidence for the alleged practice of stripping prostitutes and adulteresses. The goal of the present essay is to illustrate why I think that they cannot be read in such a manner. My

---

1. For a list of scholars who read Ezek. 16.37 and 39 as evidence of these alleged social practices, see Day 2000: 288-89 nn. 13 and 14. For passages such as Jer. 13.22, 25-27; Ezek. 23.26, 29; Nah. 3.4-5 and Hos. 2.4-5, see the standard commentaries.

primary concern is to articulate and explicate the particular fallacy that affects incorrectly maintaining that the real-life stripping of whores and adulteresses can be confidently reconstructed on the basis of these metaphorical texts. Following Shrofel (1999: 142), I shall refer to this fallacy as a *conflation* of the commonplaces associated with the constituent components of a metaphorical expression, that is, the vehicle and the tenor of the metaphor. Conflation is the medium by which commonplaces appropriate to the domain of the tenor but not the domain of the vehicle are nevertheless transferred into the domain of the vehicle, or commonplaces appropriate to the domain of the vehicle but not the domain of the tenor are nevertheless transferred into the domain of the tenor, and misconstrued as literally apposite. Biblical scholars' tendency towards conflation is, at least in part, a product of the fact that we moderns are necessarily socio-linguistic outsiders with respect to Biblical Hebrew and ancient Israel and so, to a greater or lesser extent, depending on the metaphor in question, our lack of insider knowledge about precisely how tenor and vehicle *differ* can facilitate the inappropriate transfers and consequent literalizations that characterize conflation.

In order to illustrate the error of conflation, I shall first discuss pertinent aspects of the workings of metaphor. In this discussion I will use English language examples in order to circumvent the problems inherent in being a socio-linguistic outsider that can lead to conflated misreading. Then, turning to the Hebrew Bible, I shall illustrate the fallacy of conflation by discussing the predominant scholarly interpretation of Isa. 23.17-18, a text which applies the language of whoring to the city of Tyre. As the predominant interpretation of this passage does *not* involve proposing a conflated misreading, it functions, for my purposes, to demonstrate the propriety of reading without conflation. Having established this principle, I shall explain the stripping portrayed in Ezekiel 16 and Hosea 2 without recourse to conflated misreading.

Discussions of metaphor generally illustrate its workings by using an 'A is a B' type of example. 'Man[2] is a wolf' is a standard example in which 'man' is the primary topic or *tenor* of the metaphor and 'wolf' is the subsidiary topic or *vehicle*, the word that must be understood figuratively in order to make sense of the statement as a whole. That the statement is literally untrue (or logically absurd) is what prompts the reader to recognize that 'wolf' is intended to be taken metaphorically. The reader has at his or her disposal a body of culturally conditioned common knowledge (which may or may not be true) about wolves, and it is this body of knowledge, or *associated commonplaces*,[3] that the reader mines in order to

---

2.   I have retained the term 'man' here because it is original to the metaphor under discussion. Indeed, the fact that the term 'man' focuses our attention on what is stereotypically male is intrinsic to the metaphor.

3.   I have selected this term from among several used by theoreticians of metaphor to name the phenomenon under discussion. Other terms include 'potential range of connotations', 'source domain/target domain', 'donor field/recipient field' and 'implicative complex'. For discussion and bibliography regarding theories of metaphor, see, conveniently, Galambush 1992: 4-10; Eidevall 1996: 19-41; Stienstra 1993: 17-40. That perception of metaphorical meaning is culturally conditioned is a point worth stressing. While the socio-linguistic group to which I belong shares a certain

comprehend the statement. For example, 'wolf' might evoke the culturally conditioned commonplace that wolves are predators, in which case the reader would transfer the notion of being a predator onto 'man'. This transfer hails the reader to consider 'man' in a particular way, in this case highlighting predatoriness and forcing into the background commonplaces associated with 'man' that are inconsistent with the notion of being a predator. Also forced into the background are those attributes of wolves clearly not shared by 'man' like walking on all fours, reaching maturity at about one year of age, not living in urban centers, and so on. In other words, saying that man is a wolf does not imply that 'man' and 'wolf' are the same in all respects. Rather, some degree of dissonance or *difference* between tenor and vehicle is a feature of every metaphor, as not all of the commonplaces associated with the vehicle of a metaphorical statement transfer onto the tenor (and vice versa). Thus:

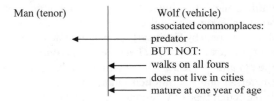

The fact that not all associated commonplaces transfer from the vehicle to the tenor (and vice versa) is the primary point to keep in mind.

In an 'A is a B' type of metaphorical statement, both the tenor and the vehicle of the respective metaphors are explicitly expressed. Not all metaphorical statements explicitly express the tenor. Consider, for example, the statement 'I'm not going to have my car fixed by the bandits down the street'. Knowing that literal bandits *qua* bandits do not engage in car repair provides the dissonance necessary to recognize that 'bandits' must be taken metaphorically, in spite of the absence of an 'A is a B' construction. In this type of metaphorical statement, the tenor, in this case 'auto mechanics', can be described as implicit rather than explicit. While the term 'auto mechanics' does not appear in the sentence, a socio-linguistic insider knows that it is mechanics and not bandits who typically engage in car repair, and so said reader would not conclude on the basis of this statement that literal bandits typically fix

body of commonplaces associated with wolves, associations can and do vary significantly across languages and cultures. Consider, for example, what an old Nunamiut man had to say about wolves (Lopez 1978: 87-88): 'Amaguk ["Wolf"] is like Nunamiut. He doesn't hunt when the weather is bad. He likes to play. He works hard to get food for his family. His hair starts to get white when he his old. Young wolves, just like Nunamiut, run around in shallow melt ponds scaring the ducks… Amaguk and Nunamiut like caribou meat, know the good places for caribou hunting. Where ground squirrels are good. Where to get raspberries. A good place for getting away from mosquitoes. Where lupine blooms first in May. Where that big rock is that looks like achlack, the grizzly bear. Where the creeks are still running in August.' Obviously, the statement 'man is a wolf' would resonate much differently in Nunamiut culture. Likewise, scholars dealing with biblical metaphors need to recognize that the commonplaces they associate with metaphorical vehicles and tenors may be very different from those evoked for the original audience of socio-linguistic insiders.

cars. In other words, and using double quotation marks to indicate a word that is to be taken metaphorically, to be able to say in a meaningful way that "bandits" fix cars does *not* imply that bandits *qua* bandits are in the business of car repair. To insist that to be able meaningfully to say that "bandits" fix cars, it must be true that bandits fix cars, fails to acknowledge a necessary difference between the tenor and the vehicle of the metaphor. It is this failure to recognize difference that I am terming conflation. Expressed in terms of associated commonplaces, conflation affects the inappropriate transfer onto the vehicle of the metaphor of a commonplace apposite only to the tenor (or vice versa). Thus:

Mechanics (tenor) | Bandits (vehicle)
associated commonplace: |
fix cars ——————————————————▶ | conflation

One final (and particularly germane) example involving an implicit tenor must suffice. Regarding the 2000 United States presidential election, the *Los Angeles Times*[4] reported a phenomenon called 'vote whoring'. The *Times* article explained that 'vote whores are paid by [political] campaigns to do favours for people in return for their absentee votes'. Given the *Times*'s explanation, the notion of payment for services is the commonplace associated with the vehicle, namely, 'whoring', that has been transferred onto the implicit tenor, namely, the activity of individuals involved in a particular type of vote-getting. In spite of the fact that literal whoring necessarily entails sexual activity, and given the *Times*'s explanation, no socio-linguistic insider would infer that the activity of these vote whores *qua* vote whores was necessarily sexual in nature. Thus:

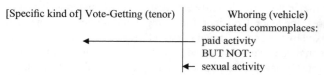

[Specific kind of] Vote-Getting (tenor) | Whoring (vehicle)
                                           | associated commonplaces:
◀—————————————————————————————————————— | paid activity
                                           | BUT NOT:
                                           | ◀— sexual activity

Concluding otherwise would entail a conflation of tenor and vehicle, such that a commonplace (i.e. sexual activity) associated with the vehicle (i.e. whoring) is mistakenly transferred onto the tenor (i.e. this specific type of vote-getting):

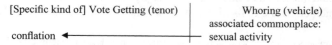

[Specific kind of] Vote Getting (tenor) | Whoring (vehicle)
                                           | associated commonplace:
conflation ◀—————————————————————————— | sexual activity

Turning to the Hebrew Bible, the error of conflated misreading can be illustrated by looking at an example in which the scholarly commentary on a statement involving an implicit tenor has acknowledged a necessary distinction between tenor and vehicle and so has *not* proposed a conflated misreading. Speaking of an envisaged future time regarding the city of Tyre, Isa. 23.17-18 reads:

> And at the end of seventy years Yahweh will attend to Tyre, and she will return to her hire ['*etnannâ*] and she will whore [*wᵉ zānᵉtâ*] with all the kingdoms of the

---

4.   The article was reproduced in the *Winnipeg Free Press* (15 December 2000), p. A15.

earth on the face of the ground. And her profit and her hire ['*etnannâ*] will be holy to Yahweh. It will not be stored up or saved, but rather her profit will belong to those who dwell before Yahweh, to eat and be sated, and for choice attire.

In the first sentence, the language of prostitution ('*etnan*, 'hire', and *zānâ*, 'whore') functions as the vehicle by which the implicit tenor, Tyre's commercial relations, is expressed. Thus, when the metaphor is extended in the second sentence to say that Tyre's hire ('*etnan*) will be holy to Yahweh, it is nevertheless, in my view, the profit from Tyre's commercial activities that the author of the passage is envisaging as becoming holy to Yahweh at some time in the future, *not* gains from literal prostitution. Analogously to the previous example involving bandits and car repair, and again using double quotation marks to indicate a word to be understood meta-phorically, to be able to meaningfully say that Tyre's "hire" will be holy to Yahweh does not imply that Tyre's hire will be holy to Yahweh, as "hire" and hire are two different things. To insist contrariwise would be an example of a conflated mis-reading since commercial "whoring", like vote "whoring" of the previous example, does not imply sexual activity.

Turning now to commentaries on Isa. 23.17-18, scholars typically maintain that, indeed, it is Tyre's commercial profit but *not* gains from prostitution that the author of the statement anticipates becoming holy to Yahweh. Several scholars (e.g. Auvray 1972: 219; Gray 1912: 396; Kaiser 1974: 171-72; Oswalt 1986: 437) are explicit about stating what I take to be the reason why scholarship in general on this passage has managed to avoid proposing a conflated misreading. These scholars point to Deut. 23.19 (Eng. v. 18), which states 'you shall not bring the hire of a prostitute ('*etnan zônâ*) or the fee of a dog into the house of Yahweh your god [in payment] for any vow, for both of them are an abomination to Yahweh your god'. This Deuteronomistic prohibition against donating gains from prostitution to Yah-weh can be described, for my purposes, as an item of socio-linguistic insider knowledge associated with harlots' pay that has impelled commentators to recog-nize that "hire" and hire are, emphatically, two different things and thus avoid a conflated misreading. For example, Kaiser (1974: 171-72) says, 'Since the profits of trade are only referred to metaphorically as the rewards of prostitution, Deut. 23.18 does not apply to them'. Likewise, Auvray (1972: 219) avers, '*Les richesses de Tyr (le "salaire de la prostituée" mais ce n'est qu'une image, et l'on ne peut objecter Dt 23, 19) seront apportées en don à Yahvé*'.[5] For Oswalt (1986: 437), '*her hire will be holy* seems to fly directly in the face of Deut. 23.18, which states that a prostitute's hire may not be given as an offering'. To resolve this seeming contradiction, Oswalt notes that 'it is necessary to remember…that prostitution is a figure here [i.e. in Isa. 23.18]'. In other words, what the above comments elucidate is that it need not be true that hire will become holy to Yahweh for "hire" to be meaningfully portrayed as becoming holy to Yahweh.

Another indicator that scholars commenting on Isa. 23.17-18 have correctly distinguished between "hire" and hire can be seen in their respective paraphrases of

---

5. 'The riches of Tyre (the "hire of a prostitute", but this is only an image, and one cannot raise Deut. 23.19 as an objection to it) will be brought as a gift for Yahweh.'

the meaning of *'etnan* in Isa. 23.18, paraphrases which correctly convey the intended meaning of the verse by making the implicit tenor explicit. Sweeney (1996: 306), for example, says of v. 18 that 'this statement focuses on the dedication of Tyre's *commercial profits* as holy to YHWH' (emphasis mine). Seitz (1993: 171) states that 'in the days following Tyre's judgement we learn that all the *merchandise* of which Tyre was so proud will "be dedicated to the Lord; her profits will not be stored or hoarded"' (emphasis mine). Blenkinsopp (2000: 345) speaks of 'revitalized *trade activity*...in the service of the Jerusalemite temple community' (emphasis mine). Further examples could be cited (e.g. Clements 1980: 196; Childs 2001: 169; Brueggemann 1998: 186). Thus, as the foregoing makes clear, when metaphorical intent is correctly apprehended it is best conveyed in a paraphrase that makes the implicit tenor explicit. My point here is not to say that such a paraphrase adequately captures the full force of the metaphor, as it most certainly does not. Rather, when paraphrasing a statement such as 'Tyre's *'etnan* will be holy to Yahweh', my point is that *'etnan* needs to be explicated in terms appropriate to the implicit tenor, namely, 'trade' or 'commercial profits' or the like, as the commentators cited above have done. Indeed, to paraphrase instead in terms appropriate to the vehicle, such as a statement like 'Tyre's whore's pay will become sacred to the Lord', would be a conflated misreading that is simply and decidedly wrong.

Having examined a passage in which scholars make an appropriate and necessary distinction between tenor and vehicle, let us now return our attention to the passages, cited above, which are routinely interpreted as evidence for stripping as a punishment for prostitution and adultery. Once again using double quotation marks to indicate a term employed as a metaphoric vehicle, and, analogous to the previous examples of metaphors in which the tenor is implicit, the stripping in these passages can meaningfully be portrayed as a consequence of "prostitution" or "adultery", but it does not imply that stripping in ancient Israel was a consequence of prostitution or adultery.[6] Indeed, in my view, the stripping is both a commonplace and a consequence associated with the implicit tenors of the respective passages, and not with the explicit vehicles of prostitution and adultery. As we learned from

---

6.   This assertion on my part is in fundamental disagreement with a statement made by Raymond Westbrook (1990: 577-78) regarding the punishment of the metaphorical adulteress, Israel, in Hos. 2. Westbrook views the stripping in v. 5 as a punishment inflicted upon an adulterous wife as part of a divorce proceeding. To support this view, he reasons that 'if God's relationship to Israel is to be explained by a metaphor drawing on the everyday life of the audience then that metaphor, to be effective, must reflect accurately the reality known to the audience. If the narrator were to invent the legal rules upon which the metaphor is based, it would cease to be a valid metaphor.' Westbrook's error here is that he has conflated "adultery" and adultery, leading him to aver that the stripping portrayed in Hos. 2.5 would be known to the ancient audience as a legal and real consequence of adultery rather than "adultery". To refute Westbrook's reasoning in more concrete terms, note, for example, Ezek. 23.1-4, where Yahweh is portrayed, in the language of the vehicle, as married, at the same time, to two sisters who are daughters of the same mother. Yet, according to Lev. 18.18, men in ancient Israel were not allowed to marry a wife's sister while that wife was still alive. The apparent contradiction vanishes when we recognize that Ezek. 23.1-4 is concerned with "marriage" (i.e. being in a covenant relationship), not marriage.

the scholars (above) whose paraphrases of Isa. 23.17-18 correctly conveyed intended meaning, we must first make the implicit tenors of adultery and prostitution explicit in order correctly to apprehend meaning. As is widely acknowledged, in Ezekiel 16 the metaphorical language of whoring and adultery has as its implicit tenor the accusations, leveled against the people of Jerusalem, of apostasy[7] (vv. 16-21) and of making inappropriate foreign alliances (vv. 24-29). The author of Hosea 2 likewise employs the language of adultery and prostitution to express the implicit tenor of apostasy (vv. 7-10), this time regarding the Northern Kingdom. Thus, to paraphrase, stripping in these two passages is portrayed as punishment for apostasy and, in Ezekiel, also for improper foreign relations, and so it is in the domains of these two tenors, and more specifically, as punishment for committing these two offenses, that, in my view, stripping must be contextualized as an associated commonplace.

Regarding Ezekiel 16, the locus of stripping as a consequence of apostasy can be found by recalling that apostasy was regarded in ancient Israel as a particularly egregious covenant transgression, and conquest by foreign nations was a particularly harsh threatened consequence of breach of covenant (e.g. Deut. 28.25, 41, 47-58; Lev. 26.16-17, 25, 38). Likewise, military incursion was a common threatened consequence of a vassal nation's improper foreign relations, which constituted a breach of the exclusive fealty due to its suzerain.[8] I submit that the practice of stripping captives of war (e.g. Deut. 28.48; Isa. 20.1-4; Sefire I A: 41; cf. Mic. 1.11)[9] and/or the conqueror's pillaging (e.g. BDB entries *bzz* and *šll*) and, in extreme cases, the razing of conquered cities (e.g. 2 Kgs 25.9; Ps. 137.7; cf. Mic. 1.6), are the commonplaces associated with the tenors that explain the depiction of Jerusalem

---

7.   That the apostasy of which Israelites and Judahites were frequently accused included participation in so-called sacred or cultic prostitution used to be a widely held view of biblical scholars. For recent, and persuasive, critiques of this position, see Oden 1987: 131-53; Bird 1989; Hackett 1989; Shrofel 1999: 70-104; cf. Beard and Henderson 1997. Expressed in terms of conflation, the very notion of cultic prostitution can be described as an inappropriate transfer onto the domain of the implicit tenor (i.e. the cult) of a commonplace (i.e. sexual activity) properly associated exclusively with the vehicle (i.e. prostitution).

8.   For this aspect of vassal treaties, see McCarthy 1981: 29-140. According to, for example, Tsevat (1959: 201-202), breach of sworn treaty loyalty is, in the book of Ezekiel, construed as a violation of the covenant with Yahweh. Tsevat's most compelling piece of evidence is Ezek. 17.11-21, in which, with the deity as putative speaker, violation of treaty loyalty is explicitly adjudged as a breach of the covenant with Yahweh. Thus, the tenor of inappropriate foreign relations may have been construed by the author of Ezek. 16, like apostasy, as a covenant violation.

9.   If we allow, as, for example, Magdalene (1995: 328-34) and Gordon and Washington (1995: 308-17) have argued, that the language of stripping in city-as-woman passages connotes rape, then biblical texts such as Lam. 5.11 and Zech. 14.2 also become pertinent to locating the action in the context of foreign invasion rather than punishment for prostitution or adultery. Along these lines, note also the seventh-century BCE succession treaty of Esarhaddon, which includes the following curse against treaty violators: 'May Venus, the brightest of stars, before your eyes make your wives lie in the lap of your enemy' (ll. 428-29; Parpola and Watanabe 1988: 46). In any event, I agree with Washington (1997: 359-60 and n. 137) that, in spite of the fact that Biblical Hebrew lacks the concept of rape, the act described in texts such as Lam. 5.11 constitutes rape.

stripped naked.[10] Regarding the breach of covenant by apostasy in Hosea 2, the threatened consequence of loss of crops and herds, either at the hands of foreign invaders (e.g. Lev. 26.15-16; Deut. 28.47-51; Jer. 5.10-17; cf. Hos. 8.4-7) or as a result of catastrophes such as drought (e.g. Lev. 26.18-20; Deut. 11.13-17; Jer. 14.1-10) or locusts (e.g. Deut. 28.38; cf. Joel 1–3), is the associated commonplace that explains Israel portrayed as stripped bare (cf. Gen. 42.9, 12; Isa. 19.7; Hos. 2.11; Joel 1.7; Ps. 29.9) and becoming like the wilderness (cf. Deut. 29.18-26). Thus, these and similar metaphoric texts cannot, in and of themselves, be used as evidence for reconstructing the social practice of stripping prostitutes and adulteresses, as the stripping is properly understood as a commonplace associated exclusively with the implicit tenors.

BIBLIOGRAPHY

Auvray, Paul
    1972   *Isaïe 1–39* (Paris: Librairie Lecoffre).
Beard, Mary, and John Henderson
    1997   'With This Body I Thee Worship: Sacred Prostitution in Antiquity', *Gender and History* 9: 480-503.
Bird, Phyllis
    1989   '"To Play the Harlot": An Inquiry into an Old Testament Metaphor', in P.L. Day (ed.), *Gender and Difference in Ancient Israel* (Minneapolis: Fortress Press): 75-94.
Blenkinsopp, Joseph
    2000   *Isaiah 1–39* (AB, 19A; New York: Doubleday).
Brenner, Athalya (ed.)
    1995   *A Feminist Companion to the Latter Prophets* (The Feminist Companion to the Bible, 8; Sheffield: Sheffield Academic Press).
Brueggemann, Walter
    1998   *Isaiah 1–39* (Westminster Bible Companion; Louisville, KY: Westminster/John Knox Press).
Childs, Brevard S.
    2001   *Isaiah* (OTL; Louisville, KY: Westminster/John Knox Press).
Clements, R.E.
    1980   *Isaiah 1–39* (NCBC; Grand Rapids: Eerdmans).
Day, Peggy L.
    2000   'Adulterous Jerusalem's Imagined Demise: Death of a Metaphor in Ezekiel XVI', *VT* 50: 285-309.
Eidevall, Göran
    1996   *Grapes in the Desert: Metaphors, Models and Themes in Hosea 4–14* (Stockholm: Almqvist & Wiksell).
Fitzmyer, Joseph A.
    1967   *The Aramaic Inscription of Sefîre* (Rome: Pontifical Biblical Institute).

10.   Understanding stripping to be a commonplace associated with war rather than a commonplace associated with literal prostitution or adultery makes better sense of another city-as-woman text, Isa. 47.1-3. In this passage, the personified city of Babylon is *not* accused of being a metaphorical adulteress or whore, but nonetheless is portrayed naked.

Galambush, Julie
    1992   *Jerusalem in the Book of Ezekiel: The City as Yahweh's Wife* (Atlanta:
                Scholars Press).
Gordon, Pamela, and Harold C. Washington
    1995   'Rape as a Military Metaphor in the Hebrew Bible', in Brenner (ed.) 1995:
                308-25.
Gray, George Buchanan
    1912   *A Critical and Exegetical Commentary on the Book of Isaiah I–XXXIX*
                (Edinburgh: T. & T. Clark).
Hackett, Jo Ann
    1989   'Can a Sexist Model Liberate Us? Ancient Near Eastern "Fertility" God-
                desses', *JFSR* 5: 65-76.
Kaiser, Otto
    1974   *Isaiah 13–39* (London: SCM Press).
Lopez, Barry
    1978   *Of Wolves and Men* (New York: Charles Scribner's Sons).
Magdalene, F. Rachel
    1995   'Ancient Near Eastern Treaty Curses and the Ultimate Texts of Terror: A
                Study of the Language of Divine Sexual Abuse in the Prophetic Corpus', in
                Brenner (ed.) 1995: 326-52.
McCarthy, Dennis J.
    1981   *Treaty and Covenant* (Rome: Biblical Institute Press).
Oden, Robert A.
    1987   *The Bible without Theology* (San Francisco: Harper & Row).
Oswalt, John N.
    1986   *The Book of Isaiah Chapters 1–39* (NICOT; Grand Rapids: Eerdmans).
Parpola, Simo, and Kazuko Watanabe (eds.)
    1998   *Neo-Assyrian Treaties and Loyalty Oaths* (Helsinki: Helsinki University
                Press).
Seitz, Christopher R.
    1993   *Isaiah 1–39* (Interpretation; Louisville, KY: John Knox Press).
Shrofel, Karin R.
    1999   'No Prostitute Has Been Here: A Reevaluation of Hosea 4.13-14' (unpub-
                lished Masters thesis, University of Winnipeg/University of Manitoba).
Stienstra, Nelly
    1993   *Yahweh is the Husband of his People* (Kampen: Kok Pharos).
Sweeney, Marvin A.
    1996   *Isaiah 1–39 with an Introduction to Prophetic Literature* (FOTL, 16; Grand
                Rapids: Eerdmans).
Tsevat, Matitiahu
    1959   'The Neo-Assyrian and Neo-Babylonian Vassal Oaths and the Prophet
                Ezekiel', *JBL* 78: 199-204.
Washington, Harold C.
    1997   'Violence and the Construction of Gender in the Hebrew Bible: A New
                Historicist Approach', *BibInt* 5: 324-63.
Westbrook, Raymond
    1990   'Adultery in Ancient Near Eastern Law', *RB* 97: 542-80.

Southern Mesopotamian Titles for Temple Personnel in the Mari Archives[*]

Daniel E. Fleming

This short article is conceived as a prospectus for future study of the temple personnel in the Mari archives, study that I would be happy to see undertaken by someone other than myself. My observations and conclusions are tentative, not based on a systematic collection and review of all references to temple personnel in the cuneiform texts found at Mari. I only realized how little we may understand temple roles in the Mari evidence when I tried to address the relationship between prophets and temple personnel in this evidence (Fleming forthcoming). In this piece I intend to describe my ignorance and to suggest a cautious approach to interpretation of Babylonian categories in Syrian settings.[1]

Outside of the specialists who make up the current Mari publication team in France, interest in religion at Mari is almost always inspired by prophecy and related phenomena. A number of scholars have recognized the essential connection between prophecy and temples (see, e.g., Van der Toorn 1998: 58-59 and Huffmon 2000: 52), but the nature of these temple institutions is generally left unexamined. The one extended treatment of Mari religion that includes the temples and their staffs was undertaken by Jean-Marie Durand, the current head of the publication project (Durand 1995). Durand observes individual contrasts between Mari usage and the Mesopotamian norm, though he offers no global evaluation of temple staffing, as visible through the Sumerian-Akkadian lens of most titles. He follows a southern Mesopotamian standard when he comments that we should think less in terms of priests (*sacerdote*) than of administrators (*administradores*) who are accompanied by a variety of specialists (Durand 1995: 435).

---

[*] I would like to express my appreciation for Herb Huffmon, who welcomed me to his neighborhood when I first moved to New York and New Jersey and began to combine studies of both the Bible and early Syrian writing. It has been a pleasure to know him and his work. I would also like to thank Bertrand Lafont for his general perspective on the problem of temple personnel in the Mari archives.

1. I will use the term 'Babylonian' to describe the entire region of southern and central Iraq that came to be identified as a single entity after Hammurabi's conquest of the Larsa kingdom. This region incorporated ancient Sumerian traditions from the southeast with various cultural streams from points upstream, to the north and west. Because the scribal definitions of temple personnel derived first of all from Sumer and Sumerian, these categories retained a strong influence even as institutional realities shifted within southern Mesopotamia.

While this may indeed be true, I am struck by how little we know of the actual staffing and responsibilities within the temples of the Mari evidence. The titles for prophets are not derived from the old Sumerian temples of southern Mesopotamia and may not even be Akkadian, especially the *āpilum/āpiltum* and the *muḫḫûm/muḫḫûtum*, the most common male/female types. Most of the permanent staff of the temples, however, bear titles that originate in that southern Mesopotamian setting, and these are usually interpreted in southern terms. My premise here is that these titles must be approached with greater caution. It is not clear that the temples of Mari and regions to its north and west served institutional structures that mirrored those of Babylonia or earlier Sumer to any great degree. These western temples were architecturally unlike those downstream, and we should expect their personnel to differ as well. The southern Mesopotamian categories appear to have been applied to local systems in ways that are bound to deceive the modern reader.

1. *Using the Mari Evidence*

Before undertaking a survey of the Mari evidence, a few methodological cautions are in order. First of all, the archives discovered at Mari represent much more than the custom of Mari itself. Many of the thousands of letters found there either were not composed at Mari or are concerned with affairs outside the seat of the Mari kingdom. The administrative documents reflect the business of the Mari palace, but this also could involve temples outside the capital.

Also, the Mari archives straddle more than one reign, and none of the documented kings could claim longstanding local ties. Yaḫdun-Lim forged a major kingdom by unifying his Binu Simʾal tribespeople under his own rule and then conquering most of the middle Euphrates River valley, establishing his capital at Mari. His son Sumu-yamam could not hold this domain against the wily Samsi-Addu, who gradually built a kingdom that spanned northern Mesopotamia, from Aššur and Ekallatum on the Tigris River to Mari and Tuttul on the Euphrates, with the Ḫabur and Baliḫ tributaries included. Samsi-Addu made Mari his western center and put his younger son Yasmaḫ-Addu on its throne. During this period, eastern influences on Mari were particularly strong. After the death of Samsi-Addu, Yasmaḫ-Addu lost Mari to the Binu Simʾal tribespeople, who crowned Zimri-Lim their king at the old royal seat of Yaḫdun-Lim. There were substantial continuities in Mari institutions across the reigns of Yasmaḫ-Addu and Zimri-Lim, but we cannot treat the evidence from each period on equal terms. For instance, the only ritual texts from the Mari archives come from the reign of Yasmaḫ-Addu and may never have been performed at Mari (Durand and Guichard 1997; Fleming 1999).

One reason for our ignorance of Mari temples is that we do not have temple archives. Almost all of the roughly 20,000 cuneiform tablets found at Mari come from the royal palace. Many of these have cultic interest, but they do not come from within any single temple institution. We do not have lists of temple personnel for either reign. In fact, it is not easy to define 'temple personnel' within strict bounds based on evidence from palace archives. The palace incorporated sanctuaries within its walls, and we do not have a clear picture of who worked full-time for a temple or whose income was entirely administered through a temple. Tablets that record disbursements from the Mari palace include oil to anoint divine statues at festivals,[2] bread and beer for royal feasts to celebrate major festivals,[3] and constant materials for sacrifice and offering at various temples.[4] These texts document the outflow from the palace, but we know too little about administration at the temples. Many prophets were identified with specific gods and evidently their temples, but we cannot assume that the primary income of these prophets came from temple service. Singers make frequent appearances in palace documents, but it is hard to know who sang for palace events, who performed for temple events, or even whether singers may have worked in multiple settings with pay from the palace or from multiple sources.[5]

Finally, language is a problem. It seems likely that most Mari scribes were bilingual. The language of written communication was Akkadian, the Semitic tongue long established downstream. Judging by the consistently high quality of the prose in the letters found at Mari, fluent Akkadian was the norm among scribes, and it is even possible that the famous prophecies were proclaimed in Akkadian (Charpin 2002: 15-16; Sasson 1994: 300 n. 5). At the same time, the letters are sprinkled with non-Akkadian Semitic words and populated by a host of characters with West Semitic names. The scribes themselves called this West Semitic language 'Amorite', and the various tribal peoples of the Mari archives seem to have spoken Amorite dialects as their first tongues (Durand 1992: 123-25; Sasson 1998: 121-22). Before the Amorites, the population of the Euphrates valley may have had its own non-Akkadian Semitic dialects. In the case of temple personnel, Akkadian titles may sometimes have enjoyed long-established use, but these were ultimately superimposed over non-Akkadian terminology. It is also possible that more recent Amorite arrivals could have substituted their own western categories for Akkadian terms in use at old centers like Mari. In addition, much of the Akkadian titulary was derived from or long equated with Sumerian words from the huge southern Mesopotamian institutions of the third millennium. We cannot read these venerable titles in Mari evidence as simple equivalents of Sumerian or southern Mesopotamian categories, even if the Sumerian or Akkadian terms were known and used.

2. *A Survey of the Temple Personnel in Mari Evidence*

If we set aside the prophets, the temple personnel attested in the Mari archives look quite southern Mesopotamian. That is, the names are generally familiar, and this makes it easy to conclude that they serve cultic systems essentially like those of contemporary Babylonia. The differences lie not in the titles themselves so much as

---

2.   For example, ARM VII 66, for Belet-ekallim at the time of *kinūnum* rite.

3.   For example, ARM XII 273, 274, and 275, for the event called 'the wagon of Nergal'.

4.   For example, the animals provided according to date and listed sacred sites in ARM XXI 15-58.

5.   All of this leaves aside the role of household agriculture or other household-based subsistence in the survival of sacred personnel.

in the distribution of their use, with apparent gaps by comparison with the Babylonian constellations of temple personnel. Evaluation of the gaps is difficult because of the limits to our evidence, but the impression of contrast persists.

Among male personnel, the most common is the *šangûm* (Sumerian sanga). This man held the primary authority in a temple, as seen in Aḫum's role in mediating the prophecy given in his temple to the Mari governor and king.[6] The *šangûm* was sometimes identified by the god of his sanctuary, such as Dada of Eštar-bišra or Iddin-ili of Itur-Mer.[7] These temple leaders appear often in texts from the reign of Zimri-Lim, but the *šangûm* also played a role in the Eštar ritual from the period of Yasmaḫ-Addu.[8] There is no question that the *šangûm* office was found in Mari sacred sites.

It is possible to find other classic southern Mesopotamian titles, but they are much rarer. The same Eštar ritual mentions the *kalûm* lamentation singer (i.10'; ii.19'; iii.7, 16) and the 'anointed' *pašīšum* priest of southern temples (iv.20, 22, 26, 31), along with the obscure *luḫšum*, known from Mesopotamian lexical lists (iv.2). A letter written to Yasmaḫ-Addu describes a devastating plague, after which an unnamed town is purified by a combination of exorcists (*mašmaššum*) and lamentation singers (*kalûm*).[9] Although texts from the reign of Zimri-Lim far outnumber those from the reign of Yasmaḫ-Addu, there is even less evidence for the southern titles during Zimri-Lim's rule. One short letter to Zimri-Lim requests that senior lamentation singers (*kalamaḫḫum*) be sent to purify the palace.[10] Asqudum, a member of Zimri-Lim's inner circle, requests some combination of specialists to perform purification rites in connection with a political negotiation. These include one broken term and the *mussirum*, if Durand's reading is correct.[11] None of the men who perform purification rites is identified by affiliation with a deity or temple, so their status as servants of specific cult centers is unproven. For all we can tell from context, they could be employed by the palace and perform their special skills in a range of settings, without temple sponsorship. Finally, the *assinnum*, a man with ambiguous gender identity, appears in connection with the temple of Annunitum, a goddess related to Eštar, who is served by the *assinnu* in southern Mesopotamian settings.[12] All of the references to the *assinnum* come from the reign of Zimri-Lim and relate to divine messages.

On the female side, by far the most common title for temple personnel is the Sumerian nin-dingir(-ra), whose Akkadian or West Semitic reading is uncertain.

6. ARM XXVI 201.7-13 (=VI 45); cf. 214.19-23 (=X 8); 235.8.

7. ARM XXVI 237.13-17 (=X 50); XXVI 238.4-6 (=X 51).

8. See the administrative texts ARM VII 10.8-9 (Yasmaḫ-Addu); 180 iv 34' (Zimri-Lim); XXII 36 rev.ii'.7' (Zimri-Lim); XXIV 6 ii.9'-10' (Zimri-Lim); and the ritual *FM* III 2 iv.20, 21, 24 (Yasmaḫ-Addu; as *šaĝĝûm*).

9. ARM XXVI 263.18-20.

10. ARM XXVI 279.10-12; cf. comment on p. 548 and n. 39.

11. ARM XXVI 44.17-20; cf. comment on pp. 185-86. The *mussirum* is otherwise known only from a lexical list. Durand restores *wāšipum*, an old form of the common *āšipu* incantation specialist, which is logical, but without precedent in the Mari evidence known to me.

12. See especially Šelebum in ARM XXVI 197.4-5; 198.3'-4'; 213.5-7; cf. Ili-ḫaznaya in 212.5-6, 10'.

These priestesses often have high status and may come from royal families. Inibšina was the daughter of Yaḫdun-Lim, and Kunšim-matum was probably the sister of Yasmaḫ-Addu.[13] Durand renders nin-dingir(-ra) 'sister of the god', though it is not clear whether the Sumerian was understood this way at Mari. The more elite dam dingir or 'wife of the god' does seem to have been read according to the Sumerian and was not taken from southern Mesopotamian institutions, which distinguished the *ēnu/ēntu* (Sumerian en) from the nin-dingir(-ra), a slightly lower rank.[14] Inibšina was a high priestess of the storm god, evidently at Mari, and her seal identifies her more exclusively as 'the wife of Addu' (dam [d][IŠKUR]).[15] Baḫlatum, another high-ranking woman in Zimri-Lim's harem, was also designated as a nin-dingir(-ra),[16] and other individuals appear in administrative lists.[17]

These references to individual priestesses, especially those of royal blood, give the impression of highest rank and elite status. Two letters, however, suggest that the term may also have had broader usage. In normal southern Mesopotamian custom, the nin-dingir(-ra) was the single leading priestess in the temple household of a god. Nevertheless, Zimri-Lim writes to Šibtu the queen about the plural nin-dingir-meš of one god, Addu of Kulmiš. The king says, 'On the tablet of plunder that I had sent, the nin-dingir priestesses of Kulmiš, along with the nin-dingir priestesses of the (other) gods separately, were inscribed one by one'.[18] In another letter, Zimri-Lim again speaks of nin-dingir priestesses as a mass: 'Now then, I have sent you some women for weaving. Among them are some nin-dingir priestesses. Identify the nin-dingir priestesses so as to assign them to the weaver-women's residence.'[19] Both times, Zimri-Lim seems to use the term nin-dingir-ra broadly, without indication of elite rank.

In early second-millennium Babylonian evidence, the term nin-dingir(-ra) designated either the *ēntum* of major temples or the *ugbabtum* of second-ranking temples.[20] Neither reading applies clearly to the nin-dingir(-ra) in the Mari texts. One letter from the governor of the Terqa district to Zimri-Lim recounts plans for housing the *ugbabtum* of Dagan, whose title is given syllabic form.[21] It is possible that in the Mari evidence the nin-dingir(-ra) title was allowed an even wider application to 'priestesses' than it had in contemporary Babylonia. Not all nin-dingir priestesses

13.   For Inibšina, see ARM VII 53.4; 54.4; XXIII 569.2; 570.3; XXIV 18.3'; XXVI 199.53; and the discussion in Ziegler 1999: 46-49. For Kunšim-matum, see Durand 1985: 396-98.

14.   See Durand 1985: 397 n. 69, for the dam dingir; for the hierarchy of southern priests, see Renger 1967.

15.   Ziegler 1999: 46-47, with restoration of the deity from her known service to the storm god in another text.

16.   Ziegler 1999: 50; e.g. ARM XXII 53.5-6; cf. 54.5-6.

17.   See, e.g., ARM VII 226.50; XXII 66.41-42; XXIV 224 i.24'.

18.   ARM X 13-16; with 'Addu of Kulmiš' said to have 'his nin-dingir priestesses' in ll. 10-11. For French translation, see Durand 2000: 352-53, no. 1169.

19.   ARM X 126.4-7; cf. Durand 2000: 349-50, no. 1166.

20.   Renger 1967: 134-35, 144-45.

21.   ARM XXVI 178.9 (=ARM III 42),[f]*ug-ba-a*[*b-tum š*]*a* d*Da-gan*. 'The previous *ugbabtum* priestess' is rendered [f]*ug-ba-*[*a*]*b-tim pa-ni-tim* in l. 12; cf. [f]*ug-ba-ab-tum* in l. 18; cf. 179.5, 10, 26, 31.

would have been designated *ugbabtum*. Among the highest ranks, some could be dam dingir ('the wife of a god'), as seen for Inibšina and Kunšim-matum. At Emar in the thirteenth century, far upstream along the Euphrates River, the standard reading of nin-dingir(-ra) according to one lexical list was *ittu*, from *ēntu*.[22] Wider use of the nin-dingir(-ra) title may not entirely reflect the inclusion of lesser priestesses in large temple establishments so much as the application of this rank to a religious landscape of smaller shrines with few permanent personnel. The evidence is too limited to permit any confident evaluation.

Other than female prophets and performers, the Mari evidence attests remarkably few other female temple personnel. A *nadītum* named Erišti-Aya sent a series of letters to Zimri-Lim from Sippar, a famous center for women devoted to the sun god.[23] One *nadītum* is mentioned in a letter to Yasmaḫ-Addu, but her place of service is not clear.[24] Durand tentatively identifies the *qaššatum* in lists of women with the *qadištum*, but it is not certain that she serves in a temple.[25] The palace harem was filled with women of various ranks and titles, including many 'singers' or musicians and women called *sekertum* ('confined') and *kezertum* (uncertain meaning). None of these was defined by temple service, and in fact their life was circumscribed by the bounds of the palace.[26]

In spite of the number and variety of titles encountered in the Mari evidence, the overall picture of temple personnel is simpler than it first seems. Most of the male and female personnel appear only in very limited contexts, such as in the Eštar ritual of Yasmaḫ-Addu's reign or in connection with prophecy, or their temple service is not clear-cut. In fact, only one male and one female category occur frequently throughout the evidence for the reign of Zimri-Lim, the *šangûm* (sanga) and the nin-dingir(-ra). Both of these titles indicate a leading male or female figure in Babylonian temple service, though the nin-dingir(-ra) was identified purely by her sacred role, and the *šangûm* was the chief administrator of a temple.

In the temples of the Mari archives, however, we cannot be sure that each figure stood at the apex of a large institutional pyramid. The fact that we are limited to palace archives makes argument from silence all the more difficult, but it is still hard to ignore certain gaps in the evidence. Extended studies by Johannes Renger and Dominique Charpin give us a good idea of what temple personnel inhabited the religious world of contemporary Babylonia (Renger 1967; 1968; Charpin 1986). No doubt the temples of Mari and its neighbors were served by any number of lesser personnel, but it is surely a mistake to transfer the whole Babylonian titulary and institutional framework onto these more western and northern sites without

---

22. See Fleming 1992: 80-82, and Emar VI.4, no. 556.47. Note that Durand (1995: 442) cites a text associated with the king of Ašlakkâ in the Ḫabur River basin that mentions 'the *ēntum* of Šamaš and the *ēntum* of Sîn', with the syllabic spelling *e-en-tam*. The Emar texts from the authorized excavations were published Arnaud 1985–87.

23. See the texts and discussion in Durand 2000: 390-402, nos. 1195-1202.

24. ARM V 82.18-21.

25. Durand, 1995: 453; see ARM IX 291, *passim*. Charpin cites one reference to a girl consecrated as a *qadištum* in the unpublished text A.1186 (1989–90: 94).

26. See the extensive treatment of sources and interpretation in Ziegler 1999: 69-89.

compelling proof, even if the scribes themselves had to try. One misses especially the male *pašīšum*, who is ubiquitous in southern Mesopotamian temples, and the *nadītum* women who are well-known at Sippar and other sites downstream.[27] The smaller the temple, the simpler may have been the staff. It is possible that minor shrines had only one male or female devotee, whom the scribes could designate a 'priest' (*šangûm*/sanga) or 'priestess' (nin-dingir-ra). Larger temples could have supported larger resident staffs, and we may have to allow for personnel who only showed up for special events.

3. *Doubting the Equation of Mari and Babylonian Temple Personnel*

The actual evidence for temple personnel is remarkably stripped down from the dozens of titles and types known to southern Mesopotamia in the same general period. Two categories dominate: the *šangûm* and the nin-dingir(-ra). The *šangûm* may have been the male head of temple affairs, but it is not clear that he always had to be the administrator of an extensive religious corporation. The reference to the nin-dingir-ra group belonging to Addu of Kulmiš would be out of place in a Babylonian setting, and there is no sign of the *gipāru*, the special residence for the nin-dingir(-ra) in southern Mesopotamia. ARM XXVI 178 and 179 even discuss problems with finding a residence for the new *ugbabtum* of Dagan, who could not move into the home of the previous priestess because it had stood empty for some time until various craftspeople occupied it (179.10). This is not a *gipāru*.

It should not be necessary to force the equation of Mari and Babylonian temple personnel. The scribes of the Mari archives were fluent both in Akkadian and in the institutional categories that accompanied a good cuneiform education in the southern Mesopotamian tradition. The religious traditions of Mari and other sites to the north and west were quite different from those of old Sumer and its Babylonian heirs. This difference is most clearly expressed in the temple architecture of these regions. Syrian temples of western and northern Mesopotamia are well known for their relatively simple and open construction, often built along one axis with a doorway looking back toward the god in the sacred *cella*. Mari itself maintained strong ties with southern Mesopotamia during the third millennium, and Yaḥdun-Lim's Šamaš temple inscription invokes the southern god Enlil instead of the local Dagan, but the excavated temples at Mari have little in common with the south. Jean-Claude Margueron observes especially the direct entries that characterize the Syrian type (1985: 506).

The relationship between temple architecture and temple staffing warrants further attention. At a simplistic level, the elaborate structures and many rooms of early southern Mesopotamia complement the major economic role of Sumerian temples. In general, the temples of the lands north and west of Sumer were much less central to economic life and did not require either the same massive space or the large administrative staff. I have not undertaken a proper exploration of the

27.   See Renger 1967: 149-70; 1968: 143-62. There is one *pašīšum* listed among the personnel of the *bītum* (temple of Dagan?) at Terqa (ARM IX 26.6).

correlations between temple form, activity and personnel, but the regional contrasts in form must be reflected in the job descriptions of personnel.

My suspicion that the Mari personnel must be understood differently from their southern counterparts derives also from my experience with the cuneiform evidence from Late Bronze Age Emar, far up the Euphrates River. Many features of Emar ritual and scribal custom have roots in the early second millennium. Emar's ritual and administrative texts attest a range of male and female sacred personnel, most with local West Semitic titles.[28] The principal place for Mesopotamian categories is as the lead 'priest' (SANGA/*šangû*) or 'priestess' (NIN.DINGIR) of an individual temple.[29]

These two titles are not misapplied in the Syrian context of Late Bronze Emar, but they cannot be interpreted solely according to the system of large southern Mesopotamian temples. The NIN.DINGIR of the storm god was a major figure in the religious life of the town, priestess of one of the most important temples, but it is not obvious that the temple had even one other person in full-time service. At her installation, the NIN.DINGIR was anointed by 'the diviner', the supervisor of a wide range of sacred sites at Emar.[30] She moved to and from the temple over several days of ritual transition in the company of singers and family members, none of whom is defined by service to the storm god. Not one of the various participants in the installation festival is defined by service to the storm god or his temple (Fleming 1992: 80-105). Tablets found in what appears to have been the storm god's temple include long lists of weapons that were assigned to listed men, along with lists for other goods and their recipients or donors, but there is no sign that any of these people served the temple on a full-time basis.[31] In the extensive collection of ritual and administrative texts from the diviner's archive in the building M₁, the only other person defined by service to the storm god is a 'slaughterer' (*zābiḫu*).[32] This man cannot be assumed to have resided in the temple, though his work did at least merit identification with the god. The NIN.DINGIR of the storm god therefore appears to have been an honored figure, but not necessarily at the head of a large temple household.

On the male side, the SANGA priest does not fulfill expectations for the Babylonian title. No SANGA (*šangû*) is attested for the temple of the storm god, and once again it may be reckless to assume his existence. Two Emar texts from outside the authorized excavations record the establishment of a new family right to occupy the

28.   See the inventory in Gary Beckman's essay on Emar religion in del Olmo Lete (ed.) 1995. Women include the *maš'ārtu* of the goddess Aštartu, the *nugagtu* lamentation priestess, and the plural *munabbiātu*, who call on the goddess Išḫara. Men include the *zābiḫu* slaughterer, the *nābû* (probably prophets), and the *wābil ilā'i* ('god-bearer'). There are male and female singers (*zammārū/zammirātu*).

29.   The 'consecrated' *qadištu* is also attested, but not as temple personnel. See Emar VI.3 124.1, where ᶠ*E-za* is NU.GIG (*qadištu*) without reference to temple service. She is married with three daughters.

30.   Emar VI.3 369.20-21; on the diviner, see Fleming 1992: 87-92; 2000: 13-47.

31.   Emar VI.3 42-62.

32.   Emar VI.3 275.1.

office of SANGA in an individual temple. In one of these, the tablet confirms the
founding of a completely new shrine for 'Nergal of the Stone', with a man and his
posterity as its SANGA priests.[33] No other personnel seems to be envisioned, and
the SANGA could be both priest and administrator without competition. Perhaps
the shrine could come to support others if it turned out to be a financial success, but
the institutional structure did not require it. Lists of barley allotments to various
named persons do not indicate much support for such SANGA priests of individual
sacred sites. They are listed among the lower tiers and do not seem to be accorded
great status.[34] It is not certain that there could only be one SANGA for each temple,
although nothing proves otherwise.

For the sacred sites encountered in the archives of the diviner housed in Emar's
building M_1, the primary 'temple administrator' may not have been the SANGA but
the diviner himself. The diviner's archive includes dozens of tablets that reflect his
administrative responsibility for many temples and shrines at Emar. One letter from
an official of the Hittite empire urges the diviner to get down to the business of
appointing a SANGA for the temple of [d]NIN.KUR, an important goddess in local
ritual affairs.[35] As a whole, the Late Bronze evidence from Emar shows that the
NIN.DINGIR and SANGA titles from the temples of southern Mesopotamia were
deeply embedded in Syrian institutions, but with distinct meanings that reflected
western religious life.

At some time in the future, the temple personnel from the Mari archives deserve
systematic evaluation of all available evidence, which is expanding continually with
the publication of new texts. This study should integrate written evidence with the
evidence for temple architecture, in order to discover how regional variation in
physical structures reflected differences in institutional roles and structures. The
temples of Syria and northern Iraq did not have the same economic and political
heritage as those from Babylonia, and especially the Sumerian situation in southern
Iraq, where each city-state was built around a massive temple complex. Because the
cuneiform scribal practices of Mari and Syria derived above all from southern
Mesopotamia, Babylonian categories were frequently borrowed in order to define
more northern and western realities. The temple terminology from this southern
Mesopotamian setting must be interpreted afresh in western texts, both at Mari and
beyond.

BIBLIOGRAPHY

Arnaud, Daniel
    1985–87   *Recherches au pays d'Aštata, Emar VI.1-4* (Paris: Editions Recherche sur les
               Civilisations).

33.   See Fleming 2000: 24 n. 33, for the details.
34.   In Emar VI.3 279, a SANGA of Dagan receives only 4 *parīsu* measures of barley, compared to the maximum of 20 or 30, and a SANGA of the moon god appears at the end of the list
with lesser recipients, though the number is lost (see ll. 21 and 48); see Fleming 1992: 91.
35.   Emar VI.3 268.

Charpin, Dominique
1986   *Le clergé d'Ur au siècle d'Hammurabi* (Geneva: Droz).
1989–90   'Compte rendu du CAD volume Q (1982)', *AfO* 36-37: 92-106.
2002   'Prophètes et rois dans le Proche-Orient amorrite: nouvelles donnèes, nou-velles perspectives', FM VI (Paris: SEPOA): 7-38.
Durand, Jean-Marie
1985   'Les dames du palais de Mari', *MARI* 4: 385-436.
1992   'Unité et diversités au Proche-Orient à l'époque amorrite', in Dominique Charpin and Francis Joannès (eds.), *La circulation des biens, des personnes et des idées dans le Proche-Orient ancien* (CRRAI, 38; Paris: Editions Recherche sur les Civilisations): 97-128.
1995   'La religión en Siria durante la época de los reinos amorreos según la documentación de Mari', *Mitología y Religión del Oriente Antiguo* II/1 (Sabadell: Editorial AUSA): 125-569.
2000   *Documents épistolaires du palais de Mari*, III (LAPO, 18; Paris: Cerf).
Durand, Jean-Marie, and Michaël Guichard
1997   'Les rituels de Mari', *FM* III (Paris: SEPOA): 19-78.
Fleming, Daniel E.
1992   *Installation of Baal's High Priestess at Emar* (Atlanta: Scholars Press).
1999   'Recent Work on Mari', *RA* 83: 160-61.
2000   *Time at Emar* (Winona Lake, IN: Eisenbrauns).
forthcoming 'Prophets and Temple Personnel in the Mari Archives', in Lester Grabbe (ed.), Proceedings of the 'Priest and Prophet' section of the 2002 Society of Biblical Literature annual meeting.
Huffmon, Herbert B.
2000   'A Company of Prophets: Mari, Assyria, Israel', in Martti Nissinen (ed.), *Prophecy in Its Ancient Near Eastern Context: Mesopotamian, Biblical, and Arabian Perspectives* (Atlanta: Society of Biblical Literature): 47-70.
Margueron, Jean-Claude
1985   'Quelques remarques sur les temples de Mari', *MARI* 4: 487-507.
Olmo Lete, Gregorio del (ed.)
1995   *Mitología y Religion del Oriente Antiguo* (Sabadell: Editorial AUSA).
Renger, Johannes
1967   'Untersuchungen zum Priestertum in der aB Zeit.1.Teil', *ZA* 58: 110-88.
1968   'Untersuchungen zum Priestertum in der aB Zeit.2.Teil', *ZA* 59: 104-230.
Sasson, Jack M.
1994   'The Posting of Letters with Divine Messages', *FM* II: 299-316.
1998   'About "Mari and the Bible"', *RA* 92: 97-123.
Van der Toorn, Karel
1998   'Old Babylonian Prophecy: Between the Oral and the Written', *JNSL* 24: 55-70.
Ziegler, Nele
1999   *Le Harem de Zimrî-Lîm* (Paris: SEPOA).

FALSE PROPHECY IS TRUE

David Noel Freedman and Rebecca Frey

The title of this paper is a bit misleading. It would probably be more accurate to say that 'failed prophecy' or 'unfulfilled prophecy' is authentic—meaning that a record of a failed prophecy is an unedited record of an actual utterance designed to predict a future event. The converse may be that 'true prophecy', or 'fulfilled prophecy', is questionable because the prophetic utterance may have been edited at a later date to conform to an event that already occurred. There is no example, to our knowledge, of anybody deliberately recording a prophecy that they mean to be false or unfulfilled. In other words, things aren't exactly what they seem—when we read a false prophecy we are reading the prophecy as it was truly given. When we read that a prophecy was fulfilled, that prophecy comes under suspicion of falsification or alteration. The evaluation of prophecies as actual, fabricated, true or false is designed to add to the body of knowledge concerning actual prophetic content, practice and form which, in turn, speaks to the entire history of Israel on socio-cultural and political levels. Such evaluation may also be used as a tool for dating texts, as it is doubtful that a prophecy was recorded after a historically attestable event had already proved it wrong.

An example of questionable true prophecy occurs in 1 Kings 13 when a prophet from Judah speaks to Jeroboam I, saying that 'a child shall be born unto the house of David, Josiah by name' who would destroy the temple at Bethel and burn men's bones on the altar. About 400 years later, in 2 Kgs 23.16, when Josiah did destroy the temple and did burn men's bones on the altar, the writer recalls the earlier prophecy and says that it happened 'according to the word of the Lord which the man of God proclaimed, who proclaimed these words'.

Such specific detail, the naming of Josiah and the burning of bones on the altar, and such temporal distance is unusual, but the prophecy is typical in that it is given as a prophecy in the name of the Lord and its fulfillment is later reported. In theory that is what is supposed to happen, but in practice many people would say that the prophecy was entirely fabricated and then interpolated into the text after the temple had already been destroyed. Some may hold a middle ground, a compromise, saying that the prophecy was given but touched up later. For instance, the original prophecy may have foretold the destruction of the temple without naming names or specifying a time, and then when the prophecy was fulfilled someone added the name of the person responsible. Such a compromise admits to the possibility of subsequent tampering while maintaining the veracity of the prophet who did, after all, predict the destruction of the temple at Beth-El. Another approach to evaluating this prophecy would have us look to the author, the famous Deuteronomic Historian, who could not resist making a point. If there was a prophecy its fulfillment was sought.

If a prophecy spells out the necessary details of what is to happen, as in the above example, it may be too good to be true, that is, it may have been embellished by the person who wrote both the prediction and its fulfillment. If a prophecy is false or goes unfulfilled then we raise doubts about the prophecy and/or the ability of that specific prophet. We have numerous examples of unfulfilled prophecy, perhaps the most famous is in Mic. 3.12 and the subsequent reference to Micah in Jer. 26.18. Micah predicts, without condition or qualification, that Jerusalem will be destroyed: 'Because of you Zion will be plowed as a field, and Jerusalem shall become heaps' (Mic. 3.12). Ultimately, we know that did happen to Jerusalem more than once, but the point is that Micah's prophecy exceeded a reasonable statute of limitations within which the fulfillment should have occurred. This is the main evidence, in our opinion, that his prophecy was given as it was recorded and as we now have it. About 100 years later the question arises as to whether his prophecy still has any validity or relevance. The question about Micah comes up because Jeremiah makes a similar prediction, only he puts it in the form of a condition: 'If they will listen and turn every man from his evil way then I may repent me of the evil which I purpose to do unto them because of the evil of their doings… If you will not listen to me…then I will make this house like Shiloh, and will make this city a curse to all the nations of the earth' (Jer. 26.3-6). Jeremiah said this in the Lord's house and all the people who heard him prophesy wanted to kill him. 'This man is worthy to die', they say, 'for he has prophesied against this city as you have heard with your ears' (Jer. 26.11). Jeremiah insists that he was truly sent by the Lord and that they can avert their misfortune if they mend their ways. Then the people say, 'This man is not worthy to die: for he has spoken to us in the name of the Lord our God'; and some of the elders recall that about 100 years earlier, during the reign of Hezekiah, Micah prophesied much the same thing and nobody killed him. On the contrary, Hezekiah and the people responded to Micah's prophecy by modifying their behavior so that nothing happened. So how do they explain this? Micah is a true prophet and he gave a true prophecy. But his prophecy does not happen. According to Deut. 18.20-22, he ought to die: 'The prophet who speaks a word in my name which I have not commanded him to speak, or who speaks in the name of other gods, even that prophet shall die'. If God commanded Micah to speak, then the city ought to have fallen as he predicted—no fallen city, no word of God. But rather than kill Micah as a false prophet, they say that his prophecy was so effective it prevented its own fulfillment. Now this is sophistication, but it provides a very useful tool with which to explain unfulfilled prophecies. If a prophecy comes true, that's easy, you have nothing to explain. If it does not, then you have to explain why it did not. So either the prophecy is fulfilled or it is not, and if it is not it could be because the prophecy itself produced its own unfulfillment.

Prophecies in the Hebrew Bible are often warnings: they are conditional even if they are not stated as conditions. The extent to which prophecy is presented as conditional is, as far as we know, peculiar to the Bible. In cultures where ecstatic prophecy was the practice, such as Phoenicia, Greece, Asia and the Hittite civilization, prophets are generally viewed as having limited access to a pool of information lying just beyond mortal grasp. Possessed by a god, they search for that bit of information particular to the one seeking it and then formulate a brief response in ambiguous language subject to interpretation on a number of different levels. For instance, the Pythia, priestess of Apollo at Delphi, does not volunteer warnings to city-states to repent before Apollo strikes them down, though she may say something concurrently or after-the-fact as to the cause of their destruction. Warnings are generally sent by way of dreams, and dreams can be purposefully false, such as the dream sent to Agamemnon urging him to attack the Trojans. Here we find another difference—Zeus has set his plan in motion and Agamemnon can do nothing to change it. In the Bible, God is influenced by the way people respond to prophecy and has the sovereign right to change the prophecy, to retract the threat. This right validates Micah and also empowers the prophecy in an unexpected way. Micah said Jerusalem would be destroyed and it did not happen. However, instead of saying Micah is a false prophet, he is seen as an even truer prophet because he is the one who relates God's warning and averts disaster.

What is striking is that Micah really gave this prophecy; he really said it. If it were not in the record there would be no need for the explanation. And nobody, the Deuteronomist or any other, would invent a prophecy and put it into Micah's mouth just to create an embarrassment by leaving the prophecy unfulfilled. Someone might say it was done in order to establish a different line of communication or action on behalf of God to achieve a result, but, such speculation aside, we have here a record that combines a prophet with a statement and an unfulfillment; that's real, that's authentic.

Prophecies often change behavior, leading God to suspend punishment. For instance, in 1 Kgs 21.28 God spares Ahab: 'Do you see how Ahab humbles himself before me? Because he humbles himself I will not bring the evil in his days, but in his son's days I will bring evil upon the house.' Similarly, in 2 Kings 22 the prophetess Huldah says that Josiah will be spared the wrath of God because, 'Your heart was tender, and you humbled yourself before the Lord when you heard what I spoke against this place and its inhabitants…and you tore your clothes and wept before me; I also have heard you…you shall go to your grave in peace'. This prophecy was false—Josiah died in battle—but the pattern of 'repent and be spared' is common enough to be appealed to when, as in the case of Micah, a prophecy has gone unfulfilled. Huldah's false prophecy is not referred to again. Nobody makes an effort to reconcile it with historical fact, although one could say that if punishment is conditional then so is reward, that is, a peaceful death is also conditional.

Huldah's prophecy is another example of accurately reported prophecy; she actually said these words, they were not added, or edited, after-the-fact because they could have been easily corrected but were not. The same applies to Jeremiah, who prophesies that Zedekiah 'shall die in peace and with the burnings of your fathers' (Jer. 34.5). Unfortunately for Zedekiah, things did not work out that way: 'And the king of Babylon slew the sons of Zedekiah before his eyes; he slew also all the princes of Judah in Riblah. Then he put out the eyes of Zedekiah; and the king of Babylon bound him in chains, and carried him to Babylon, and put him in prison till the day of his death' (Jer. 52.10-11).

The mirror image of Micah is Jonah. It is the same story, but projected onto a distant country, another name and another place. Jonah is in Nineveh warning the population to repent, just as Micah had done in Israel. 'Forty days', he says, 'and Nineveh shall be overthrown' (Jon. 3.4). The population of Nineveh repents, they fast and put on sackcloth, the king sits in ashes, and God spares them. Jonah is a true prophet, a real prophet, but he made an unfulfilled prophecy and says so himself. He suspected from the very beginning that this would be the result, that Nineveh would be spared and that he would look like a false prophet: 'I fled to Tarshish because I knew you are a gracious God and merciful, slow to anger, and of great kindness, and you repent of evil…take my life from me, for it is better for me to die than to live' (Jon. 4.2-3). Jonah, among other things, is a believer in what he thinks is justice and he thinks there was a miscarriage of justice here due to God's mercy. Micah, in the same position, may have thought similarly: 'God, what are you doing to me? I told the truth at the risk of my own life and you pull it all back and ruin my reputation and my career.' What is at work behind these prophecies is bluntly stated by the author of the book of Jonah, but put into the mouth of foreign sailors. They say, 'You, God, have done as you pleased'. That is the answer. God is not bound by any prophecy in whatever he does and Jonah analyzed it correctly from the very beginning. Within the story (the whole story may be fictional, but within the requirements of the narrative Jonah must make his prediction) he knew God's intention was to spare Nineveh and the reason he gives is not that Nineveh repents, but that God has mercy. Historically we know nothing about what Nineveh's actions were, but in the Bible this is the truth. For our purposes an unfulfilled prophecy becomes all the more important because it is unfulfilled; that means the prophet really said it, it was not inserted or tampered with later in order to augment the authority of the prophet or of prophecy.

A more important example occurs in the book of Ezekiel, because here we have a situation in which the prophet revisits his own prophecy and announces it as failed. There are scholars who assert that Ezekiel's original prophecy was at least partially fulfilled, but that does not matter. What does matter is that Ezekiel himself said that his own prophecy did not happen. He predicts, several times, that the city of Tyre will be destroyed and these predictions are all dated very carefully. Then, in the twenty-seventh year, Ezekiel is reviewing his book and comes across this unfulfilled prophecy he made 14 years earlier, that Nebuchadnezzar, the great king, would conquer Tyre and wipe it out. After 14 years he realizes that it did not happen and was not going to happen and he says, 'Nebuchadrezzar caused his army to serve a great service against Tyre; every head was made bald, and every shoulder was peeled; yet had he no wages, nor his army, for Tyre, for the service that he had served against it' (Ezek. 29.17). Nebuchadnezzar tried hard and the troops tried hard, but they all failed.

Some scholars would argue that the treaties and settlement between Tyre and Nebuchadnezzar, in which Tyre accepted certain tribute obligations, would be enough to substantiate the prophecy, but that is not what Ezekiel was talking about. His prophecy went unfulfilled and he says so flatly, and he would also deny flatly that he was a false prophet. Whose responsibility is this? Who is at fault here? Not the prophet—he got the word and delivered it. Then the responsibility rests with God. This is the converse of Classical Greece where it is the responsibility of the receiver to make the analytical leaps necessary to understand the prophecy. The Pythia at Delphi speaks the truth but the usefulness of that truth depends upon the intellectual wherewithal of the receiver to sort through the various levels of meaning and resolve the ambiguity of the prophetic utterance. Success or failure rests on that ability.

Such ambiguity is not a characteristic of Hebrew prophecy. Ezekiel said Tyre would fall, but it did not. It is God's responsibility and God takes the failure of the prophecy under consideration and gives Ezekiel a new and revised message: 'I will give the land of Egypt unto Nebuchadrezzar king of Babylon; and he shall take her multitude, and take her spoil, and take her prey; and it shall be the wages for his army' (Ezek. 29.19). For not capturing Tyre, Nebuchadnezzar can conquer Egypt. This prophecy was given in 570 and, considering all the conditions, was reasonable. In other words, prophecy is not cut and dried, fixed and settled; it is an interaction. To add a little irony, we do not know what happened to the second prophecy either. There is no comment in Ezekiel regarding Egypt, probably because he did not live long enough to make one. And there is no evidence from Egypt or Babylonia. There is a fragmentary report in the Babylonian Chronicle, written a short while after Ezekiel's prophecy, stating that the king of Babylon set out with his army for Egypt, but beyond this there is no evidence as to what happened.

Another example where the historical record does not help determine the veracity of the prophecy is reported in Amos 7.10-17. Amos, who comes to Bethel where the high priest Amaziah presides, prophesies, 'I will rise against the house of Jeroboam with a sword'. This is Jeroboam II, the king who rebuilt the Northern Kingdom. The prophecy indicates that there would be some kind of rebellion or action against the house of Jeroboam. That is a prediction that is in line with what a number of other prophets spoke against the ruling dynasty. Amaziah does not like what he hears because, as he says, this is the chapel of the king, this is the royal temple in Bethel. He sends word to the king, presumably in Samaria, that this man Amos has committed treason and threatened to kill the king.

Amos' message was different from what Amaziah reports, but Amos does not contradict him by citing the 'House of Jeroboam' instead of Jeroboam himself. It may be that by using 'House of Jeroboam' Amos was allowing himself some leeway since the revolt might not be against Jeroboam but against some successor within a certain chronological range. The point that everyone accepts is that Jeroboam was not assassinated. He died in the normal course of events. Whether that actually happened or not we do not know, but that is how the Bible recounts the end of his life. So this is a case of an unfulfilled prophecy according to the account as it was given by Amos. What really happened according to the Bible is that Jeroboam reigned for over forty years and died. His son Zechariah becomes the king, and within six months Zechariah is assassinated, and there the dynasty ends.

After that, Israel splits up, goes through a whole series of kings, and ends up being destroyed by the Assyrians. Whether Amos was correct or not, this is an authentic prophecy because there is no direct explicit fulfillment.

The book of Daniel serves as another illustration of our thesis. Most scholars would agree that the work contains a narrative recording world events over a period of 400 years presented as a series of prophecies by a man named Daniel who lived in the sixth century BCE. In fact, any real predicting concerns the last days during the persecution of the Jews by Antiochus Epiphanes. The book in its present form traces the history of empires, and Israel's relationship with those empires, all the way back to Nebuchadnezzar and the Babylonian empire. Daniel 'foresees' everything that happened after the rise of Babylon down to the critical moment at which the author is writing. The main purpose of the book is to focus on the present crisis, which has been created by the conflict between Jews and Greeks in Jerusalem and throughout the kingdom that has threatened the Temple and the worship of Yahweh. True prophecy begins at that point. The historical information for the most part is quite accurate. Inaccuracies are not due to deliberate falsification, but reflect the fact that the writer did not have access to proper historical records. In Daniel, the real prophecy comes at the end because things did not happen the way they were predicted.

We conclude by turning to the major prophets to consider the fall of Babylon in 539 BCE. The sections of Jeremiah (chs. 50–51) and Isaiah (chs. 46–48) describing the violent, cosmic destruction of Babylon are excellent examples of true/false-prophecy. These chapters must have been proclaimed and written before Babylon was handed over to Cyrus. According to the records and all the information we have, Babylon was captured with very little bloodshed. The priests of Marduk, who despised their king Nabonidus and his son Belshazzar, betrayed the city and delivered it to Cyrus. In other words, the actual capture of Babylon is entirely different in detail from the prophecies. The only explanation to account for such a difference is that these chapters must have been written before anything happened. Simply put, they are real, authentic prophecies.

ESARHADDON, SANDUARRI, AND THE ADON PAPYRUS

Alberto R. Green

The Adon Papyrus from Egypt was first published in 1945 (Saad 1945) and it immediately created a controversy about the identity of the king who purportedly had written it and when and where it had been written.[1] The papyrus is a letter to the Pharaoh in Egypt mentioning the approach of the king of Babylon. However, neither the Egyptian nor the Babylonian kings are named in the text. In the latest reconstruction of the letter (Porten 1981) almost half of the text has been broken away and only the right-hand portion has survived. It has been presumed that the name and place from which Adon wrote were in the missing portion of the text.

The problem posed by the absence of these key indicators has led to numerous interpretations of the text.[2] Most scholars who have dealt with the document have placed the activities described in the text during the Neo-Babylonian Empire and identify Nebuchadrezzar as the king who is mentioned in it.[3] Accordingly, the dates of the related actions have ranged anywhere from 605 to 597 BCE. The location of Adon himself has been placed in various cities in Phoenicia and Philistia (Porten 1981: 39-41, 49-50).

On the basis of the new photographs and readings from B. Porten, C. Krahmalkov initiated a new phase in the study of this papyrus when he observed that the name *sndwr* or Sanduarri occurs in the last line of the text. He then proposed that it was the 'messengers' of Merodach-Baladan, that is, his ambassadors, who had been sent to king Hezekiah of Judah in 702/701 BCE, rather than the 'forces' of the king of Babylon who were thought to have been approaching Philistia. Krahmalkov argued that since Sanduarri is known as the king of Kindu and Sizu in an Assyrian text

---

1. As indicated in the earliest references in Ginsberg 1948 and Bright 1949.
2. Unfortunately, the document is fragmentary and key areas where names should be found are missing. We are now left only with the right side of the document. As would be expected, there-fore, there are quite a few translations and interpretations of the text. These can be grouped together under three interpretations. First, there is Dupont-Sommer's (1948), which was subsequently modified by Ginsberg (1948). Second is the interpretation offered by Gibson (1975). Finally, the most recent has been proposed by Fitzmyer (1979 [a reprint of an article first published in 1965]).
3. On the strength of the identification of Askelon as Adon's realm by Ginsberg (1948), following the reference to the sons of Aga king of Askelon; cf. Weidner (1929: 928). Most school ars identify the presence of Babylonian troops (so, e.g., Malamat 1968; Meyer 1954: 258-59, and subsequently associate the events with the campaign of Nebuchadrezzar himself in 605/604 BCE (Malamat 1968: 142-43).

from the time of King Esarhaddon, that the Adon Papyrus was to be dated in the late eighth or early seventh century BCE (Krahmalkov 1981).

On the basis of this suggestion, Shea then followed Krahmalkov by proposing to bring the Adon Papyrus much closer in time to the inscription in which Sanduarri appears. He pointed to the imminent nature of Adon's request, and suggested that if the reason for this request was Sennacherib's march into Palestine in 701 BCE to quell the uprising of the anti-Assyrian kings of Palestine who were being instigated by Merodach-Baladan (e.g. his visit to Hezekiah of Judah [2 Kgs 20.12-19]), this would not have been evident to Merodach-Baladan, the instigator whom Krahmalkov had identified as the king of Babylon, more than a year earlier in 702. He further observed that references to this same Sanduarri are known from inscriptions of Esarhaddon dated as late as the mid-670s, suggesting that his hostility extended clear back into the reign of Sennacherib. He proposed that the developments involving Sanduarri and Adon took place a quarter of a century later, toward the end rather than at the beginning of Sennacherib's reign, and attributed the text rather to this Assyrian king's second campaign in the region in 688/687 BCE (Shea 1985).

Shea's position was not well received. Particularly on the basis of an analysis of the Demotic docket written on the outside of the text after it was received in Egypt, Yurco concluded that the text could not have been written at least before c. 650 BCE since Demotic script was not developed in Egypt before that time (Yurco 1991). On the strength of this observation, it was maintained that the 605/604 BCE date fits best with the Demotic evidence. On the one hand, such a position would seem to invalidate the possibility of dating the inscription to either 701 or 688/687 BCE. On the other hand, however, if Sanduarri is associated with the end of Sennacherib's reign according to Krahmalkov and Shea, it would seem that a reasonable argument could also be made to place the writing of the text c. 688/687 BCE even if the Demotic docket could not have been written before c. 640 at the earliest. Clearly then, a reassessment of this text is in order to determine, if possible, both when it was written and its place of origin.

The Document[4]

The transcription of the text as it now stands reads as follows:

1. *ʾl mrʾmlkn pr h bdk ʾdn mlk* . . .
2. *šmyʾw ʾrqʾwb lšmyn ʾlh* . . . . . .
3. *pr h kywmy šmyn rmyn zy* . . . . .
4. *zy mlk bbl ʾtw mḥzz . . ʾpq w* . .
5. . . . . . . *ʾḥzw* . . . .
6. *ky mrʾmlkn pr h yd ky bd(k)* . .
7. *lmšlḥ ḥyl lḥšltn(y) ʾl (y) šbqn(y)* . .
8. *wṭbth bdk nṣr wngdʾznh* . . . .
9. *pḥh bmtʾwspw šndwr sn* . . . .

---

4. See Porten 1981: 36, 42.

Translation

1. Unto the lord of kings Pharaoh, your servant Adon king of. . . .
2. Heaven and Earth and Baal Shamayin (the great) god . . . . . .
3. Pharaoh like the days of the high heavens of. . . . . . .
4. of the king of Babylon have come from Sizu (?) (unto) Aphek and
5. . . . . they have seized . . . .
6. for the lord of kings Pharaoh knows that your servant . . . . .
7. to send a force to rescue (me). Do not abandon (me) . . . . . .
8. and your servant has preserved his good relations, and his commander
9. a governor in the land, and Sanduarri they have brought to an end, . .

There are a number of ways by which documents that lack a date can be approximately dated. For example, some major lines of evidence can be derived from a study of the internal contents of the text. In the case of this particular document, there are two lines of internal evidence that can possibly give us some indication of the time when it was written.

The first has to do with the nature of the phraseology used in it and the period from which certain expression come. In the opening title, Adon addresses the Pharaoh as 'lord of kings' (*mrʾmlkn*). This Aramaic title is equivalent to the Akkadian *bēl šarrāni*,[5] and it occurs in about forty Neo-Assyrian letters addressed to Esarhaddon and Ashurbanipal, the majority to the latter and a few to the former (Porten 1981: 39). It was also current later in Imperial Aramaic (Dan. 2.47) as well as in Phoenician and Palmyrene.[6]

The second line of evidence involves Adon's faithfulness to the fulfillment of his covenant with Pharaoh. Fitzmyer (1979), following Moran (1963), has pointed out that in Adon's statement 'Your servant has guarded his good relations' (*ṭbth bdk nṣr*), the expression 'to guard good relations', is a technical phrase for the observance of treaty stipulations found especially in Assyrian texts from the time of Ashurbanipal.

In addition, there are the personal names used in the text, one for the king and another for his god. There are some onomastic parallels for the name Adon cited by Porten, and others are not listed by him. These parallels may come from the LBA and the IA down through Neo-Assyrian times, and possibly later (Porten 1981: 38-39). Regarding the name of his deity, four inscriptions mention Baal Shamayin as the name of his god, one of which comes from a Phoenician text of the tenth century, while the others derive from Neo-Assyrian and Syrian sources of the eighth and early seventh centuries.[7] None of these come from the Neo-Babylonian period sources.

If judged by the four items identified—two political phrases and two personal names—it would appear that the text belongs most directly to the Neo-Assyrian

5. See Galling 1963 and Waterman 1930.
6. It appears first in the tenth-century BCE Phoenician inscription of Yehimilk, king of Byblos. Note also the Zakkur Inscription (Dion 1995; Van Seters 1995).
7. These are noted in Donner and Röllig 1962–63: 4.3, 26. AIII. 18, 202.3, and Borger 1956: no. 69.

period of the early seventh century. These parallels are not as direct with Nebu-chadrezzar of the Neo-Babylonian period.

On the basis of this internal line of evidence, it is possible to consider the more specific line of relations of personal names and royal titles. The text identifies four rulers, some are named and others are unnamed. They are:

1.   The Pharaoh—unnamed.
2.   Adon—named, but his city name is broken away and he is unknown from other ancient Near Eastern texts.
3.   King of Babylon—unnamed.
4.   Sanduarri—named, but his city and kingdom are not named. He is known from other ancient Near Eastern texts.

Based on this line of internal evidence, Sanduarri seems to be the most direct ruler through whom to make a connection with the history of the text period. However, in view of some of the questions associated with the identification of the name San-duarri, which Yurco has argued is 'based on a questionable identification and highly dubious restoration of scant traces of Sennacherib' (1991: 41-42), it seems pertinent to make another careful examination of the text.

Sanduarri

In Porten's new epigraphic presentation of the text, aside from adding the Demotic docket which had not been noted previously, he has also provides three excellent photographs of the text; one in ordinary black and white, a second taken from above with side lighting (to eliminate the shadow), and a third with infra-red film. Beyond this we have the excellent hand copy supplied by Porten along with four transcriptions and translations of the text done by him and three other scholars. One could hardly be in a better position to evaluate this text epigraphically. Porten's accompanying commentary is lengthy and detailed. In this he deals with all aspects of this text (Porten 1981: 36-37, 41-43, 50).

Krahmalkov (1981) first identified the name *sndwr* with that of Sanduarri, king of Kindu and Sizu who had rebelled against Assyria and was subsequently captured and executed by Esarhaddon in 676 BCE. This had been read earlier by Porten, and subsequently accepted by Shea.[8] In general, it must be concluded that Porten has certainly given an accurate presentation of the document. However, a detailed read-ing of the entire text appears to reveal two places where his reading may be faulty.

In his article, Shea points out that the name Sanduarri (*sndwr*) and the *sn* [break] which follows it in the last line of the text is as clearly identified as any other part of the text. A close scrutiny of the photographs underscores Shea's point. Clearly then, there can be no doubt regarding the name. It seems, however, that there should be a correction of one letter in the word before *sndwr*. Here Porten and some earlier studies since Ginsberg have read the word as *wspr*, translating 'and the scroll

---

8.   With reference to the phrase or the name as rendered by both Krahmalkov and Porten, Shea concluded that 'the reading is quite clear and it is undoubtedly correct' (1985: 409).

(record, letter)', or the like. Others, like Gibson (1975: II, 21), have rendered this word as 'border'.

The first three letters of this word have been read correctly but the last letter has not. Having read the first three letters as *wsp* and seeing some resemblance of the last letter to reš, interpreters have commonly accepted the well-known word *seper* here. The problem is that final reš constitutes a problem here and it does not bear up under close scrutiny. The *–pr–* sequence occurs in three places in this text, in the word 'pharaoh' (*prh*) in ll. 1, 3 and 6. When we study these letter pairs it is clear that the pe has been identified correctly in l. 9, but not so the reš.

The reš in this text is a broad-brushed letter which curves to the left, and it has a broad interrupted head. The pe is like it only thinner. But the letter in l. 9 has a vertical leg with a limb at its head, which angles up to the left. It takes off from a crest of the vertical left and the crest is divided from the left leaning limb by a notch. There are at least eight examples of this letter in this text, two of them in this line. This is the letter waw. It is found at the beginning of l. 9 and it occurs again at the beginning of this very word *wsp*. In other words, the word begins and ends with a waw. The word should be read as *wspw*, not *wspr*. That makes the final waw a third person plural verbal ending, similar to what is found with *ḥzw* in l. 5. The subject there was the forces or troops of the king of Babylon, and they fit well here as the subject since they still appear to be engaged in unacceptable activity from the point of view of Adon who wrote the letter.

The Aramaic verb *swp* from which this plural perfect form has been derived has the meaning 'to end, bring to an end, terminate' (Dan. 2.44; the related noun occurs in Dan. 4.8, 19; 7.26, 28). The text thus indicates that those forces brought *sndwr* or Sanduarri to an end, either personally or in terms of his rule. In other words, this text is quite specific in terms of the dating of the action it records. It belongs to the very end of Sanduarri's reign, the time when he was deposed. We know very well when that occurred and we know who did it. The Assyrian king who defeated and deposed Sanduarri was Esarhaddon, and his inscriptions make it possible to date this event to 697 BCE during the only campaign he made that was specifically directed against Philistia (Luckenbill 1926–27). This papyrus reporting that event should therefore be dated to the year 678/677 BCE (*ANET*: 290).

The issue of the date of this papyrus can be solved by this new reading of l. 9, a date proposed earlier by Porten and Krahmalkov. First of all, Porten provided the new readings, which made the identification of Sanduarri possible. Then, on the strength of this reading, Krahmalkov took that information and made the historical connection. With the proposed new reading presented here for the verb that precedes Sanduarri's name, it is now possible to connect the text with an event at the end of his reign. This in turn makes it possible to date the text to the time of Esarhaddon and thus identify him as the king of Babylon mentioned in l. 4. This identification may be somewhat surprising as the title 'king of Assyria' might be expected instead. However, several Assyrian kings held title to the throne of Babylon, and Esarhaddon was one of them. As Yurco has pointed out, it was Esarhaddon 'who among Assyrian monarchs could best claim the title king of Babylon' (1991: 42).

Given this new reading, the text does not belong to the time of Nebuchadrezzar, nor does it belong to the second campaign of Sennacherib; rather, it belongs to the time of Esarhaddon. The political terminology of the text points in that direction. The personal name of Sanduarri, and the action of the Assyrian troops against him, bringing him or his rule to an end, makes that point specific to a particular year within Esarhaddon's reign.

The other new reading from this text could also lend some additional support to this interpretation. The fifth word in the fourth line of this text is damaged and difficult to read. Its first letter can be clearly read as a mem. The second letter has commonly been read as a ṭeth, but this is where some corrections can possibly be made. Two signs appear in this space and they are quite different. Above is a thin-lined letter with a notch and a limb extending to the left. It has a short tail but it does not extend very far down to the right, certainly not far enough to connect with the letter below it to make one letter. The letter below is but one small daub of ink. Two letters in this text come in this form—it is either a yod or a zayin. The yod, however, is triangular with a short tail extending to the left. That is not the form of this letter which must therefore be a zayin. It can be compared with examples at the end of l. 3 and the beginning of l. 4.[9]

The thin-lined letter above the zayin fits best with the two examples of the samek found in l. 9. The difference between them is that the tail of this samek does not extend as far down as the ones in l. 9. One reason for this may be that the zayin written below it interrupted its space and so it is written with a shorter tail. The reason for its thin lines could be that the scribe wrote the zayin first, in the normal line and with normal thickness of the letter. Then, having decided that letter was not the correct one, he wrote the more irregular thin-lined samek above it. What we have here, then, could be a scribal correction, the only one recognizable in the extant portion of the document.

The next letter has been read by Porten as an aleph. It is a vertical letter which curves slightly to the right, and its upper limb extends to the right. Other letters in this text and script have upper limbs which extend to the left, including kaph, mem, waw and a few others. There is only one letter in this text that has an upper limb which extends to the right, and that is the ṣade. For example, one can compare the occurrences of this letter in ll. 7 and 8. The word in l. 4 should therefore be read as *mz(!s)ṣ*. If there was a letter following the ṣade, it has been destroyed by the hole eaten there by a worm. What can be made of this word *mz(!s)ṣ*? The first letter can easily be taken as the prefixed preposition 'from'. Together with the other portion of this line, it would read '(the forces) of the king of Babylon have come from [X] [to] Aphek'. The prepositional lamedh with the next word, also a place name, probably is missing due to another break in the text. From the context, what is expected here is another place name. Can any place name be made out of *ztṣu* or *siṣu*? One possibility is that it may refer to Sizu, part of Sanduarri's combined kingdoms of Kindu and Sizu. Because of the difficulty reading this damaged name a precise

---

9.   See the accompanying copies of photographs of the papyrus made by Porten as presented in his article (1981: 36, 41, 42).

identification is impossible. Though speculative, Sizu remains a distinct possibility and should at least be given serious consideration.

Place of Origin

Having dated this text to the reign of Esarhaddon, we may now turn to the question of its place of origin. In previous studies, only Phoenicia and Philistia have been given consideration. Neither of these is a very good candidate. Phoenicia should have been ruled out long ago on the basis of language. If a Phoenician king in the pre-Persian Period was going to write to Pharaoh in Egypt, he probably would have written to him in Phoenician, not Aramaic. A similar thing can be said for Philistia. While we do have evidence of Philistine writing from Ekron, the nature of the Philistine script and alphabet continues to be a source of controversy among scholars as we wait for the discovery of documents of sufficient length to study (Dothan 1995).

Since the Phoenicians probably wrote in Phoenician and the Philistines wrote in an as yet unknown language, the Aramaic of the Adon Papyrus does not fit well with either. Where then should we locate Adon? Because the text was written in Aramaic but has some Phoenician elements mixed in (Adon, Baal-Shamen),[10] another general region is a likely place to consider. This sort of mixing took place in central and northern Syria and south central Anatolia, and it is to this area of the Neo-Hittite states that we should look for the origin of this text.[11] Locating his text in this region would also explain why the writer was so current on events in this region, for instance the fall of Sanduarri, and why this course of events should be so threatening to him.

This also says something about the location of Aphek in this text. The problem with trying to locate this site is that the name, which means 'water source', is so ubiquitous. At least four different Apheks have been given consideration in previous studies of this text (Porten 1981: 38). Most speculation has centered on the Aphek at Rosh ha- Ayin (Dupont-Sommer 1948) near the Philistine pentapolis, and the Aphek at Afga at the source of the Adonis River (Gibson 1975: II). If one had to choose between these two sites on the basis of the study of the text so far, the more northern of these two would certainly be more favored. But this does not rule out the possibility that other Apheks farther north than this should be considered. That is a distinct possibility given the more northern orientation of the text.

There is still the important matter of the text's Demotic docket, which has been read as containing the name Ekron, a reading that is far from certain. It is interesting to trace Porten's oscillations back and forth between various Demotic authorities (1981: 43-45). Some of the readings include the following:

---

10. Porten has shown that neither of these names can be considered as decisive in determining the identity of Adon (1981: 38-39).

11. Interestingly, the great majority of studies on this text have located Adon's kingdom in the region of Philistia. So, for example, for Askelon, Fitzmyer 1979: 232; for Gaza, Rainey 1975: 55-56; for Sidon, Milik 1967: 561-63, to name a few.

r. di pȝ qrn (G.R. Hughes, first reading)

r. di m bȝh pdȝ prn (K.-T. Zauzich)

r. di pȝ wr pn-Grn (or Qrn, Sqrn) (G.R. Hughes, second reading)

This range of readings hardly inspires confidence. The docket may contain the name 'Ekron' or it may not. For the time being this identification is still uncertain and may very well be a reference to some other location farther north.

Date of the Document

Shea proposed that this document could have been written as early as 688 BCE, and subsequently 678 BCE (1985: 408-10). However, Yurco (1991) has pointed out that Demotic was not written that early. Since this re-examination of the internal evidence of the text points even more strongly in the direction of an early date (678), this is more a problem for the Demoticists than for the Aramaists. It should be noted that the assumption under which Yurco is operating is that the docket was written on this document contemporaneous with its arrival in the country. However, the Pharaoh at that time (Tirhakhah) knew king Adon, with whom he was corresponding, so it was not necessary to identify the place of origin until some time later, perhaps many years after the document was received. Therefore the assumption that the docket was written on the document at the time it arrived in Egypt is open to question.

Conclusion

The results of this re-examination of the Adon Papyrus may now be summarized. The document is dated best to the year 678/677 BCE when the forces of the Assyrian king Esarhaddon defeated and executed Sanduarri. Esarhaddon is thus the unnamed 'king of Babylon' in this document, a title which he also held. Tirhakhah was the Pharaoh of Egypt to whom this document was addressed but he appears to have done little to help Adon or anyone else in Western Asia at the time. The location from which Adon wrote is still unknown, but a location in central or northern Syria is more reasonable than the Phoenician or Philistine suggestions previously proposed.

BIBLIOGRAPHY

Borger, R.
    1956   'Die Inschriften Asarhaddons Königs von Assyrien', *AfO* 9: no. 69.
Bright, J.
    1949   'A New Letter in Aramaic Written to a Pharaoh of Egypt', *BA* 12: 46-52.
Dion, P.E.
    1995   'Aramean Tribes and Nations of First Millennium Western Asia', in Sasson 1995: 1291-92.
Donner, H., and W. Röllig
    1962–63   *Kanaanaische und aramäische Inschriften* (3 vols.; Wiesbaden: Otto Harrassowitz).

Dothan, T.
1995   'The Sea Peoples and the Philistines in Ancient Palestine', in Sasson (ed.)
            1995: 1278-79.
Dupont-Sommer, A.
1948   'Un papyrus araméen de' époque saïte découvert à Saqqara', *Sem* 1: 43-68.
Fitzmyer, J.
1979   'The Aramaic Letter of King Adon to the Egyptian Pharaoh', in *idem* (ed.),
            A Wandering Aramean: Collected Aramaic Essays (Missoula, MT: Scholars
            Press, 1979): 231-42 (first published in *Bib* 46 [1965]: 41-55)
Galling, K.
1963   'Eschumanazar und der Herr der Könige', *ZDPV* 79: 148-49.
Gibson, J.C.L.
1975   *Textbook of Syrian Semitic Inscriptions* (2 vols.; Oxford: Clarendon Press).
Ginsberg, H.L.
1948   'An Aramaic Contemporary of the Lachish Letters', *BASOR* 111: 24-27.
Krahmalkov, C.R.
1981   'The Historical Setting of the Adon Letter', *BA* 44: 197-98.
Luckenbill, J.
1926–27   *Ancient Records of Assyria and Babylonia* (2 vols.; Chicago: University of
            Chicago Press).
Malamat, A.
1968   'The Last Kings of Judah and the Fall of Jerusalem', *IEJ* 18: 137-55.
Meyer, E.
1954   'Ein aramäischer Papyrus aus den ersten Jahren Nebukadnezars II', in
            W. Müller (ed.), *Festschrift für Fredrich Zucker* (Berlin: Akademie Verlag):
            251-62.
Milik, J.T.
1967   'Les papyrus araméens d'Hermopolis et les cultes syro-pheniciens en Egypte
            perse', *RB* 48: 546-622.
Moran, W.L.
1963   'A Note on the Treaty Terminology of the Sefire Stelas', *JNES* 22: 173-76.
Porten, B.
1981   'The Identity of King Adon', *BA* 44: 36-52.
Rainey, A.
1975   'The Faith of Lachish During the Campaign of Sennacherib and Nebu-
            chadnezzar', in Y. Aharoni (ed.), *Investigations at Lachish* (Tel Aviv: Uni-
            versity of Tel Aviv Press): 47-60.
Saad, Z.
1945   'Saqqarah. Fouilles royales', *Chronique d'Egypte* 39-40: 39-40, 80-82.
Sasson, J. (ed.)
1995   *Civilizations of the Ancient Near East* (8 vols.; New York: Charles Scrib-
            ner's Sons).
Shea, W.H.
1985   'Sennacherib's Second Palestinian Campaign', *JBL* 104: 408-12.
Van Seters, J.
1995   'The Historiography of the Ancient Near East', in Sasson (ed.) 1995:
            2348-49.

Waterman, L.
1930   *Royal Correspondence of the Assyrian Empire: Translations and Transliterations* (2 vols.; Ann Arbor: University of Michigan Press).

Weidner, E.
1929   'Jojachin, könig von Juda, in Babylonischen Keilschrifttexten', in P. Geuthner (ed.), *Mélanges Syriens offerts Monsieur René Dussaud* (Bibliothèque Archéologique et Historique, 30; Paris: Geuthner): 923-35.

Yurco, F.Y.
1991   'The Shabaka-Shabitku Coregency and the Supposed Second Campaign of Sennacherib Against Judah', *JBL* 110: 35-45.

Jeremiah as an Inspiration to the Poet of Job[*]

Edward L. Greenstein

The book of Job belongs to and partakes of two literary traditions. On the one hand, it may be located within the broad category of ancient Near Eastern wisdom litera- ture and, within that, the narrower class of righteous sufferer texts (e.g. Gordis 1965: 53-64; Gray 1970; Weinfeld 1988; Day (ed.) 1995; cf. Hoffman 1996: 46-83). On the other hand, Job appears to draw on and sometimes parody a wide range of genres and texts known to us from the Hebrew Bible (e.g. Segal 1949; Gordis 1965: 19-52; Dhorme 1967: clii-clxxii; Hartley 1988: 11-13; Pyeon 2003). Sometimes it would seem that the poet of Job makes use of typologies, motifs, images, and phrases that belong to the common stock of ancient Hebrew literature; but at other times it would seem that the Joban poet is drawing on a specific textual source for the purpose of allusion, parody, or elaboration. We are properly cautioned not to form facile judgments concerning how Job and another text are interrelated. It may be that one text is drawing on the other, or it may be that they are both making use of a common source (e.g. Segal 1949: 35; Tur-Sinai 1957: 46-47 n. 1; Hartley 1988: 13). One should not take for granted that similarities between Job and another text, like Jeremiah, necessarily bespeak a direct relationship. Some scholars, in con- sidering the suggestion that Job was influenced by a prophetic book like Jeremiah, find the argument 'indecisive' (e.g. Roberts 2002b: 113).

In the present essay I shall develop the thesis that the poet of Job not only made use of passages and expressions that are known to us from the book of Jeremiah, but that in several ways the character of Jeremiah and some of the discourse attrib- uted to him served as a model and even as an inspiration to the Joban poet. In mak- ing this case, I shall not confine my arguments to the delineation of linguistic and motivic parallels, extensive though some of them may be. The burden of the argu- ment will lie in my endeavor to show that some of the key concepts, figurations and rhetorical structures that distinguish the discourse of Job extend or elaborate similar ideas, images and structures in Jeremiah.

In seeking to discern the direction of influence within parallels between Job and other biblical texts, Segal (1949: 35) established an effective (though not necessar- ily exclusive) criterion. One can tell which of two texts is the source and which the

---

[*]   The present study is based on a lecture delivered in Hebrew at a symposium honoring the publication of my Israeli colleague Yair Hoffman's Hebrew commentary on Jeremiah, at Tel Aviv University, 29 May 2002. I am pleased to publish the much elaborated and written version of that lecture in honor of my American colleague Herbert Huffmon.

derivative when the language, style or content of the one appears apposite in context and where the language, style or content of the other seems somehow jarring. What I shall try to demonstrate is that the Joban poet makes extensive use of material from Jeremiah and that his appropriation of some of this material involves the transformation of something *apropos* or sensible into something not only radical but either surreal or absurd. It will make better sense, I will suggest, to argue that the poet of Job is attenuating the Jeremian source than to argue that Jeremiah is taking over but domesticating disparate texts and images from Job.

More significantly, I will endeavor to show that although there are occasional linguistic parallels between Jeremiah and Job, which could theoretically be explained as the two texts drawing on a common stock of vocabulary,[1] the use of Jeremiah in Job is not random but specific. There are, I propose, five particular areas in which the Joban poet found models or precedents in Jeremiah. This, above all, will suggest that Jeremiah served as a source of inspiration for Job. The five areas in which Jeremiah appears to have served as a model for Job are: (1) the righteous sufferer who experiences loneliness and betrayal, leading him (2) to curse the day he was born; (3) the sufferer's concern that the wicked are prospering; (4) the idea of seeking justice by litigating with God; and (5) the belief or conceit of the sufferer of being privy to conversation in the divine realm. In what follows I will discuss each of the five areas in turn.

1. *Loneliness and Betrayal*

Jeremiah, like Job, belongs to the type of the righteous sufferer (e.g. Gunneweg 1970; Polk 1984: 128-31). In his so-called 'confessions' (e.g. O'Connor 1988) or 'complaints' (e.g. Carroll 1981; Mottu 1985) Jeremiah laments his being isolated and betrayed. His social isolation is a consequence of his prophetic vocation (e.g. Jer. 15.17), but his betrayal is double: his life is threatened by his people, even by his own family (e.g. Jer. 11.18-21; 12.6); and he feels betrayed and abandoned by God (e.g. Jer. 15.18). The twin themes are brought together in a complaint such as this (Jer. 18.18-20):

1.   Examples are: Jer. 2.5 (וילכו אחרי ההבל ויהבלו) and Job 27.12 (ולמה זה הבל תהבלו); Jer. 2.22 (כי אם תכבסי בנתר ותרבי לך ברית נכתם עונך לפני) and Job 9.30-31 (אם...הזכותי בבר כפי); Jer. 17.1 (כתובה בעט ברזל) and Job 19.23-24 (בעט ברזל ועפרת...ויכתבון); Jer. 19.7 (הן אזעק חמס) and Job 20.8 (אזעק חמס ושד אקרא); Jer. 49.19 (ומי יעידני) and Job 9.19 (מי יועידני). For these and other possible examples see, e.g., Driver and Gray 1921: lxviii. Of course, in view of what I attempt to show is a very extensive impact of Jeremiah on Job, more limited parallels like those cited above may also be regarded as direct influence. For example, I tend to interpret Job 9.30-31 as a parody of Jer. 2.22 (cf. Clines 1989: 241). Instead of Judah's self-cleansing being insufficient to remove the stain of sin from God's sight, Job suspects that God would dirty (i.e. incriminate) him on purpose were Job to wash himself clean (i.e. prove himself innocent). For a useful working definition of parody see Dentith (2000: 9): 'Parody includes any cultural practice which provides a relatively polemical allusive imitation of another cultural production or practice'. He says ' "relatively" polemical because the ferocity of the attack can vary widely between different forms of parody'. For the idea that the poetic core of Job abounds in parody, see, e.g., Zuckerman 1991. For a direct connection between Jer. 20.8 and Job 19.7, see below.

Inspired Speech

They say: 'Come, let us scheme schemes against Jeremiah!
For never will the priest want for instruction, or the sage for wisdom, or the
prophet for discourse.
Come, let us strike him with the tongue,
    and let us not listen to any more of his discourses!'
'Listen, O YHWH, to me, and hear my litigious claims!
    Should (my) good be repaid by (your) evil?
    For they have dug a pit-trap for me!
Recall how I have stood before you, seeking their good,
    to remove your wrath from upon them!'

Job, the quintessential righteous sufferer, describes his isolation from family and
friends in several places and in abundant detail (e.g. Job 6.14-22; 19.13-23; 30.1-15;
cf. Habel 1977; Vinton 1978; Greenstein 1995). Job (30.1, 9), like Jeremiah (20.7),
complains of being the victim of disdain, the butt of jingles.[2] Both would 'cry out'
in distress: 'Injustice!' (זעק חמס/צ; Job 19.7; Jer. 20.8). And both attribute their
distress to the 'hand of God/YHWH' (Job 19.21; Jer. 15.17). Being subjected to
slander and mockery is a typical feature of biblical lament psalms (e.g. Pss. 44, 89),
so it is possible to ascribe the parallels between Job and Jeremiah in this vein to a
similar use of a shared literary genre (cf., e.g., Carroll 1981: 116).[3] However, a more
specific relationship between Job and Jeremiah can be invoked when comparing
two striking images that appear in both books.

At the climax of his complaint in ch. 15, Jeremiah ceases asking rhetorical questions and makes the famous accusation: 'You have been, yes, been for me like a
dried-up-wadi, unreliable waters' (היו תהיה לי כמו אכזב מים לא נאמנו, v. 18b). Job
not only takes up the same image, applying it to his disappointing companions, but
extends it into an elaborate mini-narrative embedded within a lengthy complaint:

My brothers have betrayed me like a wadi (נחל),
    Like the stream of wadis that pass.
Once dark from ice, / The frost disappears from them.
When they are seasonally scorched, they are annihilated;
    In the seasonal heat, they dissolve from their place.
They turn a twisting route, / They go into the desert and are lost.
Caravans from Tema look out (for them),
    Convoys from Sheba hold out for them.
They are disconcerted for having relied (on them),
    They arrive at the spot and are dismayed. (Job 6.15-20)

In Jeremiah the singular image of the dry wadi harks back ironically to an earlier
image in the book, where the prophet had figured YHWH as a 'source of living water'
(2.13; cf., e.g., Lundbom 1999: 746). The image in Job is elaborate, and seems in

---

2.   Pyeon (2003: 204-205) finds another parallel in Job 12.4. I regard this verse, and the ones
that follow, not as the remark of Job himself but rather as part of a series of proverbs that he quotes
(or paraphrases), introduced by the phrase, 'Who does not have such as these?' (12.3; see further
Greenstein forthcoming).
3.   For the genre of lament within Job, see Weimer 1974.

fact elaborated since the figure of the wadi as a metaphor of disappointment is developed into the story of the caravan.

Job would seem to be playing on the unique term for wadi found in Jeremiah—אכזב—when he shortly turns to his companions and swears he would never אכזב (6.28). The verb כזב in the piel conjugation ordinarily means 'to lie, deceive'. Here, however, such a meaning would be inapposite or at the least insipid.[4] Job has just accused his friends of having sold him out (6.27). It is only two verses below that Job will emphasize the veracity of his speech (v. 29). His point in v. 28 and the verses that precede it is that the companions have not acted toward him as friends should. Especially if one understands that Job is here evoking Jeremiah 15, one may better interpret Job 6.28 as: 'I would not betray you like a wadi', or simply, 'I would not be a wadi for you' (the way that you have been like a wadi for me; see vv. 15-20). This meaning of כזב is not, however, poetically fabricated. It is, in fact, the archaic meaning of the verb as attested, for example, in the Oracles of Balaam: 'El is not a man who will fail to run (like a wadi, i.e., act capriciously; ויכזב), / Or a human who will renege' (Num. 23.19; cf., e.g., Levine 2000: 182). The pointed use of אכזב in Job 6.28 in a context concerning personal disappointment would seem to depend on its source in Jer. 15.17. The image of the wadi as a metaphor for disappointment is therefore taken from Jeremiah by the poet of Job.

Yet another trope connected with the theme of betrayal that is shared between Jeremiah and Job is the motif of economic dependency. Jeremiah, in wondering aloud why he is so hated by his compatriots, illustrates the seeming illogic by observing that he has been neither a borrower nor a lender (15.10). Job, in trying to comprehend his companion's lack of support, adopts a more acute approach. He confronts his friends, asking rhetorically:

> Have I ever said, 'Hand it over to me'?[5]
> Or 'pay a bribe[6] for me with your wealth'?
> Or 'rescue me (by ransom) from an enemy'?
> Or 'ransom me from the tyrants'? (6.22-23)

In Jeremiah, the figure of the money-lender is apt because the issue that needs explanation is why people revile the prophet. There is ironically an analogy between the demands of the prophet and the demands of the lender. People don't like the demands of the one, and they don't like the demands of the other. In Job, the idea of the well-to-do and righteous Job needing his friends to pay a reward or ransom for him approaches the absurd. It may be best understood as a rhetorical take-off on Jeremiah, especially when one comes to regard this entire passage in Job 6 as inspired by Jeremiah 15.

---

4.   One could argue that we have here a double use of the verb כזב, an instance of the phenomenon of 'Janus parallelism' treated by Noegel 1996. In regard to what precedes, the sense is that of betrayal; in regard to what follows, the sense is that of lying. Noegel, it should be noted, does not include this possible example.

5.   Especially assuming the intertextual link with Jer. 15, the precise sense may be: 'Pay me back (what you owe me)!' See Zech. 11.12: הבו שכרי ('deliver [i.e. pay] my wages!').

6.   Or 'reward' (see Hartley 1988: 139).

Both Jeremiah and Job contend with their sense of loneliness and betrayal by cursing the day of their birth. This particular parallel may serve as a key test case for establishing the relationship between Jeremiah and Job.

2. *Cursing the Day of Birth*

The motif of cursing or seeking to abolish a certain day, as an expression of grief or despair, is attested from a relatively early period in Mesopotamian literature (Jacobsen and Nielsen 1992; cf. Lundbom 1999: 869-70). The notion of cursing one's own day of birth is found only in Jeremiah (20.14-18; cf. 15.10) and Job (3.1-12; cf., e.g., Newsom 1996: 366). Impressed by the structural and motivic parallels between Jeremiah 20 and Job 3,[7] most commentators have considered the nature of their relationship. Some regard Job as the source and Jeremiah as the borrower (e.g. Dillmann 1891: xxxii-xxxiii). Some find the Job passage to be dependent on Jeremiah (e.g. Driver and Gray 1921: lxvii; Terrien 1954: 889a; Dhorme 1967: clix-clx). Most believe that Jeremiah and Job are drawing on a common source or generic template (e.g. Tur-Sinai 1957: 46-47 n. 1; Clines and Gunn 1976: 406; Carroll 1981: 129; Habel 1985: 41, 103; Hartley 1988: 88 n. 2; Zuckerman 1991: 124; Hoffman 2001: 429-30). There is a widespread sense that 'literary dependence between these two passages cannot be established in either direction' (O'Connor 1988: 77-78).

I maintain that the Joban poet has reworked Jeremiah's curse and that only by adopting this position can one fully appreciate the implications of Job 3 (see Greenstein 1986, 1995). The Joban version both alters and elaborates Jer. 20.14-18 (cf. Segal 1949: 47; Terrien 1954: 889a; Dhorme 1967: clix-clx). For one thing, Job seeks to do away not only with the day of his birth but also the night of his conception (3.3, 6-10). Rhetorically, 'the series of interrogatives suggested by…Jer 20.18…is prolonged with many reverberations in the development of Job's lament' (Dhorme 1967: clx). More extraordinarily, Job replaces the individuals who attended the birth in the Jeremiah passage—the mother, the father, and the messenger—with impersonal substitutes: his father is not mentioned at all or else in the ambiguous 'knees' that received him (Job 3.12); his mother appears only as a disembodied womb[8] and breasts (vv. 10, 12); and the human messenger has been transformed into and personified as the night, which announced 'A man has been conceived' (v. 3).

For Jeremiah, the birth may now be accursed, but it was at first welcome and natural. Job's difficulty with the very idea of his birth leads him to distort its representation. Job denies there were any other people involved. Job was not, like Jeremiah, somebody's 'son' (בֵּן), but the same as he is now—a grown 'man' (גֶּבֶר,

---

7.   Although some commentators remark on the linguistic differences between the passages (e.g. Segal 1949: 45; Carroll 1981: 129; Zuckerman 1991: 124), Hakham (1981: 23) delineates several linguistic parallels as well.

8.   Note that Job refers to the womb in which he resided not as his mother's but as his own—בִּטְנִי.

Job 3.3, 23). He projects his feeling of 'radical aloneness' (Vinton 1978; cf. Greenstein 1995) as a man who has lost all his children onto his beginnings. When Job invokes a curse on the night he was conceived, he omits any reference to his parents—only, and by indirection, to the joy (רננה) that accompanied it (3.7).

Moreover, Jeremiah calls the day of his birth accursed. This may mean that he is cursing the day; but it may rather mean that he is merely describing it. That is, from the prophet's point of view, the day that would ultimately lead to his miserable life must have borne a curse—it was, he declares, an 'accursed' (ארור) day. Job attempts to do something far more extreme: he seeks to impose a curse on the night of his conception and (if that does not work) on the day of his birth in order retroactively to eliminate the day from existence (cf., e.g., Habel 1985: 107).[9] Job tries to achieve something fantastic by projecting an impossible situation—the actual elimination of something that has already been. It is difficult to imagine Jeremiah's making use of Job's radical curse and transforming it into something so relatively bland. It is quite typical of the Joban poet, however, to take a biblical passage and attenuate it *ad absurdum*. We will encounter the same general phenomenon in section 4, below.

3. *The Prosperity of the Wicked*

Job's initial grievance is altogether personal. He extrapolates from his own misery and alienation and characterizes all humankind as similarly troubled. The extrapolation becomes evident in his first discourse, in Job 3.20, where in the first colon he asks 'Why is light given to one who suffers'—in the singular—and in the second he rephrases: 'And life to the embittered of spirit'—in the plural. Job's issues are, at first, largely his own: Why does God seem to be persecuting him (e.g. 13.23-27; 19.22)? Why is he isolated and abused (e.g. ch. 19)? Here and there Job injects a more universal theological assertion, such as that of 9.21: 'It is all the same, and so I say: "The innocent and the wicked he destroys"'.

In the course of the second cycle of dialogues, however, Job generalizes at length. And he singles out for complaint the prosperity of the wicked: 'Why (מדוע) do the wicked thrive (יחיו)? (Why) do they grow strong (עתקו) and even powerful (גם גברו חיל)?' (21.7). Obviously, if the wicked succeed, it attests to the failure of the conventional biblical principle of retribution; it demonstrates the same systemic failure one finds in the suffering of the innocent (cf., e.g., Driver 1956: 410; Pfeiffer 1948: 698). This focus on the seeming injustice of the prosperity of the wicked has a parallel in Hab. 1.13 but, I would contend, its source is in Jer. 12.1-3 (so, e.g., Terrien 1954: 889a; Dhorme 1967: clvii, clxii; cf. Carroll 1986: 285).[10]

9.   Habel (1985: 103-107) goes on, following Fishbane (1971), to suggest that Job actually wants to undo the entire creation. There is nothing but a single allusion to Gen. 1.3 (יהי אור) in Job 3.4 (יהי חשך) that relates specifically to the Genesis creation narrative. Job wants to annihilate the night of his conception and the day of his birth and that is all (cf. Clines 1989: 81).

10.   The complaint of the wicked's prosperity is attested as well in the so-called Babylonian Theodicy: 'Those who seek not after a god can go the road of favor, / Those who pray to a goddess have grown poor and destitute' (Lambert 1960: 74, ll. 70-71; the translation is that of Foster 1996:

Jeremiah (12.1b), like Job (21.7), formulates his accusation as a rhetorical question—'Why does the way of the wicked succeed, / (Why) are those who break faith at ease (מדוע דרך רשעים צלחה שלו כל בגדי בגד)?' Job, too, begins with 'Why' (מדוע), but he answers Jeremiah's 'be at ease' (שלו) with 'thrive' (יחיו). The variation appears less significant once one notices that Job employs the related adjective 'at ease' (שליו) within the same discourse (21.23).[11] Moreover, Jeremiah goes on to describe the flourishing of the wicked's children, figuring them as 'fruit' (12.2), just as Job proceeds to detail the prosperity of the wicked's 'seed' (זרעם) and 'offshoots' (צאצאיהם, 21.8), adhering to the selection of metaphors from the botanical field.

Jeremiah's expression of distress over the prosperity of the wicked follows upon his account of having been the victim of an assassination plot. His accusation of God is barely removed from the personal provocation that seems to have prompted it. In this it is analogous to Job's opening complaint (ch. 3; see above). Job's apparent elaboration of Jeremiah's grievance, which takes up most of ch. 21, is directed against the traditional 'wisdom' of Zophar (ch. 20), who had delineated the ways that the wicked and their descendants get their comeuppance. However, Job does not respond to Zophar by relating to the 'joy' (רננה) and 'happiness' (שמחה) of the wicked, which were Zophar's point of departure (20.5). Job has seized rather upon the notion of the wicked's economic prosperity, which was featured in Jeremiah's depiction. The Joban poet has homed in on a brief point of Jeremiah's, removed it from its more personalized context in Jeremiah, and made it the theme of an elaborate and general reply. Such a rhetorical turn is, we are coming to see, typical of Job.

4. *Litigating with God*

In presenting his grievance against God, for prospering the wicked and their offspring, Jeremiah frames his complaint in legal terms (e.g. Carroll 1986: 284-85; Holladay 1986: 368; McKane 1986: 261): 'You would be in the right (צדיק), O YHWH, were I to litigate (אריב) against you; nevertheless, I would state my charges (משפטים) to you' (Jer. 12.1).[12] As scholars like Gemser (1960: 134) and Holladay (1963) have well observed, Jeremiah is applying the institution of the prophetic lawsuit against the people (e.g. Huffmon 1959; cf. O'Connor 1988: 88) in formulating his personal suit against God. Just as Israel is accused in the prophetic lawsuit of having breached the terms of the covenant, YHWH is accused in Jeremiah's personal suit of having broken faith with the prophet, by apparently failing to provide the support that was promised (see Jer. 1.7-12, 17-19).

---

793). Here, however, good/bad behavior is confined to the cultic sphere, in contrast to the interpersonal evil that is contemplated by Jeremiah and Job (on which cf. Lasine 2001: 182-83).

11.   The verb and adjective שלו are particularly common within the book of Job (3.26; 12.6; 16.12; 20.20; 21.23).

12.   Although the phrase את...דבר משפטים may mean 'to pass sentence' in Jer. 39.5 (Holladay 1963: 281), the usage here harks back to that in Jer. 1.16, where the sense of 'charge, indict' is apt.

Job, too, develops his grievances against the deity in the form of a lawsuit (discussion and references in Greenstein 1996). At first, Job, like Jeremiah, only entertains the idea of suing God. Jeremiah rejects the plan because, being God, YHWH would certainly be found innocent of the charges by the only magistrate who could try the case, namely, himself. Job initially rejects the idea of litigating with God for the same reason: 'How could a mere mortal be in the right (יִצְדַּק) before God?' (9.2). Job, however, cites additional apprehensions. For one thing, God would not reply to the charges (רִיב, 9.3, 15-18). For another, he would use his power to suppress any challenge (9.4, 19). More disturbingly, he would falsely incriminate an innocent Job (9.27-31). The problem at bottom, as Job sees it, is that there is no neutral arbiter who could circumvent the divine intimidation and decide the case fairly (9.32–10.2).

As the dialogues progress, however, Job increasingly realizes that he has nothing to lose by challenging God. Even upon penalty of death, he will pursue his litigation (13.15; cf. 13.3 and *passim*; 23.3-4). Job's is not a metaphorical or virtual lawsuit against God, as some have claimed (e.g. Roberts 2002c), but an actual one, and it is played out till the end (Greenstein 1996).

The idea of suing God would seem to originate with Jeremiah (e.g. Gemser 1960: 134-35; Holladay 1963; Scholnick 1975: 124-25). Jeremiah only fantasizes about such a radical move (e.g. Zuckerman 1991: 258 n. 339; Greenstein 1996: 242). Job stretches the limits of the imaginable and actually initiates a legal case against God. There are two reasons, then, for concluding that Job is in the present instance dependent on Jeremiah. First, the lawsuit framework has its natural setting in prophetic discourse. Jeremiah himself institutes a prophetic *rîb* against the people, for example, in 2.4-13 (cf. Huffmon 1959: 287-88). Jeremiah then takes advantage of the familiar lawsuit framework in setting his complaint before God. Second, the litigation with God remains in the realm of the imagination in Jeremiah. It is Job who adopts the basic idea and then carries it to a surreal extreme.

5. *Being Privy to Divine Conversation*

Job seeks to present his case directly before God. Some have seen in that desire yet another nexus between Job and Jeremiah. The prophet had enjoyed the status of one who 'stood in (God's) circle' (סוֹד,[13] Jer. 23.18, 22; and cf. 15.19). Job, it is suggested, wants to achieve a similar intimacy (Sanders 1972: 107; Pyeon 2003: 39). It is true that the prophetic lawsuit may have its native setting in the divine court (e.g. Polley 1980: 150-51). However, in the verses that are adduced in support of this interpretation of Job (13.22; 31.35), there is no more than an expression of wanting to speak to God—for which other verses could also have been cited—and no echo of the locution 'to stand in (God's) circle' or some similar locution.

A more striking parallel between Jeremiah and Job's claims to have been privy to conversation from or within the divine circle can, however, be indicated. The parallel rests on the old argument of Tur-Sinai and Ginsberg, renewed by G.V. Smith

13. Or 'council', *BDB*: 691; cf. Cross 1953: 275.

and Greenstein (references in Greenstein 1996: 258) and developed more exten-sively by Greenstein (forthcoming),[14] that the hair-raising revelation from a divine spirit in Job 4.12-21 is slightly out of place and belongs just prior to 4.1-11, as the conclusion of Job's opening discourse.[15] It was Job who received the spirit's disclosure about God's dim assessment of human potential, and it is precisely this claim of revelation by Job that Eliphaz ridicules in ch. 5 (vv. 1, 8) and derides in ch. 15 (see below).

The primary argument for the attribution of Job 4.12-21 to Job is that it is quoted by some of Job's interlocutors. It would seem to be paraphrased in the truncated speech of Bildad in 25.4-6 (cf. 4.17-19). It is cited almost verbatim by Elihu (com-pare 33.15 with 4.13). Elihu tends to quote or paraphrase the discourse of Job (e.g. Dhorme 1967: ci-ciii) and not the other friends (except when they are paraphrasing Job; Greenstein forthcoming). It is accordingly likely that Elihu is quoting Job. The clinching evidence is in ch. 15, where in vv. 14-16, Eliphaz is explicitly citing Job, and the text being closely paraphrased is 4.17-19. The verses 15.14-16 can only be understood as a quotation from Job because they are introduced by not one but two formulas found elsewhere in Job as an introduction or reference to direct discourse! The first phrase—'to return wind' (השיב רוח)—is but a more insulting version of 'to return words' (השיב מלין) attested in 35.4; and the second phrase—'to emit words from the mouth' (הוציא מלין מפה)—is but a variant of 'to emit words from the heart' (הוציא מלין מלב) attested in 8.10, introducing an entire series of proverbial sayings (cf., e.g., Hakham 1981: 63-64).[16]

Once one realizes that Eliphaz in ch. 15 is condemning Job for having claimed to have been privy to divine discourse, and that Job had made that claim in ch. 4, the rest of Eliphaz's remarks in ch. 15 become clearer. In v. 4, Eliphaz accuses Job of impiety because the latter has allegedly 'stolen (i.e. eavesdropped on) conversation before God' (ותגרע שיחה לפני אל), cf. Tur-Sinai 1957: 246-47; Ginsberg 1969: 100). When Eliphaz reiterates that Job had condemned himself with his own mouth (vv. 5-6), he is referring to Job's claim to have had a revelation. Eliphaz denies that Job has any special divine knowledge. Job was naturally not present at the creation, at which time God had made use of divine wisdom (v. 7). Nor has Job received divine wisdom by means of some later revelation (v. 8). The language of this last denial by Eliphaz is significant. In describing Job's contention, Eliphaz characterizes it as 'listening in' on the 'divine circle/council' and as 'stealing wisdom' to himself (הבסוד אלוה תשמע ותגרע אליך חכמה). Here Eliphaz makes reference to the very divine circle/council (סוד) to which Jeremiah was privy (cf., e.g., Tur-Sinai 1957: 248; Habel 1985: 253).

14. A much abbreviated English version of this Hebrew paper was presented at the annual meeting of the Society of Biblical Literature in Toronto, 24 November 2002.

15. As I explain elsewhere (forthcoming), the two passages, which are equal in size, were interchanged either in the copying process or in the attachment of the pages of papyrus or parch-ment together.

16. For לב as an organ of speech, see Ginsberg 1967: 80.

It goes without saying that the natural original biblical setting for participating in or at the very least hearing conversation in the divine assembly is prophetic discourse and not wisdom literature. There is therefore every probability that the poet of Job appropriated the motif of receiving a disclosure from the divine sphere from Jeremiah and ascribed it to the righteous sufferer Job as well. The divine speeches from the whirlwind at the end of the poetic core of Job, which are directed to Job, strongly reinforce this interpretation. Once again, the Joban poet seems to have taken his inspiration from Jeremiah and radicalized his source by endowing the righteous sufferer with a disclosure from the divine realm, possibly from a renegade spirit. The poet's move has turned the argument between Job and his companions from a contest between experience and wisdom into a confrontation between revelation and traditional knowledge.

In sum, the numerous parallels between images, motifs and structures in Jeremiah and Job lead me to conclude that the poet of Job had found inspiration in the figure and literature of Jeremiah, an earlier personality who felt betrayed and abandoned by God and by humans in spite of his outstanding loyalty to God and his ways.[17] Jeremiah made his complaints within the framework of the lament, only imagining what it would entail to sue the deity in court. Job, having suffered beyond the limits of the familiar, ventured into the realm of the surreal, seeking to eliminate the day of his birth and daring to couch his accusations of God in the form of a legal suit. By acknowledging a particular intertextual relation between Jeremiah and Job, one can more precisely appreciate the parodies, subversions of convention and figural elaborations that characterize the poetry of Job.

BIBLIOGRAPHY

Carroll, R.P.
 1981 'The Confessions of Jeremiah: Towards an Image of the Prophet', in *idem*, *From Chaos to Covenant: Uses of Prophecy in the Book of Jeremiah* (London: SCM Press): 107-35.
 1986 *Jeremiah: A Commentary* (OTL; Philadelphia: Westminster Press).
Clines, D.J.A.
 1989 *Job 1–20* (WBC, 17; Dallas: Word Books).
Clines, D.J.A., and D.M. Gunn
 1976 'Form, Occasion and Redaction in Jeremiah 20', *ZAW* 88: 390-409.
Cross, F.M., Jr
 1953 'The Council of Yahweh in Second Isaiah', *JNES* 12: 274-77.
Day, J. (ed.)
 1995 *Wisdom in Ancient Israel: Essays in Honour of J.A. Emerton* (Cambridge: Cambridge University Press).
Dentith, S.
 2000 *Parody* (London and New York: Routledge).

17. Hoffman (2001: 75-76) dates the latest stage of the formation of the book of Jeremiah to the fifth century BCE, and I surmise, on the basis of linguistic evidence, that the book of Job was not composed until the mid-fifth century BCE (Greenstein 2003).

Dhorme, E.
1967   *A Commentary on the Book of Job* (trans. H. Knight; London: Thomas Nelson).

Dillmann, A.
1891   *Hiob* (KHAT; Leipzig: Hirzel, 4th edn).

Driver, S.R.
1956   *An Introduction to the Literature of the Old Testament* (Cleveland, OH: Meridian).

Driver, S.R., and G.B. Gray
1921   *The Book of Job*, I (ICC; New York: Charles Scribner's Sons).

Fishbane, M.
1971   'Jeremiah IV 23–26 and Job III 3–13: A Recovered Use of the Creation Pattern', *VT* 21: 151-67.

Foster, B.R.
1996   *Before the Muses: An Anthology of Akkadian Literature* (2 vols.; Bethesda, MD: CDL Press, 2nd edn).

Gemser, B.
1960   'The *rîb*- or Controversy Pattern in Hebrew Mentality', in M. Noth and D.W. Thomas (eds.), *Wisdom in Israel and in the Ancient Near East Presented to Professor Harold Henry Rowley* (VTSup, 3; Leiden: E.J. Brill): 120-37.

Ginsberg, H.L.
1967   'Lexicographical Notes', in B. Hartmann *et al.* (eds.), *Hebräische Wortforschung: Festschrift zum 80. Geburtstag von Walter Baumgartner* (VTSup, 16; Leiden: E.J. Brill): 71-82.

1969   'Job the Patient and Job the Impatient', in *Congress Volume, Rome 1968* (VTSup, 17; Leiden: E.J. Brill): 88-111.

Gordis, R.
1965   *The Book of God and Man: A Study of Job* (Chicago: University of Chicago Press).

Gray, J.
1970   'The Book of Job in the Context of Near Eastern Literature', *ZAW* 82: 251-69.

Greenstein, E.L.
1986   'Professor Robert Gordis and the Literary Approach to Bible', *Proceedings of the Rabbinical Assembly* 48: 190-200.

1995   'The Loneliness of Job', in L. Mazor (ed.), *Job in the Bible, Philosophy and Art* (Jerusalem: Mount Scopus Publications): 43-53 (Hebrew).

1996   'A Forensic Understanding of the Speech from the Whirlwind', in M.V. Fox *et al.* (eds.), *Texts, Temples, and Traditions: A Tribute to Menahem Haran* (Winona Lake, IN: Eisenbrauns): 241-58.

2003   'The Language of Job and Its Poetic Function', *JBL* 122: 651-66.
forthcoming 'The Extent of Job's First Speech', in S. Vargon *et al.* (eds.), *Studies in Bible and Exegesis*. VII. *Presented to Menahem Cohen* (Ramat Gan: Bar Ilan University Press [Hebrew]).

Gunneweg, A.H.J.
1970   'Konfession oder Interpretation im Jeremiabuch', *ZTK* 67: 395-416.

Habel, N.C.
1977 ' "Only the Jackal is My Friend": On Friends and Redeemers in Job', *Int* 31: 227-36.
1985 *The Book of Job: A Commentary* (OTL; Philadelphia: Westminster Press).
Hakham, Amos
1981 *The Book of Job* (Da'at Miqra'; Jerusalem: Mossad Ha-Rav Kook [Hebrew]).
Hartley, J.E.
1988 *The Book of Job* (NICOT; Grand Rapids: Eerdmans).
Hoffman, Y.
1996 *A Blemished Perfection: The Book of Job in Context* (JSOTSup, 213; Sheffield: Sheffield Academic Press).
2001 *Jeremiah: Introduction and Commentary* (2 vols.; Mikra Le-Yisra'el; Tel Aviv: Am Oved; Jerusalem: Magnes Press [Hebrew]).
Holladay, W.L.
1963 'Jeremiah's Lawsuit with God: A Study in Suffering and Meaning', *Int* 17: 280-87.
1986 *Jeremiah. I. Commentary on the Book of the Prophet Jeremiah Chapters 1–25* (Hermeneia; Philadelphia: Fortress Press).
Huffmon, H.B.
1959 'The Covenant Lawsuit in the Prophets', *JBL* 78: 285-95.
Jacobsen, Th., and K. Nielsen
1992 'Cursing the Day', *SJOT* 6: 187-204.
Lambert, W.G.
1960 *Babylonian Wisdom Literature* (Oxford: Clarendon Press).
Lasine, S.
2001 *Knowing Kings: Knowledge, Power, and Narcissism in the Hebrew Bible* (SBLSS; Atlanta: Society of Biblical Literature).
Levine, B.A.
2000 *Numbers 21–36* (AB, 4A; New York: Doubleday).
Lundbom, J.R.
1999 *Jeremiah 1–20* (AB, 21A; New York: Doubleday).
McKane, W.
1986 *Jeremiah* (ICC; 2 vols.; Edinburgh: T. & T. Clark).
Mottu, H.
1985 *Les 'confessions' de Jérémie: Une protestation contre la souffrance* (Geneva: Labor et Fides).
Newsom, C.A.
1996 'The Book of Job', in *NIB*: IV, 317-637.
Noegel, S.B.
1996 *Janus Parallelism in the Book of Job* (JSOTSup, 223; Sheffield: Sheffield Academic Press).
O'Connor, K.
1988 *The Confessions of Jeremiah: Their Interpretation and Role in Chapters 1–25* (SBLDS, 94; Atlanta: Scholars Press).
Pfeiffer, R.H.
1948 *Introduction to the Old Testament* (New York: Harper & Brothers, rev. edn).

Polk, T.
1984   *The Prophetic Persona: Jeremiah and the Language of the Self* (JSOTSup, 32; Sheffield: JSOT Press).

Polley, M.E.
1980   'Hebrew Prophecy within the Council of Yahweh, Examined in Its Ancient Near Eastern Setting', in C.D. Evans, W.W. Hallo and J.B. White (eds.), *Scripture in Context: Essays on the Comparative Method* (Pittsburgh, PA: Pickwick Press): 141-56.

Pyeon, Y.
2003   *You Have Not Spoken What Is Right About Me: Intertextuality and the Book of Job* (New York: Peter Lang).

Roberts, J.J.M.
2002a   *The Bible and the Ancient Near East: Collected Essays* (Winona Lake, IN: Eisenbrauns).
2002b   'Job and the Israelite Religious Tradition', in *idem* 2002a: 110-16.
2002c   'Job's Summons to Yahweh: The Exploitation of a Legal Metaphor', *idem* 2002a: 117-22.

Sanders, J.A.
1972   *Torah and Canon* (Philadelphia: Fortress Press).

Scholnick, S.H.
1975   'Lawsuit Drama in the Book of Job' (unpublished PhD dissertation, Brandeis University, Waltham, MA).

Segal, M.Z.
1949   'Parallels in the Book of Job', *Tarbiz* 20: 35-48 (Hebrew).

Terrien, S.
1954   'The Book of Job', in *IB*: III, 875-1198.

Tur-Sinai, N.H.
1957   *The Book of Job: A New Commentary* (Jerusalem: Kiryath Sepher).

Vinton, Patricia
1978   'Radical Aloneness: Job and Jeremiah', *The Bible Today* 99: 1843-49.

Weimer, J.D.
1974   'Job's Complaint: A Study of Its Limits and Form, Content, and Significance' (unpublished PhD dissertation, Union Theological Seminary, New York).

Weinfeld, M.
1988   'Job and Its Mesopotamian Parallels—A Typological Analysis', in W. Claasen (ed.), *Text and Context: Old Testament and Semitic Studies for F.C. Fensham* (JSOTSup, 48; Sheffield: JSOT Press): 217-26.

Zuckerman, B.
1991   *Job the Silent: A Study in Historical Counterpoint* (New York and Oxford: Oxford University Press).

WHEN THE GOD OF ISRAEL 'ACTS-OUT' HIS ANGER:
ON THE LANGUAGE OF DIVINE REJECTION IN BIBLICAL LITERATURE

Baruch A. Levine

In an earlier study, written in honor of my teacher, Dwight W. Young, I explored the biblical doctrine that the sacrificial offerings of the unworthy are rejected by God, a theme suggested by Num. 16.15a. In the heat of the Korah insurrection, an angry Moses implored God to reject the offerings of those who were then rebelling against him: אל־תפן אל־מנחתם ('Do not turn toward their offering') (Levine 1993a: 414, 426-28; 1996). The only other biblical source that replicates the precise formula פנה אל מנחה ('to turn toward an offering') is Mal. 2.13, where the pronouncement is similarly negative: the Temple altar is covered with tears, because God does not 'turn toward' the sacrifices of the people and refuses to accept them. This theme is, however, one of broad currency in biblical literature, and the Epilogue to the Holiness Code, in its blessings, says that YHWH will turn toward his people (Lev. 26.9; cf. Ezek. 36.9). Anticipating the forthcoming discussion of Jer. 14.17-22, which will serve as our core text, we may cite 14.11-12, which precedes that very prophetic oration: 'Then YHWH said to me: Do not pray on behalf of this people for good things. When they fast, I will not listen to their chanting, and when they raise up burnt offerings and grain offerings, I will not accept them. Rather, will I do away with them by sword, and by famine, and by pestilence.' This pronouncement resonates most clearly with Isa. 1.10-15, and reflects the belief that one of the penalties inflicted upon evildoers by God (in polytheistic religions, by the gods) is the denial of cultic access and efficacy to those who are out of favor. Such cultic rejection foreshadows disastrous consequences on the ground. On this basis, a person might curse his enemies by wishing this upon them, as Moses had done.

Here, I would like to carry the inquiry further by discussing other ways of expressing divine rejection in biblical literature. It is surely more heartening, and less painful, to focus on the positive aspects of the human–divine encounter; on covenant promises, and on blessing and reward. But, truth be told, biblical literature as a whole is replete with denunciations and admonitions, sanctions and dire predictions, and with other expressions of divine anger. This aspect of biblical religion is every bit as revealing as are biblical visions of redemption and triumph, and of God's love and favor—phenomena that cannot be appreciated fully without a clear understanding of their opposites.

Methodology

A basic element of my approach to religious phenomenology has been to examine in depth the semantics of Hebrew idioms and formulas, rather than to assume that their meanings are transparent and obvious. In this vein, I have investigated 'The Language of Holiness: Perceptions of the Sacred in the Hebrew Bible' (Levine 1987b); 'Silence, Sound, and the Phenomenology of Mourning in Biblical Israel' (Levine 1993b); 'The Semantics of Loss: Two Exercises in Biblical Hebrew Lexicography' (Levine 1995) and other themes. Regarding expressions of emotion, in particular, it is noteworthy that they are often predicated on graphic, sometimes physical acts and responses, even if they become figurative or metaphorical through extended usage. One will say that he is 'desolate', in French *desolé*, when being distressed, or that he is 'crushed', or 'overwhelmed' by circumstances. In Biblical Hebrew, one who is in shock may be characterized as *šōmēm* ('desolate', 2 Sam. 13.20; Lev. 26.32), which is a graphic description in the first instance (Lam. 1.4, 16).[1]

Translators and lexicographers seem to favor 'leveled' definitions, which are more functional, and produce a smoother reading. And yet, *Grundbedeutung* and the analysis of semantic fields remain essential, and we inevitably miss something when we try to bypass them. In the context of the present discussion, this judgment aptly applies to the English verb 'reject'. It is derived from Latin *reicio* and related forms, 'to throw back, throw off, fling aside', and, by extension, 'to disdain, reject with scorn' (Cassell 1971: 510). An ancient Latin author would normally employ the verb *reicio* to express physical acts, and even in contemporary English usage, the verb 'reject' occasionally describes physical action, or reaction. Thus, one who received a transplanted organ may be said to 'reject' it subsequently. In my estimation, most of the Biblical Hebrew terms for divine rejection retain more of their graphic or physical connotations than is true of the English verb 'reject' in contemporary usage.

The task of the lexicographer and the exegete is, therefore, to determine in each specific case how verbs expressing divine rejection are being used. This will entail analysis of immediate context so as not to miss references to physical effects. Here I will study two verbs that characteristically connote divine rejection. They are known parallels, and both occur together in Jer. 14.17-22, which will serve as our core text. These are *mā'as*, usually translated 'to reject, despise', and *gā'al*, usually translated 'to spurn, reject'. I have previously discussed these verbs as they figure in the Epilogue to the Holiness Code (Lev. 26.3-46), making brief reference to Jeremiah 14 in the process (Levine 1987a, 1989). In those studies, my concern centered on the functions of these verbs in the overall composition of the Epilogue as it progressed from one stage of national crisis to another. Here it will be shown, on grounds of semantics and context, that these verbs, and others like them, convey

---

1.   An interesting treatment of emotional expression in biblical literature is that of Grushkin (2000). It was my privilege to direct this dissertation, which also benefited from the assistance of the psychology faculty.

physical or graphic effects so that their connotations are not limited to the emotional or relational dimension. Their accurate definition affects our understanding of the human–divine encounter as conceived by the many biblical authors who employed them.

A corollary consideration of a more formal nature is the syntactic environment in which the two verbs under discussion occur. We have to do with two constructions: (1) a direct-object construction, and (2) an indirect-object construction with prepositional beth. It will be my task to show that syntax affects the sense of verbs in discrete ways and is not simply a matter of alternative options or different ways of saying the same thing. As an example, I maintain that the construction *gā'al* + direct object means something different from *gā'al* + prepositional beth, and that the same is generally true with respect to the verb *mā'as*, whose analysis is admittedly more complex. Of the two principal verbs under discussion, Hebrew *mā'as* attests a cognate in Akkadian (possibly even two cognates), whose usage will prove to be relevant to our understanding of the Hebrew.

Jeremiah 14.17-22: A Prophecy of Divine Rejection

With these considerations in mind, we turn to the interpretation of Jer. 14.17-22, which will serve as our core text. Anticipating the discussion to follow, I translate this oration as follows:

> [17]May my eyes run with tears,
> day and night, let them not be still!
> For my people, the maiden daughter, has suffered
> a grievous injury, a very critical wound.
> [18]If I go out to the open country, (I) behold those slain by the sword;
> if I enter the town, (I) behold those made sick by famine;
> for both priest and prophet travel about in the land,
> at a loss to understand.[2]
> [19]Have you utterly cast off Judah (המאס מאסת את־יהודה)?[3]
> Have you become nauseated over Zion (אם־בציון געלה נפשך)?
> Why have you struck us down,
> leaving us without healing;
> Left hoping for wholeness, but without wellbeing;
> for a time of healing, but, instead, facing terror?
> [20]We acknowledge our wickedness, YHWH,
> the sins of our forefathers,
> for we have offended you.

2. The syntax of the Hebrew is somewhat strange. We normally expect that the verb *sāḥar* ('to encircle, move around') would take an accusative. As written, the sense is either that the priests and prophets roam 'to' an unknown land, or that they don't know what has happened as they wander about their own land. That is how the verse has been translated here, giving weight to the waw of ולא ידעו, as if to say, 'with the result that they failed to know'. Cf. the discussions in Bright 1962: 101-102; and Lundbom 1999: 713.

3. I am happy to agree with Bright (1962: 99), against many other commentators. He aptly translates, 'Have you utterly cast aside Judah?'

[21]Do not spurn (אל־תנאץ), for your (own) name's sake;[4]
  do not dishonor your glorious throne.
    Remember, do not breach your covenant with us!
[22]Are there any among the false gods of the nations who can bring rain?
    Can the heavens (of themselves) bring showers?
  Are you not the one, YHWH, our God?
    So (it is, that) we hope in you!
  For it is you who have made all of these things.

This poetic oration follows upon a prose section that warns the people of disaster (Jer. 14.10-16) in which the prophet is reassured that those who speak falsely in YHWH's name, promising wellbeing, are not his true messengers. In reality, the dead will be left unburied in the streets of Jerusalem! It is at this point that we encounter, in Jer. 14.17-22, the prophet's lament and supplication over the impending fulfillment of this dire prediction.

We begin with the verb *mā'as* in Jer. 14.19, whose parallel is *gā'al*. This parallelism is well established in Biblical Hebrew, but whereas the etymology of the verb *gā'al* is known, the same is not true for the verb *mā'as*. We know what *gā'al* 'means'. It starts out as a physical act, and then appropriates an extended or figurative meaning. We cannot be sure that the same is true for the verb *mā'as*, which, for all we know, may begin by describing a state of mind, or emotional disposition, and then go on to connote physical and graphic acts. Translating Hebrew *mā'as* accurately requires, therefore, that we study its usage in concrete contexts, and then proceed to the role of this verb in the human–divine encounter, where the God of Israel is variously subject and object. My first observation is that *mā'as* serves as a replacement for *hišlîk* ('to cast off, throw away'). This can be learned from a comparison of Isa. 2.20 with Isa. 31.7:

On that day, each person will throw away (ישליך) his silver idols and his golden idols, which he fashioned for himself (as objects of) worship.

On that day, they shall cast off (ימאסון), each person, his silver idols and his golden idols, which your (own) hands fashioned for yourselves in sinfulness.[5]

---

4.   As it stands, the verse either uses the verb *na'as* without an object, or intends that both verbs *nā'as* ('to spurn'), and *nibbēl* ('to dishonor') share the same direct object, namely, כסא כבודך ('your glorious throne'). Lundbom (1999: 716) cites an earlier suggestion by Dahood that we read: *lime'on šemekā*) 'the abode of your name'), written defectively with accusative lamedh. Thus, 'Do not spurn the abode of your name'. This would produce excellent parallelism. However, the pointing *l^ema'an* may be correct after all; it resonates with the earlier statement of Jer. 14.7 עשה למען שמך ('Act for your own name's sake'). That the verb *nā'as* does not always take an object may be suggested by Deut. 32.19: 'Then YHWH saw, and he spurned (וינאץ), because of the anger (ignited by) his sons and daughters (מכעס בניו ובנתיו)'. Of course, *mikka'as* may have the same adverbial sense as *beka'as* ('out of anger'), in which case we would have a direct object: 'Then YHWH saw, and angrily spurned his sons and daughters'. On balance, I would retain the Masoretic pointing in Jer. 14.21. Actually, Jer. 14.17-22 and Deut. 32 resonate with each other. One notes, in this regard, that the verb *nibbēl* ('to dishonor') also occurs in Deut. 32.15.

5.   The force of *ḥēṭ'* would seem to be adverbial, hence, 'in sinfulness', or perhaps 'as a sin'.

The scene is one of removing idols from cult-sites or from one's home, an act usually conveyed by the verb *hēsîr*, as in 1 Sam. 7.3-4. Clearly, Isa. 31.7 is a cognizant restatement of Isa. 2.20; its author seized upon the verb *mā'as* to convey the same action as did *hišlîk* in the typological source known to him. One is reminded of the parable of the Nazirite-locks in Jer. 7.29. Addressing the Israelite people, the prophet says:

> Shear your Nazirite-locks and throw them away (והשליכי)!
> Take up a lament on the foothills!
> For YHWH has cast off in abandonment (כי מאס יהוה ויטש)
> the generation of his wrath.

I hasten to cite this passage here, because it again illustrates that the verbs *hišlîk* and *mā'as* are synonymous in that they express reciprocal actions. The Israelites may just as well throw away their Nazirite-locks because YHWH has cast them off!

Several biblical attestations of the verb *mā'as* describe actual changes in physical condition. We note usage of the verb *mā'as* in an enigmatic passage, Ezek. 21.14-16, which describes the sharpened sword of YHWH:

> [14]O mortal, prophesy and declare:
> The Lord spoke as follows, Say:
> O sword, sword! Sharpened and also burnished,
> [15]to wreak slaughter has it been sharpened,
> to have a flashing blade has it been burnished...
> It can fell any tree (מאסת כל־עץ)!
> [16]It has been given over for sharpening;
> to be held in the palm of the hand.
> That sword has been sharpened and burnished,
> to be put into the hand of a killer.

A thorough, recent treatment of this problematic passage is presented by M. Greenberg (1997: 422-23). I agree with Greenberg that the bracketed Hebrew words in v. 15 are probably extraneous—although one is at a loss to know how they crept in here—or that they reflect corruption in the transmission of the text. However, Greenberg's judgment that 'the notion of a whetted sword being wielded against a tree is unlikely' may be mistaken. After all, what follows in Ezek. 21.23-25 speaks of the 'sword' of the king of Babylon advancing against Rabbat Ammon, Judah and Jerusalem: 'And clear a place (ויד ברא) at the crossroad (leading into) the town' (Ezek. 21.24). As Greenberg notes, this is what the verb ברא (piel *bārē'*) means in Josh. 17.18, speaking of cutting down trees in a forest. That this action can be accomplished with a sword is revealed in, of all places, Ezek. 23.47: 'They shall pelt them with crowd-stones, and cleave them with their swords (וברא אותהן בחרבותם)'. What interests us is the concreteness of the imagery, whereby a sword is said to be so sharp that it can cut down any tree.

Also indicative of physical condition is Lam. 3.45—'You have made us refuse and filth (סחי ומאס) in the midst of the nations' (cf. Isa. 5.25)—where there is an actual play on the meaning of *mā'as*, carrying us from the physical to the emotional in Jer. 6.29-30:

[29]The bellows puff; lead is consumed by fire;[6]
  yet the smelter smelts to no purpose.
The base elements have not been purged.
[30]They are called 'base silver' (כסף נמאס),
  because YHWH has base feelings toward them (כי מאס ה' בהם).

The context is blatantly physical, in the first instance. The prophet is employing the known metaphor of the purging fire, except that in this instance the process is ineffectual. As the previous verses tell us, Israel failed the test and has not been purged of the evildoers in its midst. In a single verse we find both the niphal and an active, indirect-object construction. The niphal is physically descriptive of low-grade silver, whereas the indirect-object construction would seem to convey YHWH's disposition. Of the latter, more is to follow.

A blending of motifs characterizes a complex description of devastation in Isa. 33.7-9:

[7]Hark! The Arielites cry out aloud,
  Shalom's (= Jerusalem's) messengers weep bitterly.[7]
[8]Highways are desolate, wayfarers have ceased.
He has broken the covenant (הפר ברית),
  he has ruined towns (מאס ערים);
  he has not shown regard for people.
[9]The land is wilted and withered (אבל אמללה),
  Lebanon is paled (החפיר) and moldering;
Sharon has become like a desert,
  and Bashan and Carmel are stripped bare.

By way of background, Isaiah 33 concludes a series of prophecies (chs. 28–33) that open with the exclamation הוי ('Hark!') and pertain to the Assyrian crisis. The prophet begins by railing against the Assyrian king, and by metonymy against the Assyrian Empire, predicting that he will meet a disastrous end (33.1). He proceeds to petition the God of Israel for deliverance, praising him as a powerful redeemer (33.2-6). Then comes the depiction of a ravaged land that was just cited (33.7-9), followed in turn by a resumption of the theme of deliverance. In poetry of unusual force and beauty, the prophet foresees YHWH arising in power to strike down the enemy. He portrays a redeemed Zion, a secure city governed in justice (33.10-24).

Our concern is with the connotation of the verb *mā'as* in v. 8, part of the accusation against the elliptical, unnamed enemy. He has broken his treaty, which harks back to the characterization of him in v. 1 as 'betrayer', and he is also referred to as a 'ravager'. Some have taken the reference to a covenant as their cue, and have accordingly followed up with emotional and legal translations. Thus, החפיר would mean 'disgraced', and ערים ('towns') might even be emended to עדים ('testimonies'), intended as a parallel word for ברית ('covenant'). It is preferable, however,

---

6. Most read מאשתם as מאש תתם (*me'eš tittōm*, 'by fire, it will be finished/consumed'), assuming haplography.

7. Read *'er'elîm*, the plural form, as suggested in NJV, and see Isa. 29.1, where *ª rî'ēl* is a poetic name for Jerusalem. This is the key to understanding *šālôm* as a veiled reference to Jerusalem, known as *šālēm* (Ps. 76.3).

to sustain the graphic imagery. After all, the verb *ḥāpar* only bears the sense of disgrace because it means 'to turn white, pale'. Curiously, both אבל and אמלל exhibit a semantic field that reaches from the graphic sense 'to wilt, dry up, wither', to the emotional sense 'to mourn, grieve, be saddened, miserable' (cf. Hos. 4.3). Furthermore, the verbs *hēpēr* and *mā'as* are acknowledged parallels, and the verb *hēpēr* means 'to break up, breach' from the root *p-r-r* (*HALAT*: 916-17). Hence, we once again take *mā'as* in its physical, graphic sense; the towns were not merely 'despised', they were ruined, or perhaps emptied of their populations. Further on, we will have occasion to discuss 2 Kgs 23.27, where Hebrew *'îr* ('town'), a reference to Jerusalem, is likewise the direct object of the verb *mā'as*.

One recalls the words of the psalmist (Ps. 118.22), 'The stone which the builders discarded (אבן מאסו הבונים) has become the primary cornerstone'. We observe masons removing a stone from the site because they regarded it as unsuitable for use. Returning to the site we find, to our amazement, that the same stone had been used as a cornerstone. A sense of movement is also conveyed in Isa. 8.6, 'Because this people has forsaken (מאס) the waters of Siloam that flow slowly'. In Ps. 89.39, *mā'as* is synonymous with *zānaḥ* ('to abandon'), and the niphal of the former in Isa. 54.6, within a metaphor of divorce, is similar in meaning:

> For, as an abandoned wife, and one sad of spirit,
>> has YHWH called you back.
> Can the wife of one's youth be cast off (כי תמאס)?

We may now proceed to the human–divine encounter, where we find the God of Israel is the subject of the verb *mā'as*, but let me first clarify the usage of the verb in Hos. 9.16-17:

> [16]Ephraim has been struck down,
>> its root is dried up;
>> they cannot bear fruit.
> Even if they do bear children,
>> I will slay their cherished offspring.
> [17]My God casts them off (ימאסם אלהי)
>> because they have not heeded him;
>> and they shall be wanderers among the nations.

In effect, this is a prophecy of exile and ethnic extinction, the punishments for disobedience to God, in which the verb *mā'as* conveys the expulsion of a beleaguered population into foreign lands, where they will not be able to settle down. To render the verb *mā'as* as merely expressive of God's rejection or dislike, in the emotional sense, ignores the graphic depictions conveyed in these oracles of doom.

That the verb *mā'as* conveys a sense of movement is subtly expressed in the beautiful prophecy of Isa. 41.8-10a, where *mā'as* serves as an antonym of *bāḥar* ('to choose, select'):

> [8]But you, Israel my servant,
>> Jacob, you whom I have selected (אשר בחרתיך);
>> the seed of Abraham, my dear friend.

> [9]You, whom I pulled in from the ends of the earth,
>   you, whom I summoned from its far recesses.
> To whom I declared: 'You are my servant!
>   I have selected you (בחרתיך), I have not cast you off (ולא מאסתיך).'
> [10a]Fear not, for I am with you.

The contrast that informs this prophecy of restoration is one of remote exile vs. nearness to God, to be regained through the ingathering of exiles. One recalls the statement of 2 Kgs 23.27, 'Then YHWH declared: Judah, as well, will I remove from my presence, just as I removed Israel. And I will abandon this town which I had selected (ומאסתי את־העיר הזאת אשר־בחרתי), Jerusalem, and the temple where I commanded: "Let my name be there!"'

There are very few instances in all of Hebrew Scripture where the God of Israel is the direct object of the verb *mā'as*. The first occurs in Num. 11.20. Numbers 11 is part of the JE narrative, which relates a dramatic challenge to the leadership of Moses on the part of the Israelites in the wilderness after the Exodus from Egypt. It records a change in governance whereby seventy of the elders, selected by Moses, are endowed with God's spirit and designated to share in the burdensome tasks of leadership. The people had demanded meat in the wilderness, finding the manna-bread nauseating, and were expressing regret over having left Egypt, where there was better food to eat. YHWH comes to Moses' aid, and angrily acquiesces to the demands of the people:

> You shall eat it (i.e. meat) not for one or two days, or for five or ten days, or even for twenty days; rather, up to a whole month of days, until it comes out of your nostrils, and is loathsome to you. For you have overthrown YHWH (כי־מאסתם את־יהוה) who is present in your midst by complaining to him, saying: 'Why did we ever leave Egypt?'

That Numbers 11 originated in northern Israel as part of the Elohist tradition is suggested by the second instance. We find similar language in 1 Sam. 8.7, part of the account of Israel's demand for a king, which is likewise presented as a challenge to God's authority. Thus, YHWH instructs Samuel, 'Heed the voice of the people in all that they say to you, for it is not you whom they have overthrown (כי לא אתך מאסו), but rather me whom they have overthrown (כי אתי מאסו) as their king'. To this, compare 1 Sam. 10.19a: 'But you, this very day, have overthrown your God (מאסתם את אלהיכם), who rescues you from all of your calamities and troubles, and have demanded, "We insist (לאכי)! Appoint a king over us!"'

In both of these passages from 1 Samuel there is poignant reference to the earlier, rebellious behavior of the Israelites in the wilderness after the Exodus from Egypt. It would appear, therefore, that in two, related contexts YHWH/God can be the direct object of the verb *mā'as*: (a) when Israel renounces God's plan to make them his people and bring them to the land, in effect, attempting to undo the Exodus and the Sinai covenant, and (b) when Israel renounces God's kingship in favor of a human king. For the rest, the direct-object construction is used most often to say that humans 'cast off' God's 'word, command' (*dābār*, 1 Sam. 15.23, 26), 'judgments' (*mišpāṭîm*, Ezek. 20.13), 'teaching' (*tôrâ*, Amos 2.4), and the like.

Is Israel, the people, or any individual Israelite ever the direct-object of the verb *mā'as*? This is so in the rhetorical question posed in the core text at Jer. 14.19. One could say that this relationship is expressed in Jer. 7.29, already cited above, where we read, 'For YHWH has cast off in abandonment (כי מאס יהוה ויטש) the generation of his wrath'. In contrast, the God of Israel elsewhere denies that he would ever do this:

> Thus spoke YHWH: 'Only if my covenant with day and night, the boundaries of heaven and earth I had not established, only then would I cast off (אמאס) the seed of Jacob, and David my servant, not selecting any of his seed as rulers over Abraham, Isaac, and Jacob, for I will surely restore their repatriates, and have compassion for them. (Jer. 33.25-26)

King Saul is the direct object of this verb (1 Sam. 15.23; 16.1) as are other potential candidates for kingship over Israel (1 Sam. 16.7-10), whereas an unnamed priest who rejected knowledge is told that he will be accordingly disqualified (Hos. 4.6). And, of course, we have Lam. 5.20-22:

> [20]Why have you forgotten us forever,
> abandoned us (תעזבנו) for so long!
> [21]Bring us back, YHWH, to you, and we will return;
> Renew our days as they were in the past,
> [22]For you have utterly cast us off (כי מאס מאסתנו),
> You have become exceedingly enraged at us.

The plea to be restored more or less confirms that the verb *mā'as* is synonymous with *'āzab* ('to abandon'). There is, however, one instance where the meaning of the verb *mā'as*, with the God of Israel as subject, is ambiguous. Amos 5.21 reads, 'I hate, I reject/brush aside (שנאתי מאסתי) your pilgrimage festival offerings, and I will not breathe in the aroma of your solemn assembly offerings'.

One could say that the offerings keep coming, but God does not accept them, thereby rendering them ineffective. Alternatively, one could assign a more active sense to the verb *mā'as* and say that the deity brushes the offerings aside, as the prophet Malachi (2.3) put it quite graphically: 'And I will strew dung on your faces, the dung of your pilgrimage festival offerings'.

The Wisdom tradition affords any number of examples where the construction *mā'as* + direct-object conveys something between an emotional disposition and an overt act. True to the distinctive vocabulary of wisdom, such usage, as subtle as it is, adds to our understanding of how this verb is used in specific contexts. A basic principle of wisdom is that we are to pursue truth and virtue, and submit to rebuke and discipline. We are to repudiate evil and sinfulness, and keep ourselves far from them. Such acts and dispositions may be expressed by the verb *mā'as* + direct object. Consider the following:

1.   Psalm 15.4, speaking of the virtuous person: 'One who is contemptible in his eyes he repudiates (ימאס), but he honors those who fear YHWH'.[8]

---

8.   It is suggested that we read ימאס instead of MT niphal נמאס to accord with the parallel יכבד, also an imperfect form.

2.   Psalm 36.5, speaking of the wicked person: 'He plots iniquity on his bed-
      stead, he stations himself on a course of doing no good; he does not
      repudiate evil (ורע לא ימאס)'.

3.   Proverbs 3.11 and 15.32 both employ the Wisdom terms *mûsār* ('disci-
      pline') and *tôkaḥat* ('rebuke') in parallelism: 'YHWH's discipline do not
      repudiate (אל־תמאס), my son; do not abhor his rebuke' (Prov. 3.11); 'One
      who breaks loose from discipline diminishes his capacity (מואס נפשו),
      but one who heeds rebuke, acquires understanding' (Prov. 15.32). Akin
      to this is Job 5.17, 'Behold, fortunate is the man whom the deity rebukes;
      do not repudiate (אל־תמאס) the discipline of Shadday'.

In the book of Job, God is at times the subject of the verb *mā'as*, as are humans
such as Job, and such passages yield interesting connotations. At one point, Job
appeals to God not to convict him: 'Does it benefit you to defraud, so that you
repudiate (כי־תמאס) the work of your hands, while approving of the designs of the
wicked?' At another point Job affirms God's justice when he says, 'For El does not
repudiate the innocent (לא ימאס־תם), and he will not give support to evildoers' (Job
8.20). Just as Job appeals to God's justice, he also affirms his own in 31.13. 'Did I
ever brush aside (אם־אמאס) the case of my servant or maid servant?' Job feels he
cannot win his suit against God despite his innocence (Job 9.20-21):

> Though I were right, my words would convict me.
> Though I were innocent, he would declare me crooked.
> I am innocent! But I am out of my mind! I repudiate my life (אמאס חיי).

In a moment of bitterness over his downfall, Job says, 'But now, those younger
than me in years mock me, whose ancestors I so shunned (אשר־מאסתי אבותם) as to
put them with my sheep dogs!' (Job 30.1)

In the book of Job there are instances where we encounter the syntax *mā'as* +
0-object, with the direct object being implied (cf. Ps. 89.39). Thus, Job 36.5: 'For
El is mighty, he would not condemn (ולא ימאס); he is mighty in strength and mind'.
In other words, he would not condemn the just. Elsewhere, Elihu poses a poignant
question to Job that uses the same construction: 'Does he (God) repay men's deeds
by your say-so, that you have denounced (כי־מאסת)?' (Job 34.33).[9] That is to say,
you have denounced the deity. The most dramatic, and the most subtle, instance of
the syntax *mā'as* + 0-object comes in Job's final statement to God, in which he
concedes that after seeing God revealed in the storm, he realizes that he is in no
position to challenge him. 'For this reason, I give up (אמאס), and reconcile myself
over being (only) earth and ashes'. In other words, Job withdraws his suit (cf. the
sense of *mā'as* in Job 31.13).

There is Akkadian evidence bearing on the Hebrew verb *mā'as*. A sure cognate
of the Hebrew is Akkadian *mêšu* ('to despise, to have contempt for, to disregard',

---

9.   The Hebrew is difficult and translates literally as 'Is it from you that he repays it?' The
verb *šillem* ('to repay'), is often used in reference to the rewards and punishments that God metes
out. The 'it' undoubtedly refers to people's deeds, what they do to incur punishment; hence, our
free translation 'men's deeds'.

hence, 'to disregard sins, to forgive', *CAD M* II: 41-42). It is frequently found in Wisdom texts of a religious character that are not too different from biblical prophecy. A second possible cognate is Akkadian *mêsu* ('to crush, squash, to trample, destroy, overwhelm', *CAD M* II: 35-36). It is said of crushing soft stone, trampling on grass and plants, and the effects of destructive weaponry. In certain of their respective realizations these two verbs, which may be totally unrelated, are homophonous and homographic, with some drifting of the –*s*– and –*sh*– sounds. They exhibit different lexical equivalents, and are used in different contexts, and yet they share a synonym in common, Akkadian *kabāsu* ('to trample'). In the case of *mêsu* ('to crush'), this is attested only in a lexical series, but as regards *mêšu* ('to despise') we have parallelism in a literary source. Thus, in the Babylonian Theodicy (Lambert 1966: 78.135) we read: *pilludê ili lu-meš // parṣi lukabbis* ('I will cast off [my] god's regulations // I will surely trample on [his] rites'—normalized *apud CAD*). Lambert translated 'ignore', but I prefer a higher degree of semantic parallelism, and therefore I render *mêšu* as 'to cast off'. In the same way, I favor a physical translation in an inscription of Esarhaddon, where *mêšu* is parallel with *abāku* ('to overturn'; cf. *CAD A* I: 8-10, s.v. *abāku* B): *ilīšina ībukama i-me-šá ištaršin* ('They overthrew their gods // they cast off their goddesses', *CAD M* II: 41-42). There are additional parallel verbs that indicate physical action.

It is relevant at this point to mention the verb *nā'aṣ* ('to spurn') which occurs in Jer. 14.21. It also attests an Akkadian cognate, *nâṣu* ('to scorn', *CAD N* II: 53), a rare verb from the West-Semitic, peripheral tradition. Its synonyms are *nadû* ('to cast off, forsake') and *ṭarādu* ('to expel'), and, like Akkadian *mêšu*, this verb also occurs in Wisdom Literature Thus, in the Babylonian Theodicy (Lambert 1966: 76.79, in my translation):

> *kitta tattadûma // uṣurti ili ta-na-ṣu*

> Rectitude—you have cast off; the designs of your god—you spurn.

Compare Ps 107.11:

> כי המרו אמרי אל ועצת עליון נאצו

> For they disobeyed the teachings of El, and spurned the designs of Elyon.

I would, therefore, apply the same reservations to the translations of Akkadian *mêšu* (and *nâṣu*) provided in the *Chicago Assyrian Dictionary* as I have to the usual translations of Biblical Hebrew *mā'as*. In many instances Akkadian *mêšu*, whose usage parallels that of Biblical Hebrew *mā'as* to a substantial degree, would be better rendered 'to cast off', rather than 'to despise'. It is significant that Akkadian *mêšu* (and *nâṣu*, for that matter) appears never to describe the actions or dispositions of gods and those in authority, but only of those who disrespect those in authority. The matter is further complicated by bringing Akkadian *mêsu* ('to crush') into the discussion. Whether *mêšu* and *mêsu* represent, respectively, two specialized offshoots of a common root, or whether they have no etymological connection whatsoever, they may have interpenetrated in Akkadian. Another possibility not to be ignored is that *mêsu* ('to crush') may be reflected in certain usages of Hebrew *mā'as*. The best candidate is the expression מאסתכל עץ ('It can fell any tree') in Ezek. 31.15. Another is מאסערים ('He has ruined towns') in Isa. 33.8. If this analysis is warranted, the Akkadian evidence has contributed indispensably to our understanding of at least two biblical passages, and in a general way to usage of the verb *mā'as*. Conversely, the fairly extensive use of the verb *mā'as* in Biblical Hebrew can enhance our understanding of its Akkadian cognate, *mêšu*.

I now turn to the verb *gā'al*, usually translated 'to spurn, reject' which occurs in Jer. 14.19 in the verbal idiom *gā'ᵃlâ nepeš* ('the stomach/esophagus vomits, ejects; becomes nauseous'), and the nominal idiom *gō'al nepeš* ('vomit of the stomach/esophagus', Ezek. 16.5). It may be that these idioms were so well known that it became unnecessary to state the subject (*nepeš*) in every case. A comparable abbreviation is the hiphil *hib'îš* ('to make foul'), short for *hib'îš rêaḥ* ('to make the odor foul'). By extension, this was a way of saying 'to give another person a bad name, to ruin a reputation' (Exod. 5.21). Thus, in Gen. 34.30 we hear Jacob saying to his two reckless sons, Simeon and Levi, 'You have sullied me, to make me foul (להבאישני) in the eyes of the inhabitants of the land, the Canaanites and Perizites' (cf. 1 Sam. 27.12). On this basis, one would similarly use the verb *gā'al*, without adding *nepeš*, to mean 'to vomit, eject, spew out'.

Except for Jer. 14.19, in the core text, remaining occurrences of this verbal root are limited to Ezek. 16.3, 45, and Lev. 26.11, 15, 30, 42, 44, in the epilogue to the Holiness Code. Ezekiel 16 is a composite text, and my parsing of it differs in some respects from most previous suggestions:

1. The caption (16.1).
2. The Hittite–Amorite *māšāl*, wherein Jerusalem is cast, in the lineage of her mother (and father), and like her sisters, Samaria and Sodom, as a wife committing תועבות ('abominations') who 'expels' or 'ejects' (the verb *gā'al*) her husband and children (16.2-3, 43b-58).
3. The metaphor of infidelity, expressed by forms of the verb *zānâ*, wherein Jerusalem is cast as the wanton harlot who gave away all of the gifts bestowed upon her by her true covenant-partner, the God of Israel, including her children, to false lovers (Ezek. 16.4-43a). Within this section, we are told that at her birth the harlot had been exposed and left to die, but was rescued, reared and cared for by God (16.4-7).
4. YHWH remains true to his covenant despite Jerusalem's violations of it, forgiving her so as to teach her the rewards of loyalty (Ezek. 16.59-63).

By way of explanation, the theme of *tô'ēbôt* ('abominations') is introduced in 16.2, and explained in terms of foreign birth in v. 3. These motifs reappear only in 16.43b, where the Amorite–Hittite metaphor resumes, whereas from 16.4-43a they are entirely absent. Ezekiel 16.4 accomplishes the switch by means of a semantic transaction on the word *môlᵉdōtayik*, which in v. 3 had meant 'place of your birth', or perhaps 'lineage'. In v. 4, which begins the harlot metaphor, it means 'the event of your birth, the time of your birth', as Ezek. 6.4 clarifies. Whereas there are two repetitive attestations of verbal *gā'al* in the Hittite–Amorite *māšāl* (16.45), there is only a single attestation of the nominal idiom *gō'al nepeš* in the depiction of exposure within the extended harlot metaphor (16.5). What is more, no matter how we interpret the nominal idiom in Ezek. 16.5, it refers to Jerusalem as the helpless victim of exposure, whereas in Ezek. 16.45 it refers to Jerusalem as the perpetrator. With this analysis in mind, let me begin by examining Ezek. 16.5, 'No one cared enough for you to do even one of these things for you, out of compassion for you. You were exposed upon the open field, in the vomit/spewing of your innards (בגעל נפשך), on the day of your birth.'

Jerusalem is cast as a female infant, exposed at birth and left to die, until God later rescues her and lovingly cares for her. The question is whether *gōʿal nepeš* either (a) describes the physical condition of the infant, herself, namely, that she is unwashed and lying in the vomit of her innards, in her own filth, or (b) whether it refers to her as the target of riddance and exposure, so that we would alternatively translate the Hebrew בגעל נפשך ('in the spurning of your person'). Each of these interpretations has a tradition in scholarship.[10] I favor the more concrete interpretation whereby the referent of the verbal noun *gōʿal* is the infant herself, not the action of whoever had spurned the child. Throughout, the child is addressed in the second person feminine, in very graphic terms describing the horrible state of her body, with umbilical chord still uncut, and without swaddling clothes. It would disrupt the powerful graphics of this description to switch suddenly to an elliptical subject, never precisely identified. Furthermore, in the few attestations of the idiom *gāʿălâ nepeš*, the term *nepeš* consistently refers to the actor, or subject, whether human or divine; it is that actor's 'stomach, esophagus' that does the regurgitating, or does whatever it is that the verb *gāʿal* connotes, in an extended sense. If this analysis is correct, we are dealing with a set of physical actions and reactions characteristic of nausea, whereby the *nepeš* rids itself of ingested content; it ejects something unwanted.

This analysis leads us directly to Ezek. 16.43b-45, where the *māšāl* of the abominable wife resumes:

> Have you not committed depravity on top of all your (other) abominations (תועבותיך)? Why, everyone who composes a *māšāl* about you, will compose the *māšāl* as follows, 'Like mother, like daughter!' You are (indeed) your mother's daughter, (one who) expels (געלת) her husband and children; and you are the sister of your sisters, who have expelled (אשר געלו) their husbands and children. For your mother was a Hittite and your father an Amorite.

The subject of the metaphor is Jerusalem, who has violated the covenant with her husband, the God of Israel. In so doing, Jerusalem has followed the precedent of her foreign mother and her two ethnic sisters, Samaria, the Northern Kingdom of Israel, and Sodom, representing Judah. The verb that connotes covenant breach is *gāʿal*. The wife has 'expelled' her husband, driven him away in anger, which in

10. For a brief review of scholarly interpretation, see Greenberg 1983: 275. I note that in principle, my interpretation is in agreement with the medieval commentator, David Kimḥi (Radaq) on Ezek. 16.5. He notes that Hebrew *nepeš* means 'body, self', and suggests that *gōʿal* refers to the blood of parturition, more generally, to the condition of the infant on the day of her birth.

turn has brought about the exile of her children, their 'ejection' from the land. It is curious that the verb *qā'â* ('to vomit, regurgitate') in its extended usage also expresses the expulsion of sinful nations by their own lands, personified; they are said to 'cough them up' (Lev. 18.25, 28; 20.22). More will be said about the force of the *gā'āl* + direct-object in Leviticus 26 as part of the discussion of syntax. Before doing so, it might be well to examine two unusual usages of the verb *gā'al*, whose proper interpretation follows from our analysis of Ezek. 16.5:

1. The niphal form *nig'al* in 2 Sam. 1.21: 'For there was the shield of heroes sullied (נגעל), the shield of Saul, no longer polished with oil'. The force of the niphal is denominative, as if to say, 'made into *go'al*, filth'. In the context of David's lament over Saul and Jonathan, which graphically depicts a mountainous battleground after the awful defeat of the Israelites, it would be abstract to translate Hebrew *nig'al* as 'rejected'. The sword of the victor is polished with oil, but that of the vanquished is sullied with blood! This connotation supports the suggestion that the form with 'ayin and the form with 'aleph, Hebrew *gā'al* ('to pollute, contaminate, defile', Mal. 1.7, 12, and elsewhere) are phonetic variants (*HALAT*: 162-63, *s.v. gā'al* II). The form with 'aleph elsewhere describes objects sullied with blood (Isa. 59.3, Lam. 4.14).

2. The hiphil form *yag'il* in Job 21.10: 'His bull impregnates (עבר) without making a mess (of its seed ולא יגעל); his cow gives birth without losing her young'. That is to say, the bull inserts his sperm inside the cow, rather than letting it go to waste, which is precisely what happened to Onan's seed (Gen. 38.9). This is also a denominative 'to make into *go'al*, filth'. This verse is part of a cynical reflection on the injustice of life, which takes up all of Job 21. In a word, everything goes well for the wicked! The present hiphil form is reminiscent of the anomalous and likewise causative-factitive 'ephal form of *gā'al* II in Isa. 63.3: 'And I sullied (אגאלתי) all of my garments'.

It bears mention that although we possess little, if any, contemporary cognate evidence bearing on the verb *gā'al*, Rabbinic Hebrew provides useful information relevant to it. The hiphil *hig'îl* conveys a privative-denominative sense, 'to remove the *gō'al*, filth; to cleanse'. This form is used to describe the scouring of kitchen utensils so as to render them ritually fit. Similarly, the piel *gi'ûl* and the hiphil *hag'ālâ* conjugations refer to this cleansing process (Levy 1963, I: 350-51, *s.v.*). Such later usage is predicated, therefore, on the concrete, physical sense of the biblical Hebrew verb *gā'al* adopted here.

The Interaction of Semantics and Syntax

Thus far, we have limited ourselves to a discussion of direct-object constructions, where physical and graphic meanings are in evidence, along with figurative connotations that express emotions. However, both *mā'as* and *gā'al* occur in indirect-object constructions with prepositional beth, as was true of the verb *gā'al* in

Jer. 14.19. The preposition beth exhibits a variety of meanings and effects, many of them subtle in character. It will be argued here that recourse to the indirect-object syntax in the cases of *gāʿal* and *māʾas* was purposeful, and that, allowing for some drift, it modulates the meaning of the verb in question.

Let us begin with the verb *gāʿal*, and idiomatic *gā ʿlâ nepeš*. In my analysis of Ezekiel 16, I have shown that the direct-object construction has active-transitive force. That is to say, the *nepeš*, as subject, regurgitates the object, either actually or figuratively. Thus, the infant wallows in the vomit that her innards have coughed up (16.5), just as, figuratively, Jerusalem ejects her husband and children who inhabited her (16.44-45). Does the indirect-object construction have a different meaning?

It is important to clarify the *Sitz im Leben* of the author by identifying the situation in Judah and Jerusalem presupposed in the prophecy of Jeremiah 14. Judah had already been stricken beyond healing, and it seemed that God had, indeed, abandoned it and ravaged it—all the things that the verb *māʾas*, in the direct-object construction, connotes. Only Zion and the temple remained. Accordingly, the prophet was pleading for the glorious throne of YHWH to be spared. Had he asked אם את ציון געלה נפשך it would have meant, 'Has your stomach ejected Zion?' In other words, 'Has God exiled the inhabitants of Zion?' At that point in time, this had not happened. Jerusalem was in a threatened state because God had become sickened by the sins of the people and its leaders. His *nepeš* had reacted to Zion in revulsion, but had not yet ejected it, so to speak; the prophet could still plead for Zion to be spared, he could still ask that God's throne not be defiled, and that God not breach his covenant for his own name's sake.

This analysis can be confirmed by studying the syntax of the verb *gāʿal* in Leviticus 26, the epilogue to the Holiness Code. In fact, Leviticus 26 resonates with Jer. 14.17-22 in a clear way. In the promise of blessing, the reward for Israel's adherence to the covenant, God declares, 'I will place my sanctuary in your midst, and I will not expel you (my stomach will not eject you ולא תגעל נפשי אתכם). Rather, will I walk about in your midst and be your God, and you shall be my people' (Lev. 26.11-12).

Contrast the words of the execration in Lev. 26.30-33, which vividly project what happens when the God of Israel finally 'ejects' Israel, the direct object of his wrath:

> And I will destroy your cult-platforms, and cut down your *ḥammānîm*, and heap your carcasses on the lifeless forms of your idols. My stomach shall eject you (וגעלה נפשי אתכם), and I will lay your towns in ruin, and make your sanctuaries desolate, and I will not savor your pleasing aromas. I will make the land desolate so that your enemies who dwell in it shall be desolate over it. And I will scatter you among the nations, and I will unsheathe the sword against you. Your land shall become a desolation, and your towns will be in ruin.

Leviticus 26.3-45 resonates as well with Ezekiel 16. This can be seen by comparing Ezek. 16.59-63 with Lev. 26.42-45. The common theme is God's faithfulness to his covenant with Israel; he remembers the covenant after Israel repents of its violation of it. Of particular interest is how this relationship is portrayed in Lev. 26.44-45:

Yet even then, when they are in the land of their enemies, I will not cast them off
and I will not eject them (לא מאסתים ולא געלתים) to destroy them, breaching my
covenant with them, for I am YHWH, their God. And I will remember in their favor
the covenant with the ancients, whom I brought out of the land of Egypt in the
sight of the nations to be their God. I am YHWH.

The difference between *gāʾal* + direct object and *gāʾal* + beth is that the former
connotes the ejection of the direct object by the subject's *nepeš*, whereas the latter
describes the subject's attitude toward the indirect object. In other words, it
conveys the experience or reaction of the subject to the indirect object. The force of
prepositional beth is close to that of *beth instrumentii* (Gesenius: 380-81, *s.v.* no.
119, q). Thus, in Jeremiah 14, Zion (= Israel) is the cause of God's nausea. It is
because of Zion's deeds that God has become nauseous. In Leviticus 26, God is
said either to eject or not to eject Israel and this is conveyed by the direct-object
construction, and the same is true in Ezekiel 16. God's anger cannot be contained.

The human–divine relationships that are conveyed by the verb *gāʾal* are not
reciprocal, however, as are those conveyed by the verb *māʾas*, soon to be discussed.
The God of Israel both 'ejects' Israel, with Israel as the direct object of the verb,
and experiences nausea at Israel's behavior, or at Zion, which is conveyed by the
indirect-object construction. As for Israel's behavior and responses, nowhere in the
Hebrew Bible is the God of Israel the direct object of the verb *gāʾal*. Israel can only
'eject, cough up' God's judgments and statutes (Lev. 26.15, 43), but not God himself. As a matter of fact, God is nowhere the indirect-object of the verb *gāʾal* either.
In other words, Israel never experiences nausea over God.

This asymmetry is not easily explained. One could say that the verb *gāʾal* can be
used only when speaking of something that has been ingested, or in an extended
sense, has been taken in, enveloped; in a word, something that is in the *nepeš* and is
now to be ejected from it. One can vomit food, of course, and figuratively, a land
can cough up its inhabitants, or a city its children. God can eject a people whom he
has brought into his land, or experience revulsion in response to the actions of a
people who are near to him, whom he has embraced. But precisely because the verb
gāʾal never loses its innate physicality, the Hebrew Bible will not say that humans
can be rid of God. They lack the power to eject him; he is not theirs to eject. Their
deeds may induce God to depart, he may become angry and abandon his people,
and there is much more that humans can do to distance themselves from God, but
God cannot be ejected!

So much for the syntax of the verb *gāʾal*. What of the verb *māʾas*, whose usage
is more complex, its semantic range broader, and its etymology unclear? We cannot
be certain, but it is reasonable to conclude that the primary meanings of *māʾas* are
'to cast off, discard, overthrow, ruin', and that its attitudinal connotations, such as
'despise, reject' are predicated upon them. In fact, one could say that the progression in meaning observable in the case of Hebrew *māʾas* resembles that of Latin
reicio ('to throw back, throw off'), an example of semantic development from the
graphic to the figurative that was cited at the outset. General usage may be stated as
follows: with respect to the verb *māʾas*, there are certain graphic and physical
connotations that are consistently expressed by the direct-object construction. One

could say that in such instances semantics govern syntax. This is illustrated by the very passages that have been studied above, all of which exemplify the direct-object construction. We are bound to ask, nevertheless, whether the same connotations are ever conveyed by the indirect-object construction.

A test case is the prophetic admonition in 2 Kgs 17.13-23. It opens with a review of the failure of northern Israel to heed prophetic calls for repentance. They have forsaken (וימאסו) God's statues and his covenant, and pursued false ways (cf. Jer. 2.5), worshipping idols and Baal, and doing everything to anger God. Yhwh became enraged at northern Israel, and removed them from his presence, so that only the tribe of Judah remained. A redactor most likely added v. 19, which states that Judah, too, eventually followed the precedent of northern Israel. 2 Kings 17.20 recapitulates, 'Then Yhwh felt hatred toward all of the seed of Israel (וימאס יהוה בכל־זרע ישראל), and he reduced them to subjugation, and handed them over to ravagers, until he cast them off (עד אשר השליכם) from his presence'.

I began the discussion by citing passages wherein the verbs *māʾas* and *hišlîk*, in the direct-object construction, are synonymous (Isa. 20.26//31.7; Jer. 7.29). But here, in 2 Kgs 17.20, we observe three stages: (1) God feels hatred toward northern Israel; (2) he then hands them over to conquerors; and (3) he finally casts them out from his presence into exile. It is my view that here the indirect-object construction focuses on the subject; it informs us of God's emotional state before anything actually happens to the indirect object. His emotions prompt his acts, but the *māʾas* + beth construction does not connote the acts themselves. In this respect, as discussed above, the force of *māʾas* resembles that of the verb *gāʾal* in the indirect-object construction. Here, however, the force of prepositional beth is spatial and relational; it expresses the notion of contact. It can be translated as 'at, toward', and even 'against'.

And yet, it seems that *māʾas* + direct object and *māʾas* + indirect object have drifted together, and that in some instances they appear to be interchangeable, with no real difference in meaning intended. This may be so in Isa. 30.12, where the people of Israel are said to show disregard for (*māʾas* + *b–*) God's word. In Ps. 78.59-60, 67-68, 70-72, we have repeated interactions between the verbs *māʾas* and *bāḥar*, with God as the subject, where there are shifts from direct- to indirect-object constructions. A perusal of usage of the verb *māʾas* in Ezek. 5.6; 20.13, 16 (cf. Lev. 26.15, 43), shows that there, too, syntax of the verb *māʾas* is fluid. For the rest, usage of the indirect-object construction seems to focus attention on the mental disposition of the subject rather than on the effects upon the object. Thus, God will punish the people for the fruits of their designs (פרי מחשבותם) because they failed to heed God's words, 'and as regards my teaching (ותורתי), they have shown disregard for it' (וימאסו בה, Jer. 6.19). Similarly, in Jer. 2.37 Israel's reliance on foreign powers will not succeed 'because Yhwh disapproves of those in whom you trust (כי מאס יהוה במבטחיך), you will not prosper through them'. On the human level, this may be the meaning of Job 19.18, 'Even youngsters have shown contempt toward me (מאסו בי)'. And of the Israelites in the wilderness it is said, 'They turned against the desirable land (וימאסו בארץ חמדה), and put no faith in his promise' (Ps. 106.24).

Conclusion

I have attempted to show that Hebrew verbs expressing rejection retain their graphic, physical meanings. By translating such verbs only as expressions of emotion or disposition we are missing an important ingredient in the biblical message. Like his human creatures, the God of Israel acts out his anger, and other negative feelings, quite graphically, often physically. His reaction to the misdeeds of his people can be visceral, and in punishing them he casts them off, ejects them, ravages them, ruins them and abandons them. An examination of the verbs *mā'as* and *gā'al* thus reveals something specific about the biblical agenda: the prophets who used these locutions to characterize God's relationship to Israel, or Israel's relationship to God, were deeply concerned about the prospect of defeat and exile, the loss of the land and its devastation, and the loss of collective identity in foreign lands after deportation. The same is true of Torah authors, biblical narrators, chroniclers and historiographers.

In contrast, the negation of divine rejection (לאגעל, לאמאס), namely, God's affirmation of his covenant and his promise of reward, are often projected as the restoration of the people to the land and the conferral of blessings upon them. Hebrew *mā'as* ('to cast off') and *bāḥar* ('to select, choose') are frequent antonyms.

BIBLIOGRAPHY

Bright, John
    1962   *Jeremiah* (AB, 21; New York: Doubleday).
Cassell
    1971   *Cassell's New Latin-English, English-Latin Dictionary* (ed. D.P. Simpson
                London: Cassell & Co.).
Lambert, William G.
    1966   *Babylonian Wisdom Literature* (Winona Lake, IN: Eisenbrauns).
Greenberg, Moshe
    1983   *Ezekiel 1–20* (AB, 22; New York: Doubleday).
    1997   *Ezekiel 21–37* (AB, 22A; New York: Doubleday).
Grushkin, Esther
    2000   'Emotions and their Effect on the Human Body as Depicted in the Hebrew
                Bible' (unpublished PhD dissertation, New York University [UMI 9970892])
Levine, Baruch A.
    1987a   'The Epilogue to the Holiness Code: A Priestly Statement on the Destiny of
                Israel', in J. Neusner *et al.* (eds.), *Judaic Perspectives on Ancient Israel*
                (Philadelphia: Fortress Press): 9-34.
    1987b   'The Language of Holiness: Perceptions of the Sacred in the Holy Bible', in
                M.P. O'Connor and D.N. Freedman (eds.), *Backgrounds for the Bible*
                (Winona Lake, IN: Eisenbrauns): 241-55.
    1989   *Leviticus: JPS Torah Commentary* (Philadelphia: Jewish Publication Society
                of America).
    1993a   *Numbers 1–20* (AB, 4; New York: Doubleday).

1993b   'Silence, Sound, and the Phenomenology of Mourning in Biblical Israel', *JANESCU* 22: 89-106.

1995   'The Semantics of Loss: Two Exercises in Biblical Hebrew Lexicography', in Z. Zevit *et al.* (eds.), *Solving Riddles and Untying Knots: Biblical, Epigraphic, and Semitic Studies in Honor of Jonas C. Greenfield* (Winona Lake, IN: Eisenbrauns): 137-58.

1996   'Offerings Rejected by God: Numbers 16.15 in Comparative Perspective', in J.A. Coleson and V.H. Matthews (eds.), *Go to the Land I Will Show You: Studies in Honor of Dwight W. Young* (Winona Lake, IN: Eisenbrauns): 107-16.

Lundbom, Jack R.

1999   *Jeremiah 1–20* (AB, 21; New York: Doubleday).

RECOVERING AN ANCIENT PARONOMASIA IN ZECHARIAH 14.5

David Marcus

At the beginning of ch. 14 of the book of Zechariah there is an eschatological passage which states that Jerusalem will be assaulted by outside nations and half of the city will go into exile. God will then come to Jerusalem's assistance and do battle with the assaulting nations. To enable the remaining inhabitants to escape from the city, the contours of the surrounding countryside will be changed. In an astonishing anthropomorphic description God is depicted as standing, like a giant, on top of the Mount of Olives, thereby splitting the mountain in two forming an enormous large valley in the middle going west and east.[1] This valley will eventually serve as a processional way for God and his holy ones advancing to Jerusalem's aid. What exactly will happen as a result of this topographical shift is uncertain because of different interpretations about one word that appears three times in v. 5. If interpreted one way the result of the seismic shift of the mountain would be to enable the population of Jerusalem to flee through this newly created valley. If interpreted another way the result of the movement of the mountain northwards and southwards would be to cause the adjacent valleys to be blocked up. Arguments can be made in favor of both interpretations which are based on different vocalizations of a key word in this verse. In this paper I will survey the development of the different interpretations which reflect three complementary, yet slightly differing, authentic traditions, and I will attempt to show that the different interpretations have developed as a result of an ancient paronomasia.

The form which is the center of the ambiguity is that vocalized in the *textus receptus* (= our MT) as וְנַסְתֶּם which occurs three times in v. 5, twice in a waw-consecutive construction (וְנַסְתֶּם) and once simply as נַסְתֶּם. The pertinent section of the verse reads: וְנַסְתֶּם גִּיא־הָרַי כִּי־יַגִּיעַ גֵּי־הָרִים אֶל־אָצַל וְנַסְתֶּם כַּאֲשֶׁר נַסְתֶּם מִפְּנֵי הָרַעַשׁ בִּימֵי עֻזִּיָּה מֶלֶךְ־יְהוּדָה. The usual translation of these lines is similar to the one adopted by the NRSV: 'And you shall flee by[2] the valley of the Lord's mountain,[3]

---

1. Hurowitz (1999) has pointed out a parallel between this remarkable picture and that in the Epic of Gilgamesh (V ii.4-5) of the fight between Gilgamesh and the monster Humbaba, guardian of the cedar forest, where it is said that 'at the heels of their feet, the ground...at their spinning around, [the mountains] Sirara and Lebanon are split apart'.

2. A preposition is implied here but apart from a couple of exceptions (Josh. 8.20; 1 Kgs 12.18 = 2 Chron. 10.18) the verb נוס when it has the meaning 'to flee to' normally takes a preposition (ל or אֶל) or terminative adverb (e.g. שָׁמָּה).

3. This translation assumes that the final yod of הָרִי is an abbreviation for the Tetragrammaton.

for the valley between the mountains shall reach to Azal; and you shall flee as you fled from the earthquake in the days of King Uzziah of Judah'. The form נַסְתֶּם is a second person plural perfect qal from the verb נוס ('to flee'). The vocalization of all three forms of this verb נַסְתֶּם as coming from the root נוס ('to flee') is the reading found in major Tiberian manuscripts, such as the Cairo Codex (Lowinger [ed.] 1971: 576), the Leningrad Codex (Freedman *et al.* [eds.] 1996: 659) and the Aleppo Codex (Goshen-Gottstein [ed.] 1976: 405). Indeed, the Masorah protects this vocalization by placing a Masorah *parva* note on this form indicating that the form with this vocalization occurs three times. The three times are elaborated in the Masorah *magna* (Weil 1971: #819) with catchwords listing our text and Lev. 26.17 where the form occurs in the phrase וְנַסְתֶּם וְאֵין־רֹדֵף אֶתְכֶם ('and you shall flee though no one pursues you'). In its own way, then, the Masorah indicates that this form must be vocalized only as וְנַסְתֶּם.[4]

Of the ancient versions, both the Vulgate and the Peshitta translate all three occurrences of the Hebrew form נַסְתֶּם as 'to flee'. The Vulgate uses forms of *fugio* ('to flee'): 'And you shall flee (*fugietis*) to the valley of my mountains, for the valley of the mountains shall be joined even to the next, and you shall flee (*fugietis*) as you fled (*fugistis*) from the face of the earthquake in the days of Ozias king of Judah'. Similarly the Peshitta uses forms of ערק ('to flee') to render נַסְתֶּם. The Peshitta translates: 'And you shall flee (ותערקון) to the valley of the mountains; for the valley of the mountains shall reach the place of disaster, and you shall flee (ותערקון) as you fled (ערקתון) from the earthquake in the days of Uzziah king of Judah'.

Taking all three verbs as 'to flee', the sense of the passage would then be that as a result of the shifting of the Mount of Olives the population of Jerusalem would be able to flee through the newly created valley. The occurrence of this form three times in the same verse is thought by Meyers and Meyers (1993: 424) to be a literary feature enabling the author to emphasize 'the concept of the escape of Yahweh's people at this apocalyptic event'. Reference is made to the people's actions during the earthquake at the time of King Uzziah (eighth century BCE), an event which is also mentioned in Amos 1.1. The implication is that during that earthquake the people fled the city, and they will do so again with this new even more devastating seismic shift of land. This interpretation is a standard one and is found in medieval commentaries such as David Kimḥi (1160–1235),[5] through modern ones such as Petersen (1995: 142-43) and Meyers and Meyers (1993: 424-27).

It is no surprise then if we recall that the 1917 Jewish Publication Society translation of the Hebrew Bible also rendered the three forms of נַסְתֶּם as 'to flee'. Its translation, which was similar to that of the KJV, reads: 'And ye shall flee to the valley of the mountains; For the valley of the mountains shall reach unto Azel; Yea, ye shall flee, like as ye fled from before the earthquake in the days of Uzziah king of Judah' (JPS 1917: 769). This translation, then, can be said to reflect the normative Masoretic reading of the text.

4.   Barthélemy (1992: 1004-1005) gives an extensive list of manuscripts where this reading and the pertinent Masorah notes are listed.

5.   In *Miqra'ot Gedolot* (1951: 9, 163).

What is surprising is that the 1985 Jewish Publication Society translation has a completely different reading. This translation takes the three forms as though they were all vocalized נִסְתַּם, a third masculine singular perfect niphal coming from the root סתם ('to block up'). Thus JPS (1985: 1098) translates: 'And the Valley in the Hills shall be stopped up, for the Valley of the Hills shall reach only to Azal; it shall be stopped up as it was stopped up as a result of the earthquake in the days of King Uzziah of Judah'. This translation is repeated in the three recent Jewish Publication Society publications: the *JPS Hebrew–English Tanakh* (1999: 1402-1403), the *Etz Hayim Torah and Commentary* (2001: 1253) and *The JPS Bible Commentary Haftarot* (Fishbane 2002: 401). Since this translation does not reflect the *textus receptus*, this translation would be one of the occasional cases[6] where the translators of the JPS have not conformed to the stated editorial policy of privileging the MT and putting alternate readings in the notes.[7] The justification for this translation stated in an accompanying note is that the editors are: 'vocalizing *[we] nistam* with Targum, Septuagint, and an old Hebrew ms'.[8] In those editions where the Hebrew accompanies the translation the editors have also added two special Hebrew notes which are attached below the text.[9] One of these notes is on נַסְתֶּם and reads: בנוסח אחר 'וְנַסְתֶּם' פעמיים כלומר שנוי תנועות ('Another version reads וְנַסְתֶּם twice, that is to say, a change of vowels'). The other note is on נַסְתֶּם and reads similarly: בנוסח אחר 'נסתַּם' כלומר שנוי תנועות ('Another version reads נִסְתַּם, that is to say, a change of vowels').[10]

The old Hebrew manuscript to which the JPS note refers is undoubtedly[11] the celebrated Codex Petrograd dated 916, often cited with its date as Codex Petrograd 916. But the original manuscript is actually numbered Firkowitsch B3 or Leningrad

6.   There are over forty such cases in the Prophets alone. These alterations sometimes involve revocalization such as וַיִּרָא for וַיַּרְא at 1 Kgs 19.3 or תִּשְׁרֹף for תִּשָּׂרֵף at Jer. 38.23. Most of the times the alterations involve a choice of different letters such וַיֶּל for וַיֵּלֶךְ at Josh. 8.13 or לֶחֶם for לָהֶם at Jer. 16.7, or of different words such as לְבָתִּים for לִגְבָרִים at Josh. 7.18; or וַתֵּבֹא for וַתֹּאמֶר at 2 Sam. 14.4.

7.   This policy is enunciated in the the 'Preface' to JPS (1985: xix-xx) and reprinted in a 'Preface to the 1985 English Edition' in JPS (1999: xxv): 'Like the translation of *The Torah*, the present translation of the prophetic books adheres strictly to the traditional Hebrew text; but where the text remains obscure and an alternation provides marked clarification, a footnote is offered with a rendering of the suggested emendation… Sometimes, however, it was deemed sufficient to offer only a change of vowels, and such modifications are indicated by "Change of vocalization yields". In all cases, the emendation is given in a footnote.'

8.   JPS (1985: 1098; 1999: 1402); and in an abbreviated form in Fishbane 2002: 401. The note continues: 'Other Hebrew mss. and printed editions read, "You [plural] shall flee [to] the Valley in the Hills, for the Valley of the Hills shall reach up to Azal. You shall flee as you fled because of the earthquake…"'

9.   These notes were composed specially by the editors of the translation and 'similar to the Letteris Bible's notes', see JPS (1999: xviii).

10.   These notes curiously enough are not found in JPS (1999: 1402), in the edition where the explanation about the Hebrew note occurs, but rather are found in JPS (2001: 1253) and in Fishbane (2002: 401).

11.   There is no other early Hebrew manuscript for which such readings are claimed.

Ms B3 (Yeivin 1980: vii). From a perusal of this manuscript[12] it can be seen that all three of the forms under discussion in our verse are pointed with Babylonian vocalization as נִסְתַּם[ו]. The Codex is usually cited from the lithographed facsimile edition originally published by Herman Strack in 1876.[13] But Strack, in his edition, indicates that these readings are secondary.[14] He explains in his notes that these vowels were originally changed from a first hand, the ḥireq over the nun was originally a pataḥ and the pataḥ over the taw of the first וְנִסְתַּם was originally a qāmeṣ (Strack 1876: 034).[15] It is not possible from an examination of the microfilm of the original manuscript to verify Strack's assertions since first-hand and second-hand readings cannot be ascertained from the microfilmed copy.[16] But if these readings are in fact secondary then the pointing in the Codex Petrograd is not as clear-cut as the JPS would have us believe.

The second witness to which the JPS appeals in support of its reading is the Targum. But this observation is plainly incorrect, for as we shall presently see, the Targum does not render נִסְתַּם[ו] the same way in all three of its occurrences. However, the third witness cited in the JPS note, the Septuagint, does represent a reading of all these Hebrew forms as וְנִסְתַּם[ו]. The Septuagint on all three occasions uses forms of the verb εὐφράσσω ('to block up') which would mean that the Septuagint interpreted all the Hebrew forms as coming from the root סתם ('to block up'). The Septuagint translates: 'The valley of my mountains shall be blocked up (ἐμφραχθήσεται), and the valley of the mountains shall be joined on to Jasol, and shall be blocked up (ἐμφραχθήσεται) as it was blocked up (ἐνεφράγη) in the days of the earthquake, in the days of Ozias king of Judah'.[17] This is also the reading of the early Greek versions such as Symmachus,[18] and the later Syro-Hexaplar (Middeldorpf 1835: *ad loc.*) which renders the Hebrew forms by the Syriac verb אסתכר, the ithpael of סכר ('to block up').

---

12. I was able to consult a microfilm copy of this manuscript from the microfilm collection in the Library of the Jewish Theological Seminary.

13. Reprinted in 1971 with an introduction by P. Wernberg-Møller. Because the text has Babylonian vocalization it was originally thought by Strack to contain a genuine Babylonian recension, but it is now widely accepted that it contains a mixed text closely akin to our *textus receptus*. See Ginsburg 1966 (1897]): 475-76; 1899: 149-88; Wernberg-Møller (ed.) 1971: xii.

14. He does this by his normal convention of placing second readings in wavy lines (Strack 1876: *explicantur signa*) or by placing a horizontal line under a secondary reading. Thus, over all three nuns the vowel for ḥireq is enclosed by wavy lines in the form of braces and there is also a horizontal line under the pataḥ of the first form (וְנִסְתַּם).

15. This would lead to an original reading of the three forms as וְנֻסְתַּם, וְנֻסְתַּם and נֻסְתַּם—a vocalization close to, though not exactly like, the eastern reading, see *infra*.

16. Saebø (1969: 111) and Barthélemy (1992: 1005) also note Strack's readings. It should be pointed out, however, that some of Strack's notes elsewhere do not accord with an examination of the microfilm. For example, Strack notes that the reading of יְהֹוָה at Amos 5.4 was originally אֲדֹנָי but this is not borne out by the microfilm. Similarly, at Ezek. 29.3, Strack notes that הַתַּנִּים originally read הַתַּנִּין, but once again the microfilm contradicts this statement for it reads הַתַּנִּים.

17. Text: Ziegler 1943: 323-24.

18. At least for the first two forms; see Field 1870: 1029; Ziegler 1943: 323-24; Saebø 1969: 111.

Reading all three verbs as 'to block up' yields the interpretation that the major result of the shifting of the Mount of Olives northwards and southwards mentioned in the previous verse is to block up the adjacent valleys. They would be blocked up as far as a hitherto unidentified town of Azal (Abel 1936: 390-92), and the blockage would be akin to one which occurred during the earthquake in the reign of King Uzziah. Such a blockage seems to be alluded to in the writings of Josephus, who, while commenting on the impious act of Uzziah as reported in 2 Chron. 26.16-21, states:

> A great earthquake shook the ground, and a rent was made in the temple, and the bright rays of the sun shone through it, and fell upon the king's face, insomuch that the leprosy seized upon him immediately; and before the city, at a place called Eroge, half the mountain broke off from the rest on the west, and rolled itself four furlongs, and stood still at the east mountain, till the roads, as well as the king's gardens, were spoiled by the obstruction. (*Ant.* 10.4; following the translation by Whiston 1857: 263).

However, there is no indication in the biblical texts, including Amos 1.1, which refers to Uzziah's earthquake, of any major blockages which occurred during that earthquake. *A priori* it is more likely that in the time of King Uzziah the population fled during an earthquake rather than that there was a blockage of valleys, block-ages which were somehow subsequently unblocked so that they could be stopped up once again in this apocalyptic vision.[19] Nevertheless, this Greek reading of the text has been adopted by some modern translations such as the NEB[20] and the JB, and by a few other scholars such as Horst (1954: 258) and Mason (1977: 125-26).

In addition to these two readings of the verse there is yet a third reading which has been handed down by other authentic witnesses. In many respects this third reading represents a combination of the two previous readings. This reading takes the first form as coming from the verb סתם ('to block up') and the next two forms as coming from the verb נוס ('to flee'). This reading is most readily found in the Targum which translates as follows: 'And the valley of *the* mountains *shall be stopped up*, for the valley of the mountains shall extend to Azal; and you shall flee as you fled before the earthquake *which came* in the days of Uzziah king of *the tribe of the house* of Judah'.[21] By reading ויסתתים (ithpeel) from סתם with waw conjunction, the Targum interpreted the first Hebrew form as coming from the root סתם ('to block up'). But by reading ותערקון and דערקתון it interpreted the follow-ing forms as coming from the root נוס ('to flee').

Because this reading was found in the Targum it gained the attention of a variety of Jewish medieval commentators who understood that the Targum's reading was based on a repointing of the MT's וְנַסְתֶּם to וְנִסְתַּם, and that the Targum was translat-ing here the verb סתם rather than נוס. For example, Rashi (Solomon ben Isaac, 1040–1105) explicitly adopted the Targum's rendering. He stated:

---

19. Reservations about such a scenario were already expressed by the medieval commentator Tanḥum Ben Joseph (see *infra*), and similar doubts are also expressed by Polak (1993: 253).

20. In his notes on the readings adopted by the translators of the NEB, Brockington (1973: 268) specifically states that the NEB translation adopted the readings of the Septuagint.

21. Text: Sperber 1962: III, 497; translation: Cathcart and Gordon 1989: 223.

Jonathan rendered 'the valley will be blocked up'. There are mountains all around Jerusalem, and there is a valley between the mountain in the north and the Mount of Olives, as well as one in the south. When half of the Mount of Olives draws toward the mountain in the north, the valley between them will be blocked up. The same [will happen with the valley] in the south.[22]

But the Targum's rendering was questioned by the medieval biblical exegete Tanḥum Ben Joseph (1220–99):

> The Targum translates the first form of וְנַסְתֶּם as ויסתתמן as though it was vocalized with a *ḥiriq* under the *nûn* as a *niphal* from סתם. This is the reading I found in some books I have, and in some of the commentators I have consulted. But I do not know what it actually means to say that the valley would be blocked up after it was opened.[23]

As it does it many other cases, the Targum's rendering here reflects an eastern or oriental reading (Komlosh 1973: 63; Geiger 1928: 482; Gordis 1971: 74-75). Eastern or oriental readings are found sporadically in our texts[24] and they are often noted by the Masoretes in their various lists and notations (Ginsburg 1966: 197-240; Yeivin 1980: 139-41; Tov 1992: 26).[25]

A number of medieval commentators similarly attribute the Targum reading to be an eastern one. For example, Joseph Qara (eleventh century) noted this variant as follows:

> There is a disagreement (מחלוקת) between oriental (בבל) and western (ארץ ישראל) texts, the oriental texts vocalize וְנַסְתֶּם, the western texts vocalize וְנִסְתַּם. Each gives a reason for their choice. According to one, when you see the mountains coming together you will flee as you fled from the earthquake in the days of King Uzziah or in the year of the death of King Uzziah as it is written 'the pivots of the thresholds shook' (Isa. 6.4). According to the other who translates according to the Targum 'the valley of the mountains will be blocked up'. One is no weightier than the other and only the Almighty can decide who is right.[26]

In a similar vein, the tenth-century Karaite Jacob Kirkisani opined that diverging textual traditions between eastern and western communities cannot be easily reconciled:

> The meanings of the two words are strikingly different. If it is וְנַסְתֶּם, then it means 'you will flee', but if it is וְנִסְתַּם, then it means 'will be blocked up'. If the Creator had intended to indicate flight he would not have inserted blocking, and if he had intended blocking he would not have put in flight. To maintain that the Almighty intended to use two *qere*s is wrong and without comprehension.[27]

---

22. In *Miqra'ot Gedolot* (1951: 9, 163).

23. Text: Shy 1991: 320.

24. *BHS* on occasion notes some of them as, for example, at Judg. 1.21, יֹשְׁבֵי for MT יֹשֵׁב; 1 Sam. 4.15, קָמוּ for MT קָמָה; Jer. 33.3, וּנְצֻרוֹת for MT וּבְצֻרוֹת; Jer. 45.4, לִי for MT's הִיא.

25. This particular reading of וְנַסְתֶּם is not noted in the Masoretic lists because these lists noted only variations in consonants, not in vowels.

26. See text in Biton 2001: 10, 529.

27. Anwar II, 17, 4. Text: Nemoy 1939: 138-39; translation: Barthélemy 1992: 1004.

Likewise Eliezer of Beaugency (twelfth century),[28] Abraham Ibn Ezra (1092–1167), and David Kimḥi (1160–1235) held that וְנִסְתַּם was a reading from the 'Easterners' (אנשי מזרח) found in a few texts. Kimḥi commented that:

> If this is the reading then the meaning would be that, after the cleaving open of the Mount of Olives, it will be shut again, an hour or hours, a day or days after, and thus the miracle will be so much the greater that it should be shut after splitting open because in normal earthquakes, the earth is split open, but it does not close again. The miracle is akin to the case of Korah and his followers when the earth was split open and the earth closed up afterwards, as it is written 'and the earth closed over them up' (Num. 16.33) and this was a great miracle.[29]

Towards the modern period, Solomon Norzi (1560–1616) in his *Minchat Shai* noticed the occurrence of this eastern reading in what he says were the most exact texts, but he stated that he himself has not seen it and, in any event, he prefers the Masoretic reading.[30] The eighteenth-century Hebraist Johann de Rossi (1785: 221) recorded that this eastern reading was to be found in three of his manuscripts,[31] and the nineteenth-century neo-Masorete, Christian David Ginsburg, in his edition of the Hebrew Bible, noted that the eastern reading occurs in one Hebrew manuscript dated c. 1300 and in one early printed edition.[32] Likewise, Strack (1876: 034) noted that this oriental reading of וְנִסְתַּם occurred in a Codex Firkowitsch 133 with Babylonian pointing.[33] This codex contains parts of the Haphtarot with a Targum and has been dated to the fourteenth century. I have also been able to attest to this eastern reading in one celebrated Tiberian manuscript and in the printed edition of the First Rabbinic Bible. The Tiberian manuscript is Codex Erfurt 3 (now known as Or. 1213), belonging to the former Prussian State Library in Berlin (now the National Library of Prussian Cultural Properties),[34] and is dated to the eleventh or twelfth century. The Erfurt manuscript in Tiberian pointing reads the form וְנִסְתַּם and has a marginal note above the text acknowledging the unusual reading by stating that 'in the book of our master (מרי)[35] it is written וְנִסְתַּם and the Targum of

28. Poznanski (ed.) 1913: 210. I thank my colleague Dr Robert Harris for this reference.

29. In *Miqra'ot Gedolot* (1951: 9, 163).

30. The observations of Norzi are printed at the back of all comprehensive Rabbinic Bibles, see *Miqra'ot Gedolot* (1951: 9, 172).

31. Manuscript nos. 264, 543, 596. In the other major collection of medieval manuscripts, that of Benjamin Kennicott (1780: II, 301), there is no variant reading on these words at Zech. 14.5.

32. Ginsburg 1926: IV, 412. In his 'Table of Abbreviations', Ginsburg identifies this manuscript as Or. 4227. However, in the detailed description of this manuscript in his *Introduction to the Massoretico-Critical Edition* (Ginsburg 1966: 721-28) he does not discuss this eastern reading. The printed edition is identified as a Pentateuch and Haphtarot from Venice 1516 but such a printed edition is not described in his *Introduction*.

33. I was able to verify this reading by consulting a microfilm copy of Firkowitsch 133 at the Library of the Jewish Theological Seminary (JTS microfilm reel, #693).

34. As checked on a microfilm courtesy of the Ancient Biblical Manuscript Center, Claremont, CA.

35. Barthélemy (1992: 1005) curiously translates 'my master י' and reports the form in the manuscript as having a qāmeṣ not a pataḥ. According to Barthélemy, the eastern reading is also to be found in a manuscript now in the Bibliotheque Nationale of Paris with a shelf mark Hebreu 3

Jonathan, with its reading (וַאִיסְתְּתִים חֵיל טוּרַיָא) supports it'. This variant is also to be found in the margin of the first edition of the Rabbinic Bible edited by Felix Pratensis (Bomberg, 1517). One of the characteristic features of this edition is that it preserves numerous variant readings in its margins (Ginsburg 1966: 937). In the right hand margin beside the word וְנַסְתֶּם, which is marked with a *circillus*, the eastern variant וְנִסְתַּם is listed.

This eastern reading is noted in modern concordances and lexicons. It is to be found in Mandelkern's *Concordance* which mentions it at the beginning of entry נוּס, and cites the reading of the Septuagint, the Targum and Ibn Ezra (Mandelkern 1896: 730). In their *Lexicon* (*sub* נוּס), Koehler and Baumgartner (2001: I, 681) state that this eastern reading with a qāmeṣ under the taw occurs in all three forms as a variant in 'eastern manuscripts' but they do not specify the manuscripts. Elsewhere in their *Lexicon* (*sub* סתם), the editors express a preference for the reading for all three cases of וְנִסְתַּם (instead of וְנַסְתֶּם), but in this entry they do not mention the eastern reading to support their preferred reading (Koehler and Baumgartner 2001: I, 771).

There are also some modern commentators who adopt this eastern reading, and these have included the classical commentaries of Nowack (1897: 383), Wellhausen (1963: 201), and Marti (1904: 451). In his ICC commentary, Mitchell favors the eastern reading and notes that the vast majority of occurrences of the verb סתם ('to block up') are with springs and wells, so he suggests that it is more likely that the subject of וְנִסְתַּם is not this or that valley, but one of the springs in the vicinity of Jerusalem, most probably Gihon (Mitchell 1912: 345). The editors of *BH*[3] and of *BHS* also indicated their preference for the reading וְנִסְתַּם, as did the editors of the RSV. The latter gave this eastern reading prominence by including it in their 1952 translation which they rendered as: 'And the valley of my mountains shall be stopped up, for the valley of the mountains shall touch the side of it and you shall flee as you fled from the earthquake in the days of Uzziah king of Judah'.

So we see that there are three readings of the text: the normative Masoretic one which reads all three forms as 'to flee', the Greek tradition which reads all three forms as 'to stop up' and the eastern tradition which takes the first form as 'to block up' but the other two forms as 'to flee'. How then can one explain the presence of these three alternate readings? Was there an original reading from which the other two developed? In his detailed study of the text of Second Zechariah, Magne Saebø examined the relationship of these three extant witnesses to this verse and concluded that one of them, the eastern reading, was the *lectio difficilior* and that the other two traditions later attempted to smooth out this difficulty. In the Greek tradition the first form, וְנִסְתַּם, was the one which influenced the following two forms and resulted in three forms of 'blocking up'; on the other hand, in the normative (western) Masoretic tradition (followed by the Vulgate and Syriac) the first form

dated 1286. But in my examination of the microfilm of this manuscript (courtesy of an inter-library loan from the Ancient Biblical Manuscript Center, Claremont, CA) I was unable to find this reading. The manuscript is a palimpsest and is very difficult to read, yet it does not seem to preserve this section of the verse.

was smoothed out to וְנָסְתֶּם to agree with the following two forms (Saebø 1969: 112-13).

According to Saebø, if the eastern reading was the *lectio difficilior* then it was most probable that it represented the original reading. I tend to agree with Saebø and would add that the claim for originality of the eastern reading is supported by the fact that this reading of the three forms, one in a different vocalization to the following two, would represent an ancient paronomasia. It is now widely recognized that paronomasia constituted an important convention of ancient Hebrew composition (Glück 1970: 50-78; Greenstein 1992: 968). Not only are a substantial number of wordplays to be found in the Minor Prophets section of the Hebrew Bible (Sasson 1976: 970), but a number of these wordplays have been identified elsewhere in the same corpus of Second Zechariah (chs. 9–14) from which our paronomasia derives (Wolters 2000: 223-30).[36] In fact, it is possible to categorize these wordplays which occur in Second Zechariah into the standard types of paronomasia such as geography, polysemy, antanaclasis, assonance, metathesis and metaphony.

An example of paronomasia involving geography is 9.3, ותבן צר מצור לה ('Tyre has built for herself a fortress'), where there is an obvious play of צר ('Tyre') and מצור ('fortress'). The paronomasia is used effectively 'to emphasize the most prominent feature of Tyre, i.e. its fortification or "bulwark"' (Meyers and Meyers 1993: 98).[37] The word מצור is also a good example of antanaclasis, which is a paronomasia where the same word is repeated with different meanings. In this verse the word מצור means 'a fortress' but in 12.2 it means 'a siege' (וגם על־יהודה יהיה במצור על־ירושלם, 'Judah shall be caught up in the siege upon Jerusalem').[38] Similar to antanaclasis is polysemy or multiple meaning of words and a good example of this form of paronomasia may be seen in the word תקוה which can mean both 'hope' and 'cord'. So the phrase in 9.12 אסירי התקוה can mean 'prisoners of hope' or 'prisoners of cord' (= 'bound prisoners').[39] An example of a paronomasia of

36. The presence of wordplays would also support the view of those who see the Second Zechariah corpus as having been influenced by 'Wisdom', a characteristic feature of which is said to be wordplay (Larkin 1994: 250).

37. Another example of a geographical paronomasia, first identified by Wolters (2000: 226), is in 9.2: וגם חמת תגבל בה ('also Hammath which borders on it'). Here there is an implicit play in the form תגבל (a denominative from גבול, 'border') with the Phoenician city גבל ('Byblos') fitting in with the context of the other North Syrian cities (Damascus, Hamath, Tyre and Sidon) which are the subject of this prophecy.

38. Other examples of antanaclasis in Second Zechariah are: (1) נגש meaning 'an oppressor' and 'a ruler'. It means 'an oppressor' in 9.8 ולא־יעבר עליהם עוד נגש ('no oppressor shall ever overrun you again'); and then 'a ruler' in 10.4. ממנו יצא כל־נוגש יחדו ('out of them every ruler'); (2) פקד meaning 'to visit (with punishment)' and 'to visit (with deliverance)' in the same verse (10.3). It means 'visit (with punishment)' in אפקוד ('My anger is roused על־הרעים חרה אפי ועל־העתודים against the shepherds and I will punish [אפקוד] the he-goats'); and once in the phrase בי־פקד יהוה צבאות את־עדרו את־בית יהודה ('for the Lord of Hosts has taken thought [פקד] in behalf of his flock, the House of Judah').

39. Discussed by Wolters 2000: 226-27. The same polysemy has been noticed in Job 7.6, see Greenstein 1992: 969.

assonance or similarity of form is in 9.5: תרא אשקלון ותירא ('Ashkelon will see and be afraid'). Here there is the well-known play on the verbs ראה ('to see') and ירא ('to be afraid'). Another example of assonance may be seen with the verbs בוש ('to shame') and יבש ('to dry up'). These verbs exhibit identical forms in their hiphil conjugation הבישו—thus allowing for a paronomasia, as can be seen in 10.5 where the meaning of הבישו is 'to put to shame' (והבישו רכבי סוסים, 'they shall put horse-men to shame') while in 10.11 the form means 'to dry up' (והבישו כל מצולות יאר, 'all the deeps of the Nile shall dry up'). An example of a paronomasia involving metathesis of consonants is in 13.7 חרב עורי על־רעי ('O sword! Rouse yourself against my shepherd'). Here there is a play between עורי ('awake') and רעי ('my shepherd')—an interchange of 'ayin and resh.

Our paronomasia is one which comes under the category of metaphony, that is, a play resulting from a different vocalization. Thus in 10.6 the *forma mixta* והושבותים could be taken either from the root ישב ('to dwell') and be vocalized וְהוֹשַׁבְתִּים ('I will make them dwell', so LXX), or from שוב ('to return') and be vocalized וַהֲשִׁבוֹתִים ('I will restore them', so Vulgate, Targum, Peshitta), as in v. 10. In 11.17, if חֶרֶב ('sword') is revocalized חֹרֶב ('heat')[40] then the phrase חרב על־זרועו ('sword on his arm') becomes 'heat on his arm', which makes a good parallel with זרעו יבוש תיבש ('his arm shall shrivel up') occurring later in the verse. Finally, in 13.5 the word אדם ('man') in the phrase אדם הקנני מנעורי ('man has possessed me from my youth') has been revocalized by translators to אָדֹם, 'red'), 'I was plied with the red stuff (אָדֹם) from my youth on' (JPS 1985); or to אֲדָמָה ('for the land has been my possession since my youth', NRSV).

The eastern reading in our verse of וְנִסְתָּם/וְנַסְתֶּם/נַסְתֶּם constitutes yet another example of metaphonic paronomasia evident in these chapters. The paronomasia not only exhibits a play on the three forms which occur in our verse but allows two interpretations to exist simultaneously in a Janus-like fashion.[41] The paronomasia enables us to bridge between the two otherwise distinct interpretations. The western reading assumes that the people will flee through the newly created valley caused by the splitting of the Mount of Olives. The Greek reading assumes that the split-ting of the Mount of Olives results in both of the split sides of the mountain moving north and south respectively and blocking up valleys in their way. The eastern read-ing represents a combination of these interpretations. The valley adjacent to the Temple Mount is blocked up and the people flee presumably either on this blocked surface or in another direction altogether but not necessarily through the newly created valley caused by the split in the Mount of Olives.

The eastern reading allows the first word to be aligned retrospectively with the previous clause, while, via paronomasia (with a play on the other forms) the first

40. Proposed by Gordis (1976: 195) and adopted by Herzberg (1981: 22-23). This recovaliza-tion was noted as a variant reading by Mandelkern (1896: 423). Sasson (1976: 969) correctly points out that 'the homonymy that allowed such punning occurred when consonants which were phonemically different in Proto-Semitic fell together in Hebrew'. Thus חֶרֶב was originally written with a ḥ, but חֹרֶב was originally written with a ḫ.

41. On many examples of Janus-type parallelism in the Hebrew Bible, see Noegel 1996: 11-38.

word can also be proleptically aligned with the following clause. So, the first meaning, that expressed in the vocalization וְנִסְתַּם ('it will be blocked up'), associates the blocking of the valley with the preceding verse describing the movement of the mountain sides whereas the play on the form would allow an alignment with the following clause which describes the fleeing of the people during the earthquake at the time of King Uzziah. The paronomasia may have been either originally intended by the author or deftly crafted by a subsequent editor of the text. As I have noted, in the course of time the paronomasia was overlooked and smoothed out. In the western normative Hebrew tradition all forms became וְנַסְתֶּם[ו], in the Greek tradition all forms became וְנַסְתֶּם[ו]. Only in the Targum and in eastern manuscripts was the original paronomasia preserved. Recognition of the original paronomasia enables us to trace the development of three complementary, yet slightly differing, authentic traditions.

BIBLIOGRAPHY

Abel, F.-M.
    1936   'Aṣal in Zechariah 14.5', *RB* 45: 385-400.
Barthélemy, Dominique
    1992   *Critique textuelle de l'ancien Testament: Ezéchiel, Daniel et les 12 Prophètes* (OBO, 50/3; Göttingen: Vandenhoeck & Ruprecht).
Biton, Daniel
    2001   *Miqra'ot Gedolot Hamaor: Nevi'im Uketuvim* (17 vols.; Jerusalem: Hamaor).
Brockington, L.H.
    1973   *The Hebrew Text of the Old Testament* (Oxford: Oxford University Press).
Cathcart, Kevin J., and Robert P. Gordon
    1989   *The Targum of the Minor Prophets* (ArBib, 14; Wilmington, DE: Michael Glazier).
Field, Fridericus
    1870   *Origenis Hexaplorum* (Oxford: Clarendon Press).
Fishbane, Michael
    2002   *The JPS Bible Commentary Haftarot* (Philadelphia: The Jewish Publication Society of America).
Freedman, David Noel *et al.* (eds.)
    1996   *The Leningrad Codex: A Facsimile Edition* (Grand Rapids: Eerdmans)
Geiger, Abraham
    1928   *Urschrift und Übersetzungen der Bibel* (Frankfurt: Madda).
Ginsburg, Christian D.
    1899   'On the Relationship of the So-called Codex Babylonicus of A.D. 916 to the Eastern Recension of the Hebrew Text', in David Gunzburg (ed.), *Recueil des travaux rédigés en mémoire du jubilé scientifique de M. Daniel Chwolson* (Berlin: S. Calvary): 149-88.
    1926   *Torah, Nevi'im u-Khetuvim* (4 vols.; London: British and Foreign Bible Society [Hebrew]).
    1966   *Introduction to the Massoretico-Critical Edition of the Hebrew Bible* (repr.; New York: Ktav [1897])

Glück, J.J.
1970   'Paronomasia in Biblical Literature', *Semitics* 1: 50-78.
Gordis, Robert
1971   *The Biblical Text in the Making: A Study of the Kethib-Qere* (New York: Ktav [1937]).
1976   *The Word and the Book* (New York: Ktav).
Goshen-Gottstein, Moshe H. (ed.)
1976   *The Aleppo Codex* (Jerusalem: Magnes Press)
Greenstein, Edward L.
1992   'Wordplay, Hebrew', in *ABD*, VI: 968-72.
Herzberg, Walter H.
1981   'Polysemy in the Hebrew Bible' (unpublished PhD Dissertation, New York University, 1979; Ann Arbor, MI: University Microfilms International).
Horst, Friedrich
1954   *Die zwölf kleinen Propheten: Nahum bis Maleachi* (HAT, 14; Tübingen: J.C.B. Mohr).
Hurowitz, Victor A.
1999   'Splitting the Sacred Mountain: Zechariah 14,4 and Gilgamesh V ii 4-5', *UF* 31: 241-45.
JPS
1917   *The Holy Scriptures According to the Masoretic Text: A New Translation* (Philadelphia: The Jewish Publication Society of America).
1985   *Tanakh: A New Translation of the Holy Scriptures According to the Traditional Hebrew Text* (Philadelphia: The Jewish Publication Society of America).
1999   *JPS Hebrew–English Tanakh* (Philadelphia: The Jewish Publication Society of America).
2001   *Etz Hayim Torah and Commentary* (New York: The Rabbinical Assembly).
Kennicott, Benjamin
1780   *Vetus Testamentum Hebraicum cum Variis Lectionibus* (2 vols.; Oxford: Clarendon Press).
Koehler, Ludwig, and Walter Baumgartner
2001   *The Hebrew and Aramaic Lexicon of the Old Testament. Study Edition* (2 vols.; Leiden: E.J. Brill).
Komlosh, Yehuda
1973   *Ha-Mikra be-Or Ha-Targum* (Tel-Aviv: Devir [Hebrew]).
Larkin, Katrina J.A.
1994   *The Eschatology of Second Zechariah: A Study of the Formation of a Man-tological Wisdom Anthology* (Kampen: Kok Pharos).
Lowinger, D.S. (ed.)
1971   *Codex Cairo of the Bible: The Earliest Extant Hebrew Manuscript Written in 895 by Moshe Ben Asher* (Jerusalem: Makor).
Mandelkern, Solomon
1896   *Veteris testameni concordantiae Hebraicae atque Chaldaicae* (Lipsiae: Veit et Comp).
Marti, D. Karl
1904   *Das Dodekapropheton* (KHC, 13; Tübingen: J.C.B. Mohr).

Mason, Rex
1977   *The Books of Haggai, Zechariah and Malachi* (Cambridge: Cambridge University Press).
Meyers, Carol L., and Eric M. Meyers
1993   *Zechariah 9–14* (AB, 25C; New York: Doubleday).
Middeldorpf, Henry
1835   *Codex Syriaco-Hexaplaris* (Berolini: Enslin).
Miqra'ot Gedolot
1951   *Miqra'ot Gedolot* (10 vols.; New York: Pardes Publishing House)
Mitchell, Hinckley G. *et al.*
1912   *Haggai, Zechariah, Malachi and Jonah* (ICC; Edinburgh: T. & T. Clark).
Nemoy, L.
1939   *Kitāb-al-Anwār wal-Marāqib: Code of Karaite Law by Ya'qūb al Qirqisān* (New York: The Alexander Hohut Memorial Foundation [Arabic]).
Noegel, Scott B.
1996   *Janus Parallelism in the Book of Job* (JSOTSup, 223; Sheffield: Sheffield Academic Press).
Nowack, D.W.
1897   *Die kleinen Propheten* (HAT, 3; Göttingen: Vandenhoeck & Ruprecht).
Petersen, David L.
1995   *Zechariah 9–14 and Malachi* (OTL; Louisville, KY: Westminster/John Knox Press).
Polak, Frank
1993   'Sefer Zecharyahu: 9–14', in Menahem Haran (ed.), *'Olam ha-Tanakh* (15/2; Tel-Aviv: Davidzon-'Iti): 230-57 (Hebrew).
Poznanski, Samuel Abraham (ed.)
1909   *Kommentar zu Ezechiel und den XII kleinen Propheten* (Warsaw: Mekize Nirdamim).
Rossi, Johannis Bern de
1785   *Variae Lectiones Veteris Testamenti* (London: Ex Regio).
Saebø, Magne
1969   *Sacharja 9–14* (WMANT, 34; Neukirchen–Vluyn: Neukirchener Verlag).
Sasson, J.M.
1976   'Wordplay in the Old Testament', in *IDBSup*: 968-70.
Shy, Hadassa
1991   *Perush Tanḥum ben Yosef ha-Yerushalmi li-Tere 'Asor* (Jerusalem: Magnes Press [Hebrew]).
Sperber, Alexander
1962   *The Bible in Aramaic* (4 vols.; Leiden: E.J. Brill).
Strack, Herman
1876   *Codex Babylonicus Petropolitanus* (St Petersburg: C. Ricker).
Tov, Emanuel
1992   *Textual Criticism of the Bible: An Introduction* (Minneapolis: Fortress Press).
Weil, Gérard E.
1971   *Massorah Gedolah* (Rome: Pontifical Biblical Institute).
Wellhausen, Julius
1963   *Die Kleinen Propheten* (Berlin: W. de Gruyter, 4th edn).

Wernberg-Møller, P. (ed.)
    1971   *The Hebrew Bible—Latter Prophets: The Babylonian Codex of Petrograd* (New York: Ktav).
Whiston, William A.M.
    1857   *The Works of Flavius Josephus* (Auburn, NY: John E. Beardsley).
Wolters, Al
    2000   'Word Play in Zechariah', in Scott B. Noegel (ed.), *Puns and Pundits: Word Play in the Hebrew Bible and Ancient Near Eastern Literature* (Bethesda, MD: CDL): 223-30.
Yeivin, Israel
    1980   *Introduction to the Tiberian Masorah* (trans. and ed. E.J. Revell; Masoretic Studies, 5; Missoula, MT: Scholars Press).
Ziegler, Joseph
    1943   *Duodecim prophetae* (Septuaginta Vetus Testamentum Graecum, 13; Göttingen: Vandenhoeck & Ruprecht).

THE ONCE AND FUTURE LAMENT:
MICAH 2.1-5 AND THE PROPHETIC PERSONA

Harry P. Nasuti

Scholars have long seen Mic. 2.1-5 as a prime example of that prophet's central social concerns. Most scholars have little difficulty in attributing the core of this passage to Micah himself. Most also agree that this passage's primary focus is on those elements of the Judean elite who built large estates for themselves by in some way oppressing others.[1] The close connection of this passage with what follows in vv. 6-11 is also widely accepted.

Despite this substantial consensus, most critical scholars of the last century also saw this passage as containing a number of features that made a unified interpretation of the text difficult. Such scholars tended to deal with these difficult elements either by eliminating them through textual emendation or by assigning them to later stages of the text's redactional history. As a result, such scholars usually achieved interpretive sense at the cost of either the integrity of the received text or a coherent synchronic understanding of that text's final form.

In contrast to these approaches, a number of more recent scholars have re-examined Mic. 2.1-5 with an eye towards achieving just such a coherent synchronic understanding. Such an approach obviously owes much to the canonical turn of the last twenty years with its concern for the final form of the biblical text. While these scholars do not completely agree on the way this passage works, they have clearly raised some fruitful new possibilities and intriguing larger questions. The present study will explore these possibilities further in an attempt to arrive at a coherent synchronic interpretation of the present text of this passage. In so doing, it will also offer some suggestions about the way this passage helps to construct the literary persona of the prophet Micah that one finds in the book that goes by his name.

Micah 2.1-5: An Overview of the Text and its Difficulties

One may begin by providing an overview of the present passage and pointing out the problem areas. In terms of both form and textual problems, the first two verses

---

1.   While few scholars accept Alt's classic study (1955) in every detail, almost all agree on the basic socio-economic issues involved here. A rare exception is the work of Andersen and Freedman (2000: 276-77, 294), which raises the possibility that national rather than domestic territorial greed is the main issue in this passage. These authors do see the imagery (especially in v. 2) as coming from the domestic sphere.

are fairly straightforward. The passage opens with a standard prophetic woe formula that moves from a הוי/participle combination (v. 1a) to a series of finite verbs in the third person (vv. 1b-2). These verses describe the blameworthy actions of those who are the objects of this oracle, namely, the powerful that plot to take away others' land. In such a way, vv. 1-2 provide the reasons for the judgment that follows. At the same time, that judgment is already to some degree anticipated by the introductory 'woe' itself, since that term's connection with the funeral lament implies that those described in these verses are considered to be already dead.[2]

Verse 3 opens the formal judgment section with a לכן and the messenger formula. This section consists of a first-person divine speech that addresses the oppressors first in the third person (על־המשפחה הזאת) and then directly in the second person plural. Commentators have often seen the על־המשפחה הזאת as a later redactional element whose purpose was to broaden the reference to the entire people at the time of the exile.[3] In contrast, some recent scholars tend to remain in the present context and see the term as a reference to the specific evildoers of vv. 1-2.[4] They also do not see the need for the specific exilic reference that commentators have often found in the phrase כי עת רעה היא at the end of v. 3.[5]

With regard to form and literary structure, the judgment oracle is basically complete in vv. 1-3. Those who are described as planning and executing evil in vv. 1-2 (חשבי־און ופעלי רע) receive the divine announcement of God's plans of evil against them in v. 3 (רעה...הנני חשב). Nevertheless, the oracle continues in v. 4 by means of the phrase ביום ההוא, which scholars have often seen as indicating later redactional activity. Earlier scholars also saw redactional activity in other aspects of vv. 4-5, as well as arguing that the text of these verses is in some disrepair.[6]

More recent scholars do not necessarily dispute the later origins of all or part of vv. 4-5.[7] They are, however, more interested in the way that these verses can now be understood in relation to what has gone before in vv. 1-3. Particularly important for such scholars are the pervasive references to the covenantal nature of land possession that one finds throughout all of vv. 1-5. These references include the accusation of coveting and stealing fields and houses in v. 2, which recalls the language of the prohibitions in both the Decalogue and Leviticus.[8] The terms נחלה (v. 2), משפחה (v. 3) and the root חלק (twice in v. 4) have an important place in the land division traditions of Numbers, Deuteronomy and Joshua, as do the terms חבל, גורל and שלך in v. 5.[9] Some of this language also appears in the specific case of Naboth's

2.   Reference to the extensive literature on the prophetic 'woe' form may be found in most commentaries on this passage. For an important study of the larger metaphorical background of this and related forms, as well as their use in eighth-century prophecy, see Hardmeier 1978.

3.   So, e.g., Jeremias 1971: 333; Wolff 1990: 69.

4.   See, e.g., Niccacci 1989: 11; Kessler 1999: 128. Cf. also Allen 1976: 290.

5.   Compare, e.g., Wolff 1990: 69; Kessler 1999: 118.

6.   See McKane 1997 for a useful survey of these scholars.

7.   Thus, Kessler (1999: 98) sees all of vv. 4-5 as a later addition.

8.   For the חמד in v. 2, cf. Exod. 20.17; Deut. 5.18. For the accusations of the second half of the verse, cf. Lev. 19.13 (also the related Lev. 5.21-23), as well as Jer. 21.12; Ezek. 18.18; 22.29.

9.   References to נחלה and משפחה are found throughout Numbers and Joshua with reference to the hereditary, inalienable property of the tribes and their subdivisions. For the related use of חלק,

vineyard, where the issues of land usurpation are quite similar to those of the pre-sent passage.[10] Even the often-emended term יָמִיר may be seen to fit in this cove-nantal land context.[11] One can obviously make the case that later redactors have artfully crafted their additions to cohere with the language (and literary structure) of the original oracle. However, it is clear that this consistent use of language from a specific tradition also facilitates synchronic attempts to understand the entire pas-sage as a cohesive unit.

The contrast between earlier and more recent commentators is perhaps most striking in the way that at least some of the latter have understood v. 4. This verse has two parts: the third-person description of the taking up of a מָשָׁל and the lament-ing of a נְהִי 'on that day' in v. 4a, and a first-person lament in v. 4b. According to a near consensus of earlier commentators (as well as some more recent commenta-tors), the natural speakers of the lament in the second part of that verse are those whose oppressive behavior has just been condemned in vv. 1-3 and who will suffer as a result.[12]

This reading is, however, complicated by the first part of the verse which addresses the oppressors in the second person and envisions a lament being spoken עֲלֵיכֶם. Because of this, a number of scholars see other lamenters as the 'subjects' of the introductory third-person singular verbs of v. 4a, which they understand as indefinite forms bearing either a plural or a passive sense (so, e.g., Hillers 1984: 31). Such lamenters are seen as using the oppressors' own words as part of their lamenting over them. Along these lines, a parallel is sometimes seen to the profes-sional mourners of Amos 5.16-17 and Jeremiah 9 (so Mays 1976: 65).

This view of v. 4b as a lament either by or over the oppressors accords reasona-bly well with the reference to a נְהִי in v. 4a. It is, however, less clear how such a view fits with the parallel reference in v. 4a to a מָשָׁל. To address this issue, scholars usually point to what they see as similar passages elsewhere in the prophetic litera-ture (Isa. 14.4; Hab. 2.6; Jer. 24.9) in support of understanding the מָשָׁל as a 'taunt

see especially Num. 18.20; Josh. 14.4; 15.13; 18.5, 6, 7, 9; 19.9 (cf. Deut. 10.9; 12.12; 14.27, 29; 18.1; Josh. 18.7). For חלק as a verb, cf. Num. 26.53, 55, 56; Josh. 13.7; 14.5; 18.2, 5, 10; 19.51; cf. Ezek. 47.21. (In Num. 26.53, 56; Josh. 13.7; 18.2; and Ezek. 47.21-22, it is used with נחלה.) In light of what follows in v. 5, it is obviously significant that the mechanics of this land division usually involve the casting of lots (גורל), as in Num. 26.55, 56 (following the enumeration of the people by משפחה; cf. Num. 33.54; 34.13; 36.2, 3); Josh. 14.1-5; 18.5-6, 10; and 19.51 (cf. also 14.2; 15.1; 16.1; 17.1, 14, 17; 21; Judg. 1.3). One should also note Josh. 18–19, which describes a specific casting of lots by Joshua (and in 19.51 by Eleazar the priest) before God at Shiloh. Josh. 18.8, 10 uses the verb שלך in connection with this casting of lots. The term חבל is found in a similar context in Josh. 17.5, 14; 19.9; Ps. 78.55; and Ezek. 47.13.

  10.   See especially the reference to נחלה in 1 Kgs 21.3-4.
  11.   Cf. the use of this verb in Ezek. 48.14 (which prohibits the selling or 'changing' of the land reserved for God in the restored community) and Ps. 15.4 (where one of the attributes of the right-eous person is that that person does not 'change'; note the social nature of the other assertions in the psalm). Cf. also the derived noun in Ruth 4.7 and the discussion of Cathcart (1988: 192-95) who has suggested a possible ancient Near Eastern background of the term with reference to the land.
  12.   Cf. McKane (1998: 68) who sees this speech as being 'put in the mouths' of the oppressors.

song'. They thus envision a group of 'mourners' who mock the (now judged and landless) oppressors by quoting their own first-person lament against them (Hillers 1984: 33; Mays 1976: 60, 65).

The problems with this approach to v. 4 have often been noted, even by those scholars who have adopted it as the best alternative for a difficult text. First of all, there is nothing about the quote in v. 4b that would indicate that it is a mocking taunt song or anything other than a sincere and heartfelt lament (Kessler 1999: 121). The examples of נהי that are usually cited in this regard are clearly straightforward examples of actual grief.[13] Similarly, there are no other examples of a משל that employ a sarcastic or ironic use of someone's own lament to rub salt in that person's wounds. Both Isa. 14.4 and Hab. 2.6 are quite explicit with regard to their 'taunting' nature, in that both openly revel in the downfall of the objects of their משל and confront those objects with a description of their faults and fallen condition.

Another problem with relating the quote in v. 4b to the נהי/משל of the first part of the verse has to do with the perfect verb אמר that connects the two parts of the verse. The fact that this is a perfect verb would seem to indicate that the action of the second half of the verse took place in the past, while the נהי/משל is to take place at the time of the future judgment. Almost every scholar emends this verb in accord with the versions (which do not entirely agree), again at the expense of the received form of the MT (cf. McKane 1997: 17-19).

Yet another problem with this view of v. 4 is that the speech in v. 4b contains a number of elements that do not easily fit in the mouth of the oppressors or those that quote them. Thus, for example, many scholars have noted the awkwardness of attributing the term עמי to these figures. In the view of most earlier scholars, this term seems to imply an identification of the speaker with the entire nation, an identification that most feel is inappropriate in the present context.

Scholars deal with this problem in a number of ways. Some see the first person singular here as the voice of the oppressed (or the prophet or God) breaking into the oppressors' lament.[14] More common is the redactional approach that sees this part of the verse as an exilic addition meant to express the stricken situation of the entire nation (so Jeremias 1971: 334; Wolff 1990: 70). While this solution may explain the diachronic development of the present text, it does not make sense of it in a synchronic way. It is telling that the עמי is seen to be so difficult in the mouths of the oppressors that even some more recent scholars see this phrase as implying an addressee that goes beyond those of the literary context to the later 'rereaders' of the text (so Ben Zvi 1999: 90; 2000: 48).

A similar difficulty is raised by the לשבב of the quote's final section. If the speakers are the oppressors or those who are quoting them, it is clearly awkward that

13.   So Amos 5.16; Jer. 9.9, 17, 18, 19; 31.15, though the verbal use of this root in Ezek. 32.18 does fit a taunt situation. On the last of these passages, see further below.

14.   Thus, McKane (1997: 17, 22) sees the voice of the oppressed as breaking through here (and in the לשבב) at the cost of literary consistency. Mays (1976: 65) attributes the first-person form of עמי to the fact that God quotes the lament here. Allen (1976: 290) sees an 'ironic echo' of the lament of the previous victims now turned against the oppressors. In keeping with his view of this prophetic book as a drama, Utzschneider (1997: 24; 1999: 107) sees this section as an 'aside'.

they should see their fields as being given to an 'apostate'. This is especially the case since those who are taking away their fields are usually seen to be a foreign enemy for whom 'apostate' is not really an appropriate term. Once again, scholars have attempted to deal with this problem by either emending the text or attributing the phrase to a later redactional level.[15]

A final problem with seeing the oppressors or those who quote them as the speakers of v. 4b has to do with the implications of this view for the following verse. As has often been noted, the לכן with which v. 5 opens seems to indicate that that verse is in some way the consequence of what has gone before (so Kessler 1999: 121). In more specifically form-critical terms, the announcement of judgment introduced by the לכן should be grounded in some sort of 'invective' or description of offenses in the preceding verse.

The problem is that v. 4 does not seem to provide such a rationale for the judgment of v. 5. Instead, the נהי/משל of v. 4 seems to presuppose such a judgment or to be part of such an announcement of judgment in its own right. This has prompted a number of scholars to see all of v. 5 as a redactional addition that disrupts what they see as the tight a-b-a'-b' structure of vv. 1-4 (so, e.g., Wolff 1990: 70). This eliminates the troublesome double לכן, at least for what such scholars posit as the original oracle. Once again, however, it does so at the cost of understanding the final form of the text.

A number of more recent scholars have attempted to avoid these difficulties by seeing the speaker of v. 4b not as the oppressors (or those who quote them) but rather as the victims of v. 2.[16] For such scholars, the speech in v. 4b is not a mocking taunt but the sincere and legitimate lament of the oppressed. Such a view was, to a certain degree, anticipated by those who saw the voice of the oppressed as breaking through in the first person singular, though the more recent scholars argue for a more consistent reading of the entire quote as belonging to this voice.

This understanding of the lament has several points in its favor. First of all, those who see the lament as spoken by the oppressed are able to make much more sense out of the עמי and the לשבב that posed such problems for those who see the lament as relating to the oppressors (cf. Niccacci 1989: 100). This is in keeping with the fact that at least in chs. 1–3 of the book of Micah, עמי seems to refer almost exclusively to the part of the people that are oppressed by the powerful.[17] Similarly, the lament that the speaker's land has been given to an 'apostate' is more appropriate if the speaker has lost land to a fellow Israelite who is perceived as violating the demands of the covenant.

15. See the survey of approaches in McKane 1997: 15-21.

16. These scholars include Niccacci 1989: 99-101; Kessler 1999: 121-22; Andersen and Freedman 2000: 278-88. Their views will be considered further below.

17. This is in contrast to the term 'this people' in 2.11 and 'this family' in 2.3, both of which refer to the oppressors. Cf. Stansell 1988: 117-20; Lescow 1972: 53. Also cf. Niccacci (1989: 103) who sees such a reference for the speeches of condemnation in chs. 2–3. One should, however, also note the ambiguity in the MT of 2.8. On the latter, cf. Willis 1970: 81-87 and Williamson 1997: 360-64.

Secondly, seeing the lament as part of a description of the crimes of the oppressors allows v. 4 (or at least v. 4b) to function as a reason for the judgment that is announced in v. 5. As such, it sets up a standard two-part judgment oracle in which the לכן of v. 5 plays its normal role (just as in vv. 1-3). Because of the wrongs described in the complaint of those who have had their land wrongly taken from them, those who have perpetrated such wrongs will have no share in the future re-division of the land.

Thirdly, seeing the oppressed as the speaker of the lament makes sense out of the often-emended ימיר in v. 4. The charge that someone has changed חלקעמי fits very nicely with the specific accusations against the oppressors in v. 2, as well as with the covenantal language of the rest of this passage. As noted above, the story of Naboth's vineyard seems to provide a clear parallel to the situation envisioned in this charge.

In the view of this interpreter, such arguments seem fairly compelling, especially since they provide a relatively straightforward understanding of the MT without resorting to drastic emendations or excessive speculation about the text's redactional history. It should, however, be noted that even scholars who agree on seeing the oppressed as the speaker in v. 4b differ as to the nature and setting of this speech and the way the two halves of v. 4 relate to each other. At the root of many of these differences are different perceptions of the temporal dynamics of this passage. It is to the latter issue that this analysis now turns.

The Once and Future Lament:
Some Unresolved Temporal Questions in Micah 2.1-5

One of the most important consequences of the recent focus on the final form of Micah has been a more consistent attention to the temporal dynamics of the book.[18] Unlike earlier commentators who primarily understood the specific parts of the text in the context of the different historical periods of their origins, more recent commentators are also interested in the internal chronology of the text itself. Thus, even though some of these scholars also attempt to locate a historical context for the text's composition/redaction, what distinguishes them from earlier commentators is their interest in the temporal point of view of the literary context.

Such scholars tend to agree that the basic point of standing for the book of Micah is set by the superscription in 1.1. This means that in the present passage vv. 1-2 should be seen as the words of Micah concerning those who are 'presently' (that is, in the time of the literary persona set forth in the superscription) engaged in planning for and accomplishing the usurpation of others' land.[19] In v. 3, Micah takes on the role of God's messenger (using the standard messenger formula) and delivers

18. See especially Utzschneider 1997; 1999; Kessler 1999.

19. Whether one sees these verses as directly addressed to such evildoers depends on whether one reads them in connection with v. 3. Thus, Ben Zvi (2000: 42) sees the participles as vocatives. Utzschneider (1999: 105-106) sees a change of scene in vv. 3-4, though he also sees these verses as closely related to vv. 1-2.

God's words to these figures. These words reveal that God is also 'presently' engaged in planning evil against them. That evil, however, will take place at a time future to the exchange described in the verse, even though it may be past from the perspective of the reader of the book.[20]

While most recent interpreters would agree on the temporal dynamics described so far, that agreement breaks down with the move from v. 3 to v. 4 effected by the ביום ההוא. On the 'day' in question, a משל and a נהי will be taken up and lamented 'over' or 'against' the evildoers. The interpretive question is how 'that day' and the speech that is to be made on it are to be understood.

Along these lines, one may first consider the view of Niccacci, who pioneered the argument for seeing the oppressed as the speaker of v. 4b. For Niccacci, the lament of v. 4b was originally vocalized by the oppressed during the time described in vv. 1-2. However, v. 4 itself does not relate the original speaking of that lament. Rather, that verse relates the future *repetition* of a 'past' lament in the aftermath of the judgment described in v. 3 (which is itself future to the time of Micah's prophecy).[21] At that time, Niccacci (1989: 100) envisions an assembly that will re-divide the land (v. 5). During that assembly, the 'repetition' of the 'past' lament of those whose land had been taken will function as an accusation that will result in the oppressors' loss of all their land, not just the land they had usurped.[22]

One will note that Niccacci sees the lament as occupying two places in the timeline of this passage. The first results from and is roughly contemporary with the 'present' events described in vv. 1-2. The second is subsequent to the 'future' events of v. 3 and results in the 'also future' judgment of v. 5. In Niccacci's view, the latter event may be past from the point of view of the actual reader, even as it is 'future' to the time of the literary character Micah who is speaking in vv. 1-2.

Kessler (1999: 121-23) agrees with Niccacci that the lament of v. 4b was once the lament of the victims of vv. 1-2 that will be repeated as an accusation against their oppressors in a future assembly. For him, however, the 'day' on which this assembly takes place is not during Micah's own time, but rather in a post-exilic re-division of the land under the Persians.[23] In terms of the literary timeline of the text itself, Kessler is able to extend this reference into the more distant future because of the way he sees the ביום ההוא. While Niccacci understands 'that day' as a simple

---

20. Cf. Utzschneider (1997: 26) who sees the future references of this scene as 'Erinnerungen an die Zukunft'.

21. Note Niccacci's translation of the ונהה נהי נהיה as, 'e si ripeterà il lamento passato (?)', (1989: 12). He takes the difficult נהיה as a 'participio nifal di haya con il senso di "passato", referito a "lamento"' (1989: 13). This is in contrast to the usual understanding of this word as either a dittography, part of a superlative or a niphal perfect that indicates that what was predicted has come to pass.

22. Unlike many scholars, Niccacci does not see the judgment in question as that of the Babylonian exile. For him it is instead to be found in the Assyrian period. See, for example Niccacci 1989: 98.

23. On the redaction-critical level, Kessler supports this understanding by arguing for a post-exilic understanding of the term קהל יהוה (in contrast to Niccacci who notes its pre-exilic possibilities). One will recall that Kessler sees vv. 4-5 as a product of the Babylonian–Persian period that goes beyond the horizon of the original of chs. 1–5.

reference to the events of v. 3, Kessler takes the term as a technical eschatological expression capable of a more distant future interpretation.[24]

Like Niccacci, Andersen and Freedman also see the lament in v. 4b as spoken by the victims of the crimes described in vv. 1-2.[25] They also see these victims as the speakers in v. 4a, though they differ from Niccacci in arguing that vv. 4a and 4b represent 'two different occasions in different situations and in different moods'. Specifically, Andersen and Freedman argue that v. 4b actually relates the lament that took place at the time of the past oppression (vv. 1-2), and they support this argument by taking seriously the tense value of the usually emended אמר. In contrast, they see the speech of v. 4a as taking place in the future (after the judgment announced in v. 3), when the oppressed will taunt their former oppressors.

Andersen and Freedman thus agree with Niccacci and Kessler that one should see a twofold 'lament' in v. 4 and that the oppressed are the speakers in each case. They also agree that the victims' 'lament-complaint' in v. 4b results in the verdict of v. 5 (2000: 293). Nevertheless, there are some important differences here. The most obvious of these is that Andersen and Freedman see the future lament of v. 4a as a taunt rather than an accusation. In this, they continue the interpretation of earlier scholars who attempted to account for the reference to both a משל and a נהי in v. 4a (so 2000: 279, 283). In contrast, Niccacci and Kessler do not see this as the significance of the משל of v. 4a.

Andersen and Freedman's differences with Niccacci and Kessler on this point have to do with how they understand the temporal dynamics of the passage. The two latter scholars see a consistent temporal progression in vv. 1-5. The evildoers plan and execute evil in vv. 1-2, which leads to God's planning and executing evil against them in v. 3. This will lead (in v. 4) to the repetition of the victims' lament as an accusation at the time of a future assembly that will follow the judgment of v. 3, as well as to the oppressors' exclusion from the land in v. 5. That is to say, the actual time value of v. 4b is future with regard to Micah's speech in vv. 1-2, as implied by what they see as an introductory v. 4a. Verse 4b is a 'repetition' of the original lament, whose existence at an earlier time is assumed here.

For Andersen and Freedman, on the other hand, the actual time value of v. 4b is past, as indicated by the perfect verb אמר. These scholars see v. 4b as a 'flashback to the misery of the victims of the actions catalogued in vv. 1 and 2' (2000: 283). They see the entire passage as a woe oracle/accusation with a two-part sentence (vv. 3-5) in which the first לכן describes the action of God and the second describes the consequences of that action.

One will note that these scholars continue the interpretation of earlier scholars in certain ways and break with them in others. Thus, Niccacci and Kessler agree with earlier scholars in seeing the speech in v. 4b as that which was introduced by v. 4a, even though they disagree with these scholars in their view of the nature of that

---

24. Kessler (1999: 38) argues that this expression should not be separated from the 'end of days' in 4.1 and that it introduces a list of events that will occur before the end.

25. Cf. Andersen and Freedman (2000: 278-92), though one will recall that they raise the possibility that the actors here are tribal and national rather than individual.

speech, who is speaking it and when it is spoken. On the other hand, Andersen and Freedman agree with earlier scholars about the 'taunt' nature of the speech in v. 4a, though they reject an identification of that speech with what follows in v. 4b.

This continuing critical diversity leaves little doubt that Mic. 2.1-5 still offers an interpretive challenge. Nevertheless, the scholars considered in this section have clearly opened up some new possibilities for understanding this text. The next section will attempt to follow up on their work in the interest of a more consistent reading of the present text of this passage and a better understanding of its role in the larger book of Micah.

Towards a Synchronic Reading of Micah 2.1-5

One may begin this analysis by agreeing with recent scholars that the book's superscription implies a literary context for this passage in an exchange between Micah and certain of his contemporaries.[26] In this context, the passage describes a first-person speech in which the prophet Micah laments those whom he describes as usurping others' land. Micah then continues his speech by directly confronting these evildoers with the divine message of judgment.

Taking this literary context seriously has its first real interpretive impact in v. 3. As noted above, earlier redaction-critical scholars saw the phrase על־המשפחה הזאת as a later reference to the fate of the entire nation at the exile. It is, however, clear that whatever the origins of this phrase, the passage itself does not *require* the reader to move beyond the literary context set forth above. Instead, the more natural reading of the המשפחה in the present context is one that is in line with the covenantal imagery of land possession that is found throughout vv. 1-5. In this context, the characterization of the evildoers as המשפחה leads naturally to the threat of exclusion from the land distribution of v. 5.

Similarly, there is nothing about the 'evil time' at the end of v. 3 that *requires* a specifically exilic reference. It is certainly possible that this phrase (like the המשפחה) allowed a 'rereading' in light of the exile (so Ben Zvi 2000: 48). Nevertheless, its primary reference belongs to the literary context of v. 3, which describes events that are future to the prophetic address of vv. 1-2 but in the past to the reader.

In the absence of any explicit indication of a change in speaker, it seems best to see v. 4 as a continuation of the divine speech of v. 3, rather than a return to the specifically prophetic voice of vv. 1-2.[27] Similarly, the fact that what follows is an

---

26. It is worth emphasizing that the acceptance of such a context neither makes an actual historical claim for these verses nor denies their relevance to other readers at a later time. It does, however, mean that one should not assume a direct (as opposed to an indirect) appeal to a later readership unless it is impossible to read the text in accordance with its literary context. On these different contexts, see Dempsey 1999: 117-18.

27. That this is not incompatible with the possibility that the prophet's voice is present in v. 4b (as a number of scholars have suggested) will be seen below. Seeing a continuation of the divine speech here does mean, however, that the temporal formula in v. 4a should not be seen as introducing part of a narrative *nebentext* that establishes a framework for the discourse of the text

announcement of judgment with a direct second-person address means that such a speaker is also likely for v. 5.[28] As a result, the most natural reading is to see all of vv. 3-5 as a single divine speech introduced by the כה אמר יהוה of v. 3. It is to the last two verses of this speech that this analysis now turns.

Time and Identity in Micah 2.4a

Verse 4 clearly poses the most difficult interpretive questions in this passage. The first of these is how to understand the temporal implications of its opening phrase, ביום ההוא. As noted above, this phrase may either link what follows closely to what has preceded in v. 3 or it may introduce a prediction of the distant future. Both of these are possible options for the reader, although it is clear that the latter more radically stretches the temporal context established in vv. 1-3. While this stretch is possible, both in the literary context and in the context of a later rereading, it is certainly not required. As De Vries has shown, what follows in v. 4 can quite naturally be seen as taking place in the 'proximate future' of the events of v. 3. Indeed, De Vries sees this verse as 'a call for an appropriate (quasi-)liturgical response' to those events.[29]

Another interpretive decision is called for by the unspecified nature of the subjects of the third person singular verbs in v. 4. Since the עליכם in that verse rules out the oppressors as the speakers of the נהי/משל within the timeframe of v. 4a, scholars have suggested a variety of other possible speakers, including a foreign enemy, anonymous (possibly professional) 'mourners', and the victims described in v. 2. Crucial for determining their identity are the related questions of how one conceives of the nature of the נהי/משל, whether the נהי/משל is a repetition of a past speech (and, if so, for what purpose), and whether the נהי/משל of v. 4a is to be linked with the speech of v. 4b.

In answering these questions, much depends on the degree to which one attempts to interpret the present MT. Thus, for example, Andersen and Freedman (2000: 279) refuse to emend (or minimize) the perfect verb אמר that is now found in v. 4 of the MT. As a result, they do not follow the lead of most scholars and identify the speech of v. 4b with the נהי/משל of v. 4a, even though they see the same speaker in each case. Since one of the major problems in understanding v. 4 has always been the

without being a part of it. (Cf. Utzschneider 1999: 19, for this possibility.) In this regard, one might note that the other two examples of the phrase ביום ההוא in Micah (4.6; 5.9) are clearly marked as divine speech by the phrase נאם־יהוה and the first-person pronoun.

28. The third-person reference to the קהל־יהוה is not a problem for seeing a continuation of the divine speech here (so Utzschneider 1999: 110). The second person singular לך in v. 5 is at variance with the plural reference in vv. 3-4 and is usually taken as either a haplography (with the first letter of the משליך that follows) or an indication of a different redactional hand. Either is possible, though it is also possible to read it in the present context as a reference to the singular oppressor in the lament of v. 4b. Utzschneider's attempt (1999: 109) to see a reference to the singular addressee in 1.16 seems difficult in light of the difference in gender.

29. So De Vries 1995: 44, 53. In keeping with most scholars, De Vries identifies the נהי/משל with what follows in v. 4b (by emending the אמר). It will be argued below that neither this identification nor this emendation is necessary.

fact that the speech in v. 4b does not really fit the מְשַׁל designation of v. 4a, it would appear that the MT-oriented approach of Andersen and Freedman deserves some further attention.

What this means is that the נהי/מְשַׁל of v. 4a describes something that will take place on a 'day' future to the prophetic speaking of this oracle, most probably in conjunction with the judgment announced in v. 3. Andersen and Freedman (2000: 279) see this as a 'taunt', in keeping with the parallel usage of the phrase נשׁא מְשַׁל in Hab. 2.6. Since they also argue that those speaking this taunt against the now suffering oppressors of v. 3 are the latter's original victims, they see a certain poetic justice in this taunting activity.

There is, however, another aspect of this verse that has important implications for the way one understands the larger passage and its role in the book. This aspect becomes apparent when one looks again at the Isaiah and Habakkuk parallels, which, it may be recalled, introduce explicit taunts of an oppressor with the fact that that oppressor had now received exactly what that oppressor had previously done to others.

As has often been noted, the most exact parallel to this passage is to be found in Hab. 2.6-17. In that passage, the introduction of the מְשַׁל is followed by four woe oracles in the הוֹי + participle form. Three of these oracles continue with a second-person direct address, in which the principle of reciprocity plays a key role.[30] All of these elements are to be found in Mic. 2.1-5.

In both the present passage and Hab. 2.6-17, the oppressors are taunted as a result of a coming judgment. The difference between the two passages is that in the Habakkuk passage the נשׁא מְשַׁל introduces a (future) woe oracle, whereas in Mic. 2.1-5 a (present) woe oracle precedes the נשׁא מְשַׁל. The significance of this difference becomes apparent when one notes that in the Micah passage it is the prophet that verbalizes the woe 'taunt'. In Habakkuk, the prophet sees this woe taunt as being spoken by others at the time of the future judgment. For Micah the future judgment (with its appropriate reversal of the oppressors' situation) is so certain that the prophet can address the oppressors (in vv. 1-2) as if they are already dead.

What v. 4a adds to this picture is the assurance that on the 'day' of judgment (described in v. 3) others will do exactly what the prophet has just done. That is to say, one should understand the מְשַׁל of v. 4a not on the basis of v. 4b but rather on the basis of vv. 1-3. Indeed, like the Isaiah and Habakkuk parallels, these verses constitute a very appropriate מְשַׁל in that they make a comparative statement quite in keeping with at least one possibility for that word's root meaning.[31] What makes looking to vv. 1-3 for an understanding of v. 4a an even more attractive alternative is the fact that the former verses are just as appropriate as a נהי as they are as a מְשַׁל.

As scholars have often noted, the rhetorical force of the type of 'woe' found in vv. 1-2 depends on its roots in the ceremony of lamentation over the dead.[32] The

---

30. Thus, in Hab. 2.8 those that plundered many nations will be plundered by the remnant of those nations, while in Hab. 2.15-16 those who made others drink from the cup of wrath will have to drink from God's cup.

31. Cf. the discussion in Crenshaw 1974: 230.

32. So Krause 1973; Wolff 1990: 77.

prophet is able to mourn the oppressors as if they are already dead, since the divine verdict has already been given. Such a personal lament on the part of the prophet is, however, also a נהי in that it proleptically laments a collective disaster.[33] On the 'day' when that disaster actually takes place, others will join the prophet in this נהי that is also a משל.

This picture of wider lamentation by others certainly helps to flesh out the poetic description of the judgment that the prophet is announcing in vv. 1-3. However, taking note of the connection between this more general lamentation and that of the prophet also brings out another important aspect of these verses, namely, the way they contribute to the construction of the prophetic persona in the book as a whole. In this passage, Micah is not only depicted as a prophet who proclaimed the word of God at a particular point in time. Rather, Micah is here presented as someone who both anticipates and specifies the future behavior of others.[34] That is to say, Micah is presented here as someone who functions as a model for the latter's behavior.

Such a view of the prophetic persona is, in fact, in keeping with what one finds elsewhere in the book. Thus, even though the book of Micah is, for the most part, lacking in narrative material about the prophet, a number of scholars have noted that Micah is a prominent figure there, especially in his presence as a first-person speaker.[35] Such scholars have further argued that the prophet is presented through-out as a model for imitation, one that is depicted in contrast with other less praise-worthy figures.[36]

What makes this possibility particularly suggestive for the present passage is the fact that lamentation seems to be a prominent aspect of Micah's prophetic persona throughout the book.[37] Such lamentation takes on a number of different aspects. Thus, for example, Mic. 1.8-9 presents a picture of the prophet lamenting (in the first person) over the fate of Samaria and the upcoming similar judgment of Jerusalem.[38] Given the dynamic suggested here for Mic. 2.1-5, it is significant that this description of the prophet is immediately followed by an exhortation to others to lament in a similar fashion (1.10-16).[39] At the other end of the book, one may note

33. Cf. Hardmeier (1978) who notes the role of the eighth-century prophets in bringing together elements of the personal *Leichenlied* (קינה) with those of the political *Untergangslied* (נהי). This makes possible the *Promische-Gebrauch* of קינה and נהי in Jer. 9.9, 19, and Ezek. 27.32 (p. 338). For an example of a prophetic lament/taunt, cf. Ezek. 32.18 (which uses the verb נהה).

34. One will recall De Vries's view of v. 4 as a call for an appropriate (quasi-)liturgical response (1995: 44). According to Utzschneider (1999: 103), the speaker wants to carry off his audience (both *textinterne* and *textexterne*) into a mourning scene.

35. For Wolff (1990: 95), the first-person style 'runs through these passages like a red thread'.

36. Thus, for example, Shaw (1993: 55, 120, 187) notes that such first-person passages as 1.8-9; 3.8; and 7.1-7 constitute an 'ethical appeal' to the audience.

37. Cf. Renaud (1977: 79) who notes that Micah manifests a certain propensity for the genre of lamentation.

38. This accepts the scholarly consensus that 1.8-9 is to be seen as the speech of the prophet, rather than the argument of Beal (1994) who attributes this speech to God. See also Ben Zvi (2000: 33) and Runions (2001: 125) who note the ambiguity of the speaker here.

39. Utzschneider (1997: 25-26; 1999: 101) has also noted the relevance of 1.8-16 for the present passage, though his different view of vv. 4-5 leads him to somewhat different conclusions. Cf. also 4.9-10 for another call for others to lament.

what is usually taken to be the prophet's lamentation in 7.1-7, whose concluding expression of confidence is picked up in the speech (apparently of the city) that follows.[40]

The move from the prophet's apparently sincere lamentation in 1.8-9 to his accusatory lamentation in 2.1-2 constitutes a significant development in the description of the prophetic persona, as well as in the literary dynamics of the book. While the day of judgment for the evildoers is still in the future (so v. 3), it is so certain that the prophet's lament over them is taking place *now*. The anticipatory nature of that lament, the negative description of those being lamented and the concluding announcement of judgment give that lament a very different tone from the previous lament in 1.8-9.[41] While the imperatives of ch. 1 are apparently a call to imitate the prophet in the type of lament found in 1.8-9, the future announced in v. 4a envisions that others will join him in the נהי/משל of vv. 1-3.

The Lament of Micah 2.4b

If the argument of the previous section is valid, the first-person speech of v. 4b no longer needs to be forced into the mold of a נהי/משל. One can now read this speech as a straightforward lament whose language is fully consistent with the estrangement of the land from its rightful owners in violation of its covenantal distribution. As such, the present MT is most naturally seen as a speech of the individual(s) mentioned in vv. 1-2, and the actions described in this speech provide the reasons that lead to the judgment described in v. 5. This would also mean that such victim(s) are the subject of the אמר that introduces that speech and that the perfect verb would fit well with the past oppressive actions that occasioned the entire oracle.

Despite the attractiveness of this understanding of v. 4b, there are some elements of this speech that require further analysis. Among these is the alternation of the singular and plural subjects. Given the singular verb אמר that introduces the speech, one would naturally expect all of its first-person references to be in the singular as well. The fact that the victims of v. 2 are both individuals and representatives of larger units is one possible explanation for the presence of both the singular and the plural, or at least one possible way of understanding the present text (beyond attributing it to different redactional levels). Recent scholars have often noted the chiastic arrangement of singular and plural in this speech, which is reinforced by a similar chiasm in the language (so, e.g., Andersen and Freedman 2000: 279).

---

40. It is of interest that the LXX and the Syriac of v. 6 interpret the masculine plural negative imperative אל־תטפו as an exhortation not to lament. One wonders whether this reflects an understanding of the previous oracle (as well as 1.10-16) as concerned with lamentation. Along these lines, the addressees of this imperative are being cautioned not to do what the prophet has already done (in 1.8-9 and 2.1-2), as well as what the prophet exhorts the cities in ch. 1 to do and what he foresees others as doing at some point in the future (in 2.4).

41. It is significant that the actions of 1.8-9 are temporally ambiguous, admitting of either a present or future time value. The actions of Mic. 2.1-2, on the other hand, are clearly taking place in the book's present (though this is the reader's past).

Related to this numerical question is the presence of the term עמי in this speech. As noted above, it was the presence of this term that presented problems for earlier attributions of this speech to the oppressors. It should be noted, however, that this term may also complicate seeing too simple an identification of the speaker of the lament of v. 4b with the victim(s) of v. 2.

As was noted above, עמי has a fairly specific reference in the book of Micah, especially in its first three chapters, where it usually refers to the oppressed. What complicates the question of the identity of the speaker of v. 4b is the fact that this term's first-person suffix is usually seen to refer to the prophet himself or even to God. In the present case, the reference is more likely to the prophet, since, if vv. 4-5 continue the divine speech, the first-person reference is also the subject to whom God refers in the third-person אמר.

Such a view would not necessarily invalidate the arguments of those scholars who see the speech of v. 4b as the speech of the oppressed victims of v. 2. It would, however, mean that the lament of these victims is presented as being spoken by the prophet himself. Such a view would, of course, be consistent with the stance of a great number of scholars who have seen Micah as the spokesperson for a particular group whose rights were being violated. Such a view also provides another way to make sense of the alternation of singular and plural in this verse.[42]

What makes this picture of the prophet particularly interesting for the present analysis is, of course, the fact that the text once again seems to be providing a picture of the prophet as someone who laments on behalf of his people. However, unlike the accusatory lament over the oppressors in vv. 1-2, this lament is a straightforward expression of solidarity with those who have suffered at these oppressors' hands. Indeed, it is this lament that leads to the judgment of the oppressors and the vindication of the oppressed that is described in v. 5.[43]

One final point is worth noting. If vv. 4-5 continue the divine speech of v. 3, it is in fact God who is presenting the prophet as a model here. This third-person divine approval of the prophet reinforces the validation of the prophet that is implicit in the first-person prophetic speech found throughout the book. That such a third-person divine presentation of the prophet may not be unique in the book is suggested by the well-known verse, Mic. 6.8. The unspecified subject of that verse's opening הגיד is, of course, the topic of much critical debate. Nevertheless, it is certainly suggestive that Micah's important first-person defense of himself in 3.8 uses precisely this verb to describe his prophetic role with regard to Israel. This may well indicate that the reference in 6.8 is to the work of the prophet, especially if that verse resumes the divine speech of vv. 3-5. Such a reference to Micah's prophetic activity in a divine speech would serve to validate the prophetic persona in a way similar to what seems to be the case in 2.4.

---

42. Thus, for example, Niccacci (1989: 100) sees the prophet as being identified with the people here.

43. Wolff (1990: 78-79) sees a similar dynamic at work in the move from the woe of vv. 1-2 to the לכן-introduced announcement of judgment in v. 3.

Conclusions: Micah 2.1-5 and the Prophetic Persona

This essay is clearly supportive of the standard view of Mic. 2.1-5 as a prophetic condemnation of social injustice and oppression. However, it has also tried to argue that the final form of this passage has the additional function of highlighting the role of the prophet himself and so contributing to the picture of the prophetic persona that the book is at pains to construct. This passage presents Micah as someone who is in solidarity with the oppressed and who laments over the oppressors. It also presents the prophet as someone whose present behavior anticipates the future behavior of others. Indeed, both here and throughout the larger book, the prophet is presented as someone who is in some respects a model for others, both in his own time and in that of the later readers of his book.

While recent scholarship has increasingly noted the emphasis on the prophetic persona in the book of Micah, the contribution of Mic. 2.1-5 towards the construction of that persona has not usually been recognized. This may be in part because the role of the prophet only becomes prominent once one works with the present MT of the passage, rather than a version that one has arrived at by means of either emendation or redaction-critical reconstruction. While this essay does not claim to have solved all the problems of an obviously difficult passage, it is hoped that it has at least highlighted one relatively neglected but possibly important aspect of the present text.

BIBLIOGRAPHY

Allen, L.C.
    1976   *The Books of Joel, Obadiah, Jonah, and Micah* (NICOT; Grand Rapids: Eerdmans).
Alt, A.
    1955   'Micha 2, 1-5 ΓΗΣ ΑΝΑΔΑΣΜΟΣ in Juda', in N.A. Dahl and A.S. Kapelrud (eds.), *Interpretationes Ad Vetus Testamentum Pertinentes Sigmundo Mowinckel Septuagenario Missae* (Oslo: Land og Kirche): 13-23.
Andersen, F.I., and D.N. Freedman
    2000   *Micah: A New Translation with Introduction and Commentary* (AB, 24E; New York: Doubleday).
Beal, T.K.
    1994   'The System and the Speaking Subject in the Hebrew Bible: Reading for Divine Abjection', *BibInt* 2: 171-89.
Ben Zvi, E.
    1999   'Wrongdoers, Wrongdoing and Righting Wrongs in Micah 2', *BibInt* 7: 87-100.
    2000   *Micah* (FOTL, 21B; Grand Rapids: Eerdmans).
Cathcart, K.J.
    1988   'Micah 2.4 and Nahum 3.16-17 in the Light of Akkadian', in Y.L. Arbeitman (ed.), *Fucus: A Semitic/Afrasian Gathering in Remembrance of Albert Ehrman* (Amsterdam/Philadelphia: John Benjamins Publishing): 191-200.

Crenshaw, J.L.
1974 'Wisdom', in J.H. Hayes (ed.), *Old Testament Form Criticism* (San Antonio: Trinity University Press).

De Vries, S.J.
1995 *From Old Revelation to New: A Tradition-Historical and Redaction-Critical Study of Temporal Transitions in Prophetic Prediction* (Grand Rapids: Eerdmans).

Dempsey, C.J.
1999 'Micah 2–3: Literary Artistry, Ethical Message, and Some Considerations about the Image of Yahweh and Micah', *JSOT* 85: 117-28.

Hardmeier, C.
1978 *Texttheorie und biblische Exegese: zur rhetorischen Funktion der Trauermetaphorik in der Prophetie* (Beiträge zur evangelischen Theologie, 79; Munich: Chr. Kaiser Verlag).

Hillers, D.R.
1984 *Micah: A Commentary on the Book of Micah* (Hermeneia; Philadelphia: Fortress Press).

Jeremias, J.
1971 'Die Deutung der Gerichtsworte Michas in der Exilzeit', *ZAW* 83: 330-54.

Kessler, R.
1999 *Micha* (HTKAT; Freiburg: Herder).

Krause, H.-J.
1973 '*hôj* als profetische Leichenklage über das eigene Volk im 8. Jahrhundert', *ZAW* 85: 15-46.

Lescow, T.
1972 'Redaktionsgeschichtliche Analyse von Micha 1-5', *ZAW* 84: 46-85.

Mays, J.L.
1976 *Micah: A Commentary* (Philadelphia: Westminster Press).

McKane, W.
1997 'Micah 2.1-5: Text and Commentary', *JSS* 42: 7-22.
1998 *The Book of Micah: Introduction and Commentary* (Edinburgh: T. & T. Clark).

Niccacci, A.
1989 *Un profeta tra oppressori e oppressi: Analisi esegetica del capitolo 2 di Michea nel piano generale del libro* (Studium Biblicum Franciscanum Analecta, 27; Jerusalem: Franciscan Printing).

Renaud, B.
1977 *La Formation du Livre de Michés: Tradition et Actualisation* (Paris: J. Gabalda).

Runions, E.
2001 *Changing Subjects: Gender, Nation and Future in Micah* (Playing the Texts, 7; London: Sheffield Academic Press).

Shaw, C.S.
1993 *The Speeches of Micah: A Rhetorical-Historical Analysis* (JSOTSup, 145; Sheffield: JSOT Press).

Stansell, G.
1988 *Micah and Isaiah: A Form and Tradition Historical Comparison* (SBLDS, 85; Atlanta: Scholars Press).

Utzschneider, H.

1997   'Michas Reise in die Zeit. Ein Werkstattbericht', in W. Sommer (ed.), *Zeitenwende—Zeitenende: Beiträge zur Apokalyptik und Eschatologie* (Theologische Akzente, 2; Stuttgart: W. Kohlhammer): 11-44.

1999   *Michas Reise in die Zeit: Studien zum Drama als Genre der prophetischen Literatur des Alten Testaments* (Stuttgarter Bibelstudien, 180; Stuttgart: Katholisches Bibelwerk).

Williamson, H.G.M.

1997   'Marginalia in Micah', *VT* 47: 360-72.

Willis, J.T.

1970   'Micah 2.6-8 and the "People of God" in Micah', *Biblische Zeitung* 14: 72-87.

Wolff, H.W.

1990   *Micah: A Commentary* (trans. G. Stansell; Minneapolis: Augsburg-Fortress).

THE CONTEXT, TEXT, AND LOGIC OF ISAIAH 7.7-9*

J.J.M. Roberts

Despite a relatively clear historical and literary context, Isa. 7.7-9 has remained a crux for interpreters from very early times. Verse 7 offers a promise to the Judean royal court that the hostile plans of Aram and Israel will not be realized, and vv. 8-9, introduced as they are by a causative כִּי, appear to give the reason(s) why Ahaz and his court can believe this divine promise, but the logic of the prophetic reasoning is not immediately apparent. Moreover, as almost all modern scholars recognize, there has been a textual disruption in vv. 8-9 that has made the logic of the original argument less clear than it once was. This paper is an attempt at resolving the crux by a new look at the context, text, and logic of these verses.

Context

In discussing the context of these verses one must discuss both the literary context and the historical context. Both are important for the interpretation of this crux.

Literary Context

Isaiah 7.7-9 is part of the literary complex made up of Isa. 7.1–8.18. This complex contains a series of oracles all closely connected to the Syro-Ephraimitic war of 735–732 BCE. Several of these oracles give prominence to three children who bear symbolic names: Shear-jashub (7.1-9), Immanuel (7.10-17), and Maher-shalal-hash-baz (8.1-4). Given the similarity between these oracles, the common prophetic practice of giving their children symbolic names (cf. Hos. 1.3-8), and the fact that Isaiah refers to the children whom God gave him as signs and portents in Israel (8.18), it is probable that all these children with symbolic names were Isaiah's children (Roberts 1985). The message of all these children oracles is basically the same. Judah and its Davidic dynasty should trust God's promises and not be afraid of the combined armies of Israel and Damascus, because within a very short time these two enemy states will be destroyed. The oracles follow one another in temporal progression just as the children are born in temporal progression, and one can sense something of the passage of time in the way in which the prophet progressively shortens the time until the expected destruction of the enemy. Because of the

* It is with great pleasure that I dedicate this study to Herb Huffmon, a very stimulating fellow-student of prophecy, long-time colleague in the Biblical Colloquium, and dear friend.

textual disturbance in Isa. 7.8, the present text of this verse makes it difficult to ascertain how quickly the prophet expected the destruction of Israel and Damascus, but the following Immanuel oracle expects their demise in two to three years (7.15-16), and the Maher-shalal-hash-baz oracle looks for their destruction in one to two years (8.4).

Curiously enough, given the prominence of the symbolic names in these oracles, only the Maher-shalal-hash-baz oracle contains an explicit interpretation of the symbolic name. There is other material that appears to have been displaced from its original historical setting, however, which does offer explicit interpretations of the other two names. Thus the explanation of the name Shear-jashub found in Isa. 10.20-22, though it is now found in a much later context, can aid in the interpretation of 7.1-9. Isaiah 8.5-10 also seems to have been displaced from its original context, though not as far. Since it provides an explanation for the name Immanuel, historically it should have preceded the oracle about Maher-shalal-hash-baz in 8.1-4. In any case, it can contribute to the interpretation of the famous Immanuel passage in 7.10-17. Finally, 8.16-18, which has close ties to 8.1-4 and refers to Isaiah's children as signs and portents, should be taken as the original conclusion of this material.

Historical Context

Isaiah 7.1-3 makes it very clear that the historical context for the oracle that Isaiah gives to Ahaz and his advisors in vv. 4-9 is at the very beginning of the Syro-Ephraimitic War. Rezin, the Aramean king of Damascus, was attempting to create a new south-Syrian league, modeled on the relatively successful league of the ninth century, to resist the continuing southern expansion of Tiglath-pileser III's Assyrian hegemony into Aramean and Phoenician territory. Israel under Pekah had joined the Aramean league, and the same seems to have been true of the Phoenician and Philistine cities as well. The major holdout appears to have been Judah, which in the final days of Jotham's reign and in the beginning days of his successor Ahaz, refused to commit to this defensive alliance. The league needed Judah's support for its success against Assyria on its northern front and was understandably nervous about being sandwiched between Assyria moving down from the north and a potentially hostile ally of Assyria to the south. Thus Rezin decided to win Judah's support by force, by a surprise attack on Jerusalem that would isolate it from the rest of Judah long enough for the Aramean troops and their allies to breach the walls of the city and replace Ahaz with a new king over Judah who would bring Judah into their anti-Assyrian league.

Verse 1, as it presently stands as a kind of historical summary of the whole affair, already indicates that the Aramean move was a failure, but that was hardly obvious to the participants at the time. A major portion of v. 1, beginning with 'Rezin king of Aram', is taken from 2 Kgs 16.5 and probably represents a considerable expansion of Isaiah's original account by the later collector. Isaiah would have had little reason to provide detailed historical background information for his contemporaries who were as familiar with the events as he. If Isa. 6.1 provides a model, Isaiah's account probably began more modestly: 'In the days of king Ahaz, the house of David was told...' The later collector, however, needed to include background information so that later readers could understand the context. His quotation from 2 Kings provides that information, but it also confuses the issue by indicating the outcome of the crisis at the very beginning of the account. At the time Isaiah met Ahaz inspecting Jerusalem's water supply, the city was not yet under siege. As v. 2 specifies, the Davidic house had just become aware of the plans of the Aramean–Israelite coalition, and the simple report of those plans was enough to send both king Ahaz and his people into a panic. It was certainly not yet clear that the coalition's assault on Jerusalem would fail.

In this context of Jerusalem's panic, uncertainty, and feverish preparation to resist a siege, Yahweh sent Isaiah together with his son, Shear-jashub, to meet king Ahaz (v. 3). The reason for the presence of Isaiah's son is undoubtedly because Isaiah, just as Hosea before him, had given his son a symbolic name. Unfortunately, this passage neither gives us the age of the child at this encounter nor does it interpret his symbolic name for us. If the child had been given this symbolic name at some earlier point as seems likely from the wording of the command to Isaiah (7.3), the presence of the child was probably intended to remind Ahaz of an earlier oracle associated with the naming of the child in which his symbolic name was explained. On the other hand, if, despite the wording of the text, the child was actually named on this occasion, it is likely that the naming was accompanied by an oracle explaining the name.

In either case, such an explanatory oracle may be preserved in a pericope from this period that was reused in the later Assyrian crisis. Isaiah 10.21-22 interprets Shear-jashub, 'A-Remnant-Will-Return', to suggest that only a remnant of the northern kingdom, called 'Jacob' and 'your people Israel' (10.20-22) in contrast to Judah, called 'my people who dwell in Zion' (10.24), would survive the Syro-Ephraimite war. They would return to Yahweh and to El-gibbor, 'Mighty God', a title for the Davidic king of Judah (Isa. 9.6 [Heb. 5]). In other words, the surviving northerners would return to the kingdom of Judah. This explanation of the name is very closely tied to the Syro-Ephraimite war, so either the child was given this name a relatively short time before Isaiah's meeting with Ahaz, or the name was reinterpreted at this time with specific reference to this war. At any rate, the presence at the meeting of this child with his symbolic name was intended to underscore Isaiah's message of salvation.

Isaiah's actual oracle to Ahaz begins in v. 4 with a command to Ahaz to beware, calm down, not to fear, and not to let his heart grow fearful at the anger of his two main enemies, Rezin king of Aram and the king of Israel, whose name he treats as unworthy of mention, referring to him merely as the son of Remaliah. These two enemies of whom Ahaz was in terror, Yahweh dismisses as nothing more than the smoking stubs of two burnt out sticks, absolutely nothing of which to be afraid.

In v. 5 Yahweh then refers to the evil plan of these two states, and in v. 6 God specifies what that plan was by giving a direct quotation of the enemy. Literarily this has a close parallel in Ps. 2.1-3, where again the enemies' evil plan is spelled out in a direct quotation put in the mouth of the enemies. According to v. 6, Aram and Israel planned to go up against Judah, cut her off,[1] breach her for themselves,[2] and install as king within her the son of a certain Tab'al. The 'her' of the object suffixes on the two verbs and the preposition can hardly be Judah, since the country Judah is normally construed as masculine.[3] Though Jerusalem is a more remote antecedent (7.1), it is likely that the city is the understood antecedent, not only for grammatical reasons, but because both the strategy, involving a surprise attack specifically on Jerusalem (7.1), and the normal meaning of the verbs used, 'to cut off' and 'to breach', fit better with a city as the object than with a country. The identity of this son of Tab'al is uncertain, partly because the name Tab'al, 'Good for Nothing', appears to have been intentionally skewed. A number of suggestions have been made, but one of the most attractive is Vanel's suggestion followed by Asurmendi (1982: 54) that Aram's candidate for the throne was a son of the Tubail (= Ittoba'l) of Tyre mentioned in Tiglath-pileser III's tribute list from 737 BCE (Vanel 1974: 18, for the identification of the name see p. 23 n. 3). At any rate, nothing in the text suggests that the candidate was a Davidide from a secondary line of the royal Judean family.

After citing the enemy plan, God then reassures Ahaz in v. 7 that the plan will neither stand nor come to pass. Then vv. 8a-9a are introduced with the causal conjunction כי, and appear to give the reason why Ahaz and his court can trust the promise God gave in v. 7:

כי ראש ארם דמשק וראש דמשק רצין   8a
ובעוד ששים וחמש שנה יחת אפרים מעם   8b
וראש אפרים שמרון וראש שמרון בן־רמליהו   9a

---

1.   The meaning of ונקיצנה is disputed; I assume a by-form of the root קצץ ('to cut off'). The derivation from קוץ ('to terrify'), seems less satisfying as the tactical objective of an attack on Jerusalem. The LXX translation of the verb is too free to offer much help: καὶ συλλαλήσαντες αὐτοῖς ('and having consulted with them...'). Based on the LXX, Driver suggested that the Hebrew root was cognate with Arabic *qāḍa* ('to negotiate'), and thus the verb should be translated 'let us open negotiations with them' (Driver 1968: 39). Even if this root existed in Hebrew, however, the proposed meaning hardly fits with the meaning of the following verb 'to breach'.

2.   LXX renders ונבקענה אלינו as ἀποστρέψομεν αὐτοὺς πρὸς ἡμᾶς ('let us turn them aside to us'), but the normal meaning of בקע is 'to breach'. The closest syntactical parallel to this passage is found in 2 Chron. 32.1, where Sennacherib entered Judah, encamped against the fortified cities, and commanded/thought to breach them for himself (ויאמר לבקעם אליו).

3.   The object suffixes on the verbs and the suffix on בתוכה are all feminine singular in the MT. The Syriac follows the MT. LXX and the Targum translate the two object suffixes on the verbs as masculine plurals referring to the people, but even they translate the suffix on בתוכה as a feminine singular, which suggests that their rendering of the object suffixes on the verbs is free translation and not evidence of a different *Vorlage*. In the books of Kings and in the eighth-century prophets the name of the country יהודה, 'Judah', is consistently construed as masculine (1 Kgs 5.5; 14.22; 2 Kgs 14.12; 17.19; 24.2; 25.21; see Isa. 3.8; 11.13 for the Isaianic usage; and cf. Hos. 4.15; 5.5, 13; 6.4, 11; 8.14; 10.11; 12.1). The usage in the seventh century and later is more mixed (for the masculine construal see Jer. 2.28; 11.13; 31.23, 24; for the feminine construal see Jer. 14.2; 23.6; 33.16), perhaps due to the influence of the metaphor of Judah and Israel as unfaithful women (see Jer. 3.7-11).

For the head of Aram is Damascus, and the head of Damascus is Rezin;
And within sixty-five years Ephraim will be shattered from being a people,
And the head of Ephraim is Samaria, and the head of Samaria is the son of Remaliah.

Text

Needless to say, the logic of this formulation is not crystal clear. Some of the lack of clarity may stem from textual corruption, as there are clear signs of a disturbed text. The order of the three lines is quite odd. Verse 8b intrudes between and disrupts the clear parallelism between 8a and 9a. In v. 8b an impending judgment is announced on Ephraim, but in v. 8a only Damascus has been mentioned; Ephraim is not mentioned until v. 9a, after the announcement of judgment. The temporal phrase in v. 8b, 'within sixty-five years', gives too long a time period to fit the context as a reassurance to Ahaz. Faced with more immediate problems, Ahaz could hardly be particularly concerned with what would happen sixty-five years later. He could not expect to be around to see a judgment on his enemies that was delayed that long. Moreover, the time limits indicated in the following oracles involving the other children with symbolic names are much shorter. With Immanuel in 7.16 the promise is that before the child can choose his own food, that is, before he is weaned (about three years after birth), the land of these two kings will be deserted; and with Maher-shalal-hash-baz in 8.4 the promise is that before the child can say 'Mommy' or 'Daddy' (about a year after birth), the booty of these two enemy countries will be carried away to Assyria. One might expect a time limit of five to six years, since that would correspond to time limits of three to four and one to two, but a time limit of sixty-five years falls completely out of any meaningful sequence.

For these reasons it is fairly common for scholars to bracket out v. 8b as a later intrusive gloss. This move gets rid of the problem of the interruption of the parallelism between v. 8a and v. 9a, but it has its own difficulties. Why would any later interpreter introduce such a gloss in so awkward a manner? Why would a glossator intentionally disrupt a clear parallelism in the text, mentioning only the weaker of Judah's two enemies and inserting his comment in the text prior to its reference to that enemy? Unless one assumes that ancient glossators were by definition stupid, it is hard to explain the disrupted text as the result of a simple misplaced gloss. There is no known historical event that transpired sixty-five years after 735 BCE, that is c. 670 BCE, involving the destruction of Ephraim that could reasonably provoke such a gloss. Moreover, if one deletes this whole line as a gloss, one removes the only clear announcement of judgment on Judah's enemies found in the whole Shear-jashub oracle, though the parallel Immanuel oracle (7.17) and Maher-shalal-hash-baz oracle (8.4) both have clear announcements of judgment on Aram and Israel. Finally the vocabulary and syntax of this supposed gloss are distinctly Isaianic. Despite Wildberger's assertions to the contrary (Wildberger 1991: 285), it is not at all clear that the use of חתת in 7.8, 'to be shattered', is different from its use in 8.9. The fate of the enemies gathered together against God's people and his chosen city is not merely to be terrified, but to be shattered and dispersed just as they are in the related passages in Isa. 17.12-14 and 29.1-8. The translation 'be shattered' is more appropriate in 8.9 than the translation 'be terrified'. The sense 'to be shattered' fits Isa. 7.8; 8.9; 9.3; 30.31, while a greater emphasis on fear fits 20.5; 31.4, 9; 37.27—but the two usages are simply two poles of an external-internal continuum and do not suggest two different writers. One should also note that the idiom–verb of destruction + PN + מן + noun, 'PN will be destroyed from being something'—is extremely rare in the Old Testament. It is found only here, in the genuine Isaianic oracle from the period of the Syro-Ephraimitic war in 17.1, perhaps in a slightly altered form in Isa. 25.2, and in Jer. 48.42. It is hard to believe that a late glossator came up with such a rare idiom.

These observations suggest one try a different approach at solving the textual problem. One should note that the significant amount of repetition in vv. 8-9 invites textual corruption by haplography. Indeed, if one looks at the textual traditions for all of 7.1-9, one finds a significant number of haplographies in the various textual traditions.

In v. 2, MT's לבבו ולבב עמו ('his heart and the heart of his people') is reduced by haplography in 1QIsa[a] to לבב עמו ('the heart of his people'). In v. 4, a major corruption in the LXX's *Vorlage* leads to a significantly different reading than MT's

בחרי־אף רצין וארם ובן־רמליהו, 'at the fierce anger of Rezin and Aram and the son of Remaliah'.

LXX appears to read

כי בחרי־אף ארפא ובן ארם ובן־רמליהו, 'for when my (God's) fierce anger has passed, I will again heal. And as for the son of Aram and the son of Remaliah…' (ὅταν γὰρ ὀργὴ τοῦ θυμοῦ μου γένηται, παλιν ἰασομαι. καὶ ὁ υἱὸς τοῦ Αραμ καὶ ὁ υἱὸς τοῦ Ρομελιου,…).

This corruption in v. 4, because it has removed the syntactical connection between the concluding proper names and the earlier part of the verse, leads to a major omission of all the proper names in v. 5, since the leftover names in v. 4 have now become the subject of the now plural verb in v. 5:

MT:
יען כי־יעץ עליך ארם רעה אפרים ובן־רמליהו לאמר, 'because Aram counseled evil against you (along) with Ephraim and the son of Remaliah, saying…'

LXX:
יען כי־יעצו עליך] [רעה] לאמר, ('And as for the son of Aram and the son of Remaliah [v. 4]—because they counseled evil against you, saying…' (ὅτι ἐβουλεύσαντο βουλὴν πονηρὰν περὶ σοῦ λέγοντες…).

Finally, and most telling of all, one should note that the LXX has omitted the last half of v. 8a by a haplography caused by the recurring repetition of phrases:

MT:
כי ראש ארם דמשק וראש דמשק רצין, 'because the head of Aram is Damascus and the head of Damascus is Rezin'

LXX:

[ ] כי ראש ארם דמשק, 'because the head of Aram is Damascus' (ἀλλ' ἡ κεφαλὴ Ἀραμ Δαμασκός,).

This pattern of haplographies in the text suggests that one look for the disruption in vv. 8a-9a as the result, not of the awkward insertion of an incomprehensible gloss, but as the result of a major haplography and its attendant corruptions. Working from these presuppositions, I will suggest a plausible reconstruction of the original text and then explain how it was corrupted into the present text of the MT. The original text, presumably written in the script and orthography of pre-exilic Hebrew with its lack of distinctive final forms and most internal *maters*,[4] ran something like the following:

כי ראש ארם דמשק וראש דמשק רצין	8a
וראש אפרים שמרן וראש שמרן בנ־רמליהו	9a
בעוד חמש שנה יחת אפרים מעם	8b
ובעוד שש מסר דמשק מעיר	8c

For the head of Aram is Damascus and the head of Damascus is Rezin,
  and the head of Ephraim is Samaria and the head of Samaria is the son of Remaliah;
within five years Ephraim will be shattered from being a people,
  and within six Damascus will be removed from being a city.

The restoration of the numbers assumes the common stylistic motif in which a number is cited and then that number plus one is mentioned (see especially Prov. 6.16; Job 5.19; Amos 1.3, 6, 9, 11, 13; 2.1, 4, 6; but cf. also Exod. 20.5; 34.7; Num. 14.18; Deut. 5.9; 2 Kgs 13.19).[5] That Isaiah made use of this pattern is clear from two occurrences of the pattern in Isa. 17.6: שנים שלשה ('two or three'), ארבעה ...חמשה ('four or five'). The restoration of מסר דמשק מעיר in the reconstructed line is based on the occurrence of the similar expression הנה דמשק מוסר מעיר ('Damascus is about to be removed from being a city') in Isa. 17.1, another oracle against Damascus and Ephraim coming from the time of the Syro-Ephraimitic war.

---

4.   The significance of this assumption for the proposed reconstruction is that in pre-exilic orthography final forms of the letters were not distinguished from medial and initial forms, and internal *maters* were not normally used, particularly not to mark the masculine plural form of nouns. For example, the later form of the plural אנשים ('men'), or אנשיו ('his men'), was written in pre-exilic orthography without the yod or the distinguishing form of the final mem: that is, אנשם ('men', Arad 24 rev. 8) and אנשו ('his men', Lachish 3 rev. 2). Thus, orthographically the only difference between ...שש מ ('six...') and ששם ('sixty'), would be the spacing, and spacing is often not clearly enough marked to avoid a misreading. For the spelling of עוד, see Siloam 1.2; and for the spelling of עיר, see Arad 24 rev. 6.

5.   Both Procksch (1930: 116) and Wolff (1962: 22) saw that ששים וחמש was somehow a corruption of the numbers 'six' and 'five', and Procksch even noted they should occur in the other order, 'five' and 'six', but neither was able to offer any explanation how such a corruption could have taken place. Wildberger's rejection of their insight on the basis that 'pre-exilic prophets did not work with such exact dates' (1991: 285) just shows that Wildberger has not grasped the real significance of the time limits in Isa. 7.16; 8.4; and 37.30, all of which work with dates just as exact as 'five or six years'.

If one begins with this as the original text, it is easy to see how it could have been corrupted into the present MT. The scribe copied the first line[6] without any problem, but when he looked back to his *Vorlage*, because of the repetitive nature of the lines, his eyes skipped over the second line and landed on the second ובעוד. The scribe then copied the first few words of 8c—ובעוד ששמ, mistakenly taking the initial מ– on מסר as the final letter of the numeral. At this point he looked back to his *Vorlage* and saw the numeral חמש following the first בעוד, so he continued writing, thus conflating the beginning of 8c with the end of 8b: ובעוד ששמ חמש שנה יחת אפרים מעמ, thus omitting entirely the end of 8c, just as the LXX omitted the end of 8a. At this point, however, the scribe looked back to his *Vorlage* and noted that he had omitted 9a, so he added it at the end. Thus, with the perhaps subsequent addition of final consonant forms, internal *maters*, and a stylistic ו before חמש, one finally arrives at what is essentially the present MT. All the posited errors are plausible and reflective of the kind of mistakes actually attested in the textual traditions for this section of First Isaiah.

Logic

If one accepts my reconstruction of the original text, the logic of the oracle is at least clearer, and an attempt to grasp the deeper significance of the repetitive mention of the various 'heads' becomes possible. I have already alluded to a certain literary parallelism between Isa. 7.5-9 and Psalm 2, but the parallelism between these two passages reaches much deeper; they share a common theology. In Psalm 2 the foreign enemies are portrayed as restive vassals plotting to throw off the hegemony of Yahweh and his anointed, that is, the Davidic king in Jerusalem (Ps. 2.1-3). But the divine suzerain laughs at their plans and scoffs at them (Ps. 2.4), much as Yahweh belittles Rezin and the son of Remaliah in Isa. 7.4. Then God speaks to these enemies and terrifies them with the assertion, 'I have set my king on Zion my holy mountain' (Ps. 2.5-6). The Davidic king then goes on to cite God's covenantal promise to him, 'You are my son, today I have given birth to you. Ask of me, and I will give you the nations as your inheritance, the ends of the earth as your possession. You will shepherd/shatter [*double entendre*] them with a staff of iron; you will smash them like a potter's vessel' (Ps. 2.7-9). In view of these promises, the king warns the rebellious vassals, 'Now O kings be wise; be warned O rulers of the earth. Serve Yahweh with fear and kiss his feet with trembling,[7] lest he grow angry and you perish from the way; for his anger is very close to flaring up' (Ps. 2.10-12).

In short, the machinations of these enemy kings in Psalm 2 will come to naught precisely because God has chosen the Davidic king as his anointed and legitimate representative on earth, and he has chosen Zion/Jerusalem as his holy abode on earth. The same tradition of this double election of the Davidic line and the city

---

6.   I refer to 'lines' only for clarity. The manuscript from which the scribe was copying was probably written as prose without any clear indication of poetic line divisions.

7.   Reading with the common emendation of vv. 11b-12a as ורגליו נשקו ברעדה.

Jerusalem is also reflected in Ps. 132.10-18, and it was a fundamental part of the Zion theology cultivated at the royal court in Jerusalem and in which Isaiah was also steeped (see my discussion in Roberts 1982: 136-38).

Once one begins to think in Zion Tradition categories, the logic of the oracle becomes clear. The threat from Aram is not serious because the head of Aram is Damascus and the head of Damascus is merely Rezin. Damascus is not Yahweh's chosen city Jerusalem, and Rezin is not Yahweh's anointed Davidide. In the same way, Samaria is not God's chosen city, and the son of Remaliah is certainly not Yahweh's anointed. Since Yahweh has chosen Jerusalem and David, Aram's presumptuous plan to seize Jerusalem and replace the Davidic line is contrary to the will of the divine suzerain and doomed to failure. Moreover, its failure will have disastrous consequences for the two ringleaders of the plan. Within the relatively short time span of five to six years Ephraim will cease to exist as a people, and Damascus will be destroyed as a city. In effect, Isaiah is urging Ahaz and the Davidic court to take seriously their own royal theology, and as a sign that the promise is reliable, Isaiah assures Ahaz that, if he will only stand firm, he will see the promise fulfilled within six years.

Isaiah concludes this oracle with a warning, however, that is also rooted in the same royal Zion theology. Playing on the root אמן, a root used in the promises made to David that Yahweh would build him a firm house בית נאמן (1 Sam. 25.28; 2 Sam. 7.16) and establish for him a firm covenant ברית נאמנת (Ps. 89.29; cf. Isa. 55.3), Isaiah warns Ahaz and his court אם לא תאמינו כי לא תאמנו ('If you do not believe, surely you will not be established'). The best commentary on this phrase is found in an admonition King Jehoshaphat gives to the people of Judah and Jerusalem just prior to an expected battle with a far more numerous enemy in 2 Chron. 20.21:

האמינו ביהוה אלהיכם ותאמנו
האמינו בנביאיו והצליחו

> Believe in Yahweh your God and be established;
> believe in his prophets and succeed.

The admonition is in response to an earlier prophetic oracle by Jahaziel in which God urged the people not to be afraid, but to go forth to meet the enemy in the confidence that God was with them, because God promised that he would personally defeat the enemy and that the people need only to stand and observe the salvation of Yahweh (vv. 14-17). It is clear that the belief spoken of in 2 Chron. 20.21 is quite particular; it is the belief in the promise God had just given through his prophet. In the same way, the belief Isaiah speaks of in Isa. 7.9 is quite particular; it is belief in the promised deliverance from the threat of Aram and Ephraim that God has just given through Isaiah, based on the long standing promises made to the Davidic house and Jerusalem so emphasized in the royal Zion theology. Just as in Isa. 28.16-17, the implication seems to be that Yahweh's foundational commitments will remain firm and unmovable, providing security for the one who trusts Yahweh, but the one who attempts to find security on some other foundation will be washed away (Isa. 28.17-19). Whether Isaiah intended this as a threat to the continuance of the whole Davidic line may be doubted. Given his fundamental commitment to the Zion theology, it is more likely that the threat was more particular and more limited, directed only to Ahaz, the reigning Davidide, and his advisors.

BIBLIOGRAPHY

Asurmendi, J.M.
  1982   *La Guerra Siro-Efraimita: Historia y Profetas* (Valencia: Institución San
               Jerónimo para la Investigación Biblica; Jerusalén: Instituto Español Bíblico
               y Arqueológico).
Driver, G.R.
  1968   'Isaiah I–XXXIX: Textual and Linguistic Problems', *JSS* 13: 36-57.
Procksch, Otto
  1930   *Jesaia I: übers. und erklärt* (KAT, 9.1; Leipzig: Deichert).
Roberts, J.J.M.
  1982   'Isaiah in Old Testament Theology', *Int* 36: 130-43.
  1985   'Isaiah and his Children', in Ann Kort and Scott Morschauser (eds.), *Biblical
               and Related Studies Presented to Samuel Iwry* (Winona Lake, IN: Eisen-
               brauns): 193-203.
Vanel, A.
  1974   'Tâbe'él en Is VII 6 et le roi Tubail de Tyr', in *idem*, *Studies on Prophecy*
               (VTSup, 26; Leiden: E.J. Brill): 17-24.
Wildberger, Hans
  1991   *Isaiah 1–12: A Commentary* (Minneapolis: Fortress Press).
Wolff, Hans Walter
  1962   *Frieden ohne Ende: Jesaja 7, 1-17 und 9, 1-6 ausgelegt* (Biblische Studien,
               35; Neukirchen Kreis Moers: Neukirchener Verlag).

THE EYES OF ELI:
AN ESSAY IN MOTIF ACCRETION

Jack M. Sasson

ואני אמרתי נגרשתי מנגד עיניך אך אוסיף להביט אל־היכל קדשך

As for me, I ponder, 'Driven from your sight, might I yet keep gazing at your holy sanctuary?' (Jon. 2.5)

We are told in 1 Sam. 3.1-2 about Eli that one evening, as the old priest went to lie on his couch within reach of God's ark in Shiloh, 'his eyes (*ketiv* eye) becoming dull, he no longer could see'.[1] This is a touching description about an elderly man who, as we learn from previous chapters, had lost God's trust and so hardly needed this infirmity to render him less suitable for ministering to God (as per Lev. 21.18). The notice about Eli's loss of sight will soon be repeated with minor variation at

---

1.   Unless otherwise stated, all biblical references are from 1 Samuel. The literature on the first chapters of Samuel is immense and I have consulted a broad range of commentaries and secondary literature. Although I do not always cite it, Fokkelman's analytical *tour de force* (1993) has proven very useful. Both of us have found the same passages to be protean, but our treatments of them differ appreciably. As is well-known, the received Hebrew text of Samuel has its fair share of difficulties and appeal to the versions from which to enhance our comprehension is fairly standard in the literature. The issue of the relative merits of Greek and Hebrew, debated heavily since the mid-nineteenth century, came back in full force with the recovery of Qumran fragments of Samuel with many readings that match the Greek better that the Hebrew and some readings not found in either version. Ever since, how to treat the differences and whether to use them to restore a better original of Samuel have been hotly debated, with Pisano (1984: 1-12) offering a good (yet not the last) review of the positions. Barthélemy (1982: 137-53) has good judgment on the significance of crucial differences in the chapters relevant to this essay. Aside from the book of Pisano, there is much profit in also consulting Ulrich 1978 and Tov (ed.) 1980. The unity of 1 Sam. 3 is also discussed in the literature, with much interest in whether or not 4.1a belongs to it or not. See, for example, Spina (1991), who defends the latter view. In recent literature one meets with the curious assumption that if components of a narrative can be shown to fall into an elegantly balanced format (chiasms, ladders, rings or the like), it is evidence of a unity or integrity of construction. In turn, this unity of construction is deemed strong evidence that a composition has reached us in its original form, written or oral (see, e.g., Radday 1971). Most of the arrangements I have seen are highly accommodating to personal sensibilities. The opposite is also plausible: insertions and manipulations achieve harmonious configurations.

On the historicity of the material reported in the Samuel chapters relevant to this paper is concerned, my notion is that there is truth in every scene but the real facts are less reliably conveyed.

4.15. Even if we grant the allusion its metaphoric dimension of moral or ethical blindness, there is nothing in either context for which the quality of Eli's sight is a plot element, and so the question becomes why was its mention necessary at this juncture.[2] The matter is by no means critical to a better comprehension of the story or to evaluating the origins and adaptations of the Shiloh traditions. Yet, in this paper, dedicated to my good friend Herb Huffmon, the references to Eli's eyes will allow the exploration a literary device not often charted in the vast scholarship on the Bible as literature—sometimes a phrase displays accretion on its repetition across a narrative to convey intensification of meaning. I am calling it 'motif accretion' but any appropriate label will do. Because the paper means to please Herb, it will be about a prophet (but not about prophecy) and, of course, it will call on Mari texts to enrich the thesis.

Pregnant Phrases

Samuel's growing intimacy with God is developed over 1 Samuel 2 and 3, playing counterpoint (at 2.12-17, 22-25, 27-36) to the increasing deterioration of Eli's standing with God.[3] 1 Samuel 2.11 is itself pivotal in charting this development, its language replaying in two other contexts, 2.18 and 3.1. Superficially, the phrase contains the same information about Samuel ministering to Eli; yet it carries new dimensions of meaning at each of its reappearances:

2.11:   והנער היה משרת את־יהוה את־פני עלי הכהן

2.18:   ושמואל משרת את־פני יהוה נער חגור אפוד בד

3.1:   והנער שמואל משרת את־יהוה לפני עלי

At 2.11, the clause is an insert, neither preceded nor succeeded by details about Samuel himself. Syntactically it reveals much that has unfortunately been obscured by translations. The participle משרת in fact controls two direct objects, God and Eli, for, as we learn from 3.1 and from Est. 1.10, the idiom is the same whether construed with the particle את or the compound את־פני. So, rather than following the LXX in treating the phrase as describing two phases of the same act (καὶ τὸ παιδάριον ἦν λειτουργῶν τῷ προσώπῳ κυρίου ἐνώπιον Ηλι τοῦ ἱερέως, 'the child ministered in the presence of the Lord before Heli the priest'), we should recognize that at this juncture the boy had two distinct chores: 'The youth was serving the

---

2.   This is in contrast to what is said about Isaac (Gen. 27.1), Jacob (Gen. 48.10), Ahijah (1 Kgs 14.4), and Tobit (2.10). Not relevant are the occasions in which individuals are blinded temporarily. Such blindness is said to strike individuals either as punishment or because of anxiety; for which see Holden 1991: 132-36.

3.   There is much discussion in the literature about the weaving of independent narratives into 1 Sam. 2, allegedly originating in Samuel (some imagine Saul) and Eli traditions. See the commentaries and the papers of Peter-Contesse (1976), Ilan (1985–86) and Koorevaar (1997). Brettler (1997) wields a harsh scalpel to restore a text that fits his notion of the original that he deems consisted of 1.1-28, 2.11a, 2.18-21, and 3. Happily, this sort of speculation is not of immediate interest to this paper.

Lord *as well as* Eli, the priest'. The implication is that the child was learning his craft of attending on God by waiting on Eli. Not incidentally Eli is here for the last time titled as priest.[4]

This reference to Eli the כהן serves to introduce the crimes of Eli's sons, themselves כהנים (2.13), priests at Shiloh before the birth of Samuel (see 1.3). 'They did not "know" the Lord (לא ידעו את־יהוה)' contrasts with what is soon said about Samuel (at 3.7) and so also highlights their incapacity to experience the divine presence.[5] In addition to their crime against worshipers, the sons of Eli were also compromising the purity of their own apprentices.[6] The contrast with the apprentice (נער) Samuel in the verse immediately following (2.18) is sharpened by replay of את־פני יהוה, a phrase that is syntactically awkward in v. 17 but perfectly idiomatic in v. 18.

From this point, Samuel begins to take control, not just of the name his mother had given him (1.20), but also of the priesthood, for he is said to wear a linen ephod.[7] Hannah's yearly gift to her son is certainly an indication of her continuous attachment to the child she vowed to God: yet we may notice that the ephod, which can be girt by means of a band (חשב, see Lev. 8.7) also required a מעיל ('tunic', Exod. 28.31; 29.5, etc). We may imagine, then, that Hannah took a role in supplying her son with priestly accouterment. A nice touch is that the Samuel that the sybil at Endor conjures is wrapped in a מעיל (28.14). The rendering '(girded by) just an ephod' for אפוד בד, proposed in Banwell (1989), would be unidiomatic. The rise of Samuel is itself monitored by what Jonathan Magonet calls the 'growing phrase':[8]

2.21: ויגדל הנער שמואל עם־יהוה

Meanwhile, young Samuel rose in God's esteem.[9]

---

4. Eli's title is recalled in a notice about his grandson Ahiya, a priest under Saul (1 Sam. 14.3) and, indirectly, in 1 Kgs 2.27, when the curse against his priesthood is fulfilled as Solomon dismisses Abiathar from his office.

5. The phrase לדעת את־יהוה has a broad range of meanings (see the dictionaries), almost invariably treated as cause for God's rejection or punishment. The offenses of Phinehas and Hophni were many: venality, greed and (we learn later) depravity among them. But in coveting what is God's, among them the fat of sacrifice (see 2.20), they rendered unfit for consumption the portion normally available to the sacrificers and their family, if not also all of Israel. There is much debate in the commentaries, inspired by the versions, whether vv. 13-14 described abuses, as did clearly vv. 15-16.

6. Consequently, 'The sin of the attendants was enormous in the Lord's judgment' (ותהי חטאת הנערים גדולה מאד את־פני יהוה, 2.17).

7. 'Samuel was serving the Lord, an attendant girt in a linen ephod' (ושמואל משרת את־פני יהוה נער חגור אפוד בד).

8. Magonet (1983: 31-33, 40-42) builds on the works of L. Fränkel and G.H. Cohn.

9. Hardly: 'Young Samuel meanwhile grew up in the service of the LORD' (JPSV [Tanakh]) or '…in the presence of the LORD' (RSV, i.e., at his sanctuary). Such renderings are unduly influenced by the versions, as for example, McCarter (1980: 80), 'Reading *lpny yhwh* with LXX and 4QSamᵃ. The reading of MT ('*m yhwh*, 'with Yahweh') has been influenced by '*m yhwh* in v. 26, where it is certainly original.' Why is there such certitude and why might the influence not have gone the opposite way?

2.26:   והנער שמואל הלך וגדל וטוב גם עם־יהוה וגם עם־אנשים

Young Samuel kept gaining stature and esteem, with God as with people.[10]

The first of these verses brings to a satisfying end the story of Samuel's parents (2.19-21a). As Hannah becomes progressively absorbed by her large brood, Samuel is taken into God's shelter. The second (2.26) occurs after a pitiful display of Eli's collapsed authority (2.22-26) and so serves to underscore Samuel's rising fame in Israel. Rather than sharp condemnation or pitiless punishment, Eli had engaged his sons in rhetoric too subtle for their ears.[11] In any case, they could not have heeded their father, for 'the Lord was resolved to kill them (כי־חפץ יהוה להמיתם)'. This means that God had already decided to end Eli's priestly line. For this reason, the narrator could indulge in bringing Samuel out of his keeper's shadow before turning once more to the fall of Eli's house.

In this last indictment of Eli, at 2.27-36, a man of God reveals to Eli the cost of sinning: withdrawing the promise to sustain his line; premature death for the living; humiliation for the survivors; the deaths of Hophni and Phinehas on the selfsame day; and the anointing of a new leader. The loss to Eli was immense, for beyond his priestly functions inherited from Aaron, Eli was also Judge in Israel (4.18) and while that particular office was not hereditary, it brought prestige and honor on its holder. Distanced from God, he no longer was privileged to see divine holiness. Still, God was relatively kind to Eli, basically a decent, if weak-willed, priest, not revealing to him yet the greatest calamity that was to befall Israel under his watch: the loss and exile of the ark, and with it God's presence in Israel, until David's time.

At 3.1 occurs the final manifestation of the growing phrase I originally cited above ('Young Samuel was serving God, before Eli [והנער שמואל משרת את־יהוה לפני עלי]'), the impression being that as Samuel attended to God, Eli was likely an otiose observer. This distancing of Eli from Samuel no less than from God is, in fact, the controlling motif in the story of Samuel's rise, the old priest being clearly faulted for having lost Israel's contact with its God as expressed in two clauses that follow immediately the statement about Samuel: ודבר־יהוה היה יקר בימים ההם אין חזון נפרץ.[12] It is natural to assume that the two clauses complement each other, jointly referring to the dearth of communication from God. This is reflected in many translations, including that of the Tanakh, 'In those days the word of the LORD was rare; prophecy was not widespread'. Yet the two clauses are not redundant, for they distinguish between two distinct manifestations, the first aural ('An oracle from the Lord was rare in those days [ודבר־יהוה היה יקר בימים ההם]'), and the second

---

10.   See 2 Sam. 5.10 (= 1 Chron. 11.9), 'David kept growing stronger, for the Lord God of Hosts was with him (וילך דוד הלוך וגדול ויהוה אלהי צבאות עמו)'.

11.   'If people sin against each other, God might mediate for them. But if it is against the Lord that people sin, who could intercede for them?' This statement is clearly drawing on a proverb, but other interpretations of its meaning and setting are also possible; see Ward 1977 and Houtman 1977.

12.   The Masoretic punctuation attaches בימים ההם at the end of the first clause. It could just as correctly have opened the second clause with these words.

visual ('no vision was had [נפרץ חזון אין]').[13] The theophany accorded Samuel will be developed along these distinct paths, setting up the hope that before the story ends, there will be reversal of either or both of these lacks. Actually, references to the senses of hearing and sight resonate throughout the stories about Eli and Young Samuel, serving not merely as figures for obedience and morality, but also as guideposts in the fortunes of God's servants.[14] The eyes and ears of Eli chart this fall; those of Samuel are emblematic of his rise.

The Eyes (and Ears) of Eli

It is a pity that we never meet Eli until he had already been replaced as priest of Shiloh by his sons.[15] He is aged and likely no longer playing a vital role in the conduct of the affairs of Israel. Yet, as we know from Scripture, it is death and not age or power that retires servants from their duty to God. What we learn about him is framed by two scenes in which Eli sits on a chair: in one he is near God's temple (1.9), and in the other by the town's heights (4.13).[16] We first meet him watching but not hearing Hannah as she prays. His eyesight is excellent, for seated by the doorposts of the היכל (where later Samuel will have his fateful encounter with God at 3.3), Eli scrutinizes the lips of Hannah (ועלי שמר את־פיה) as she prays, likely in the חצר ('courtyard'), just beyond the אולם ('vestibule'), that is, at a fair distance away. Once he realizes that Hannah is no drunkard, Eli's judgment, no less than his eye, is sharp and clear. He could not have acted more properly than when he eased Hannah's anxiety (1.17). Eli remains in favor despite what God must surely have known about his sons' inequity, for he delivers an effective blessing upon the couple's delivery of their child to God (2.21).

Eli's hearing is still unaffected by old age when he sets forth to reprimand his sons. Ostensibly he is driven to do so because he hears about their abuse of women attending to the Tent of Meeting (2.22), a crime that Eli could have witnessed when seated at God's temple. But his rebuke harks back to the cleavage the sons created between God and Israel. We notice how often the root שמע is replayed in very few

---

13. More commonly, the verb ראה (qal or niphal) is attached to חזון ('vision'). There is discussion in the literature on how to understand נפרץ, a niphal, because the Greek διαστέλλουσα is a present active particle (see Gnuse 1984: 123). פרץ in the qal has an appropriate meaning when its subject is דבר (2 Chron. 31.5) and there is no reason why a niphal form (reflexive rather than passive) could not be connected with חזון ('vision'), since this noun is commonly construed with the niphal of ראה. (See the dictionaries.)

14. For some interesting remarks on the conjunction of hearing and seeing at Sinai, see Carasik 1999.

15. Josephus makes Eli an immediate successor of Samson and nestles the story of Ruth under his rule as judge (*Ant.* 5.9). He backtracks and retells, with deviations, the familiar text of Samuel in 5.10-11.

16. Although many passages in the HB link seats to God, kings and even priests (Zech. 6.13), they are also cited as belonging to lazy women (= Folly, Prov. 9.14) and as articles of home furnishing (2 Kgs 14.10). It is possible that Eli's seat is one of honor given to judges; but, aside from providing perfect brackets for the Eli's story, I would not read too much into its mention here, as does Spina 1991.

verses (2.22-25). Deterioration of Eli's position (as well as the health of his senses) begins at this point, because God had already decided to end the old man's line (2.25).

A good many allusions to sight (less obviously also, to hearing) are embedded in the condemnation the Man of God brings to Eli. It opens on an argument that is pregnant with potential: 'Have I shown myself to the house of your ancestors (הנגלה נגליתי אל־בית אביך) when, in Egypt, they belonged to the house of Pharaoh?' (2.27). The question is rhetorical and hardly benefits from a widely adopted emendation to remove the interrogative.[17] God's pronouncement is about bodily appearance to (אל) someone; for elsewhere the niphal of גלה is about exposure of the body (Exod. 20.26; 2 Sam. 6.20; Isa. 47.3) or parts thereof (Isa. 53.1; 40.5).[18] This is emphasized in 3.21 where the same point is made twice, 'The Lord resumed being seen in Shiloh, for the Lord revealed himself to Samuel in Shiloh, in oracular matters (ויסף יהוה להראה בשלה כי־נגלה יהוה אל־שמואל בשלו בדבר יהוה)'. So, from the outset we are dealing with whether or not God allows himself to be seen by the favored, a theme that will be featured in ch. 3.[19]

The charge found in 2.29-30 is partially obscured by difficult language, but it reflects on the sons (treating sacrifices despicably) as well as on the father (Eli honors those who dishonor the sacrifice).[20] It is interesting that for 2.29a the Greek (LXX[B]), looking ahead to the penalty segment of the oracle (at 2.32), proposes ἵνα τί ἐπέβλεψας ἐπὶ τὸ θυμίαμά μου καὶ εἰς τὴν θυσίαν μου ἀναιδεῖ ὀφθαλμῷ ('Why have you looked at my incense and meat offering with a wanton eye?'). In this way it carries forward the theme of sight that we are following.[21]

The doom predicted for Eli resumes:

2.32:   ...והבטת צר מעון בכל אשר־ייטיב את־ישראל

You will look *anxiously*...at all that profits Israel.

2.33:   ואיש לא־אכרית לך מעם מזבחי לכלות את־עיניך ולאדיב את־נפשך

But I shall remove for you no one from my sacrificial altar to empty your eyes and dry your throat.

17.   See the excellent remarks of Driver 1913: 36.

18.   Most relevant is Gen. 35.7, where Jacob consecrates an altar at Bethel, 'For God himself appeared to him (כי שם נגלו אליו האלהים) as he fled from his brother'. It is also used metaphorically, about justice (Isa. 56.1), sin (Ezek. 16.57; 21.29; Prov. 26.26) and, as we shall soon see, God's word (3.7). See Zobel 1975: 479-80.

19.   Exod. 24.9-11 is the classic text, much debated, about the capacity of people to see God (or parts thereof) without themselves being prophets or the like.

20.   Proposals for emending this verse are not lacking in the commentaries, some more facile in resolving the problems than others.

21.   There is also a play on כבד, albeit across stems, in that God honors those who honor him (2.30, כי־מכבדי אכבד) rather than those Eli misguidedly honors (2.29, ותכבד את־בניך), and Eli dies too obese (4.18, כי־זקן האיש וכבד) to survive a fall.

No less than in the previous verses, the language in 2.32-33 is unusual and difficult, attracting a broad array of emendations.[22] Here, however, we need only notice how the eyes of Eli control them. In 2.32 Eli is to gaze at something, for the hiphil of נבט has that meaning when construed with a direct object. While the textual difficulties prevent us from knowing what Eli is observing (concretely or figuratively), the oracle obviously frustrates his hopes by adding 'there shall never be an elder in your house'.

More directly personal is the prediction revealed in 2.33. 'Emptying the eye' and 'drying up of the throat' are idioms for distress, referring to endless tears and deep anxiety.[23] The idioms occur, singly or jointly (here *italicized*) in the Hebrew Bible. Almost exclusively (see Job 31.16), they represent afflictions that are either due to God (*Lev. 26.16*; Deut. 28.32; Jer. 31.12, 25; Lam. 2.11; 4.17; figurative, Jer. 14.6) or the result of (vainly) awaiting signs of grace (*Pss. 69.4*; 119.82, 123; Job 11.20; 17.5). We need not reconstruct their pathology or detail their symptoms to recognize how they are to affect Eli. What Eli hears is indeed brutal, but not without its measure of mercy: while his line is ending, Eli himself will witness neither the extermination of those around his altar (meaning Samuel?) nor the death of newborns in his household (meaning perhaps Ichabod and Ahituv). The death of sons may indeed be a brutal sign, even when he knew them to be immoral; but for now Eli is spared hearing about the greatest calamity of all: the capture of the divine Ark.

Eli's eyes and what they can no longer see open the next major scene.[24] One day, we are told, Eli was lying down at his customary place, in the temple, presumably fairly close to the הכל, the sanctuary where the Ark was kept and where Samuel had his cot. We suppose the time was night, but not because Eli and Samuel are said to lie down (שכב). In fact, Hebrew uses other verbs when sleep is specifically mentioned (McAlpine 1987: 59-62). We presume that it was night-time because at the conclusion of the drama Samuel is said to rise in the morning (3.15), and not because the drama unfolds when 'God's lamp was yet to be trimmed (ונר אלהים טרם יכבה)' (3.2). Sanctuary lamps were to be lit perpetually (תמיד, Exod. 27.20; Lev. 24.2; possibly otherwise in Exod. 27.21; Lev. 24.3), but they were kept alive for their capacity to burn (incense or the like) rather than to give light.[25]

---

22. Most proposals try to conciliate with Greek readings that obviously have gone their own way.

23. On the first idiom, see Gruber 1980: 390-400, with Ugaritic equivalent. On the second, see Gruber 1987. Of the many emendations proposed for this verse, none is as gratuitous as attributing the distress to a third person rather than to Eli; see, for example, McCarter 1984: 88-89, who also misunderstands the idiom הכרית with accusative and ל, always very negative (among others, see 1 Kgs 14.10; 21.21; 2 Kgs 9.8; Isa. 14.22); see Barthélemy 1982: 149-50.

24. Polzin (1989: 49-54) has good remarks on this topic as it concerns ch. 3.

25. In fact, the instruction in Exod. 30.7-8 was to stoke (להיטיב) rather than to trim lamps in the morning for burning aromatic incense. In 2 Sam. 21.17, 'trimming the lamp of Israel' is a metaphor for the death of David (see also 1 Kgs 11.36). It is possible that the statement about God's lamp in 3.2 suggests that the vision of Samuel came at a very opportune moment.

From Eli's perspective, however, night was no longer about darkness, for 'his eyes had begun to dull so that he could not see, החלו כהות לא יוכל לראות [*qere* ועינו [ועיניו'. Hebrew has several words to describe deterioration of vision.[26] It may well be that כהה was intentionally selected to foreshadow the censure Eli was again to suffer (3.13).[27] Eli's infirmity is not immediately germane to the plot; yet without it what will soon be said about Samuel might lose its power.

The Eyes (and Ears) of Samuel

Lying by the Ark, young Samuel—Josephus makes him twelve-years old (*Ant.* 5.10)—hears a call and answers twice: first from his cot (3.4), then as he draws near Eli (3.5). In this and two subsequent instances, neither he nor Eli was sleeping or awakening from sleep since the narrative lacks the vocabulary for either condition (ישׁן, נום, רדם or יקץ, עור). Neither was Samuel dreaming, for the appropriate language (חלום, חלם) is also missing.[28] In fact, as we shall see, fully awake protagonists are necessary to bolster their acceptance of God's destiny.

In his third trip to Eli's couch, Samuel took back to his resting place Eli's instruction. Should God call him again, he is to answer (3.9), 'Speak Lord, for your servant is listening (דבר יהוה כי שמע עבדך)'. The language seems perfectly suited for the occasion, but in fact it is unique to this story (at 3.9, 10). Elsewhere, when God calls someone by name (once, but often twice), a 'Here I am' (הנני) suffices to initiate delivery of divine instructions.[29] As pointed out by my student David

---

26. The vocabulary for Eli's infirmity, as that attached to other personalities, is interesting but hardly diagnostic. It may be accidental that the two instances mentioning Eli lack coordination between subject and verbs. The verbs used are: (1) כהה ('to go dim'; see Akkadian *apû, barāru, dalāḫu*, and derivatives), said of Eli's eye(s) (1 Sam. 3.2) and of Isaac's (Gen. 27.1, '...his eyes were too dim to see [ויהי כי־זקן יצחק ותכהין עיניו מראות]'); (2) כבד ('to become heavy'), said of Jacob's eyes (Gen. 48.10, 'Israel's eyes drooped with age; he could not see [ועיני ישראל כבדו מזקן לא יוכל לראות]'); (3) קום (to 'stand, freeze'), said of the eyes of Eli (1 Sam. 4.15, '...his eyes were fixed and he could not see [ועיניו קמה ולא יכול לראות]') and of Ahijah (1 Kgs 14.4, 'Ahijah could no longer see for his eyes were fixed from old age [ואחיהו לא־יכל לראות כי קמו עיניו משיבו]').

It is not clear to me whether what is said about Leah belongs here: her eyes were רכות ('tender', Gen. 29.17). Because what is said about her contrasts with how her sister is described ('shapely and beautiful [יפת־תאר ויפת מראה]'), it is natural to think it a euphemism about an unattractive or abnormal appearance; compare to Akkadian *damqam-īnam*, literally 'fine of eye' (CAD D, 67a; Ṣ, 236a). At any rate, in Genesis nothing further is made of Leah's eyesight; rather, it is Jacob whose eyes fail, in the wedding tent (Gen. 29) and later also when in Egypt (Gen. 48).

27. Eli knew about his sons' sacrilege, yet he did not rebuke them (ולא כהה בם). The pun is noted by many, most forcefully by Fishbane 1982: 202.

28. Despite the efforts of Gnuse (1984: 133-52; modified in 1996: 83-84, see 83 n. 197, 'mixed genre of dream report and prophetic call'), we should resist locating a dream theophany anywhere in this narrative.

29. The formula generally includes three parts: (1) detailing the circumstances (may specify the caller, God or angel); (2) naming the called (once—God to Abraham, Gen. 22.1; angel to Jacob [recalled], Gen. 31.11; twice—angel to Abraham, Gen. 22.11; God to Israel/Jacob, Gen. 46.2; to

Calabro, it remains unclear whether הנני of 3.4 is attributable to Samuel ('When the Lord called Samuel, he said "I am here"') or to God ('When the Lord's called Samuel, saying "I am about to..."'). If the latter, we recall that in 3.11 God finally gets to give a speech that begins with הנה אנכי. Here, however, narrative logic frustrates the formulation in favor of a progression of appeals, moving from no name (3.4), to one name (3.6, 8), to two names (3.10).[30] The episode itself scarcely deploys any of the expected elements common in calls to prophecy.[31] It is doubtful that it aims to deliver comically about Samuel's inability to discriminate between the voices of God and Eli. Rather, it focuses on the pathetic moment when Eli realizes that God was bypassing him (ויבן עלי כי יהוה קרא לנער).[32]

Yet Eli has not completely given up, for his were the unique and anomalous words he taught Samuel to say, 'Speak, Lord, for your servant is listening (דבר יהוה כי שמע עבדך)'. The old priest may well have hoped that Samuel would not fully confirm the indictment brought by the prophet of God (2.27-36).[33] Here, the principle at play is that discordant versions of an oracle may compromise the potential of its fulfilment.[34] A well-known illustration (whatever its historical worth)

Moses, Exod. 3.4); (3) responding, 'Here I am'. The formula is the same when individuals (normally with authority) summon others, as when Eli calls Samuel at 3.16.

30.   Commentators who privilege the Greek or Qumran versions do not always recognize this narratological logic and feel called upon to restore vocatives in defense of a more 'original' text; see, for example, McCarter 1980: 95.

31.   As seen, for example, in the calls to Moses (Exod. 3), Isaiah (6.1-3), Jeremiah (1.1-10) and Ezekiel (1.1-28). Missing from the present scene are such core elements as the confrontation, the reluctance of the prophet, divine reassurance, divine commission and (probably) confirmatory sign; on all this, plus a good bibliography on the issue, see Gnuse 1984: 133-40. That 1 Sam. 3 does not transmit a call narrative has been seen by many commentators, most clearly by Simon (1981, 1997). However, he reads the story as a paedea, the education of Samuel by a loving and kindly old man. Note that it is not a lack of intelligence that prevents Samuel from understanding what Eli does comprehend but rather a profound psychological block. Is it possible that God is calling him rather than Eli the priest? Conversely, Eli apprehends what Samuel fails to see, not because of superior intelligence or experience, but because he lacks the inhibitions generated by self-interest. Nothing deters him from assuming that God might turn to the young servant and pass over the old priest! In this way, Eli's humility compensates for Samuel's (1997: 66).

32.   In this sense, its emotional equivalent is Saul's acceptance of his fate at Endor when, through Samuel's ghost, God brutally shreds his illusion about creating a dynasty (1 Sam. 28.17).

33.   In this sense, the revelation brought by Samuel was by no means superfluous, as thought by Polzin 1989: 51. In Mari, diviners could even badger heaven into auspicious responses. Omens identified the perfect place in which to house an *ugbabtum*-priestess (ARM 3 42 = ARMT 26 178 = LAPO 18 958, p. 105). When this residence did not prove convenient (it was needed for other purposes), new rounds of omen-taking located another place, just as perfect (ARM 3 84 = ARMT 26 179 = LAPO 18 959, pp. 105-106).

34.   This is not the same as confirming a prophecy through its fulfillment, an issue that exercised the Deuteronomist (Deut. 18.15-22). There are several illustrations of this principle, including fine examples of it embedded in the Ahijah of Shiloh narratives (1 Kgs 11.29-30 fulfilled in 12.15; 1 Kgs 14.7-16 fulfilled in 14.17 and 15.29).

It grieves me to remove from consideration an alleged Mari parallel as adduced by Hurowitz (1994). On the basis of a protocol for diviners published as ARMT 26 1, Hurowitz weaves a fanciful scenario in which Eli's plea to know God's message (just four words in 3.17!) is deemed evidence

of this notion is in the 1 Kings 22 account about Micaiah ben Imlah. Jehosaphat insisted on obtaining from him confirmation about the victory the prophets of Ahab were predicting (ובינה לו במראה).[35] This principle itself is venerable and is already known from the Mari archives, from which I cull four examples, all from the reign of Zimri-Lim (eighteenth century):[36]

1. *A dream and a prophecy coincide*: Addu-duri (mother or aunt of Zimri-Lim) communicates her dream, brimming with sinister portents about the wellbeing of the king and his dynasty. She immediately cites the prophecy of an ecstatic that urges caution to the king. ARMT 10 50 (= ARMT 26 237 = LAPO 18 1094, pp. 278-79).[37]

2. *Separate omen-takings match*: Zimri-Lim writes to his wife: 'About the omens about which you wrote me, "I have had omens taken for the welfare of my lord: the enemy is delivered into my lord's hand". What you wrote me is exactly the same here too, as in my own omens: the enemy is delivered into my hand'. ARMT 10 124 (= LAPO 18 1170, pp. 353-55).

3. *Prophecy and a provoked oracle correspond*: Queen Shiptu transmits a prophecy (unfortunately lost in a break) brought by a berdache (*assinum*), Ili-ḫaznaya. The queen had extracted oracles of victory from mediums she intoxicated. She adds, 'Even before the message of Ili-ḫaznaya that (the goddess) Annunitum sent through him—5 days ago in fact—I myself posed (a similar) query. The message which Annunitum sent you and the information I obtained are one and the same'. ARMT 10 6 (= ARMT 26 212 = LAPO 18 1146).

4. *Message, repeated more specifically the second time*: Kibri-Dagan, governor of Terqa reports that a servant had a dream in which God warns, 'You must not build this ruined house. If this house is built, I will dump it in the river.' The dream not having been reported immediately, the servant received another dream the night after, 'You must not build this house. If you build it, I will dump it in the river.' The second message is more specific about who must not engage in rebuilding. By not

for the imposition of oaths requiring prophets to reveal all to their masters. Hurowitz tries hard to explain why this oath is imposed on Samuel *after* he had received a prophecy when in the Mari settings oaths made sense only when administered *before* omen-taking. Hurowitz proposes that Eli calls Samuel, 'my son' (בני), because they belonged to a prophetic guild (as in Amos 7.14 and often in 2 Kgs 2). Eli himself was a judge and not a prophet.

35. In apocalyptic literature a divine message may pass understanding and has to be delivered through another medium; see Dan. 10.1, 'In the third year of Cyrus, king of Persia, an oracle was revealed (דבר נגלה) to Daniel, who was called Belteshazzar. That oracle was true, but it was a great task to understand the prophecy; understanding came to him through the vision.'

36. The principle is not to be confused with the many instances in which Mari dreams and prophecies were accompanied by snippets of hair and garment from the medium. These items were not taken to control the 'authenticity of the prophetic word' (as our esteemed jubilar asserted recently in Huffmon 2000: 50), but to make certain that in the first place there was a message to communicate.

37. See the commentary of Sasson 1983: 286.

identifying the house as 'in ruin (*ḫaribātum*)', the second dream also removes any potential excuse for rebuilding. ARMT 13 112 (= ARMT 26 234 = LAPO 18 935, p. 85).[38]

The Presence of God

The narrator felt the need to report, after Samuel's second visit to Eli's couch, that the youth 'had yet to experience the Lord; the Lord's oracle was yet unrevealed to him' (3.7). This information may seem redundant, given the earlier (3.1) statement about the dearth of oracles and revelation; yet its formulation moves the knowledge of God from the general to the specific, finding completion in 3.21 (cited above), 'The Lord resumed being seen in Shiloh, for the Lord revealed himself to Samuel, in oracular matters'. More, it anchors a series of statements about the presence of God in Shiloh that draws all internal movements into one integral unit, so intensifying the developing intimacy between Samuel and God, the rising isolation of Eli, and the return of God to his Ark in Shiloh.

3.1: ודבר־יהוה היה יקר בימים ההם אין חזון נפרץ

3.7: ושמואל טרם ידע את־יהוה וטרם יגלה אליו דבר־יהוה

3.21: ויסף יהוה להראה בשלה כי־נגלה יהוה אל־שמואל בשלו בדבר יהוה

Noticeable in this progression, too, is an increasing gravitation toward sight rather than hearing; so much so that דבר־יהוה ('The Lord's oracle') gradually loses it syntactic (consequently also its semantic) placement such that it hardly belongs to 3.21.[39] By then, however, the focus had shifted to the appearance of God.

Samuel calls what he experienced a מַרְאָה (3.15), a term that applies to anything seen, whether in a dream (see Num. 12.6) or in a vision, whether during the night (Gen. 46.2, our passage) or not.[40] In 3.10, we read that, 'The Lord came, held himself upright, and called out as in each previous instance, "Samuel, Samuel"... (ויבא יהוה ויתיצב ויקרא כפעם־בפעם שמואל שמואל)'. The sequence involves three

---

38. This particular house may have belonged to an *ugbabtum* priestess (about which see n. 34) or to a deceased administrator. Malamat (lastly 1998: 76, 99) has read the story of young Samuel (and of other prophets) into this document, tying the repetition of the Terqa dream to the inexperience of the servant. In the Mari texts, *ṣuḫārum* is not necessarily a youngster (Finet 1972), and he had no problem receiving divine messages. Kibri-Dagan explains why this particular servant had not relayed his first message: he was ill. (I would not read a psychological disorder here.)

39. LXX[B] does not reflect בדבר יהוה, but instead expands with the following, 'Samuel was accredited to all Israel as a prophet to the Lord from one end of the land to the other. Heli was very old, and his sons kept advancing in wickedness, and their way was evil before the Lord.' See Pisano 1984: 29-34, who also cites the debate about what to do with בדבר יהוה in 3.21, the closest parallel usage for which are in 2 Chron. 20.12 and 1 Kgs 13.5.

40. This particular form (מַרְאָה, *mar'â*) is feminine; but the better-attested masculine form (מַרְאֶה, *mar'ê*) can have a similar range of meaning. In Dan. 8.26 we find that it can occur at any time and is equated it with חזון. The term can be related to a comatose state (תרדמה, as in Job 4.12) and so must not be confused with dreams; see Vetter 1976: 699-700. Both forms occur in the Num. 12 passage quoted above.

acts: first, God is said 'to arrive' when twice earlier his presence is not physical.[41] Third, there is explicit mouthing of Samuel's name when earlier it was implicit. In between, God יתיצב, an act that must not be treated hendiatically with what follows (as in McCarter's AB commentary's 'stood calling'). The hithpael of יצב connotes taking a stand determinedly and without falter, often in assemblies or facing an enemy.[42] But when God or his angel is the subject, it attests to their physical presence at crucial and sensitive occasions. There is a striking example of such a context in Num. 12.4-8, albeit the verbs used there are ירד and עמד, with הלך completing the staging. God seeks to suppress a rebellion against Moses:

> Suddenly, the Lord told Moses, Aaron, and Miriam, 'Come out, you three, to the Tent of Meeting'. The three of them went out. Descending (וירד) in a pillar of cloud, the Lord stood (ויעמד) at the entrance of the Tent and called out, 'Aaron and Miriam!' When both of them came out he said, 'Listen to my words: If there is a prophet among you, I may make myself known to him as Lord in a vision or I may make speak to him in dream (יהוה במראה אליו אתודע בחלום אדבר־בו)'. Not so with my servant Moses, who is trusted over my entire household. I converse with him mouth to mouth, visually (ומראה) and never parabolically; he may even look at the Lord's form (ותמנת יהוה יביט). So, why did you not fear maligning my servant Moses?' Having expressed his anger against them, he left (וילך).[43]

In our passage, however, Samuel's role is not yet prophetic. He is given no commission; he has no opportunity to cajole (as occurred repeatedly with Moses) or intercede (as does Abraham regarding Sodom). This situation is corrected in 4Q160 ('Vision of Samuel'), a fragment in which Samuel prays on behalf of Israel. We find a similarity of prophetic constraint in Amos 9.1-4, a passage that opens with a vocabulary that is highly reminiscent of ours, 'I saw my lord standing upright over the altar, saying... (ראיתי את־אדני נצב על־המזבח ויאמר)'.[44] Given the narrative

41. Elsewhere the Lord (YHWH) is said to arrive only in an apocalyptic passage (Zech. 14.5). All other arrivals of God (Elohim) occur in dream sequences: Abimelech in Gen. 20.3, Laban in Gen. 31.24, and Balaam in Num. 22.9, 20.

42. The verb occurs under two forms: יצב in the hithpael, נצב in the piel and niphal. There is likely a merging of two separate, semantically related verbal roots, each with only fragmentary attestation; compare their paralleling use in Num. 22.23, 31 (niphal) and 22.22 (hithpael). The niphal of נצב has a somewhat similar range of meanings, as in Gen. 28.13, '[Jacob dreams of a ladder with angels], The Lord was suddenly upright (נצב עליו) over him, saying...'. It is possible that the narrator selected יצב/נצב in recall of Hannah's words in 1.26, 'I am the woman who stood here by you (הנצבת עמכה בזה) praying to the Lord'.

43. In Hebrew poetry God is often placed in the center of combat (often in Song at the Sea, Habakkuk, and the Psalms, esp. Ps. 18). In prose texts too, God (or his intermediary, an angel) can be said to 'arrive' (בוא, Gen. 20.3; 31.24; Num. 22.9, 20) or 'appear' (נראה) to individuals (1 Kgs 3.5)'; to 'descend' (ירד) within a cloud (Exod. 34.5; Num. 11.25; 12.5) or not (Gen. 11.5; 18.21; Exod. 19.11, 20; Isa. 31.4), and to show himself (niphal of גלה, see above). In apocalyptic literature divine beings are often said to stand (עמד) by the seer (Ezek. 43.6; Zech. 1.8-11; 3.5; Dan. 10.16).

44. See also 7.7. In most renderings of Exod. 34.5, God stands with Moses as he reveals to him his divine attributes; for example the JPSV's 'The LORD came down in a cloud; He stood with him there, and proclaimed the name LORD (וירד יהוה בענן ויתיצב עמו שם ויקרא בשם יהוה)'. This understanding is sustained by Exod. 33.19 where can be found the only other reference out of about

genre in which such appearances are embedded (tales and the like), and given that the Hebrew language readily constructs anatomic metaphors when expressing divine feelings or emotion—God has a human anatomy and displays human emotions—we cannot always determine whether we are dealing with figurative language about the nearness of God or with stated belief in ancient Israel about the visibility of God.[45] Whatever its practical implications, the presence of God in the delivery of messages was a literary convention in ancient Israel. This is especially obvious in recording dreams because their delivery gains in authority when deities personally relay warnings or encouragement.[46] However, the presence of gods during a recipient's wakened state is less commonly reported, whether to transmit prophecies, grant a vision, or channel an omen.[47] One Mari text exceptionally brings these matters to the fore.

FM 7 39 (A.1121+A.2731 = *LAPO* 18 984, pp. 130-33) is one of the more complex of prophetic documents in the Mari archives in that the writer (Nur-Sin, writing from Kallassu, near Aleppo) had compiled two separate oracles: the first attributed to the local Addu and delivered during omen taking; the second fabricated from the aural recall of another oracle (A.1968, attributed to Addu of Halab) that Nur-Sin had earlier sent to Zimri-Lim.[48] The portion in which we are interested covers ll. 13-33:

> *ina têrētim*, Addu, Lord of Kallassu is upright (*izzaz*), saying, 'Am I not Addu, Lord of Kallassu, who has raised him between my thighs and have restored him to his ancestral throne? Having restored him to his ancestral throne, I decided also to

twenty where God is the subject of קרא בשם יהוה. Yet, given that Moses had been instructed to present himself (נצבת לי) atop Sinai, it is possible that Moses is the subject of ויתיצב עמו. So it is not just euphemism that motivated the Vulgate to replace the ambiguous pronouns in 34.5 with 'Moses'. This is also the understanding of a number of translations, including the Jerusalem Bible, the German *Lutherbibel* (1984) and the French *Traduction Oecuménique de la Bible* (1988).

45. Whether or not these manifestations of a superbeing betray Hebrew credence in anthropomorphism or they confirm an image-centered worship in Israel are major issues that cannot be developed here. The literature on these topics is hirsute. Aside from the articles on 'anthropomorphism' or 'imagery' in good Bible dictionaries, I can refer readers to two recent collections of essays, van der Toorn (ed.) 1997 and Gittlen (ed.) 2002. On Mesopotamia, see the remarks by a master historian of art, Amiet 1997.

46. Best detailed in Oppenheim 1956: 18, and repeated in Gnuse 1996: 41-43, 73-74; Weinfeld 1977: 185-87.

47. The 'Ritual to Obtain an Oracular-Decision (*purussûm*)' (from the second millennium on, see Butler 1998: 349-77) includes incantations and instructions on cajoling a personal god to deliver oracles (see pp. 366-67). The repertoire of techniques differs little when provoking dreams. It is interesting that the vocabulary for deities stepping forth in dreams (Akkadian *tebûm*, *izuzzum*) is often attached to the delivery of divine messages (as in 'The prophet from Dagan of Tuttul rose and told me...', ARM 26 209.6-7), probably as an extension of the phenomenon of divine appearance. For a listing see Durand 1988: 389-90, repeated by others, for example van der Toorn 2000: 80-81. I should note, however, that in such contexts the verb *tebûm* ('to rise') acts as an auxiliary (much as does Hebrew קום) and so may not be taken literally.

48. See the exposition in Sasson 1994: 314-16. Nur-Sin writes about delivering animals for a ritual and gives reasons for his zeal in posting oracles to the king. The text has been re-edited in Lafont 1984. A.1986 is edited in Durand 1993.

give him a dwelling place. Now since I restored him to his ancestral throne, I shall take from his household a property in perpetuity. If he does not hand (it) over, I—the lord of throne, land, and cities—can take away what I have given. But if it is otherwise, and he does hand over what I am requesting, I shall give him throne upon throne, household upon household, land upon land, city over city; I shall give him a territory, from its eastern to its western (corners)'.

This is what the *āpilū* said, with (Addu) remaining upright (*ittanazzaz*) there *ina têrētim*. Therefore, the *āpilum* of Addu, Lord of Kallassu, is demanding the shrine at Alaḫtum as property in perpetuity. My lord should know this.

I have left the phrase *ina têrētim* untranslated because the term *têrtum* (a derivate of *wârum*, 'to go, move on', so plausibly a cognate to תורה) is elusive in this context. In the phrase *têrētim epēšum*, it normally means 'to take omens (on the organs of animals)'; such a meaning is obvious even when the verb is not expressed (AHw, 1350-51). In Mari of the Zimri-Lim period, the term also stood for 'divine message'.[49] Therefore, how to translate it is at issue.[50] At stake is whether there is a coincidence of messages through separate routes (omen-taking and oracle, mutually confirming each other) or simply the delivery of just one oracle. In Mesopotamian lore, deities are said to be upright during sacrifice (e.g. ARM 26 3.1, 18), during the taking of omens, or at the granting of visions. Therefore, however skeptical we might be about such manifestations, for Nur-Sin the god Addu was *physically* present at that fateful omen-taking (*izzaz* in l. 14, *ittanazzaz* in l. 30).

The Eye(s) of God

The Mari material that reports the physical presence of a deity at the delivery of oracles merely bolsters what sensitivity to the accretion of sight and hearing motifs in 1 Samuel 3 imposes: awake, Samuel actually saw God.[51] We notice, too, that, having seen God, Samuel did not need to call him by name, as Eli instructed (3.10). God delivered a condemnation that was so precisely targeted at Eli that Samuel

49.   Construed with *nadānum* (ARM 26 6) and/or *qabûm* (ARM 26 206.28-34). The same can be said about *wûrtum* (ARM 26 199.52, 206.28-34) and *egerrû*, on which see Durand 1988: 384-86.

50.   Pongratz-Leisten (1999: 66-69) reviews the diverse opinions, among them those of Anbar (1981), Durand (1982: 46-47), and Lafont (1984: 12). Deities are said to stand by during the taking of omens ('Šamaš and Adad are duly present'; cited in CAD K 385a), their absence being an inauspicious sign ('At the prayer of the diviner, the god was not upright'; cited from CAD N/2 295a). The appearance of a deity during omen taking may be documented in FM 7 50. An official writes Zimri-Lim about the illness of Abban, son and heir of king Hammurabi of Aleppo: 'Regarding Young Abban who is ill. When Dadi-ḫadu wrote to my lord, I was traveling through Tuttul, so I have had omens taken about this child, and the god Itur-Mer came up to/for me (*ilêm*), In Abattum I had the *pirikkum* of Itur-Mer dropped in Abattum and the child made a sacrifice. Now the child has recovered, the God of my lord having helped him.' Itur-Mer occasionally seems to act as one of the Hebrew *terāpîm* (Sasson 2001: 417-21). It is difficult to decide what 'coming up' implies when said about a deity.

51.   It may be this privilege, rather than just their capacity to intercede with God, that helped link Moses and Samuel in Jer. 15.1; see also Ps. 99.6.

could scarcely keep it to himself.[52] When in the morning Samuel opens the temple doors—whose manipulation elsewhere is symbolic for submission (Hezekiah, 2 Chron. 29.3) or rebellion (Ahaz, 2 Chron. 28.24)—Eli hardly needed to put him under oath (3.17) to hear the report he was dreading all night long: the protocol of prophecy demanded full disclosure (Jer. 42.4).

Eli accepts his fate by declaring, 'The Lord is who he is, and he will act as he pleases (יהוה הוא הטוב בעינו יעשה)'.[53] The sentiment is personal, but it draws on an accepted notion of the sovereignty of God (Judg. 10.15; 2 Sam. 10.12 = 1 Chron. 19.13) and of kings (Saul: 2 Sam. 19.19; David: 2 Sam. 24.22). Yet Eli could have used other perfectly venerable musings, such as what we find in Jon. 1.14 (see also Pss. 115.3; 135.6: 'You are the Lord, and accomplish what you desire [כי־אתה יהוה כאשר חפצת עשית]'), and we may therefore wonder whether this particular expression allowed the narrator to focus once more on the dilemma of a practically sightless man for whom God's unclouded vision (עין) carries such a foreboding promise. Ostensibly the story should shift to Samuel, declared in the next couple of verses to be God's choice (3.19–4.1a).[54] In fact, Samuel soon disappears from the ensuing story of the Ark, not to re-emerge until 7.3, vacating the stage for God's terrible vendetta against the house of Eli.

Sightless in Shiloh

In the HB (but not in the LXX), the war against the Philistines is launched suddenly, perhaps even by Israel itself, in two phases, neither of them following consultation with God who might, in any case, have egged it on.[55] (Throughout the hostilities, the Philistines display a sharper appreciation of God's powers than do the Hebrews.) The results were preordained and so predictable: a devastating defeat for Israel. The news certainly tingled the ears of those who heard it (3.11), including those of Eli who sat on a chair awaiting news of the Ark's fate and what it might portend for Israel, and for him as well. The Greek text is easiest to follow, 'Heli was upon the seat by the gate looking along the way'.[56] The Hebrew, however, is much more interesting for us, reading at 4.13: והנה עלי ישב על־הכסא (*qere* יד) יך דרך מצפה. If we accept the *qere* as a shortened form of יד השער of 4.18 and vocalize the last word as מְצַפֶּה (the commentaries are full of alternate suggestions), we might make

---

52. והגדתי לו כי־שפט אני את־ביתו עד־עולם ('And I declare to him [perfect with waw conversive] that I am judging his house for ever', 3.13). We should not follow the readings of the LXX ('I have told him [καὶ ἀνήγγελκα αὐτῷ]') or of Driver ('and you [Samuel] will tell him [והגדת]'). God derives wicked pleasure in conveying to Eli his loss of prestige.

53. בעינו (*ketiv*) is singular, as it is in 2 Sam. 12.9 (God's); 19.19; 24.22 (David).

54. This is perceived by later readers, for the LXX expands on 3.21–4.1a, 'And the Lord manifested himself again in Selom, for the Lord revealed himself to Samuel; and Samuel was accredited to all Israel as a prophet to the Lord from one end of the land to the other. And Heli was very old, and his sons kept advancing in wickedness, and their way was evil before the Lord.'

55. To march out against an enemy (4.1) is not necessarily a defensive action; see, for example, Num. 21.23; 1 Sam. 17.55.

56. καὶ ἰδοὺ Ηλι ἐκάθητο ἐπὶ τοῦ δίφρου παρὰ τὴν πύλην σκοπεύων τὴν ὁδόν.

a reasonable rendering, 'Now Eli was sitting on a chair by the Mizpah-road Gate'.[57] The Masoretes, however, vocalized that word as a piel participle, מְצַפֶּה ('watching'), and so continued the exegesis implied by the LXX. It is true that this form does not necessarily imply the use of sight, as in Ps. 5.4, said of a worshiper awaiting (on signs from God?), and Mic. 7.7, said of the prophet, waiting in expectation; but it does sharpen our appreciation of how the motif of vision and sight remains in control of the story.

Samuel's vision had confirmed to Eli God's utter contempt for him; yet there was still the matter of the dignity of God when facing the enemy. So Eli sat 'watching' and listening for the ululations that would accompany the return of a triumphant army (Exod. 15.20-21; Judg. 11.34; 1 Sam. 18.6-7). He could neither see the bedraggled bearer of the horrible news, for his eyes had become fixed into a sightless stare (ועיניו קמה, 4.15 [on which see n. 26]), nor could he distinguish any longer between the sound of triumph and of despair. As he falls backward and cracks his neck, sightless Eli has time to hear about the defeat of Israel, the great slaughter accompanying it, the death of his sons, and the exile of God.

Looking Back at God

When Hannah made plans to deliver her son to God at Shiloh, she said, 'As soon as the child is weaned, I shall bring him, ונראה את־פני יהוה, he will live there for good' (1.22). The phrase I have not translated has been a crux for generations. As punctuated by the Masorites, the verbal form is a niphal, with Samuel the presumed subject, translatable something like '...*he shall appear before God*...' The phrase itself occurs half a dozen times in Hebrew Scripture, with the verb ראה vocalized as a niphal in all but two cases (Gen. 32.10, 30). Yet in all instances the phrases can make good sense when the verbal form is a qal. It is therefore tempting to translate 1.22, '...I shall bring him and we shall look at face of God'.[58] If so, we would be dealing with a metaphor (or more likely with a calque) from neighboring cultures where 'to look at the face of God' (e.g. Akkadian *pān ilim naplusum*) simply meant to worship.[59] However, whether or not Hannah wanted her son to be

---

57. Mizpah, we learn from 7.11-12, is on the road leading to Eben-Ezer, possibly at Izbet Sertah, and archaeologists look for it at Nebi Samwal or Tell an-Nasbeh. Halpern (1999) tries to solve the problem by studying the architecture of gates. In his opinion the narrative dates from the tenth century.

58. Much has been written on this phrase, most recently in Wilson 1995, where he also gives the history of the debate. His use of Akkadian material, however, is faulty; see Veenhof 1995.

59. Thus in ARM 10 143 (= LAPO 18 1100) Zimri-Lim writes his aunt (or mother) Addu-duri, '...I will head to Ziniyan the day after (posting) this tablet of mine. On getting there, I shall repeatedly worship (lit. "keep on seeing the face of") Dagan of Ṣubatum. Additionally, I shall unstintingly give him whatever he requests as his donation. I am well. News of your wellbeing should keep on reaching me.' In Gen. 32.31 Jacob at the Yabbok praises himself, 'I have met God face to face, yet I have survived (כי־ראיתי אלהים פנים אל־פנים ותנצל נפשי)'. On meeting his brother the next day, Jacob tells him, '(If you favor me, kindly accept this gift from me,) inasmuch as I have seen your face as seeing the face of God, in your acceptance of me (כי על־כן ראיתי פניך כראת פני אלהים ותרצני)'. No doubt, the narrator is indulging in one more wordplay on the place

seen by God or simply to look at God, just a few years later Samuel indeed does see God, thereby sharpening his own vision about his role as mediator.

By then, however, Eli's eyes had already lost their capacity to focus on God and on the grinding demands God's service required.

BIBLIOGRAPHY

Allegro, J.M.
   1968   *Dead Sea Scrolls: 4Q. Selections* (DJD, 5; Oxford: Clarendon Press).
Amiet, P.
   1997   'Anthropomorphisme et aniconisme dans l'antiquité orientale', *RB* 104: 321-37.
Anbar, M.
   1981   'Comments', *RA* 75: 81.
Banwell, B.
   1989   'A Possible Meaning of *'pwd bd* in 1 Sam 2.18', *Old Testament Essays* 2: 73-74.
Barthélemy, D.
   1982   *Critique textuelle de l'Ancien Testament. I. Josué, Juges, Ruth, Samuel, Rois, Chroniques, Esdras, Néhémie, Esther* (OBO, 50/1; Göttingen: Vandenhoeck & Ruprecht).
Brettler, M.
   1997   'The Composition of 1 Samuel 1–2', *JBL* 116: 601-12.
Butler, S.A.L.
   1998   *Mesopotamian Conceptions of Dreams and Dream Rituals* (AOAT, 258; Münster: Ugarit-Verlag).
Carasik, M.
   1998   'To See a Sound: A Deuteronomic Reading of Exodus 20.15 [20.18, MT]', *Prooftexts* 19: 257-76.
Durand, J.-M.
   1982   *Archives royales de Mari*, XXI (Textes cunéiformes de Mari, 5; Paris: Guenther).
   1993   'Le combat entre le Dieu de l'orage et la Mer', *MARI* 7: 41-70.
   2002   *Le Culte d'Addu d'Alep et l'affaire d'Alaḫtum* (FM, VII; Mémoires de N.A.B.U, 8; Paris: SEPOA).
Driver, S.R.
   1913   *Notes on the Hebrew Text and the Topography of the Books of Samuel: With an Introduction on Hebrew Palaeography and the Ancient Versions and Facsimiles of Inscriptions and Maps* (Oxford: Clarendon Press, 2nd edn).
Finet, A.
   1972   'Le *ṣuḫārum* à Mari', in D.O. Edzard (ed.), *Gesellschaftsklassen im alten Zweistromland und in den angrenzenden Gebieten. XVIII. Rencontre assyriologique internationale, München, 29. Juni bis 3. Juli 1970* (Munich: Verlag der Bayerischen Akademie der Wissenschaften): 65-72.

name פנואל. Certainly, there is here a psychological factor at work as Jacob flatters a brother he had reasons to fear. But it is also likely that we dealing with an idiom by which Jacob equates the joy of seeing his brother with that of worshiping God.

Fishbane, M.
1982   '1 Samuel 3: Historical Narrative and Narrative Poetics', in K.R.R. Gros Louis and J.S. Ackerman (eds.), *Literary Interpretations of Biblical Narratives* (Nashville: Abingdon Press, 1984): II, 191-203.

Fokkelman, J.P.
1993   *Narrative Art and Poetry in the Books of Samuel: A Full Interpretation Based on Stylistic and Structural Analyses* (Studia Semitica Neerlandica; 20; Assen: Van Gorcum).

Gittlen, B.M. (ed.)
2002   *Sacred Time, Sacred Place: Archaeology and the Religion of Israel* (Winona Lake, IN: Eisenbrauns).

Gnuse, R.K.
1984   *The Dream Theophany of Samuel: Its Structure in Relation to Ancient Near Eastern Dreams and its Theological Significance* (Lanham, MD: University Press of America).
1996   *Dreams and Dream Reports in the Writings of Josephus: A Traditio-Historical Analysis* (AGFU, 36; Leiden: E.J. Brill).

Gruber, M.I.
1980   'Chiasm in Samuel', *Linguistica Biblica* 1: 21-31.
1987   'Hebrew נפש דאבון "Dryness of Throat": From Symptom to Literary Convention', *VT* 37: 365-69.

Halpern, B.
1991   'Eli's Death and the Israelite Gate: A Philological-Architectural Correlation', in B.A. Levine *et al.* (eds.), *Frank Moore Cross Volume* (Eretz-Israel, 26: Jerusalem: The Israel Exploration Society): 53*-63*.

Holden, L.
1991   *Forms of Deformity* (JSOTSup, 131; Sheffield: Sheffield Academic Press).

Houtman, C.
1977   'Zu I Samuel 2.25', *ZAW* 89: 412-17.

Huffmon, H.
2000   'A Company of Prophets: Mari, Assyria, Israel', in Nissinen (ed.) 2000: 47-70.

Hurowitz, V. (A.)
1994   'Eli's Adjuration of Samuel (1 Samuel III 17–18) in the Light of a Diviner's Protocol from Mari (AEM I/1, 1)', *VT* 44: 483-97.

Ilan, Y.
1985–86   'The Literary Structure of 1 Sam 2.11-2', *Beit Mikra* 31: 268-70 (Hebrew).

Koorevaar, H.J.
1997   'De macrostructuur van het boek Samuël en de theologische implicaties daarvan', *Acta Theologica* 17: 56-86.

Lafont, B.
1984   'Le roi de Mari et les prophètes du dieu Adad', *RA* 78: 7-18.

Magonet, J.
1983   *Form and Meaning: Studies in Literary Techniques in the Book of Jonah* (Bible and Literature, 8; Sheffield: Almond Press).

Malamat, A.
1998   *Mari and the Bible* (SHCANE, 5 (Leiden: E.J. Brill).

McAlpine, T.H.
 1987 *Sleep, Divine and Human, in the Old Testament* (JSOTSup, 38; Sheffield: JSOT Press).
McCarter, P.K.
 1980 *1 Samuel: A New Translation* (AB, 8; New York: Doubleday).
 1984 *2 Samuel: A New Translation* (AB, 9; New York: Doubleday).
Nissinen, M. (ed.)
 2000 *Prophecy in its Ancient Near Eastern Context: Mesopotamian, Biblical, and Arabian Perspectives* (SBLSymS, 13; Atlanta: Society of Biblical Literature).
Oppenheim, A.L.
 1956 *The Interpretation of Dreams in the Ancient Near East: With a Translation of an Assyrian Dream-Book* (Transactions of the American Philosophical Society, 46/3; Philadelphia: American Philosophical Society).
Peter-Contesse, R.
 1976 'La structure de 1 Samuel 1–3', *BT* 27: 312-31.
Pisano, S.
 1984 *Additions or Omissions in the Books of Samuel: The Significant Pluses and Minuses in the Massoretic, LXX and Qumran Texts* (Orbis Biblicus et Orientalis, 57; Fribourg: Univeritätsverlag, 1984; Göttingen: Vandenhoeck & Ruprecht).
Polzin, R.
 1989 *Samuel and the Deuteronomist: A Literary Study of the Deuteronomic History, pt. 2: 1 Samuel* (San Francisco: Harper & Row).
Pongratz-Liesten, Beate
 1999 *Herrschaftswissen in Mesopotamien: Formen der Kommunikation zwischen Gott und König im 2. und 1. Jahrtausend v. Chr.* (SAAS, 10; Helsinki: The Neo-Assyrian Text Corpus Project).
Radday, Y.T.
 1971 'Chiasm in Samuel', *Linguistica Biblica* 1: 21-31.
Sasson, J.M.
 1994 'The Posting of Letters with Divine Messages', in D. Charpin and J.-M. Durand (eds.), *Florilegium marianum*. II. *Recueil d'études à la mémoire de Maurice Birot* (Mémoires de *N.A.B.U.*, 3; Paris: SEPOA): 299-316.
 1983 'Mari Dreams', *JAOS* 103:283-93.
 2001 'On Reading the Diplomatic Letters in the Mari Archives', *Amurru* 2: 329-38.
Simon, U.
 1981 'Samuel's Call to Prophecy: Form Criticism with Close Reading', *Prooftexts* 1: 119-32.
 1997 'Young Samuel's Call to Prophecy: The Servitor Became a Seer', in *idem*, *Reading Prophetic Narratives* (Indiana Studies in Biblical Literature; Bloomington, IN: Indiana University Press): 51-72.
Spina, F.A.
 1991 'A Prophet's "Pregnant Pause": Samuel's Silence in the Ark Narrative (1 Sam 4.1–7.2)', *HBT* 13: 59-73.
Toorn, K., van der
 2000 'Mesopotamian Prophecy between Immanence and Transcendence: A Comparison of Old Babylonian and Neo-Assyrian Prophecy', in Nissinen (ed.) 2000: 71-87.

Toorn, K., van der (ed.)
  1997   *The Image and the Book: Iconic Cults, Aniconism, and the Rise of Book Religion in Israel and the Ancient Near East* (Contributions to Biblical Exegesis and Theology, 21; Leuven: Peeters).

Tov, E. (ed.)
  1980   *The Hebrew and Greek Texts of Samuel* (Jerusalem: Academon).

Ulrich, E.C.
  1978   *The Qumran Text of Samuel and Josephus* (HSM, 19; Missoula, MT: Scholars Press).

Veenhof, K.R.
  1995   '"Seeing the Face of the God": The Use of Akkadian Parallels', *Akkadica* 94–95: 33-37.

Vetter, D.
  1976   ראה, *r'h*, sehen', in *THAT*, II: 691-701.

Ward, E.F., de
  1977   'Superstition and Judgment: Archaic Methods of Finding a Verdict', *ZAW* 89: 1-19.

Weinfeld, M.
  1977   'The Hymn to Samas', *Shnaton* 2 (1977): 60-81.

Wilson, E.J.
  1995   'The Biblical Term *lir'ot 'et penei yhwh* in the Light of Akkadian and Cultic Material', *Akkadica* 93: 21-25.

Zobel, H.-J.
  1975   '*gālāh*; *gôlāh*; *gālûth*', in *TDOT*, III: 476-88.

FROM THE MOUTH OF THE PROPHET: THE LITERARY
FIXATION OF JEREMIAH'S PROPHECIES IN THE
CONTEXT OF THE ANCIENT NEAR EAST

Karel van der Toorn

In the comparative study of ancient Near Eastern prophecy, Herbert B. Huffmon is
a name that counts. Many scholars of the younger generation (to which I consider
myself to belong) owe him a debt of gratitude for the ground-breaking work he has
done. It is a pleasure to dedicate this contribution to him—a scholar, a friend and a
much-respected colleague.

Introduction

The study of ancient Near Eastern prophecy, biblical prophecy included, is based
entirely on the testimony of written texts. No modern researcher has ever witnessed
an actual performance of a Babylonian or Israelite prophet. Yet if the written
sources show us one thing, it is that prophets were originally orators rather than
writers.[1] Prophecy as a literary genre—the only form under which ancient prophecy
is accessible to us—represents a secondary development. This state of affairs raises
a number of questions. The present article will focus on the transition from oral to
written prophecy, probe for the reasons behind the transformation, look at the
actors involved and assess some of its consequences. The issue is a complex one
and is best addressed, I believe, by studying a case in point. The book of Jeremiah
presents a promising avenue of investigation on account of the various references it
contains to the fixation of prophecy in writing. As there is little doubt that the historical Jeremiah was an exponent of prophecy as an oratory phenomenon, the book
that bears his name may be taken as a witness to the transition from the oral to the
written.

The Extra-Biblical Evidence

Judging by the extra-biblical evidence from the ancient Near East, there were basically two motives for committing prophecy to writing: (a) as a means of transmitting

---

1.   The notion of the early prophets as oral performers was laid out by Hermann Gunkel in a
ground-breaking essay from 1915 (Gunkel 1915: XXXVIII). Gunkel proceeded to demonstrate that
biblical prophecy eventually became a literary genre, yet its roots in the oral tradition have never
been seriously contested.

a prophecy received (and usually pronounced) at one place to a contemporary audience present at a different place; (b) as a means of preserving an oracle for future use. The literary fixation served the purpose of either transmission in space or transmission in time. The two types of transmission command their own forms: the letter or letter report in the first case, the memorandum or oracle collection in the second.

Transmission of an oracle from place A to place B is amply attested in the Old Babylonian 'prophetic letters'. These letters, which exhibit all the traits of ordinary letters, are qualified as 'prophetic' by their modern editors because they quote prophecies and often contain a summary description of the circumstances under which the prophecy was delivered. Most of these letters have been written (or rather, dictated) by a deputy of the king who sees it as his responsibility to inform his master of the oracles uttered in the sanctuaries outside the capital. Only rarely does the one who gave the oracle take the initiative to convey the message in writing to the king. In fact, there is only one letter known to date that has been written by an *āpilum* (who supposedly made use of the services of a scribe for the purpose).[2] There are a few other letters couched as messages from one or more gods to the king that were supposedly dictated by prophets, but in these cases their mediation is only tacitly implied.[3] Finally, there are those instances where a prophet, whether a lay person or a cultic functionary, delivers a prophecy to the royal deputy and urges the latter to transmit it to the king.[4] Although some of the tablets contain a series of oracles of different gods,[5] the Old Babylonian prophetic letters differ fundamentally from the Neo-Assyrian oracle collections in that their messages are relevant to only one specific occasion.

The Neo-Assyrian oracle collections, a millennium younger than the Old Babylonian material, are a different matter. The collections, easily accessible in the edition by Parpola (1997, nos. 1-4), contain about twenty prophecies, each followed by the name of the prophetess or prophet that delivered it (*šapīNN*). Although the historical circumstances of the individual prophecies can often be plausibly surmised, there is no explicit reference to them in the texts or their subscriptions. The tablets in question are relatively large, containing two or three columns on each side. This tablet type (known as *ṭuppu*) was used for treaties, census lists and inventories, as well as for collections of all sorts, including royal decrees. They were specifically drawn up for archival storage and reference purposes. There is evidence to the effect that the information recorded on the oracle collection tablets was copied from smaller tablets (so-called *u'iltu*s) containing individual prophetic oracles. Once the latter had been copied, they were routinely destroyed. Three out of the four oracle collections presently known were compiled by the same scribe, whereas the reports of individual prophecies (the *u'iltu* tablets) are from the hands

---

2.   ARM 26 no. 194: 'Speak to Zimrilim: Thus says the *āpilum* of Shamash: Thus says Shamash...'

3.   ARM 26 nos. 192 and 193; FLP 1674 and 2064, published by Ellis 1987.

4.   ARM 26 nos. 197.4-5, which seems to refer to no. 198; 210.12; 220.20; 221.14-15.

5.   E.g. ARM 26 nos. 192 and 194.

of different scribes. These facts point to a deliberate policy on the part of the royal bureaucracy to preserve a least a fair number of individual prophecies for secondary use.

The nature of this secondary use is, to some extent, a matter of speculation. A number of considerations, however, point to a use of these documents as revelations relevant beyond their original historical context. The lack of information on chronology or historical circumstances does not favor the idea that they were being kept as merely archival documents. The general tenor of the texts, which refer to 'your enemy' rather than naming one, and the pervasive presence of a dynastic ideology are two elements that are conducive to a second life of the oracles. The occurrence of quotations of older oracles, both in new prophecies (Weippert 1997) and in letters addressed to the king (Nissinen 1998: 120-25), corroborates the hypothesis according to which the Neo-Assyrian prophecies were believed to retain their validity well after their first utterance. There is reason, then, to concur with Martti Nissinen in concluding that 'the prophecies were no longer disposable *ad hoc* utterances concerning a special case but became part of the written tradition, a reference record that could be used and interpreted by succeeding generations' (Nissinen 1998: 172).

Much closer geographically to the world of the Israelite prophets is the so-called Balaam text from Deir Alla, written in an early form of Aramaic and generally dated between 800 and 750 BCE. The plaster inscription was found, broken into fragments, in one of the rooms of a large sanctuary in the East-Jordan Valley of Succoth. The fragments came in two groups and could be pieced together into two combinations, of which only Combination I yields a more or less coherent text; the damages to Combination II are too serious to allow a reliable textual reconstruction. The layout of the text follows the model of a scroll (Millard 1982: 149): it is written in ink, arranged in columns (probably two rather than one; cf. Lemaire 1991: 42), and contains rubrics, that is, titles and key passages, marked in red. The plaster on which it was written has apparently come off of the wall. What we have, then, are most likely the remains of a monumental mural inscription copied from what must have been a literary collection of oracles attributed to, and narratives about, a seer called Balaam (Weippert 1991: 177-78).

The contents of Combination I bear some remarkable analogies to what we find in the prophetic collections from the Bible. The text is headed by a rubric: '[This is] the book (*spr*) of [Ba]laam, [son of Beo]r, a seer of the gods'. It then opens with a description of the gods visiting the seer at night and communicating to him an oracle of El. The following morning Balaam is greatly distressed and tells his people, in reply to their questions, what the gods are about to do. His prophecy is one of doom, implying that the conditions of both the natural realm and human society will go through such dramatic changes that a kind of counter-order will prevail. Several details of the announcement have parallels in the Hebrew Bible and other ancient Near Eastern literature; they need not detain us here. The main point in the present connection is the light the Deir Alla text throws on the formation of prophetic 'books' in the North-West Semitic linguistic area. The master text behind the plaster inscriptions shows that the practice of compiling the words and deeds of someone invested with prophetic authority goes back to the ninth century BCE. There were people in the close vicinity of Israel, if not in Israelite territory, that produced such texts, read them and studied them. The status of the book of Balaam was such, moreover, that excerpts of it could be written on the wall for public display. Clearly this is a case, and a remarkable one at that, of prophecy written down for future use.

References to Prophetic Writing in the Book of Jeremiah

The book of Jeremiah is an important reference point in the study of the scripturization of Hebrew prophecy because of the various references it contains to the fixation in writing of oracles received by the prophet. I will summarize the relevant passages and reassess their meaning and significance for the history of prophecy as a literary genre. The ancient Near Eastern evidence presented above will serve as data for comparison. The scope of this contribution does not allow an extended reconstruction—by necessity hypothetical—of the composition of the book as we have it in either the Masoretic or the Septuagint version. A critical analysis of the references to Jeremiah as a writer-prophet enables us, however, to sketch the motives and the development which ultimately led to the book of Jeremiah.

There are four instances in the book of Jeremiah where the prophet is said to have written, or dictated, a single oracle or a collection of oracles. First, in chronological order, is the account of the scroll that Baruch wrote, at Jeremiah's dictation, containing the oracles which the prophet spoke from the beginning of his career until the fourth year of King Jehoiakim, that is, 605:

> Get a scroll (*m^{e}gillat sēper*) and write upon it all the words that I have spoken to you—concerning Israel and Judah and all the nations—from the time I first spoke to you in the days of Josiah to this day [i.e. the fourth year of King Jehoiakim] (…) So Jeremiah called Baruch son of Neriah; and Baruch wrote down in the scroll (*'al-m^{e}gillat-sēper*), at Jeremiah's dictation (*mippî yirm^{e}yāhû*), all the words which he LORD had spoken to him. (Jer. 36.2, 4)[6]

A year later, Jeremiah instructs Baruch to read the scroll to the men of Judah when they are gathered for a fast in the temple. Immediately afterwards, Baruch is summoned to the chamber of the royal scribe, reads the scroll once again, and explains that Jeremiah himself spoke the words which he wrote on the scroll in ink (*'al-hassēper badd^{e}yô*, Jer. 36.18). The king is informed, has the scroll read to him, tears up the scroll in pieces of three or four columns (*šālōš d^{e}lātôt w^e'arbā'â*), and throws them into the fire of his brazier. After the king has burned the first scroll, Jeremiah is instructed to get another one:

> Get yourself another scroll (*m^{e}gillâ 'aḥeret*), and write upon it the same words that were in the first scroll that was burned by King Jehoiakim of Judah… So Jeremiah got another scroll and gave it to the scribe Baruch son of Neriah. And at Jeremiah's

---

6.   All biblical references in the paper are taken from the NJPS translation.

dictation, he wrote in it the whole text of the scroll that King Jehoiakim of Judah had burned; and more of the like was added (w*e 'ôd nôsap 'alêhem de bārîm rabbîm kāhēmmâ*). (Jer. 36.28, 32)

It is presumably this scroll that is referred to in Jer. 25.13 and 45.1.

The second written message by the prophet is the letter addressed to the Judaean exiles in Babylon (Jer. 29). On the occasion of the diplomatic mission to Babylon, in the year 594, Jeremiah entrusted his letter to Elasah son of Shaphan and Gemariah son of Hilkiah, members of the mission, the one a cousin and the other a brother of the prophet.[7] The purpose of the mission was a demonstration of the loyalty of the Judaean vassal king to his Babylonian overlord.[8] The contents of Jeremiah's letter were consonant with the intention of King Zedekiah to convince Nebuchadnezzar of his acceptance of the Babylonian supremacy. The prophet enjoined his compatriots not to cherish hopes of an imminent change in their situation, but to prepare themselves for a life on foreign soil and to integrate themselves in the Babylonian society.

According to 51.59-64, Jeremiah used the same occasion to send a second written prophecy of a very different sort to Babylon:

> The instructions that the prophet Jeremiah gave to Seraiah son of Neriah son of Mahseiah, when the latter went with King Zedekiah of Judah to Babylonia, in the fourth year of [Zedekiah's] reign. Seraiah was quartermaster. Jeremiah wrote down in one scroll (*sēper 'eḥād*) all the disaster that would come upon Babylon, all these things that are written concerning Babylon. And Jeremiah said to Seraiah, 'When you get to Babylon, see that you read out all these words. And say "O LORD, You Yourself have declared concerning this place that it shall be cut off, without inhabitant, man or beast; that it shall be a destruction for all time". And when you finish reading this scroll, tie a stone to it and hurl it into the Euphrates. And say "Thus shall Babylon sink and never rise again, because of the disaster that I will bring upon it. And [nations] shall have wearied themselves [for fire]"'. Thus far the words of Jeremiah.

There is general agreement among commentators that the redactor(s) of the book of Jeremiah meant to imply that this second letter (or scroll—the term *sēper* allows both translations) contained the anti-Babylon prophecies presently found in Jeremiah 50–51.

The fourth and last reference to the writing activities of Jeremiah concerns what might be called the 'Book of Consolation for Israel and Judah' (Jer. 30–31):

---

7.   Elasah b. Shaphan, was brother of Ahikam b. Shapan (Jer. 26.24), son of Shaphan the scribe of King Josiah (2 Kgs 22.3). Gemariah and Jeremiah both had Hilkiah as father (Jer. 1.1; 29.3), who should most likely be identified with the chief priest in the reign of Josiah (2 Kgs 22.4). According to Ezra 7.1-5, the high priest Hilkiah was a descendant of Shallum, whose name occurs in the variant form Meshullam in Neh. 11.11. Since the scribe Shaphan was a grandson of this Meshullam (2 Kgs 22.3), the high priest Hilkiah and the scribe Shaphan, two central figures in the reform of Josiah, have a common priestly ancestry, traced back in Ezra 7.1-5 to Aaron.

8.   See Ahlström 1993: 792; Albertz 2002: 26.

> The word which came to Jeremiah from the LORD: Thus said the LORD, the God of Israel: Write down in a scroll (*sēper*) all the words that I have spoken to you. For days are coming—declares the LORD—when I will restore the fortunes of My people Israel and Judah, said the LORD; and I will bring them back to the land that I gave their fathers, and they shall possess it. (Jer. 30.1-3)

It is clear from the motive clause in the divine command ('For days are coming…') that the written prophecies here referred to are oracles of salvation—quite different in tenor from the messages of doom for which Jeremiah was known by his contemporaries.

Jeremiah as a Writer-Prophet: A Critical Reassessment

When we try to use the reports on the writing activities of Jeremiah in order to establish to what extent and for what motives Jeremiah was a writer-prophet, we must weigh the historical plausibility of each case separately. Let us first look at Jeremiah's letter to the exiles. The historical credibility of the story is enhanced by the fact that there can be little doubt that Zedekiah did indeed send a diplomatic mission to Babylon (whether he went there himself is questionable[9]) to protest his loyalty after the aborted insurrection against Babylonia by various neighboring states. Since two officials of the mission carried the letter and were responsible for its dissemination among the exiles, it must be assumed that Jeremiah's message had the approval of the king. This is in keeping with the position of the prophet in the first years of Zedekiah's reign. The contents of the letter, moreover, reinforced the intended effect of the mission, which was to show the Babylonian administration that Judah was a loyal vassal and accepted the exile of part of its citizens as a *fait accompli*. On this view, the seventy years prophecy of vv. 10-14 must be considered a redactional interpolation, as it would seriously undermine Jeremiah's call for submissiveness.

If there is good reason to assume the historical reliability of Jeremiah's letter to the exiles, it follows that the prophet used the written medium to reach a contemporary audience which he could not address in person. This is a prophetic letter, then, not unlike the Old Babylonian ones, even though its format is more in the nature of a pamphlet than that of a simple letter or letter report. The prophet had recourse to the written word not to preserve his message for posterity, but as a means of communication over a physical distance.

The story of the scroll which Baruch wrote at Jeremiah's dictation is another matter. On the face of it, the chapter reads like an account that means to authenticate and legitimize a scroll of collected oracles attributed to Jeremiah, presumably a forerunner of the book as it eventually took shape. This helps to explain the emphasis on the divine order to write, the comprehensiveness of the collection, the faithfulness of Baruch in transcribing every word 'from the mouth of Jeremiah', and such details as the use of ink and the disposition in columns. The fact that the first scroll was destroyed and that the second one contained an addition of 'many words

---

9.   See Volz 1928: 442.

like these' reflects an awareness on the part of the author that the written collection he had at his disposal was not an original and had gone through a stage, or various stages, of amplification.

The apologetic motives of the story are too obvious to regard it as historically credible. In its present form, the story focuses on Jehoiakim's burning of the first scroll. Here is a king who hears the words of God, written down from the mouth of the prophet, and throws them into the fire, much to the dismay of some of his courtiers. This motif portrays Jehoiakim as the negative counterpart of his father Josiah; whereas the latter rent his clothes at the reading of the scroll of the teaching (*sēper hattôrâ*) discovered in the temple (2 Kgs 22.11), the former tears up the scroll of God's prophet and burns it. Under the leadership of a king so obviously unwilling to hear the word of God, the impending fall of Jerusalem could not be avoided.

Although the theological overtones of the story are inversely proportional to its historical plausibility, it hardly belongs entirely to the realm of fiction. Several elements sound genuine enough, such as the role of Baruch, the names of Jehoiakim's courtiers and their different attitudes, and the popular fast in the temple, as well as the withdrawal of the prophet into hiding. The latter fact provides the historical clue of the story. Since Jeremiah could not speak his message in the open, he had it put down in writing and used Baruch as his mouthpiece. The written word allowed his voice to be heard in a situation where otherwise he was reduced to silence. Though the story in its present form, then, pictures the scroll of Baruch as a means of preserving the collected prophecies of Jeremiah for future use, the historical basis of the legend implies that Jeremiah wrote without some future audience in mind, but as an alternative to oral communication—even though the people in the temple did not read his words, but heard them from the mouth of Baruch.

Both the letter of Jeremiah and his written message to the crowd in the temple are indicative of the authority Jeremiah enjoyed with his contemporaries. In 604, even though Jeremiah had fallen into disgrace with the royal administration, his words, transmitted by Baruch on the basis of a written text, commanded the attention of the worshippers. And some ten years later, in 594, it was the authority of Jeremiah which King Zedekiah used to convince his subjects in exile that there was no room for rebellion. In both instances Jeremiah comes across as a man invested with the authority of a spiritual leader—despised by some, but venerated by many. His influence goes beyond that of a temple scholar, a mere priest or a technician of divination. As the figurehead and ideologue of a religious movement that went back to the days of the reform of Josiah, his descent from the high priest Hilkiah and his personal charisma combined to make Jeremiah a spiritual authority of extraordinary proportions.

The story of the scroll of Jeremiah intimates that Baruch son of Neriah was instrumental in the recording and public reading of Jeremiah's prophecy. Many biblical scholars assume that in fact much of the early material in the book of Jeremiah, speeches attributed to the prophet as well as accounts of Jeremiah in the third person, is from the hand of Baruch. The plausibility of this hypothesis depends in large measure on the relationship obtaining between Jeremiah and Baruch.

The account of the property transaction between Jeremiah and his cousin Hanamel in 588 throws light on the position of Baruch. When the deed of sale was written, sealed and witnessed, Jeremiah publicly charged Baruch to put it into an earthen jar, which was, at the time, the usual mode of official archival (Jer. 32.6-15). The discovery of a bulla of 'Berekhyahu son of Neriyahu the scribe', originally attached to a cord tied around a folded papyrus and deposited in a royal archive, suggests that Baruch was serving as an official scribe in the royal administration (Avigad 1986: 28-29, 125-30). This is consonant with the fact that his brother Seraiah served as minister in Zedekiah's administration (Jer. 59.64). Baruch was accredited by the court, and the apposition of his seal served to validate the deed. If Jeremiah used his services to commit to writing one or more of his oracles, and had him subsequently read them to an audience he himself could not reach in person, it may have been primarily because of Baruch's reputation as an official scribe of integrity and reliability.

Other indications in the book of Jeremiah, however, suggest that Baruch was more to Jeremiah than a respected professional whose accuracy and faithfulness were not in doubt. According to Jer. 43.2-3, some people suspected Baruch to be the evil genius of Jeremiah:

> Azariah son of Hoshaiah and Johanan son of Kareah and all the arrogant men said to Jeremiah, 'You are lying! The LORD our God did not send you to say, "Don't go to Egypt and sojourn there!" It is Baruch son of Neriah who is inciting you against us, so that we will be delivered into the hands of the Chaldeans to be killed or to be exiled to Babylon!'

Irrespective of its validity, such an allegation presupposes that the association between Jeremiah and Baruch was more than occasional. The two men must have developed a close collaboration, as a result of which they became companions in adversity; together they were forced to go to Egypt (Jer. 43.6-7); Baruch's complaint (45.3) echoes similar misgivings by Jeremiah (especially 20.7-18). Whether Baruch's commitment to the cause of Jeremiah means that he had at some point 'left his official position and joined Jeremiah in his struggle' (so Avigad 1986: 130) is doubtful; Baruch's role in the validation of Jeremiah's deed of purchase shows that he was still functioning in 588.

For some 20 years at least, then, Jeremiah relied on the services and support of an official scribe from the royal administration. As a partisan of the movement for which Jeremiah acted as a spokesman, and being a close companion of the prophet, Baruch was well-placed to write down the words and deeds of Jeremiah. An early Jewish tradition about the origin of the book of Jeremiah, reflected in Jeremiah 36, regards Baruch indeed as the writer of the Jeremiah scroll. The reference to the addition of 'many similar things' in Jer. 36.32 as well as the position of the oracle to Baruch at the end of the earliest edition of Jeremiah (Jer. 45 = 51.31-35 LXX; note the *inclusio* through the motif of 'overthrowing' [*hrs*] and 'uprooting' [*ntš*] in 45.4 which echoes 1.10) indicate that Baruch's authorship was believed to extend to the book of Jeremiah in its entirety. Though modern biblical scholarship rejects the latter claim, it generally follows the early Jewish tradition in ascribing substantial parts of the book to Baruch.

The hypothesis of Baruch being the author of the oldest nucleus of the book of Jeremiah is not without difficulties, however. First, Jeremiah's logion concerning the empty wisdom of the wise who boast the possession of the Torah of Yahweh is informed by a distrust of scribal culture when applied to the transmission of sacred lore: 'Behold, the deceitful pen of the scribes has turned it into a lie' (Jer. 8.8). It would be strange for a man of such views to consent to the fixation in writing of his oracles. Second, the two times when Jeremiah used writing as a means to communicate his message, he did so to reach a contemporary audience from which he was physically removed. The purpose of the book of Jeremiah when stripped down to its nucleus is different: the collected words and deeds of the prophets are meant for the instruction and edification of future generations. Nothing suggests that Jeremiah ever pursued such a goal. Third, the very insistence in Jeremiah 36 on the fact that every word in Baruch's scroll was 'from the mouth' of Jeremiah and that the written text had come into being at the explicit order of God arouses suspicion about its authenticity. How could Jeremiah have a *verbatim* recall of all the oracles he had delivered over a period of more than twenty years? Obviously an early collection of Jeremiah prophecies came into circulation at some point. But precisely because its authenticity was subject to doubt did the author of Jeremiah 36 feel the need to stress its extraordinary origin.

All of the above arguments could be countered by assuming that Baruch wrote the nucleus of the book of Jeremiah at his own initiative and without the consent of the prophet. But the rebuttal bites its own tail: if Baruch is believed to be the author, it is because of his intimacy with Jeremiah; yet in order to maintain the hypothesis of his authorship, we must presume that he betrayed the trust of the prophet.

In order to explain the existence of an early compilation of the words and deeds of Jeremiah we are therefore forced to assume the activity of a third party: it was neither Jeremiah nor Baruch who produced such a collection, but an anonym who used Baruch as his alias. The Baruch hypothesis strikes one as a simple solution to a complex problem; the solution proposed here complicates the matter once again. It assumes that Jeremiah did indeed call upon Baruch to put one or two of his oracles into writing for the specific purpose of communicating them to a contemporary audience he could not address in person; but that, in addition, others were responsible for the preservation in writing of his early oracles, and that a later editor—an adept, presumably, of a Deuteronomistic school of thought—brought the separate pieces together in a collection to which he added recollections (or inventions) of his own making. The Baruch hypothesis implies that we possess, in the nucleus of the book of Jeremiah, the account of a contemporary witness from the close vicinity of the prophet. Upon closer scrutiny, however, this hypothesis is untenable; we should therefore reckon with a greater distance, with respect to both time and familiarity, between the historical Jeremiah and the authors responsible for the various components of the book.

So far the anti-Babylon prophecies in Jeremiah 50–51 and the Book of Consolation in Jeremiah 30–31 have been left out of the discussion. Jeremiah 51.59-64 intimates that Jeremiah wrote the anti-Babylon prophecies from 50.1 through 51.58

on a scroll which he entrusted to Seraiah the brother of Baruch, quartermaster of the diplomatic mission to Babylon in 594.[10] Unlike his letter to the exiles (Jer. 29), this message of Jeremiah was to remain secret. Seraiah was instructed to read the scroll during his visit to Babylon and hurl it, with a stone attached, into the Euphrates. The gesture is heavy with symbolism, as it prefigures the 'sinking' (*šq'*) of Babylon. The text does not say that the reading was to be public; the reader is led to assume that no audience was present. The prophetic announcement of Babylon's downfall, read aloud by Seraiah, is presented as a performative speech-act that possessed self-efficacy; the disposal of the scroll into the Euphrates underscored the fact that henceforth Babylon's doom was inescapable. By the same token, the act ensured that the oracles would remain secret.

Various commentators have observed that the passage under consideration is 'inauthentic', that is, a late addition to the Jeremiah material (see, e.g., Volz 1928: 441-43). Its historical reliability seems nil. The significance of the tradition which these verses reflect lies in the notion of a secret mission of Jeremiah. On this view, Jeremiah wrote down secret prophecies, hidden from the profane, alongside the ones designed for public delivery. This notion allowed later authors to claim the authority of Jeremiah for literary oracles quite at odds with the preaching for which the prophet was known. It is by virtue of this later doctrine that the seventy-years oracle could be inserted in Jer. 25.11-14 and 29.10-14. The *post eventum* prediction that Babylon's supremacy would end after seventy years (counting from the fourth year of King Jehoiakim, that is, 605; see Jer. 25.1) was thus retrospectively put in the mouth—or rather the scroll—of Jeremiah, who was thus turned into a prophet of both Babylon's rise and fall.

The Book of Consolation (Jer. 30–31), a collection of salvation oracles for Israel and Judah, falls into the same category. The divine order to 'write down in a scroll all the words that I have spoken to you' (30.2) is patterned after 36.2—an indication of the secondary nature of this fictitious scroll. What follows are predictions of a return of both the Judaean and the Israelite exiles, the restoration of the Davidic kingship, the unification of Ephraim and Judah, and the rebuilding of Jerusalem. These were hopes and expectations that were cherished by many in the early post-exilic period; there are no grounds for assuming that the historical Jeremiah entertained a similar vision of the future. The insertion of these prophecies by a post-exilic redactor is meant to legitimize the aspirations of the post-exilic community in Judah by putting them under the authority of Jeremiah. But for all their appeal, Jeremiah never had such dreams (31.26). Though the author of these chapters does not refer to Jeremiah as a source of secret prophecies, the introduction in 30.3 does imply that the prophet was the author of oracles concerning the distant future which he put into writing for future reference. The prophet, in this view, is not only the man of the day but—unbeknownst to the historical prophet—the man of the future as well.

---

10.   Note the quotation of the closing word of the anti-Babylon oracles (51.58e) in 51.64, which subtly points to the contents of the scroll.

Conclusion

It is time to return to our initial question: In what way was Jeremiah a writer-prophet? The analysis of the passages which cast him in that role compel us to conclude that the only times when Jeremiah actually wrote his message—or had Baruch write it down from dictation—he did so in lieu of an oral delivery. When circumstances prevented him from addressing his audience in person, he resorted to the means of written communication. Jeremiah was a spiritual leader, an advisor to the king, a priest whose intercessory prayer was credited with special efficacy—but he was no literary author. On the few occasions when he wrote he had no intention of laying down his message for future generations, but of getting the attention of a contemporary audience which he could not reach otherwise.

The early collection (or collections) of Jeremiah oracles that was circulated—presumably during the lifetime of prophet—goes back to one or more anonymous authors. At a later stage of the tradition, another author—anonymous as well—reworked much of this material substantially so as to give it a Deuteronomistic slant and added narratives about the prophet. This compilation was then ascribed to Baruch and legitimized by the fiction according to which the prophet himself, at the order of God, had dictated every word. The anonymous author was congenial with the scholars responsible for the ultimate (or penultimate) shape of the Deuteronomistic History. Various literary oracles that date from the early post-exilic period found their way into this Deuteronomistic edition of the Jeremiah material, expanding it substantially, under the cover of the notion that Jeremiah was the source, too, of various secret prophecies which pertained to a time yet to come.

Insofar as Jeremiah himself did write, he should be compared to the Old Babylonian prophets who wrote their prophecies, or had them reported, to bring them to the attention of the king. The early collections of Jeremiah prophecies, on the other hand, compare to the Neo-Assyrian oracle collections. The Deuteronomistic forerunner of the book of Jeremiah, finally, resembles *qua* genre the postulated scroll of Balaam, extracts of which were found on the Deir Alla plasters.

Although Jeremiah was not a writer-prophet but a prophet of the spoken word, the fact that on occasion he did use writing as a means of communication allowed those responsible for the successive stages of the book of Jeremiah to present their literary activity as his work. Already in the early exilic period, then, Jeremiah came to be perceived as a writer-prophet. However remote from the historical truth, this was the image that would eventually shape a new conception of what it is to be a prophet. The fiction of Jeremiah as a writer-prophet created the reality of the writer-prophet. Ezekiel is the earliest case in point, and various other writer-prophets would follow in his footsteps. Though the phenomenon of prophecy as an oratory and performing art did not disappear, it had to share the stage with prophecy—and, not much later, apocalyptic—as a literary genre. In this respect, then, Jeremiah was a pivotal figure; and the book that bears his name at once attests to and brought about a transformation of Hebrew prophecy.

BIBLIOGRAPHY

Ahlström, Gösta W.
1993   *The History of Ancient Palestine from the Palaeolithic Period to Alexander's Conquest* (JSOTSup, 146; Sheffield: Sheffield Academic Press).
Albertz, Rainer
2002   'Die Zerstörung des Jerusalemer Tempels 587 v. Chr.: Historische Einordnung und religionspolitische Bedeutung', in Johannes Hahn (ed.), *Zerstörungen des Jerusalemer Tempels: Geschehen – Wahrnehmung – Bewältigung* (WUNT, 147; Tübingen: Mohr Siebeck): 23-39.
Avigad, Nahman
1986   *Hebrew Bullae from the Time of Jeremiah: Remnants of a Burnt Archive* (Jerusalem: Israel Exploration Society).
Ellis, Maria deJong
1987   'The Goddess Kititum Speaks to King Ibalpiel: Oracle Texts from Ishchali', *MARI* 5: 235-66.
Gunkel, Hermann
1915   'Die Propheten als Schriftsteller und Dichter', in H. Schmidt (ed.), *Die grossen Propheten* (Göttingen: Vandenhoeck & Ruprecht): XXXVI-LXXII.
Hoftijzer, J., and G. van der Kooij (eds.)
1991   *The Balaam Text from Deir 'Alla Re-Evaluated: Proceedings of the International Symposium held at Leiden, 21-24 August 1989* (Leiden: E.J. Brill).
Lemaire, André
1991   'Les inscriptions sur plâtre de Deir 'Alla et leur signification historique et culturelle', in Hoftijzer and van der Kooij (eds.) 1991: 33-57.
Millard, Allan R.
1982   'In Praise of Ancient Scribes', *BA* 45: 143-53.
Nissinen, Martti
1998   *References to Prophecy in Neo-Assyrian Sources* (SAAS, 7; Helsinki: Helsinki University Press).
Parpola, Simo
1997   *Assyrian Prophecies* (SAAS, 9; Helsinki: Helsinki University Press).
Volz, Paul
1928   *Der Prophet Jeremia* (KAT; Leipzig: A. Deichertsche Verlagsbuchhandlung D. Werner Scholl).
Weippert, Manfred
1991   'The Balaam Text from Deir 'Alla and the Study of the Old Testament', in Hoftijzer and van der Kooij (eds.) 1991: 151-84.
1997   '"Das Frühere, siehe, ist eingetroffen...": Über Selbstzitate im altorientalischen Prophetenspruch', in J.-G. Heintz (ed.), *Oracles et prophéties dans l'antiquité: Actes du Colloque de Strasbourg, 15-17 juin 1995* (Paris: De Boccard): 147-69.

THE METAPHORS OF 'CANAANITE' AND 'BAAL' IN HOSEA

Lyn M. Bechtel

Although the Hebrew Bible is often read as if ancient Israel has only one uniform, non-conflictual Yahwist theology, namely Deuteronomic theology (e.g. Sternberg 1985: 36-37, 156), it is my contention that there are *two aristocratic*[1] *Yahwist theologies*. First, there is 'Deuteronomic theology',[2] which is dominant when the Hebrew Bible reaches it final formulation. It is represented in Exodus through Kings,[3] Psalms, Proverbs, Lamentations, Esther, Daniel, Ezra through Chronicles and the prophets.[4] Prophecy in the Hebrew Bible only advocates adherence to Deuteronomic theology, *not general faith in YHWH*. Second, there is what I call 'non-Deuteronomic theology', represented in Genesis, Ruth, Job and Ecclesiastes.[5] Each of these two theologies has numerous versions, stemming from different contexts with slightly different agendas, and each challenges, critiques and polemicizes the *other*. At the heart of the difference between the two theologies are different perceptions of *divine functioning* and the structuring of *human power/control*. When interpreters assume only one unified theology, then all opponents are considered evil *outsiders*, and the ongoing religious/political/economic struggle for dominance, power and control within *Yahwist Israel* goes unrecognized.

In general, Deuteronomic theology justifies a power structure in which there is centralized political, judicial, military and religious power within the *aristocratic leadership in Jerusalem*.[6] The focus is on exercising rigid *control* by removing

---

1. As in most societies, the only theological traditions preserved in the Hebrew Bible are those of the upper class. Upper class people have the resources to employ scribes to articulate their theologies. They are willing to invest in the project because their theology supports *their claim* to power and control. Peasants have neither power nor the luxury of laying out their theological traditions.

2. I use the term 'deuteronomists' generically for all people who adhere to general Deuteronomic theology. Traditionally, 'Deuteronomic' has indicated writers of the book of Deuteronomy and 'deuteronomistic' the writers of the tradition from Joshua through 2 Kings. I assume that the compilers of the books I have identified as 'Deuteronomic' are all deuteronomists, who reflect their theology as it responds to different points in time.

3. I will refer to Joshua through Kings as 'Deuteronomic tradition', rather than 'Deuteronomic History', which is common in historical/critical interpretation. Joshua through Kings is not intended to be historical material, though it may at times inadvertently reflect some history.

4. Micah is the possible exception.

5. Song of Songs may fit into this theology, but its content and issues are so different that categorizing it is more difficult.

6. The theology is commonly set in a centralized monarchy supported by YHWH as a way of advocating their power structure. The setting is not necessarily intended to be historically accurate,

power from the local communities, isolating the nation from outside relations and influences and drawing strong boundaries around themselves—even separating themselves from fellow Yahwists. In order to sustain this power structure, YHWH is imaged as exercising *absolute political* (as King), *judicial* (as Judge) *and military* (as Commander) *power*. At times YHWH is portrayed as a controlling husband who expects complete obedience and loyalty from his wife, Israel. This imagery spills easily into sexual violence to obtain submission, as seen in such prophets as Hosea, Jeremiah and Ezekiel. Of course, although Deuteronomic theology projects absolute control onto YHWH, control is most often placed in the hands of the Deuteronomic kings/leaders, who strive to administer for YHWH.

In contrast, non-Deuteronomic theology[7] justifies the power structure of the local agrarian communities, where there is a desire for mutual distribution of power between the local communities *and* the central government. Their focus is on the *continuation of life* through child and food producing, which requires interrelatedness, cooperation and mutuality among males, females and the divine. In their image of the divine, YHWH is the *creator and sustainer of life*, the *natural* power of fertility and the relational power of connections/unity. These are the powers granted by Elohim to the heavens, the earth and all living entities in Genesis 1, where life is co-generated and there is a repeated refrain to 'Be fruitful, multiply and fill the earth'.[8] Since humanity is created in the image of Elohim (Gen. 1.26), humanity's greatest power is life sustaining and producing.[9] Thus, when the deuteronomists use images of fertility and the continuation of life for their opponents, they may be pointing to this Yahwist theology.

---

but to provide a backdrop for the presentation of Deuteronomic theology. One exception is the book of Judges, which is set within the power structure advocated by the non-deuteronomists. Judges ridicules and denigrates this structure as leading to corruption, anarchy and division, thus demonstrating the need for a centralized Deuteronomic theology structure. It is not a monarchy *per se* that is advocated, but a centralized power structure based on the Deuteronomic theology law corpus. Because the structuring of human power is an issue at any point in time, locating its origins in the past justifies the deuteronomists' claim to power in the present.

7.   The general characteristics of non-Deuteronomic theology are foundationally laid out subtly in the book of Genesis.

8.   It is interesting that in ancient religions the Goddess symbolizes a continuous process of life and death, permanence and change, sexuality and renewal. In Goddess religions, birth and death are equivalent and mutually supportive aspects of existence. In these religions, for life to proceed and renew itself, it must also be destroyed. Death is loss of vitality, but it is also creative and renewing (see Whitmont 1982).

9.   Therefore, in Gen. 4.1, creative mutuality among Eve, Adam and YHWH, as procreator, is foundational. In addition, YHWH is the foundational oneness of reality, being described metaphorically as 'breath/air' (*ruah*), moving in unity with the foundational 'waters' (Gen. 1.2). Air penetrates everything and is essential to sustain all existence, so it best symbolizes basic qualities of Elohim. All living beings are completely dependent on and integrated with air; nothing can be separated from air or stand independently on its own. Apparent separation of entities is more conceptual than physical; what appears to be separate can only exist within the inclusive oneness of YHWH. Any division (e.g. dualism or prejudice) creates disunity and violates the oneness of YHWH. Like air, YHWH Elohim is the mutual, determinative, interconnected, cooperative and non-domineering.

Within the context of these two theologies, I am proposing that the terms 'Canaanite' and 'Baal' are *metaphors* used by the deuteronomists to *represent and denigrate*[10] the non-deuteronomists, who perceive YHWH's power differently. These threatening opponents are called 'Canaanites' or 'baalists'—as if they were not Yahwists—and are placed in a category of indigenous 'others', who are considered evil enemies worthy of being destroyed (*ḥrm*).[11] In the book of Genesis (non-Deuteronomic theology), for instance, there are no polemics against baalism and the 'Canaanites' are generally viewed positively or, at least, neutrally. They are woven together with the other nations of the world to form one interdependent family, which is the *foundation* of Israel.[12]

The use of the terms 'Canaanite' and 'Baal' *in the Bronze Age* is fundamental to my argument. In the parlance of the ancient world, the term 'Canaanite' is a collective name, referring to *all* the people who inhabit the geographical area called Canaan *under a particular political structure*[13] (Drews 1998: 46-49). The political structure of the area entails monarchies within a variety of powerful, semi-independent, *agrarian* cities with regional differences, a degree of mutual distribution of power and loose control between the leaders of the cities *and* the central government of the Egyptian Empire.

The theology of these people is never uniform, but has many local variations and is congruent with their agrarian orientation. Their theology envisions 'Baal' as the creator, sustainer, husband, who *promotes* the continuation of life generation after generation, season after season, similar to Genesis 1. It is the general dynamics of this kind of political structure, and the congruent theology, to which the deuteronomists point with the metaphors 'Canaanite' and 'Baal'.

When there is a change in political structure in this geographical area during the Iron Age, the former semi-independent cities are incorporated into two monarchies[14] and under this new structure the people are then called 'Israelites' and 'Judahites'. The people do not significantly change, only the political structure. Logically, there is a corresponding modification of theology. As the political structure evolves, Baal

---

10.   Ironically, though the deuteronomists denigrate Baal's/non-Deuteronomic theology's continuation of life, in Hosea they try to incorporate it into their theology's divine image.

11.   Since theology is always political (i.e. related to human power/control) and shaped in conflict, it serves power interests that are endlessly in dispute within the human community.

12.   YHWH is the giver of the land in both non-Deuteronomic and Deuteronomic theologies, but in Deuteronomic theology the land is acquired by conquest and by killing the indigenous people (see the books of Deuteronomy and Joshua). In non-Deuteronomic theology, land is acquired by cooperating and sharing with the indigenous people (see the book of Genesis). The 'family model' speaks *against* establishing exclusionary boundaries and *supports* foreign trade and relations, openness to others, acceptance of difference and the mutual distribution of power among all people. A sense of inclusiveness, with openness to others and acceptance of difference, is essential.

13.   These groups of people never use the term as a self-designation; it is always applied by outsiders (Lemche 1991: 152).

14.   A 'united kingdom' is probably an *ideal* for which the deuteronomists strive, rather than a historical kingdom that at the *beginning of this new political development* commences at the pinnacle of its development.

religion evolves into different forms of Yahwism (e.g. non-Deuteronomic[15] and Deuteronomic theology). During the monarchical period and beyond there is archaeological evidence of diversity within Yahwism and the appropriation of Baal sanctuaries, but not of a continuing, separate Baal cult[16] (e.g. Mays 1965: 39). Since differences in theology are portrayed by using different names for the divine,[17] the change of name from 'Baal' to 'YHWH' is not unlike the change from 'Jacob' to 'Israel'. Name changes point to a transformation of character or theology, not to different persons or deities.

Consequently, since the previous political structure no longer exists and since there is no support for a continuing, separate Baal cult, the terms 'Canaanite' and 'Baal' should *no longer be appropriate*. Nevertheless, these terms continue to be utilized, and their persistence implies that they have been *reformulated as metaphors for a particular distribution of power*. During the monarchy, some Yahwists prefer centralized power only in the Jerusalem kingship (deuteronomists) and some prefer mutual distribution of power between local leaders and the monarchy (non-deuteronomists). The fact that the deuteronomists continue to use Canaanite/Baal metaphors well into the Persian period and beyond points to a continuous ideological clash with non-deuteronomists.

Unfortunately, because of lack of understanding of the deuteronomists' use of the 'Canaanite'/'Baal' metaphors, many scholars in their enthusiasm to prove the superiority of Israel's religion have uncritically embraced Deuteronomic polemics and denigrated the idea of fertility. Moreover, they have assumed that Baal is a separate God.[18] Identifying these two conflicting Yahwist theologies and understanding the deuteronomists' use of the 'Canaanite'/'Baal' metaphors may clarify the polemics in the book of Hosea.

---

15.   During the Iron Age, local sanctuaries (i.e. high places), such as Dan, Hazor, Megiddo, Beth Shean, Shechem and Arad, are Yahwist, though their theology is different from that of the temple in Jerusalem (there is no archaeological evidence from the Jerusalem temple itself). Arad is a particularly good example.

16.   The Jews of Elephantine in Middle Egypt in the fifth century BCE worship YHWH with Anat and Asherah as wives/sisters (Snaith 1953: 33; Wolff 1974: 49).

17.   People replicate and justify their own desires and perceptions of reality by projecting them onto the divine.

18.   Based on misreading of various biblical texts and with no Canaanite archaeological or extra-biblical textual evidence, scholars have further disparaged the natural powers of reproduction by imagining 'sacred prostitution' in the outlying sanctuaries or 'high places', which are probably Yahwist sanctuaries other than the official Deuteronomic theology temple in Jerusalem. The idea is generated by picking up the theme of sacred marriage from Canaanite religion (Anderson 1979: 85). Denigration of sexuality is a modern problem, not an ancient one (cf. Brueggemann 1990: 159, for the details of this polemic). In his commentary on the book of Hosea, Wolff lists examples of cultic prostitution in Canaanite and Babylonian culture, and because of the profusion of Canaanite fertility cults with orgiastic sexual rites in ancient Israel, he feels Israelite bridal rites are taken from Canaanite bridal rites of initiation (Wolff 1974: 14; cf. Andersen and Freedman 1980: 160). The evidence comes from classical Roman and Greek society, where in a puberty rite a father dedicates his daughter to the deity to make her fit for marriage (Andersen and Freedman 1980: 163).

Hosea 2–3

It is my claim that Hosea uses prostitution and adultery[19] as metaphors for fellow Yahwists who *turn away from* Deuteronomic and *to* non-Deuteronomic theology. An underlying issue is adult maturation, which gives people the capacity to 'know' good and bad.[20] In the dualistic worldview of the deuteronomists, 'good' and 'bad' are absolutely separate and unchanging, so 'knowing' entails choosing 'good', which is deuteronomic theology and its *torah*/law.[21] To embrace such understandings of reality is tantamount to the 'wisdom'[22] of YHWH. Once Deuteronomic theology has been chosen, then *unquestioning* obedience follows and leads to 'rightness'. If people choose 'good', the 'right path' (Deuteronomic theology), YHWH rewards them for their loyalty (*ḥesed*) to *torah* with material prosperity, protection, favor, honor and long life (cf. Proverbs). However, if people choose 'bad', the 'wrong path' (non-Deuteronomic theology), they commit the egregious sin of 'turning away' from obedience to Deuteronomic theology. It is a crime determined in the law court and YHWH must punish[23] the disobedient with adversity and deprivation.[24] Because of the possibility of swift punishment, 'fear of YHWH' is essential (cf. Proverbs). 'Fear' is not awe or respect, as some scholars have proposed, but genuine 'fear' related to judgment and punishment (Harper 1905: 223). The setting behind Hosea 1–3 is a law court where the husband is the plaintiff and represents YHWH. The wife and children are wayward deuteronomists and the lovers are another Yahwist theology (non-Deuteronomic).

Non-Deuteronomic theology holds a different perception of adult maturation. Maturation should give people the capacity to discern good and bad, but since reality is a constantly changing differentiated unity of oppositional forces, good and bad are always simultaneous and ever fluid. 'Good and bad' have to be discerned in

19.   Prostitution and adultery should be investigated as metaphors of deeper issues, not as literal events.

20.   The capacity to discern/know is not a capacity of children (Deut. 1.39; 2 Sam. 19.35; Isa. 7.15), but something that should be acquired when a person matures into adulthood. The adult capacity is essential for 'good' deuteronomists (1 Kgs 3.9), particularly rulers, messengers/prophets (2 Sam. 14.17) and priests (Lev. 27.12, 14).

21.   Some have assumed that *torah* refers to Genesis through Deuteronomy or the Pentateuch. It is my contention that *torah* refers to the law corpus of Deuteronomic theology, found in Exodus, Leviticus, Numbers and Deuteronomy. There are *no* references to *torah* in non-Deuteronomic theology (Genesis, Ruth, Ecclesiastes) and the book of Job mentions *torah* only because the book contains a series of 'Deuteronomic theology characters' who feel that Job is being punished for a violation of *torah*. Job contends he has not violated *torah* and that he is being unfairly punished. Of course, from the beginning Elohim has proclaimed Job an exemplary deuteronomist who has not violated *torah*.

22.   It is not broad understanding of life or general knowledge.

23.   YHWH, a severe judge, who tolerates no disobedience and slips easily into anger and vengeance, normally punishes with naturally occurring famine, pestilence, earthquake, drought, blight and death (e.g. Deut. 30.15-20)—all of which are under the absolute control of YHWH. YHWH's 'rightness' relates to YHWH's adhering to these requirements.

24.   Of course, it is often humans who actually carry out the supposed judgment of YHWH (e.g. Isa. 29.5-7).

each changing situation and require situational ethics, critical thinking and questioning. Law can be a guide, but it is not flexible enough to correspond to changing
circumstances. Consequently, the metaphor of a law court does not function and
the idea of absolute obedience, reward and punishment is unworkable. Prosperity
and deprivation are most often generated by social, political, religious or economic
systems or by an arbitrary interplay of oppositional forces, irrespective of human
behavior. These are some of the ideas against which the deuteronomists are
reacting:

> 'And on that day', says YHWH, 'you will call (me) my *'iš* (husband)[25] and you will
> not call me my *ba'al* (husband). I will remove the names of the *ba'alîm* (husbands)
> from her mouth and they will not be called by their name again'. (Hos. 2.16-17
> [Heb. 18-19])

In order to denigrate the word *ba'al*, scholars (e.g. J.L. Mays) feel that *'iš* connotes
a 'husband' who has mutuality with his wife and *ba'al* connotes a 'husband' who
owns or has authority over his wife (1965: 48). However, this distinction is not
valid. The Deuteronomic image of YHWH as an *'iš*/husband to Israel in Hosea and
other prophets is anything but one of mutuality. YHWH is imagined as all-control-
ling, expecting absolute obedience from his wife, Israel. YHWH clearly has authority over his wife, takes her to court and then severely punishes her with sexual
violence for 'turning away'.

Instead of mutuality and its lack, this verse focuses on a change in the woman's
choice of theology, indicated by a different name. Both *'iš* and *ba'al* mean 'man' or
'husband', although *ba'al* is typically used for marital relationships and is related to
the verb *b'l* ('to marry').[26] In Deuteronomic theology *'iš* is commonly used for deuteronomists, while *'adam* and *ba'al* are frequently used for non-deuteronomists.
Although *ba'al* may have been as common as *'iš* to indicate marriage and hus-
bands, it is used negatively by the deuteronomists as a deprecating name, since it
has an association with the Canaanite cult. The switch in names preserves the focus
on 'husband', but substitutes a word associated with Deuteronomic theology for a
word associated with non-Deuteronomic theology. It does not indicate a change in
Gods, but a change in Yahwist theology:[27]

> For their mother prostitutes (*znh*); she conceives them in shame. For she says, 'I go
> after my lovers, who give me my food and water, my wool and my flax, my oil and
> my drink'. (2.5 [Heb. 7])

According to von Rad, 'prostitution' points to Israel being entangled in and block-
aded by the despotic power of evil (1968: 110, 114), while Wolff suggests the

25. This passage contradicts 2.2 where YHWH says, 'Accuse your mother!... I am not her
husband'.
26. YHWH, a severe judge, who tolerates no disobedience and slips easily into anger and
vengeance, normally punishes with naturally occurring famine, pestilence, earthquake, drought,
blight and death (e.g. Deut. 30.15-20)—all of which are under the absolute control of YHWH.
YHWH's 'rightness' relates to YHWH's adhering to these requirements.
27. The phrase 'on that day', implies this is a future, possibly ideal, event, implying this is a
hoped for turning back to Deuteronomic theology, but not necessarily one that occurs.

problem is depraved fornication, not soliciting prostitution (Wolff 1974: 12-13). Most scholars (e.g. Mays 1965: 36; Andersen and Freedman 1980: 116) feel that like the Israelites the mother is a prostitute and shames herself by performing ritual sexual acts in the Canaanite fertility cult. Since a separate Canaanite cult no longer exists, the interpretation of this verse needs to concentrate on the metaphorical use of 'prostitution', particularly since there is no indication of overt sexual activity. When scholars condemn her relationship as sexual depravity, they are not reading the clues in the text carefully.[28]

Marriage is both the location of the perpetuation of human life and an important part of the social control system. Among other things, marriage limits people's freedom of choice in the use of their sexuality and places people under societal control. In contrast, a prostitute is a woman whose sexuality is not under the control of the institution of marriage. She determines what she does with her sexuality. This makes her an *independent* woman, who *thinks for herself*.[29] Since Deuteronomic theology strives to keep people under control, independence is threatening. Many of the references in the Hebrew Bible to women being prostitutes may simply be derogatory ways of labeling women as independent of the rigid controls of society, rather than as women who are professional prostitutes. Because non-Deuteronomic theology advocates critical thinking (thinking for oneself), rather than absolute obedience, the deuteronomists can deprecate and shame fellow deuteronomists, who think for themselves, become independent of the control of Deuteronomic theology and choose non-Deuteronomic theology,[30] by calling them 'prostitutes'. Since prostitutes have low social standing, calling an aristocrat with wealth and high status a prostitute is status-reducing and shameful. In addition, marriage commitment is used to symbolize allegiance to Deuteronomic theology. Prostitutes and adulterers do not commit to their partners nor do their partners commit to them. Lack of commitment is shameful and, therefore, calling a person a prostitute and adulterer is doubly shameful. Consequently, when the woman conceives, she does so in shame.

Another of the characteristics of Deuteronomic theology is prejudice, which epitomizes dualistic thinking. Prejudice establishes categories of *absolute* separation between people. One group is perceived as completely good and elevated over the other, which is regarded as completely bad and belittled. The deuteronomists

---

28. It could be that many of the references to women being prostitutes are simply derogatory ways of labeling women as independent of the rigid controls of society, rather than as women who are professional prostitutes.

29. In contrast, Anderson suggests that 'a wild and reckless passion' drives the woman to abandon her true husband and become a prostitute (Anderson 1979: 86).

30. 'Turning away' (*šûb*) from Deuteronomic theology to non-Deuteronomic theology is referred to as 'going after other elohim'. The word *elohim* is a name for the divine used by both Deuteronomic and non-Deuteronomic theologies. It can also refer to the perception of the divine in other religions; then it is normally translated 'gods', as if it is a separate God. In fact, the idea of a multitude of separate gods is a modern misunderstanding of ancient thinking. Different names for the divine represent different dimensions of the divine reality or different theologies or images of the divine.

place themselves in the category of 'good', 'right' and 'pure'. People who are different are placed in a category of 'evil', 'wrong' and 'impure'; they are demonized. In this case, they are called 'prostitutes' or 'adulterers'. Demonizing 'others' unifies the deuteronomists by providing them with a clear identity and distinct boundaries of animosity[31] between themselves and 'others'.[32] Within *torah* YHWH requires the utter destruction (*ḥerem*[33]—e.g. Lev. 21.2, 3; 18.14; Deut. 2.6; 3.6; 7.2; 13.15; 20.17) of indigenous people, who do not adhere to Deuteronomic theology (i.e. fellow Yahwists). There are to be no relationships, covenants, marriages or compassion for these people.[34] Holy war ideology gives divine backing to intolerance, brutality and killing, and the deuteronomists are most often the instrument of divine punishment.

Proverbs provides a relevant example of demonizing 'others'. The path[35] of Deuteronomic theology (i.e. *torah*) is represented by the woman Wisdom. The path of another theology (non-Deuteronomic theology) is symbolized by the 'other' woman. Both categories of women are attractive and seductive, but those who follow Wisdom gain reward, protection and long life. Those who turned aside to the 'other' woman/theology are evil and are punished. In Hosea, the imagery is similar, except the 'other' woman is called a 'prostitute' or 'adulteress'.

Since the imagery implies the woman has turned to another husband/man (*ba'al*), the use of the word 'lover' is interesting. In modern society, the word 'love' is used so frequently that it has virtually lost its meaning. In contrast, the Hebrew Bible uses *'hb* so sparingly that it needs to be taken seriously. A 'lover' is someone who has a strong emotional tie to the loved one and may or may not be a legal husband. Since men who use the services of a prostitute do not normally 'love' them, the 'lover' acts more like a husband than a client of a prostitute.[36]

In addition, it is the duty of a husband to feed and cloth his wife (Mays 1965: 41) and this is what the 'lover' does. The woman assumes that he gives her the basic necessities of life—food, water, wool and flax (for warm and cool clothing), oil and

---

31. Consequently, during the monarchy and the provincial period the deuteronomists constantly use the refrain 'to completely destroy' (*ḥrm*) the Canaanites and the worshipers of Baal.

32. The struggle is envisioned as a battle for superiority and dominance. For example, in the Elijah story (1 Kgs 18.20-40) people turn away from Deuteronomic theology, so the story portrays a struggle between YHWH, who represents Deuteronomic theology, and Baal, who may represent non-Deuteronomic theology.

33. The *ḥerem* provides the legal justification for atrocities against and the elimination of the enemy; it is the hallmark of a tyrannical regime. As Dr Martin Luther King Jr said, 'The ultimate weakness of violence is that it is a descending spiral begetting the very thing it seeks to destroy. Instead of diminishing evil, it multiplies it.'

34. The deuteronomists' constant call for the elimination of these people throughout Israel's history testifies to the simultaneous presence of these two power structures and theologies.

35. It should be noted that straight paths are made by humans; they are contrived, not natural. They reflect a human need for control over the environment. Things in nature do not grow in straight lines or rows. Natural paths undulate and fit the contours of the land.

36. Of course, the text never labels the woman as a *zona*/prostitute (Andersen and Freedman 1980: 224).

drink (a wine mixture). The issue is *who* provides these necessities—that is, which theology? Mays contends that Baal is 'fruitless' (e.g. Mays 1965: 39); Harper assumes that the 'flagons of wine' indicate debauchery (1905: 218); others posit that the materialistic woman engages in pagan sexual rituals, so that these items are rewards for sexual service[37] (e.g. Myers 1959: 15; Mays 1965: 39; Andersen and Freedman 1980: 220, 230). All of these responses are attempts to denigrate Canaanite religion rather than react to clues in the text:[38]

> She does not know that it is I who gives her the grain, the wine and the oil and who lavishes silver and gold on her, which they use for (her) husband/man (*ba'al*). Therefore, I will take back my grain in its time and my wine in its season. I will take away my wool and my flax, which cover her nakedness. Now I will expose her shame in the eyes of her lovers and no one will rescue her from my hand. (2.8-10 [Heb. 10-12])

Deuteronomic theology normally emphasizes the military, political and judicial power of YHWH more than the natural creative power central in non-Deuteronomic theology. This verse seems to be an attempt to usurp this non-Deuteronomic theology characteristic. Although the woman assumes the 'lover' (non-Deuteronomic theology) provides the basic necessities, the deuteronomists claim it is actually Deuteronomic theology. Since Deuteronomic theology also provides silver and gold,[39] a sense of competition regarding who offers the best is interjected. Of course, the lovers give freely, while for the deuteronomists YHWH offers these things as reward for obedience, but withdraws them for disobedience. Withdrawal carries a sense of vengeance; not only are the basic necessities withdrawn, but also the woman is shamed publicly by her nakedness and psychological vulnerability. Mays proposes that God is gracious because YHWH does not decree the death penalty (1965: 39). However, YHWH strips her naked and leaves her arid like the wilderness, so that she nearly dies of thirst; this is not compassion, but revenge:

> I will end her celebrations: her feasts, her new moons, her Sabbaths and all her appointed feasts. I will ravage her vines and her fig trees, of which she says, 'These are my pay which my lovers have given to me'. I will make them into a forest and the wild beasts of the field will devour them. I will punish her for the feast days of the *ba'alîm* when she burns offerings for them and dresses herself with rings and jewelry and goes after her lovers and forgets me', says YHWH. (2.11-13 [Heb. 13-15])

---

37. Does the text indicate sexual activity? Deuteronomic theology uses a large number of sexual metaphors in association with the divine and many scholars feel the marriage between YHWH and Israel is trans-sexual (Wolff 1974: 15). Why are the metaphors different?

38. It is interesting that the deuteronomists consider 'reward' for obedience acceptable, but the same 'reward' from a lover is deplorable.

39. Mays feels that food, water, wool, flax are basic nourishment and clothing, but oil and wine he feels are luxuries of the good life (1965: 39). This shows lack of understanding of the basics of life in the ancient world. Oil is necessary for both life and cooking and wine is usually a mixture of wine and water that provides a safe, but ordinary drink (plain water often carries dangerous bacteria).

One of the strongest indicators that the woman is turning to another Yahwist theology (i.e. non-Deuteronomic) is the mention of new moons,[40] sabbaths, appointed feasts and burnt offerings. In particular, sabbaths and appointed feasts are *not* part of Bronze Age Canaanite worship, but central to both Yahwist theologies. The woman may be worshiping YHWH and giving thanks through her celebrations, but within non-Deuteronomic theology at an outlying sanctuary, not at the 'chosen' Jerusalem temple of Deuteronomic theology (see Deut. 12[41]).

Since there is nothing in the law code that prohibits dressing with rings and jewelry, and since the deuteronomists claim that YHWH provides the silver and gold for jewelry, the problem lies in wearing gifts attributed to the reward from one theology to celebrate another theology. Of course, the fact that the woman has the silver and gold implies that she was once a 'good' deuteronomist who was rewarded for her obedience.

Anderson and Freedman posit that the devastation of vines and fig trees is a return of the earth to pre-creation chaos (1980: 251). However, changing the entire world to punish one disobedient human implies that nature has no other function or value except as tools of YHWH's reward and punishment. It reflects an extremely egotistic worldview. On the other hand, the implied threat of turning the cultivated (i.e. human controlled) vines and fig trees into a forest with wild beasts involves the removal of human control. In Deuteronomic theology, the natural state *without human control* is considered chaos, which is either eliminated by YHWH or used to punish people for disobedience to Deuteronomic theology.[42] Punishment is expressed metaphorically as the removal of human control:

> And YHWH says to me, 'Again go and love a woman who is loved by a friend and
> is an adulteress, as YHWH loves the sons of Israel, though they turn (their) faces to
> other Elohim and love raisin cakes.' (3.1)

Now, the 'prostitution' metaphor changes. Hosea is told to 'love' a woman who is loved by another, an 'adulteress'. Some scholars feel that the problem lies in the fact that Israel has a *personal* relationship with YHWH, but not with Baal (e.g. Mays 1965: 39). Yet the passage says that the woman is 'loved' by a friend. Again, 'love' is indicative of a strong *personal* relationship. However, the command to Hosea to

---

40.   According to Wolff, new and full moon celebrations are sexual ritual (1974: 34).

41.   Deut. 12 uses typical Deuteronomic theology polemical language for their non-Deuteronomic theology opponents. There is mention of Asherim and green trees that are symbolic of the continuation of life season after season or generation after generation, as in Gen. 1. The passage also commands the destruction of images made by human hands, which provide religious symbolism to everyone regardless of whether they can read or not. Deuteronomic theology supports images made by the human tongue—words—despite the fact that words separate the unity of reality and, therefore, are not congruent with reality. Since the average person cannot read, the religious symbolism of 'words' is controlled by the deuteronomists.

42.   Yet in non-Deuteronomic theology, chaos is essential to creation and cannot be eliminated. For example, in Job 41, Leviathan (chaos) is a symbolic creature, who lives in the *tehom* (foundational waters, v. 32e) and is an element of creation that cannot be controlled or eliminated, even by Elohim who is proud of Leviathan (v. 12). 'There is not on the dust his like, a creature without fear. He sees everything high; he is king over the sons of arrogance' (41.33-34e).

love a woman 'as YHWH loves the sons of Israel' implies that it is to be a relationship of reward for her complete obedience and punishment for disobedience; Hosea is to be in control and a judge of her behavior. The outlook does not look good for mutuality in their relationship!

Again, her behavior simply has the quality of adultery, which violates the exclusivity and limited use of marital sexuality. Since the adulterer decides how to use his/her sexuality, adultery is another metaphor for independent thinking and another derogatory metaphor for turning away from the control of Deuteronomic theology:

> And I say to her, 'For many days you must dwell as mine and not prostitute (*znh*) or belong to another and also I am with you.' For many days, the sons of Israel will dwell without a king and prince, without sacrifice and pillar, without ephod and teraphim. Afterward, the sons of Israel will turn back and seek YHWH their Elohim and David[43] their king and they will come in fear of YHWH and his goodness in the latter days. (3.3-5)

After a life of depravation as punishment and without prostituting (independence), Hosea takes back the woman, which is parallel to the deuteronomists turning away from their theology, being exiled from Jerusalem and, then, turning back with fear to Deuteronomic theology.[44] When they turn back, they will return to an ideal Deuteronomic theology with an ideal political, religious, judicial and military structure, represented by the paradigmatic David. The phrases 'afterwards' and 'in the latter days' point to the fact that this is an ideal, not a reality. Deuteronomic theology creates three paradigms (exodus, conquest and the Davidic monarchy), which are projected into the past. This passage refers to the Davidic monarchy, which functions as ideal united Deuteronomic theology monarchy. During Saul, there is mutual distribution of power between the government and the local communities, but YHWH rejects this structure.[45] Next, a Deuteronomic monarchy[46] is established with centralized, unilateral political/religious/judicial power in an ideal Deuteronomic king (David); this structure receives divine backing. Power is removed from the local communities, and the divine election of the Jerusalem temple/Zion makes it the sole location of Deuteronomic power.[47] This ideal Davidic monarchy

---

43. Mays (1965: 40) and others assume the reference to David comes from a later redactor, which is the classic solution to something that a scholar does not understand. Since scholars interpret historically, this seems to be the only option. But it may be that the prophets as a whole are a later product that warn of the dangers of turning away from Deuteronomic theology by being situated in an earlier time of crisis and loss.

44. Snaith (1953: 49) posits that only the remnant deuteronomists will repent.

45. The book of Judges denigrates this alternative structuring of power, advocated by non-Deuteronomic theology.

46. Of course, the idea of a monarchy rising up to its zenith within a few years of its origins flies in the face of logic, and there seems to be little archaeological evidence that such a 'united' kingdom ever existed. The historicity of David or lack of it is immaterial to this paradigm. Though it should be kept in mind that the figure of David is reformulated by the deuteronomists at a later time in the books of Chronicles, as is the figure of Solomon.

47. Interwoven in this paradigm is a covenant found in 2 Sam. 7, which grants adopted sonship to the Deuteronomic theology leaders, who are the firstborn 'sons of Elohim' and inherit the land

is followed by the Solomonic Deuteronomic kingship, in which outside alliances, trade and influences are prominent. This emphasis leads to conflict and division. Only David[48] is portrayed as a 'good', obedient deuteronomist, who sins, is punished, repents and never loses his power.[49] It is an ideal that is striven for, but probably never achieved.

Conclusion

When the prophets are viewed as a whole, the focus of their message is to provoke wayward deuteronomists to turn back to Deuteronomic theology. Part of the motivation involves accusing them of prostitution, adultery, being a Canaanite and worshiping Baal. Since archaeology does not substantiate a continuing Baal cult or the existence of a separate 'Canaanite' group during the monarchy and onward, the woman's turning to a depraved Bronze Age sexual cult is illogical. However, the characteristics of non-Deuteronomic theology seem to be congruent with the theology to which the woman is 'turning'. Thus, she is being charged with changing to another Yahwist theology, not changing Gods.

BIBLIOGRAPHY

Andersen F.I., and D.N. Freedman
        1980   *Hosea: A New Translation with Introduction and Commentary* (AB, 24; Garden City, NY: Doubleday).

Anderson, B.W.
        1979   *The Eighth-Century Prophets: Amos, Hosea, Isaiah, Micah* (London: SPCK).

Brueggemann, W.
        1990   *First and Second Samuel: Interpretation—A Bible Commentary for Teaching and Preaching* (Louisville, KY: John Knox Press).

Cross, F.M.
        1973   *Canaanite Myth and Hebrew Epic: Essays in History of the Religion of Israel* (Cambridge, MA: Harvard University Press).

Drews, R.
        1998   'Canaanites and Philistines', *JSOT* 81: 39-61.

and authority of Elohim (a land-grant/adoption treaty; cf. Cross 1973: 257-64; Kruse 1985; Brueggemann 1990). This represents a major shift in land control, which has significant economic implications. The covenant also establishes the military and political power of the deuteronomists, in the form of a guarantee of a continuing 'dynasty', 'kingdom' and 'throne' (the seat of political power).

    48.   It should be noted that the only references there are to David as the paradigmatic Deuteronomic theology king are found in the Deuteronomic theology tradition—non-Deuteronomic theology tradition does *not* mention him.

    49.   According to later deuteronomists, the reason why their theology does not offer protection against the destruction of Jerusalem and exile of some of its aristocracy is that many deuteronomists 'turned away from' Deuteronomic theology and its political structure.

Harper, W.R.
1905 *A Critical and Exegetical Commentary on Amos and Hosea* (Edinburgh: T. & T. Clark).

Kruse, H.
1985 'David's Covenant', *VT* 35.2: 139-64.

Lemche, N.P.
1991 *The Canaanites and their Land: The Tradition of the Canaanites* (JSOTSup, 110; Sheffield: JSOT Press)

Mays, J.L.
1965 *Hosea* (OTL; Philadelphia: Westminster Press).

Myers, J.
1959 *Hosea to Jonah* (Layman's Bible Commentaries; London: SCM Press).

Rad, G. von
1968 *The Message of the Prophets* (London: SCM Press).

Snaith, N.
1953 *Mercy and Sacrifice: A Study of the Book of Hosea* (London: SCM Press).

Sternberg, M.
1985 *The Poetics of Biblical Narrative: Ideological Literature and the Drama of Reading* (The Indiana Literary Biblical Series; Bloomington: Indiana University Press).

Whitmont, E.C.
1982 *Return of the Goddess* (New York: Crossroad).

Wolff, H.W.
1974 *Hosea: A Commentary on the Book of the Prophet Hosea* (ed. P.D. Hanson; trans. Gary Stansell; Hermeneia—A Critical and Historical Commentary on the Bible; Philadelphia: Fortress Press).

What's in a Name? Cyrus and the Dating of Deutero-Isaiah[*]

Milton Eng

The Cyrus oracle of Isa. 44.24–45.7 is unique among the classical prophets and has had a long and interesting history of exegesis. It is unique not simply because it prophesies the coming of a deliverer for Israel in exile but because it is the only prophetic oracle to do so by giving the literal name of the deliverer in advance! Even the great oracle at Delphi would only refer to Cyrus as 'a mule who would rule over Media' (Herodotus, *Hist.* 1.55).[1] Calvin, however, marvels at the specificity of the biblical prophecy, 'This is a remarkable passage…[h]ere "Cyrus" was named long before he was born' (Calvin 1948: 390).

Some interpreters are not as sanguine as Calvin regarding the naming of Cyrus in Isaiah. It occurs in only two places in the entire book (Isa. 44.28; 45.1), in the exact same syntactical phrase, לכורש, and in immediately contiguous verses. More importantly, it is uncharacteristic of biblical prophecy in general to announce the names of individuals ahead of time.[2] Thus, one approach to the problem has been to view the mentions of the name as later interpolations or explanatory glosses.[3]

Chief among such interpreters have been C.C. Torrey and James D. Smart, to whom modern commentators often refer. In his 1928 commentary on Deutero-Isaiah, Torrey begins by arguing that the occurrence of לכורש in Isa. 45.1 is anomalous and breaks the 3|3 meter of the verse and of those following it (Torrey 1928: 40-41) and it therefore reflects the hand of a later writer. To prepare the way for this later insertion, the same interpolator added a second gloss in the previous verse (Isa. 44.28a). Indeed, since many commentators (including Duhm) consider 44.28b a later insertion, Torrey considers the entire verse suspect and the work of the later interpolator. Looking back on this analysis, biblical scholars today no longer regard emendations based *metri causa* to be strong arguments. Even the question of

---

  [*]   It is my pleasure and privilege to contribute to this volume of essays in honor of Dr Huffmon, who has not only been a long-time mentor and friend but fellow minister in the 'coastlands' of the presbytery of northern New Jersey.

1.   Cyrus was born c. 590 of a Persian father and a Median mother.

2.   This is notwithstanding the announcement of Josiah's name by the man of God from Judah against the altar at Bethel in 1 Kgs 13.2 (fulfilled in 2 Kgs 23.16-18). Most interpreters see evidence here of Deuteronomic redaction.

3.   See, e.g., Baltzer 2001: 223, who views the names as coming from Deutero-Isaiah himself. Even the conservative scholar R.K. Harrison felt compelled to view the occurrences as textual glosses (Harrison 1969: 794-95).

whether meter exists in the Hebrew Bible (as a characteristic feature) is a highly disputed one at the present time.[4] One must also take into consideration Torrey's overall program in his understanding of Deutero-Isaiah. He argues for the unity of chs. 40–66 (including chs. 34–35) coming out of a Palestinian milieu in the late post-exilic period (1928: 53). In order to do so, he not only argues against the references to Cyrus's name but also against the references to 'Babylon' and 'Chaldea' in Isa. 43.14, 48.14 and 20, thereby removing any clear linguistic connections to a Babylonian setting. In Torrey's view, these latter occurrences are also insertions by the same interpolator. Needless to say, Torrey's emendations are far too many for most scholars today to be comfortable with and it appears that the theory is shaping the text more than the text the theory.

Another interpreter who is often cited to justify the excision of the Cyrus cognomen is James D. Smart, whose commentary is remarkably similar in its conclusions to Torrey's. He too suggests that chs. 40–66 (including only ch. 35) are a unity and come out of Judah in approximately 550–538 BCE (Smart 1965: 32). Smart argues that the two instances of Cyrus's name represent later insertions (early fifth century) that were added when the notion of Cyrus as great benefactor of the Jews would have been prevalent and an 'obvious' fulfillment of the text. Arguing more on theological grounds, he holds that the Cyrus insertions represent an unnecessary historicizing of what is essentially an eschatological prophecy of a totalizing character. The insertions actually confuse the unity of Deutero-Isaiah and muddy the waters, for Cyrus does not and could not fulfill all the expectations raised in the text. The acts of the Persian king do not 'prove to all men that Yahweh was the only true God (Isa. 45.6)' (Smart 1965: 120). How is it conceivable that all nations would bow down and pray to Cyrus and utter the words 'God is with you alone, and there is no other' (45.14) (Smart 1965: 121)? Concerning 44.27-28 specifically, Smart believes these two verses are later insertions because the climax of the pericope has already been achieved at v. 26. He believes the two verses are incongruent, repetitive and out of place in the development of the oracle. Moreover, לכורש in 45.1 exceeds the line length of the bicolon verse. Like Torrey, Smart also believes the references to Babylon/Chaldea in 43.14, 48.14 and 20 are later insertions. While not employing the argument from meter, he appears unnecessarily rigid in discounting any possibility of a historical framework within which eschatological language works. The question is not *either/or* but *both/and* and Smart is not even sensitive to the possibility of hyperbolic language.[5] Historical events are often the inspiration for eschatological and apocalyptic visioning. In any case, like Torrey, Smart appears overly programmatic in his approach to the material.

---

4. See the comments of Berlin 1996: 302, 308-309; see also Longman 1982. In a careful analysis of the syntax, versification and structure of the Cyrus oracle, Fokkelman (1997: 315) demonstrates quite the opposite: that is, that the presence of the name of Cyrus is necessary to the careful balance of rhyme, alliteration and assonance in 45.1a! The same is true for the Cyrus name in 44.28, although he does not hesitate to delete 44.26c on similar grounds.

5. He presses the *all* in 'he (Cyrus) shall carry out *all* my purpose' (Isa. 44.28) much too far (Smart 1965: 117).

By contrast, the vast majority of scholars accept the naming of Cyrus as original with the Hebrew text and crucial for the dating of Deutero-Isaiah.[6] Whybray's comments (1975: 20) are typical of this view:

> In the case of chapters 40–55 the occurrences (44.28; 45.1) of the name Cyrus, which can only refer to the first Persian king of that name, the conqueror of Babylon in 539 BC (or, in theory, to one of his successors) are not, as was suggested quite arbitrarily by Torrey, later additions to the text, but rather pointers to the interpretation of these chapters as a whole.

Most commentators agree that even if the Cyrus name is removed from the text, the image of Cyrus as raised up by Yahweh is clearly in view in the key chapters of Isaiah 40–48 (Blenkinsopp 2002: 248). Most see the allusions to a great conqueror from the east ('Who has roused a victor from the east', Isa. 41.2) and the north ('I stirred up one from the north', Isa. 41.25) as references to the early military successes of Cyrus (Childs 2001: 318). Some have even tried to connect these allusions to specific events in the career of the Persian king. Isaiah 41.1-5, for example, points to Cyrus's conquest of Sardis in 547 BCE (see Blenkinsopp 2002: 92; Baltzer 2001: 30 n. 153; Westermann 1969: 4).[7] It is also quite clear that when the reader arrives at the naming of Cyrus in 44.28 and 45.1, one is arriving at the very center and climax of the entire section of chs. 40–48 (see Childs 2001: 348; Blenkinsopp 2002: 92). Thus, a number of scholars have pointed out that the very mention of the Persian king *by name* is crucial to the entire flow of the prophetic argument and cannot therefore be easily excised from the passage. Yahweh frustrates the omens and prognostications of the Babylonian wise men (Isa. 44.25) but 'confirms the word of his servant and fulfills the predictions of his messengers' (44.26) and to prove that beyond a shadow of a doubt, Yahweh literally names the human instrument of his deliverance![8]

If most scholars accept the naming of Cyrus as part of the original prophecy, it becomes a primary datum for locating Deutero-Isaiah in its historical context.[9] In chs. 40–48, the early allusions point the reader to Cyrus's accomplishments *in the past*, while the later references are predictions of his conquest of Babylon *in the future*: 'The LORD loves him; he *shall* perform his purpose upon Babylon, and his

---

6.   See, e.g., Seitz 2001: 315. This does not prevent the same commentators from excising other portions of the Cyrus oracle when they do not make literary or theological sense. Isa. 44.28b is commonly deleted or inserted into 44.26 (cf. Muilenberg 1956: 520-21; Westermann 1969: 152-53; Whybray 1975: 104).

7.   See also the rather extreme but now unaccepted interpretations of Sydney Smith (1944: 49-75).

8.   'Second Isaiah did not play it safe by hiding behind theological generalities. He responded with specificity and poignancy: God has chosen *Cyrus*' (Hanson 1995: 98 [emphasis in original]).

9.   There are those, of course, who accept the originality of the Cyrus name but believe the entire prophecy (or at least much of it) comes from a later post-exilic period. Coggins argues from ideological, sociological and historical reasons that Deutero-Isaiah may not have emanated from a 'hypothetical' exilic situation in Babylon but simply reflects such an ideological *Tendenz* from a later period (Coggins 1998).

arm *shall be* against the Chaldeans' (48.14b [my emphasis]). Thus, the *termini a quo* and *ad quem* are usually assessed at 550–539 BCE, the last decade of the Neo-Babylonian empire (Blenkinsopp 2002: 93). According to Whybray:

> Since Deutero-Isaiah regards him [Cyrus] as already a great conqueror, the prophet's career must fall within the years 550–538. Further precision, however, is hardly attainable. Deutero-Isaiah himself, in some of his oracles, regarded the capture of Babylon as imminent, but the actual event may have been delayed somewhat longer than he anticipated. (Whybray 1975: 23)

A corollary of this assessment is that most scholars therefore understand these later Cyrus prophecies as predictive in some sense. S.R. Driver reflects this view:

> The prophecy opens at some date between 549 and 538: for the conquest of Babylon is sill future; but the union of the Medes with the Persians appears to have already taken place. It introduces us therefore to the time while Cyrus is pursuing his career of conquest in N.W. and Central Asia. The prophet's eye marks him in the distance as the coming deliverer of his nation: he stimulates the flagging courage of the people by pointing to his successes (41$^{2-4}$), and declares that he is God's appointed agent, both for the overthrow of the Babylonian empire and for the restoration of the chosen people to Palestine. (Driver 1972: 231)

As if to make himself perfectly clear, he adds, 'It need only be added (for purposes of precluding misconception) that this view of its date and authorship in no way impairs the theological value of the prophecy, or reduces it to a *vaticinium ex eventu*' (Driver 1972: 243).

The only question remaining is how much earlier than Cyrus' defeat of Babylon were chs. 40–48 of Deutero-Isaiah composed. At the early end of the spectrum, Driver cites A. Dillmann, who believes that chs. 40–45 were written during the height of Cyrus's successes in 545 BCE (Driver 1972: 244). Many scholars mention 540 as a year but only in a rather general manner. Some suggest more specifically the spring of 539 BCE, just six months or so before the fall of Babylon in October when Cyrus invaded the Diyala plains region east of Babylon: 'It is presumably during the time that Cyrus had occupied the Diyala Plain that those Jews exiled in Babylon began to sense the hand of God in shaping this unexpected change in world destiny' (Hoglund 2000: 306).

T. Cuyler Young suggests that Isaiah may have found inspiration in certain anti-Nabonidus propaganda circulated by the Persians in Babylon in the years prior to the taking of the city (Young 1992; 1988: 36-37). This would have taken place some time between 547 and 539 when Cyrus was engaged in campaigns to the east and northeast of Babylon.[10] Morton Smith writes that 'Cyrus was famous for his use of subversion and is commonly thought to have used it for his capture of Babylon' (M. Smith 1963: 418). Thus, he believes (as Young) that the Cyrus oracles in Isaiah 40–48 received their 'inspiration' from 'propaganda put out in Babylonia by

---

10. Though our sources are silent about these years of Cyrus's career, Young argues that this is a reasonable conclusion (1988: 35-36).

Cyrus' agents' (M. Smith 1963: 417).[11] In his recent commentary, Blenkinsopp also sees Isaiah 40–48 against this backdrop:

> Read in the context of international events, Isa 40–48 emerges as the Judean version of current anti-Babylonian and pro-Persian propaganda...both the biblical text and the [Cyrus] Cylinder reflect pro-Persian propaganda circulating in the Near East, including the various ethnic groups settled in Babylonia and in the city of Babylon itself during the decade before the fall of the city. (Blenkinsopp 2002: 207, 249)

It is clear that conditions were ripe for such propaganda early on. There are indications that Babylon had been Cyrus's ultimate target as early as 547. Young writes, 'As already suggested, *strategically* Cyrus' conquest of Babylon began with the campaign against Lydia, which resulted in the increased isolation of Mesopotamia' (Young 1992: 36 [my emphasis]). Citing several Persian incursions into Babylonian territory as early as 547, Amélie Kuhrt concludes, 'Taking this together... should perhaps encourage us to see the Persian moves against Babylon as a much more protracted affair, involving perhaps several attacks on the area to the north east of Babylonia and the establishment of Persian control of important routes, especially the Diyala' (Kuhrt 1988: 123). We know that by 543 Nabonidus had already returned to the city from Teima to begin preparations for war with Cyrus (Dandamaev 1989: 41; Hoglund 2000: 306). Among the texts cited as evidence for propaganda is the so-called 'Verse Account of Nabonidus', an Akkadian inscription which Dandamaev describes as a pamphlet-like poem intended for public circulation that criticizes the last Babylonian ruler of all sorts of crimes against the gods and people (*ANET*: 312-15). In addition, there is also the famous Cyrus Cylinder whose first part accuses Nabonidus of neglect of the worship of Marduk and oppression of the people (*ANET*: 315-16). While these texts are later than the fall of Babylon, it is generally accepted that they reflect earlier propaganda either of Cyrus or the anti-Nabonidus sentiment of the Marduk priesthood (M. Smith 1963: 415, 418).[12] It is well-known that this last Babylonian king was resented for his devotion to the worship of the moon-god Sin and his neglect of Babylon's patron deity.[13]

Much of the foregoing revolves around the issue of the relationship of the Cyrus Cylinder to the Cyrus oracles of Deutero-Isaiah and there are indeed some rather uncanny verbal parallels between the two. For example, when Yahweh speaks in Isa. 45.4 of electing Cyrus as his instrument, 'For the sake of my servant Jacob, and Israel my chosen, *I call you by your name*', this is often related to the Cylinder's

---

11. While holding to the general premise, Smith seems to suggest that the propaganda campaign took place much closer to the time of the fall of Babylon, probably within the year 539.

12. But note the cautions of Dandamaev: 'Almost all the texts, however, which praise Cyrus, have the character of propagandistic writings and demand a very critical approach, as they were composed by Babylonian priests at a time subsequent to the fall of their country to the Persians, at the command, either of their new king, or of some of his following' (Dandamaev 1989: 53; see also Kuhrt 1988: 123).

13. The Babylonian Chronicle makes note of his residence in Teima and consequent inability to celebrate the Babylonian *Akitu* festival (cited in Young 1988: 38).

statement that having found Nabonidus unacceptable, Marduk '...scanned and looked through all the countries... Then he *pronounced the name of Cyrus*, king of Anshan, *pronounced his name* to become the ruler of all the world' (*ANET*: 315 [my emphases]). The act of grasping the hand in Isa. 45.1, 'Thus says the LORD to his anointed, to Cyrus, *whose right hand I have grasped* to subdue nations before him', is often connected with the text, '[Marduk] scoured all the lands for a friend, seeking for the upright prince whom *it would have to take his hand*' (*DOTT* 92). Scholars have seen a reference here to the Babylonian New Year's festival where the king annually seizes the hand of Bel in a cultic ritual to renew the kingship from the gods. Most commentators, however, agree with Kittel's initial assessment that neither text is dependent upon the other but that each draws upon well-known traditions of Babylonian court protocol and ceremony (Kittel 1898; Whybray 1975: 105; Childs 2001: 350). M. Smith disagrees, believing that the literary allusions are much too specific and must therefore depend directly on propaganda materials circulated prior to the fall of Babylon (so also Blenkinsopp 2002: 249).[14]

The use of propaganda is judged to explain in part the surprisingly swift defeat of Babylon in 539, the most important city of the world during that period.[15] It has been suggested that in addition to Nabonidus's lack of support, the city was handed over to Cyrus's forces with the cooperation of the Marduk priesthood. The same type of thing had already occurred when the Persian ruler had conquered the kingdom of the Medes in 550. The Median general Harpagus, having been duly insulted and alienated from Astyages, conspired with the nobility and went over to the side of Cyrus in the very first battle.

Cyrus's fame may have spread as early as 556 BCE. Young mentions a certain text of Nabonidus which refers to a dream he had in the first year of his reign predicting the end of the Median empire (Young 1988: 30-32). In it, the gods Marduk and Sin stand before Nabonidus and the former deity commands him to build a temple for Sin in Harran in upper Mesopotamia. The king hesitates, stating that the Medes are presently attacking the city and their army is very great. Then Marduk replies, 'The *Umman-manda* [i.e. the Medes] of whom you spoke, they, their country and all the kings, their allies, shall cease to exist!' (Oppenheim 1956: 250). After the narrative of the dream itself, Nabonidus goes on to speak of its fulfillment:

14. Smith finds it 'incredible' that the Persian document might be dependent upon Deutero-Isaiah. Nor does he believe that Deutero-Isaiah can be dependent upon the Cyrus Cylinder since he believes that it was written before the fall of Babylon and is therefore not *ex eventu* prophecy (M. Smith 1963: 417). At the end of his article, Smith cites Elias Bickerman 'who suggests that the source of the material common to II Isaiah and the Cyrus inscription may have been a Persian prophecy promising Babylon to Cyrus in the name of Ahura Mazda, the creator of heaven and earth' (420).

15. Dandamaev describes the city as having had a population of 200,000 and being very well fortified with a surrounding moat and double walls of 12 and 22 feet in thickness and 26 and 36 feet in height (Dandamaev 1989: 45). Cyrus would later write on his cylinder that he entered Babylon 'without any battle' (*ANET*: 315).

> And indeed when the third year came to pass, he [Marduk] made rise against them
> Cyrus, king of Anshan, his young servant, and he [Cyrus] scattered the numerous
> *Umman-manda* with his small army and captured Astyages, king of the *Umman-manda* and brought him in fetters into his [Cyrus's] land. (Oppenheim 1956: 250)

Young suggests the following chronology by bringing into consideration the Baby-lonian Chronicle, which dates the war with Media in the king's sixth year (Young 1988: 32). If taken at face value, the dream of Nabonidus would have taken place in his first year of 556, the Medo-Persian war then breaking out in his third year of 553. With an ongoing campaign taking two to three years, the war would have ended in 550 per the Chronicle. Young notes, 'Isaiah's tone, if not his words, is reminiscent of the Dream Text of Nabonidus' (Young 1988: 37). More importantly, Blenkinsopp adds:

> As at other great turning points in the history of the Near East, there seems to have
> been a flurry of prophetic activity during the declining years of the Neo-Babylo-nian Empire; compare the prophecies addressed to Zimri-lim of the kingdom of
> Mari on the eve of its conquest by Hammurapi in the early seventeenth century
> BCE more than a millennium earlier. (Blenkinsopp 2002: 206-207)

Cyrus's fame after his death in 530 became legendary in the ancient world. Within a decade's time, he had conquered three of the four great empires of the time from Media in the east to Lydia in the west, creating a kingdom unlike any before it.[16] Through his son, Cambyses, Persia would eventually include the fourth great king-dom of Egypt in its vast empire. At his death, Cyrus died still fighting to expand his empire against the tribe of the Massagetae to the northeast (Herodotus, *Hist.* 1.201-14). If not altogether historical, the founder legends of his origins testify to his significance (see Briant 2002: 14-16). Among the Greeks, the Persian king was greatly admired both for his achievements and his character as a righteous man (see Baltzer 2001: 223-24). Xenophon's *Cyropaedia* is a work based on Cyrus's life as a model of the ideal ruler. Alexander himself is said to have visited Cyrus's tomb and ordered that it be restored. But Cyrus's fame must have spread during his own lifetime with the defeat of Asytages and the Medes in 550 and the defeat of Croesus of Lydia and all of Asia Minor c. 547. The only major kingdom remaining in the immediate orbit of Persia was Babylonia. To have risen to such great power in so short a time from relative obscurity as prince of the Persian tribe of the Pasargadae must have sent reverberations throughout the entire ancient Near East.

BIBLIOGRAPHY

Baltzer, Klaus
    2001   *Deutero-Isaiah: A Commentary on Isaiah 40–55* (Hermeneia; trans. M. Kohl;
                Minneapolis: Fortress Press).
Berlin, Adele
    1996   'Introduction to Hebrew Poetry', in *NIB*: IV, 301-15.

16. Young (1988: 43) observes, 'Equally challenging was the fact that no king of the Near East had ever ruled so much, or been so powerful as Cyrus'.

Blenkinsopp, Joseph
2002   *Isaiah 40–55* (AB, 19A; New York: Doubleday).
Boardman, J., N.G.L. Hammond, D.M. Lewis and M. Ostwald (eds.)
1988   *Cambridge Ancient History Volume Four: Persia, Greece, and the Western Mediterranean* (Cambridge: Cambridge University Press, 2nd edn).
Briant, Pierre
2002   *From Cyrus to Alexander: A History of the Persian Empire* (trans. P.T. Daniels; Winona Lake, IN: Eisenbrauns).
Calvin, John
1948   *Commentary on the Book of the Prophet Isaiah*, III (trans. W. Pringle; 4 vols.; Grand Rapids: Eerdmans).
Childs, Brevard
2001   *Isaiah* (OTL; Louisville, KY: Westminster/John Knox Press).
Coggins, Richard J.
1998   'Do We Still Need Deutero-Isaiah?' *JSOT* 80: 77-92.
Dandamaev, M.A.
1989   *A Political History of the Achaemenid Empire* (trans. W.J. Vogelsang; Leiden: E.J. Brill).
Driver, S.R.
1972   *An Introduction to the Literature of the Old Testament* (repr., Gloucester, MA: Peter Smith).
Fokkelman, J.P.
1997   'The Cyrus Oracle (Isaiah 44,24–45,7) from the Perspectives of Syntax, Versification and Structure', in J.T.A.G.M. van Ruiten and Marc Vervenne (eds.), *Studies in the Book of Isaiah: Festschrift Willem A.M. Beuken* (Leuven: Peeters): 303-23.
Hanson, Paul D.
1995   *Isaiah 40–66* (Louisville, KY: John Knox Press).
Harrison, R.K.
1969   *Introduction to the Old Testament* (Grand Rapids: Eerdmans).
Hoglund, Kenneth G.
2000   'Cyrus', in D.N. Freedman (ed.), *Eerdmans Dictionary of the Bible* (Grand Rapids: Eerdmans): 305-306.
Kittel, R.
1898   'Cyrus und Deuterojesaja', *ZAW* 18: 149-62.
Kuhrt, Amélie
1988   'Babylonia From Cyrus to Xerxes', in Boardman, Hammond, Lewis and Ostwald (eds.) 1988: 112-38.
Longman, Tremper
1982   'A Critique of Two Recent Metrical Systems', *Bib* 63: 503-10.
Muilenberg, James
1956   'The Book of Isaiah: Chapters 40–66', in G.A. Buttrick (ed.), *Interpreter's Bible* (12 vols.; New York: Abingdon Press): III, 381-773.
Oppenheim, A. Leo
1956   *The Interpretation of Dreams in the Ancient Near East with a Translation of an Assyrian Dream Book* (Transactions of the American Philosophical Society, New Series, 46, Part 3; Philadelphia: American Philosophical Society).

Seitz, Christopher R.
    2000   'The Book of Isaiah 40–66', in *NIB*: VI, 309-552.
Smart, James D.
    1965   *History and Theology in Second Isaiah: A Commentary on Isaiah 35, 40–66*
                (London: Epworth Press).
Smith, Morton
    1963   'II Isaiah and the Persians', *JAOS* 83: 415-21.
Smith, Sydney
    1944   *Isaiah Chapters XL–LV: Literary Criticism and History* (Schweich Lectures;
                Oxford: Oxford University Press).
Torrey, C.C.
    1928   *The Second Isaiah: A New Interpretation* (New York: Charles Scribner's
                Sons).
Westermann, Claus
    1969   *Isaiah 40–66* (trans. D.M.G. Stalker; OTL; Philadelphia: Westminster Press).
Whybray, R.N.
    1975   *Isaiah 40–66* (NCBC; Grand Rapids: Eerdmans).
Young, T. Cuyler
    1988   'The Early History of the Medes and the Persians and the Achaemenid Em-
                pire to the Death of Cambyses', in Boardman, Hammond, Lewis and Ostwald
                (eds.) 1988: 1-52.
    1992   'Cyrus', in *ABD*, VI: 1231-32.

WHAT DID ELIJAH DO TO HIS MANTLE?
THE HEBREW ROOT *GLM*

John Kaltner

Elijah's mantle (*'adderet*) is mentioned five times in the Hebrew Bible (1 Kgs 19.13, 19; 2 Kgs 2.8, 13, 14), and in each case it is touched or somehow manipulated by a person, usually Elijah himself. In 1 Kgs 19.13 he uses it to cover his face (*wayyālet*) as he stands outside a cave near Mt Horeb. Six verses later he throws it (*wayyašlēk*) over Elisha while the latter is plowing. The third reference to Elijah's mantle, which will be the focus of this essay, describes him taking (*wayyiqqaḥ*) the cloak and doing something to it prior to striking the waters of the Jordan, which then divide, allowing him and Elisha to pass over on dry land (2 Kgs 2.8). The Hebrew verb used in this verse to describe what Elijah does to his garment is *yiglōm*, and it will be discussed in detail below. Immediately after this scene Elijah is taken up into the sky in a chariot of fire. The final two references to the mantle are found in 2 Kgs 2.13 and 14 when Elisha first picks it up (*wayyārem*) and then takes it (*wayyiqqaḥ*) in order to strike the waters of the Jordan as Elijah had done earlier.

This essay is concerned with the meaning of the verb *yiglōm*. What does Elijah do to his mantle as he and Elisha stand on the bank of the Jordan? A perusal of commentaries and translations suggests that the answer to that question is a very obvious one: Elijah rolled up or bundled together his mantle prior to striking the water with it. This is the way the verb is typically rendered in translation and there is virtual agreement among commentators that the word describes the act of rolling up or bundling something.[1] But study of the Hebrew root *glm* and the evidence from comparative Semitic lexicography suggest that there may be another meaning for the verb that better fits the context of the passage.

Only two other words etymologically related to the verb in 2 Kgs 2.8 are found in the Hebrew Bible, and neither is particularly helpful in explaining what Elijah did to his mantle. The plural form of the noun *gᵉlōm* appears in Ezek. 27.24 (*gᵉlômê tᵉkēlet*), where it is part of a list of items traded on the international market and is usually translated as 'clothing' or 'garments'. The other word is *gōlem* in Ps. 139.16, which is usually rendered 'embryo, unformed substance'. This latter word and meaning are sometimes cited as support for the translation 'bundle together' in

---

1. Most commentators do not emend the text and see the verb as coming from the root *g-l-m*. A rare exception is Gray (1963: 422), who translates it as 'rolled up' from the root *g-l-l* but acknowledges that this reading is 'unsupported by any version'.

2 Kgs 2.8, but the fact that the verb in 2 Kings 2 is a *hapax legomenon* makes it extremely difficult to ascertain its meaning through simply appealing to potentially related words within Hebrew. The problem is compounded by the lack of contextual clues in the passage that might assist the reader in determining the precise nature of Elijah's action—as he stands at the Jordan and takes the mantle in his hand there is no way of knowing what he might do next.

Comparative Semitic lexicography offers a promising, if rarely traveled, avenue to uncovering the meaning of this Hebrew verb. The only Semitic language with a relevant etymological equivalent to Hebrew *glm* is Arabic, which has the root *jalama*.[2] The *HALOT* entry for the Hebrew root lists this Arabic cognate (it is the only cognate listed), but it does so in a somewhat imprecise way and it is clear that the Arabic root is not taken into account as the editors attempt to establish the meaning of the usage in 2 Kgs 2.8. I propose that the Arabic evidence has direct relevance for the Hebrew and that proper attention to it can shed new light on Elijah's actions prior to crossing the Jordan.

The meaning of the Arabic verb *jalama* is listed as 'to cut off' in *HALOT*, but this is not a completely accurate reflection of what is contained in the Arabic dictionaries.[3] The verb can convey this sense, particularly when it is used in relation to shearing the wool off an animal, but the first meaning contained in the lexicons is the more general 'to cut'.[4] In other words, it does not describe only the act of cutting something in order to remove it or detach it, as the citation in *HALOT* suggests, but it can refer to any act of cutting. The difference is a crucial one when considering the possible relevance of the Arabic root for the Hebrew one. The meaning 'to cut off' does not smoothly fit the context of 2 Kgs 2.8. What would it mean to say that Elijah 'cut off' his mantle? The image runs counter to common sense and experience since people normally take off, not cut off, their garments. But to say that he cut his mantle makes perfect sense and actually fits the context better than the meaning 'to roll up, bundle together'.[5]

Elijah's mantle has at least two functions in the biblical text. On the one hand, it is the vehicle through which power and authority are transferred from Elijah to Elisha. This is clearly seen in the role the garment plays in their relationship. 'The mantle which is cast on Elisha and which provides a magical act of Elisha's

---

2.   See Cohen 1993: 129; the root does not exist in Akkadian or Ugaritic, and the meanings given to it in post-Biblical Hebrew all derive from the presumed meaning 'to roll up' for the verb as well as the meaning 'embryo, formless shape' for *gōlem*. See Jastrow (1950: 222, 250) for a discussion of these words in the post-Biblical literature. Meanings related to 'cut' are attested in Ethiopic, where Tigre *gälma* means 'break off, cut into pieces' (Leslau 1991: 191). It will be mentioned below (see n. 5) that the same meaning also appears to be present in Punic.

3.   *HALOT*, I: 194.

4.   The verb can also mean 'to cut off flesh from a bone'. See Lane (1980: II, 445) and Ibn Manẓūr (1968: XII, 102-103); the latter dictionary, originally compiled in the fourteenth century, is a particularly comprehensive and valuable resource for Arabic lexicography.

5.   The Arabic meaning 'cut off' has been cited recently to translate the previously enigmatic word *hglm* in Punic. According to Krahmalkov the phrase *bd 'štrt 'lm hglm* means 'Mute Bostar, the shearer' (2000: 240).

adoption as an apprentice and servant of Elijah, changes in the story of Elijah's ascent heavenwards to a mythical sign of Elisha's confirmation as Elijah's heir' (Weisman 1981: 234; cf. Cogan and Tadmor 1988: 34).

The second function of the mantle is hinted at in Weisman's reference to a 'magical act'. There is an element of the magical to Elijah's cloak that is most fully expressed in the scene at the Jordan when it is the instrument by which he is able to defy the laws of nature and part the waters of the river.[6] Thomas Overholt has studied stories that describe events he refers to as 'acts of power', which he defines as 'reported actions of prophetic figures which in their narrative context appear somewhat unusual, extraordinary or miraculous' (Overholt 1982: 3). More than sixty such acts of power have been identified by Overholt in 1 and 2 Kings and the prophetic corpus, and only a small group of them (most of them in the Elijah/Elisha cycle) abrogate the laws of nature by describing feats that are normally impossible for a person to do. Not surprisingly, Elijah's action in 2 Kgs 2.8 falls under this latter heading (Overholt 1982: 23).

Elijah's parting of the waters of the Jordan clearly qualifies as an act of power, but how did the verb *yiglōm* acquire the meaning 'roll up', especially since there is no solid lexicographic support for it? The reason may well be Elijah's identification with Moses, another figure in the Hebrew Bible who was able to stop the flow of water. Moses' staff is mentioned repeatedly in the Bible: when he is first called by God (Exod. 4.17); when the plagues are sent on Egypt (Exod. 9.23; 10.13); during the battle with the Amalekites (Exod. 17.9); at the waters of Meribah (Num. 20.8-11); and, most germane to our discussion, at the crossing of the sea during the Israelites' escape from Egypt (Exod. 14.16). In each of those passages, he wields his staff (usually at God's request) in a way that allows him to perform some 'act of power' that is beyond the ability of a normal person to accomplish. Scholars have often commented on the underlying dimension of magic in many of these texts, where Moses' staff appears to be the equivalent of a magician's wand (Tarragon 1995: 2075).

The similarity between their two acts naturally leads to an association between the staff of Moses and Elijah's mantle, which both have an instrumental function in an act of power.[7] But the connection between the two should remain on the functional level and not result in an attempt to interpret Elijah's mantle as somehow physically resembling or duplicating Moses' staff. This may be what has led to the translation of the Hebrew verb *yiglōm* as 'roll up, bundle together'. According to that view, Elijah's cloak, as a true replica of Moses' staff, must be shaped in a way

6. Its magical quality is expressed in Fohrer's designation of Elijah's cloak as a *Wundermantel* that can divide waters (1968: 11). Fohrer calls attention to the same quality in his discussion of 1 Kgs 19.19-21, where he says Elisha is empowered with *magnetischer Kraft* after Elijah's mantle is thrown over him (1968: 115).

7. Wilson notes that 'the similarities between Moses and Elijah are obvious and have long been recognized' (1980: 197). A good discussion of the parallels between the Moses story and the Elijah/Elisha traditions is presented by Carroll (1969: 411-15). Other scholars who cite the connection between the two figures include Brueggemann (2000: 294-95), Cohn (2000: 13), Robinson (1976: 23-24) and Wiseman (1993: 195).

that approximates its dimensions, and the easiest way to do that with an article of clothing is to roll it up.[8] The fact that there is an etymological equivalent in Hebrew (*gōlem*) whose meaning 'embryo, formless mass' allows for an improper extension of meaning to 'roll up' only facilitates the attempt to establish a physical resemblance between Elijah's mantle and Moses' staff.

A meaning for *yiglōm* based on its Arabic cognate's well-attested meaning 'to cut' is on a firmer foundation and it preserves the magical element that many commentators have noted is a central component of the scene: 'In its broadest sense, "magic" is a form of communication involving the supernatural world in which an attempt is made to affect the course of present and/or future events by means of ritual actions (especially ones which involve the symbolic imitation of what the practitioner wants to happen)' (Scurlock 1992: 464). By cutting his mantle, Elijah rends it and splits it apart in a way that anticipates what will soon happen to the waters of the Jordan. This dimension of his action is lost if his mantle is rolled up rather than cut.

In addition, two problems are resolved if the verb is translated as 'cut' rather than 'roll up'. In the first place, there is the question of why Elijah would want to roll up his mantle and what such an action would result in. The suggestion put forward above that the translation 'roll up' is due to a desire to realize a physical similarity between the mantle and Moses' staff is a plausible explanation that has no basis in the text. It might explain the motives of translators, but it sheds no light on Elijah's purpose. Furthermore, even if we adopt the meaning 'roll up' for the verb, what does it mean? Can a rolled up mantle really look like or represent a staff, or will it just look like a rolled up mantle? Either way, why does Elijah have to give it that shape before hitting the water with it? Translating the verb as 'cut' has the advantage of establishing a connection between the prophet's manipulation of the mantle and the act of power he is about to perform, a connection that is not possible with the translation 'roll up'.

Translating *yiglōm* as 'cut' also helps to explain a curious omission in the passage. After Elijah is taken from him in the chariot of fire, Elisha retrieves the mantle and returns to the Jordan: 'Wielding the mantle which had fallen from Elijah, he struck the water in his turn and said, "Where is the LORD, the God of Elijah?" When Elisha struck the water it divided and he crossed over' (1 Kgs 2.14 NRSV). The first part of this verse is an almost word-for-word repetition of what Elijah had done six verses earlier when he and Elisha were on the other side of the river. In the earlier scene, three verbs are used to describe Elijah's actions: *yiqqah*, *yiglōm* and *yakkeh*. In v. 14 the second verb is not present; Elisha takes the mantle and he hits the water, but he does not *yiglōm*. The omission may be a scribal mistake, but it is also possible that the verb is not there because of the meaning it conveys. If it means 'roll up' or something similar, we should expect to find it repeated in v. 14 since it was an integral part of the act of power that Elijah performed in v. 8 that must now be re-enacted by Elisha so that he can cross the river. The double reference to the

---

8. Tarragon (1995: 2076) makes this connection when, in the context of a discussion of rods with magical powers, he states that Elijah's 'rolled cloak' permitted him to cross the Jordan.

mantle falling to the ground when Elijah ascends (vv. 13, 14) also supports the inclusion of the verb 'to roll up' here since it suggests that the mantle is no longer in the exact shape it had assumed after Elijah rolled it up. But if the verb means 'cut' there is no reason to repeat it. Once Elijah has cut the mantle it stays cut and there is no need for Elisha to cut it again. This translation therefore resolves the problem of the missing verb.

The prophetic drama that Elijah enacts at the Jordan River, like many such acts, contains a level of ambiguity: 'There may be some sense in which the performance of a drama represents an escalation in expression, but it is by no means always an escalation in clarity' (Stacey 1990: 266). In this instance, while the meaning of the event is fairly clear, there is a rarely noticed lack of clarity in the words used to describe the event. The lexicographic evidence suggests that the usual way of understanding what Elijah did to his mantle has little support and might be in need of revision.

BIBLIOGRAPHY

Brueggemann, Walter
    2000   *1 & 2 Kings* (Macon, GA: Smyth & Helwys).
Carroll, Robert P.
    1969   'The Elijah-Elisha Sagas: Some Remarks on Prophetic Succession in Ancient Israel', *VT* 19: 400-15.
Cogan, Mordechai, and Hayim Tador
    1988   *II Kings* (AB, 11; Garden City, NY: Doubleday).
Cohen, David
    1993   *Dictionnaire des racines sémitiques*, III (8 vols.; Leuven: Peeters [1993–99]).
Cohn, Robert L.
    2000   *2 Kings* (Berit Olam; Collegeville, MN: Liturgical Press).
Fohrer, Georg
    1968   *Die symbolischen Handlugen der Propheten* (ATANT, 54; Zürich: Zwingli Verlag, 2nd edn).
Gray, John
    1963   *I & II Kings* (OTL; Philadelphia: Westminster Press).
Ibn Manẓūr
    1968   *Lisān al-'Arab* (15 vols.; Beirut: Dār lil-Ṭibā'a wal-Našr).
Jastrow, Marcus
    1950   *A Dictionary of the Targumim, the Talmud Babli and Yerushalmi and the Midrashic Literature* (New York: Pardes Publishing House).
Krahmalkov, Charles R.
    2000   *Phoenician–Punic Dictionary* (Leuven: Peeters).
Lane, Edward W.
    1980   *Arabic–English Lexicon* (8 vols.; Beirut: Librairie du Liban [first published 1863–93]).
Leslau, Wolf
    1991   *Comparative Dictionary of Ge'ez* (Wiesbaden: Otto Harrassowitz).

Overholt, Thomas W.
  1982   'Seeing is Believing: The Social Setting of Prophetic Acts of Power', *JSOT*
                  23: 3-31.
Robinson, J.
  1976   *The Second Book of Kings* (Cambridge: Cambridge University Press).
Scurlock, J.A.
  1992   'Magic, ANE', in *ABD*, IV: 464-68.
Stacey, W. David
  1990   *Prophetic Drama in the Old Testament* (London: Epworth Press).
Tarragon, Jean-Michel de
  1995   'Witchcraft, Magic, and Divination in Canaan and Ancient Israel', in Jack
                  M. Sasson (ed.), *Civilizations of the Ancient Near East* (4 vols.; New York:
                  Charles Scribner's Sons): III, 2071-81.
Weisman, Ze-ev
  1981   'The Personal Spirit as Imparting Authority', *ZAW* 93: 225-34.
Wilson, Robert R.
  1980   *Prophecy and Society in Ancient Israel* (Philadelphia: Fortress Press).
Wiseman, Donald J.
  1993   *1 and 2 Kings* (Leicester: Inter-Varsity Press).

WORD EVENT IN JEREMIAH: A LOOK AT THE COMPOSITION'S 'INTRODUCTORY FORMULAS'

John I. Lawlor

Speaking of the prophet Jeremiah in a similar volume, this book's honoree observed that 'Jeremiah is the most accessible of the prophets; Jeremiah is the most hidden of the prophets' (Huffmon 1999: 261). Not only might that be said of the prophet, but also of the composition which bears his name. The book exudes reality and authenticity in many of its narrated events; various issues and theological themes are immediately apparent even to the casual reader. But how all the pieces of the 'Jeremiah puzzle' fit together remains enigmatic.[1] Among the issues to which the book draws attention is the 'word event'—the 'happening of the word of Yahweh' to Jeremiah;[2] 44 times[3] the book notifies the reader of this. Minimally, such frequent occurrence of an expression in a written composition qualifies it as a 'repetitious motif'; but less apparent is the overall purpose of this repetition, that is to say, how this repetitious motif functions in the final composition. The motif raises additional questions: Why does the motif occur so often in the book? Why are several different versions of the motif employed? Are certain formulas used in certain types of textual settings? Is there any correlation between certain versions of the expression and the sources commonly accepted as represented in the work's final editing? These are but a few of the issues still unresolved. This revisiting of the subject does not purport to resolve all these nagging questions; rather, it is a modest attempt to acknowledge previous work that has been done on the topic, to introduce into the discussion some fresh questions, and to offer a slightly different approach to understanding better the contribution of this literary phenomenon to the Jeremiah composition.

Previous Analyses of the Problem

Three particular studies have focused attention on the matter: Neumann (1973), Seidl (1979), and Bretón (1987). While each makes its own contribution, the purposes and approaches of each differ significantly, resulting in something less

---

1. See Stulman 1998 for a recent incisive reading of the Jeremiah composition. This work represents the type of analysis that 'teases out of the text' some of its less obvious issues and theological themes.

2. While several different forms of the expression are represented in the text, one of the more commonly used and representative is הדבר אשר היה אל־ירמיהו.

3. The present study is based on the MT. Seventeen of the 44 occurrences have alternative readings or associated text critical matters; 14 of the 17 involve the LXX text. See Lundbom 1999: 62.

than a consensus. Neumann's investigation is confined to Jeremiah 1–25, and thus produces a truncated perspective.

Seidl's study is more comprehensive in approach, including the entire Jeremiah composition. His treatment, however, is marked by its omission of the formulas accompanied by a date line (*Datierungsformel*), having examined these in an earlier study (Seidl 1977). Furthermore, Seidl includes two texts containing formulas which do not fit the pattern of the others: Jer. 46.13 and 50.1 (Seidl 1979: 23, 31).[4]

The most recent study is Bretón's modified dissertation which has as its larger purpose the examination of prophetic formulas relating to the prophetic call and mission; the scope of the work is the entire Hebrew Bible. Chapter 2 of this very useful contribution to the subject focuses particularly on the 'word as event formulas' (Bretón 1987: 31). Breton's two-part organization is based on grammatical phenomena: '*wayyiqtol* form'—first and third persons (Bretón 1987: 34-35); and '*qatal* form'—with or without אשר (Bretón 1987: 36-37). All 44 occurrences in Jeremiah are subsumed under this template, although variations are recognized. Certainly, Bretón's classification based on the use of the *qatal* form of היה is legitimate, but his sub-division based on the presence or absence of an אשר clause seems somewhat simplistic.

These three studies encourage serious contemplation of the Jeremiah formulas; nevertheless, each writer's classification of the various forms generates questions. Neumann's limited focus results in omission of some forms that are located predominately or exclusively in chs. 26–52; Seidl's classification seems more function- than form-oriented, and Bretón's tends to be too generic.

The Formulas

Label	Formula	Use	References
A	אשר היה דבר־יהוה אליו	1×	1.2
B	ויהי דבר־יהוה אלי לאמר	9×	1.4, 11, 13; 2.1; 13.3, 8; 16.1; 18.5; 24.4
C	הדבר אשר היה אל־ירמיהו מאת יהוה	10×	7.1; 11.1; 18.1; 21.1; 30.1; 32.1; 34.1, 8; 35.1; 40.1
D	אשר היה דבר־יהוה אל־ירמיהו	4×	14.1; 46.1; 47.1; 49.34
E	הדבר אשר־היה על־ירמיהו	1×	25.1
F	היה דבר־יהוה אלי	2×	25.3; 32.6
G	היה הדבר הזה מאת יהוה	1×	26.1
H	היה הדבר הזה אל־ירמיה מאת יהוה	2×	27.1; 36.1
I	ויהי דבר־יהוה אל־ירמיהו	12×	28.12; 29.30; 32.26; 33.1, 19, 23; 34.12; 35.12; 36.27; 37.6; 42.7; 43.8
J	אל־ירמיהו היה דבר־יהוה	1×	39.15
K	הדבר אשר היה אל־ירמיהו	1×	44.1

No less than eleven different formulas or variations confront the reader of Jeremiah.[5] Shown above is a list of the formulas in the order in which they first

---

4.   Jer. 46.13 and 50.1 use the expression הדבר אשר דבר יהוה אל־ירמיהו. The piel form of the root דבר is used rather than the noun; the verb היה is not used, either in the prefix or suffix form.

5.   Additional variations will be observed for the following formulas: B 1.13; 13.3 show שנית before לאמר; C 7.1; 11.1; 18.1; 30.1 end with לאמר; D 46.1; 47.1; 49.34 (all OAN uses) conclude

appear in the text; shown also is the number of times the formula is used and the texts where it is located. Five basic patterns emerge, based on common grammatical/syntactical features:

A—אשר היה דבר־יהוה אליו and D—אשר היה דבר־יהוה אל־ירמיהו

These two versions reflect association on the basis of the use of the introductory אשר; furthermore, each refers to the prophet in the third person:

B—ויהי דבר־יהוה אלי לאמר and I—ויהי דבר־יהוה אל־ירמיהו

Only these two versions make use of the prefix form of היה. Although the B formula is first person and the I formula is third person, it should be observed that the former is used exclusively in Jeremiah 1–25 while the latter appears exclusively in chs. 26–52. Collectively, B and I comprise nearly one-half (21/44) of the occurrences of these formulas in the Jeremiah composition:

C—הדבר אשר־היה על־ירמיהו מאת יהוה, E—הדבר אשר היה אל־ירמיהו, and
K—הדבר אשר היה אל־ירמיהו

Characteristic of this pattern is the definite noun followed by the relative clause. E's use of the preposition על is to be observed, although several manuscripts read אל (*BHS*, Jer. 25.1, note). While neither E nor K specify that the word is 'from Yahweh' (מאת יהוה), as does C, the context of each clarifies that such is the case:

G—היה הדבר הזה אל־ירמיה מאת יהוה and H—היה הדבר הזה מאת יהוה

Distinguishing these formulas from the others, but establishing commonality between them, is the adjectival use of the demonstrative in the attributive position. The only difference between the two versions is G's omission of the prepositional phrase אל־ירמיה:[6]

F—אל־ירמיהו היה דבר־יהוה and J—היה דבר־יהוה אלי

The association between these last two forms is less firm than in the preceding four groupings. Common to this pair is the core assertion היה דבר־יהוה. The two first-person uses of the F formula (25.3; 32.6) occur in the context of third-person narration, in which the prophet's assertion concerning the word of Yahweh is reported. The J formula also appears in third-person narration (39.15), but it is the narrator who makes the assertion. The expression היה דבר־יהוה appears precisely in this form elsewhere only in the A/D pairing; but there it follows the particle אשר, which distinguishes that pattern from the present one.

---

with הנביא + the preposition על/אל + nation; F 32.6 ends with לאמר; H 27.1 note spelling of prophet's name as ירמיה; I 29.30; 32.26; 33.19, 23; 35.12 end with לאמר; 33.1 ends with שנית; 34.12 concludes with the prepositional phrase מאת יהוה + לאמר; 37.6 concludes הנביא לאמר; 43.8 ends with בתחפנחס לאמר.

6. The spelling of the prophet's name in the formulas of 27.1 and 28.12 differs from its spelling in other formulas; see also 28.5, 6, 10, 11, 15; 29.1. Holladay (1989: 114) suggests that the spelling of 27.1 and 28.12 may represent a 'later spelling'.

Reduction of the eleven formulas to five seems appropriate but does not address the basic issue of the use of a particular formula in a given context. Stated another way, is insight to be gained from pursuing the possibility of commonality among the texts that use a particular expression or group of expressions? It is to that question that attention is next turned.

The Expressions in Context

It is not possible, given the limitations of the present study, to address all five groupings with respect to the potential function of each in the Jeremiah composition. However, within the guidelines for this work, another, possibly more productive, approach is to focus on the 21/44 texts that make use of the B (9)/I (12) versions—texts in which the prefix form of היה is used.[7] The exclusive use of the first-person B expression in Jeremiah 1–25 coupled with the exclusive use of the third-person I expression in Jeremiah 26–52, already noted above, is a point not to be too quickly dismissed. This restriction of the first-person B expression to chs. 1–25 is consistent first with the proposal, initially put forward by Duhm (1901) and developed by Mowinckel (1914), that the 'A' material of the book is situated in Jeremiah 1–25; it is also consistent with the general consensus that the first scroll, the preparation of which involved Jeremiah as a direct participant (Jer. 36), is imbedded in, though perhaps not synonymous with, that portion of the composition (Lundbom 1999: 93). This is not to suggest, of course, that only those texts to which the B expression is attached are to be viewed as original to Jeremiah or that all of chs. 1–25 is to be understood as 'A' material.

The third-person I expression's use solely in texts of the second half of the book (chs. 26–52) is also deserving of comment. This version appears to be an intentional follow-up to the B version, by virtue of its common pattern; yet it appears to be intentionally distinct from it, by virtue of its use of the third person. It is the combination of this 'distinct-yet-related' association and the distinctive locus of each use that evokes further probing. In addressing the matter of the relationship between the two Jeremiah scrolls (chs. 1–25, 26–52), Stulman argues for a 'formal and definitional discontinuity', but goes on to observe that, '...the data also indicate that the second scroll is essentially dependent upon the first scroll as prolegomenon' (Stulman 1998: 62).

What is striking to this writer is the fact that the sequence of texts employing the B/I pattern begins immediately after the editorial introduction to the entire composition (1.1-3), which uses its own, distinct, form (A). Indeed, the use of B appears three times in the initial chapter: at the beginning of the 'commissioning narrative' (1.4), and at the initiation of each of two vision accounts (1.11, 13) which accompany the 'call scene'. Holladay draws attention to the fact that 'the phrase...covers both verbal and visionary material' (Holladay 1986: 32). The use of the expression

---

7.   Of these 21 occurrences, seven show alternative readings in the LXX; 4/9 uses of the B formula and 3/12 uses of the I formula.

in Jer. 24.4 is also associated with a vision; however, there it introduces a follow-up divine explanation of the vision, rather than introducing the vision itself.

A 'final-form reading' of the Jeremiah composition[8] sees Jeremiah 1 as the foundational component of the composition. As a 'prologue' it is not unusual that it would initiate themes, issues and diction that will be encountered later in the composition and, when encountered, encourage the reader to return to the point of beginning for a reminder of the later text's foundation in the earlier text. It is that dynamic that is here suggested to be operative in the sequence of Jeremiah texts which make use of the B and I expressions.

The B Expression in Jeremiah 1–25[9]

This expression is not unique to Jeremiah; it appears 41 times in Ezekiel[10] and four times in Zechariah.[11] In neither of those books is it exclusive to a particular section of the book or paired with the third-person version (I in Jeremiah), as in Jeremiah. Lundbom comments that the first-person form conveys, 'the impression that Jeremiah is giving direct testimony to a revelatory experience' (Lundbom 1999: 230). Holladay understands the emphasis of the expression somewhat differently, asserting that, 'The phrase carries with it the whole paradoxical experience of the overwhelming inbreaking of God's revelation into the consciousness of the one who is to speak and act for God' (Holladay 1986: 32). Beginning with the prologue occurrences, continuing in the 2.1 use, where it introduces the first macro-structural movement of the book (Stulman 1998: 39; Sweeney 1999: 208) and continuing through the remaining five occurrences (13.3, 8; 16.1; 18.5; 24.4), the phrase conveys a sense of divine invasion into the psyche of the prophet; and through the prophet, into the experience of the nation. Furthermore, each of these contexts takes the reader back to the prologue (1.4-19) in one way or another.

The narrative concerning the linen loincloth employs the expression twice (13.3, 8). In the first instance, subsequent to the prophet's compliance with initial divine directions (introduced by כה־אמר יהוה אלי) to acquire and put on the garment, the expression introduces further, more elaborate, instructions to hide it in a crevice of a rock in Parah (13.3-4).[12] Again, Jeremiah obeys; further divine word calls for

8.   For a brief, but useful, account of scholarship's gradual move toward this literary approach to the book, see Stulman 1998: 25-32.

9.   Neumann (1973: 173-91) suggests that this expression's use in chs. 1–25 signals the divine change of a concrete situation. This proposal is not without its difficulties; in addition to its being too general an observation, one might ask of some of the texts: What has been changed as a result of Jeremiah's encounter with the divine word?

10.   3.16; 6.1; 7.1; 11.14; 12.1, 8, 17, 21, 26; 13.1; 14.2, 12; 15.1; 16.1; 17.1, 11; 18.1; 20.2; 21.1, 6, 13, 23; 22.1, 17, 23; 23.1; 24.1, 15; 25.1; 27.1; 28.1, 11, 20; 30.1; 33.1, 23; 34.1; 35.1; 36.16; 37.15; 38.1. The third-person version (I) is not used in Ezekiel; other versions employing the suffix form of היה are used an additional nine times.

11.   Zech. 4.8; 6.9; 7.4; 8.18. The third-person version (I) is used two times in Zechariah (7.8; 8.1); other versions employing the suffix form of היה are used an additional three times.

12.   Here, as in 1.13, the formula makes use of the feminine ordinal שנית.

retrieval of the loincloth, which is accomplished. The second use in this context introduces the divine explanation of this elaborate procedure (13.8-11). Included in the indictment of the nation is the characteristically Deuteronomic explanation (Brueggemann 1988: 122; Holladay 1986: 394) that 'they have gone after other gods to serve them and to bow down to them' (וילכו אחרי אלהים אחרים לעבדם ולהשתחות להם). This recalls the Jer. 1.16 rhetoric of divine indictment, 'and they burned sacrifices to other gods and bowed down…' (ויקטרו לאלהים אחרים וישתחוו). Reading 1.15 as a divine summons to northern peoples to come against Judah and lay siege against its cities (Lundbom 1999: 243-44; Thompson 1980: 154-55; cf. Holladay 1986: 40), 1.16 then anticipates that Yahweh would 'speak…judgments' against Judah. The linen loincloth incident and the accompanying word from Yahweh (Jer. 13.1-14) can be understood as one such instance. The 'spoiling' of the linen loincloth seems to anticipate the 'spoiling' of the nation. Furthermore, פרתה ('Euphrates', NRSV) as the temporary hiding place for the linen loincloth, appears to function as a double entendre. Most likely, Jeremiah enacted the instructions at 'Parah', a village just a few kilometers northeast of his own Anathoth (Bright 1965: 96; Friebel 1999: 105-107); however, that the term elsewhere in the Hebrew Bible specifies 'Euphrates' seems intended to serve as an allusion to 'the land of the north' from which invasion would come (1.13-15).

Jeremiah 16 records Yahweh's invasion of the prophet's experience by the announcement that he was to remain celibate and without sons or daughters; the B version introduces this message. These instructions are linked to Yahweh's anticipation that the nation would be 'hurled' from its land into a land which it did not know (16.13). While 16.14-15 anticipates restoration, it would be restoration from the 'land of the north' (הדיחם מארץ צפון...אשר). The initiation of such 'northern oriented' rhetoric is located in Jeremiah 1 with emphasis (1.13, 14, 15). Consequently, the celibacy scenario of Jeremiah 16 is best engaged with awareness of its textual roots in the second vision of 1.13-16.

The remaining two texts in Jeremiah 1–25 that make use of the B expression (18.5; 24.4) share a common link to the prologue of 1.4-19 by nuancing the formative 1.10 terminology. There, the first four infinitives set a 'dismantling direction' for Jeremiah's assignment (לנתוש ולנתוץ ולהאביד ולהרוס); however, the final two infinitives (לבנות ולנטוע) anticipate reversal. Furthermore, the last term, ולנטוע, seems particularly intended to reverse לנתוש, the first term, while לבנות relates similarly to לנתוץ (see Holladay 1986: 36-37). In several strategically located texts in both halves of the book (not all appear in conjunction with a use of the B formula) these theologically loaded terms are used in fresh ways, but always with the expectation that the reader will bring an understanding of the commissioning narrative (1.4-10) and its paradigmatic rhetoric to the subsequent text. Brueggemann suggests that 'this range of six verbs provides the essential shape of the book of Jeremiah in its present form (cf. Jer. 18.7-10; 24.6; 31.27-28; 42.10; 45.4)' (Brueggemann 1991: 25-26).

Jeremiah 18 places Jeremiah at the potter's house by Yahweh's direction (18.1-4). After the spoiling of one vessel, the potter remade the clay into a vessel that 'seemed right'. Introduced by the B version, the ensuing expression of sovereign word (דבר, vv. 7, 9) over nations or kingdoms outlines two possible scenarios. The first expresses the divine intention to dismantle a nation or kingdom deserving of judgment—לנתוש ולנתוץ ולהאביד (18.7). Such devastation can be avoided, however, if that nation or kingdom turns from evil. The second considers the opposite situation in which a nation or kingdom might be established—לבנות ולנטוע (18.9). This might be reversed if such nation or kingdom is disobedient to the voice of Yahweh. Five of the six infinitives first encountered in 1.10 are engaged in this word of Yahweh, and they are found in the same sequence. For some, the inclusion of ולהאביד is an 'expansive intrusion' (Holladay 1986: 658), presumably because its presence brings asymmetry to the passage; however, one might rather draw attention to the curious omission of ולהרוס. Additional diction of Jeremiah 1, prominent in this text as well, calls the reader's attention to the appropriateness of reading ch. 18 in light of ch. 1. Two specific examples include the reference to the 'speaking' (דבר; a root used 11 times in Jer. 1) of Yahweh (18.7, 9) concerning 'nations and kingdoms' (גוי...ממלכה, 18.7, 9; cf. 1.10). Holladay, likewise, sees the latter pairing as a 'reflex' of the 1.10 pairing (Holladay 1986: 516).

The commissioning narrative of Jer. 1.4-10, coupled with the two visions (1.11-12, 13-16) and the ensuing challenge and encouragement (1.17-19), clarify the point that the 'work' outlined in the six infinitives of 1.10 would be accomplished as Yahweh 'put his word in Jeremiah's mouth' (1.9), as Jeremiah 'spoke all that Yahweh commanded him' (1.7, 17), and as Yahweh 'watched over his word to accomplish it' (1.12). The word of Yahweh which 'happened to Jeremiah' as recorded in Jer. 18.5-12. theologizes about how that divine word works in relation to the response of nations or kingdoms—Judah, as well as gentile nations. The role of Jeremiah in this process—as anticipated in Jeremiah 1 and reiterated here—is captured in the concluding lines of the paragraph: 'Now speak…saying, "Thus says Yahweh"…' (18.11).

Jeremiah 24.4 reflects a dual association with the prologue. It involves both a vision similar to that in Jeremiah 1 ('What do you see, Jeremiah…?', 1.11, 13), and the nuancing of 1.10 terminology. In a reversal of the direction of the 1.10 rhetoric, Yahweh anticipates a reversal of Judah's captivity in Babylon when he asserts, 'I will build them up (ובניתים) and not overthrow (לא אהרס) and I will plant them (ונטעתים) and not pluck up (לא אתוש)' (24.6). Somewhat unexpected in this context is the slightly different pairing of terms than that found in the initial text. There, נתש is reversed by נטע and נתץ is reversed by בנה; in the present text בנה is seen as the opposite of הרס, while the association between נטע and נתש is retained. The diction of the prologue is not merely reused here; its usage at the close of the first scroll eloquently images a reversal of its initial use.

Each of these Jeremiah 1–25 texts reflects a rhetorical dependence on some aspect of the material in the composition's prologue. They do not represent mere repetition of terminology already employed in Jeremiah 1; rather, each appears to be consciously crafted so as to advance the dynamics of the conversation initiated in 1.4-19. Each encourages, indeed requires, comparison with Jeremiah 1 in order to gain the full and intended impact of the respective texts.

The I Expression in Jeremiah 26–52

Stulman presents a viable case for the appropriateness of recognizing a distinct 'literary and symbolic world' for each of the Jeremiah scrolls (Stulman 1998: 62). However, his reminder that, 'Jeremiah 1 serves as a functional introduction not only to chs. 2–25 but to the entire book' (Stulman 1998: 59; see also Hobbs 1984: 184, 188) is cogent. Perhaps the relationship between the B and I expressions is something of an appropriate micro-structural corollary to the macro-structural relationship of Jeremiah 2–25 and 26–52.

The nature of the texts employing the I expression in chs. 26–52 is, like the expressions themselves, somewhat different from that of the texts in chs. 2–25. That difference is largely because of the issues they address as well as the manner in which they relate to Jeremiah 1. While several second-scroll texts also relate to Jeremiah 1 through repetitive and paradigmatic rhetoric, others interact with the prologue through theological dynamics which the prologue anticipates. Deuteronomy 18-like diction employed in Jer. 1.7, 9, together with what are most certainly other intentional Mosaic analogies (the demurring of the prophet, for example), pair up in the 'call narrative' to image Jeremiah as a 'Moses-like prophet' (Deut. 18.15, 18; see Thompson 1980: 150; Carroll 1986: 99). The prologue thus sets the stage for the numerous confrontations between Jeremiah and contemporary prophets (Carroll 1981: 52). The first two uses of the I version in the second scroll appear in narratives of this genre.

Jeremiah 27–28 narrates the collision of contradictory prophetic words—the words of Hananiah and Jeremiah. What appears to be a council of rebellion against Babylon by the king of Judah and neighboring kings (27.3) is confronted by the yoke-related word of Yahweh through Jeremiah (27.5-11). This word is, essentially, to 'wear the yoke of Babylon; it is Yahweh's doing'. In ch. 28, Hananiah dramatically confronts the word of Jeremiah by removing Jeremiah's yoke and by offering a contradictory message which he purports to be the word of Yahweh (28.2). Two-thirds of the way through the narrative, after Jeremiah withdraws from public confrontation, the I expression appears for the first time in the second scroll (28.12). This 'word event' addresses the immediate narrative situation and anticipates the ultimate triumph of Jeremiah's word. Immediately, the text redirects attention to Jeremiah 1, where the prophetic paradigm was projected. Jeremiah's declaration that Hananiah would die, and the subsequent notation that he did, fit the Deut. 18.19-22 paradigm of true prophecy (Bright 1965: 203; Holladay 1989: 129; Lundbom 1997: 151).

Likewise, the Jer. 29.30 use occurs in a context in which Shemaiah, the prophet in Babylon (29.31), opposes Jeremiah's word. Hence, it continues to nuance the dynamic of true vs. false prophets. The divine word, introduced by the I expression and addressed to the exiles, publicly confirms the legitimacy of Jeremiah (29.31) and anticipates Shemaiah's demise (29.32). Domeris agrees that Deut. 18.18-22 type prophetic legitimization is an important component of this text (Domeris 1999: 250). In this respect, this text resonates with the Jeremiah 27–28 scenario and with Jeremiah 1. Setting up this prophetic clash, conducted through correspondence, is

Jeremiah's counsel to the exiles which employs the two 'positive' terms of Jer. 1.10. Jeremiah instructs them to 'build houses' and 'plant gardens' (29.5, 28). A segment of the divine blueprint for Judah, anticipated in the prologue, was an 'uprooting' from their land and a 'breaking down' of their houses to go into exile. Their exile would be of sufficient duration as to make it appropriate for them to 'build houses' and 'plant gardens'.

The language of Jer. 1.15-16 seems to anticipate a siege of Jerusalem and the cities of Judah—leading to conquest—as judgment for the nation's turning away from Yahweh. It is not surprising, therefore, that the I version appears in several second-scroll contexts in which a Babylonian siege is not merely anticipated, but is a reality. The example in Jer. 32.26 is striking both because of the historical setting of the narrative (32.2) and because of the expression's placement in the narrative— between 'two discussions' regarding the siege. In 32.16-25, Jeremiah prays to Yahweh after he had purchased a piece of property and obtained a deed of purchase (32.1-15). The prayer ends with the prophet describing the present siege and drawing Yahweh's attention to the seemingly contradictory instructions to purchase a piece of property (32.24-25). It is as though this 'word event' is intended to interrupt the prayer with, 'Look! I am Yahweh, God of all flesh (כל־בשר)! Is anything (כל־דבר) too difficult for me?' (32.27), whereupon Yahweh returns to the subject of the Babylonian siege and impending destruction of Jerusalem (32.28-29). The explanation given includes a description of Judah's forsaking Yahweh and going after other gods (cf. 1.16). The deed of purchase, however, is appropriate because of the ultimate divinely arranged return to the land.

Jeremiah 33 contains three 'word events' in vv. 1, 19, 23. In 33.1, the expression ties what follows to the preceding sequence by specifying that the prophet was 'still confined' (cf. 32.2) and by the addition of שנית at the end. The latter two (33.19, 23) introduce covenant discussions, both of which involve David and which anticipate future restoration. Although the first also looks forward to a reversal of Judah's present situation, it begins with recognition of the status quo, both for Jeremiah (confined) and Jerusalem (besieged). Siege and destruction are unavoidable realities, but both prophet and people are called upon to look beyond the inevitable on the basis of Yahweh's identity and activity—'maker, fashioner, establisher'. Not to be overlooked in this context is the somewhat ironic use of the root נתץ to describe the 'tearing' of houses in order to create siege defenses (33.4) while the root בנה is used in 33.7 to anticipate the 'rebuilding' of the nation.

Brueggemann (1991: 104-20) argues convincingly for reading Jeremiah 34–35 as a pair of intentionally juxtaposed narratives which present contrasting case studies in fidelity; each makes use of the I expression (34.12; 35.12). The first involves an initial commitment by the people of Jerusalem to a covenant concerning the freeing of all debt slaves; their subsequent reneging elicits a 'word event' from Yahweh to the prophet (34.12). The resulting message from Yahweh reiterates the return of Babylon to Jerusalem[13] and the ultimate destruction of the city, as anticipated in

---

13. This seems to correlate with Jer. 37, which alludes to a Babylonian withdrawal from Jerusalem and also anticipates a Babylonian return resulting in the destruction of the city.

Jer. 1.15. The contrasting study focuses attention on the Rechabites who have remained fiercely loyal to a command from an ancestor regarding abstention from consumption of wine, building houses, sowing seed and planting vineyards (35.6-7). Yahweh's word in this situation guarantees that they will have perpetual progeny. This scenario, like the prophet's instructions in his letter to the exiles (29.1-9) seems intended to 'play off' the rhetoric of 1.10. In the case of the Rechabites, not 'building' and not 'planting' is evidence of an appropriate fidelity to a commitment, and is rewarded. The residents of Jerusalem's infidelity to covenant will result in uprooting and overthrow.

Jeremiah 37 narrates an event which appears to precede the Jeremiah 32–33 sequence; Jeremiah had not yet been imprisoned (37.4) and the Babylonian siege had been temporarily lifted (37.5). The prophet is approached by a delegation of the king to enlist his intercession on behalf of the nation (37.3). In this situation, the word from Yahweh to Jeremiah reiterates the certainty of the city's destruction at the hands of the Babylonians, notwithstanding the temporary break in the siege.

Jeremiah 36 has received extensive attention in scholarship from various perspectives.[14] The chapter is well known for its narration of the preparation of a scroll containing 23 years of oracles given to Jeremiah for the nation and the subsequent destruction of that scroll by Jehoiakim. The majority of the narrative is devoted to detailing what has just been summarized above; it is only the final few verses (36.27-32) which preserve the account of the preparation of a second scroll in response to the instructions of Yahweh, preceded by the I expression. While there appears to be no specific rhetorical links between ch. 36 and ch. 1, a significant relationship between the two portions of the composition appears to revolve around the nature of Jeremiah's prophetic role. The entire emphasis of Jeremiah 1 is on Jeremiah's 'speaking' the words of Yahweh. Nothing in 1.4-10, 1.11-14 or 1.15-19 hints at the turn of events that has been preserved in this engaging narration. What has heretofore focused attention on the oralization of the word of Yahweh, here describes the inscription of that word. Jeremiah, the bearer of Yahweh's word, has been barred from the place where it would normally be announced (32.5); but that will not obviate the divine purpose of its confronting those who must be confronted by it. As Brueggemann (1991: 129) observes, 'It is the book (scroll), and not the presence of the prophet, which becomes decisive in resisting the king'. Destruction of the scroll elicits another 'word event' (36.27) and leads to a second, fuller, edition (36.32). The scroll has its own authority (Brueggemann 1991: 130) inasmuch as it contains the word 'which happened to Jeremiah'. Although Jeremiah's commissioning, as recorded in 1.4-19, does not specifically make reference to 'writing' the word of Yahweh, the roots for such are there inasmuch as it is Jeremiah who is commissioned and it is the word of Yahweh which is to be communicated. For Jeremiah, what is common to 'speaking' and 'writing' is the encounter with divine word, communicated through the 'happening of the word' to the prophet.

---

14. Kessler 1966: 389-401; Holladay 1980: 452-67; Hicks 1983; Dearman 1990; Hoffman 1996.

Part of a larger, macro-structural section of the second scroll,[15] Jeremiah 42–43 constitutes another extended narrative in which Jeremiah is approached about inquiring of Yahweh on behalf of a remnant associated with Johanan and Azariah. In language unprecedented in the book for its commitment to obedience, the group pledges to obey whatever word the prophet may receive from Yahweh for them. The word from Yahweh in this textual setting interacts with several earlier texts, all of which are dependent on 1.10: 'If you will surely remain in this land I will build you (ובניתי אתכם) and not overthrow (לא אהרס), I will plant you (ונטעתי אתכם) and not uproot (ולא אתוש)...' (42.10). The diction of this word is very similar to that of 24.6 with its pairing of terms. Contrary to their emphatic avowal of obedience, they accuse Jeremiah of lying (43.2) and depart Judah for Egypt—apparently taking Jeremiah and Baruch with them. Ironically, this final 'word event' occurs while Jeremiah is in Tahpanhes with the disobedient remnant; thus the expression's final use brings the reader back to its first use in conjunction with the commissioning of 1.4-10.

Conclusion

Jeremiah's 'word events' may be 'formulaic' but they are not mere 'formulas'. They are strategically located 'texted word events' which represent the incursion of potent, sovereign word into the life of prophet and nation. Specifically, the exclusive use of B in Jeremiah 1–25 and I in chs. 26–52 with their individual textual settings allied with their collective dominance, suggests that this 'paired expression' creates a skeletal network of texts which consciously build on and advance the prologue's seminal theological dynamics. At appropriate locations in the composition, the reader encounters these particular 'word event expressions' and is thus encouraged to read the immediate text as a dynamic development of core issues of the prologue.

BIBLIOGRAPHY

Bretón, S.
    1987   *Vocación y missión: Formulario profético* (AnBib, 111; Rome: Biblical
                Institute Press).
Bright, John
    1965   *Jeremiah* (AB, 21; Garden City, NY: Doubleday).
Brueggemann, Walter
    1988   *To Pluck Up, To Tear Down: A Commentary on Jeremiah 1–25* (ITC; Grand
                Rapids: Eerdmans).
    1991   *To Build, To Plant: A Commentary on Jeremiah 26–52* (ITC; Grand Rapids:
                Eerdmans).

15. Brueggemann (1991: 121) reads Jer. 36 and 45 as 'the brackets' around the 'Baruch Document'; see also Stulman 1998: 88-93.

Carroll, Robert P.

1981   *From Chaos to Covenant: Prophecy in the Book of Jeremiah* (New York: Crossroad).

1986   *Jeremiah: A Commentary* (OTL: Philadelphia: Westminster Press).

Dearman, J. Andrew

1990   'My Servants the Scribes: Composition and Context in Jeremiah 36', *JBL* 109: 403-21.

Diamond, A.R., K.M. O'Connor and L. Stulman (eds.)

1999   *Troubling Jeremiah* (JSOTSup, 260; Sheffield: Sheffield Academic Press).

Domeris, W.R.

1999   'When Metaphor Becomes Myth', in Diamond, O'Connor and Stulman (eds.) 1999: 244-62.

Duhm, Bernard

1901   *Das Buch Jeremiah* (KHAT; Tübingen and Leipzig: J.C.B. Mohr).

Friebel, Kelvin G.

1999   *Jeremiah's and Ezekiel's Sign-Acts* (JSOTSup, 283; Sheffield: Sheffield Academic Press).

Hicks, R.L.

1983   '*Delet* and *Megillah:* A Fresh Approach to Jeremiah xxxvi', *VT* 33: 46-66.

Hobbs, T.R.

1984   'Some Remarks on the Composition and Structure of the Book of Jeremiah', in L.G. Perdue and B.W. Kovacs (eds.), *A Prophet to the Nations: Essays in Jeremiah Studies* (Winona Lake, IN: Eisenbrauns): 175-91.

Hoffman, Y.

1996   'Aetiology, Redaction and Historicity in Jeremiah xxxvi', *VT* 46: 179-89.

Holladay, William L.

1980   'The Identification of the Two Scrolls of Jeremiah', *VT* 30: 452-67.

1986   *Jeremiah. I. A Commentary on the Book of the Prophet Jeremiah Chapters 1–25* (Hermeneia; Philadelphia: Fortress Press).

1989   *Jeremiah. II. A Commentary on the Book of the Prophet Jeremiah Chapters 26–52* (Hermeneia; Minneapolis: Fortress Press).

Huffmon, Herbert B.

1999   'Jeremiah of Anathoth: A Prophet for All Israel', in R. Chazan, W.W. Hallo and L.H. Schiffman (eds.), *Ki Baruch Hu: Ancient Near Eastern, Biblical and Judaic Studies in Honor of Baruch A. Levine* (Winona Lake, IN: Eisenbrauns): 262-71.

Kessler, M.

1966   'Form-Critical Suggestions on Jer. 36', *CBQ* 28: 389-401.

Lundbom, Jack R.

1997   *Jeremiah: A Study in Ancient Hebrew Rhetoric* (Winona Lake, IN: Eisenbrauns, 2nd edn).

1999   *Jeremiah 1–20: A New Translation with Introduction and Commentary* (AB, 21A; Garden City, NY: Doubleday).

Mowinckel, Sigmund

1914   *Zur Komposition des Buches Jeremia* (Kristiania: Dybwad).

Neumann, Peter K.D.

1973   'Das Word, das geschehen ist…, Zum Problem der ortempfangsterminologie in Jer. i-xxv', *VT* 23: 171-217.

Seidl, T.
    1977   'Datierung und Wortereignis', *Biblische Zeitschrift* 21: 25-44, 184-99.
    1979   'Die Wortereignisformel in Jeremia: Beobachtungen zu den Formen der
                Redeeroeffnung in Jeremia, im Anschluss an Jer. 27, 1.2', *BZ* 23: 20-47.
Stulman, Louis
    1998   *Order Amid Chaos: Jeremiah as Symbolic Tapestry* (The Biblical Seminar,
                57; Sheffield: Sheffield Academic Press).
Sweeney, Marvin A.
    1999   'Structure and Redaction in Jeremiah 2–6', in Diamond, O'Connor and
                Stulman (eds.) 1999: 200-18.
Thompson, J.A.
    1980   *The Book of Jeremiah* (NICOT; Grand Rapids: Eerdmans).

VISIONS OF PEACE IN ISAIAH

David A. Leiter

Introduction

The Hebrew Bible conveys the notion of peace in various literary forms such as narrative, legal collections, prophetic oracles, psalms and wisdom literature. In the prophetic literature, one specific way in which the concept of peace emerges is in the form of a vision. In most cases the vision of peace describes a situation, often in the future, of harmony and hope where *shalom* will be present. Of all the prophetic books, the vision of peace occurs most frequently in the book of Isaiah. What is striking about a majority of these visions in Isaiah is that they emerge without forewarning. In most cases there is a pronouncement of judgment and destruction and then, with no prior notice, there is an abrupt shift to a vision of peace, harmony and hope. The purpose of this essay is to identify the primary visions of peace in Isaiah and to ascertain how they function within the book as a whole.

The visions of peace to be discussed in this essay are Isa. 2.1-4; 8.23–9.6 (Eng. 9.1-7); 11.1-9; 32.1-20; 35.1-10; 55.1-13; 60.17-22 and 65.17-25. Five of these eight visions occur in First Isaiah while the remaining visions occur in Second and Third Isaiah. The starting point for dating the book of Isaiah normally involves the three standard divisions of the book: chs. 1–39, 40–55 and 56–66. Ever since the work of Bernhard Duhm, who first identified these three divisions, there has been considerable debate about the structure of the book of Isaiah (Duhm 1892). Although technical discussions continue to emerge regarding the dating of specific passages in Isaiah as well as that of redactional additions, the traditional dating of Isaiah 1–39 to the pre-exilic period, Isaiah 40–55 to the exilic period and Isaiah 56–66 to the post-exilic era will be followed here in a general fashion.

Whereas the visions of peace in chs. 40–66 are usually viewed as relatively late, there is considerable debate regarding the visions in Isaiah 1–39. Some writers maintain that the dating of the visions in this section is consistent with the overall provenance of the section, namely the pre-exilic period (Wildberger 1991: 86-87, 389-90). Others view the visions of peace in Isaiah 1–39 as later additions because of their intrusive character and because they seem to speak more directly to the exilic and post-exilic periods (Pleins 2001: 224, Wolff 1992: 117-18; Kaiser 1983: 51). While the historical setting of the visions of peace in Isaiah 1–39 may be of importance in certain instances, the primary concern in this essay is how these visions function in the book as a whole, regardless of whether they are of pre-exilic, exilic or post-exilic origin.

Isaiah 1–39

A clue to the literary function of the visions of peace in Isaiah 1–39 lies in their thematic shift from judgment to hope and peace (Dempsey 2000b: 161). One can recognize this pattern in each of the five visions. Isaiah 1 proclaims the rebellion of Judah in the midst of Assyria's power and destruction. There is a call to refrain from evil and to seek good and justice. In addition, this chapter includes warnings, condemnations and images which portray evildoers as burning like kindling and wood. There is a hint of restoration and respite in this chapter but it will be realized only after the described destruction occurs. Following the closing words of Isaiah 1, with its images of destruction, the message of ch. 2 quickly changes to one of hope and peace. This vision makes the point that judgment is not the final word (Goldingay 2001: 42). The vision focuses upon Mt Zion and describes nations gathering at the mountain to learn God's *Torah*. God's role will be that of judge and arbiter, and the peoples and nations will transform their weapons into farming implements; indeed, war will be a thing of the past. Although the word *shalom* is not used in the passage, the primary expectation is one of peace (Wildberger 1991: 96). Whether or not one views this vision as eschatological (Chester 1989: 471; Seitz 1993: 39) or addressing present circumstances (Wolff 1992: 119-20), it is a vision that looks to peace among countries and nations that at one time used violence and power to control one another (Dempsey 2000a: 122; Lind 1990: 176).

The next peace vision is also introduced by words of judgment and gloom (Isa. 8.23–9.6). The prophet uses the image of flooding to portray the message that Assyria will overpower Judah. The chapter concludes by describing an atmosphere of gloom and darkness. Isaiah 8.23 provides a transition from the darkness and gloom specified in ch. 8 to the message of hope and peace delineated in 9.1-6. Brevard Childs views 8.23 as a bridge from the darkness described in the previous verses to that of light and hope (Childs 2001: 79). Hans Wildberger suggests that this verse serves as an announcement that the turning point from darkness to peace is at hand (Wildberger 1991: 392). Regardless of the specific role of 8.23, an abrupt transformation has taken place from what transpires in Isaiah 8 to what is described in Isa. 9.1-6 (Hanson 1986: 192; Watts 1985: 135). This transformation involves a dramatic shift from gloom and darkness to a vision that describes continual peace, justice and righteousness for David's throne.

Following the vision of peace in Isa. 8.23–9.6, the message reverts back to one of judgment and destruction in the remainder of ch. 9 and into ch. 10. Beginning with Isa. 10.12, the message moves from one of judgment against Judah to judgment against Assyria. The prophet also indicates that God's wrath upon Judah will not last forever and that a remnant will indeed survive. Chapter 10, however, concludes with graphic imagery indicating that Assyria will be cut down like trees in a forest. A shift then occurs from destruction to hope and peace as Isa. 11.1-5 revisits the remnant theme to describe the new ruler who will lead Judah. The message of peace becomes prominent in Isa. 11.6-9, which portrays a paradisical vision of what life will be like under this new leadership (Dempsey 2000a: 123). In this vision predatory animals will coexist with animals that are normally their prey. The scene also involves a child leading such animals as well as other children playing in close proximity with dangerous creatures. Instead of destruction, danger, pain and injury, the land will be filled with enduring peace. This is a very different picture from the destruction and ruin portrayed in chs. 9 and 10.

The move from judgment to hope in Isaiah 31–32 comes about in a gradual fashion. Isaiah 31 begins with prophetic oracles against Egypt and Assyria. Isaiah 32.1-8 envisions a time when rulers will govern with integrity and justice, but then there is a shift to judgment as vast destruction is described for Judah (32.9-15). The message in Isa. 32.16-20 dramatically shifts back to justice, righteousness and peace. At first glance, it appears that the destruction and judgment could be enduring and everlasting (Goldingay 2001: 182-83). The transformation from destruction to righteousness and peace actually begins with v. 15, which serves as the primary link between vv. 9-14 and 16-20 (Childs 2001: 241). A state of confusion and anarchy is transformed into a situation of peace and justice (Leclerc 2001: 84). People will live in secure and peaceful houses and will be able to plant their fields near sources of water where the ox and the donkey can roam freely.

The last vision of peace in chs. 1–39, Isa. 35.1-10, follows words describing God's wrath against sinners in Zion and words against the surrounding nations of Judah, especially Edom. The vision in 35.1-10 describes the wilderness and the desert as places of gladness and rejoicing. Blind persons will see. Deaf persons will hear. Those unable to walk will leap as gracefully as deer and those who cannot speak will sing. A highway will emerge in the desert and wilderness, and those traveling on this road will not go astray but will journey with joy and gladness to Jerusalem.

There are several ways to interpret the shift from judgment to peace in Isaiah 33–35. Some see the movement as abrupt and unexplained (Goldingay 2001: 196). Others view chs. 36–39 as a historical appendix that stands on its own and thus they consider ch. 35 to be the conclusion to First Isaiah. Accordingly, it is possible to view chs. 34 and 35 as a redactional bridge that combines First Isaiah with Second Isaiah (Childs 2001: 253). David Pleins goes a step further and sees the judgment in Isaiah 1–34 as culminating in the peace and hope of Isaiah 35. He argues that in the midst of the struggle between desolation and peace that occurs frequently in the first 35 chapters, the message of peace in Isaiah 35 ends up being the final word (Pleins 2001: 252).

What has been evident so far in the analysis of the peace visions in Isaiah 1–39 is that there is a consistent movement from judgment to peace and hope. In four of the five peace visions there is an abrupt change from judgment to peace. The vision in Isa. 2.1-4 emerges without any hint or indication that a new way of life involving the transformation of military tools into farming implements will be described. In a similar way the peaceful visions in 8.23–9.6 and 11.1-9 emerge in an abrupt fashion after words of judgment. The peace vision in 35.1-10 also seems to come out of nowhere but it is a fitting end to First Isaiah as a whole. The one exception in the group of five visions is the gradual movement in Isaiah 32 to a scene of justice, righteousness and peace in vv. 16-20. This chapter is interspersed with messages of judgment and hope and culminates in the final scene of peace. So what can be said about the recurrent movement from judgment to hope and peace in the first part of Isaiah?

From a literary standpoint the transition represents the juxtaposition of two drastically different genres. Prophetic oracles of judgment are placed alongside visions of peace. Not only are these two genres different by design but they send two distinct and contrary messages. Robert Alter discusses the fact that prophetic literature contains these two types of genres at various points. He identifies the two genres as monitory poems or prophecies of doom and prophecies of consolation (Alter 1985: 151-62). Although Alter does not deal with the abrupt shift between the monitory poems and the poems of consolation in Isaiah 1–39, he does suggest that a connection exists between the two genres in prophetic literature as a whole. In one sense, the prophecies of consolation offer a balance to the prophecies of doom. This balance occurs because the poems of consolation contain antithetical imagery and rhetorical strategies that are analogous to the monitory poems:

> The monitory poems of the prophets are dominated by images of wasteland, uprooting and burning, darkness, enslavement and humiliation, stripping of garments, divorce and sexual abandoning, earthquake and storm. The poems of consolation are dominated by images of flourishing vineyards and fields, planting and building, shining light, liberation and regal dignity, splendid garb, marital reconciliation and sexual union, firm foundations and calm. (Alter 1985: 156)

Thus the poems of consolation point to a society filled with harmony while the monitory poems speak of situations of primitive chaos. By focusing on the antithetical imagery that is displayed in each combination, Alter's scheme of contrast can help us understand the five pairs of oracles of judgment and visions of peace in Isaiah 1–39.

The prophecy of judgment in Isaiah 1 speaks of a desolate land (1.7-9) while the vision of peace in Isaiah 2 describes an established mountain. The former speaks of aliens devouring the land while the latter sees nations coming to the mountain of Yahweh to learn God's *Torah*. Similarly, the oracle of judgment in Isaiah 8 utters words of darkness, gloom and anguish while the vision of peace in 8.23–9.6 looks to a transformation from the darkness to the light. The words of judgment lament the fact that those in the land will be distressed and hungry (8.21), while the vision of peace speaks of rejoicing during the harvest (9.3).

In the third contrast between judgment and peace in First Isaiah, Isa. 10.33-34 illustrates the destruction of the Assyrians upon Judah through the imagery of the toppling of tall and majestic trees and the leveling of the thickest parts of a forest. On the other hand, new life is symbolized through the branch that emerges from the stump of Jesse in 11.1. In addition, 9.17 notes that God did not have compassion upon the young, orphans and widows, namely the poor, but 11.4 notes that the poor will be judged with righteousness and the meek with egalitarian measures.

The contrast between judgment and consolation by way of antithetical imagery becomes even more vivid in the comparison of 32.9-14 and 32.15-20. Isaiah 32.10 discusses a time in the near future when the vintage will fail and a bountiful fruit harvest will not come, while v. 15 envisions the transformation of the wilderness into a fruitful field. The former judgment speech depicts thorns and briers coming up from the soil while the latter peace vision looks to righteousness in a field that is ripe for the harvest. Isaiah 32.14 speaks of a deserted city while 32.18-19 anticipates people living peacefully in secure and quiet houses.

The final contrast between judgment and peace in First Isaiah occurs in 33.7-12 and 35.1-10. The first section refers to crying and weeping in the streets (v. 7) and deserted highways that no longer carry travelers (v. 8). In addition, the land mourns as the mountainous area of Lebanon fades away, the plain of Sharon becomes a desert and the trees and vegetation of Bashan and Carmel lose their leaves. Isaiah 35.1-10, however, tells an altogether different story. Instead of crying and weeping there is rejoicing and gladness in the wilderness, dry land and the desert (v. 1). Instead of the decline and demise of Lebanon, Sharon and Carmel, these areas enjoy glory and majesty (v. 2). Instead of deserted highways, there is now a highway where travelers cannot become lost as they find their way into the city with much rejoicing (vv. 8-10). All of the five visions of peace in Isaiah 1–39 offer a contrasting and divergent message to the speeches of judgment that precede each vision.

If one follows Atler's scheme, which seems appropriate in the context of Isaiah 1–39, then the visions of peace balance the preceding prophecies of doom. In most cases of the five examples outlined here, the visions of peace occur immediately after the speeches of judgment. Therefore, not only does the message of peace provide literary symmetry, it also offers the final word. Because of the arrangement of the contrasting genres the notions of peace and harmony punctuate the text and eclipse judgment and despair. The fact that the shift from judgment to peace is somewhat abrupt in these five examples further reinforces the fact that the final compiler of Isaiah 1–39 saw peace and harmony as notions that transcend and surpass that of judgment. Judgment is temporary but peace and harmony will be everlasting and unending. Thus the visions of peace tend to soften the explicit messages of judgment. In some cases the words of judgment are fairly forceful, leaving the reader or hearer with the impression that perhaps the described judgment will indeed prevail. The visions of peace come along and provide the notion that judgment is not the final word and that hope for the future is indeed a possibility. The presentation of visions of peace after potent judgment oracles lessens the intensity of perpetual judgment and opens up the door for the prospect of a perpetual and everlasting peace.

When addressing the texts in question in Isaiah 1–39 from a socio-historical perspective, it becomes evident that the writer looks to hope during a time of oppression. The various periods of the pre-exilic era addressed by First Isaiah involve economic deprivation and local and national destruction by military powers such as Assyria. The writer has hope that such deprivation and destruction will not last forever and that a time will occur in the future in which liberation, restoration and rebuilding will take place. The visions of peace follow the words and oracles of judgment in an effort to provide hope to the people that oppression and foreign domination will not last forever.

Finally, the vacillation back and forth throughout the first section of the book of Isaiah between judgment and peace sends the message that unless the community is able to find long-lasting ways to live in harmony with one another there is no reason to assume that this vacillation will not continue in the future. What we have here is a subtle exhortation to work for harmony and peace. Peace is preferred over judgment and the idyllic and peaceful visions serve as inspiration to promote a situation of peace that will exhibit a sense of longevity. For example, a vision that describes predatory animals coexisting with their prey and little children playing with dangerous reptiles (Isa. 11.6-9) presents imagery that suggests that although a certain type of peace and harmony under usual circumstances may seem unlikely, such peace and harmony is something to work toward.

Isaiah 40–66

The visions of peace in Isaiah 40–66 differ from those in Isaiah 1–39 in some respects. First of all, the historical context is different. Instead of facing the impending disaster and destruction that occurred at the end of the pre-exilic period, the writers of chs. 40–66 have already experienced this disaster and are looking forward to a time of restoration and rebuilding. A second difference is that oracles of judgment are virtually non-existent in Isaiah 40–66. In other words, the visions of peace in the latter portion of the book are not preceded by poems of judgment and doom, but rather find themselves placed alongside other prophetic genres that are characteristic of the late exilic and post-exilic periods. The result is that the peace visions in Isaiah 40–66 function in a very different manner than those in Isaiah 1–39.

Isaiah 55.1-13 is the first of three visions of peace in Isaiah 40–66. It begins by inviting those who are thirsty and without money to come and eat. Food, wine and milk are freely available. The author links this invitation to food and drink, essentially life, to the everlasting covenant. The covenant of David is transferred to the people and becomes a present reality to them (Childs 2001: 435). The vision concludes with imagery of peace that results in rejoicing and gladness. The mountains and the hills sing. The trees break into applause. Instead of thorns and briers, the cypress and the myrtle spring forth. This imagery of life and peace provides a sign that the covenant will be long lasting and serve the people well into the future. This vision constitutes a fitting conclusion to Second Isaiah. It attempts to inspire hope in dispirited exiles in Babylon and, more importantly, contributes to the future social construction of restoration and rebuilding (Birch 1991: 302).

The second vision of peace in this section occurs in Isa. 60.17-22. As in Isaiah 40–55, the transformation from desolation to hope has not yet taken place. This vision contrasts present conditions and those yet to come. The disparity of the present and the future is seen in the building materials for the new Jerusalem. New materials such as gold, silver, bronze and iron will replace bronze, iron, wood and stones used in the construction of Solomon's city. The rulers of the new community, moreover, will be peace and righteousness, while violence, devastation and destruction will come to an end. Light will no longer come from the sun and the moon but from God. And this transformation, the text claims, will occur in the very near future.

Isaiah 65.17-25 is the final peace vision in the book. Verses 17-19a announce that peace is about to come and vv. 19b-25 describe what this peace will entail (Westermann 1969: 407). The imagery contained in the latter section offers a vivid contrast to what the exilic and post-exilic communities had experienced. Something new is on the horizon. This new peace will not involve the crying and weeping that was so prevalent in the exilic period. Food and other resources will be plentiful enough that infants will not die a few days after birth and people will live long and healthy lives. Additionally, this peace will ensure the equal distribution of resources. The powerful will not inhabit the land of the powerless and the 'haves' will not eat the food of the 'have-nots'. The vision concludes by revisiting the animal imagery from ch. 11 where predators coexist peacefully with their prey. The final statement of the vision resounds with power and a long-lasting effect as God proclaims that those who inhabit the holy mountain will not hurt or destroy one another.

The literary context of these three visions of peace is different from the visions of peace in Isaiah 1–39 because they are not juxtaposed immediately alongside oracles of judgment. However, this does not mean that the contrast between despair and peace does not exist in the later visions. When looking at the book of Isaiah as a whole, the contrast between earlier prophecies of doom and the later poems of consolation is consistently found. However, as we move to the latter part of the book the judgment oracles drop out and the message of peace takes precedence. As such, it becomes the final and overriding message. The visions of peace no longer serve to balance the oracles of judgment as they did in Isaiah 1–39; instead, the strategic placement of these visions in Isaiah 40–66 strengthens the message of peace and harmony found in earlier parts of the book.

As mentioned previously, Isa. 55.1-13 serves as a fitting conclusion to Second Isaiah. Chapters 40–55 bring a message of hope to the exiles in Babylon with a surplus of salvation oracles. These oracles challenge the Babylonian gods; they exploit the Exodus theme to anticipate the return of the exiles to Judah; and they speak of liberation as well as Yahweh's servant. These important themes culminate in a vision of peace that solidifies the message of hope for the future. In a similar fashion, Isa. 65.17-25 serves as a proper conclusion to the book of Isaiah as a whole. It is not a mere coincidence that the final compilers of the book of Isaiah chose to end the book with a message of peace. Peace and harmony are the themes that are designed to help move the community forward from despair to hope, from desolation to restoration, from ruin to rebuilding. The message of peace occurs at various points in the book but its presence at the end is strategic: it makes this particular message the ultimate claim of the tradition. It sets the stage for a brighter future for the people of God, a future that will lead to a transformation from violence to peace and from domination and injustice to liberation and justice.

The content of Isaiah 40–66 makes it quite clear that although this transformation has not yet taken place, it is something that the exiles in Babylon and remnant in Judah could work toward and look forward to. As with the peace visions in Isaiah 1–39, the three visions of peace in Isaiah 40–66 pulsate with idealism. The transformation from violence and destruction to peace and harmony clearly has a utopian flavor to it. The message here for contemporary readers is not to dismiss the visions because of their idealism but to allow the images of transformation and a new world order to inspire us to work towards their fulfillment in our own local contexts (Dempsey 2000b: 181). Free food and drink are not readily available as depicted in Isa. 55.1-13, and predators cannot amicably coexist with their prey without causing considerable disruption in the ecological food chain (65.17-25). But the imagery portrayed in these visions motivates readers and hearers to join God in creating a peaceful world. It also serves to instill hope in those whose lives look bleak and hopeless. People of faith are invited to find ways to develop and maintain a new creation that involves peace and harmony for all persons.

Conclusion

These identified eight visions of peace in Isaiah are not arbitrary and random visions that simply appear in the book. They are visions that are strategically placed in the first part of the book alongside oracles of judgment to offer a necessary balance to the message of judgment and destruction. Peace visions are also placed at the end of particular sections such as Second Isaiah and the book as a whole to leave the reader with the hope that peace and harmony shall overcome judgment and doom.

This study has argued that the message of peace has a distinct purpose in Isaiah. If this is the case then similar studies applied to other books in the Hebrew Bible may be helpful in identifying how interpretive communities used the concept of peace to influence their respective settings. Contemporary faith communities tend to overlook the message of peace in the prophetic literature of the Hebrew Bible because of the many judgment oracles. What is often unnoticed is the message of peace has the last word.

BIBLIOGRAPHY

Alter, Robert
  1985   *The Art of Biblical Poetry* (New York: Basic Books).
Birch, Bruce C.
  1991   *Let Justice Roll Down: The Old Testament, Ethics, and Christian Life* (Louisville, KY: Westminster/John Knox Press).
Chester, Andrew
  1989   'The Concept of Peace in the Old Testament', *Theology* 92: 466-81.
Childs, Brevard
  2001   *Isaiah: A Commentary* (OTL; Louisville, KY: Westminster/John Knox Press).
Dempsey, Carol J.
  2000a   *Hope Amid the Ruins: The Ethics of Israel's Prophets* (St Louis: Chalice Press).
  2000b   *The Prophets: A Liberation-Critical Reading* (Minneapolis: Fortress Press).
Duhm, Bernhard
  1892   *Das Buch Jesaia* (Göttingen: Vandenhoeck & Ruprecht).

Goldingay, John
    2001   *Isaiah* (Peabody, MA: Hendrickson).
Hanson, Paul D.
    1986   *The People Called: The Growth of Community in the Bible* (San Francisco: Harper & Row).
Kaiser, Otto
    1983   *Isaiah 1–12: A Commentary* (OTL; Philadelphia: Westminster Press).
Leclerc, Thomas L.
    2001   *Yahweh is Exalted in Justice: Solidarity and Conflict in Isaiah* (Minneapolis: Fortress Press).
Lind, Millard C.
    1990   'Perspectives on War and Peace in the Hebrew Scriptures', in *idem*, *Monotheism, Power, Justice: Collected Old Testament Essays* (Text Reader Series, 3; Elkhart: Institute of Mennonite Studies): 171-81.
Pleins, David J.
    2001   *The Social Visions of the Hebrew Bible: A Theological Introduction* (Louisville, KY: Westminster/John Knox Press).
Seitz, Christopher R.
    1993   *Isaiah 1–39* (Interpretation; Louisville, KY: Westminster/John Knox Press).
Watts, John D.W.
    1985   *Isaiah 1–33* (WBC, 24; Waco, TX: Word Books).
Westermann, Claus
    1969   *Isaiah 40–66: A Commentary* (OTL; Philadelphia: Westminster Press).
Wildberger, Hans
    1991   *Isaiah 1–12: A Commentary* (Minneapolis: Fortress Press).
Wolff, Hans Walter
    1992   'Swords into Plowshares: Misuse of a Word of Prophecy?', in Perry B. Yoder and Willard M. Swartley (eds.), *The Meaning of Peace: Biblical Studies* (Louisville, KY: Westminster/John Knox Press).

'YAHWEH HAS GIVEN THESE THREE KINGS INTO THE HAND OF MOAB': A SOCIO-LITERARY READING OF 2 KINGS 3

Jesse C. Long, Jr, and Mark Sneed

Along with other former and current students of Herb Huffmon, the authors have a high regard for him as a teacher, scholar and mentor. We have been impressed with his scholastic rigor, unwavering sense of fairness and general good humor. Most of us also have vivid images of our distinguished professor's impassioned exposition of Scripture—at times as if he were in an ecstatic state—particularly if our course of study was in the prophetic literature. For some of us, prophetic voices in Scripture even occasionally wear his face. We do not recall, however, that he ever had to call for a musician, as did the prophet Elisha in 2 Kings 3; his passion for the prophets was always at his beck and call. In his honor, the following article sets out to resolve one of the critical issues in the prophetic narrative of 2 Kings 3, the ambiguity that especially characterizes the conclusion to the story.

Methodology

We are proposing a socio-literary methodology for interpreting the text. Both sociological and literary approaches have recently become popular among biblical scholars. As frequently pointed out, both are reactions to the liabilities of the historical-critical method. Sociological criticism reacts by focusing on the entire society assumed by biblical material rather than just the royalty and elites. Biblical literary criticism, which is primarily synchronic and attentive to the final form of the text, reacts to the unending fragmentation that characterizes the older source criticism.

As heirs of historical criticism, sociological and literary critics of the Bible share common ground. Unfortunately, they have made little effort to unite their respective approaches. To one extreme are literary critics like Robert Alter who views the sociological issues surrounding the text as too speculative to control (Alter and Kermode 1987: 5-6; Alter 1981: 21). To the other extreme are sociological critics who pay little attention to the literary features of the text. For example, Victor Matthews and Don Benjamin characterize Jephthah's offering of his daughter as a heroic act in the eyes of the people (Judg. 11); its context within the DtrH[1] is not

---

1.   DtrH = Deuteronomistic History; Dtr = Deuteronomist or Deuteronomistic; D = Deuteronomic; in using this terminology, we are referring to the consensus that an author or school of

considered (Matthews and Benjamin 1993: 19-21). A careful, literary reading of the story reveals that the actual hero of the story is Jephthah's daughter, who, without a murmur submits to the tragic consequences of her father's rash vow; thus, the daughter serves as a disturbing foil to highlight the tragedy of Jephthah's actions.[2]

Several scholars attempt to bridge the gap between literary and sociological approaches (Jobling [1991, 1992],[3] Gottwald [1992], Clines [1995], Yee [1995, 1999, 2001] Boer [1996] and Coote [1992]). Their studies are essentially synchronic, they involve a close reading of texts, and they investigate how biblical literature functioned ideologically within the contemporary society.

Coote's edited volume of socio-literary readings of the prophets Elijah and Elisha deserves special attention (Coote 1992). And two authors in the anthology are especially noteworthy for their literary and sociological integration. The essay by Judith Todd (1992) provides a close reading of the Elijah–Elisha narratives that incorporates sociological concerns. Todd argues that the narratives represent the disenfranchised *vis-à-vis* the Omrides. She maintains that the Elijah and Elisha stories were taken up together to authenticate Elisha and his role in the Jehu rebellion. Jehu's authority was, by necessity, charismatic, since his emergence as king was not dynastic (i.e. *coup d'état*). Thus, he needed either prophetic or popular support to legitimate his takeover. Todd's analysis would have been more true to literary criticism, however, if she had gone beyond a pre-Dtr stage of the composition and to consider how the Dtr actually uses this material. The Dtr composition does not characterize Jehu's reign as positively as she speculates for the pre-Dtr stage of composition (2 Kgs 10.28-31; cf. J.C. Long 2002: 283-86). The other essay of interest is by Wesley Bergen (1992). Bergen takes an ideological, or, specifically, a Foucaultian approach to the Elisha narratives. He focuses on Elisha's encounters with royalty to explore how the text reflects a societal conflict between two alternative forms of power: monarchic and prophetic. Bergen's focus is on the final form of the text.

Ideological criticism seems to be at least part of the answer to the socio-literary dilemma (see Gottwald 1999b: 256-57). Its methodology largely overlaps with that of sociological criticism (see Aichele *et al.* [eds.] 1995: 272-308), of which it might

authors composed Joshua through 2 Kings, using the criteria of the D code (Deut. 12–16) to judge the various Israelite and Judean kings. In using this terminology, we are referring to the final form of the history, which is usually dated to the exilic or post-exilic period.

2.   Sneed similarly critiques Fry (2000), who tries to argue that David was not senile when Adonijah attempted to make himself heir-apparent to the throne (1 Kgs 1–2). He argues that David desired to save his own skin by delaying his designation of the next king for as long as possible. Essentially, he played the two sons (Adonijah and Solomon) off each other to see which would emerge as the most competent heir-apparent. Solomon was literally a 'little child', and Bathsheba, his mother, was the cunning instigator of Solomon's eventual selection. However, Fry essentially imposes the political, anthropological theory of Robbins Burling onto the Succession Narrative, and is not sensitive to the literary intent of the Dtr to portray Adonijah as a potential usurper of the throne (Sneed 2000).

3.   In fact, Jobling (1997) critiques Gottwald's (1985) *The Hebrew Bible: A Socio-Literary Introduction* because it fails to synthesize the two methodologies in a sophisticated way.

be considered a subcategory.[4] Ideological criticism is usually more suspicious of the text than sociological criticism per se.[5] It is almost synonymous with Marxist criticism. And it begins with a close reading of the text, a truly formalistic enterprise, with emphasis on contradictions that might indicate deeper ideological tensions that the text attempts to hide.[6]

Fredric Jameson, perhaps the foremost of Western Marxist literary critics, offers a version of ideological criticism that has become increasingly popular.[7] Jameson's readings have been frequently touted for their formalistic finesse. His close analysis of a text becomes the basis of his sociological interpretation. Jameson's method is not the stereotypical Marxist approach that views literature, an example of the superstructure, as naively reflecting its social and economic base. He sees the relationship as more complex, with the superstructure actually affecting the base, a truly dialectic symbiosis. Sometimes literature occludes its social matrix rather than simplistically reflecting it.

While our reading of 2 Kings 3 is not strictly Jamesonian, it does follow Jameson's general sequential order of literary-sociological. We maintain that a close literary critique of a biblical text is logically and temporally prior to sociological analysis. It establishes the parameters within which sociological investigation can occur, placing the investigation on inherently firmer ground. The more careful and detailed the literary analysis, the better the sociological analysis.

2 Kings 3 is an ideal text for demonstrating the potential of a socio-literary reading. It is an intriguing story that often baffles scholars. In brief, the narrative portrays the escapade of the northern king Jehoram, son of Ahab, Jehoshaphat, the Judean king, and the king of Edom to regain territory of the Moabites lost to Israel. In the process, the armies become incapacitated in the desert due to lack of water. They consult the prophet Elisha, who delivers an oracle of Yahweh predicting water for the troops and victory over the Moabites. Just as it appears that the prophecy is about to be fulfilled, the tables are turned. Mesha, the Moabite king, sacrifices his own son, and the attacking armies make a hasty retreat.

Through a careful literary analysis, the unexpected and perplexing ending can be unraveled, which also situates the episode in the larger composition. A sociological analysis, then, calls attention to the social location of the Dtr and brings out his concerns, which serves to reinforce the results of the literary investigation of the text.

Before beginning our analysis of the text, we will survey some of the literary-critical and source-critical explanations of the story's unexpected ending, especially

---

4.   For a brief introduction to ideological criticism and a sample, see Lye 1997 and 1999.

5.   Gorman (2001: 22) classifies ideological criticism as a type of existential exegesis that is suspicious of the text.

6.   The methodology is laid out nicely for biblical scholars, with an example, by Yee (1995). She begins with an 'extrinsic analysis' that investigates the socio-historical setting of the text. Then follows 'intrinsic analysis', which is what we would describe as literary analysis.

7.   Jameson's seminal text is *The Political Unconscious* (1981). Because it is such a difficult reading, the introductions to his method are quite helpful (Dowling 1984; Roberts 2000). For a biblical scholar's adaptation of his method, see Boer 1996.

as it relates to Elisha's unfulfilled prophecy (2 Kgs 3.27). Among the literary proposals, there are seven main strategies:

1.   The defeat is simply part of the Dtr's retributive interpretation of Israel-
     ite history (Satterthwaite 1998: 12; Provan 1995: 184; Hobbs 1985: 38).
2.   More specifically, the Israelite coalition is punished for the way it con-
     ducted the attack (Seow 1999: 183-85; Brichto 1992: 201-209). The
     campaign against Moab does not adhere to the Deuteronomic injunction
     not to fell fruit trees in a foreign campaign (Deut. 20.19-20; for different
     interpretation of the command, see Hobbs 1985: 37) and, as a conse-
     quence, suffers a setback.
3.   In light of the story of Micaiah and the lying prophets (1 Kgs 22), Elisha
     is viewed as having been used by Yahweh to entice Jehoram to go into
     battle (Provan 1995: 184; Gray 1970: 485; Satterthwaite 1998: 11).
4.   The prophecy technically comes to pass (vv. 20-25a; Provan 1995: 183).
5.   Verses 18-19, which assert that Yahweh will deliver Moab into Israel's
     hand, represent Elisha's words rather than Yahweh's (Kissling 1996:
     185-86).
6.   The coalition gives up (McConville 1989: 40), thus placing responsibil-
     ity on the people and not the prophet or Yahweh.
7.   The ending is confusing and unresolved (Brueggemann 2000: 315;
     B.O. Long 1991: 44).

Among source-critical solutions, David N. Freedman (personal correspondence
cited in Cogan and Tadmor 1988: 52 n. 8) believes the author changed the actual
prophetic account that originally recorded the fulfillment of the prophecy in order
to prevent an Omride from having 'an undiluted victory'. Like Freedman, Cogan
and Tadmor (1988: 48, 51) see vv. 26-27 as a redactional attempt to treat the
tension between a prophetic (Israel won) and a (Israel lost) historical tradition. The
'sudden divine wrath' solves the dilemma: it is punishment for some undisclosed
sin on Israel's part. More recently, Susanne Otto (2003: 496, 502) dissects 2 Kings
3 into vv. 2-3 (Dtr) and vv. 4-27 (post-Dtr, mid-sixth century) because these verses
contain, in her view, differing evaluations of Jehoram. The redactional approach,
however, is less than satisfactory since it fails to appreciate the literary artistry in
the composition.

    In the analysis to follow, aspects of these various approaches can be seen, espe-
cially in viewing 1 Kings 22 against the background of 2 Kings 3. However, our
reading will attempt to demonstrate that 2 Kings 3 is a sophisticated literary work
that participates in the Dtr's grand scheme of justifying the actions of Yahweh—in
this case, by validating the word of the prophet and reasserting the theme of
delayed retribution. Our literary reading focuses on the final form of the text and
locates the story within the context of the Dtr's intent. The literary analysis is reinforced and framed in our subsequent sociological analysis.

Literary Analysis

A synchronic reading of 2 Kings 3 places the episode of the campaign of Jehoram of Israel against Mesha of Moab into its larger context and suggests an overarching literary design. In particular, a literary reading calls attention to structural and verbal cues that clarify tensions unresolved by traditional, source-critical analyses of this passage. As most commentators bring out, the promise of Elisha's oracle against Moab (vv. 16-19) is unrealized by the close of the story. While Moab is devastated by Jehoram's coalition, Mesha retains hegemony over Moab with the sacrifice of his eldest son on the wall of Kir-hareseth. The narrative's chiastic structure highlights this tension:

vv. 1-3 'Jehoram does evil in the eyes of Yahweh' (framing verses).

A.   vv. 4-5: Mesha rebels.

  B.   vv. 6-8: Jehoram asks Jehoshaphat to fight with him against Moab.

    C.   vv. 9-12: There is no water, and the kings respond by going down to Elisha.

      X.   vv. 13-19: Elisha reproaches Jehoram and gives an oracle of victory over Moab.

    C'.   vv. 20-23: Water flows, and the Moabites respond by going against Israel.

  B'.   vv. 24-25: Israel 'fights' Moab.

A'.   vv. 26-27: Mesha sacrifices, and the coalition withdraws.

At the center of this structure ('X'), the prophet's oracle appears to suggest a coalition victory over Mesha. However, parallel segments 'A' and 'A'' indicate otherwise. The story ends at its beginning, with Mesha in rebellion and in control of his own territory. One can imagine the Moabite king praising his god Chemosh for giving him victory, in the words of the Mesha Stela, 'over all my adversaries' (*ANET*: 320). As Yahweh later rescues Jehoram from Ben-Hadad (2 Kgs 7) and Hezekiah from Sennacherib (2 Kgs 19), Mesha is delivered from Jehoram of Israel (Nelson 1987: 168).

Contrasting statements by Jehoram and Elisha reinforce the conflict between the word of Yahweh in the mouth of his prophet Elisha and the last scene in the story. To Jehoram, the prophet declares, '[Yahweh] will give Moab into your hand' (ונתן את־מואב בידכם, v. 18). Twice, Jehoram expresses the opposite view: 'Yahweh has called these three kings to give them into the hand of Moab' (כי־קרא יהוה לשלשת המלכים האלה לתת אותם ביד־מואב, vv. 10, 13). Jehoram's dialogue is introduced in v. 10 with the interjection אהה ('Alas!') and in v. 13 with the negative אל ('No'). On a literary level, this repetition of Jehoram's statement—first, in response to the coalition's dire situation without water and, second, in response to Elisha's invective against Jehoram—calls attention to the king's point of view. When Elisha, with the 'hand of Yahweh' upon him, asserts the opposite, the reader suspects that Jehoram must be mistaken. When Jehoram's assessment turns out to be true, the prophet of Yahweh is called into question.

The resolution to this tension, at least in part, comes in recognizing that there are larger literary patterns at work. The story of Ahab's campaign against Ben-Hadad at Ramoth Gilead lies in the background and frames of 2 Kings 3 (see J.C. Long

2002: 300-307). Like his father before him, Jehoram calls Jehoshaphat king of
Judah to join him in battle. When the narrator has Jehoshaphat quote himself from
1 Kings 22, 'I am as you are; my people are your people; my horses are your horses'
(כמוני כמוך כעמי כעמך כסוסי כסוסיך, v. 7; cf. 1 Kgs 22.4), the reader recalls the
earlier story. When Jehoshaphat asks, 'Is there no prophet of Yahweh here, through
whom we may inquire of Yahweh' (האין פה נביא ליהוה ונדרשה את־יהוה מאותו,
v. 11—also a quotation from 1 Kgs 22.7), the reader is prepared to overhear an
oracle of doom against the king of Israel, as Micaiah prophesied that Ahab would
be defeated. The fact that Elisha sees victory for the coalition does not deter a
careful reader, for Micaiah also prophesied victory for Ahab, before revealing the
scene in heaven with the lying spirit (1 Kgs 22.15). Is it possible that the prophet
Elisha is also enticing Jehoram to go up against Moab?

Allusions to 1 Kings 22 suggest the following outline for 2 Kings 3:

1 Kings 22	*2 Kings 3*
vv. 1-3: Will you go up? Ahab to Jehoshaphat	vv. 4-8: Will you go up? Jehoram to Jehoshaphat
vv. 5-6: Inquiring of the word of Yahweh	*Scene missing* (implied in vv. 9-10, 13)
	vv. 9-10: 'Yahweh called these three kings'
vv. 7-8: 'Is there a prophet of Yahweh?'	vv. 11-12: 'Is there a prophet of Yahweh?'
vv. 9-28: Micaiah and Ahab	vv. 13-19: Elisha and Jehoram
vv. 19-23: Scene in heaven	*Scene missing*
(vv. 6, 12, 15: 'Into the hand of the king')	(v. 18: 'Into your hand')
vv. 29-40: Battle report, a defeat	vv. 20-27: Battle report, a defeat

Both the parallels *and* the omissions recommend reading 2 Kings 3 in light of
1 Kings 22. The coupling in 2 Kings 3 of a son of Ahab with Jehoshaphat of Judah,
aligned in battle against a common foe, along with the verbatim quotations of the
king of Judah, conjure up the 1 Kings 22 battle narrative. The requests for a prophet
and the somewhat contentious interactions between a prophet of Yahweh and the
king of Israel (cf. 1 Kgs 22.16, 26-28; 2 Kgs 3.13-14) also buttress the connections
between the stories. But the missing scenes (i.e. the intentional gaps) also link the
two narratives. When Jehoram opines, 'Alas, Yahweh has called these three kings
to give them into the hand of Moab' (v. 10), a careful reader realizes that the kings
of Israel and Judah must have received a prophetic sendoff—similar to the thresh-
ing floor scene in Samaria (cf. 1 Kgs 22.10-12)—which is missing in the Jehoram
narrative.[8] The repetition of Jehoram's exclamation in v. 13 to Elisha emphasizes
the gap and reinforces this reading. The kings of Israel and Judah had received a

---

8.   Provan (1995: 182) misses the intentional gap in the narrative (framed by 1 Kgs 22) when
he suggests that Jehoshaphat ('his memory suddenly restored') should have requested a word from
Yahweh 'at the start'. Brichto (1992: 205) recognizes the implication that Yahweh had been consulted, but argues that it is hyperbole and does not actually mean that Yahweh 'instigated the war'.

word of victory from prophets of Yahweh, which Jehoram now suspects was a word of enticement to give them into the hand of the king of Moab.

At this point, the statement by the narrator in v. 2 that Jehoram was not as evil as his father and mother comes into play. By implication, Jehoram is a Yahwist who, with Jehoshaphat, sought the favor of Yahweh before commencing the campaign against Mesha. Filling in the intentional gap in the narrative, the reader surmises that Jehoshaphat must have seen no reason to question the word of Jehoram's prophets, as he did the four hundred prophets of Jehoram's father Ahab in the earlier narrative. Only when the survival of the coalition is threatened by thirst in the wilderness does Jehoshaphat request another prophet of Yahweh. Now, along with Jehoram, the king of Judah has reason to question the word of Yahweh that has apparently sent them into the hand of Moab, as he had reason to question the prophets of King Ahab. In 1 Kings 22, Jehoshaphat was apparently suspicious of the behavior of Ahab's 'yes-men' prophets. In 2 Kings 3, he only becomes suspicious when his men and animals are dying of thirst. The almost verbatim repetition of his request for a prophet of Yahweh (cf. 1 Kgs 22.7; 2 Kgs 3.11) secures the connection between the stories.

When the prophet Elisha, 'who used to pour water on the hands of Elijah' (v. 11), in an ecstatic state ('bring me a musician', v. 15), speaks in the name of Yahweh (using the appropriate messenger formula, 'Thus says Yahweh' [twice, vv. 16-17]), both kings' suspicions are apparently assuaged. However, Elisha's word is the same as Ahab's prophets who had a lying spirit and the same as the initial, deceptive word of Micaiah in 1 Kings 22. The prophets of Ahab declare, 'Go up, *for Yahweh* will give it [Ramoth Gilead] into the hand of the king' (עלה ויתן אדני ביד המלך, 1 Kgs 22.6). Following the lead of the prophet Zedekiah, this becomes, 'Go up against Ramoth Gilead and be victorious, *for Yahweh* will give it into the hand of the king' (עלה רמת גלעד והצלח ונתן יהוה ביד המלך, 1 Kgs 22.12), which is then echoed, almost word for word, by the prophet Micaiah (v. 15). It is only after Ahab's skeptical response that Micaiah relates the throne-room-in-heaven scene and prophesies that the king would not return from the battle in peace (vv. 17-28).

To Jehoram, Elisha proclaims, 'This is an easy thing in the eyes of Yahweh; he will give Moab into your hand' (ונקל זאת בעיני יהוה ונתן את־מואב בידכם, 2 Kgs 3.18). The somewhat ambiguous phrase from 1 Kings 22, 'into the hand of the king', becomes, 'into your [plural] hand'. Elisha promises victory for the kings of Israel and Judah and in so doing mirrors both the prophets of Ahab and the prophet Micaiah. Only, in Elisha's oracle Micaiah's account of the scene in heaven and his revised oracle of defeat—not victory—are missing. Nevertheless, the connections between 2 Kings 3 and the episode with Micaiah and the lying prophets are clear. Has Elisha enticed Jehoram to go up against Moab? Does this explain the unexpected defeat at the end of the story (2 Kgs 3.27)?

By means of an ingenious use of structural irony, with 1 Kings 22 framing 2 Kings 3, it looks as if Yahweh, through his prophet Elisha, has sent Jehoram to defeat. With verbal irony,[9] the narrator confirms this reading. Elisha prefaces his

---

9. For definitions of types of irony in Kings (i.e. the Elijah narrative), see Fredenburg 2003: Chapter 2.

word of victory over Moab with, 'This is an easy thing in the eyes of Yahweh' (ונקל זאת בעיני יהוה, 2 Kgs 3.18). Is it just a coincidence that Elisha employs the word קלל ('be trifling/to curse')? In the story that immediately precedes the account of the campaign against Moab, the prophet of Yahweh at Bethel curses (קלל) children who are jeering him, with the effect that 42 of them are mauled by bears (2 Kgs 2.23-25). The term קלל conjures up the preceding story and suggests that Elisha may be cursing Jehoram. In context, Elisha's words to Jehoram are irony. On one level, it 'is an easy thing' (קלל) for Yahweh to provide water for the coalition and give them victory over Moab (vv. 16-19). But, on another level, what Jehoram is trying to do is trivial/accursed (קלל) in the eyes of Yahweh. The king of Israel is attempting to maintain the empire of his father Ahab, who was also קלל before Yahweh (Hobbs 1985: 38-39; see 1 Kgs 16.29-33; 20.1–21.29).

With 1 Kings 22 in the background and with the resulting defeat of Jehoram by Mesha in v. 27, Elisha may in fact be cursing (קלל) Jehoram when he entices the king to continue his plans against Mesha of Moab. In fact, the double meaning is consistent the prophet's rather ambiguous 'this' (זאת, v. 18). And, by using verbal irony the narrator cues the reader that Elisha is not an unwitting false prophet with a lying spirit, like the four hundred prophets of Ahab. With קלל in the mouth of the prophet, the storyteller subtly indicates that Elisha is in on the deception. Like Micaiah, he is a reliable prophet of Yahweh, who speaks for Yahweh, even when it is a word of deception. Ironically, King Jehoram twice verbalizes one of the key themes in the story: 'Yahweh has called these three kings to give them into the hand of Moab' (vv. 10, 13; J.C. Long 2002: 307). With subterfuge, Elisha lures the king of Israel into what will in the end be an unsuccessful campaign—into the hand of Mesha of Moab!

With the keyword עלה ('to go up'), the storyteller also intimates Yahweh is defeating the king of Israel. The root עלה has already been established as a *Leitwort* in preceding narrative scenes. In 2 Kings 1, עלה (vv. 3, 4, 6 [twice], 7, 9, 13, 16; along with עליה ['upper room', v. 2]) functions with ירד ('to go down' [vv. 4, 6, 9, 10 [twice], 11, 12 [twice], 14, 15 [twice], 16]) as a 'going up/coming down' motif to highlight that Ahaziah (the first son of Ahab to reign in Samaria) would 'go up' upon his sickbed but not 'come down' (J.C. Long 2002: 282).[10] The motif resurfaces in 2 Kings 2, when Elijah 'goes up' (עלה, vv. 1, 11) to heaven in a whirlwind, and, then, when children from Bethel sarcastically cajole Elisha to 'go up' (עלה, v. 23 [4 times]) like Elijah (J.C. Long 2002: 296). In 2 Kings 3, עלה brings to mind these scenes and connects Jehoram's incursion into Moab once more with Ahab's military campaign against Ramoth Gilead, where the prophets of Ahab and Micaiah counseled the king to 'go up' (עלה) against Ben-Hadad (1 Kgs 22.6, 12, 15; see also vv. 20, 29, 35). Jehoshaphat agrees to 'go up' (עלה) with Jehoram against Moab (vv. 7-8), and the Moabites hear that the three kings have 'gone up' (עלה) against them (v. 21).

However, it is with the two references to offerings (with עלה) that the narrator implicates Yahweh in Jehoram's defeat—and clarifies the reason for the coalition's

---

10. A careful reader expects Jehoram to 'go up' against Moab and not return (see below).

retreat at the end of the story. When the God of Israel miraculously provides water for the coalition, which the Moabites mistake for the blood of their adversaries, the storyteller pinpoints the arrival of the water with the time of the morning sacrifice—literally, 'in the morning at the *going up* (עלה) of the offering' (בבקר כעלות המנחה, v. 20). The timing of the flood with the morning offering indicates that Yahweh is responsible for the event, just as Elisha had predicted (vv. 16-17). At the end of the story, Mesha literally 'causes [his firstborn son] to *go up* (עלה) as a burnt offering (עלה)' (v. 27). With the preposition על, the narrator calls attention to the offering: '[Mesha] took his firstborn son, who would reign in his place, and offered him (עלה) as a burnt offering (עלה) upon (על) the wall. The wrath was great against (על) Israel. So, they withdrew from against (על) it [Kir-hareseth] and returned to the land' (v. 27). Framed by the reference to Yahweh's mighty act at the morning offering, this emphasis on Mesha's offering suggests that Yahweh participates in the coalition's retreat. The two offerings frame Yahweh's acts, on behalf of the coalition (including Jehoshaphat of Judah), and against Israel—that is, against Jehoram!

Recognizing this rather brilliant rhetorical strategy helps clear up what has been a difficult problem for many commentators. In v. 27, the 'great wrath' (קצף-גדול) against Israel is ambiguous. Is this the wrath of Jehoshaphat, Chemosh, or Yahweh? Since קצף is often used for Yahweh's anger (Cogan and Tadmor 1988: 47; cf., e.g., Num. 18.5; Deut. 29.27; Josh. 9.20; 22.20) and it is inconceivable that the Dtr would entertain a victory of Chemosh over Yahweh, it is reasonable—in context—to interpret this as the wrath of God.[11] The resonance between the two offerings, the morning offering and the offering of Mesha's son, endorses this reading. Yahweh orchestrates the events that transpire following each of the offerings—the water flowing from Edom and the retreat of the coalition.

However, this by itself does not completely elucidate the storyteller's strategy. With the creative use of על/עלה in v. 27 (implying careful design), the ambiguity in the concluding scene must be intentional. The reader might fill in the gap by imagining Jehoshaphat's wrath against Jehoram for this unpleasant turn of events. He might also see Elisha's deception and recognize that Yahweh has most likely defeated Jehoram. Nevertheless, by only indirectly involving Yahweh in the act, the text withholds unequivocal judgment on Jehoram. Since Yahweh is not explicitly mentioned in these events, we are left to ponder the fate of the king who is not as bad as his parents, Ahab and Jezebel. The ambiguity serves larger themes in Kings. The king of Israel is defeated, but there is not yet a final verdict on his reign (see below).

The storyteller's use of point of view reinforces this reading. 2 Kings 3 is a web of differing perspectives. In the framing verses, and in the voice of the narrator, the Dtr gives his assessment of the reign of Jehoram, and, in so doing, proffers Yahweh's point of view. The king of Israel has done evil in the eyes of Yahweh (v. 2, a refrain in Kings for the northern kings; cf., e.g., 2 Kgs 10.29; 17.22). However, in a caveat introduced with רק ('only'), the narrator allows that Jehoram's indiscretions

---

11.   Cohn (2000: 24) conjectures that v. 27 may reflect Moab's point of view; Nelson (1987: 169-70) suggests that the ending may intimate Yahweh uses gods like Chemosh.

are not as bad as his parents. Jehoram is a reformer, a rarity among the kings who reign in Samaria. This son of Ahab removes (סור) the pillar of Baal that his father had made (v. 2; cf. 1 Kgs 16.32-33). The narrator's word choice is conspicuous. סור is the Dtr's word for the kings of Israel who 'turn away' from the way of Yahweh and follow their forefathers in evil.[12] A rather stark contrast is set up, then, with the narrator's next statement. Nevertheless (once more with רק), Jehoram 'clings' (דבק, reflecting Deuteronomistic language; cf. Deut 10.20; 11.22; 13.4 [MT 5]; 30.20; Josh. 23.8, 12; 1 Kgs 11.2; 2 Kgs 18.6) to the sin of Jeroboam, who caused Israel to sin (a refrain in Kings; cf., e.g., 1 Kgs 14.16; 15.26, 30, 34; 2 Kgs 10.29, 31) and does not *turn aside* (סור) from them—as his father Ahab considered it קלל ('trivial') to walk in the sins of Jeroboam (1 Kgs 16.31). So, by means of two caveats, the framing words are ambiguous. The parallel statements with רק and סור indicate intentional ambiguity (see the figure below). Jehoram of Israel is evil in the eyes of Yahweh, but his actions are both good and bad.

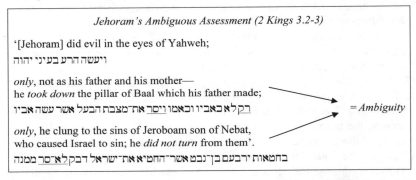

Jehoram's Ambiguous Assessment (2 Kings 3.2-3)

'[Jehoram] did evil in the eyes of Yahweh;
ויעשה הרע בעיני יהוה

only, not as his father and his mother—
he *took down* the pillar of Baal which his father made;
רק לא כאביו וכאמו ויסר את־מצבת הבעל אשר עשה אביו

only, he clung to the sins of Jeroboam son of Nebat,
who caused Israel to sin; he *did not turn* from them'.
בחטאות ירבעם בן־נבט אשר־החטיא את־ישראל דבק לא־סר ממנה

= *Ambiguity*

In the story that follows, various points of view are reflected. Jehoshaphat's point of view toward Jehoram appears in dialogue with 'I am as you are...' (v. 7). Even if the wording reflects his treaty obligations as a vassal to the king of Israel or just court etiquette (see J.C. Long 2002: 262, 300; cf. Cogan and Tadmor 1988: 44; Cogan 2001: 489), his response to Jehoram surely reflects a somewhat positive attitude toward the proposed military mission. When events turn sour in the wilderness to the south, Jehoshaphat's altered perspective appears in his query about a prophet of Yahweh (v. 11). Jehoram reflects a similar, changed view when he laments that Yahweh has delivered them into the hand of Mesha (vv. 10, 13). His lamentation also characterizes him negatively. Jehoshaphat's point of view toward Elisha, 'the word of Yahweh is with him' (v. 12), serves to characterize the king of Judah favorably in a story that does not end successfully. On another level, it also subtly validates the prophet and labels the forthcoming oracle as a 'word of Yahweh', obviously reflecting the narrator's view of Elisha (see below). The storyteller also

12.   For example, the Dtr appears to make a play on סור when he says that Josiah did not 'turn (סור) to the right or to the left' in walking in the ways of his father David (2 Kgs 22.2), as did the kings of Israel, and then records Yahweh saying, 'I will also remove (סור) Judah from my presence as I removed (סור) Israel' (23.26; see J.C. Long 2002: 501, 518; cf. 453).

allows the reader to overhear Elisha's view of Jehoram, which is colored by his stance toward the idolatries of the king's parents (v. 13)—and may color the oracle that follows. On the surface, the oracle itself reflects the point of view of Yahweh; the prophet introduces his word with the appropriate messenger formula ('thus says Yahweh', [twice] vv. 16-17), and the narrator avers, 'the hand of Yahweh came upon him' (vv. 15-16). In v. 20, a הנה clause (והנה־מים באים מדרך אדום, 'All of a sudden, water came from the way of Edom') describes, from Israel's point of view, the miraculous appearance of the water promised by Yahweh. The drama intensifies as the Moabites 'hear' (שמע, v. 21) and 'see' (ראה, v. 22) the flood, but their perception is distorted. At the end of the story, Mesha sees (ראה, v. 26) that the battle is against him, and he sacrifices his son (v. 27).

Of interest at this juncture, the Mesha Stela (*ANET*: 320-21) directly reflects the point of view of the Moabite king. J.A. Emerton (2002: 490-91) confirms the general historicity of the Moabite stone (contra T.L. Thompson), arguing that 2 Kings 3 is a variant of the struggle between Moab and Israel. Concerning Jehoram, he observes that the Mesha Stela says nothing of this Israelite king, though it implies that he was unsuccessful in recapturing lost territory. Emerton concludes, 'The most plausible way of accounting for the differences between the two stories is to suppose that neither was written from a purely objective point of view, and that each left out events that were not to its credit' (2002: 491). We would add that the two accounts (i.e. 2 Kgs 3 and the Mesha Stela) highlight the literary character of the Dtr's account and that 2 Kings 3 is not framed to put Israel in a 'positive light'. As a theodicy, the storyteller's main concern is putting Yahweh in the best light possible. While not directly addressing Mesha's point of view that Chemosh wins, the Dtr does so indirectly by explaining the perplexing prophecy of Elisha (see below).

The various perspectives in 2 Kings 3 have the literary effect of shaping the reader's external point of view. In particular, they highlight the tension existing between the questions the two kings have about their mission (once their plans start to unravel [vv. 9-11]) and Elisha's prophecy that Yahweh would give Moab into their hand (v. 18). Yet, statements by the narrator/characters that endorse the prophetic voice, and the dramatic irony which arises because of information the narrator has supplied to the reader as the Moabites misperceive events, lull the reader into accepting at face value the anticipated victory of the coalition. With Jehoram and Jehoshaphat, a first-time reader may also be deceived about the outcome of the campaign! The prospect of victory is challenged when the unexpected turn in the plot creates dissonance for the reader. The resulting ambiguity raises the specter of Yahweh's perception of events. There is 'great wrath against Israel' (v. 27), but in whose eyes? The phrase 'in the eyes of Yahweh' (בעיני יהוה) appears twice in 2 Kings 3, once in the narrator's voice of exposition (v. 2) and once in the prophet's oracle of deliverance (v. 18). Jehoram has done evil in the eyes of Yahweh, and an ambiguous 'this' (זאת) is קלל in his eyes. As already indicated, קלל is ironic, indicating Elisha is in fact cursing Jehoram's campaign against Moab. It follows that the great wrath against Israel/Jehoram must be the wrath of Yahweh (reinforced by the use of על/עלה in v. 27; see above), although the storyteller chooses not to state this explicitly. It is as if the qualified appraisal of Jehoram by the Dtr (vv. 1-3) resurfaces in the indirect way the storyteller indicates Yahweh's disapproval of Jehoram's mission. Bolstered by the use of the narrative technique of point of view, the chapter ends where it began—in ambiguity!

The perspective of Jehoram's servant, who identifies Elisha as the one 'who poured water on Elijah' (v. 11), also stands out in the story. Provan (1995: 185) observes, 'It is a pronounced feature of the Elisha stories in 2 Kgs. 3–8 that it is characteristically the politically powerless who are in touch with and open to what God is doing through Elisha, while the powerful (especially the kings) reveal only ignorance and arrogance, refusing to adopt a humble and respectful attitude towards him'. The fact that the king's servant knows the whereabouts of Elisha is consistent with this outline. In addition, episodes in the Elisha cycle alternate between the prophet's dealings in international settings, with kings and high officials, and his interactions on a local, personal level, often with those on the periphery of society, as follows (adapted from J.C. Long 2002: 347):

> A. The king of Israel's campaign against Moab (3.1-27)
>
> > B. The miracles of the widow's oil, the Shunammite's son, death in the pot for the sons of the prophets, and feeding the people (4.1-44)
>
> A. The healing of an Aramean general, a leper (5.1-27)
>
> > B. The miracle of the floating ax head for one of the sons of the prophets (6.1-7)
>
> A. The Aramean army trapped by Elisha and the siege of Samaria (6.8–7.20)
>
> > B. The Shunammite's property restored (8.1-6)
>
> A. The 'anointing' by Elisha of the kings of Aram and Israel (8.7–9.13)

The upshot of this pattern is that 2 Kings 3, however indirectly, participates in the composition's ethical concern for social justice in Israel (see J.C. Long 2002: 309).

Even though the story ends in ambiguity, the Dtr has carefully laid out a strategy for validating the prophet. Part of the strategy revolves around the key word נכה ('to strike/smite'). Occurring six times in 2 Kings 3 (vv. 19, 23, 24 [3 times], 25; including the *qere* in v. 24), נכה represents the primary verb in the prophet's declaration of what Israel would do to Moab—'strike/smite' all of the fortified and choice cities of Moab. The coalition would also cut down every good tree, stop up all of the springs, and cover every good field with stones (v. 19). Following the prophet's word of 'victory', water comes and fills the land, at which time the Moabites mistake the reflection of the sun on the water as blood: 'The kings must have attacked and smote (נכה) each other' (v. 23). When they approach the camp of Israel, 'the Israelites rise up and strike (נכה) them', whereupon they flee, but the coalition 'continues to strike (נכה) Moab' (v. 24). In v. 25, the Dtr, in his typical prophecy–fulfillment pattern (cf. 1 Kgs 17.14-16), chronicles the fulfillment of the oracle in the words of the prophet (v. 19; i.e. in dialogue-bound narration; see Alter 1981: 65). Only, there are noticeable differences: 'All the fortified cities' and 'all the choice cities' simply become 'the cities', which are 'torn down' (הרס). The verb change (from נכה) stands out. The narrator then recounts the actions outlined in Elisha's oracle (v. 19) in reverse order (Kissling 1996: 185), as follows:

2 Kgs 3.19:

  A.   'You will strike (נכה) all of the fortified and all of the choice cities'
      (והכיתם כל־עיר מבצר וכל־עיר מבחור);

      B.   'You will fell all the good trees' (וכל־עץ טוב תפילו);

          C.   'You will stop up all of the springs of water'
             (וכל־מעיני־מים תסתמו);

             D.   'You will ruin with stones all of the good fields'
                (וכל החלקה הטובה תכאבו באבנים).

2 Kgs 3.25:

  A'.   'They tore down (הרס) the cities' (והערים יהרסו);

          D'.   'Each man threw his stone on all the good fields until they
              were covered'
             (וכל־חלקה טובה ישליכו איש־אבנו ומלאוה);

        C'.   'They stopped up all the springs of water'
           (וכל־מעין־מים יסתמו);

      B'.   'They felled every good tree'
         (וכל־עץ־טוב יפילו);

  E.   'Until Khir-Hareseth remained with its stones intact'
      (עד־השאיר אבניה בקיר חרשת);

  A''.   'The slingers surrounded it and struck (נכה) it'
      (ויסבו הקלעים ויכוה).

This inverted arrangement sets up the reader for a surprise. The coalition was not able to take Kir-hareseth (item 'E'). However, in 'A''' the narrator records that the slingers 'struck' (נכה) the city. The reader has been brought back to Elisha's initial statement (v. 19). Israel did 'strike' (נכה) all of the cities of Moab. Technically, the words of the prophet come true (Provan 1995: 186; see J.C. Long 2002: 304-305). Elisha is a prophet of Yahweh whose word is reliable.

The storyteller's indirect literary stratagem explains the defeat of Jehoram. With the allusions to 1 Kings 22, Yahweh has, in the words of the king of Israel, 'given the three kings into the hand of Moab' (vv. 10, 13). Elisha entices Jehoram to go up against Mesha of Moab. However, 1 Kings 22 also establishes expectations for the reader that indicate Yahweh's judgment on Jehoram is measured. With the promise of Yahweh that Ahab's dynasty would end in the days of his son (1 Kgs 21.28-29), the framing scenes of Ahab's demise create the prospect of Jehoram's death in Moab. A careful reader anticipates this outcome.

After the episode of Naboth's vineyard (1 Kgs 21.1-16), Yahweh instructs Elijah to pronounce judgment on Ahab of Israel: 'In the place where the dogs licked the blood of Naboth, dogs will lick up your blood' (v. 19). Moving beyond Yahweh's instructions, the overzealous prophet of Yahweh, assuming the divine voice without signaling messenger speech (Kissling 1996: 127-32; Olley 1998; J.C. Long 2002: 253-56) instead announces the destruction of the whole house of Ahab: 'I will consume those who come after you and cut off from Ahab every male, whether slave or free' (v. 21). In response, Ahab repents—tearing his clothes, donning sackcloth, fasting, and walking around sullenly (v. 27, in stark contrast with his demeanor when Naboth would not sell the king his vineyard [v. 4]). Yahweh responds with a word for the prophet: the destruction of Ahab's house will happen in the days of his son (v. 28). Nevertheless, when a 'stray arrow' fatally pierces the king at Ramoth Gilead (22.34), Yahweh's designs for Ahab materialize—but his royal house carries on.[13]

As soon as Elijah decrees that Ahab's son Ahaziah will not come down from his sickbed after falling through the lattice of his upper room (2 Kgs 1.2-6), the reader anticipates the end of the house of Ahab. However, at the death of Ahaziah the storyteller interjects, for the first time, that Ahab has another son who now reigns because the deceased king has no heir (v. 17). For the reader, this is an unexpected delay; the storyteller has withheld information for dramatic effect (Provan 1995: 169; J.C. Long 2002: 285-86). In 1 Kgs 16.34,[14] the Dtr frames the account of Ahab with the note that during his reign Hiel rebuilds Jericho with the loss of his two sons (as a foundation deposit?), which happens according to the curse that Joshua spoke against the city of Jericho (Josh. 6.26). With Elijah's judgment and Yahweh's altered word against the king of Israel (1 Kgs 21.19, 29), Joshua's curse now looms as a shadow over the house of Ahab—and foreshadows the loss of his two sons (Conroy 1996: 213-15).

When the campaign against Moab mirrors the failed campaign against Ramoth Gilead, in which Ahab lost his life, the reader anticipates the end of the house of Ahab, the death of Jehoram. Yahweh's altered word against the house of Ahab, 'in the days of his son', reinforced by the framing note about the death of Hiel's two sons, must now be about to come down. As Micaiah promised Ahab that he would 'go up' (עלה, 1 Kgs 22.15) but not 'return' (שוב, v. 28), so the storyteller has used allusion to create the expectation that the house of Ahab will now end. That expectation, however, does not materialize. Jehoram goes up (עלה) against Moab, enticed by the prophet Elisha, but when Mesha sacrifices his son, the coalition 'returns (שוב) to the land' (v. 27). For the reader who sees the connections between 1 Kings 22 and 2 Kings 3, this is a surprise, a reversal.[15] Mesha's son dies as an offering on the wall of Kir-hareseth—instead of the reigning son of Ahab!

The prophet Elisha has enticed the son of Ahab to go up against Moab in what will be a failed campaign, but Jehoram returns with his life and reign intact. The king who is better than his parents receives a reprieve. Resolution of the prophetic oracle against the house of Ahab is set in abeyance, and this reinforces the

13.   Dogs lick his blood in Samaria, not Jezreel (vv. 37-38), but the word of Yahweh comes to pass when Jehoram, symbolically as Ahab, is assassinated with an arrow by Jehu and thrown, now as a lifeless corpse, on the plot that belonged to Naboth the Jezreelite (2 Kgs 9.24-26; see J.C. Long 2002: 366-68).

14.   For the issues involved in a diachronic reading of 1 Kgs 16.34, see Conroy 1996: 210-11, 216-18 and references there.

15.   For the reader who does not see the allusions to 1 Kgs 22, the surprise is that Elisha's prophecy does not come to pass, which creates a problem that is only solved by recognizing the storyteller's strategy of framing 2 Kgs 3 with 1 Kgs 22.

important theme in Kings of delayed retribution.[16] The delay in retribution on the house of Ahab in the time of Elijah (1 Kgs 21.29) reappears in the ambiguous conclusion to the Jehoram-Mesha episode (which echoes the ambiguity in the Dtr introduction to the narrative [vv. 1-3]). Yahweh is working against Jehoram, but the reader must wait to see if Jehoram's less idolatrous policies will avert Elijah's word of judgment on the house of Ahab.

Sociological Analysis

Four Facets of a Sociological Analysis: 2 Kings 3

Having completed a close literary analysis of our passage, we will now explore four significant sociological facets of 2 Kings 3, which flow out of and frame our preceding literary observations and which call attention to the social location and theological concerns of the Dtr.

(1) *Theodicy*. Theodicy was a central concern for the Dtr in the exilic/post-exilic community. A major factor in composing the DtrH was in exonerating Yahweh from the idea that he had lost to the Assyrian and Babylonian gods. To address the perception that Yahweh had lost power and prestige, DtrH employs a retributive understanding of reality. Military victories, for instance, are explained as rewards for compliance to the D Code. Conversely, defeats in battle are understood as punishments for disobedience to the D code. 2 Kings 3.1-3, which is typically acknowledged as the actual words of the Dtr, depicts Jehoram as a generally evil king, though, in comparison with his father, not quite so bad. The assessment of his reign is mixed, though more evil than good. This characterization fits the results of the battle remarkably well. The mixed character of Jehoram's reign is reflected in the mixed but ultimately faulty outcome of the story. Though Elisha's prophecy technically comes true, Mesha's royal city remains intact (vv. 24-27). The failure to take the city casts a dark shadow over the whole incident. That all Israel 'returns' shows that the narrow victory was no victory at all.

The mixing of categories is also seen beyond the introduction (vv. 1-3). Jehoram is depicted as a despairing, pessimistic complainer when confronted with a crisis (v. 10). Jehoshaphat, on the other hand, is characterized as decisive and knowledgable about proper protocol, that is, the need to consult a prophet for help (v. 11). And when he hears the name 'Elisha', he knows that he is a true prophet (v. 12). Elisha, at first, hesitates to have anything to do with Jehoram. Only for the sake of

---

16. In the larger story of Kings, the delay in retribution for the house of Ahab foreshadows the delay in retribution/judgment on Judah and Jerusalem. When Josiah humbles himself (כנע, 2 Kgs 22.19) before Yahweh, as did Ahab (1 Kgs 21.29), judgment on the house of David is delayed to the time of his son Zedekiah (Provan 1995: 272; see J.C. Long 2002: 257-59; cf. 151-52, 271-72; 543). Knoppers (1997: 405-409) contends that 'transgenerational punishments' characterize Kings, in contrast with the Chronicler's more cyclical 'sequence of punishments and rewards'. From a Deuteronomic perspective, 'it is a mark of divine leniency to impose the punishment due to the father upon the son'.

Jehoshophat does Elisha intervene and seek an oracle from God. That Jeshoshaphat is southern and depicted as a generally good king (cf. 1 Kgs 22.43-44) could explain any advances the coalition of troops is able to make (2 Kgs 3.23-26). However, in spite of his good qualities, the king of Judah is willing to align himself with a northern Israelite king, which, according to the Dtr, is a major fault (1 Kgs 22.44). At any rate, we have here a generally bad, northern king, but not as bad as Ahab and Jezebel, and a generally good, southern king whose main fault is his alignment with evil northern kings. So it comes as no surprise that their joint venture would have mixed results.

(2) *True and false prophecy*. The issue of true and false prophecy is another societal problem. Skillfully, the storyteller has constructed a well-orchestrated strategy of validating the prophet, with the following features (see also the literary analysis above):

1. With naming/description: in the mouth of Jehoshaphat, 'Is there not a prophet of Yahweh here...?' (v. 11); and 'The word of Yahweh is with him' (v. 12). In the mouth of the officer of the king, 'He used to pour water on the hands of Elijah' (v. 11).
2. In the attitude that Elisha expresses toward the parents of Jehoram and their deities (vv. 13-14).
3. With incubation and messenger speech: 'While the harpist was playing, the hand of Yahweh came upon Elisha, and he said, "Thus says Yahweh..."' (vv. 15-16, the messenger formula repeated in v. 17).
4. With 1 Kings 22 as a frame, which indicates that Elisha is enticing Jehoram.
5. With the careful repetition of the prophet's oracle, in reverse order, to indicate that the words of the prophet are technically true.

(3) *Incubation, ecstasy, and anthropology*. Elisha is portrayed as using the process of incubation to elicit a response from Yahweh concerning the crisis. This is a cross-cultural phenomenon that varies in particular manifestation. What is interesting is how the Dtr carefully uses the description of this phenomenon for his own purposes. Both Robert Wilson and Thomas Overholt have described the tension between the Elijah/Elisha narratives and the Dtr ideology, and this is especially true concerning the ecstatic behavior of prophets (see Wilson 1996: 418-20; Overholt 1996: 28-39). Ecstasy or bizarre behavior was one way that those on the periphery of society could gain prestige and power for themselves (Wilson 1980: 69-70). Its non-rationality could potentially threaten the stability of society. The Dtr, then, has a tendency to downplay this aspect of prophecy, even though he needs such behavior to legitimate particular prophets. Ancient Israelite society expected prophets to exhibit stereotypical patterns of behavior to demonstrate their authenticity. While playing the lyre is not in itself ecstatic behavior, it was a means of eliciting such behavior and the communicative process of possession, the typically ancient Near Eastern variety (see Overholt 1996: 48).

The Dtr dealt with the tension between the potentially threatening facets of ecstasy and its necessity for legitimation by distinguishing between two types of ecstasy: controlled and uncontrolled (Wilson 1996: 412-21). Saul exemplifies the uncontrolled aspects, when he is filled with the evil spirit and needs music for relief, and when, under its influence, attempts to kill David with a spear (1 Sam. 18). Elijah and Elisha represent the controlled kind of ecstasy, and our story has Elisha acting in a very controlled manner. The details of ecstasy are carefully avoided and the emphasis is set on the incubation's effectiveness. This careful balancing act of the Dtr is also characteristic of the next important sociological facet of our story.

(4) *Social class conflict*. Drawing on the insight of Fredric Jameson, our text can be conceived as a battleground between social classes. As noted earlier, Jameson is well known for qualifying the typical Marxist position that literature, as part of the superstructure, simply reflects its economic base. Jameson emphasizes that literature often itself extends an influence in the opposite direction, from superstructure to base. In other words, literature and art react to the base and attempt to mitigate its liabilities, while simultaneously emerging from it. Literature and art are a society's main venue for treating social ills. Literature often attempts to repress or compensate for societal conflict.

How might our text do such a thing? Jameson looks for contradictions or tensions in the text as places where his analysis begins. Wesley Bergen has laid the groundwork for our analysis (1992). He argues that the tension in the Elisha narratives is between the monarchy and prophecy as two opposing types of authority. He argues that the Elisha narratives indicate that the narrator uses the prophetic material to critique the wicked behavior of kings, especially from the north, but without critiquing the viability of the monarchy as a system. Bergen relies on Foucault for his method, but it is essentially Jamesonian in its attention to contradictions in the text and the assumption that a dominant voice suppresses minor ones.

Bergen addresses 2 Kings 3 by pointing out that Elisha represents an alternate form of power to the king (1992: 130-31). This is inherently threatening, but the narrator is careful to portray the prophet as subject to the rule of the king. He aids the king in need but becomes subordinate to his authority. Bergen concludes that Jehoram is made to look bad in this story because of the failed attempt to overtake Mesha. At the same time, the monarchy is not questioned as a system.[17]

Bergen fails to consider directly the dimension of social class conflict, though it is implied, and the social location of the Dtr is an elite. Tamis Rentería (1992) goes beyond Bergen here. She suggests that the Elijah/Elisha block of material originally functioned as a lower class, peasant polemic against the upper class hegemony of the Omride dynasty. However, the actual instigators of this polemic were rural Israelite

17.   What Bergen does is strikingly similar to Roland Boer, who uses a Jamesonian approach to analyze 1 Kgs 11–14. He argues that the post-exilic Dtr has co-opted dissident, prophetic material to critique the previous monarchy, while simultaneously legitimating the new, 'declassed', ruling class (1996: 147-76, 192).

elites who resented the Omrides. They supported Jehu and used the Elijah/Elisha stories, which reflected societal resentment, to justify Jehu's *coup d'état*.[18]

Going beyond Rentería and focusing on the final form of the text, we suggest that the Dtr in this block of material bolsters his own retributive strategy for the exilic/post-exilic community. For the Dtr, the Elisha material represents a lower class ethos, and he uses this to call into question the Omrides. Thus, the Omrides are not only discredited in the eyes of the reader because of their idolatrous activities, but also because of their social injustice. In the DtrH, the Omrides represent a significant factor in God's decision to allow Samaria's destruction at the hands of the Assyrians.

Though our story does not focus explicitly on the social evils of Jehoram, it does critique the king by virtue of the mere presence of Elisha in the story. Also, that information about Elisha's whereabouts comes from the king's servant (v. 11) further confirms the class conflict represented in the story.

What is interesting from a Jamesonian perspective is what the Dtr does not discuss, what gets occluded in this story. As Bergen has pointed out, the monarchy itself is never impugned in the Elisha narratives. This is also true for Kings and even the DtrH as a whole, though anti-monarchic sentiment may be present in Samuel.[19] Instances of egregious acts of injustice committed by particular kings are the things that are brought into question (e.g. Ahab's obtaining Naboth's vineyard [1 Kgs 21]). This means that the inherent, oppressive character of monarchic systems, no matter how 'just' they may appear, is never an issue; it gets repressed. The Dtr detaches the egregious acts from the polity of the monarchy as a whole. It is not the monarchy that is unjust but only particular kings who rule unjustly. And it is not a stratified society *per se* that is questioned—only ones with ruthless, ungodly kings.

The Dtr is blind to such questioning because of his own, privileged position as an elite priest or scribe within the exilic/post-exilic community. Even though there was no monarchy during the days of the Dtr, he lived within a highly stratified society whose leaders, whether governors or priests, assumed essentially the same powerful role as a king. As a highly educated elite of that society, the Dtr would do nothing to question the stratified society that provided for his comforts and allowed him the leisure time to compose such a tome as the DtrH (cf. Clines 1995: 38). And, thus, by focusing on defending Yahweh's integrity with his theodicy strategy and by undermining the credibility of wicked kings in northern Israel but also in Judah, the Dtr occludes dealing with the similar social realities of his own day and avoids implicating himself and the social class to which he belongs as part of an oppressive

18.   White (1997) argues that the Elijah narratives are largely fictive and are based on the Elisha stories. She believes they were concocted to further legitimate Elisha and that the Elijah/Elisha material was used to legitimate Jehu's bloody coup.

19.   Amit concludes that since the books of Samuel put the prophet above the king and seem less Dtr than Joshua and Kings, this demonstrates that they are an example of 'prophetic historiography' (1999: 48). Though this may be true, the fact that the books of Samuel have been framed by more heavily Dtr works (i.e. Joshua, Judges, and Kings) suggests that the anti-monarchic sentiment has been co-opted in service of the larger agenda of the Dtr to discredit wicked kings.

system.[20] The faint hope of a future Davidide, represented in the release of Jehoia-chin from prison at the end of the history (2 Kgs 25.27-30), further confirms our suspicions about the Dtr's 'blind spot' (cf. Boer's assessment of the regnal material in 1 Kgs 11–14 [1996: 168]).

Conclusion

Our socio-literary reading of 2 Kings 3 demonstrates the following:

1. A synchronic, literary reading explains the difficult ending to the story and exposes the Dtr's larger strategy. The ambiguity in the text is inten-tional. Out of his wrath, Yahweh entices the king who followed in the sins of Jeroboam into a failed campaign against Moab, but in his grace allows the king who was also better than his parents to retain his throne. Final judgment on the house of Ahab in the narrative must await the further character development of Ahab's second son to reign in Samaria.

2. The Dtr has a well-developed strategy of validating the word of Elisha. If Floyd (2002: 401-22) is correct that מַשָּׂא (typically understood as 'ora-cle') in the mouth of Jehu (2 Kgs 9.25-26) carries the nuance of the reinterpretation of past prophecies that were in some way problematic, 2 Kings 3 may be understood as מַשָּׂא (without carrying the designation), as part of the intervening narrative between 1 Kings 21 and 2 Kings 9. The story of the Moabite campaign is also מַשָּׂא in the sense that a prob-lematic prophecy of Yahweh's prophet Elisha is being 'reinterpreted' by the Dtr for an exilic/post-exilic context. That problem episode is recon-strued in a way that upholds the prophet and explains Yahweh's action/lack of action (the king is defeated but does not die) against Jehoram of Israel.

3. The Dtr's overarching concern is with justifying the acts of Yahweh; Kings is fundamentally a theodicy! However, his retributive strategy for explaining Yahweh's judgment on Israel and Judah is tempered by the theme of delayed retribution—for the Dtr, an expression of grace—which is clearly reflected in the account of the house of Ahab, including Jehoram's failed campaign against Mesha of Moab.

4. The Dtr critiques the Omrides and calls attention to issues of social injus-tice in Israel, but, as an elite, he does not see the abandonment of the monarchy as a possibility for Judah's future. As an elite, he is blind to the possibility of his own involvement in oppression.

5. There should be a dynamic interplay between sociological and literary approaches to biblical texts. Sociological readings must be filtered through literary analysis. Literary readings can be validated by sociologi-cal analysis. Our reading of 2 Kings 3 illustrates the interplay.

---

20. Referring to the Elijah/Elisha sections, Hill writes, 'All biblical prophets are in the canon because they can be seen as, or used in, supporting the Temple or post-Temple cult… Specifically, the prophet must be depicted as favoring the canonizers and opposing their enemies' (1992: 38).

BIBLIOGRAPHY

Aichele, George *et al.* (eds.)
1995   *The Postmodern Bible: The Bible and Culture Collective* (New Haven: Yale University Press).
Alter, Robert
1981   *The Art of Biblical Narrative* (New York: Basic Books).
Alter, Robert, and Frank Kermode
1987   'General Introduction', in R. Alter and F. Kermode (eds.), *The Literary Guide to the Bible* (Cambridge, MA: Belknap): 1-8.
Amit, Yairah
1999   *History and Ideology: An Introduction to Historiography in the Hebrew Bible* (trans. Y. Lotan; The Biblical Seminar, 60; Sheffield: Sheffield Academic Press).
Bergen, Wesley J.
1992   'The Prophetic Alternative: Elisha and the Israelite Monarchy', in Coote (ed.) 1992: 127-37.
Boer, Roland
1996   *Jameson and Jeroboam* (SBLSS; Atlanta: Scholars).
Brichto, H.C.
1992   *Toward a Grammar of Biblical Poetics: Tales of the Prophets* (Oxford: Oxford University Press).
Brueggemann, Walter
2000   *1 & 2 Kings* (Macon, GA: Smyth & Helwys).
Clines, David J.A.
1995   *Interested Parties: The Ideology of Writers and Readers of the Hebrew Bible* (JSOTSup, 205; Gender, Culture, Theory, 1; Sheffield: Sheffield Academic Press).
Cogan, Mordechai, and Hayim Tadmor
1988   *II Kings: A New Translation with Introduction and Commentary* (AB, 11; New York: Doubleday).
Cogan, Mordechai
2001   *1 Kings: A New Translation with Introduction and Commentary* (AB, 10; New York: Doubleday).
Cohn, Robert L.
2000   *2 Kings* (Berit Olam; Collegeville, MN: Liturgical Press).
Conroy, Charles
1996   'Hiel between Ahab and Elijah-Elisha: 1 Kgs 16,34 in its Immediate Literary Context', *Bib* 77: 210-18.
Coote, Robert (ed.)
1992   *Elijah and Elisha in Socioliterary Perspective* (SBLSS; Atlanta: Scholars Press).
Coote, Robert, and Mary P. Coote
1990   *Power, Politics, and the Making of the Bible* (Minneapolis: Fortress Press).
Dowling, William C.
1984   *Jameson, Althusser, Marx: An Introduction to The Political Unconscious* (Ithaca, NY: Cornell University Press).
Emerton, J.A.
2002   'The Value of the Moabite Stone as an Historical Source', *VT* 52: 483-92.

Floyd, Michael H.
    2002   'The משא (*Maśśa'*) as a Type of Prophetic Book', *JBL* 121: 401-22.
Fredenburg, Brandon L.
    2003   'With Horns of Irony: The Implications of Irony in the Narrative of Ahab's
             Reign (1 Kings 16.29–22.40)' (unpublished PhD dissertation, University of
             Denver and the Iliff School of Theology).
Fry, Keith
    2000   'Following the Leader: Political Anthropology and the Hereditary Succes-
             sion of Judean Kings' (unpublished paper presented at the annual meeting of
             the SBL, Nashville, TN).
Gorman, Michael
    2001   *Elements of Biblical Exegesis: A Basic Guide for Students and Ministers*
             (Peabody, MA: Hendrickson).
Gottwald, Norman K.
    1985   *The Hebrew Bible: A Socio-Literary Introduction* (Philadelphia: Fortress
             Press).
    1992   'Social Class and Ideology in Isaiah 40–55: An Eagletonian Reading',
             Semeia 59: 43-71.
    1999a   'The Expropriated and the Expropriators in Nehemiah 5', in M. Sneed (ed.),
             Concepts of Class in Ancient Israel (South Florida Studies in the History of
             Judaism 201; Atlanta: Scholars Press): 1-19.
    1999b   'Response: Twenty-Five Years and Counting', *Semeia* 87: 255-65.
Gray, John
    1970   *I & II Kings: A Commentary* (OTL; London: SCM Press, 2nd edn).
Hill, Scott D.
    1992   'The Local Hero in Palestine in Comparative Perspective', in Coote (ed.)
             1992: 37-73.
Hobbs, T.R.
    1985   *2 Kings* (WBC, 13; Waco, TX: Word Books).
Jameson, Fredric
    1981   *The Political Unconscious: Narrative as a Socially Symbolic Act* (Ithaca,
             NY: Cornell University Press).
Jobling, David
    1991   '"Forced Labor": 1 Kings 3–10 and the Question of Literary Representa-
             tion', *Semeia* 54: 58-76.
    1992   'Deconstruction and the Political Analysis of Biblical Texts: A Jamesonian
             Reading of Psalm 72', *Semeia* 59: 95-127.
    1997   'Sociological and Literary Approaches to the Bible: How Shall the Twain
             Meet?', in D. Chalcraft (ed.), *Socio-Scientific Old Testament Criticism: A
             Sheffield Reader* (The Biblical Seminar, 47; Sheffield: Sheffield Academic
             Press): 34-42.
Kissling, Paul
    1996   *Reliable Characters in the Primary History: Profiles of Moses, Joshua,
             Elijah and Elisha* (JSOTSup, 224; Sheffield: Sheffield Academic Press).
Knoppers, Gary N.
    1997   'Solomon's Fall and Deuteronomy', in L.K. Handy (ed.), *The Age of Solo-
             mon: Scholarship at the Turn of the Millennium* (Leiden: E.J. Brill): 392-410.
Long, Burk O.
    1991   *2 Kings* (FOTL, 10; Grand Rapids: Eerdmans).

Long, Jesse C., Jr
    2002   *1 & 2 Kings* (The College Press NIV Commentary; Joplin, MO: College Press).

Lye, John
    1997   'Ideology: A Brief Guide' <http://www.brocku.ca/english/jlye/ideology.html>.
    1999   'Ideological Reading: Aunt Jennifer's Tigers' <http://www.brocku.ca/english/courses/4F70/aunt.html>.

McConville, J.G.
    1989   'Narrative and Meaning in the Book of Kings', *Bib* 70: 31-49.

Matthews, Victor H., and Don C. Benjamin
    1993   *Social World of Ancient Israel: 1250–587 BCE* (Peabody, MA: Hendrickson).

Nelson, Richard D.
    1987   *First and Second Kings* (Interpretation: A Commentary for Teaching and Preaching; Louisville, KY: John Knox Press).

Olley, John W.
    1998   'YHWH and His Zealous Prophet: The Presentation of Elijah in 1 and 2 Kings', *JSOT* 80: 25-51.

Otto, Susanne
    2003   'The Composition of the Elijah–Elisha Stories and the Deuteronomistic History', *JSOT* 27.4: 487-508.

Overholt, Thomas
    1996   *Cultural Anthropology and the Old Testament* (Minneapolis: Fortress Press).

Provan, Iain W.
    1995   *1 and 2 Kings* (New International Biblical Commentary; Peabody, MA: Hendrickson).

Rentería, Tamis Hoover
    1992   'The Elijah/Elijah [*sic*] Stories: A Socio-Cultural Analysis of Prophets and People in Ninth-Century B.C.E. Israel', in Coote (ed.) 1992: 75-126.

Roberts, Adam
    2000   *Fredric Jameson* (Routledge Critical Thinkers; London: Routledge).

Satterthwaite, Philip E.
    1998   'The Elisha Narratives and the Coherence of 2 Kings 2–8', *TynBul* 49/1: 1-28.

Seow, Choon-Leong
    1999   'The First and Second Books of Kings: Introduction, Commentary, and Reflections', in *NIB*: III, 1-295.

Sneed, Mark
    2000   'A Response to Keith Fry's "Following the Leader: Political Anthropology and the Hereditary Succession of Judean Kings"' (unpublished paper presented at the annual meeting of the SBL, Nashville, TN).

Todd, Judith A.
    1992   'The Pre-Deuteronomistic Elijah Cycle', in Coote (ed.) 1992: 1-35.

White, Marsha C.
    1997   *The Elijah Legends and Jehu's Coup* (BJS, 311; Atlanta: Scholars Press).

Wilson, Robert R.
    1980   *Prophecy and Society in Ancient Israel* (Philadelphia: Fortress Press).

1996   'Prophecy and Ecstasy: A Reexamination', in C. Carter and C. Meyers (eds.), *Community, Identity, and Ideology: Social Sciences Approaches to the Hebrew Bible* (Sources for Biblical and Theological Study, 6; Winona Lake, IN: Eisenbrauns): 404-22.

Yee, Gale A.

1995   'Ideological Criticism: Judges 17–21 and the Dismembered Body', in *idem*, (ed.), *Judges & Method: New Approaches in Biblical Studies* (Minneapolis: Fortress Press): 146-70.

1999   'Gender, Class, and the Social-Scientific Study of Genesis 2–3', *Semeia* 87: 177-92.

2001   ' "She is not my Wife and I am not her Husband": A Materialist Analysis of Hosea 1–2', *BibInt* 9/4: 345-83.

THE SPIRITUAL JOURNEY OF JONAH:
FROM THE PERSPECTIVE OF C.G. JUNG'S ANALYTICAL PSYCHOLOGY

Jongsoo Park

Introduction

Traditionally, Jonah has been regarded as one of the prophets in ancient Israel. Some unrealistic elements of the book of Jonah, however, guide us to look at it differently from other historical or prophetic books. The fantastic elements—Jonah's staying in the belly of a big fish, 'a godly scale' of Nineveh (Simon 1999: 28), repentance of the whole people of the Ninevites, and the fast growing and withering of a mythical plant (*qîqāyôn*)—reveal Jonah not as one of the traditional prophets (Zimmermann 1991: 580), but as an imaginary and symbolic figure. Another peculiar characteristic of Jonah that sets him apart from other prophets is his attitude toward his divine vocation. Prophets accept God's call, despite their reluctance and conflicted attitudes (see, e.g., Jer. 1.4-10; Isa. 6.1-13). Jonah, however, is 'a parody or caricature of a prophet, refusing to accept the call to be Yahweh's messenger' (Payne 1988–89: 131). When he heard the words of God, 'Jonah set out to flee to Tarshish from the presence of the Lord' (Jon. 1.3). It is probable that the dreaded image of Nineveh made him instinctively resist the prophetic call. Here, the author of the book of Jonah poses the question of what to do in a desperate situation.

In addition to the unrealistic features of the story of Jonah, other aspects of the text lead us to approach the book of Jonah psychologically as well as symbolically. The first aspect is the frequent use of mythical elements. The great fish (*dāg gādôl*) in the book can be compared to sea monsters, such as Rahab (Isa. 51.9) and Leviathan (Isa. 27.1; Job 3.8; 41.1), that appear as adversaries of Yahweh (cf. McKenzie 1963: 129). The fast growing-plant (*qîqāyôn*) also has a mythical element through which Jonah could see himself. For C.G. Jung, myth is a tool that announces the unconscious and enables humans to experience it (*CW* 13, par. 199; Segal 1998: 18). The story of Jonah may represent a therapeutic myth, which has 'a helpful and loosening effect, even when the patient shows not a trace of conscious understanding' (*CW* 11, par. 292). According to Jung (*CW* 14, par. 751), 'In order to secure its co-operation the religions have long turned to myths for help, or rather, the myths always flung out bridges between the helpless consciousness and the effective *idées forces* of the unconscious'. By using mythological motifs, the author of Jonah drew out the collective unconscious of the readers who had similar experiences to those of Jonah. In this case, 'Myth is the natural and indispensable intermediate stage between unconscious and conscious cognition' (Jung 1961: 343).

The second aspect is found in the structure of the book. The prayer in ch. 2 leads to the end of the first scene, where Jonah seems to experience rebirth. But he does not maintain his integration in the following chapters. The chiastic structure (chs. 1–2 and chs. 3–4) suggests that two different layers of Jonah were merged into one story. For this reason, Zimmermann (1991: 584) is of the opinion that 'there are two different personalities of Jonah. Actually, when the compiler composed two traditions about Jonah, he mistakenly put one before the other'. His idea is based on two personalities: the immature Jonah and the spiritually born-again Jonah (Zimmermann 1991: 585). The whole picture of Jonah, however, does not appear even at the final stage.

Some scholars are still in favor of the symmetrical structure of Jonah (Craig 1990: 111; Simon 1999: 25). But such a view does not explain the position of the prayer in ch. 2 and the incomplete ending of ch. 4. From the reader's point of view, the ending may be appropriate as it is. The lack of Jonah's answer makes 'the reader create both an ending for Jonah and an ending for him- or herself' (Crouch 1994: 107). Assuming that Jonah is the psychological projection of the author, the incomplete ending of ch. 4 reflects the process of ongoing life. This psychological understanding of Jonah gives us an opportunity to look back upon ourselves, who may be on the same track of our life journey.

The third aspect appears in the regressive behavior of Jonah. When he sees the repentance of the Ninevites and their salvation from calamity Jonah responds, 'O Lord, please take my life from me, for it is better for me to die than to live' (Jon. 4.3).[1] Zimmermann argues that Jonah was afraid of being the scorn of his people, who would have regarded him as a false prophet whose message was not realized (1991: 585). This opinion, however, does not explain the spiritual state of Jonah. When the fast growing plant withered in a day, Jonah was again in a state of death, saying, 'It is better for me to die than to live' (Jon. 4.8). How can we explain such an overreaction? It seems to be an outward expression of his unconscious.

The story of Jonah, in sum, may be a kind of 'unconscious drama of the psyche which becomes accessible to man's consciousness by way of projection—that is, mirrored in the events of nature' (*CW* 9 Part 1, par. 7). Jonah was not just a prophet who carried out his prophetic vocation in a historical context. More importantly, as a character that is psychologically projected by the author, he is a symbolic figure who represents someone in the process of being directed by God. In the experience of self-realization (individuation), Jonah was being guided by God. Jonah, who was terribly upset in the beginning, finally calmed down before God (Simon 1999: 48), although he was still on the borderline between consciousness and the unconscious. This paper is an attempt to explore the psychological dimension of the book of Jonah.

---

1.   Jonah was excessively attached to a death wish just as the prophet Elijah was (1 Kgs 19.4). Cursing the day of his birth Job also said, 'Why did I not die at birth, come forth from the womb and expire?' (Job 3.11)

Jonah's Reluctant Journey to a New World

The name Jonah appears in 2 Kgs 14.25, where he is called a prophet. Except for the statement that he is the son of Amittai, there is no other information about him. It is not clear whether there is any relationship between the Jonah in 2 Kgs 14.25 and the prophet Jonah in the book that bears his name. The historical book reports that Jonah, being contemporary with King Jeroboam II (788–748 BCE), carried out his prophetic vocation in the second half of the eighth century BCE, while the book of Jonah describes him as a prophet who announced God's message to the people of Nineveh in the last quarter of the seventh century (612 BCE). The gap of more than 150 years in the two reports indicates that there is no direct relationship between the two Jonahs. It is possible that the author of Jonah adopted the familiar name in order to attract readers' attention. Along with the historical uncertainty surrounding the book of Jonah, the date of its writing is also controversial. Although Limburg (1993: 31) holds that dating the book of Jonah is an impossible task, quite a number of scholars are in agreement that Jonah was probably written in the late Persian or early Hellenistic period (Alexander 1985: 117; Wolff 1986: 78; Lacocque and Lacocque 1990: 36).[2]

If we accept the dating of the book in the late period between the fourth and third centuries BCE, then the destruction of Nineveh, the capital of Assyria, was already known to the people of Israel. What made the author choose Jonah as the prophet who delivered God's message to the old city? As a symbol of 'the antithesis to Jerusalem' (Bolin 1995: 115), Nineveh elicited strong emotion from the Israelites. The unfamiliar expression the 'king of Nineveh' (4.6) also exemplifies the symbolical function of the city.[3] Almost forgotten but still continuing to exit in the unconscious, the name 'Nineveh' was enough for the people of Israel to recall the past threat of Assyria. Jonah's immediate reaction to run away was, in all likelihood, accelerated by this image of Nineveh.

The story of Jonah begins with the prophet's uncomfortable encounter with God. While God's command is urgent (1.2),[4] Jonah's reaction is contrary to normal expectations. Without responding to God's will, Jonah hastily fled from God's presence. What made Jonah flee to Tarshish? In the last scene, Jonah reveals the reason why he had to flee: 'That is why I fled to Tarshish at the beginning; for I knew that you are a gracious God and merciful, slow to anger, and abounding in steadfast love, and ready to relent from punishing' (4.2). God's message of doom (1.1) implies the fall of Nineveh. However, Jonah did not accept the oracle as it was. He already realized the real meaning of God's message, which was not intended to destroy the city of Nineveh. In effect, Jonah was confronted with another image of

2.   Lacocque and Lacocque (1990: 14, 35) argue that the use of late Hebrew, Aramaic terms and Hellenistic influence as seen, for example, in the term *qîqāyôn*, support dating the book in the Hellenistic period.

3.   Bolin (1995: 118) points out that 'the title "king of Nineveh", which the Assyrian kings never used for themselves, is found in Jonah and the Greek writings'.

4.   'Go at once to Nineveh, that great city, and cry out against it, for their wickedness has come up, before me' (NRSV).

God, who was urging him to do something impossible. The two Gods in Jonah made him torn; one God is in the consciousness of the law, and the other God is hidden in the unconscious. Upon receiving his unexpected call, Jonah was so conflicted that he fled to Tarshish without having any reasonable solution. Jonah's awareness of two different Gods meant that two opposite responses were present in his psyche: he could either run away from Nineveh, or he could attempt to assist the gentiles in the city.[5] Without fully understanding the opposing forces within him, Jonah was still wandering between the two Gods. Jonah's case suggests that the human condition lies on the border between two choices: one is to keep his/her conventional way of thinking, and the other is to hear the inner voice, the Truth.[6] This reality seems to be the primary subject of the story of Jonah.

This psychological reading of the text is also supported by the names of Jonah and his father. The name Jonah means 'dove' in Hebrew. In the story of Noah, a dove appears as a symbol of salvation—through the role of the dove, Noah knew when his family could safely leave the ark (Gen. 8.6-12). In his story, however, Jonah did not act according to his name since he was neither peaceful nor compassionate to the gentiles. Instead of delivering good news, he preferred to abandon the Ninevites, who had traditionally been regarded as the enemies of his people. By contrasting these images of Jonah, the author directs the reader's attention to the psychological component of the text. Similarly, Jonah was the son of 'Amittai', a name that is etymologically related to the Hebrew word for 'truth' (*'emet*). As the son of 'truth', Jonah should hear and follow the Truth. Ironically, however, he stood between the not-yet-truth and the real Truth (cf. West 1984: 238). Kahn (1994: 89) argues that, 'Indeed, the tension between Yonah and Amittai articulates a basic conflict in the book, the conflict between love and justice'. Although his problem does not lie in differentiating love from justice yet, Jonah leaves the divine task unaccomplished.[7]

Jonah ran away almost instinctively to avoid the given task. What made him reluctant to follow God's will? In terms of Jung's analytical psychology, the shadow—the dark side of the personality—made Jonah avoid the divine call. At the same time, the shadow stimulates the consciousness so that one hears the voice of the unconscious. To see one's shadow is the starting point of individuation:

> The individuation process is invariably started off by the patient's becoming conscious of the shadow, a personality component usually with a negative sign. This 'inferior' personality is made up of everything that will not fit in with, and adapt

5. Simon (1999: 27) states, 'Thus the symmetrical structure of the book unites two seemingly contradictory aspects of the character of God, the conjoining of which is the paradoxical theme of the book'.

6. The two personalities can be compared to Jung's ideas of the Ego and the Self. When the Ego in the consciousness meets the Self in the center of the unconscious, according to Jung, the personality keeps integration that unites the opposites (cf. Jung 1961: 235, 371). 'An individual who has a conscious connection to the Self, since there is a reconciliation of opposites within him, is likely to promote harmony in his environment' (Edinger 1986: 103).

7. Wolff (1986: 172) also states that 'his first expression of unwillingness was also deeply rooted in self-pity, not in genuine concern about the validity of God's word and his justice'.

to, the laws and regulations of conscious life. It is compounded of 'disobedience' and is therefore rejected not on moral grounds only, but also for reasons of expediency. (*CW* 11, par. 292)

Jonah was accustomed to the God who had been familiar with his people. The God of Israel was regarded as the God of law, love and justice. In other words, God should always stand by the people of Israel. To be sure, the Ninevites should have been punished due to their wrongdoings. The call to Jonah, however, asked him to have a different understanding of God. True vocation is 'to go his/her own way and to rise out of unconscious identity with the mass as out of a swathing mist' (*CW* 17, par. 299; Edinger 1986: 26). Jonah, identified with the mass of Israel, is confronted with a strange God, who asks him to turn away from his old way. Jonah's tendency to run away resurfaces on the way to Tarshish. While the sailors are busy overcoming a mighty storm, Jonah goes down into the hold of the ship and falls asleep (1.5). How could he sleep in such a dangerous situation? It is another example of his running away (Lacocque and Lacocque 1990: 81) as he falls into a numb state without any thought. Faced with an unpleasant and undesirable duty, Jonah chooses death rather than go into Nineveh. How many people follow the same track as Jonah! In particular, Jonah's situation is similar to that of the author, who had to live with his enemies.

The sea is a symbol of threatening power to be overcome, while the great fish is a means of salvation. In the story of Moses, the sea also functions as a hostile power, while his staff is a means of salvation (Exod. 14). Similarly, the Canaanite myth of Baal and Anat describes a conflict between the power of the sea and a deity (Matthews and Benjamin 1991: 157). The sea often functioned as a mythical power of violence for the ancient Israelites. At the same time, the sea must surrender to the power of Yahweh. The fish in Jonah appears as a bridge between death and life. Therefore, 'sea and fish as symbols of death and rebirth' lead Jonah to enter into his unconscious (Lacocque and Lacocque 1990: 78).

The fish in Jonah, however, is understood differently from other kinds of fish in mythology, most of which are defeated by heroes. In the Redskin myths, the sea monster swallows the hero. In the belly of the monster, the hero, unlike Jonah, cuts off some of its internal organs (*CW* 7, par. 160; Segal 1998: 164). The Hebrew Bible also presents sea monsters (Rahab, Leviathan or sea dragons) as creatures to be vanquished (Isa. 27.1; 51.9; Job 3.8; 41.1). The author of Jonah does not present the typical path of a mythical hero, a powerful man or a god-man who vanquishes all kinds of evil power (*CW* 18, par. 548). Instead, the author utilizes a mythical archetype in his literary work by changing the stereotypical structure (cf. Bolin 1997: 94). The fish in Jonah is not a hostile creature. Rather, it is described as the means of giving Jonah a chance to uncover his hidden sight, the unconscious. The mention of the temple in Jonah's prayer (2.7)[8] implies that the fish guides Jonah to the place of God. Jung explains, 'Jonah entered its mouth just as a man enters the

---

8.   'As my life was ebbing away, I remembered the Lord; and my prayer came to you, into your holy temple' (NRSV).

great synagogue' (*CW* 5, par. 509).[9] The fish, as a 'womb' symbol of death and life, connects Jonah's consciousness to the unconscious (cf. Zimmermann 1991: 582).

Continuing Process of Individuation

The structure of the book of Jonah is still problematic, especially regarding the prayer in ch. 2. Wolff suggests, 'the narrator whose work we read today has independently fused traditional material that had already taken on more or less fixed shape' (1986: 131). He seems to differentiate the final redactor from the original author or collector, regarding the psalm/prayer as 'a literary interpolation' (Wolff 1986: 131). Craig argues that readers have 'opportunities to construct a framework for establishing connections' (1990: 104). He is of the opinion that the prayer of ch. 2 'fits quite harmoniously with the surrounding prose narrative, both in terms of physical-psychological portrayal and in terms of structural symmetry' (Craig 1990: 111). Woodard also points out that the mood of the prayer is related to other chapters (1991: 9). Lacocque and Lacocque, who approach the story of Jonah psychologically, also hold that 'the psalm has been inserted where it now stands by the author himself' (1990: 12-13), drawing on Allen's view of the symmetrical structure of Jonah: (1) a Hebrew sinner is saved (1.1–2.10); (2) heathen sinners are saved (3.1–4.11) (1976: 197).

Allen's reading, however, does not sufficiently highlight Jonah's role. In my opinion, the second part concentrates on Jonah rather than on the Ninevites, who serve to develop further the main character (Payne 1979: 7-8). Jung's theory of individuation (self-realization) process can be helpful in determining the intention of the author who wants to share his psychological journey with the reader. Actually, Jonah's problem does not center on the salvation of the Ninevites, but on himself who cannot accept the unimaginable (Wolff 1986: 172). How is it possible that the Ninevites can repent and be saved? How could evil and good coexist? After the fall of Jerusalem, the Israelites were faced with a most critical problem: how to get along with Gentiles. It was necessary for those who lost their land to learn how to live with others, including their enemies.

Faced with the difference between the lived reality (consciousness) and the ideal (the unconscious), one was not free to go one's way. The more attached to traditional ideologies, the more threatened an Israelite would feel by the new demands. Jonah was one of those who were caught up in the common understanding of God as the Redeemer of the chosen people. His immediate reaction to run away came out of his unconscious. Entering into a new world is risky and dangerous, but risk is inherent in the process of self-realization. In the process of individuation, one has to overcome the former ideology, including 'painful' psychological and physical experiences (Edinger 1986: 79).

The book of Jonah describes a continuing process of individuation, which shows two aspects: (1) Jonah's entering into the unconscious (1.1–2.10); (2) Jonah's

9.   Midrash compares Jonah's entering the fish's mouth to a person entering a great synagogue (Kahn 1994: 91).

self-realization by God (3.1–4.11). While running away, he looked back on his vocation and saved the Gentile sailors by sacrificing himself (1.12). Jonah's ego, in terms of Jung's psychology, starts to meet the self, the inner voice of the unconscious. Both the sea and the fish give Jonah an opportunity to experience death and rebirth (Lacocque and Lacocque 1990: 109). The belly of the fish, as a womb of the truth, is the place where Jonah sees God. There, 'Jonah became transformed, free of guilt and cleansed of sin' (Zimmermann 1991: 582-83). At least at this moment, he became a self-realized man of integration who was ready to follow the divine call. Chapter 2 seems to close the first scene, although its incomplete ending leads the reader to imagine the next step.

The Jonah of chs. 3–4 is a different person than the Jonah of ch. 2. He went to Nineveh and delivered the message of doom (3.3-4) and, faced with the unexpected event of the Ninevites' repentance, he regressed to the former ego (4.1-4). All of a sudden, the born-again image of Jonah disappears in ch. 4. This has led some scholars to suggest the possibility of there being two different Jonahs in the book (Zimmermann 1991: 584). The literary inconsistency between the psalm (ch. 2) and the prose section (ch. 3), along with Jonah's unusual behavior, leaves the reader puzzled (Wolff 1986: 128). Nonetheless, the fact that Jonah went back to his original state does not seem overly strange since human beings often revert to their former ways at critical moments. It is not unusual for opposite sides to exist in one person. The author is not solely concerned with producing literary art, but with reflecting on the existential reality of the human condition.

Despite the experience of rebirth in ch. 2, Jonah's personality does not make absolute or irreversible progress. Rather, his emotions become more complex than before. Jonah was shocked by unbelievable happenings such as the Ninevites' faith in God, their repentance, and the fast of their entire community, including the animals (3.5-9). While such events changed God's mind so that calamity was not brought upon them (3.10), Jonah himself was not changed. He already knew how and when God would save the enemies, and this is the reason Jonah fled to Tarshish (4.2). When he understood what was happening, Jonah was angry not because of his role as a prophet (cf. Zucker 1995: 364), but because of his excessive attachment to the conventional way of thinking. The contrast between God and Jonah shows that it is not easy for humans to change their minds even after experiencing rebirth. Jonah's anger arose as a result of the hidden side of God that is beyond conventional ideologies.

The fact that Nineveh was saved by God led Jonah to a despondent psychological state. When he realized that his message of doom would not be realized Jonah said, 'O Lord, please take my life from me, for it is better for me to die than to live' (4.3). As Simon explains, 'Psychologically, he was motivated by the death wish that assails him whenever the course of his life reaches the end of a blind alley' (1999: 34). This is not the only time Jonah was in such a suicidal state. When the shadow-giving plant withered and the sun beat down on his head, Jonah desperately uttered similar words: 'It is better for me to die than to live' (4.8). The loss of his familiar belief system made Jonah ready to give up his life. Caught in a serious inner conflict he has become suicidal. At the moment he is most in need of help, God becomes a counselor and healer for him.

The appearance of the mythical plant (*qîqāyôn*)[10] allows Jonah to take a look at himself. The fast-growing and withering plant reflects the unstable psyche of Jonah, who easily becomes happy and all of a sudden falls into depression (cf. Wolff 1986: 171-72). God helped Jonah to discover who he really was by showing him the symbolical plant. It mirrors the image of a complex psyche. Even after realizing who he was Jonah could not answer the last question of God, 'Should I not be concerned about Nineveh, that great city, in which there are more than a hundred and twenty thousand persons who do not know their right hand from their left, and also many animals?' (4.11)

The story of Jonah seems to end without a conclusion, but some scholars see this as part of its attraction (Lacocque and Lacocque 1990: 164). Wolff echoes this sentiment when he explains, 'Since the final question (v. 11) is left open, the reader sees himself in the end challenged to think about the problem and to find his own answer' (1986: 162). Lacocque and Lacocque (1990: 164) believe that the story of Jonah returns to its beginning and that, 'perhaps the hero is still to live other exhausting experiences before he understand God's will'. Another possibility is that Jonah found himself and finally achieved self-realization. Jonah's silence at the last moment could be his confession, 'Yes, I will follow you, although I am still in need of your help'. If 'Jonah once again finds himself at a dead end' (Simon 1999: 35), it is the state of the mythical union of the opposites Jonah (the ego) and God (the self) (cf. *CW* 14, par. 542; Edinger 1986: 100). From this point of view, the book of Jonah reflects his spiritual journey to find himself as well as to see the God who appears differently from what Jonah had imagined. In this way, Jonah is a representative of all of us, including the ancient Israelites. Like him, all human beings stand at the border between what they have been and what they will become.

Conclusion

Jonah's suicidal desires imply that he was experiencing severe mental conflict. He needed help. The Lord responded to his situation and helped Jonah to see himself and be transformed into a new being. He represents those who experience mental and spiritual difficulties, and his story offers an important message for them. Although his personality is consistent throughout the story, Jonah was on the track of self-realization toward rebirth after death.

The importance of the story of Jonah, from this point of view, relies neither on its historicity nor on its literary structure, but on the fact that anyone can be in his situation. The intention of the author is to share with his contemporaries his personal experience of a death wish. Caught between the existential reality and the demand of the divine (unconscious), Jonah had to decide what to do. Decision making is not easy in a situation that is religiously or psychologically desperate. Even

---

10. Jonah's *qîqāyôn* plant is often interpreted as 'any sort of fast-growing and shade-giving bush' (Robinson 1985: 396).

God could not force Jonah to do something. Jonah needed an opportunity to see himself and make harmony between the opposites in his psyche. This is why we do not have to interpret the story of Jonah in only theological terms. The universal God, open to all people, should not be confined to any religion or ideology. If the story of Jonah is understood only as a message about God's love and justice in the reconciliation with Gentiles, its value will be greatly diminished. There is a clear psychological component to the text and Jonah's message may be beyond our consciousness.

BIBLIOGRAPHY

Alexander, T. Desmond
    1985   'Jonah and Genre', *TynBul* 36: 35-59.
Allen, Leslie C.
    1976   *The Books of Joel, Obadiah, Jonah, and Micah* (Grand Rapids: Eerdmans).
Bolin, Thomas M.
    1995   '"Should I Not Also Pity Nineveh?": Divine Freedom in the Book of Jonah', *JSOT* 67: 109-20.
    1997   *Freedom beyond Forgiveness: The Book of Jonah Re-Examined* (JSOTSup, 236; Sheffield: Sheffield Academic Press).
Craig, Kenneth M., Jr
    1990   'Jonah and the Reading Process', *JSOT* 47: 103-14.
    1993   *A Poetics of Jonah: Art in the Service of Ideology* (Columbia: University of South Carolina Press).
Crouch, Walter B.
    1994   'To Question an End, To End a Question: Opening the Closure of the Book of Jonah', *JSOT* 62: 101-12.
Edinger, Edward F.
    1986   *The Bible and the Psyche: Individuation Symbolism in the Old Testament* (Toronto: Inner City Books).
Hall, Calvin S., and Vernon J. Nordby
    1973   *A Primer of Jungian Psychology* (New York: Mentor Books).
Jung, C.G.
    1961   *Memories, Dreams, Reflections* (trans. Richard and Clara Winston; Glasgow: Fontana Press).
Kahn, Paul
    1994   'An Analysis of the Book of Jonah', *Judaism* 43: 87-100.
Lacocque, André, and Pierre-Emmanuel Lacocque
    1990   *Jonah: A Psycho-Religious Approach to the Prophet* (Columbia: University of South Carolina Press).
Limburg, James
    1993   *Jonah: A Commentary* (Louisville, KY: Westminster/John Knox Press).
Matthews, Victor H., and Don C. Benjamin
    1991   *Old Testament Parallels: Laws and Stories from the Ancient Near East* (New York: Paulist Press).
McKenzie, John L.
    1963   *Myth and Realities: Studies in Biblical Theology* (Milwaukee: The Bruce Publishing Company).

Payne, David F.
1979   'Jonah from the Perspective of its Audience', *JSOT* 13: 3-12.
Robinson, Bernard P.
1985   'Jonah's Qiqayon Plant', *ZAW* 97: 390-403.
Segal, Robert A.
1998   *Jung on Mythology* (Princeton, NJ: Princeton University Press).
Simon, Uriel
1999   *Jonah* (Philadelphia: The Jewish Publication Society of America).
West, Mona
1984   'Irony in the Book of Jonah: Audience Identification with the Hero', *Perspectives in Religious Studies* 11: 233-42.
Wilt, Timothy Lloyd
1992   'Lexical Repetition in Jonah', *Journal of Translation and Textlinguistics* 5: 252-64.
Wolff, Hans Walter
1986   *Obadiah and Jonah* (Minneapolis: Augsburg).
Woodard, Branson L.
1991   'Death in Life: The Book of Jonah and Biblical Tragedy', *GTJ* 11: 3-16.
Zimmermann, Frank
1991   'Problems and Solutions in the Book of Jonah', *Judaism* 40: 580-89.
Zucker, David
1995   'Jonah's Journey', *Judaism* 44: 362-68.

Harder than Flint, Faster than Eagles: Intensified Comparatives in the Latter Prophets*

Eric A. Seibert

In my first semester of doctoral studies at Drew University, I had the good fortune of being a student in a class Dr Huffmon was teaching on the books of Amos and Hosea. The course was designed to consider these prophetic works through the lens of persuasion. Having never seriously considered prophetic literature from that angle of vision, I found it most enlightening. As the course progressed, I was particularly intrigued by the vast array of persuasive techniques the Israelite prophets had at their disposal and command.

Since that time, I have continued to be impressed by the versatility of the prophets in their role as persuasive speakers. This versatility is evidenced by their creative use of personification, hyperbole, rhetorical questions, similes, metaphors, and numerous other forms of rhetoric. While several of these have been studied in some detail, one that has been neglected, and to my knowledge not clearly identified, is what I will be referring to as an 'intensified comparative'.[1] Broadly speaking, an intensified comparative is an expression comparing two 'items'[2] which both display a high degree of some quality, by stating that the first 'item' exhibits that quality to a greater degree than the second. To illustrate, consider these familiar words:

> Faster than a speeding bullet! More powerful than a locomotive! Able to leap tall buildings in a single bound! Look! Up in the sky! It's a bird! It's a plane! It's Superman![3]

*   This essay is warmly dedicated to Dr Huffmon. His unique ability to bring prophetic texts to life has profoundly impacted my appreciation for and understanding of this rich corpus. It was his comments about 'impossible words' in Jeremiah and elsewhere (see now Huffmon 1999) that inspired me to begin collecting intensified comparatives many years ago. May this knowledge of the impact his teaching had upon me bring him more satisfaction than a shipment of new books. I would like to express my gratitude to Terry L. Brensinger for taking the time to discuss this topic with me and for reading and commenting on an earlier draft of the essay.

1.   For example, I see no recognition of 'intensified comparatives' as a unique figure of speech in the classic work of Bullinger (1968 [1898]) or in Caird's (1997 [1980]) and Gibson's (1998) more recent treatments of biblical language.

2.   As we will see, these 'items' can be people, animals, objects, etc.

3.   Wright (2001: 13), quoting the words spoken by the announcer at the beginning of the radio episodes devoted to this superhero. I wish to express a special word of thanks to Matt Kustenbauder for calling to my attention the Superman connection.

The first two sentences of this description may be classified as intensified comparatives. While this kind of rhetoric obviously shares much in common with a simile, it is imprecise to regard it as an equivalent expression—a common practice among biblical scholars. Rather than using a simile and saying Superman is '*as fast as* a speeding bullet', the intensified comparative claims he is faster. And rather than simply likening Superman's might to a locomotive, the intensified comparative declares that Superman is even more powerful than that! Such heightened rhetoric is intended to impress the hearer with the amazing abilities of this superhuman superhero.[4]

Given the evocative potential of intensified comparatives, it is not surprising that Israelite prophets utilized them in their efforts to persuade. The present study is devoted to a comprehensive examination of this form of rhetoric in the Latter Prophets.[5]

Definitions and Methodology

To begin, it is necessary to define carefully this unique figure of speech. Intensified comparatives utilize comparative מִן in a way corresponding to what Waltke and O'Connor call a 'positive comparison'.[6] This is a comparison in which 'both the subject and the thing compared possess the quality expressed by the adjective, with the subject possessing it to a greater degree' (§14.4d). Usually this results in language such as 'A is harder, faster, etc. than B' or 'A is rarer, more wicked, etc. than B'.[7] In order for an expression to be classified as an intensified comparative it must contain at least three basic elements: a subject,[8] an intensified quality, and a comparative object[9] with מִן. Notice, for example, the presence of these elements in Hab. 1.8a, 'Their horses are swifter than leopards'.[10] Additionally, all intensified comparatives share two other essential features: (1) the comparative object exhibits/exemplifies the quality under consideration to a very high degree[11] (leopards are

---

4. Examples of this form of speech in common usage include: 'higher than a kite (on the Fourth of July)', 'slower than molasses in January', 'crookeder than a dog's hind leg', 'larger than life' and 'deader than a doornail'. Note also Jim Croce's song 'Bad, Bad Leroy Brown' which describes Leroy Brown, a hardened man from the south side of Chicago, as being 'Badder than old King Kong…meaner than a junkyard dog'.

5. Defined as Isaiah, Jeremiah, Ezekiel, and the twelve minor prophets.

6. For a discussion of other uses of comparative מִן, see Waltke and O'Connor (1990) §14.4e-f. Cf. GKC §133a-e and Davidson §§ 33-34.

7. Isa. 40.17 is not discussed since the subject exhibits *less* rather than more of the qualitative category. Cf. Mic. 7.4 and see the note below.

8. To qualify as an intensified comparative, there must be a clearly defined subject which keenly possesses the intensified quality. For this reason, passages like Ezek. 8.15b, 'You will see still greater abominations than these', and Ezek. 36.11b, 'I…will do more good to you than ever before', have not been included in the following discussion.

9. I am using the term 'object' in a grammatical sense. Comparative objects may be either animate or inanimate.

10. All biblical citations are from the NRSV unless otherwise noted.

11. This rules out a passage like Isa. 54.1b, 'For the children of the desolate woman will be

very fast);[12] (2) the subject is said to exhibit/exemplify this same quality to an even higher degree than the comparative object (Babylon's [war]horses are described as being even faster!).[13] If one or both of these conditions is not satisfied, the expression should not be classified as an intensified comparative.

With these parameters in mind,[14] the following investigation will proceed along two tracks. First, I will provide a chart containing an overview of the passages under consideration. On the basis of this information, preliminary conclusions will be drawn about the frequency, distribution, and content of this form of speech in the prophets. The second half of the study attempts to answer certain kinds of questions related to prophetic persuasion. For example, 'How do intensified comparatives function persuasively?' and 'What patterns or connections can be detected in this regard?' The resultant answers will allow us to draw some broader conclusions about the nature and function of intensified comparatives in prophetic speech.

Assembling the Data

To my knowledge, the chart opposite displays every undisputed example of an intensified comparative (as defined above) in the Latter Prophets:[15]

---

more than the children of her that is married', since the emphasis is not on the enormous number of children born to the married woman. Similarly, I have chosen not to discuss Isa. 10.10 since there is no discernable stress on the greatness of Israel's 'images'.

12.   Though the prophets' primary goal was not to preserve Israel's perception of the hardest natural substances or the fastest animals—prophets were, after all, concerned with more pressing matters—in many cases intensified comparatives do just that, giving us with windows into the world of ancient Israel. See Berlinerblau's (1996: 38-40) treatment of tacit assumptions for a theoretical discussion of this phenomenon whereby the writers of the Bible tell us more than they realize.

13.   This disqualifies Amos 6.2 and Nah. 3.8 from consideration. While both passages utilize comparative מן as part of a rhetorical question (twice in Amos), the point is that Israel is *not* better than Hamath or Gath and that Nineveh is *not* better than Thebes. These references represent another form of persuasion whereby prophets recalled historical disasters to shake people out of their complacency and false security. Cf. Jeremiah's use of Shiloh (Jer. 7.12-15; 26.4-9).

14.   It should also be noted that the subject and comparative object of intensified comparatives are typically quite dissimilar (such as [war]horses and eagles). In the Latter Prophets, this distinction is least pronounced in Jer. 7.26 and 16.12, verses that compare the wickedness of Jeremiah's generation to that of its ancestors.

15.   The references in canonical order are as follows: Isa. 13.12; 56.5; Jer. 4.13; 5.3; 7.26; 15.8; 16.12; 46.23; Ezek. 3.9; 5.6-7; 16.47, 51-52; 23.11; 28.3; Nah. 3.16; Hab. 1.8. There are two passages that have been excluded from consideration due, in part, to textual uncertainties. In Mic. 7.4, MT's ישר ממסבוה may be corrupt. Wolff (1990: 200-201; cf. Mays 1976: 149) regards this as an example of wrong word division and proposes ישרם מסבוה ('the most upright [like] a thorn hedge'). This eliminates the comparative preposition, regarding it as a third masculine plural pronominal suffix of the previous word. For attempts to retain the MT, see Waltke and O'Connor's (1990: § 14.4d) translation, 'The most upright person (is *worse*) than a thorn hedge', and cf. GKC §133e; L.C. Allen 1976: 383 n. 4. Secondly, I have not included Jer. 48.32a, 'More than for Jazer I weep for you, O vine of Sibmah!' Holladay (1989: 343) reads מִבְּךָ ('fountain') for MT מִבְּכִי, following Landes and Mansoor. For an alternate view, see McKane (1996: 1185) who retains the reading in the MT and contends the revocalization 'should not be entertained'.

General Category	Reference	Subject	Intensified Quality	Comparative Object
Abundance	Jer. 15.8	Jerusalem's widows	more numerous than	the sand of the seas
	Jer. 46.23	Babylonians	more numerous than	locusts
	Nah. 3.16	Nineveh's merchants	increased more than	the stars of the heavens
Hardness	Jer. 5.3	the faces of Jerusalem's inhabitants	harder than	rock
	Ezek. 3.9	Ezekiel's forehead	harder than	flint
Scarcity	Isa. 13.12	human beings	rarer than	fine gold/the gold of Ophir
Speed (and destructiveness)	Jer. 4.13	an invading army's horses	swifter than	eagles
	Hab. 1.8	Babylon's horses	swifter than/more menacing than	leopards/wolves at dusk
Wickedness	Jer. 7.26; 16.12	Jeremiah's generation	did worse than	their ancestors
	Ezek. 5.6-7	Jerusalem	more wicked than/more turbulent than	the nations and the countries all around/the nations…all around
	Ezek. 16.47, 51-52	Jerusalem	more corrupt and abominable than	Samaria and Sodom
	Ezek. 23.11	Oholibah (Jerusalem)/her lusting and whorings	more corrupt than/worse than	her sister = Oholah (Samaria)
Wisdom	Ezek. 28.3	prince (king) of Tyre	wiser than	Daniel
Worth	Isa. 56.5	a monument and a name better than	better than	sons and daughters

Table 1. *Intensified Comparatives in the Latter Prophets*

The following conclusions can be drawn from these examples:

1. Intensified comparatives occur relatively infrequently in the Latter Prophets,[16] and are almost exclusively located in the Major Prophets, the only exceptions being Nah. 3.16; Hab. 1.8 (twice).
2. Intensified comparatives occur almost exclusively in poetic sections.[17]
3. The most common intensified quality, accounting for more than one-third of all occurrences, is 'wickedness'. The second most frequent category, having three examples, is 'abundance'. Every other category contains only one or two examples.
4. In almost every instance, the subject is—or is related to—a person or group of people.[18]
5. Comparative objects are never duplicated except in those cases where Jeremiah compares his generation to its ancestors and Ezekiel compares Judah to the nations or to her northern neighbor. Otherwise, the closest comparative objects are a rock (Jer. 5.3) and flint (Ezek. 3.9).[19]
6. Every comparative object is, or represents, a human being(s), animals/insects, or an element from the natural world.

Rhetorical Function and Persuasive Event

With the foregoing preliminary observations in hand, we are now ready to explore the rhetorical function of these intensified comparatives, paying special attention to their persuasive possibilities. Due to limitations of space and the number of passages to be considered, only brief attention can be devoted to any single example. We begin with several occurrences related to future judgment.

Judgment

Imminent Danger

There are two passages in the Latter Prophets (Hab. 1.8; Jer. 4.13) which contain intensified comparatives emphasizing both the imminence and inevitability of judgment. Following Habakkuk's complaint about the delay in punishing wicked Judah (Hab. 1.2-4), the Lord replies, 'A work is being done in your days that you would not believe if you were told. For I am rousing the Chaldeans' (1.5b-6a). Many Judahites apparently did not consider Babylon a threat given its great distance from

---

16. In contrast to more than 500 prophetic similes (Brensinger 1996: 4), there are only 21 clear examples of intensified comparatives in 18 verses in the Latter Prophets.

17. The only exceptions are Ezek. 3.9 and the references under the general category of wickedness.

18. Exceptions include (1) (war)horses in Jer. 4.13 and Hab. 1.8, though these may be understood metonymically as references to foreign invaders, and (2) the reference to 'a monument and a name' (Isa. 56.5) which is, incidentally, given to a group of people (eunuchs).

19. While eagles (Jer. 4.13) and leopards (Hab. 1.8) are both very fast, and sand (Jer. 15.8) and stars (Nah. 3.16) are both great in number, the comparative objects themselves are obviously quite different.

their homeland coupled with the 'security' they felt as a result of their current geo-political situation.[20] Persuasion was needed to drive home the reality of this rather audacious claim. This was accomplished, in part, through the use of two consecutive intensified comparatives[21] deployed in reference to the coming Chaldeans. 'Their horses are swifter[22] than leopards,[23] more menacing[24] than wolves at dusk;[25] their horses charge. Their horsemen come from far away; they fly like an eagle swift to devour' (Hab. 1.8).

By describing Babylon's (war)horses as 'swifter than leopards' and 'more menacing than wolves at dusk', both the amazing speed and frightening destructiveness of the encroaching army are effectively emphasized. Such dramatic imagery, emphasizing that judgment is coming fast and furiously, seems especially apropos given the prophet's complaint about God's slowness!

A similar example is found in Jer. 4.13. In this verse, notice how each expression depicts increasing speed, climaxing with an intensified comparative. 'Look! He comes up like clouds, his chariots like the whirlwind; his horses are swifter than eagles—woe to us, for we are ruined!'

Like the examples in Hab. 1.8, this intensified comparative was designed to emphasize the imminence and inevitability of judgment.[26] Yet despite this similarity, Jeremiah uses this imagery for a considerably different purpose. He deploys it in an effort to help people realize their desperate condition—which they do—so that they might change their ways (cf. Jer. 4.14).[27] Habakkuk holds out no such hope.

Utter Helplessness

A somewhat different emphasis can be detected in two passages which use intensified comparatives to stress a nation's utter helplessness against coming destruction. Unlike the previous two examples, both of these occur in oracles against foreign nations. In Jer. 46.13-24, Egypt's helplessness in the face of the Babylonian

---

20. So Robertson 1990: 152.

21. The use of two consecutive intensified comparatives is extremely rare in the Latter Prophets. It occurs only here and in Isa. 13.12 and Ezek. 23.11 (cf. Isa. 56.5 and Ezek. 5.6, which have compound comparative objects). Cf. 2 Sam. 1.23 where David reportedly eulogizes Saul and Jonathan as being 'swifter than eagles...stronger than lions'. See Lam. 4.7 for three consecutive intensified comparatives followed by a fourth at the beginning of v. 8.

22. For additional examples of intensified comparatives utilizing קלל, see 2 Sam. 1.23 (noted above); Jer. 4.13 (discussed below); Lam. 4.19; Job 7.6; 9.25.

23. It seems likely that the choice of leopards is governed, in part, by a desire to emphasize the destructiveness of this animal (cf. Roberts 1991: 96-97). Of the six references to נמר in the Hebrew Bible (Song 4.8; Isa. 11.6; Jer. 5.6; 13.23; Hos. 13.7; Hab. 1.8), this is the only one that emphasizes the leopard's speed.

24. The meaning of חדד is not entirely clear. Cf. Ezek. 21.14-16 where it has the connotation of sharpening.

25. Roberts (1991: 92 n. 8) proposes emending ערב ('evening') to עתבה ('steppe'). This reading would not substantially affect the meaning of the intensified comparative.

26. In this case, the identity of the invading army is unspecified (see Jer. 4.6).

27. For a discussion of the call to repentance as a later addition, see Carroll 1986: 164.

onslaught is repeatedly emphasized. The Apis bull has fled (v. 15), Egypt's 'mercenaries' are useless (v. 21), and Egypt herself makes 'a sound like a snake gliding away; for her enemies march in force' (v. 22). Egypt's inability to save herself is further emphasized by an intensified comparative which occurs toward the end of the oracle. 'They [the Babylonians] shall cut down her forest, says the LORD, though it is impenetrable, because they are more numerous than locusts; they are without number' (Jer. 46.23).

The basic meaning of the intensified comparative is clear enough. Locusts are used to depict the Babylonian army as an innumerable[28]—and, by implication, unstoppable—fighting force. Less clear is the meaning of the preceding statement, 'they shall cut down her forest...though it is impenetrable'. Most commentators interpret the reference to 'her forest' metaphorically. As such, it may refer to the people of Egypt or the country itself (Keown, Scalise and Smothers 1995: 294). According to Holladay (1989: 32), this phrase 'represents the pride of Egypt, perhaps her public buildings in which wood is used, and perhaps the multitude of her army as well'. Thompson (1980: 693), observing a connection between vv. 22-23, writes, 'The snake hides in the forest, and since the woodcutters cannot search the forest to find it, they cut the forest down'. Whichever interpretation is accepted, the essential point remains: Egypt doesn't stand a chance. The Egyptians will be conquered and there is absolutely nothing they can do to save themselves given the enormous number of Babylonian soldiers who will swarm over their land.

Assuming this oracle was intended for Judah's ruling elite, it would seem that its persuasive intentions are directed toward those who looked to Egypt for help against the Babylonians. According to Keown, Scalise and Smothers (1995: 289), 'This oracle, if delivered at some point in the events of 604–588, would have served to discourage government leaders from placing unwarranted reliance upon the failed power of the Pharaoh'.[29] Since Egypt is depicted as falling helplessly before the invading Babylonians, trusting her for military assistance would be sheer folly.

A similar example of an intensified comparative highlighting a nation's helplessness appears in the final chapter of the book of Nahum, a chapter devoted to displaying the destruction of Nineveh: 'You increased your merchants more than the stars of the heavens. The locust sheds its skin and flies away' (Nah. 3.16). Using the stars of the heavens[30] as the comparative object, Nahum claims that Nineveh has merchants beyond number. Once again, what is less clear is the rhetorical function of this intensified comparative. According to Maier (1987 [1959]: 349), this verse is intended to demonstrate 'that the wealth and foreign connections produced by Nineveh's commerce have not been able to restrain the flight of its

---

28. For similar examples of the figurative use of locusts to describe large numbers, see Judg. 6.5; 7.12; Ps. 105.34; Jer. 51.14; Joel 1.6.

29. Cf. Holladay 1989: 333.

30. This image is routinely used to describe the innumerability of Israel's descendants (Gen. 22.17; 26.4; Exod. 32.13; Deut. 1.10; 10.22; 28.62; 1 Chron. 27.23; Neh. 9.23; cf. Gen. 15.5). The only exception is this reference to Nineveh's merchants which, incidentally, is the only instance in which the image is used as an intensified comparative.

people'.[31] While Maier believes the locusts in v. 16 represent the general Ninevite population, others think they only refer to the merchants.[32] In either case, 'v. 16 …together with vv. 15 and 17, contains a remarkable prediction of the hopelessness of destroyed Nineveh' (Maier 1987 [1959]: 352). Given Assyria's strength and dominance, Nineveh's total collapse must have seemed highly unlikely to Nahum's audience. The use of this intensified comparative, along with a variety of other persuasive techniques, was intended to help them believe the impossible by assuring them that Nineveh would fall and that the Assyrians could do nothing to stop it.

Enormous Destruction
Still another variation on the theme of coming judgment involves two examples which both emphasize the magnitude of destruction. While these examples share certain similarities with the foregoing categories, here the emphasis falls on the scope of judgment rather than its imminence or inescapability. Consider Jer. 15.8, which, like the previous two examples, utilizes an image of innumerability: 'Their widows became more numerous than the sand of the seas; I have brought against the mothers of youths a destroyer at noonday; I have made anguish and terror fall upon her suddenly'. If Judah's widows—and by implication her dead soldiers—are to be even more numerous than the sand of the seas,[33] the coming destruction is envisioned as being of epic proportions. The use of this particular comparative object is especially interesting since it is used elsewhere to describe the vast number of descendants promised to the patriarchs (Gen. 22.17; 32.13 [12][34]). How ironic that the same expression once used to describe Israel's enormous population is now used to describe its depopulation! 'It is a terrible reversal of the great promise to Abraham and Jacob' (Holladay 1986: 442). To make matters worse, this image of enormous destruction resides in an oracle which indicates there is nothing that can be done to avert it (Jer. 15.1-9).[35]

Similarly, Isa. 13.12 also stresses the enormity of divine destruction. This verse, which is part of a judgment oracle against Babylon, describes the general devastation all nations will experience on the day of the Lord: 'I will make mortals more rare than fine gold, and humans than the gold of Ophir'. The image here is one of extreme scarcity.[36] Gold of any sort was rare, and fine gold, particularly the kind

31. As Achtemeier (1986: 28) puts it, 'A multitude of riches and armies are not sufficient to save'.
32. So, e.g., Roberts 1991: 75-76.
33. The sand of the sea(s) is arguably the most common image used in the Hebrew Bible to represent a large quantity of something.
34. Verse numbers in square brackets refer to the English verse number.
35. This is especially clear from Jer. 15.1, 'Then the LORD said to me: Though Moses and Samuel stood before me, yet my heart would not turn toward this people. Send them out of my sight, and let them go!' Even the combined intercessory power of Israel's two greatest mediators would not be enough to avert destruction in the present situation. Brueggemann's (1988: 136-37) suggestion that 15.7-9 represents a call to repentance similar to Amos 4.6-11 is not convincing.
36. Pss. 19.11 [10]; 119.127 use similar intensified comparatives, though in these instances it is gold's value rather than its scarcity that is emphasized.

that would come from Ophir,[37] was even more so.[38] The only mention of the 'gold of Ophir' coming to Israel, for example, is during Solomon's reign. If, on the day of the Lord, humans are going to be even scarcer than this kind of gold, the devastation will be extensive indeed!

Justified Punishment

The most numerous set of passages related to future judgment appear aimed at justifying it by accentuating the wickedness of those under condemnation. In a judgment oracle against Jerusalem, Jeremiah describes the entire community as being completely resistant to the will of the Lord, lacking even 'one person who acts justly and seeks truth' (5.1). What's worse, the people have even failed to respond positively to the Lord's discipline: 'O LORD, do your eyes not look for truth? You have struck them, but they felt no anguish; you have consumed them, but they refused to take correction. They have made their faces harder than rock; they have refused to turn back' (Jer. 5.3).

By describing the people's faces as 'harder than rock'—a condition of their own making—the prophet powerfully illustrates their obstinacy and recalcitrance, an understanding confirmed by the following line, 'they have refused to turn back'. Jeremiah deploys this image to convince his audience that the coming judgment is both just and necessary in light of their sinfulness and refusal to return to the Lord (see Jer. 5.9).

There are also several passages in the books of Jeremiah and Ezekiel that demonstrate the depths of Judah's wickedness via an intensified comparative declaring the people of Judah more sinful than other groups of wicked people.[39] In Jer. 7.22-26 the prophet describes the Israelites—from the Exodus generation onward—as a disobedient group who did as they pleased, 'looked backward rather than forward', and who failed to respond positively to the prophetic word (Jer. 7.24-25). Yet Jeremiah's generation[40] 'did worse (הרעו) than their ancestors did (7.26). A similar evaluation is made in Jer. 16.10-12:

> And when you tell this people all these words, and they say to you, 'Why has the
> LORD pronounced all this great evil against us? What is our iniquity? What is the
> sin that we have committed against the LORD our God?', then you shall say to
> them: It is because your ancestors have forsaken me, says the LORD, and have

---

37.   1 Kgs 9.28//2 Chron. 8.18; 1 Kgs 10.11//2 Chron. 9.10; though cf. 1 Chron. 29.1-4(!). Jehoshaphat's gold-seeking fleet never makes it out of port (1 Kgs 22.49 [48]).

38.   On this construction, see Robert Alter's (1985: 19) discussion of 'semantic parallelism' in which he observes that 'the characteristic movement of meaning [from one verse to the next] is one of heightening or intensification…of focusing, specification, concretization, even what could be called dramatization'. Thus, while fine gold is already quite rare, the gold of Ophir is rarer still.

39.   Jer. 7.26; 16.12; Ezek. 5.6-7; 16.47, 51-52; 23.11. Unlike the other examples of intensified comparatives we have considered thus far, the comparative objects here are not *fundamentally* different from their subjects. Rather than saying something like, 'you are worse than rotten fruit', Jeremiah and Ezekiel cite a group of wicked people and proclaim that Judah's wickedness exceeds theirs.

40.   In support of reading this verse in reference to Jeremiah's generation, see Holladay 1986: 263; McKane 1986: 175.

gone after other gods and have served and worshiped them, and have forsaken me and have not kept my law; and because you have behaved worse than your ancestors, for here you are, every one of you, following your stubborn evil will, refusing to listen to me.[41]

Interestingly, both of these references follow an unusual divine interdiction. In the first instance, Jeremiah is forbidden from interceding on behalf of the people (7.16), while the second finds Jeremiah barred from marriage and family, symbolic of the death that awaits all Judah (16.1-4). These contexts further underscore the extreme seriousness of Judah's predicament which has been precipitated by their flagrant and frequent violations of God's law. As such, they reinforce the justness of the divine judgment which Jeremiah says is on its way, judgment characterized by death, destruction and exile (7.33-34; 16.4, 13).

Ezekiel takes a slightly different approach, though the effect is the same. Rather than comparing Judah to past generations of unfaithful Israelites, he compares her to the surrounding nations—and finds her wanting! 'But she [Jerusalem] has rebelled against my ordinances and my statutes, becoming more wicked than the nations and the countries all around her, rejecting my ordinances and not following my statutes' (Ezek. 5.6; cf. v. 7).

Ezekiel also deploys a series of intensified comparatives accusing Judah of being worse than her 'sisters', Israel to the north and Sodom to the south: 'Samaria has not committed half your sins; you have committed more abominations than they, and have made your sisters appear righteous by all the abominations that you have committed' (Ezek. 16.51; see also Ezek. 16.47, 52; 23.11). By accusing Jerusalem of committing 'more abominations' than Samaria and Sodom, the latter being 'the archetype of wickedness in Israelite tradition' (Block 1997: 509), the prophet attempts 'to present as negative a picture of Jerusalem as possible' (Block 1997: 510). If you're 'badder' than the 'baddest', you're really bad! Judah's judgment, therefore, is fully justified.

One additional intensified comparative from the book of Ezekiel should be mentioned at this point, though it differs considerably from the foregoing examples since the subject is a foreign ruler, namely, the king of Tyre. Ezekiel says of the king, 'You are indeed wiser than Daniel; no secret is hidden from you; by your wisdom and your understanding you have amassed wealth for yourself, and have gathered gold and silver into your treasuries' (Ezek. 28.3-4). It seems best to follow those who regard Daniel as the non-biblical figure known from the Aqhat Epic.[42] This is the only intensified comparative in the Latter Prophets that names a particular individual as the comparative object. While other references to Daniel in the book of Ezekiel cite him, along with Noah and Job, as being a person of exceptional *righteousness* (צרקה),[43] this is the only reference to Daniel's extraordinary

41. Holladay (1986: 475) wonders in what sense the present generation did worse and answers, 'The present passage does not say clearly, but Jrm's discourse elsewhere suggests that it is because the present generation has not heeded the prophets (7.25)'.

42. For discussion, see Day 1980.

43. Ezek. 14.14, 20; cf. also Ezek. 14.16, 18. The prophet claims that even if these three 'supersaints' were living in Judah, the land God had destined to destroy, their extreme righteousness

wisdom.[44] Given its present context, it may be that this intensified comparative is intended to be taken sarcastically in reference to the king of Tyre.[45] It was the king's unparalleled wisdom that brought him wealth, yet his wealth led to pride, and his pride was the cause of his destruction. This passage affirms the conventional belief that wisdom brings wealth and with it the attendant danger of hubris and self-reliance. Being wiser than Daniel may result in great riches, but it carries even greater risks.

Empowerment and Promise

Divine Strengthening

The final two intensified comparatives are more 'positive' in form and function than those we have examined thus far. Earlier, we observed Jeremiah's description of his contemporaries as people who 'have made their faces harder than rock'. A similar image is used by Ezekiel,[46] though with very different effect. The Lord says to Ezekiel, 'Like the hardest stone, harder than flint, I have made your forehead; do not fear them or be dismayed at their looks, for they are a rebellious house' (Ezek. 3.9). In this instance, it is God rather than Judah who is responsible for the hardening and the image is used to describe just one individual rather than a whole group. Moreover, in Ezek. 3.9 hardness symbolizes the strength to carry out the divine will rather than suggesting some type of resistance to it. Flint was one of the hardest and most durable natural substances known in ancient Israel[47] and its usage here is intended to convey the divine strengthening given to Ezekiel for the exceedingly difficult task that lay ahead of him.[48] Since the prophet has been given the fortitude to accomplish his task, he can minister without fear.[49]

Divine Promise

Another example of an intensified comparative describing what God will do for someone occurs in Isa. 56.5. In this instance, however, it is a group of people (eunuchs), rather than just one individual, who is the beneficiary of God's activity:

would have no vicarious effect on the inhabitants of that land. This persuasive technique, like Jer. 15.1 (see above), is used to demonstrate the absolute certainty of divine judgment.

44.   Day (1980: 180-81) makes the case that the Aqhat Epic depicts Daniel as being especially wise. If one rejects this tenet, the reference no longer functions as an example of an intensified comparative. For another example of an extraordinarily wise individual, see 1 Kgs 4.31, and note the two consecutive intensified comparatives used to describe Solomon's unmatched wisdom.

45.   While J.P. Allen (1997: 93) believes the הנה at the beginning of the verse 'has an ironic force' meaning 'obviously', Zimmerli (1983: 80) sees the connotation as one of 'sincere admiration'.

46.   There are some linguistic differences between Jeremiah/Ezekiel in terms of what is hardened—faces (פנים)/forehead (מצח)—and the comparative object itself—stone (סלע)/flint (צר).

47.   Cf. Isa. 5.28, which contains a simile likening the hardness of horses' hoofs to flint.

48.   Cf. Jer. 1.18, which reports a similar act of divine strengthening for Jeremiah, though, as Zimmerli (1979: 138) points out, 'Whereas in Jeremiah's similes of the fortified city and the wall of bronze we can trace indirectly a reference to the protection of the prophet by divine power, with Ezekiel the hardening is introduced into the personality'.

49.   For a similar reference to prophetic resolve, see Isa. 50.7, where the prophet speaks of setting his face like flint (חלמיש).

'I will give, in my house and within my walls, a monument (יָד) and a name (וָשֵׁם) better than sons and daughters; I will give them an everlasting name that shall not be cut off'. The meaning of the phrase יָד וָשֵׁם is not entirely clear. According to Westermann (1969: 314), '"Monument and name" is to be taken as hendiadys—the name of the person concerned is preserved for the generations to come in the monument erected to him within the precincts of the temple: it is continuously in the mind of the community that speaks of its ancestors and remembers them'.[50] One of the pre-eminent ways people were remembered in the ancient world was through their offspring. Since a monument was even more enduring than descendants—who would eventually perish—such a memorial was clearly superior.

Others prefer to treat יָד and שֵׁם separately and translate the former term as 'share'.[51] Taking this approach, Japhet (1992: 78) believes this verse emphasizes the eunuchs' secure position since it 'opens with a confirmation of the eunuchs' basic right to belong to the community, and goes on to state the permanence and endurance of this right'. This fits nicely with the larger context which emphasizes that both eunuchs and foreigners who observe the sabbath and keep the Lord's covenant are assured a permanent place in the community of faith. As such, it is a word of great promise. Of all the intensified comparatives in the Latter Prophets, this one is by far the most positive and hopeful.

Conclusions

In this essay I have proposed that intensified comparatives be regarded as a distinct form of rhetoric, a distinction which has previously gone unnoticed. Though comparable to similes in certain respects, the intensified comparatives in the Latter Prophets are generally best understood as a particular form of hyperbole.[52] Nineveh's merchants were not actually more numerous than the stars of the heavens, nor were Babylon's (war)horses really faster than leopards. Such language, which revels in exaggeration and overstatement, was clearly used for rhetorical effect.[53] I have therefore attempted to demonstrate how the prophets used intensified comparatives in their efforts to persuade their hearers by creating powerful images and impressions.[54]

50. Cf. Whybray 1990 [1975]: 198, and see 2 Sam. 18.18. For the rationale behind this interpretation, see Oswalt 1998: 459 n. 37.

51. Robinson 1976, followed by Japhet 1992.

52. One might argue that the intensified comparatives used to demonstrate the depth of Judah's/Jerusalem's wickedness are 'accurate' and thus not hyperbolic, though I suppose this would be a matter of perspective. Likewise, one might contend that what God does for the eunuchs (Isa. 56.5) actually is 'better than sons and daughters'.

53. Ryken (1987: 177) defines hyperbole as 'conscious exaggeration for the sake of effect'. In his discussion of hyperbole, Gibson (1998: 14) notes that 'the Old Testament...habitually lets it hair down and exaggerates and overstates with considerable aplomb'. For additional discussions of hyperbole, see Bullinger 1968 [1898]: 423-27; Eybers 1970; Caird 1997 [1980]: 110-17, 133; Watson 1984: 316-21; Schökel 2000 [1988]: 168-69.

54. As Ryken (1987: 177) observes, 'We all use hyperbole when we feel strongly about a matter or when we are trying to be persuasive'.

Based on the discussion in the second part of this paper, the following conclusions can now be added to those made earlier. (1) Intensified comparatives occur most frequently in judgment oracles against Judah.[55] While this is not surprising given the disproportionate number of judgment oracles in the prophets, it does raise questions about whether their frequency in these contexts reflects the considerable difficulty prophets had persuading their audiences that disaster was at hand. Did the prophets feel compelled to use extraordinary rhetoric in their efforts to convince people of the seriousness of their situation? Presumably. The use of such forceful speech would seem to indicate that many people simply found it hard to believe they were in any real danger or that disaster was so near at hand. (2) The rhetorical effect of intensified comparatives varied widely. Sometimes intensified comparatives were deployed to emphasize the imminence or comprehensive scope of divine judgment. On other occasions, intensified comparatives accented a doomed nation's helplessness. Most frequently, this form of rhetoric was used to demonstrate the depth of Judah's/Jerusalem's wickedness and to justify the coming judgment. (3) The prophets could use qualitatively similar intensified comparatives for very different persuasive purposes. For instance, while both Jer. 5.3 and Ezek. 3.9 use the imagery of extreme hardness, in one case it represents obstinacy and in the other, fortitude. Similarly, while both Jer. 4.3 and Hab. 1.8 depict the speed of an approaching army, Jeremiah uses this to persuade the people of their dire predicament in hopes of eliciting their repentance while its use in Habakkuk, at least in part, seems more intent on settling a question of divine justice. Thus, even though the basic rhetorical effect is similar in each of these instances, the persuasive function is significantly different. This ability to use similar images for quite different ends, along with the wide range of rhetorical effects produced by intensified comparatives, stands as a testimony to the great versatility of the prophets as creative and persuasive communicators.

The limited scope of this study and the relatively small number of intensified comparatives in the Latter Prophets has restrained me from drawing overly broad conclusions. I am hopeful that future studies will build upon the work done here, enhancing and clarifying our understanding of this type of hyperbolic language. For example, a better understanding of the form and function of intensified comparatives could be gained by investigating other appearances of this form of rhetoric throughout the Hebrew Bible.[56] Given the high frequency of intensified comparatives in the Psalms, that collection would be a logical place to begin. It would also be instructive to explore ancient Near Eastern materials—prophetic and

---

55. In three instances, the intensified comparatives appear in oracles against the nations (Jer. 46.23; Ezek. 28.3; Nah. 3.16). Only rarely were intensified comparatives used to emphasize constructive divine activity, in one instance describing divine strengthening (Ezek. 3.9) and in another conveying a divine promise (Isa. 56.5).

56. For selected examples, see Gen. 49.12; Judg. 2.19; 2 Sam. 1.23; 1 Kgs 5.11 [4.31]; Job 6.3; 7.6; 9.25; 11.8-9, 17; Pss. 4.8 [7]; 19.11 [10]; 40.13 [12]; 51.9 [7]; 55.22 [21]; 62.10 [9]; 63.4 [3]; 69.5 [4], 32 [31]; 93.4; 108.5 [4]; 119.72, 103, 127; 130.6; 139.18; Prov. 3.14-15; 5.3; 8.11, 19; 16.32; 21.3; 27.3; 31.10; Song 1.2; 4.10.

otherwise—to determine the extent to which intensified comparatives were used in those writings and to what end.[57]

Whatever quarrels the reader may have with certain particulars of the foregoing analysis, it is hoped that this study has demonstrated the uniqueness of the intensified comparative and its persuasive potential. Although just one technique among many, the prophetic use of this form of rhetoric powerfully illustrates the linguistic extremes to which prophets were willing to go as they attempted to persuade people to hear and heed the divine word.

BIBLIOGRAPHY

Achtemeier, Elizabeth
    1986   *Nahum-Malachi* (IBC; Atlanta: John Knox Press).
Allen, James P.
    1997   'The Celestial Realm', in David P. Silverman (ed.), *Ancient Egypt* (New York: Oxford University Press).
Allen, Leslie C.
    1976   *The Books of Joel, Obadiah, Jonah, and Micah* (NICOT; Grand Rapids: Eerdmans).
Alter, Robert
    1985   *The Art of Biblical Poetry* (New York: Basic Books).
Berlinerblau, Jacques
    1996   *The Vow and the 'Popular Religious Groups' of Ancient Israel: A Philological and Sociological Inquiry* (JSOTSup, 210; Sheffield: Sheffield Academic Press).
Block, Daniel I.
    1997   *The Book of Ezekiel: Chapters 1–24* (NICOT; Grand Rapids: Eerdmans).
Brensinger, Terry L.
    1996   *Simile and Prophetic Language in the Old Testament* (Lewiston, NY: Mellon Biblical Press).
Brueggemann, Walter
    1988   *To Pluck Up, To Tear Down: A Commentary on the Book of Jeremiah 1–25* (ITC; Grand Rapids: Eerdmans).
Bullinger, E.W.
    1968 [1898] *Figures of Speech Used in the Bible: Explained and Illustrated* (Grand Rapids: Baker Book House).
Caird, G.B.
    1997 [1980] *The Language and Imagery of the Bible* (Grand Rapids: Eerdmans).
Carroll, Robert P.
    1986   *Jeremiah: A Commentary* (OTL; Philadelphia: Westminster).
Davidson, A.B.
    1901   *Introductory Hebrew Grammar: Hebrew Syntax* (Edinburgh: T. & T. Clark, 3rd edn).

---

57. Consider, for example, this description of Amun from ch. 200 of the Leiden Papyrus: 'He is hidden from the gods, and his aspect is unknown. He is farther than the sky, he is deeper than the Duat' (J.P. Allen 1997: 126-27).

Day, John
    1980   'The Daniel of Ugarit and Ezekiel and the Hero of the Book of Daniel', *VT*
                    30: 174-84.
Eybers, I.H.
    1970   'Some Examples of Hyperbole in Biblical Hebrew', in I.H. Eybers and
                    J.J. Glück (eds.), *Semitics* (10 vols.; Pretoria: University of South Africa
                    Press, 1970–89): I, 38-49.
Gesenius, W.
    1910   *Gesenius' Hebrew Grammar* (ed. and enl. by E. Kautzsch; 2nd English edn
                    by A.E. Cowley; Oxford: Oxford University Press).
Gibson, J.C.L.
    1998   *Language and Imagery in the Old Testament* (Peabody, MA: Hendrickson).
Holladay, William L.
    1986   *Jeremiah. I. A Commentary on the Book of the Prophet Jeremiah Chapters
                    1–25* (Hermeneia; Philadelphia: Fortress Press).
    1989   *Jeremiah. II. A Commentary on the Book of the Prophet Jeremiah Chapters
                    26–52* (Hermeneia; Philadelphia: Fortress Press).
Huffmon, Herbert B.
    1999   'The Impossible: God's Words of Assurance in Jer 31.35-37', in Stephen L.
                    Cook and S.C. Winter (eds.), *On the Way to Nineveh: Studies in Honor of
                    George M. Landes* (Atlanta: Scholars Press): 172-86.
Japhet, Sara
    1992   'יד ושם (Isa. 56.5)—A Different Proposal', *Maarav* 8: 69-80.
Keown, Gerald L., Pamela J. Scalise and Thomas G. Smothers
    1995   *Jeremiah 26–52* (WBC, 27; Dallas: Word Books).
Maier, Walter A.
    1987 [1959]   *Nahum* (St Louis: Concordia).
Mays, James Luther
    1976   *Micah* (OTL; Philadelphia: Westminster Press).
McKane, William
    1986   *Jeremiah*, I (ICC; Edinburgh: T. & T. Clark).
    1996   *Jeremiah*, II (ICC; Edinburgh: T. & T. Clark).
Oswalt, John N.
    1998   *The Book of Isaiah: Chapters 40–66* (NICOT; Grand Rapids: Eerdmans).
Roberts, J.J.M.
    1991   *Nahum, Habakkuk, and Zephaniah* (OTL; Louisville, KY: Westminster/John
                    Knox Press).
Robertson, O. Palmer
    1990   *The Books of Nahum, Habakkuk, and Zephaniah* (NICOT; Grand Rapids:
                    Eerdmans).
Robinson, G.
    1976   'The Meaning of יד in Isaiah 56.5', *ZAW* 88: 282-84.
Ryken, Leland
    1987   *Words of Delight: A Literary Introduction to the Bible* (Grand Rapids: Baker
                    Book House).
Schökel, Luis Alonso
    2000 [1988]   *A Manuel of Biblical Poetics* (trans. Adrian Graffy; SubBi, 11; Rome: Ponti-
                    fical Biblical Institute Press).

Thompson, J.A.
    1980   *The Book of Jeremiah* (NICOT; Grand Rapids: Eerdmans).
Waltke, Bruce K., and M. O'Connor
    1990   *An Introduction to Biblical Hebrew Syntax* (Winona Lake, IN: Eisenbrauns).
Watson, Wilfred G.E.
    1984   *Classical Hebrew Poetry: A Guide to its Techniques* (JSOTSup, 26; Shef-
                field: JSOT Press).
Westermann, Claus
    1969   *Isaiah 40–66: A Commentary* (Philadelphia: Westminster Press).
Wolff, Hans Walter
    1990   *Micah: A Commentary* (trans. Gary Stansell; Minneapolis: Augsburg–
                Fortress).
Whybray, R.N.
    1990 [1975]   *Isaiah 40–66* (NBC; Grand Rapids: Eerdmans).
Wright, Bradford W.
    2001   *Comic Book Nation: The Transformation of Youth Culture in America*
                (Baltimore: The Johns Hopkins University Press).
Zimmerli, Walther
    1979   *Ezekiel 1: A Commentary on the Book of the Prophet Ezekiel, Chapters 1–24*
                (trans. Ronald E. Clements; Philadelphia: Fortress Press).
    1983   *Ezekiel 2: A Commentary on the Book of the Prophet Ezekiel, Chapters*
                25–48 (trans. Ronald E. Clements; Philadelphia: Fortress Press).

Jeremiah as a Polyphonic Response to Suffering

Louis Stulman

At five in the afternoon.
It was exactly five in the afternoon.
A boy brought the white sheet
    at five in the afternoon.
A frail of lime ready prepared
    at five in the afternoon.
The rest was death, and death alone...
At five in the afternoon.
A coffin on wheels in his bed
    at five in the afternoon...
The wounds were burning like suns
    at five in the afternoon...
Ah, that fatal five in the afternoon!
It was five by all the clocks!
It was five in the shade of the afternoon! (Lament for Ignacio Sanchez Mejias)

Death has come up into our windows,
    it has entered our palaces,
to cut off the children from the streets
    and the young men from the squares...
Human corpses shall fall like dung upon the open field,
    like sheaves behind the reaper,
    and no one shall gather them. (Jer. 9.21-22)

Startling images of death and destruction! The first lament derives from the modern poet and dramatist Federico García Lorca who 'at five in the afternoon' beheld the death of Ignacio Sanchez Mejias, a death which symbolized the violence that would engulf the country he passionately loved. The second is associated with the biblical prophet Jeremiah, who, in the late seventh and early sixth centuries BCE, witnessed his own country ravaged and occupied by enemy forces. Although Lorca and Jeremiah lived in entirely different worlds, they stand together in the company of poets, artists, dissidents, saints and seers whose images of human tragedy have forever seared our minds and hearts. In our modern context, one thinks of the haunting cries from the killing fields of Auschwitz, Cambodia, El Salvador, Hiroshima, Kosovo, and Rwanda, to name only a few. From survivors' literature, we know that such massive, gratuitous suffering not only causes physical and emotional devastation but it also evokes probing questions about ultimate reality. Where is God?

How can such random and obscene acts of violence occur? Does evil go unpunished? Is it possible to live through the darkness and embrace life again? The testimonies of survivors to the multifaceted configurations of evil and the silence of God shatter all neat and cohesive understandings of life.

The witness of the book of Jeremiah is no exception. Its fifty-two chapters—comprising the largest writing of the prophetic literature in the Hebrew Bible—come face to face with human suffering and moral ambiguity. Jeremiah, or more precisely, the book that bears his name, depicts the unraveling of a culture that many perceived to be indestructible. With graphic imagery and unflinching courage, and often with thick, symbolic language, this prophetic writing 'chronicles' the dismantling of Judah's sacred and social world. In a relatively short span of time, the imposing neo-Babylonian military machine under King Nebuchadrezzar (605–562 BCE) delivered three crushing blows to Judah and its capital city Jerusalem. According to the biblical narratives, the first military assault resulted in the loss of Judah's independence and in the deportation of many of its leading citizens (597 BCE). The siege and capture of Jerusalem in 587 BCE took the greatest toll on the nation. This incursion ended in death, displacement, and the breakdown of Judah's social and political order. The Babylonian army burned to the ground the Jerusalem temple and the royal palace complex. In order to squelch signs of insubordination in the years following the fall of Jerusalem, Babylon attacked in 582 BCE and carried a third wave of Judean citizens to Babylon. In less than two decades, long-standing institutions associated with God's blessings and protection, cherished belief systems, and social structures in place for centuries all came to an abrupt and screeching halt.

The book of Jeremiah is a complex and multifaceted response to these tragedies. It dares to speak of the horrors of war and of people whose lives are wracked with unspeakable pain. The text bears witness to a 'moment' so terrible that it defies ordinary categories. Walter Brueggemann calls the crisis the end of Judah's known world (1986: 3-7). Pete Diamond refers to it as the 'end of a culture' (2001). Kathleen M. O'Connor speaks of the devastation as the 'colossal collapse' of Judah's world (2002b). I have used the term 'cosmic crumbling' to depict Judah's undoing (Stulman 1998: 54). For the Judean people the fall of Jerusalem and the series of deportations to Babylon represented nothing less than the 'end of history', the dissolution of the created order (e.g. Jer. 4.23-27). And Jeremiah, written by and large in the shadow of the wreckage, attempts to make symbolic sense of the upheaval and help survivors cope with the devastation.[1] More precisely, the book's plurality

---

1. When reading the book of Jeremiah it is important to make a distinction between *Jeremiah the prophet* and *Jeremiah the book*. While the two are obviously interrelated, they represent distinct stages in the development of the tradition. Based on virtually all of the prose sections in the book, it is safe to assume that *Jeremiah the prophet* was most active from the inauguration of Jehoiakim (609) to the fall of Jerusalem (587). During this time, his oracles focused largely on the devastation to come and the lasting impact it would have on the character of the Judean nation. *Jeremiah the book* took shape by and large after the tragic events and addressed the focal concerns of the Judean community in exile and perhaps the repatriates who returned to Judea in the late sixth and fifth centuries. In contrast to those who first 'heard' Jeremiah prophecies and supposedly had the chance

of voices and claims, representing various sectors of the community, converge in prose and poetry to come to terms with war, invasion, exile, and the accompanying existential dilemmas.

Although the Jerusalem establishment and its proponents insisted that the royal-temple structures would endure the onslaught of invasion, the interpretive community of Jeremiah maintained from the outset that the crisis would permanently change the character of the nation. In the first half of the prophetic drama, chs. 1–25, for instance, the text *predicts* the collapse of the temple and its liturgical systems (7.1-15), the covenant relationship between Yahweh and Israel (11.1-17), the election tradition (18.1-12), the Davidic dynasty (21.1–23.40), as well as the capital city and ancient land claims. The text asserts that the old world and its configurations of reality, social and symbolic, would go down to destruction. And nothing would remain to prop up its vestiges. The second part of Jeremiah, chs. 26–52, *depicts* the dismantling, while sustaining the reader with hope for coming restoration. Together the two 'acts'—Jeremiah 1–25 and 26–52—announce the end of Judah's once safe and stable world. Alongside the suffering nation, moreover, stands the prophet who also experiences unspeakable hardship. The book portrays its hero as one who suffers *with* his fellow citizens and *because of* their impassioned opposition to God's message. Even God is not above the fray in Jeremiah. God is beset by pain. Every divine word and act is entrenched in suffering (e.g. O'Connor 1998). Because of the slain people of Judah, God weeps day and night and is inexorably embroiled in the ordeal (9.1-2). Thus, all three major participants in the prophetic drama—Judah, Jeremiah and Yahweh—are drenched in tears.

In this essay, dedicated to my esteemed teacher and dear friend Herb Huffmon, I will argue that the book of Jeremiah is a labyrinth of thick theological interpretations of suffering. I will consider three of these claims. The first and perhaps governing assertion in the book is that, despite Judah's ordeal, the world is orderly and congruent, moral and stable, exacting punishment on wrongdoers and, by implication, promising blessing to the faithful. In support of this reading of reality, a surplus of prose and poetic texts contend that Judah—and especially its leaders—is responsible for its own demise. Judah's infidelity to God, its mistreatment of the poor, and its royal policies of brutality and greed have brought down the walls of the city. Consequently, insiders, not dangerous outsiders, constitute the principal protagonists in the fall of Judah. Furthermore, God's people, not God, are culpable. While a host of passages in Jeremiah 1–25 reflect such a view, this essay will focus on 11.1-14, a representative prose sermon with a distinctly Deuteronomic texture.

The second theological response to Judah's plight is far more at home in a dissonant and morally ambiguous universe. In the Joban tradition, this formulation looks to the 'innocent' suffering of Jeremiah as a way to work through the devastation. Here we encounter one who is faithful to God and yet is not granted immunity

---

to circumvent disaster, the exiles in Babylon (as well as later communities) could only look back on fallen worlds in hope that they would not make similar mistakes. These oral and written stages of the tradition are further complicated by the emergence of two textual witnesses of *Jeremiah the book*: a Hebrew *Vorlage* of the Old Greek and the later MT of Jeremiah (for the implications of these lines of text traditions, see Stulman 1986: 49-146).

from the sorrow of his country. Like innocent Jerusalemites, Jeremiah endures enormous hardship and pain for no fault of his own. Thus, in the prophetic persona, we discover that suffering is not always punitive, that the world bristles with conflict and danger, and that clearly defined categories do not do full justice to the scope of human pain. And now permission is granted to grieve the community's profound losses. While one can discern this Joban *Tendenz* throughout the book, it is most transparent in the so-called 'Confessions of Jeremiah' and in much of the 'Baruch Narrative'. Both literary units depict their hero as a tormented and conflicted prophet whose suffering is not wholly manageable, at least from a rational standpoint.[2] To outline Jeremiah's theology of protest, we will look briefly at three of the 'Confessions'[3] (11.18–12.6; 15.15-18; 20.7-18).

The third theological interpretation of Judah's crisis—particularly the suffering of the post-587 Judean community—is not as sweeping as the first two but no less significant. Here the interpretive community of Jeremiah distances, indeed extricates, Yahweh and Yahweh's spokesperson from the gratuitous violence. As such, divine silence and divine absence play a central role. The most stunning example of this bold overture is found in the account of Gedaliah's failed government (40.7–41.18). This segment of the 'Baruch Narrative' details the brutal death of Gedaliah and the pilgrims en route to Jerusalem without reference to God or Jeremiah.

The First Strategy for Addressing Judah's Plight:
Moral Order Amid the Chaos

The dominant voice in the book of Jeremiah maintains that Judah is to blame for its troubles, that life is not spiraling out of Yahweh's control, and that the world is by and large orderly and morally manageable. Although the prose sermons in Jeremiah do not hold a monopoly on these claims, they articulate them most forcefully while organizing a range of poetic and prose texts that make similar and counter assertions (Stulman 1999; see also Wilson 1999). Influenced to a large measure by Deuteronomic theology, the prose sermons declare that Judah's political and social devastation is a direct consequence of its own actions. By 'his servants the prophets'[4] Yahweh had warned Israel to turn from its evil ways and keep the commandments;

---

2.   Admittedly, there is a strong tendency in the present form of the book of Jeremiah to use the suffering of Jeremiah and his prayers of protest to reinforce symmetrical moral categories. The Deuteronomic prose tradition exploits the rejection and harsh treatment of Jeremiah to demonstrate the guilt of Judah: Judah rejects Yahweh and the words of Yahweh's messenger Jeremiah and therefore deserves divine judgment. In this way Jeremiah's suffering 'makes sense'. Such an interpretive strategy is only partially successful for it is unable to silence the force of Jeremiah's cries and those he represents. Thus, both theodicy and anti-theodicy strands co-exist and create a rich theological tension.

3.   Scholars often treat Jer. 20.7-18 as the fifth and sixth confessions of Jeremiah. Concerns for determining literary boundaries, however, need not occupy our attention because the same argument can be made whether the unit comprises one or two of Jeremiah's laments. For a discussion of these critical issues see Diamond 1987: 101-25.

4.   For a recent examination of the phrase 'my servants the prophets' and its implications for the composition of Jeremiah, see Sharp 2003: 41-80.

however, Israel rejected this message and therefore suffered divine judgment (see, e.g., 7.25-34; 25.4-11; 26.4-6; 29.17-19; 44.4-6; cf. 2 Kgs 17.13-18). Consequently, Judah's disobedience exonerates God of injustice and mismanagement: the destruction of Jerusalem and the exile to Babylon are Judah's responsibility. God acts only in accordance with the covenant demands.

Jeremiah 11.1-14 is one of many texts that represent such understandings. In the prose sermon Jeremiah indicts Israel and Judah for breaking the covenant. Not unlike the first ten chapters of the book, it asserts that the people of God have been unfaithful and therefore must brace themselves for Yahweh's judgment. Jeremiah 11.1-14, however, expresses this motif in the language, style, and theology of Deuteronomy. Similar to Deuteronomy, the language of Jer. 11.1-14 is verbose and repetitive. Its prose is parenetic and rhetorical. A number of words and phrases in the text are virtually identical to those found in Deuteronomy (e.g. Jer. 11.3 = Deut. 27.26; Jer. 11.4 = Deut. 4.20; Jer. 11.5 = Deut. 7.8; 8.18; 9.5; Jer. 11.7 = Deut. 4.30; 8.20; Jer. 11.8 = Deut. 29.1, 9; Jer. 11.10 = Deut. 8.19; 11.28). Moreover, the prose sermon reflects the Deuteronomic belief that divine blessing accompanies obedience whereas disaster results from disobedience (e.g. Deut. 28). If Israel complies with the stipulations of the covenant, wellbeing and prosperity will follow. If Israel does not heed Yahweh's commandments, judgment will ensue. The structure of Jer. 11.1-14 is also strikingly similar to speeches in the Deuteronomistic corpus (e.g. 2 Kgs 17.7-18): it includes an introduction (11.1-2), the word of Yahweh in the imperative, that is, the commandments (11.3-6), a statement of disobedience (11.7-10), and the pronouncement of divine judgment (11.11-14).

In the prose sermon Yahweh addresses Jeremiah four times with four distinct commands (11.2-5, 6-8, 9-13, 14). Couched in the negative, the first follows the letter of Deuteronomy 27–28 (11.2-5): 'All are cursed who do not obey the terms of this covenant' (11.3). God instructs Jeremiah to summon the people of Judah to obey the terms of the covenant. The demand for obedience grows out of the exodus story; that is, obedience is supposedly the joyous response to God's gracious act of liberation from oppression, 'when I brought them out of the land of Egypt, from the iron-smelter…' (11.4). God freed the Israelites from Egyptian bondage so that they might obey a benevolent suzerain and enjoy a special relationship with this divine king. God's covenant with Israel is a gift and a great privilege, but it does not offer Israel a free ride. Privilege involves responsibility. God expects Israel to obey its covenant obligations, and in large measure Israel's continued status as God's people is dependent upon such fidelity. Obedience is thus in no way ancillary but is the very centerpiece of the covenant relationship. To remain in the land and enjoy the blessings of the covenant, Judah must be a faithful vassal (11.3-5). In other words, the blessings of the covenant are not entitlements: they are dependent on observing the terms of the solemn agreement.

The second admonition (11.6-8) builds on the harsh tone of the previous verses. Jeremiah implores the people of Judah to 'hear the words of this covenant and do them' (11.6). Earlier communities had their chance to obey the terms of the covenant but adamantly refused: 'They did not obey or incline their ear, but everyone walked in the stubbornness of an evil will' (11.8). Yahweh therefore brought upon them 'all the words of this covenant'. This historical synopsis is another somber warning for the contemporary community. It characterizes Israel's entire history as one of incessant disobedience and infers from this judgment that the present hearers will likely do little to change it. Interestingly, the Septuagint almost entirely omits vv. 7-8. The shorter Greek text states succinctly, 'The Lord said to me...hear the words of this covenant and do them, *but they did not*'. Whereas the Hebrew text uses the ancestors' disobedience as a rhetorical device to coax the contemporary people of God into obedience, the Greek text hones in only on the unwillingness of the contemporary community to heed Yahweh's word. Both the Hebrew and Greek texts agree that violating the stipulations of the covenant carries grave consequences.

Next, Yahweh informs Jeremiah of a 'conspiracy' brewing among the people of Judah and the inhabitants of Jerusalem (11.9-13). What makes the conspiracy so dangerous is that it is against God! The Judeans have resolved to follow their ancestors' example of disobedience. The first two verbs in v. 10 convey the nature of the 'revolt' in stereotyped language: the people of Judah have *turned back* (שוב) to the iniquities of their ancestors...and have *gone after* (הלך) other gods to serve them. The third verb is less common: the house of Israel and the house of Judah have *broken* (פרר) *the covenant* made with their ancestors. For the first time in the book, Jeremiah *explicitly* accuses the nation of breaking the covenant. The precise language to 'break covenant' occurs five times in Jeremiah (11.10; 14.21; 31.32; 33.20, 21), and two of these references identify Judah as the covenant breaker (11.10 and 31.32). Jeremiah 31.32, a principal text for the construction of exilic and post-exilic Judaism, states that the establishment of a 'new covenant' is necessary since Israel has broken the covenant that God made at Sinai. The reference in Jeremiah 11 is significant because it refers to a breach that places the future of the house of Israel and the house of Judah in grave danger. This text asserts that one cannot write off the covenant demands without suffering grave consequences, even more so since the people's love affair with 'many gods' violates the very cornerstone of the covenant relationship: 'you shall have no other gods before me'. Furthermore, by associating covenant breaking with the conspiracy against Yahweh (11.9-10), Jeremiah declares that the people's disobedience is a formal and brazen renunciation that will result in the covenant curses (11.11-13).

Last, Yahweh prohibits Jeremiah from interceding on behalf of the community (11.14). The command not to intercede is essentially a repetition of Jer. 7.16. The people have 'not listened' to Yahweh (11.8) and now it is Yahweh's turn 'not to listen' (11.14). By betraying their covenant obligations, the people of Judah have forfeited their covenant claim upon God and their right to enter Yahweh's house (11.15). No prophetic intercession or priestly offerings can thwart God's plans to strip away Judah's world (11.14-15). This final admonition serves to intensify the scope of God's judgment and prevent loopholes.

The covenant sermon accuses Judah of fracturing the ancestral covenant and bringing upon itself inescapable judgment. As such Jeremiah's diatribe is couched in retributive terms. The prophet predicts that the covenant curses shall befall the nation (such as exile and military defeat) as a penalty for its moral failure and breach of covenant obligations. Just as the ancestral community disobeyed the conditions of the covenant and reaped the consequences of its conduct, so the present nation runs the same risk of suffering the consequences of covenant disloyalty. Such arrangements dispel any trace of ethical ambiguity. The lines that separate good from evil are clear and well defined. A correlation between conduct and condition is distinctly drawn; acts have prescribed consequences, and thus life is manageable and predictable. In a universe controlled by a just God who is a faithful covenant partner, evildoers are punished for their wrongdoing, even if they are God's people. In a universe with a meaningful ethical code, suffering is explicable and never beyond the scope of God's just governance. National crisis and personal suffering are thus not the product of an arbitrary and chaotic world.

Clearly informed by Deuteronomic categories, Jer. 11.1-14 articulates a coherent and symmetrical *Weltanschauung*, which attends to the construction of a morally exacting universe. In this world, blessing and punishment are purposefully meted out according to conduct. The righteous enjoy blessing from God (cf. Deut. 28.1-14) while evildoers are punished for their wrongdoing (Deut. 28.15-68). In this morally unequivocal universe, Judah's devastating circumstances are not value-neutral. The nation brings exile and destruction upon itself by refusing to comply with its covenant obligations. God only holds Judah accountable for its behavior.

This well-proportioned and balanced view of social and symbolic reality is certainly not distinctive to Jeremiah or the Deuteronomic literature. A number of torah, wisdom, and creation psalms reflect a similar orientation. Psalm 1, for example, speaks of two clearly defined ways of life, each with clearly defined consequences: the way of the righteous, which is blessed, and the way of the wicked, which leads to ruin. In addition, conventional wisdom generally construes the world as having straightforward moral categories. Proverbs 4.18-19 says it this way: 'the path of the righteous is like the light of dawn...the way of the wicked is like deep darkness'. Also informed by such assumptions are Job's friends who are absolutely certain that the sufferer has committed some moral failing. For these defenders of conventional wisdom, Job must have done something to bring on his problems or else their relatively unambiguous worldviews would crumple—which, of course, they did. These various sources, including Jer. 11.1-14, are for the most part crystal clear about life and its workings.

The Second Strategy for Addressing Judah's Plight: Jeremiah's Suffering and Moral Chaos

The portrayal of Jeremiah's prophetic experience, especially his suffering, calls into question and then shatters these stable and congruent categories. The interpretive community of Jeremiah presents the prophet as one who is faithful to God and yet is attacked, ostracized, ridiculed, and rejected. Immediately following the covenant sermon, for instance, Jeremiah cries out to Yahweh concerning his own unjust treatment at the hands of evildoers (Jer. 11.18–12.6). He has done nothing except obey God, yet he is maligned and persecuted. He sees himself as innocent and naïve, as 'a gentle lamb led to the slaughter' (11.19). As a result, he appeals to Yahweh for protection and for the punishment of his persecutors. Although Yahweh responds to the prophet's complaint with the assurance of eventual retribution (see, e.g., 11.21-23), Jeremiah is still caught in the chaotic interim before justice materializes. And so, he accuses Yahweh of wrongdoing and collusion with his enemies (12.1-2). During the interim, between the 'already and not-yet', Jeremiah bears witness to the disturbing reality of undeserved suffering and the apparent indifference of God. In stark contrast to his clear-cut proclamation, Jeremiah *lives* in a social environment in which the righteous are denied justice and the innocent encounter real evil. Jeremiah's first confession describes this dangerous world without offering an explanation or justification for evil. Here there is no cover-up, no denial of the randomness of suffering, and no easy answers that anesthetize people to the deeply fissured universe. Even innocent prophets, who represent a myriad of tormented people, suffer abuse, bitter opposition, and failure. Thus, Jeremiah has only questions, and these reveal his conflicted character as well as his bold courage to look moral ambiguity in the eye without flinching.

In Jer. 15.15-18, another of Jeremiah's laments, the battered and tormented prophet again cries out to Yahweh. Jeremiah reaffirms his dedication to his prophetic call: 'Your words were found, and I ate them and your words became to me a joy and delight to my heart; for I am called by your name, O Yahweh, God of hosts' (15.16; see also Ezek. 3.1-3). The prophet, who is Yahweh's voice, has done all God expects of prophets (15.17-18). He has internalized the divine message (15.16), avoided 'the company of scoffers' (15.17; cf. Ps. 1.1), and 'sat alone under the weight' of Yahweh's hand (15.17b). Nonetheless, he suffers excruciating pain and persecution. *For the distraught prophet, God has failed.* Thus, he likens the Lord to a 'deceitful brook' (15.18), a figure that draws on the image of a desert mirage which tricks a parched wanderer into believing there is water when the wadi is dry. Yahweh has sorely disappointed and such disappointment leaves the prophet deeply wounded (15.18).

Jeremiah 20.7-18 employs perhaps the most scandalous words in the book to depict Jeremiah's address to God. In this passage the prophet accuses God of being unreliable and deceptive. With raw emotion and astonishing boldness, Jeremiah holds Yahweh responsible for his abuse. In anguish and anger, he accuses God of 'betraying/enticing/seducing' and 'overpowering' him (see Diamond 1987: 101-13; Heschel 2001: 144-46; O'Connor 1988: 70-75):

> O Lord, you have *enticed* me
>> and I was enticed;
> You have *overpowered* me,
>> and you have prevailed.
> I have become a laughingstock all day long;
>> everyone mocks me. (Jer. 20.7)

This language pushes the lament genre to the limits. Although other laments dare to question the reliability of Yahweh, none does so in such a frontal manner. The verb 'overpower' (חזק in the hiphil) in v. 7 has a wide semantic range, which includes seizing, compelling, strengthening, taking hold of, and even raping (Deut. 22.25). The Hebrew word translated as 'deceive/entice/seduce' (פתה), depending on the

English translations, has a more narrow range. It occurs in about twenty-five texts in the Old Testament and generally means to 'trick', 'deceive', or 'seduce'.

With this language Jer. 20.7 conveys the idea of being duped and besieged by the power and purposes of God, forces over which Jeremiah has little control (e.g. 20.9). At the outset of his prophetic ministry, Yahweh had assured him that 'kings, princes, priests, and the people of the land' (1.18-19; cf. 15.20) would not 'prevail' (יכל) against him. But now it seems that all prevail against him. Priests beat and imprison him, his enemies slander and mock him (20.7c-8), and his 'close friends' attack him (20.10). Even Yahweh, his ally and covenant partner, has 'crushed' him and 'prevailed' (20.7b). All this evokes a deep sense of rage and betrayal. And Jeremiah does not hesitate to confront Yahweh with his doubts and misgivings. Yet at the very same time he acknowledges Yahweh's trustworthiness. The prophet affirms that Yahweh is with him 'like a dread warrior' and as a result his 'persecutors will not prevail' but 'will be greatly shamed' (20.11). He declares that Yahweh has 'rescued the needy from the hands of evildoers' (20.13), which harkens back to the divine promise at his commissioning (see 1.8, 19). These turbulent responses defy logic but show raw human emotion.

According to the final words of ch. 20 (vv. 14-18), Jeremiah plunges into the depths of despair as his hopelessness reaches its most critical level. Now the term 'curse' (ארר) no longer depicts disobedient Israel (11.3) or the one who 'trusts in mere mortals' (17.5). Now Jeremiah, like Job, curses the day of his birth (20.14-17). Now we see what von Rad calls the 'lowest point in the suffering of Jeremiah' (von Rad 1983: 96). 'Night has now completely enveloped the prophet' (von Rad 1983: 95). All hope for equilibrium is gone. Alongside the nation's descent to destruction is a prophet who is not granted immunity.

Jeremiah functions in these texts as an archetypal or representative figure. In the tradition of the righteous sufferer Job, Jeremiah assumes a larger-than-life identity whose experiences and piety transcend his own solitary experience (e.g. Reventlow 1966). As such, he not only speaks for himself, articulating his own disappointment and brokenness to God, but also for those living in the aftermath of Jerusalem's demise whose suffering was inexplicable. In this way, Jeremiah's obedience, his devotion to God, and his hardship take on paradigmatic force. His suffering service and surrender to God in defeat and utter trust become a model of faithful living.

As an exemplary righteous sufferer, Jeremiah finds himself in a place of extreme vulnerability. His social environment is harsh and dangerous with few structures in place to protect him. He endures great hardship at the hands of adversaries; he is ridiculed and cries to Yahweh for help. The prophet seeks vengeance on his persecutors, and even curses the day of his birth (20.14-18). He faces scorn, abject humiliation, and reproach. The opponents of the prophet threaten to kill him unless he abandons his prophetic mission (11.18-23). They conspire against him (18.18-23; cf. 11.9) and dig pits to trap him (18.22). Those who pursue Jeremiah attempt to 'prevail' over him (20.7-13), they ban him from the temple precincts (36.5), and eventually arrest and imprison him (20.1-6; 37.11-16). This lack of protection and moral symmetry results in anxiety and sorrow, so much so that Jeremiah longs for death (20.14-18). Yet, like Job and the embattled psalmists, in the face of adversity and persecution Jeremiah declares his innocence, maintains his personal/prophetic integrity, and takes an active stance against oppressors and evildoers (11.20; 12.3; 15.15; 17.18; 18.21-22; 20.12).

As one who suffers in solidarity with God and those deprived of justice, Jeremiah gives voice to an alternative understanding of suffering. Suffering is not a shameful consequence of wrongdoing or evidence of divine injustice. On the contrary, in the '*body*' of Jeremiah suffering becomes a witness of faithful service to God (von Rad 1983). In the prophet's pleas for justice and in his cries of protests, Jeremiah aligns himself with the poor and oppressed. His scandalous confessions speak for the alien, the orphan, and the widow, as well as for women and men whose innocent blood was shed (7.6). Consequently, Jeremiah becomes a symbol of hope for those whose distress is unintelligible and borne in obedience to God.

It is important to note that the final form of the text does not privilege the suffering of the prophet over the well-defined arrangements of his prophetic message. Instead, it holds both in abeyance. Wild, explosive, and at times cynical outbursts are located alongside texts that are absolutely sure about the workings of the universe. The portrait of a tormented prophet, which accentuates the failure of rational understandings to account for human evil, does not quash conventional arrangements of divine retribution. Voices that pulsate with internal anxiety and testify to the fractured human condition join the chorus with those that insist that the fall of Judah is a sure consequence of the people's rebellion. Such dissonance creates an engaging cacophony which at the end of the day concedes that Judah's wreckage is too massive for any singular explanation.

The Third Strategy for Addressing Judah's Plight:
Silence and Divine Absence

Another strategy for dealing with Judah's disaster is buried in a story about the post-war era. It is a response of silence, divine silence. The composer of the Baruch Narrative (Jer. 36–45) tells the story of Gedaliah's failed government without reference to Jeremiah or Yahweh (40.7–41.18). In fact, this narrative is the only one in the book where neither the prophet nor Yahweh is present. Until recently, historical categories have governed most explanations of the lacuna. Jeremiah is absent, it is often argued, because he wasn't there! That is to say, the text merely reflects the authorial conviction that Jeremiah does not play a prominent part in the Gedaliah administration, even though an earlier account places him in the custodianship of the governor (40.1-6). In his OTL commentary, Robert Carroll takes a somewhat different slant, although informed by similar assumptions. Carroll suggests, 'the story of Gedaliah's assassination and the break-up of the community is told without reference to Jeremiah *because the editor had it in this form*' (1986: 701 [italics are mine]). That the material was handed down in this way may be well and good but it says little about the artistic and theological significance of the missing God and prophet. It may be that the missing God and prophet have less to do with objective presentation than literary representation, less with history than theology. As such, their absence functions as a meaningful part of the narrative! The missing voice, the silence of God, speaks with eloquence about gratuitous suffering.

In order to determine how this 'silence' functions we turn to the story itself. The central character of Jer. 40.7–41.18 is introduced in the preceding text where he is appointed governor of post-war Judah. Gedaliah, son of Ahikam, is the one on whom the people of Judah come to depend for continued land occupation. The news of his leadership reaches those who have been in hiding since Babylon's victory and soon Judeans return home to rally around him (40.7-12). The first to arrive at Mizpah, the provincial capital, are 'freedom fighters' who had fought against Babylon's incursion and subsequently retreated to the Judean hills. Gedaliah demands loyalty of the commanders for the assurance of welfare and amnesty. They must only stay in the land and submit to the current government and 'it shall go well' with them. Like Joseph's kind treatment of his brothers (Gen. 50.19-21), Gedaliah encourages the Judean nationalists and provides for their needs. This is no time for reprisals. There has already been enough suffering for a lifetime. Now is the time for rebuilding and restoration, for breaking the vicious cycle of violence. Soon refugees from the trans-Jordan and elsewhere join the commanders and their units. All are united in the land under the care of Gedaliah. And the governor responds to their needs by inviting them to partake in a bountiful harvest of wine and summer fruits. This portrait of abundance has an idyllic quality (40.12).

But there is trouble in the air. Johanan and other leading military figures approach Gedaliah with news of a plot on his life (40.13–41.3). According to the report, the king of the Ammonites is behind the conspiracy, and Ishmael, one of their compatriots, is about to execute the plan. The syntax of the interrogative, 'Aren't you aware' (הידע תדע) suggests that the governor should know about conspiracy (40.14). This is a time of intense political power struggles. There are enemies near and far. Gedaliah must surely be privy to such dangers. Nonetheless, he dismisses the warning as unfounded. Even after a clandestine meeting in which Johanan volunteers to take matters into his own hands, he refuses to act: 'You are telling a lie (שקר) about Ishmael' (40.16). Gedaliah will have no part in a pre-emptive strike, and so he forbids Johanan from slaying Ishmael.[5] Before long it becomes apparent that Johanan's concerns are well founded. Gedaliah's refusal to listen will cost him his life and the remnant of Judah their hopes for a future in the land.

The report of the assassination of Gedaliah is succinct (41.1-3). The narrator relates the actions without dialogue or embellishment. Ishmael, the subject of the previous conversation, shows up at Mizpah with ten men. The reference to his royal ancestry (41.1; cf. 36.12, 20, 21) and Gedaliah's Babylonian loyalties (41.2) suggests that the meeting is laden with political and ideological anxiety. Perhaps Ishmael harbors aspirations for the throne. If so, Gedaliah, a 'Babylonian pawn', is the only thing that stands in his way. Even with these signs of trouble and Johanan's previous warning, the parties sit down together. The meal they share represents a gracious act of hospitality. Hospitality, says Henri Nouwen, overcomes hostility and bears the seeds of community (1975: 65-109). However, not in this case! Under the guise of covenant friendship and the banner of patriotism, Ishmael and his

---

5.   Critical assessments of the governor's actions are as different as night and day; some commentators consider him a 'saint' while others see him as inept, at best.

cohorts betray their unsuspecting host. During the meal, they rise up and strike down Gedaliah with the sword. To complete their coup, Ishmael murders all the Jews who are with the governor as well as the Babylonian soldiers stationed at the garrison.

The massacre does not end with the death of Gedaliah and his cadre (41.4-10). Ishmael eyes eighty pilgrims from the northern cities of Shechem, Shiloh, and Samaria en route to Jerusalem. With beards shaved, cloths torn, and bodies gashed as a sign of mourning, presumably over the tragic events of 587, they bear gifts to present to God at the temple. (Apparently, the narrator assumes that some form of worship continued at the temple site after the fall of the city.) Ishmael intercepts the pilgrims, feigns solidarity, persuades them to meet Gedaliah, and then carries on his killing rampage in the middle of the city. He spares only ten men because they had hidden 'stores of wheat, barley, oil, and honey in the fields' (41.8). After throwing the corpses into a cistern built by King Asa, desecrating a holy place, Ishmael takes off with hostages in hand.

Johanan and his brigade hear of the bloodbath and set out in pursuit. They eventually overtake Ishmael near the great waters in Gibeon, six miles northwest of Jerusalem (41.11-18). The pool of Gibeon had been the site of an earlier civil war between Israel and Judah (2 Sam. 2.12-17). Now, some four hundred years later, it is the field of Ishmael's last stand. But Ishmael does not even engage in battle. Beset by the Johanan's forces, he and his men abandon their hostages and escape to Ammon (41.15). At that point Johanan gathers the captives and sets out towards Egypt. He resolves to go there because he is afraid of Babylonian reprisals. Before leading the remnant south, Johanan stops at a village near Bethlehem where Jeremiah re-enters the picture (42.1-6).

Jeremiah 40.7–41.18 is probably the most grisly section in the book. It is saturated with violence, brutality, and duplicity. The death of Gedaliah and his company as well as the mass murder of the seventy pilgrims flood the streets of Mizpah with innocent blood. All are victims of cunning and cruelty. Whether fueled by patriotic zeal or sheer madness, the murderous acts are indefensible. One can hardly read of the carnage without shock (see Judg. 20–21 for an earlier text set at Mizpah that is equally savage). To make matters worse, the killers go unpunished. They flee unharmed to the Ammonites. Clearly, the text presents to us a historicized world in total disarray (cf. 4.23-27 for a poetic counterpart). As the story of the Judean remnant winds down, communal life falls into a downward moral and religious spiral that reaches its lowest point. The social order is broken down, all forms of civility disappear, evildoers run rampant, and innocent people are butchered. And, perhaps most perplexing, Yahweh and Jeremiah are absent! Where is the prophet whom Nebuzaradan had entrusted into Gedaliah's care? And more importantly, where is Yahweh?

Initially, Gedaliah's policies, like those of King Josiah, may have rendered Jeremiah's prophetic speech unnecessary.[6] The text portrays Gedaliah as a hero, a benevolent leader, who accomplishes what the last kings of Judah could not. This

---

6.   An insight from Pete Diamond.

Babylonian appointee cares for the vulnerable in the land, 'men, women, and children, those of the poorest of the land'. He attracts Judean survivors 'from all the places to which they had been scattered' (40.12). When the refugees return, he calms their fears, attends to their needs, and serves as their advocate before the Babylonians. Gedaliah wins the hearts of the survivors and creates a sense of optimism for the future of the community in Judah. Here is one who at last complies with Jeremiah's instructions, submits to Babylonian rule, and whose speech to the gathering of the remnant echoes Jeremiah's oracles and program for sustained life in the land.

But then all goes awry. It is at this critical point, when the post-war community falters and its social world collapses, that the silence of God is most troubling. Why does the narrator exclude Yahweh and Yahweh's prophet from Judah's darkest hours? Put differently, how does 'divine silence' function in the narrative and serve as a response to Judah's wreckage? Although the story provides no direct explanation or commentary, it nonetheless resonates with interpretive possibilities. Only three will be noted below.

First, the absence of the book's two major characters may imply that neither Yahweh nor Jeremiah has anything to do with the coup of the nationalists. In particular, Yahweh does not figure in the bloodbath of Ishmael, nor belong there! Yahweh has no part in the treachery, betrayal, or brutal fanaticism of the Judean nationalists. The militants may think Yahweh does, they may even act in Yahweh's name. But Yahweh does not show up, and certainly does not sanction the brutality, whether in the guise of patriotism or religion. Thus, there is no divine voice or presence, no divine intrusion or prophetic witness. In a bold and daring literary move, the narrator distances Yahweh and Jeremiah from the politics of violence. They are missing because they are not involved in the savage acts.

Admittedly, the book is replete with the rhetoric of violence, indeed with theo-political violence. It pulsates with the conviction that Yahweh is 'plucking up and pulling down, destroying and overthrowing' Judah and its capital city. Jeremiah asserts that Babylon is the *divine* instrument charged with executing the dangerous dismantling. Yet, when the armies *actually* pounce on Judah, as described in Jer. 39.1-14 and 52.3b-30, the narrators become far more reticent to use God-language. Rather than seizing the moment to corroborate the prophetic message (see Deut. 18.21-22; cf. Jer. 28.17), the tellers merely present an 'objective' account of the events, without theological commentary or evaluation. As in the Gedaliah fiasco, the account of the fall of Jerusalem is told without explicit reference to God. Consequently, Yahweh is neither implicated nor exonerated. Yahweh is just missing.

Second, the absent God (and prophet) helps to refute the theodicy argument in the book. The events surrounding the death of Gedaliah are not only tragic but are also theologically embarrassing. The unimaginable evil flies in the face of principal tenets of the book: that life makes moral sense, that acts have consequences, that the universe is a morally coherent place. As we have seen, these claims are used to make the destruction of Judah rationally manageable. Judah's recalcitrance, as demonstrated in its abject rejection of the word and person of Jeremiah, gives rise to its present predicament. In traditional terms, Judah's woes are divine punishment for sin. Gedaliah's death and God's absence, however, challenge these fundamental assumptions. Again, here is one who obeys Yahweh's word, and yet dies without cause. Despite being a custodian of Jeremiah and being a part of a pious family—his grandfather Shaphan and Ahikam played prominent roles in King Josiah's reform (2 Kgs 22.3-14) and his father was instrumental in saving Jeremiah's life (26.24)—Gedaliah is slaughtered. His death makes no sense.[7] It contradicts moral logic and exposes holes in the conventional understandings of suffering.

Yet, by facing the ethical chaos head on, the narrative shows remarkable courage. By refusing to clean up the mess with oracular speech, the story honors moral ambiguity. It courageously rejects easy answers and clear-cut systems. Slain Gedaliah and the massacred worshippers, alongside a hostage prophet, subvert congruent and symmetrical views of suffering. The counter-theodicy concedes, perhaps even asserts, that the righteous *do* suffer, that God is sometimes silent, that the world is indeed a dangerous place. In a haunting manner, this text mirrors the world in which we live, a world that seems at times to be morally irrational and expressly evil. Gedaliah's death, Ishmael's coup, the slaughter of the innocent, the escape of the murderer, and the silence of God all shatter illusions of moral certitude.

Last, the silence of God is necessary from a literary and human perspective. It 'speaks' on behalf of the innocent. It allows the voices of the brutalized to be heard. It preserves their story and their memories. Any prophetic utterance would risk trivializing the losses. Divine silence is therefore absolutely essential.[8] In Chaim Potok's *The Chosen*, Reb Sauders says it this way: 'You can hear the pain of the world in silence'. Kathleen O'Connor recently explores the 'missing voice' in Lamentations and concludes that

> Lamentations' haunting power lies in its brutal honestly about the Missing Voice; its brilliance is that it does not speak for God… It prevents us from sliding prematurely over suffering toward happy endings. It gives the book daring power because it honors human speech. God's absence forces us to attend to voices of grief and despair, and it can reflect…our own experiences of a silent God… If God spoke, God's words would diminish the voices of pain, wash over them, and crowd them out. Even one word from God would take up too much space in the book. (2002a: 86)

Similarly, Jer. 40.7–41.18 allows the testimony of a slain leader and murdered worshippers to linger and the cruelty of the killers to haunt us. It refuses to clean up the 'mess'. The cries of the innocent must be heard and embraced before life can go on. No wonder Eli Wiesel remained silent for so many years after the years of darkness at Auschwitz. Words—although essential for testimony—would only diminish

---

7. The story of Josiah's untimely death in 2 Kings reads as a stunning narrative analogy. It should also be noted that the Gedaliah fiasco likely serves the interests of the Judean exiles in Babylon. The failure of Gedaliah and his administration to provide a viable alternative in the land provides further 'proof' that the Babylonian exiles are true heirs of the divine promises.

8. From a pastoral point of view, the silence of Job's friends (Job 2.11-13) is surely their most compassionate posture. When they eventually open their mouths, the author transforms Job's friends into enemies. With words as weapons they do violence to the sufferer and to all those crushed by life's injustices.

the unspeakable horror of the camps. And no wonder Christians see the silence of God in the death of Jesus Christ (see, e.g., Mt. 27.45-46).

Conclusion

The three theological responses explored in this essay cannot by themselves account for the collapse of Judah's world. The wreckage is too massive, complex, and unmanageable. The losses and resultant despair are beyond ordinary patterns of speech. Instead, the three voices expose the inadequacy of monolithic assertions and assured assumptions. They also contribute to the book's cacophony of claims and counter-claims, testimonies and opposing testimonies, arrangements and dissymmetrical arrangements. Since the groundbreaking work of B. Duhm (1901) and S. Mowinckel (1914), Jeremiah research has spent enormous energy attempting to tame this complex and chaotic character. To make Jeremiah more 'intelligible', countless articles and monographs have privileged one genre, tradition, or source in the book over all others.[9] Such efforts have had mixed results. While they have failed to domesticate Jeremiah's chaos—the book is just too unwieldy to control— they have, unfortunately, been more successful in dismissing marginal voices.[10] Walter Brueggemann has recently proposed an alternative approach to the textual dissonance. Instead of disparaging the chaos, he suggests that we read it as 'a meditation upon the abyss, into it and out of it' (2002: 350).[11] As such, Jeremiah's ruptured and chaotic literary shape 'makes sense' as a window into Judah's profound loss 'for which we have no ready categories' (Brueggemann 2002: 350). If Brueggemann is correct, the book's many undulations, including the three voices examined above, present to us another sign of Judah's unbearable pain.

BIBLIOGRAPHY

Biddle, M.E.
    1996   *Polyphony and Symphony in Prophetic Literature: Rereading Jeremiah 7–20* (Studies in Old Testament Interpretation, 2; Macon, GA: Mercer University Press).
Brueggemann, Walter
    1986   *Hopeful Imagination: Prophetic Voices in Exile* (Philadelphia: Fortress Press).

9.   Until recently, the poetry of Jeremiah or the so-called 'A' source/tradition was viewed as the authentic witness of the book. This material was read not only as Jeremianic but also as engaging, dynamic, and original. In start contrast, the 'C' material was interpreted as impoverished, dull, and legalistic (see, e.g., Mowinckel 1914: 36-39). Following Mowinckel's lead, the majority of scholars have disparaged the prose literature in Jeremiah. For a different view, see Stulman 1998; 1999: 34-63; 2005).

10.   Robert Carroll has made an incisive case for the importance of listening to 'something rich and strange' in Jeremiah (see Carroll 1999: 423-43).

11.   O'Connor says it this way: 'First and foremost, the book of Jeremiah names the disaster, reveals its contours, and mirrors it back to the audience. It depicts the totality of the destruction, speaks of pain and bitter grief, and articulates the rawness of the world in which the survivors find themselves' (2002c: 370).

2002   'Meditation upon the Abyss: The Book of Jeremiah', *Word & World* 22/4: 340-50.

Carroll, Robert P.

1986   *The Book of Jeremiah* (OTL; Philadelphia: Westminster Press).

1999   'Something Rich and Strange: Imagining a Future for Jeremiah Studies', in Diamond, O'Connor and Stulman (eds.) 1999: 423-43.

Diamond, A.R.

1987   *The Confessions of Jeremiah in Context: Scenes of Prophetic Drama* (JSOTSup, 45; Sheffield: JSOT Press).

2001   'Deceiving Hope: The Ironies of Metaphorical Beauty and Ideological Terror in Jeremiah' (a paper presented at the international meeting of the Society of Biblical Literature, Rome).

Diamond, A.R. Pete, Kathleen M. O'Connor and Louis Stulman (eds.)

1999   *Troubling Jeremiah* (JSOTSup, 260; Sheffield: Sheffield Academic Press).

Duhm, B.

1901   *Das Buch Jeremia* (Tübingen: J.C.B. Mohr).

Heschel, Abraham

2001   *The Prophets* (New York: HarperCollins).

Mowinckel, S.

1914   *Zur Komposition des Buches Jeremia* (Kristiania: Jacob Dywad).

Nouwen, Henri J.M.

1975   *Reaching Out* (New York: Doubleday).

O'Connor, Kathleen M.

1988   *The Confessions of Jeremiah: Their Interpretation and Role in Chapters 1–25* (SBLDS, 94; Atlanta: Scholars Press).

1998   'The Tears of God and Divine Character in Jeremiah 2–9', in Tod Linafelt and Timothy K. Beal (eds.), *God in the Fray: A Tribute to Walter Brueggemann* (Minneapolis: Fortress Press): 172-85

2002a   *Lamentations and the Tears of the World* (Maryknoll, NY: Orbis Books).

2002b   'Jeremiah and Formation of the Moral Character of the Community' (a paper presented at the annual meeting of the Society of Biblical Literature, Toronto).

2002c   'Surviving Disaster in the Book of Jeremiah', *Word & World* 22/4: 369-77.

Rad, G. von

1983   'The Confessions of Jeremiah', in James L. Crenshaw (ed.), *Theodicy in the Old Testament* (Philadelphia: Fortress Press): 88-99.

Reventlow, H.G.

1966   *Liturgie und prophetisches Ich bei Jeremia* (Gütersloh: Gütersloher Verlagshaus).

Sharp, Carolyn J.

2003   *Prophecy and Ideology in Jeremiah: Struggles for Authority in the Deutero-Jeremianic Prose* (OTS; London and New York: T&T Clark International).

Smith, M.S.

1990   *The Laments of Jeremiah and their Contexts: A Literary and Redactional Study of Jeremiah 11–20* (SBLMS, 42; Atlanta: Scholars Press).

Stulman, Louis

1986   *The Prose Sermons of the Book of Jeremiah* (SBLDS, 83; Atlanta: Scholars Press).

1998   *Order Amid Chaos: Jeremiah as Symbolic Tapestry* (The Biblical Seminar, 57; Sheffield: Sheffield Academic Press).

1999   'The Prose Sermons as Hermeneutical Guide to Jeremiah 1–25: The Decon-struction of Judah's Symbolic World', in Diamond, O'Connor and Stulman (eds.) 1999: 34-63.

2005   *Jeremiah* (AOTC; Nashville: Abingdon Press).

Wiesel, Eli

1960   *Night* (New York: Bantam Books).

Wilson, Robert R.

1999   'Poetry and Prose in the Book of Jeremiah', in Robert Chazan, William W. Hallo and Lawrence H. Schiffman (eds.), *Ki Baruch Hu. Ancient Near East-ern Studies in Honor of Baruch A. Levine* (Winona Lake, IN: Eisenbrauns): 413-27.

THE ROYAL FAMILY IN THE JEREMIAH TRADITION

Alex Varughese

When social, economic, political or religious structures collapse, it is appropriate to raise the question of culpability. The question of culpability is more critical than the questions of 'how and why' because such disasters often result from the irresponsible behavior of a particular individual or a social group, or the abuse of power by those who were responsible for the social order and proper structure of community life. Stulman, in his insightful study of the literary structure of the book of Jeremiah, raises the question, 'Who is to blame?' for the Judean national tragedy of 587 (Stulman 1998: 120-36). The Jeremiah tradition[1] does not portray the invading army of Babylon as the real enemy or the culprit of Judah's disaster. The Babylonians, the 'dangerous outsiders', are indeed Yahweh's instrument of judgment against the wicked and faithless 'insiders' in Judah (Stulman 1998: 120-28). Stulman correctly observes that Jeremiah places the blame on the upper layer of the social structure—the priests, the false prophets, and members of the royal administration—for the dissonance and disintegration of the Judean social, religious and political life (Stulman 1998: 128-29).

Throughout the two major sections of the text of Jeremiah (i.e. chs. 1–25 and 26–52),[2] we see ample evidence of the prophet's finger pointing at the nation as a whole, but, more importantly, at the priests, the false prophets and the kings, often accompanied by scathing criticism and pronouncement of Yahweh's judgment.[3] The Babylonian threat against Judah and the dangerous and precarious situation that faces the city of Jerusalem are Yahweh's work to bring an end to a nation that stubbornly rejected divine instructions. However, Jeremiah places greater culpability for the nation's departure from Yahweh squarely on the priests, the shepherds and the prophets. All three groups have one thing in common: each in its own way

1. This essay does not attempt to deal with the questions of the literary character, structure and composition of the book of Jeremiah. Many scholars have attempted to deal with these questions. More recently, Stulman has attempted to show that there is enough evidence in the book to suggest an intentionally executed literary strategy behind the final form of the book that is aimed to bring literary and theological balance to a text that at the surface level seems to be chaotic and disorganized. For a summary of more recent attempts to study the literary structure, see Stulman 1998: 25-98.

2. Here I am following the two-part structure of the book (chs. 1–25 and 26–52) adopted by most recent commentators. See, for example, the commentaries of Brueggemann (1988; 1991), Holladay (1986; 1989), and McKane (1986; 1996).

3. See Jer. 1.18; 2.8, 26; 8.1; 13.13; 17.25; 32.32; 44.17, 21.

failed to promote fidelity to Yahweh (see 2.8).[4] The specific charge against the rulers is that they rebelled against Yahweh's established patterns of governing the people. Jeremiah often designates the political leaders, particularly the kings, as shepherds of God's people (i.e. members of the Davidic dynasty; see 23.1-4, 5-6).[5]

This paper aims to show that though the priests, the (false) prophets and the kings all share the responsibility for Judah's demise, the Jeremiah tradition singles out the Davidic kings who were the 'trustees' and defenders of the nation from 'internal corruption and external attack' (Johnson 1967: 136-37) and members of the royal family as the primary architects of the national calamity of 587. In Jeremiah's thinking, the ultimate blame for the national catastrophe belongs to those kings who had violated the terms of the Davidic covenant. The book not only challenges but also invalidates the conventional schemes of Israel's royal ideology in numerous places. We shall briefly analyze and evaluate the crucial texts that deal with God's judgment of the Davidic kings and the royal family, and the role they have played in bringing dissonance and disintegration to Judean national and community life.

The Jeremiah tradition begins with the prophet's commission to announce the removal of the established throne of Judah and Jerusalem (1.15). Yahweh's appointment of the foreign political kingdoms of the north signals the divine determination to bring an end to the political rulers who belonged to the Davidic dynasty. Foreign kingdoms receive the divine appointment to set up their thrones at the entrance of the capital of the Davidic kingdom. The royal ideology that promoted the irrevocable relationship between the Davidic kings and Yahweh is at the outset suspended by the text.[6] Neither the city nor the Davidic throne enjoys any special favor. Both are on the verge of being destroyed and overtaken by forces at the command of the deity who once established these symbols of stability and security for his people.

The theme of failed leadership is the focus of Jer. 2.14-19. Though political leaders receive no specific mention in 2.18, it is obvious that they were the architects of Judah's past and present political alliances with foreign powers that resulted in the ruinous state of the nation.[7] The Deuteronomistic rejection of Judah's alliances with foreign nations is clearly evident in 2.14-19 (Carroll 1986: 128). Political alliances with foreign powers meant rejection of loyalty to Yahweh with whom this nation had made a covenant treaty at Sinai (Exod. 20–24). The people and their religious and political leaders pursued the path of religious apostasy and idolatry, and the consequence is shame and disgrace that would come upon the whole nation, including the leaders (Jer. 2.26-27). Political alliances initiated by the ruling kings

---

4.   Carroll sees in the book of Jeremiah a frequent echoing of the themes of 'the corrupt nation and the corrupting leadership'. Carroll also correctly points out that in chs. 26–29 and 34–39, 'the folly of the leaders...eclipses the role of the nation in the disaster of 587' (Carroll 1986: 125).

5.   See Jer. 3.15; 10.21; 12.10; 23.1-4; 25.34-36. Also see 2 Sam. 5.2; 7.7.

6.   See the royal psalms, but Ps. 89.19-29 in particular.

7.   The text of 2.18 does not offer sufficient evidence to identify a specific historical situation. Carroll notes that Egypt and Assyria are poetic 'word-pairs' that simply convey the idea of Judah's 'past history of political alliances with the great powers of Egypt and Assyria' (Carroll 1986: 128-29).

inevitably lead to the loss of national and political identity and the dismantling of social order and community life.

The Jeremiah tradition completely reverses the dominion of the Davidic kings over the kings and nations of the earth in the royal ideology (Ps. 72.8-11). The Davidic kings have neither world dominion nor strength to sustain even their own subjects. They are no longer the symbols of national fortitude; rather, they are symbols of failed strength. They are just as terrified as the nation before the invading army (Jer. 4.9).[8] The identity of the king in 4.9 is not clear. McKane, citing Kimchi, suggests the possibility that it might be Zedekiah (McKane 1986: 93).

The judgment speech in 7.30–8.3 does not mention the Judean kings by name; however, the fate of the city and its population is certainly the direct consequence of idolatry and child sacrifice in the valley of Ben Hinnom promoted by the Davidic rulers (see 8.1 where kings are mentioned along with officials, priests, and prophets). Both Ahaz and Manasseh were patrons and promoters of idolatry in the temple and the cult at the valley of Ben Hinnom (McKane 1986: 180). Kings and their officials, religious leaders and the inhabitants of Jerusalem are given no hope of peace and rest even after their death. The invading army will humiliate and dishonor them by bringing their bones out of their tombs.

The lament in Jer. 10.19-20 portrays intense pain and brokenness because of the displacement of the community from its home. We cannot be certain whether the lament is expressed in anticipation of the disaster to come (vv. 17-18), or if it follows the events of 597/587. Verse 21 is a theological explanation of the destruction of the community life. The lament places the blame for the disintegration of the community on the shepherds who are not only foolish, but who also make decisions that affect the welfare of their flock without consulting Yahweh. It is clear that the shepherds are the Davidic rulers who have reneged on their covenantal responsibility to offer protection and wellbeing to the nation.

Yahweh's speech in 12.7-13 has two key elements: (a) Yahweh's decision to forsake his house and hand the people into the hands of their enemies (Yahweh's anger/judgment theme in vv. 7-9, 12-13); and (b) the destruction of Yahweh's vineyard by 'many shepherds' (vv. 10-11 NRSV). The shepherds mentioned in this text are clearly a reference to foreign rulers (Thompson 1980: 358). Though this label is traditionally used in Jeremiah for the Davidic kings, here it is applied to Yahweh's agents of Judah's destruction and desolation. Though the Davidic kings are not mentioned in this text, their role in the desolation of the land is clear. Yahweh's shepherds (Davidic kings) failed to care for the vineyard. Therefore Yahweh is angry and has turned over the vineyard to be made desolate by shepherds of other nations who would wield Yahweh's sword throughout the land (v. 12).

The text of Jer. 13.12-14 uses the figurative language of intoxication to portray Yahweh's judgment upon all the kings, priests, prophets and inhabitants of Jerusalem. Kings are specifically identified in this text as those who sit on the throne of David (Carroll 1986: 320). The imagery of this passage vividly portrays Yahweh's wrath upon the nation and its leaders in the upper social stratum. There is no

---

8.   See Jer. 4.5-8 for the metaphorical description of the invading army.

particular reason given in 13.12-14 for Yahweh's role in the intoxication and subsequent destruction of the kings, priests, prophets and inhabitants of Judah. Carroll suggests a connection between this text and the idolatry of the nation in 13.10 (Carroll 1986: 299).

The lament in Jer. 13.18-19 lacks specificity and we cannot locate this text to a particular historical situation. Most commentators identify 'the king and the queen' as Jehoiachin and his mother Nehushta (2 Kgs 24.8-17), and the events of 597 as the occasion of the lament. Other likely candidates could be Jehoiakim and his mother (Carroll 1986: 301). The dethronement and the exile of the royal family and the population of Judah is the subject of the lament. Verse 19b ('all Judah is taken into exile, wholly taken into exile' [NRSV]) is hyperbolic since the exile of the whole nation did not take place until 587. The lament not only portrays the dismantling of the royal power, but also implicates the royal family members as the responsible parties for their own self-destruction and abdication of power and the exile of their citizens.[9]

Jeremiah 15.1-4 is an oracular response to the people's lament in 14.19-22. However, the divine response is not what the nation hoped to hear; instead of the promise of salvation, the nation hears Yahweh's rejection of any attempt of mediation on behalf of the nation, even by such great mediators as Moses and Samuel. The nation is now faced with the prospect of total destruction. Carroll observes here a 'reversal' of the exodus theme (1986: 320). Yahweh, who commanded Pharaoh to give freedom to Israel (Exod. 5.1), declares without any gesture of compassion, 'send them out of my sight and let them go' (Jer. 15.1). Yahweh withdraws all pity and compassion from the people as death, famine and captivity face the nation. Yahweh will make the kingdom of Judah an object of extreme repugnance to all other earthly kingdoms, and the blame for this shameful and tragic fate of Judah is placed on Manasseh, son of Hezekiah (2 Kgs 21.1-16). The Jeremiah tradition singles out here the most villainous, cruel, and corrupt Davidic ruler as the responsible party for the nation's ruin. Yahweh's word of judgment upon Judah and Jerusalem because of Manasseh's wickedness (see 2 Kgs 21.12-13) is about to become a reality. Though Manasseh was not the only irresponsible Davidic king, it is likely that he represents all the wicked kings of Judah who were ultimately responsible for bringing Yahweh's judgment upon their nation.

The primary addressees of 17.19-27 are the kings of Judah, while Judah and the inhabitants of Jerusalem are secondary addressees. The strict observance of the Sabbath is the key to the future of the Davidic dynasty.[10] Not only the stability and

---

9.   The stories of Maacah, grandmother of Judah's king Asa (1 Kgs 15.13), and Athaliah, mother of Judah's king Ahaziah (2 Kgs 11.1-20), give us a glimpse of the powerful religious and political influence of queen mothers. See also Brueggemann's note (n. 16) on the role of 'competing queen mothers' (1998: 131).

10.   Though there are significant parallel between Jer. 17.19-27 and Neh. 13.15-22, we cannot with any certainty place this text in the post-exilic period. The argument that 17.19-23 implies the violation of the Sabbath law as the cause of the 587 disaster cannot be sustained in light of the fact that the text that follows (vv. 24-27) presumes the existence of the Davidic dynasty and the 'palaces of Jerusalem' (v. 27). The text contains a promise and a threat: the promise of the continuation of

continuity of the Davidic dynasty, but the existence of the whole nation depends on their faithful adherence to the Sabbath command.[11] The kings and the nation as a whole are given a strong warning of the impending disaster. The reference to the disregard of the Sabbath laws by the ancestors is both a warning and an instruction (מוסר, v. 23) not to repeat the sins of the fathers. Destruction of the city and removal of the Davidic throne would be the outcome of the rejection of this instruction. The ultimate responsibility for the future of the nation thus depends on the seriousness with which the royal family would pay attention to the Sabbath law and enforce it in the land.

The impending fall and destruction of Jerusalem is the subject of the sermon in 19.1-13. Here, too, the primary addressees are the kings of Judah while the people of Jerusalem are secondary addressees. The text seems to focus on Yahweh's irrevocable word of judgment, which would result in the irreparable destruction of Judah. The cult at Topheth, which promoted pagan forms of worship in the valley south of the temple mount, is the cause of divine judgment (see also 7.30–8.3). Worship at this place incorporated into the Israelite religion elements from pagan religions including rituals to appease foreign gods and human sacrifice. The cult at Topheth was permitted, promoted and even participated in by the kings of Judah (see vv. 4-5). The charge against the kings includes forsaking Yahweh, participation in pagan worship and burning children as offerings to Baal. Yahweh's judgment is directed primarily against the political powers who were clearly the architects and promoters of pagan worship in the backyard of the temple. The judgment would result in the total defilement and destruction of the houses of the kings of Judah (v. 13).

Jeremiah's most forceful and unequivocal anti-royal statements are found in 21.1–23.8. Stulman labels 21.1–24.10 the 'final macro-unit' in the first part of Jeremiah (chs. 1–25) in which the focus is on the 'dismantling of royal ideology' (1998: 31, 49-52). The presence of other oracles in this block of material addressed to the people and the prophets (21.8-10, 13-14; 22.8-9, 20-23; 23.7-8, 9-40; 24.1-10) shows the somewhat chaotic arrangement of the section. Oracles addressed directly to the royal family fall within 21.1–23.8.[12]

The word to Zedekiah is placed at the beginning of this block, perhaps to show that he and his predecessors are responsible for the disaster of 587 (Carroll 1986: 404). The setting seems to be around 588/587 in the context of the Babylonian threat. The king, who hoped for Yahweh's intervention as the divine warrior fighting a holy war to save his people just as he did in the past, is given an ominous word. Yahweh will indeed come as the divine warrior, only this time not on the side of the Davidic king but on the side of the enemy. Just as Yahweh's enemies

---

the Davidic dynasty and stability of the nation, and the threat of the destruction of the city and the royal palaces. However, those who place the text in a post-exilic climate see in the text a reflection of the development of the Sabbath law after the fall of Jerusalem (see Carroll 1986: 368-69).

11. See McKane (1986: 416) on Kimhi's view of the special responsibility of the king to maintain Sabbath observance and to reprove the nation when the Sabbath law is violated.

12. See Holladay's evaluation of the structure and composition of 21.1–23.8 (1986: 568).

were totally annihilated in the ancient traditions of holy war, the inhabitants of Jerusalem will be totally annihilated and their king will be delivered into the hands of the Babylonian king. Brueggemann observes in this text the 'nullification of God's old commitments' (1998: 190). The special relationship that God had with the city and with the Davidic dynasty has come to an end.

Jeremiah 21.11-12 is a word addressed to an unidentified king of Judah. The royal family is urged to promote justice in the land by putting an end to all forms of oppressive behavior in the land. The result of continued injustice will be Yahweh's fire that will destroy the power structure that failed to guarantee justice to the people. Brueggemann connects these two verses with Zedekiah's request to Jeremiah in 21.2 (1998: 192). The prophet offers escape to the nation but the offer is conditional upon the commitment to do justice—the fundamental character of the covenant community. The oracle's placement in this section seems to serve a crucial purpose since it explains that the failure of the kings to administer justice in the land is the cause of the fire of 587.

The royal obligation to provide justice and righteousness in the community is also the theme in Jer. 22.1-5. Again, no specific king is identified in the text. The oracle is applicable to any king and to any historical context. Verses 4 and 5 focus on the conditionality of the Davidic covenant. Brueggemann notes in these verses the attempt to bring the monarchy under the authority of the Torah (1998: 196). The oracle ends with a promise and a threat: the promise of the perpetuity of the Davidic kingdom for obedience and the threat of the desolation of the royal family for its failure to carry out its covenantal responsibility to the nation. Again, as in the previous oracle, we find the royal family as the cause not only of the nation's destruction but also of its own tragic demise.

The desolation of the royal house is reiterated in Jer. 22.6-7 where Yahweh threatens to remove the royal house from its favored status. Various metaphors in this poem completely reverse the once cherished royal ideology. Its connection to the previous oracle is clear. Though the poem does not preserve conditionality, the conditional nature of this threat is clear from its association to the previous oracle.[13] The royal family may escape from its road to self-destruction by its positive response to the prophetic word, but if it reneges on its moral and ethical responsibility, it will be destroyed by the invading army.

The lament in Jer. 22.10 and the following explanation in vv. 11-12 portray exile as the inevitable destiny of the royal family. Shallum's deportation and the word about his impending death in exile signal the tragic fate of the royal family. The uprooting and displacement of the royal family has already begun and the poem anticipates a similar fate for others who follow Shallum on the Davidic throne.

Jeremiah's critique of the monarchy reaches its climax in 22.13-19. The first part of this section is a woe oracle (vv. 13-17) addressed to an unnamed power structure that exploits the poor and practices extreme social injustice. The lack of (a) specific name(s) in this text has led some to conclude that the original oracle was a critique

---

13. Carroll notes that the oath form in this poem makes the threat absolute and thus inescapable (1986: 419).

of corrupt and unjust social practices (Carroll 1986: 427). The second part is a funeral lament for Jehoiakim (vv. 18-19). In the present arrangement of the text, it is clear that the subject of vv. 13-17 is Jehoiakim and that 'your father' (v. 15) is Josiah. The indictment shows that Jehoiakim broke all the rules of kingship. His concern was only for his own wellbeing and luxury of life. The prophet makes clear that living an affluent life in a luxurious palace does not make a person king. Jehoiakim failed to learn the fundamental rules of kingship from his father Josiah, who promoted justice and righteousness in the land. The self-serving king will die in total disgrace. The dishonorable death and burial of Jehoiakim is yet another step in the dismantling of the royal house and the royal ideology.

The next member of the royal family to receive the announcement of a disgraceful end is Coniah, also known as Jehoiachin (Jer. 22.24-27, 28-30). Though he was the symbol of any hope of the continuation of the Davidic dynasty, the royal line will come to an end with him. Yahweh will 'tear' him off, and remove his claims of royal power. Yahweh's decision to exile the king and his mother to a foreign country signals the end of the royal history. Any hope of a future succession of the Davidic descendants on the throne of David is categorically dismissed in this text. Brueggemann sees in this text a termination of the royal promise in 2 Sam. 7.13-16 (Brueggemann 1998: 205). The royal house that failed to keep the principles of the monarchy brought not only its own demise but also the exile of the nation.

Jeremiah 23.1-2 is a general charge against 'shepherds', namely, the kings of Judah. The accusation is that they have brought about the disruption of the community and its scattering (exile is probably intended here). The text ends with a threat against the shepherds: God will punish (פקד) those who have not attended (פקד) to their flock. This text is an introduction to the promise of God's gathering of the community from its exile (Jer. 23.3-4).

The cycle of oracles against the royal family ends with a word against Zedekiah and the population that was left in the land after the first deportation of Judah in 598 (24.8-10). The text very clearly 'delegitimate(s) the rule of Zedekiah' (Brueggemann 1998: 219). The dynastic line ended with Jehoiachin's exile and Zedekiah does not represent the Davidic dynasty; neither does he represent God and his people. He sits on the throne of David by default.[14] Utter destruction of the land is what awaits the pseudo-king and his people who regard themselves as God's favored people. The good fig/bad fig imagery in ch. 24 depicts the shocking reversal of fortune. Those who are making the claim that they are Yahweh's chosen people (good figs) are mistaken about their future. In reality, Yahweh's chosen (good figs) are those who are in exile, and the bad figs are those who are left in the land.

The final blame for the national catastrophe is placed on Zedekiah, who refused to submit to the yoke of Babylon (27.12-13). The yoke of Babylon is clearly the yoke of Yahweh; submission to Babylon is submission to Yahweh's will. The only hope for Judah's escape is Zedekiah's crucial decision to submit to a political

---

14. 2 Kgs 24.17 and Jer. 37.1 indicate that Zedekiah was 'made king' by Babylon. The end of the royal line prompted the Babylonians to seek a survivor from the house of Josiah to act as their puppet ruler over Judah.

power that is now decisively acting as Yahweh's agent. The events of 587 show that Zedekiah chose the alternative—that is, resistance to Babylon and thereby to Yahweh's will.

Jeremiah 29.16-19 is a word about the utter destruction of Jerusalem and its population. This word directly contradicts the words of the (false) prophets who supported and encouraged the royal policy of resistance against Babylon. Yahweh's curse is on Zedekiah who sits on the throne of David and those who held on to their false confidence. The king and the nation are indicted for their total rejection of Yahweh's word spoken by his true prophets.

Their covenant breaking and lack of fidelity to the poor are added reasons for Yahweh's judgment upon Jerusalem's inhabitants (Jer. 34.8-22). We do not know what prompted Zedekiah and the leadership to make a proclamation about the release of slaves. What seemed to be a humanitarian act was soon reversed; the sudden policy change and the enslavement of those who were released show a total disregard for the plight of the poor in the land. Zedekiah and his officials stand under indictment in this text for their irresponsible leadership and covenant disloyalty to Yahweh.

Jehoiakim burned Yahweh's word and ordered the arrest of the prophet and his scribe (36.1-26). No other kings of Judah showed such blatant disregard for Yahweh's word. The king's plan was not only to destroy any evidence against him but also to destroy his accusers. Yahweh's response is a punishment that fits the crime. Jehoiakim's sons shall not sit on the throne; his city and its population will suffer disaster and destruction (vv. 29-31). The placement of this narrative in the fourth year of Jehoiakim shows the royal family already in direct confrontation with Yahweh and his will in 605. The king's defiance and the burning of Yahweh's word thus set the course that ultimately led to the burning of the city by the Babylonians in 587.

Jeremiah 37–39 graphically portrays Zedekiah's covenant disloyalty, ineptitude and political indecisiveness.[15] Chapter 37 begins with the general indictment that Zedekiah and his officials did not listen to Yahweh's word that came through the prophet (37.1-2). Zedekiah is Babylon's puppet ruler, but the Judean king is still a subject of Yahweh's Torah. His rejection of the prophetic word is a sign of his claim to autonomy and freedom from Yahweh's rule over his people. Nonetheless, the disloyal king seeks a word from Yahweh. But Yahweh's word does not give Zedekiah any hope (37.3, 6-10); the king who shifted political loyalty to Egypt will be utterly disappointed. The Babylonian army will return and utterly destroy the city, and God will accomplish this even if only a few wounded soldiers are left in the ranks of the Babylonian army. The destruction of the city is Yahweh's judgment upon the king who refused to listen to God's word.

Neither the land nor Zedekiah will escape the Babylonian invasion. This is the message of the prophet, who is in prison on charges of treason (37.16-21).

15. Brueggemann concludes that chs. 37–45 ('Baruch document') contain a 'pro-Babylonian ideology' that clearly establishes Judah's surrender to Babylon as surrender to Yahweh's will. This ideological and theological shift recognizes Yahweh as the one who is acting decisively and purposefully in the larger historical political realities of the ancient Near East (1998: 338-44).

Zedekiah, who rejected the words of Yahweh's true prophet, must now live with the disastrous consequences of listening to false prophets who advocated an anti-Babylonian policy and a political process contrary to Yahweh's will. Yahweh's will is to hand over not only the land but also the king into the hands of the Babylonian king (37.17).

Chapter 38 once again portrays Zedekiah's crucial role in bringing Yahweh's death verdict on Jerusalem and the end of the Davidic dynasty. The king, who maintains a very delicate balance of power, is afraid of the princes who are capable of influencing the public to turn against him. He knows the reality of Yahweh's word; yet, he acts in a cowardly way to maintain power, and gives approval to the mistreatment of the prophet by those who consider the prophetic word to be treason. Jeremiah is unwavering in his word about surrender to Babylon as the only way of escape for the king and his people. The prophet is keenly aware of the king's intention; though the king seeks a word from Yahweh, he is determined not to listen to him (37.15). At this point, as far as Zedekiah is concerned, the real threat is neither God nor Babylon, but the political powers in the land that may turn against him. So he gains a guarantee from the prophet, under the threat of death, that the prophet will not disclose the truth to the princes (37.24-25).

The Jeremiah tradition seeks to give no further explanation for the disaster of 587. All evidence points toward the royal family as the responsible parties. Those who stood against the call to surrender to Babylon were ultimately destroyed, the palaces were burned down and the people were taken into exile. The defiant king himself stood before Nebuchadnezzar and watched the murder of his sons by the Babylonians. He was taken to exile, blinded and chained, with no hope of return.

Jeremiah 41 narrates the continued villainous acts by the surviving members of the royal family. The narrative vividly portrays Gedaliah's murder and the murder of a large number of unsuspecting Judeans by Ishmael, a member of the royal family. He is not only ruthless, but also unprincipled and lacking basic qualities of trust, hospitality and compassion.[16] For a brief moment, there was hope that Gedaliah might bring some stability to the extremely fragile conditions of the surviving population, but Ishmael's action forced the surviving Judeans to flee their homeland out of fear of reprisal by the Babylonians. Ishmael's act of treachery once again proved that even in the death and the destruction of national life the members of the royal family were consumed with a self-serving ideology and total contempt for the concerns of justice and righteousness in the land.

Conclusion

Except for a few brief statements about a future Davidic ruler and Yahweh's covenant with David, the two major parts of the book contain virtually no reference to

---

16. Brueggemann suggests the possibility that 'Ishmael may be an extreme case of the enduring, self-destructive power of the royal ideology which has already provoked the (Babylonian) empire and brought destruction upon the city', and that he 'will risk yet another imperial intrusion into Jerusalem for the sake of his ideology and his ambition' (1998: 383).

the sacral relationship between God and the ruling members of the Davidic dynasty.[17] No other prophetic book contains such extensive treatment of the royal family as malevolent, irresponsible and unrighteous rulers who have broken the conditions of the covenant, the theological foundation of their claim to the Davidic throne. As a result, they have not only placed their kingship in jeopardy, but also have brought about the destruction of the fabric of Judah's social and political existence. The Jeremiah tradition thus flatly rejects the conventional royal ideology that claimed an irrevocable and sacrosanct relationship between God and the descendants of David. It is very likely that the polemic against the royal family in the Jeremiah tradition is a true reflection of the deuteronomistic criticism of the Davidic rulers who miserably failed to uphold the terms of the Davidic covenant. What then is the future of the Davidic kingship in the Jeremiah tradition? For an answer, one must turn to those few passages that imagine and hope for the resurrection of the Davidic kingship under a future Davidic ruler.[18]

BIBLIOGRAPHY

Brueggemann, W.
    1988   *To Pluck up, To Tear Down: A Commentary on the Book of Jeremiah 1–25* (ITC; Grand Rapids: Eerdmans; Edinburgh: Handsel Press, 1988).
    1991   *To Build, To Plant: A Commentary on the Book of Jeremiah 26–52* (ITC; Grand Rapids: Eerdmans).
    1998   *A Commentary on Jeremiah: Exile and Homecoming* (Grand Rapids: Eerdmans).
Carroll, R.
    1986   *Jeremiah: A Commentary* (OTL; Philadelphia: Westminster Press).
Holladay, W.L.
    1986   *Jeremiah. I. A Commentary on the Book of the Prophet Jeremiah Chapters 1–25* (Hermeneia; Philadelphia: Fortress Press).
    1989   *Jeremiah. II. A Commentary on the Book of the Prophet Jeremiah Chapters 26–52* (Hermeneia; Philadelphia: Fortress Press).
Johnson, A.R.
    1967   *Sacral Kingship in Ancient Israel* (Cardiff: University of Wales Press).
McKane, W.
    1986   *A Critical and Exegetical Commentary on Jeremiah 1–25* (ICC, 1; Edinburgh: T. & T. Clark).
    1996   *A Critical and Exegetical Commentary on Jeremiah 26–52* (ICC, 2; Edinburgh: T. & T. Clark).
Stulman, L.
    1998   *Order Amid Chaos: Jeremiah as Symbolic Tapestry* (The Biblical Seminar, 57; Sheffield: Sheffield Academic Press).
Thompson, J.A.
    1980   *The Book of Jeremiah* (NICOT; Grand Rapids: Eerdmans).

17.   For texts that deal with the Davidic covenant and a future Davidic ruler, see 23.5-6; 33.14-16, 17, 19-22, 23-26.

18.   See the previous footnote.

Part III

OTHER STUDIES

NEW LIGHT ON THE STORY OF ACHSAH

William W. Hallo

Ten years ago I received the manuscript of a paper entitled 'The Wisdom of Achsah: A Reading of Judges 1:11-15' (Beem 1993). The author was Beverly Beem, then chair of the Department of English at Walla Walla College in the state of Washington. She had been a member of my fourth and last Summer Seminar for College Teachers in 1990. The following year, her seminar paper was published, along with ten others, in volume 4 of the series *Scripture in Context* under the title 'The Minor Judges: A Literary Reading of Some Very Short Stories' (Beem 1991). I was thus familiar with her as a sensitive reader and literary critic of the book of Judges. As I wrote her at the time:

> I read your paper with interest which escalated to excitement when I came to p. 22. As soon as I read your note 19, I found myself quoting my favorite proverb: 'The leech has two daughters: Gimme! Gimme!' (my translation of Prov. 30.15a). (Letter of 10 August 1993)

What was it that sparked my interest and led to the peculiar association of Achsah with the proverb? The story of Achsah in Judg. 1.11-15 recounts how Othniel, first of the judges, won the hand of Achsah, the daughter of Caleb, by conquering Devir. It has a virtually verbatim parallel in Josh. 15.15-19. The principal differences are these: in Joshua, the pericope is part of a larger section dealing with Caleb (beginning two verses earlier, at v. 13), whereas in Judges it is inserted awkwardly into the story of Jehudah (beginning with v. 1); the opening word, 'and he went' (*wayyēlek*) instead of 'and he went up' (*wayya'al*) still implies Jehudah for an antecedent. In v. 13, Othniel ben Qenaz the brother of Caleb is further identified as 'younger (smaller) than him'. In v. 14, 'field' becomes 'the field'. Most importantly for my purpose here, in v. 15 Achsah uses the Aramaism *hāvā-lî* ('give me'), for *tᵉnā-lî* ('give me'), in Joshua. The verse—and the pericope—ends with 'and Caleb gave her the upper (singular) *gullōt* and the lower (singular) *gullōt*' instead of 'and he gave her the upper (plural) *gullōt* and the lower (plural) *gullōt*' (*wayyitten lah ēt gullōt 'illiyyōt wᵉ 'ēt gullōt taḥtiyyōt*).

What those *gullōt* were bears a moment's notice. In Judg. 1.15a, LXX translates *gullōt māyyim* by *lutrōsin hudatos*, or 'spring of water' according to Liddell and Scott—citing exclusively this passage for this sense of *lutrōsis*, which otherwise (and frequently) is attested in the meaning 'ransom, redemption'. In Josh. 15.19a, LXX doesn't translate at all, instead treating all three occurrences of *gullōt* as toponyms: *Golathmain* or, in some MSS, *gōlathmaim*. BDB offers three different but related English equivalents: basins, pools, or possibly wells. Marvin Pope, in discussing Song 4.12, and defending the reading *gal* (for proposed *gan*) there, cites with approval J.P. Brown's linking of 'Hebrew *gullāh*, Ugaritic *gl*, Akkadian *gullat* with Greek *gaulos*, "bowl"' (Pope 1977: 488 end). I might add Sumerian *gal* ('cup') and its possible association with *lugal* ('king') conventionally analyzed as 'great man', but which I prefer to derive from an original 'man of the cup, i.e master of the house(hold)' (Hallo 1996: 191-92).

In an earlier section of her paper, Beem had quoted Butler's commentary on Joshua to the effect that Achsah had used 'her feminine charms to gain his [Othniel's] acceptance of her proposition' that he ask her father for a field (Beem 1993: 12-14). And in n. 19 she had expanded on this: 'Within the course of two verses, she (Achsah) speaks with the voice of a wily *femme fatale* and a spoiled child'. To quote Butler again, in approaching Caleb, 'she did not try to turn on the feminine charm with her father. Rather, she returned to the child's role: "Give me, daddy, give me. I've been cheated, daddy. It's not fair"' (Butler 1983: 186).

Given Butler's reading, it is not too far-fetched to think of the enigmatic passage in Proverbs. There, it is true, we hear of two daughters, not just one. But they too address their parent in Aramaicizing Hebrew: *hav-hav* ('give, give'), or, to use a comparable American colloquialism, 'gimme, gimme'. The imperative here is not strengthened by the cohortative *â*-ending, nor is it followed by the dative of the first person singular (or plural), but it *is* in the masculine, even though the parent addressed has a feminine form. That parent, oddly enough, is the leech (*'alūqâ*), and that brings me to the conclusion of Beem's paper.

The story of Achsah revolves around 'Devir, formerly known as Qiryath Sefer' (Judg. 1.11 = Josh. 15.15). This is a city of the Shephelah, the region which lies between Beer-Sheva and Jerusalem; more specifically, it is identified with Khirbet Rabud, little more than 20 km (15 miles) north-northeast of Beer-Sheva and half that far southwest of Hebron. The identification was first suggested by Moshe Kochavi in 1974 (Kochavi 1974) and accepted by Yohanan Aharoni, *inter aliis*.[1] According to Kochavi, there are to this day two wells of subterranean depth about 2.5 km north of the site in question, and in Arabic they are known—*mirabile dictu*—as the upper well of the leech (*Bīr el-'Alaqah el-Fōqāni*, or *el-'Alyeh* in the local vernacular) and the lower well of the leech (*Bīr el-'Alaqah et-Taḥtāni* or *et-Taḥtā* in the local vernacular), respectively (Kochavi 1974: 2 and pl. 1). The Arabic word for leech is *'alaqa* or *'alaq*, cognate with Akkadian *ilqu, ilqitu*, Syriac *'elaqta* and Hebrew *'alūqâ*!

The Hebrew word is a *hapax legomenon*, that is, it occurs only once in the Bible, and it is thus duly listed by Chaim Cohen in his dissertation on the subject of biblical *hapax legomena* (1978). But since it is not a verb, perhaps—in his opinion—not even a common noun, it does not rate his special attention. That is too bad, considering what some commentators have done with it. Here are some of the 'solutions' offered in the past (cited from McKane 1970: 652-54); (a) instead of *la'alūqâ* read *lā'ū laqqū*, 'lick and lap' (Gemser 1937: 80; 1963: 104); (b) it is a proper name (Ringgren 1947); (c) it means 'erotic passion' based on Arabic *'alaqa*

---

1.   Aharoni 1979: 215, 279 n. 78, 346, 354, and 383 n. 93.

= 'copulation'; for good measure there are two girls of burning desire, reading *ḥbb* instead of *hab hab* (Gluck 1964, following LXX).

About the only thing the commentators seem agreed on is that *if* the word means 'leech' then the two daughters allude to the two suckers, one at each end, with which the leech typically fastens on its prey; they would then represent the epitome of insatiability, 'a parable of grasping greed in human society' (McKane 1970: 654).

What we have then is, on the one hand, an enigmatic proverb about two insatiable leeches, and, on the other, the story of Achsah importuning her father for a blessing and receiving upper and lower pool(s) or well(s) near the city of Devir (= Khirbet Rabud) which to this day is located near 'the upper well of the leech' and the 'lower well of the leech', respectively.

This remarkable collocation of coincidences calls for an explanation. I can think of several. (1) The Arabic toponyms preserve an older tradition in which comparable names in their West Semitic guise identified these basins or pools or wells. In such guise they could actually go back to pre-conquest times, and the story of Achsah could be an etiology designed to account for them. The proverb would then represent a popular saying—perhaps even a riddle—preserving the ancient name. Whether it was meant to be attributed to 'Agur the son of Yaqe the Massa(ite)'[2] remains a matter of dispute, with Sauer (1963: 92-112) and Gottlieb (1991: 280-81) arguing for it, and Crenshaw (1990: 211) and Whybray (1994: 148-53) against. (2) The story of Achsah is older than the toponyms and the latter are deliberate attempts to find and name an 'upper' and a 'lower' basin or pool or well with existing twin sources of water in the vicinity of Khirbet Rabud. Such names for a water source would be no more remarkable than, for example, the name Par'osh ('flea'), that used to be attached to one of the sources of the Jordan.[3] The proverb would then represent the 'missing link' between the story and the toponyms. (3) The proverb is the oldest element in the equation and the story of Achsah is an attempt, perhaps via the toponyms, to account for it. We have many parallels to this sort of literary sequence, whether for straightforward proverbs or for riddles, the latter the subject of a brief but incisive note by Moshe Held (1985: 93-96).[4] Most commentators would argue, for example, that the 'riddle' of Samson (Judg. 14.14) is older than the story which represents at the same time its solution. Or again, in the case of the proverbial expression, 'Is Saul too among the prophets?', we have no less than two discrete stories to account for it (1 Sam. 10.11-12 and 19.24). When the proverb is particularly apposite we may not even recognize it as such; when it sticks out like a sore thumb, it gives itself away—as when proverbs are quoted in cuneiform epic (Hallo 1990).

2.   On the tribe of Massa see Eph'al 1982: 10, 218-20.

3.   Or so I was told during my first visit to the site (1951), though I have been unable to verify it since. Chaim Cohen notes the 'sons of Par'osh' in Ezra and Nehemiah, comparable to the 'daughters of Aluqah' (letter of 5 May 2000).

4.   For 'the semantic parallel between BH *mašal* and Akk. *tēltum* as demonstrated by the semantic correspondence between I Sam 24.13 and ARM I, 5.10-11' (quoted by Held 1985: 94-95; cf. already *idem apud* Cohen 1982: 319 [letter from Chaim Cohen, 7 May 2000]).

One could easily think of other permutations and combinations based on the presumed chronological order of the three elements, or on other grounds. But I would rather move on to a further coincidence. In the Judges version of the story, Achsah says to her father: 'give me a blessing' (*hāvā lî bᵉrākâ*, 1.15; cf. Josh. 15.19: *tᵉnā lî bᵉrākâ*), and he responds by giving her the upper and lower *gullōt*. So the blessing (*bᵉrākâ*) that she asks for turns out to be a pool (*bᵉrēkê*). Is this an intentional pun? Or an error in transmission? That certainly appears to be the case in Ps. 84.7, where we read (with NJV):

> They pass through the Valley of Baca,
>> regarding it as a place of springs,
>> as if the early rain had covered it with blessing.

But NEB translates rather:

> As they pass through the thirsty valley
>> they find water from a spring;
>> and the Lord provides even men who lose their way
>> with pools to quench their thirst.

In Mandelkern's concordance all three passages are discussed under *bᵉrākā* ('blessing'), but the suggestion is to understand all of them as implying *bᵉrēkâ*, respectively *bᵉrēkōt* ('pool[s]'). A 'pool of water' is like a blessing in its fullness and richness, just as its antithesis, a shortage of water, is like a curse (Mandelkern 1978: 239).

That a pun is intended in Judg. 1.15a (= Josh. 15.19a) seems likely in light of Judg. 1.15b (= Josh. 15.19b), the conclusion of the pericope. Counting the Greek, there are four versions of this half verse. The shortest is the Hebrew of Josh. 15.19b, 'and he gave her the upper *gullōt* and the lower *gullōt*'. In the Hebrew of Judges and the Greek of Joshua we find 'And Caleb gave her the upper *gullōt* (respectively *Golathmain*) and the lower *gullōt* (respectively *Golathmain*)'. The longest version is the Greek of Judges, which has: 'And Caleb gave her according to her heart the high-lying *lutrēsin* and the low *lutrēsin*'. The plus represented by 'according to her heart' (*kata ten kardian autēs*) must go back to a Hebrew *Vorlage* which had *kᵉlibbâh* (so *Biblia Hebraica* [3rd edn] *ad loc.*)—clearly a play on the name Caleb that immediately precedes it.

The following conclusions can thus be drawn from the pericope. The two wells at Khirbet Rabud, 20 km north of Beer-Sheva, and known to this day as the wells of the upper leech and the lower leech respectively, are linked on the one hand with the proverb: 'the leech has two daughters: Gimme! Gimme!' and on the other with the story of Achsah who importuned her father Caleb for a blessing (*bᵉrākâ*) in the form of a pool (*bᵉrēkâ*) and received from him the upper *gullōt* and the lower *gullōt*, described in the LXX variously as *golothmaim/n* or *lutrōsin hudatos*, a spring of water. And, we may add with the LXX to Judges, Caleb gave them to her *kelibbâh* ('according to her heart').

Addenda

Rainey (1984: 88) notes that Achsah's request is motivated by the fact that he gave her 'Negeb-land', interpreted in the Talmud (*Temura* 16a) as 'a house dry (devoid) of all goodness (wealth)'. He refers to the 'Negeb of Caleb' and the 'Calebites' (1984: 89, 99) but not specifically to Devir or Khirbet Rabud.

Fewell (1995) notes additional puns in the pericope, beginning with Achsah's name.

Younger (2002) find a Phoenician parallel for a transfer of real estate linked to marriage in an inscription from seventh-century Anatolia.

For a recent photograph (by Robert Maxwell) of a leech 'on the medicinal comeback trail', see the cover (and p. 4) of *The New York Times Magazine* for 16 March 2003.

BIBLIOGRAPHY

Aharoni, Yohanan
1979   *The Land of the Bible: A Historical Geography* (Philadelphia: Westminster Press).
Beem, Beverly
1991   'The Minor Judges: A Literary Reading of Some Very Short Stories', in Younger *et al.* (eds.) 1991: 147-72.
1993   'The Wisdom of Achsah: A Reading of Judges 1:11-15' (unpublished seminar paper).
Butler, Trent C.
1983   *Joshua* (WBC, 7; Waco, TX: Word Books).
Cohen, Chaim
1978   *Biblical* hapax legomena *in the Light of Akkadian and Ugaritic* (SBLDS, 37; Missoula, MT: Scholars Press).
1982   'Some Overlooked Akkadian Evidence Concerning the Etymology and Meaning of the Biblical Term *MŠL*', in B. Uffenheimer (ed.), *Bible Studies Y.M. Grintz in Memoriam* (Te'uda 2) (Tel Aviv: Hakibbutz Hameuchad [Hebrew]): 315-24.
Crenshaw, James L.
1990   'The Sage in Proverbs', in John G. Gammie and Leo G. Perdue (eds.), *The Sage in Israel and the Ancient Near East* (Winona Lake, IN: Eisenbrauns): 205-16.
Eph'al, Israel
1982   *The Ancient Arabs: Nomads on the Borders of the Fertile Crescent 9th–5th Centuries BC* (Jerusalem: Magnes Press; Leiden: E.J. Brill).
Fewell, Danna Nolan
1995   'Deconstructive Criticism: Achsah and the (E)razed City of Writing', in Gale A. Yee (ed.), *Judges and Method: New Approaches in Biblical Studies* (Minneapolis: Fortress Press): 119:45.
Gemser, Berend
1937   *Sprüche Salomos* (HAT, 1; Reihe, 16; Tübingen: J.C.B. Mohr [2nd edn, 1963]).

Gluck, J.J.
1964 'Proverbs XXX 15a', *VT* 14: 367-70.
Gottlieb, Claire
1991 'The Words of the Exceedingly Wise: Proverbs 30–31', in Younger *et al.* (eds.) 1991: 277-98.
Hallo, William W.
1990 'Proverbs Quoted in Epic', in T. Abusch, J. Huehnergard and P. Steinkeller (eds.), *Lingering Over Words: Studies in Ancient Near Eastern Literature in Honor of William L. Moran* (HSS, 37; Atlanta: Scholars Press): 203-17.
1996 *Origins: The Ancient Near Eastern Background of Some Modern Western Institutions* (SHCANE, 6; Leiden: E.J. Brill).
Held, Moshe
1985 'Marginal Notes to the Biblical Lexicon', in A. Kort and S. Morschauser (eds.), *Biblical and Related Studies Presented to Samuel Iwry* (Winona Lake, IN: Eisenbrauns): 93-103.
Kochavi, M.
1974 'Khirbet Rabud = Debir', *Tel Aviv* 1: 2-33.
Mandelkern, Solomon
1978 *Veteris Testamenti Concordantiae Hebraicae atque Chaldaicae* (Jerusalem/ Tel Aviv: Schocken Books).
McKane, William
1970 *Proverbs: A New Approach* (OTL; Philadelphia: Westminster Press).
Pope, Marvin H.
1977 *Song of Song* (AB, 7C; Garden City, NY: Doubleday).
Rainey, A.F.
1984 'Early Historical Geography of the Negeb', in Z. Herzog (ed.) *Beer-Sheba II: The Early Iron Age Settlements* (Tel Aviv: The Institute of Archaeology and Ramot Publishing): 88-104.
Ringgren, Helmer
1947 *Word and Wisdom* (Lund: Håkan Ohlssons Boktryckeri).
Sauer, Georg
1963 *Die Sprüche Agurs* (BWANT, 84; Stuttgart: W. Kohlhammer).
Whybray, R.N.
1994 *The Composition of the Book of Proverbs* (JSOTSup, 168; Sheffield: Sheffield Academic Press).
Younger, K.L., Jr, *et al.* (eds.)
1991 *The Biblical Canon in Comparative Perspective* (Scripture in Context, 4; Ancient Near Eastern Texts and Studies, 11; Lewiston, NY: Edwin Mellen Press).
2002 'Cebel Ires Daği', in W.W. Hallo and K.L. Younger, Jr (eds.), *The Context of Scripture*. III. *Archival Documents from the Biblical World* (Leiden: E.J. Brill): 137-39.

BATHSHEBA'S SILENCE (1 KINGS 1.11-31)

Michael S. Moore

Bathsheba plays a pivotal role in Israel's first successful attempt at genetic dynasty, but the contours of her character remain blurry and indefinite.[1] Certainly one of her roles is that of *mediator*,[2] but the biblical text's reticence to give details about this role has frustrated interpreters.[3] With George Nicol we might compare this story with other texts in the biblical Bathsheba tradition and wonder here about the relative level of ambiguity (Nicol 1988). Yet we might also wonder about the 'deep aesthetic qualities' lying beneath this ambiguity and whether contemporary scholarship has fully grasped its source.[4] Because this is the final chapter of the deuteronomistic succession narrative (2 Sam. 11–1 Kgs 2), the Bathsheba story appears at a critical moment in Israelite history and a critical point in the history of Israelite literature. For this reason alone we can ill afford to ignore it, regardless of whether we read it as a unified composition (Rost 1982) or as a lately edited amalgamation (Würthwein 1974).[5] Historical, literary, and even ideological approaches have told us much about Bathsheba, but we still know little about why she plays this mediatorial role.

This study will read the story of Bathsheba alongside another, similar story from its immediate Syro-Palestinian context, the legend of *Aqhat* (*KTU* 1.17–19). My primary goal will be to tease out of this comparison some of the more obvious similarities and dissimilarities and thereby try to situate Bathsheba's character within a more plausible socio-literary context. My secondary goal is to demonstrate the enduring value of comparative intertextual analysis, particularly the kind which employs both historical and literary methods as complementary (not antithetical)— a holistic program long championed by the recipient of this *Festschrift*.[6]

---

1.   For a recent sampling of interpretations from widely different perspectives see Levenson and Halpern 1980; Augustin 1983; Bal 1987; Yee 1988; Nicol 1988; Exum 1993; Ogden Bellis 1994; Berlin 1994; Moore 1995; Stone 1996; and Nicol 1997.

2.   Margalit (1989: 476-85) notes that female characters often enact roles as initiators in ancient Syro-Palestinian stories, and I offer a survey of female mediators in my dissertation (under Huffmon's guidance; see Moore 1990: 20-65).

3.   Ambiguity is characteristic of biblical narrative. Only rarely will a biblical narrator explicitly expose a character's inner thinking—what Stanley Hopper calls 'inscaping' (Hopper 1978: 63).

4.   Gunkel 1901: 2. In this paper there is no need to assume that attention to literary themes and characters automatically precludes, dismisses or even speaks to questions of history and/or historiography.

5.   Seiler (1998: 3-26) helpfully summarizes the discussion since Rost.

6.   Over thirty years ago my *Doktorvater* pointed out that the decision to read the Bible

Even if we accept Rost's thesis that the throne succession narrative is a unified composition,[7] this tells us little about Bathsheba. We can, by suturing two passages together, conclude that she is (a) the daughter of a man named Eliam (2 Sam. 11.3), and (b) that a man named Eliam is the son of Ahithophel, one of David's most influential counselors (2 Sam. 23.34). But whether these Eliams are one and the same person is impossible to say, and the fact that her name later changes to 'Bathshua' only complicates the problem.[8]

Bathsheba thus remains swathed behind a veil of mystery, and this has led many readers to 'fill in the gaps' and colorize her character.[9] Alice Ogden Bellis, for example, portrays her as 'an innocent victim of (David's) lust', though the text itself is conspicuously silent (Ogden Bellis 1994: 149).[10] Jon Levenson and Baruch Halpern imagine her not as a victim, but as a politician shrewd enough to entrap David sexually and replace him with the fruit of this entrapment, Solomon (Levenson and Halpern 1980). Samuel ben Naḥmani argues that David never commits adultery at all because the soldiers in David's army were required to write 'bills of divorcement' before going into battle (*b. Shab.* 56a). The Torah says nothing about this 'law', however, and this makes Naḥmani's interpretation look like several other attempts to beatify David.[11]

Roger Whybray condescendingly labels Bathsheba 'a good-natured, rather stupid woman who was a natural prey to more passionate and cleverer men' (Whybray 1968: 40), but this remark has done little more than enrage feminists. Elizabeth Wurtzel, for example, insists that Bathsheba is a prime example of 'those sexually compelling Bible women' (like Jael and Delilah) who represent the kind of sexual independence which frightens men (Wurtzel 2000: 43). Esther Fuchs uses darker colors. Explaining Bathsheba's silence before David's 'rape', she argues that it is to be expected because the Bible portrays *all* women—as a class—as slaves (Fuchs 2000: 14-16). Cheryl Exum pushes this ideological argument a step further by accusing the biblical narrator of deliberately 'withholding her point of view', because he likes 'disrobing Bathsheba' as much as David does. Exum calls this behavior a 'crime', and labels as 'criminal' the interpretations of all contemporary (predominantly male) commentators who 'perpetuate' this opinion (Exum 1993: 173-74).

Adele Berlin's reading, however, relies less on political ideology than literary insight (Berlin 1982). With Levenson and Halpern she too sees a certain amount of

through parochial instead of holistic lenses has led in recent history to some rather horrifying theological and political consequences (Huffmon 1969).

7.   Seiler (1998: 326) prefers Rost's analysis to Würthwein's.

8.   'Bathshua' probably means 'daughter of error' (1 Chron. 3.5).

9.   'Gap-filling' is not in itself unacceptable or inappropriate unless it becomes a substitute for holistic interpretation (Sternberg 1985: 186-229).

10.   Ogden Bellis, however, distinguishes between the 'flat' character in 2 Samuel and the 'developed' character in 1 Kings.

11.   Brueggemann (1985) documents several other attempts to rescue David's reputation. Van Seters (1987: 244) reminds us that 'some [rabbis] attempted to exonerate [David], but those who found him guilty of wrongdoing saw a divine purpose in the events; namely that David was to be an example of contrition and repentance to give hope and encouragement to Israel when it sinned'.

shrewdness in Kings, but in Samuel she agrees with Ogden Bellis that Bathsheba operates only as a 'flat' character (Berlin calls her an 'agent'). In Samuel her function is simply (a) to be a married woman and (b) to have adulterous sex with David. Later, when Abishag enters the picture, Bathsheba's character becomes considerably more complicated and Berlin traces this complexity to the literary irony triggered by the second mention of Abishag in v. 15. In short, 'Bathsheba, who was once young and attractive like Abishag, is herself now aging, and has been, in a sense, replaced with Abishag, just as she comes for the purpose of replacing David with Solomon' (Berlin 1994: 28). Later, when Adonijah comes to ask for Abishag's hand (doubtless as his own 'agent' to win back the throne), Berlin notes the ambiguity in Bathsheba's response, but fails to offer a convincing explanation for it. Is it because Bathsheba is feigning naïveté before Adonijah's request? Is it because she still fears this Davidic prince and the potential harm he might do to her son? Is it because Bathsheba wants to use Adonijah, like Medea in Euripides' famous play,[12] to wreak revenge against a philandering husband?[13]

It is unfortunate that so few interpreters have tried to examine Bathsheba's behavior against other female characters in ancient Near Eastern literature because this approach has great potential for unraveling some of these questions. Jack Sasson recognizes the potential of comparative literary analysis in his study of Ruth and notes that in its place we often find 'a pervasive tendency to rely too much on a *deus ex machina*…to unravel the plot of the tale' (Sasson 1995: viii). Neal Walls also recognizes the potential of the comparative approach, employing it effectively to situate Anat's character against several other 'virgin goddesses' (Walls 1992). This leads him to deeper reflection on 'the enigmatic quality of her (Anat's) symbolic identity' within 'the complexities of ancient myths and mythic characters' (Walls 1992: 2). Sasson's approach has not yet been fully engaged by biblical scholarship, but Walls's has been hailed as 'original', full of 'common sense' (Pardee 1994) and a 'model' for further research (Parker 1994).[14]

The fourth column of the third tablet of the Ugaritic poem of Aqhat (*KTU* 1.19.iv.18-61) has a heroic character named Daniel (Nathan) 'empowering' (Ug. *mrr*, iv.33) a female character named Paghit (Bathsheba) to use outright deception in response to a horrible injustice—one with which El (David) has passively refused to get involved (*KTU* 1.18.i.1-19).[15] In an act of savage violence El's daughter Anat

---

12. Like Bathsheba, Medea makes sure that her protector (Aegeus, king of Athens) takes an oath: 'Dear woman…if you come to my country, I shall in justice try to act as your protector… (this) I swear by Earth, by the holy light of Helios, and by all the gods' (Euripides, *Medea* 719-53). Unlike Medea, however, Bathsheba does not sacrifice her child in a fit of rage, imagining that 'this will sting my husband the most' (817).

13. Commentators are divided. Berlin (1994: 29) sees Bathsheba as 'cunning' and 'jealous', but Gunn (1978: 137) sharply disagrees. Fokkelman (1981: I, 394) characteristically looks for a mediating position.

14. See Moore (2003) for (a) an intertextual connection between the Anat and Jehu traditions, and (b) an interpretation of the latter as a Yahwistic parody of the former.

15. Clifford (1975: 300) speaks of the 'David-like charms of Baal in the heavenly court', but the aging David looks more like El than Baal.

has hired an assassin named Yatpan (Joab) to attack Daniel's son Aqhat (Solomon)[16] and steal away from him his 'bow' (the throne).[17] While it may not seem obvious at first, the primary elements of this story resonate deeply with the primary elements of the Bathsheba story. Both traditions use similar characters, manipulate similar plotlines, and highlight strikingly similar themes in order to address the same problem—the problem of genetic dynastic succession. The following chart breaks down these parallels into three subcategories: *characterization*, *plot*, and *theme*:[18]

Succeeding David (1 Kings 1–2)	*Succeeding Daniel (KTU 1.17–19)*
Characterization	
David	El
Nathan	Daniel
Solomon	Aqhat
Bathsheba	Anat/Paghit
Abishag/(Adonijah)	Anat/Paghit
Benaiah	Yatpan
Plot	
David is impotent	Daniel is impotent
Solomon is 'longed-for'	Aqhat is 'longed-for'
Solomon rides David's mule	Aqhat receives the divine bow
Abishag replaces Bathsheba	Anat steals the bow
Adonijah steals the throne	Anat steals the bow
Nathan employs Bathsheba	Daniel employs Paghit
Bathsheba falls down before David	Anat falls down before El
Bathsheba impugns David's integrity	Aqhat impugns Anat's integrity
Bathsheba impugns Adonijah before David	Anat impugns Aqhat before El
David impugns Joab before Solomon	Anat impugns El
Bathsheba 'deceives' Adonijah	Anat 'deceives' Aqhat
Solomon's reign becomes plagued	Aqhat's bow becomes 'lost'
Solomon warns Adonijah	Anat warns Aqhat
Solomon gives Adonijah options	Aqhat gives Anat options
Bathsheba responds to threat to Solomon	Paghit responds to threat to Aqhat
Solomon lives	Aqhat lives
David curses his enemies	Daniel curses cities near Aqhat's death
Themes	
dynastic ambition is universal	dynastic ambition is universal
old age and death are inevitable	old age and death are inevitable
throne/power/virility is temporal	'bow'/power/virility is temporal
female mediation is complex	female mediation is complex
female mediation is necessary	female mediation is necessary

16. Is she attacking Aqhat to defend Baal, like she attacks Mot (*KTU* 1.6.ii.30-37)?

17. That Aqhat's bow represents his virility is a logical conclusion as long as we recognize the broader implications (Hillers 1973). Virility is only one of the requirements for effective leadership (Stone 1996: 102-107).

18. This study proceeds, as does my study of the Jehu tradition (Moore 2003), on the presumption that most Syro-Palestinians are at least nominally aware of these stories, characters, plots, and themes.

Characterization

Like *Aqhat*, the biblical succession narrative works with a stock cast of characters, what Vladimir Propp calls the *dramatis personae* (Propp 1968: 21-23). Leadership vacuums, whether in the divine (El) or human realms (David), cannot exist indefinitely. The world has to go on and the people in this world have to be competently shepherded. Malevolent forces are always anxious to fill up these vacuums. Ambitious usurpers always stand waiting in the wings to seize power and take control. Thus impotent leaders, for all their experience and wisdom, eventually become a problem, and how this problem is addressed becomes the stuff of succession narrative.

Like Naomi in the book of Ruth, the characters Daniel in Aqhat and Nathan in the Bible serve as 'dispatchers' (Sasson 1995: 201), individuals whose function is to react to this perennial crisis of impotence/aging/death. They have to arise because the potential successor—the character Propp calls the 'sought-for person' (Aqhat in *Aqhat*; Solomon in 1 Kings; Obed in Ruth)—stands in dire need of help. Not having any power of his own, he stands in a very liminal, precarious situation. When leadership vacuums lead to leadership conflicts (Adonijah vs. Solomon; Abishag vs. Bathsheba; Anat vs. Aqhat), wise heroes must arise to fill in these vacuums, especially if the crisis is driven by true 'villainy' (Anat; Adonijah; Joab). Often these roles become fluidly interchangeable as the characters in the *dramatis personae* interact and interface with each other and narrators become creative, sometimes splitting roles in half or making several characters enact the same role.[19] But to varying extents these ancient tales always work with a stock cast of characters, and it is in the defining of the phrase 'varying extent' that effective characterization replaces ineffective characterization, genius replaces mediocrity, and pan-cultural celebration replaces localized memory.

Plot

Plots are interesting only when they make effective use of surprise and suspense and lead to truly satisfying conclusions. Without these elements a plotline becomes lifeless and slow, and therefore easily forgotten. With a good story, though, plotting the points of the action is like connecting the dots on a map. Sometimes the shortest distance is not necessarily the best path. Sometimes it is more important to take the long way around to build suspense, or introduce a subplot, or test a character's mettle. In *Aqhat*, El is not *truly* impotent (see *KTU* 1.23), but Daniel is, and so is David (and Kirta and Abraham). David's impending death, like Elimelech's in Ruth, is the engine which drives the plot, the catalyst for everything which follows. The crisis of Daniel's impotence is what drives everything in *Aqhat*, however twisted or violent or strange or bizarre. Everything in these plotlines begins with an

---

19. De Moor (1969: 170-71) and Taylor (1982) note this phenomenon in the 'twin' Ugaritic goddesses Anat and Athirat, and Taylor points to similarities in the portrayals of Deborah and Jael in *Judges*.

initial crisis, the 'childless patriarch' being one of the more common in androcentric cultures (Bauckham 1997). One cannot imagine David's sons fighting for the throne under the watchful eye of an engaged David. Neither can one imagine Anat taking advantage of Aqhat apart from El's *laissez faire* aloofness.

As we watch the potential successors square off (Amnon vs. Absalom, Adonijah vs. Solomon, Anat vs. Aqhat), the depth of their dilemma comes painfully into focus. The very existence of succession narratives reminds us that dynastic succession is hard and dangerous. It is easy for postmoderns to forget this, but stories like these, so universal, so ubiquitous, testify to the difficulty of the problem and the persistence of the ancients to address it. Zadok anoints Solomon only after the shedding of much royal blood. Aqhat arrives as El's gift to Daniel only after much fervent prayer and careful priestly ritual.[20] Paghit goes to reclaim her brother in the same spirit Isis goes to reclaim Osiris (Griffiths 1980) or Anat goes to reclaim Baal (*KTU* 1.5.vi.25). That these conflicts can and must involve both heaven and earth is never questioned because the cosmos is not segregated into neatly stacked cubicles. Anat's attack against Aqhat is an attack on El because it so savagely assaults his devotee Daniel, the mortal whose name means 'judgment of El'. Anat attacks Aqhat for the same reasons Adonijah attacks Solomon—not just because she wants power, but because conflict is necessary to advance the plot. This attack must sufficiently motivate a response from the *dramatis personae*.

Whether power is symbolized by a 'bow' (Ug. *qšt*)[21] or a 'beautiful girl' (Heb. *na'ªrâ yāpâ*, 1 Kgs 1.3) or a 'ring' (Tolkien 1954) is inconsequential—what is important is that this power be symbolically portrayed in such a way that would-be usurpers truly 'long' for it—like Anat 'longs' for Aqhat's bow (*KTU* 1.17.vi.13— Ug. *ṣb*), like Amnon 'longs' for Tamar (2 Sam. 13.2). Whether this symbol is manipulated or stolen by one or more anti-hero forces is irrelevant—what is more important is that this language grab the soul of the narrator's audience and squeeze hard. It has to drive them to their knees in terror, and lift them to their feet in hope. Whether the 'longed-for' successor eventually survives or not is peripheral—what is more important is that peace be restored to the cosmos. Whether this attack is from clearly benevolent or clearly malevolent sources is also peripheral—what is more important is that it sufficiently motivate a 'dispatcher' to arise and empower a 'mediator'. Even whether the method used by this 'mediator' is 'ethical' or 'unethical' is secondary to the plot of the story—what is more important is that equilibrium be competently restored via this mediator's mediation. Thus Bathsheba uses deception just as surely as Paghit deceives Yatpan, or Jael deceives Sisera, or Tamar deceives Judah.

In fact, it is in the execution of this deception that female mediators really show off their skills (Thompson 1932–36; Williams 2001). In Judith, for example, the

---

20. The literature on Ugaritic ritual is growing: see de Tarragon 1980; Wright 2001; Pardee 2002.

21. Hillers' thesis is appropriate as long as the focus remains on Anat's desire for sexual *power* over Aqhat, not just sexual intercourse (Hillers 1973: 72-74). Walls seems to miss this point when he limits her motivations only to sexual drive vs. confused sexual identity (Walls 1992: 190).

narrator takes great pains to show off Judith's ability to deceive Holofernes.[22] In Ruth, Naomi takes great pains to adorn Ruth before she goes to Boaz and convinces him to intervene (Moore 2000: 347-53). In Aqhat (*KTU* 1.19.iv.43-46), Paghit takes great pains to deceive the murderer of her brother, Yatpan:

She puts a hero's outfit (underneath)	*t*[ḫt] *tlbš . npṣ . ġzr*
She places the knife in her belt	*tšt . ḫ*[lpn] *bnšgh .*
She places the sword in its scabbard	*ḥrb . tšt . b t* '*r*[th]
And over (it) she puts a woman's outfit	*w* '*l . tlbš . npṣ . aṭt.*[23]

So effective is this ruse, the men in Yatpan's camp call her 'the woman who hired us', an obvious reference to Anat as the androgynous deity who hired them to assassinate Aqhat. What Paghit does after this preparation is unclear because the tablet breaks off, but doubtless she does what all mediators do. She restores equilibrium to a volatile situation by any means at her disposal. Deception is not a secondary role in the repertoire of female mediators. Even 'old woman' priestesses in Anatolia must use it (Moore 1990: 20-29). The whole point of homeopathic ritual is to create a likeness of something or someone in order to trick one's attackers into going after the likeness instead of the person imitated by the likeness. That Bathsheba does the same thing when she plants the 'likeness' of a promise in David's mind can be concluded from two simple facts: (a) we have no textual evidence for such a Davidic promise, and (b) female mediators habitually use deception in such situations. Bathsheba's deception may look muted when compared to, say, the deceptions of Paghit or Judith or Anat or Esther, but this is probably because the narrator does not want to portray David as a total 'dupe' (*pace* Marcus 1986).

Themes

From this brief analysis of characterization and plot we might now list a few of these narratives' more dominant themes. One of the reasons for preserving succession narratives is to assure future generations that succession crises, no matter how difficult, are not the end of the world. If managed appropriately they can eventually be weathered, scars and all. Dynastic ambition is never going to go away because the desire for power is a universal human longing. Jeroboam wants just as desperately to sire a dynasty as does David or Daniel—that is why Ahijah's condemnation of him is not simply of him, but of his entire *house* (1 Kgs 14.10). Baal, too, wants his own 'house' (*KTU* 1.3–4) just as David wants his own 'house' (2 Sam. 7.1-16). Leaders everywhere, when faced with their mortality, become highly motivated to think about the legacy they will leave for the next generation. In succession narratives it is the *realization* of this mortality which often drives aged leaders into action, however passive or reticent they may be to relinquish their power to a successor.

---

22.   Craven (1983: 121) remarks that 'only the book of Ruth offers a parallel' to Judith's behavior, but Craven does not look at the Ugaritic evidence.

23.   On Anat's androgyny see de Moor (1987: 264 n. 250) and Walls (1992: 154-59).

Yet power itself is temporal and fleeting and David dies just as certainly as Aqhat's bow becomes lost and Utnapishtim's 'special plant' falls from Gilgamesh's hands (*ANET*: 96).[24] In some situations God/the gods punish(es) these leaders for clinging to power too long and/or withholding it from legitimate successors (Hanson 1996). In others they send (or allow) mediators to pry it out of their hands. In the story of David, Bathsheba succeeds in loosing David's grip by 'reminding' him of a promise he probably never made, but one which he probably should have made long before. Female mediation is one of the most traditional, most common, and most effective ways to force this issue with recalcitrant, desperate, and/or suffering leaders.

Conclusion

Marvin Pope says of Anat that she 'embodies the tensions and paradoxes of feminine power in an androcentric world' (Pope 1994: 350). The same might be said for Bathsheba. In rabbinic legend, the triad of David–Bathsheba–Uriah become symbols for Adam, Eve, and the serpent, but this kind of interpretation does little to situate her character in its socio-literary context (Stern 1987). Neither do contemporary analyses which read her character through ideological and theological lenses while ignoring the ancient literature to which this story owes its basic shape. Doubtless the foregoing suggestions will not answer every question about her character, but at least they attempt to situate her character in a plausible socio-literary context. Apart from some understanding of this context the temptation to colorize her character will remain too strong to resist, and Bathsheba will continue to remain silent.

BIBLIOGRAPHY

Augustin, M.
1983   'Die Inbesitznahme der schönen Frau aus der unterschiedlichen Sicht der Schwachen und der Mächtigen', *BZ* 27: 145-54.
Bal, M.
1987   *Lethal Love: Feminist Literary Readings of Biblical Love Stories* (Bloomfield, IN: Indiana University Press).
Bauckham, R.
1997   'The Book of Ruth and the Possibility of a Feminist Canonical Hermeneutic', *BibInt* 5: 29-45.
Berlin, A.
1982   'Characterization in Biblical Narrative: David's Wives', *JSOT* 23: 69-85.
1994   *Poetics and Interpretation of Biblical Narrative* (Winona Lake, IN: Eisenbrauns).
Brueggemann, W.
1985   *David's Truth in Israel's Imagination and Memory* (Philadelphia: Fortress Press).

24. Note that Utnapishtim's wife is responsible for Utnapishtim's decision to offer Gilgamesh the 'special plant'.

Clifford, R.
1975   'Proverbs IX: A Suggested Ugaritic Parallel', *VT* 25: 298-306.
Craven, T.
1983   *Artistry and Faith in the Book of Judith* (SBLDS, 70; Chico, CA: Scholars Press).
Exum, J. Cheryl
1993   *Fragmented Women: Feminist (Sub)Versions of Biblical Narratives* (JSOTSup, 163; Sheffield: JSOT Press).
Fokkelman, J.P.
1981   *Narrative Art and Poetry in the Books of Samuel* (2 vols.; Assen: Van Gorcum).
Fuchs, E.
2000   *Sexual Politics in the Biblical Narrative: Reading the Hebrew Bible as a Woman* (JSOTSup, 310; Sheffield: Sheffield Academic Press).
Griffiths, J.G.
1980   *The Origins of Osiris and His Cult* (NumenSup, 40; Leiden: E.J. Brill).
Gunkel, H.
1901   *The Legends of Genesis* (Chicago: Open Court Publishing).
Gunn, D.M.
1978   *The Story of King David: Genre and Interpretation* (JSOTSup, 6; Sheffield: JSOT Press).
Hanson, K.C.
1996   'When the King Crosses the Line: Royal Deviance and Restitution in Levantine Ideologies', *BTB* 26: 11-25.
Hillers, D.R.
1973   'The Bow of Aqhat', in H. Hoffner (ed.), *Orient and Occident* (AOAT, 22; Kevelaer: Butzon & Bercker): 71-80.
Hopper, Stanley
1978   'The "Terrible Sonnets" of Gerard Manley Hopkins and the "Confessions" of Jeremiah', *Semeia* 13: 29-73.
Huffmon, H.B.
1969   'Israel of God', *Int* 23: 66-77.
Levenson, J., and B. Halpern
1980   'Political Import of David's Marriages', *JBL* 99: 507-18;
Marcus, D.
1986   'David the Deceiver and David the Dupe', *Prooftexts* 6: 163-71.
Margalit, B.
1989   *The Ugaritic Poem of AQHAT: Text, Translation, Commentary* (BZAW, 182; Berlin: W. de Gruyter).
Moor, J.C. de
1969   'Studies in the New Alphabetic Texts from Ras Shamra I', *UF* 1: 170-71.
1987   *An Anthology of Religious Texts from Ugarit* (Leiden: E.J. Brill).
Moore, M.S.
1990   *The Balaam Traditions: Their Character and Development* (Atlanta: Scholars Press).
1995   'Wise Women in the Bible: Identifying a Trajectory', in C.D. Osburn (ed.), *Essays on Women in Earliest Christianity* (2 vols.; Joplin, MO: College Press): 87-103.

2000   *Ruth* (NIBCOT, 5; Peabody, MA: Hendrickson).
2003   'Jehu's Coronation and Purge of Israel', *VT* 53: 97-114.
Nicol, G.
1988   'Bathsheba, A Clever Woman?', *ExpTim* 99: 360-63.
1997   'The Alleged Rape of Bathsheba: Some Observations on Ambiguity in
              Biblical Narrative', *JSOT* 73: 43-54.
Ogden Bellis, A.
1994   *Helpmates, Harlots, Heroes: Women's Stories in the Hebrew Bible* (Louis-
              ville, KY: Westminster/John Knox Press).
Pardee, D.
1994   Review of *The Goddess Anat in Ugaritic Myth* (SBLDS, 135; Atlanta:
              Scholars Press, 1992), by N. Walls, in *JBL* 113: 505-506.
2002   *Ritual and Cult at Ugarit* (Atlanta: Society of Biblical Literature).
Parker, S.B.
1994   Review of *The Goddess Anat in Ugaritic Myth* (SBLDS, 135; Atlanta:
              Scholars Press, 1992), by N. Walls, in *RSR* 20: 139-40.
Pope, M.H.
1994   Review of *The Goddess Anat in Ugaritic Myth* (SBLDS, 135; Atlanta:
              Scholars Press, 1992), by N. Walls, in *CBQ* 56: 349-51.
Propp, V.
1968   *Morphology of the Folktale* (Austin: University of Texas Press).
Rost, L.
1982   *The Succession to the Throne of David* (Historic Texts and Interpreters, 1;
              Sheffield: Almond Press).
Sasson, J.
1995   *Ruth: A New Translation with a Philological Commentary and a Formalist-
              Folklorist Interpretation* (The Biblical Seminar, 10; Sheffield: Sheffield
              Academic Press).
Seiler, S.
1998   *Die Geschichte von der Throngefolge Davids [2 Sam. 9–20; 1 Kgs 1–2]:
              Untersuchungen zur Literarkritik und Tendenz* (BZAW, 267; Berlin and
              New York: W. de Gruyter).
Van Seters, J.
1987   'David', *ER* 4: 242-44.
Stern, D.
1987   'Afterlife: Jewish Concepts', *ER* 1: 120-24.
Sternberg, M.
1985   *The Poetics of Biblical Narrative* (Bloomington, IN: Indiana University
              Press).
Stone, K.
1996   *Sex, Honor and Power in the Deuteronomistic History* (JSOTSup, 234;
              Sheffield: Sheffield Academic Press).
Tarragon, J.-M. de
1980   *Le Culte à Ugarit d'après les textes de la pratique cunéiformes alphabé-
              tiques* (CRB, 19; Paris: J. Gabalda).
Taylor, J.G.
1982   'The Song of Deborah and Two Canaanite Goddesses', *JSOT* 23: 99-108.

Thompson, S.
    1932–36   *Motif-Index of Folk Literature* (Helsinki: Suomalainen Tiedeakatemia).
Tolkien, J.R.R.
    1954   *The Lord of the Rings* (London: Allen & Unwin).
Walls, N.
    1992   *The Goddess Anat in Ugaritic Myth* (SBLDS, 135; Atlanta: Scholars Press).
Whybray, R.
    1968   *The Succession Narrative* (SBT Second Series, 9; London, SCM Press).
Williams, J.
    2001   *Deception in Genesis: An Investigation into the Morality of a Unique Biblical Phenomenon* (Studies in Biblical Literature, 32; New York: Peter Lang).
Wright, David P.
    2001   *Ritual in Narrative: The Dynamics of Feasting, Mourning, and Retaliation Rites in the Ugaritic Tale of Aqhat* (Winona Lake, IN: Eisenbrauns).
Würthwein, E.
    1974   *Die Erzählung von der Thronfolge Davids* (Zurich: Theologischer Verlag).
Wurtzel, E.
    2000   *Bitch: In Praise of Difficult Women* (New York: Doubleday).
Yee, G.A.
    1988   'Fraught with Background: Literary Ambiguity in 2 Samuel 11', *Int* 42: 240-53.

A Quest for the Divine and...the Tourist Dollar: The Dilemma Faced by Contemporary Dervish Orders

Mary-Louise Mussell

I owe a debt to Herbert B. Huffmon for introducing me to the reality of modern dervishes and their sacred dance. Being keenly aware of H.B. Huffmon's dislike of opinion-based scholarship, I will attempt to craft an anthropological/ethnographic report on the subject. This paper should be considered a starting point only, with its aim to discuss the religiosity of the modern day public rites/performances of the dervishes. Should we view these rites/performances as expressions of the sacred or are they merely theatre?

The Dervish

The term *dervish* refers to a number of Sufi *tariqa*s (orders, from an Arabic word meaning 'way' or 'path') which use music and dance as a means to approach unity with the divine. The dance is a series of bodily movements linked to a thought and to a sound or sounds. The sound fuses thought and movement together, leading to an ecstatic state or *hal* that orients the dancer toward the divine (Burke 1975: 49). Dervish orders include the Bektashi, the Alevi and the Mevlevi, who are the focus of this article. The Mevlevi are predominantly Turkish, but include Kurds, Syrians and others; Middle Eastern locales which have a Turkish community are often home to dervishes who may or may not be Turkish (Elias 1995: 77). The Mevlevi have gained a particularly strong following among non-Turks in the West.

Public rites/performances of the dervish *sema* (see below) can readily be found; a group was performing in Cairo during the spring of 2002. The group had been performing for a lengthy period of time after having initially performed in the Khan al-Khalili bazaar. In May of that year I attempted to see a rite/performance, but the group had moved to the Citadel in Cairo where it performed to, according to a number of accounts, 'techno', not traditional, music.

The Mevlevi (Arabic Mawlawiyah)

The order was founded in the city of Konya by the thirteenth-century poet Celâled-dini Rumî (Arabic, Muhammad Jalal al-Din Rumî), and the leadership of the group has usually remained within his family until today. Much of the founder's poetry has been translated into English from the original Persian (see bibliography).

Jalal al-Din was born in the Afghan city of Balkh. He moved, with his father, at a young age to Konya, a city in Turkey even now known for its piety. Despite what some biographers suggest, the family had fled their home in the wake of Mongol invaders, journeying to Damascus and then making the pilgrimage to Mecca before returning to Damascus. From there they moved to Konya to live under the protection of the Seljuk sultan. The family's residence in Anatolia (Rum) would lead to Jalal al-Din being referred to as *Rumî*. Rumî stepped into the shoes of his father Bahad Walad, the noted legal scholar and preacher, upon the latter's death. Rumî began his formal Sufi training in 1232 when Burhan al-Din al Tirmidhi, a disciple of Bahad Walad, arrived in Konya. Despite nine years of study with the Sufi scholar, Rumî appears to have had little involvement with mystical matters. His active involvement began with the arrival in Konya of Shams al-Din, also known as Shamsi Tabrizi.

Shams al-Din became Rumî's medium for gaining mystical knowledge. He was also a source of jealousy for Rumî's students and family. The jealousy reached a fever pitch with Shams al-Din being forced to flee to Damascus. Rumî sent his son Sultan Walad to Damascus to bring his dear friend back to him. Shams al-Din vanished soon after returning to Konya, probably murdered by Sultan Walad and/or Rumî's students.

With the disappearance of the object of his affection, Rumî retired to concentrate on his mystic poetry. The missing Shams al-Din became the focus of Rumî's work with the name of Shams al-Din inserted into the works as if he were the poet (see Arberry 1975; Nicholson 1964). The followers of Rumî, or *Mevlana* (Arabic, *mawlana*, 'our master') as they called him, would eventually become known as the Mevlevi, but during the lifetime of their master they appear to have been known as Jalaliyah, after his given name Jalal al-Din. With *Mevlana*'s death in 1273, leadership of the order passed to Salah al-Din Zarkub, a disciple of Burhan al-Din al-Tirmidhi, who had been Rumî's mystical focal point after the disappearance of Shams al-Din. Leadership then passed to Husam al-Din Çelebi and finally to Sultan Walad, though the first seven years of his leadership were under the guardianship of Karim al-Din ibn Bektimur. As noted above, leadership has, for the most part, remained in the family ever since (Elias 1995: 77). The current leader is Faruk Hemden Çelebi, the thirty-third member of the family to lead the order (visit <www.mevlana.net>).

Mevlevi followers are organized into *tekke* or lodges, all responsible to the governor (Turkish, *çelebi*) in Konya. Beginning in the seventeenth century, the Mevlevi began to play a role in Ottoman politics. For example, in the nineteenth century they functioned as the 'girders of the sword' at enthronement ceremonies. This high-profile duty led to the Mevlevi having influence on the social development of the upper classes of Ottoman society (Mardin 1995: 102).

Modern Mevlevi

With the rise to power of Mustafa Kemal Attaturk and the establishment of the Republic of Turkey came the closing of the religious orders in 1925 (Kreiser

1986: 47). But the closing of the Mevlevi lodges did not lead to the end of the order. Rather, it, along with others, became a type of secret society. Burke recounts his efforts to find dervishes in Istanbul and, when he succeeded, their efforts to insure he was not a government spy (1975: 55-56). It should be noted that Burke does not identify the order with which he made contact, but the description of their gathering suggests they were Bektashi.

Mevlevi practices became public once more in 1953 when tourist-oriented performances started at Konya (Norton 1992: 188). Transported outside Turkey, the performances gained great popularity in North America and Western Europe where the 'Whirling Dervishes' became crowd pleasers. The popularity of the Mevlevi performances can be seen in the number of Internet websites related to the group (visit, e.g., <www.mevlana.net>; <www.bdancer.com/med-guide/culture/dervish. html> and <www.dankphotos.com/whirling/>). Mevlevi music is also widely available throughout the world, and public performances are given in many places, including Turkey. For example, the Mevlevi currently perform most evenings at the Sarihan Kervansaray-Culture and Exhibition Centre near Goreme in Cappadocia (Çelebi), about a three-hour drive from Konya.

The Sarihan Kervansaray dates to 1249 and is an architectural gem worthy of the twenty or more busloads of tourists that visit nightly, dervishes or not. From the east, an alignment typical of a Roman fortress, one enters an open courtyard with a central fountain. The court is flanked on two sides (north and south) by covered, raised, platforms which originally would have provided sleeping space for caravan drivers while their animals slept in the courtyard. Today the raised platform provides a seating area for tired tourists who wish to enjoy tea. The small guardrooms flanking the entrance are now used as gift shops. Opposite the entrance is a large doorway leading to a covered court. This second smaller court and its flanking rooms mirror the first court but the center of the second court now contains a raised wooden platform used by the dervishes for performances. Seating for spectators is available in the flanking rooms, which are open to the court.

The Sema *(Arabic,* Sam'a*)*

The *sema*, or audition, as the performance is known, is a type of meditation. Parts of the *sema* can be traced to the time of the founder, but features were added until the time of Sultan Walad's great grandson, Adil Çelebi, who died in 1490 (Elias 1995). The Mevlevi provide a description of the *sema* in pamphlet form to all who attend their ceremonies. The text of the pamphlet, composed by the late Dr Celaleddin B. Çelebi, can be found at <www.mevlana.net>.

The Mevlevi see the *sema* as a mystical journey to the 'Perfect'. In order to reach the 'Perfect' the dervish must desert his ego and nature, so as to love all, no matter their religion, class or race (Çelebi). The culmination of the journey should be the state of *hal* or loss of consciousness. While observing a non-Mevlevi dervish order, Burke noted that nine of eleven dervishes reached *hal* in a span of time ranging from six minutes to two hours. He reports that all dervishes showed no sign of life and had shallow breathing. Their eyeballs did not turn back when the eyelid was raised and their pupils did not react to light (Burke 1975: 52). A number of photos of Mevlevi in an ecstatic state can be seen at <www.dankphotos.com/whirling>. The pamphlet distributed by the Mevlevi describes the *sema* at Sarihan Kervansary in detail, but it does not correspond with the account of the Mevlevi *sema* published by Elias. The inconsistencies discussed below may be an indication that Mevlevi public performances are not religious acts.

The Dervishes arrive dressed in tall headdresses (the ego's tombstone) and black *khirqah* or cloaks over white tunic and skirts (the ego's shroud). They kneel with arms crossed to await the start of the ceremony. Çelebi divides the Mevlevi rite/performance into seven units:

A. Eulogy to the prophet
B. Drum sound symbolizing the command of creation: 'Be!'
C. Improvisational music (*taksim*) with a reed *ney* to symbolize Divine Breath
D. Greeting
E. Whirling
F. Reading from the Koran
G. Prayer, after which the dervishes return to their cells for meditation

Elias provides extra details concerning the beginning of the rite/performance. He describes the entry of the presiding Mevlevi (*meydanci dede*), who places a pelt or skin on the floor. The skin will be the seat of the *shaykh*. Once the skin is placed, the call to prayer signals the arrival of the *shaykh* and the other dervishes. They pray, they gather around the *shaykh* to listen to hymns and readings from the *Masnavi* (a collection of Rumî's works) accompanied by music. This segment of the rite/performance is concluded by the *shaykh* reciting the prayer of the skin (Elias 1995: 78). The greeting portion of the ceremony (D) then follows.

Unit D is a ritual of greeting in which all of the dervishes (*sema zen*) acknowledge each other while completing the *devri veleh* or circular walk three times to accompanying music (Çelebi). Elias is more specific, noting that all participants in the rite/performance take part in the greeting. Still wearing their cloaks, with arms folded under, each dervish walks in a circle toward the skin. When the dervish reaches the skin he bows to the person in front of him. He faces the skin as he passes it and then turns to face the next participant, who bows to him. After receiving the greeting the dervish turns forward after three steps and continues to walk with head bowed and eyes down. The greeting concludes when the *shaykh* takes his seat on the skin (Elias 1995: 78).

Unit E, the whirling, can be divided into four salutes or *selam*:

1. Man's birth to truth, representing his concept of the divine
2. The nature of man in light of creation
3. Complete submission and the annihilation of self
4. Termination of the spiritual journey and return to subservience (Çelebi)

Elias adds a few details. The cloaks are removed before the whirling begins. The *shaykh* sits upon the skin to signal the beginning of the whirling. The dervishes move counter-clockwise, arms extended with the right palm facing upwards and the left downwards. The left foot is used as a pivot, as the dervishes move through the cycles (salutes to Çelebi) or *devre* (Arabic, *dawra*). The upturned right hand symbolizes the dervish's receipt of divine grace, while the downturn of the left hand represents the passing on of God's gifts to humanity (Elias 1995: 78).

For Çelebi, the next part (F) of the *sema* is the reading of the Koran, in particular v. 15 of chapter 2, known as the 'chapter of the cow' (Arabic, *surat al-baqara*). Elias makes no reference to unit F or to unit G, the prayers for the peace of the souls of all prophets and believers (Çelebi; Elias 1995: 78).

Observations

These observations stem from two different performances of the *sema*. The first was on 22 July 2002 at a ceremony witnessed by myself and an economist employed by the Canadian government. The second performance occurred on 2 October 2002 and was viewed by two retired librarians, both former employees of the Government of Canada. While this is a small sample of observers, it does represent a starting point.

The layout of the *sema* differed slightly from that described by Elias (1995: 78). He describes a platform that is circular, while the platform of the Sarihan Kervansarayi is rectangular. The shape of the platform does not affect the performance or rite in any way, as can be seen in the photos of Daniel Kramer (<www.dankphotos.com/whirling>). What can also be seen in the photos at that website is the presence of more than one *meydanci dede* and/or *shaykh*. A photo shows four standing figures in the centre of the dance and no seated figure. At the Kervansarayi rites/performances there was one standing figure, and no one remembers a seated figure corresponding to Elias' *shaykh*. Obviously, some flexibility is permitted in the ritual. The *meydanci dede* appears to function as a director, and can be seen watching the movement of the dance as a choreographer might be seen watching the performance of a Broadway show.

Elias makes no reference to the gender of the dancers. All dancers at the Kervansarayi rites/performances appeared to be male, but the photos by Kramer seem to show female dancers. Some dervish orders, such as the Alevi, include women in their rituals. However, the Shi'ite Alevi are often criticized for this inclusion by the Sunni majority (Mandel 1992: 421). The Mevlevi are Sunni and they may not wish to include women in public 'performances'. That is to say, women take part in the rituals, but not in front of tourists. The women of the Kramer photos may be Western, certainly one appears to be blond, and another is identified as 'Dakota', certainly not a Turkish or Arab name. It may be that a western woman performing in public does not violate Mevlevi sensibilities. It should be noted that other Sufi orders, such as the Naqshbandiyya, admit women to their ranks, with some female members becoming *shaykhs*. Other orders have enrolled women in women's circles to preserve the traditional gender divisions (Veinstein 1986: 294).

The whirling appears almost effortless. The dancers pivot on their left foot while the right makes a heel to toe motion, not unlike the rhythmic action of a skate boarder. The ease of the movement is aided by low, leather-soled boots that appear to be soft and supple. The dervishes glide almost effortlessly between positions. One must realize that the whirling is not static *per se*. The dervishes move around the floor space after completing, on average, seven rotations. A number of the dervishes appear to employ a spotting technique to maintain their equilibrium. That is to say, they fix their gaze on one spot and return their gaze to it as quickly as possible while they turn. Dancers, gymnasts and figure skaters commonly employ this technique to control their balance. However, the use of spotting defeats the purpose of whirling; losing control is a necessary part of obtaining an ecstatic state.

None of the dervishes in either performance was seen to enter a state of *hal*. The whirling lasted at least half an hour, and if Burke's observations hold true some of the dervishes present should have been in a trance (see Burke 1975: 55-56). The state of the dervishes appeared quite the opposite; all appeared alert, and some were observed straightening their clothing before donning their black cloaks in preparation to withdraw for private meditation. One older man appeared flushed and hot, but otherwise little reaction to the dance was evident. After the main performance a few dervishes returned to whirl for photographs, and, in some cases, talk with the audience.

Conclusion: A Working Theory

The question is whether this activity should be categorized as a rite or a performance. The evidence clearly points to this type of public *sema* being a performance. The dervishes do not reach a state of *hal*, and so the goal of the *sema* has not been reached. Furthermore, the failure to attain a state of *hal* appears to be a purposeful decision. There are three possible explanations for why the dervishes do not wish to reach *hal*.

The first possible reason is that the dervishes may consider their rite too sacred to be revealed to tourists. Konya, the spiritual centre of the Mevlevi, is a very conservative city. Women, Turkish and non-Turkish, are routinely harassed if they are not correctly dressed: heads covered, upper arms covered, skirts below the knee, clothing loose and opaque and no trousers. Such treatment is rare in most of Turkey. Against this theory is the fact that dervishes performing the rite outside of Turkey do enter *hal* and have been photographed (see <www.dankphotos.com/whirling/>). It may be that the location of the performance is the problem.

The second possibility takes into account that the performance is taking place in Turkey. The *tekke*s have been illegal since 1925 (Kreiser 1986: 50), but the Mevlevi received permission in 1953 to revive their whirling for reasons of tourism. The Bektashi received this permission in 1964, and the officials in charge of the Bekstashi three-day festival present it as a tourism initiative, not a religious festival (Norton 1992: 187-88). The achievement of *hal* is the core of the religious rite and, therefore, not for tourists.

The third possibility precludes neither reason one nor two. Elias notes that during the reign of Selim III (1789–1807) the frequency and occasion of the *sema* changed (1995: 78), telling us that the religious rite of *sema* is performed only on certain days. The Kramer photos document one of the occasions, the celebration of the birth of Rumî on 17 December. The dervishes perform in Konya on that day, having gained permission for a festival geared for tourists (Norton 1992: 188). At this time, I have no information concerning the dervish reaching *hal* at the December festival. The two performances upon which this study is based did not fall upon days when the *Mevlevi* would normally celebrate the *sema*.

The public performances of the dervish have kept alive their *tariqah*. Despite laws against them, they thrive and earn capital in hard currency, US Dollars preferred, in a country almost crippled by inflation. By failing to complete the *sema* through reaching *hal*, they keep strictly within the law, and at the same time preserve their culture and delight foreign audiences.

BIBLIOGRAPHY

Arberry, A.J. (ed. and trans.)
    1975   *Discourses of Rumi* (repr.; London: John Murray)
Burke, Michael Omar
    1975   *Among the Dervishes: An Account of Travels in Asia and Africa, and Four Years Studying the Dervishes, Sufis and Fakirs by Living Among Them* (New York: E.P. Dutton).
Çelebi, Celaleddin B.
    n.d.   *Semâ the Universal Movement* (n.p.n.e.)
Elias, Jamal J.
    1995   'Mawlawiyah', in Esposito (ed.) 1995: 77-78.
Esposito, John L. (ed.)
    1995   *The Oxford Encyclopedia of the Modern Islamic World*, III (New York: Oxford University Press).
Kreiser, Klaus
    1986   'Notes sur le present et le passé des ordre mystiques en Turquie', in Popovic and Veinstein (eds.) 1986: 47-62
Mandel, Ruth
    1992   'The *Alevi-Bektashi* Identity in a Foreign Context: The example of Berlin', *Revue des Etudes Islamiques* LX: 419-26.
Mardin, Serif
    1995   'Melevi', in Esposito (ed.) 1995: 102.
Nicholson, Reynold A. (ed. and trans.)
    1964   *Rum Poet and Mystic (1207–1273): Selection from his Writings Translated from the Persian with Introduction and Notes* (London: George Allen & Unwin, 3rd edn).
Norton, John David
    1992   'Development of the Annual Festival at Hacibektash, 1964–1985', *Revue des Etudes Islamiques* LX: 187-96.
Overholt, Thomas W.
    1986   *Prophecy in Cross-Cultural Perspective* (SBL Sources for Biblical Study, 17; Atlanta: Scholars Press).
Popovic, A., and G. Veinstein (eds.)
    1986   *Les Ordres Mystiques dans l'Islam: Cheminements et Situation Actuelle* (Paris : Edition de l'Ecole des hautes études en sciences sociales).
Veinstein, Gilles
    1986   'Un essai de synthèse', in Popovic and Veinstein (eds.) 1986: 293-310.

DISSONANT PIETIES: JOHN CALVIN
AND THE PRAYER PSALMS OF THE PSALTER

Paul A. Riemann

1. *Introduction*

Some years ago one of Calvin's writings on prayer found its way into the syllabus for a course I taught on the book of Psalms. It was this work which provided the point of departure for the present study.[1] What first drew my attention was his keen sense that many of the prayers of the Psalter do not follow his own guidelines for due and proper prayer, and his directness in saying so. This is a notably candid assessment, far less common in the interpretive tradition than it ought to be. In spite of all he was able to say in praise of the Psalter, when all was said and done he could not commend it to his readers as a book of model prayers they needed only to imitate. When he praised it he had other uses in mind, as we shall see. There is no doubt either that his judgment was correct; taken as a group, the prayer psalms[2] do not conform to his own convictions about the proprieties to be observed in prayer.

I have come to the conclusion that the piety implicit in the prayer psalms and the piety Calvin himself endorsed and espoused differ significantly. They embody fundamentally different perceptions of prayer, what it is, why one engages in it, what one hopes to achieve by it. From what I have said thus far it may appear that this was also his view. It was not. The purpose of this study is to learn why it was not, and to trace some of the more important consequences.

Calvin did not work in splendid isolation, to be sure. He was a figure of his time, his approach was shaped by the interests and conflicts of the period, and he was of course building upon the work of others. He was drawing upon the rich traditions of the ancient and medieval Church, and the work of other reformers who were his predecessors and contemporaries, Luther above all. In the case of the book of Psalms he was making use of many sources, and may well have been influenced by

---

1. This study first took shape as a matriculation address for Drew Theological Seminary, September 1987. A more developed version was presented in August 1991, to the Colloquium for Biblical Research. I am especially grateful to Suzanne Selinger, who graciously read a later version and offered many helpful comments.
2. By 'prayer psalms' I refer to those psalms biblical scholars classify as *Klagelieder* (in English, current usage favors 'complaint psalms' rather than 'laments'; my own preference would be 'plaint psalms'). There are more psalms of this type in the Psalter than of any other. They share many conventional elements; among those which are almost always present are plaint and petition.

the commentary of Martin Bucer of Strassburg in particular.[3] He was well read in Augustine, whom he greatly revered, and the introspective character of Augustine's writings doubtless encouraged him in a reading of the psalms in the same mode, even though the fourth-century bishop had no comparable interest in the Psalter's historical setting and Calvin is frequently critical of his exegetical judgment.[4] In view of recent studies which have shown how extensively scholars of this period drew upon their predecessors in the late medieval period as well as each other, it cannot simply be assumed that he was solely responsible even for those insights which most shaped his understanding of Psalter piety.

For the purposes of the present study we shall focus our attention upon Calvin and his own historical setting, leaving aside the matter of antecedents and forerunners. The clarity of his thought makes it relatively easy to see what led him to take the stance he did and, more important, how he managed to work it out and justify it. There is at least a hint, as we shall see, that he did not do this all at once, that there was something about the psalms he had to ponder for some time before he was willing to commit himself in writing. But at least by the time he published his Commentary on the Psalms he had found a way to disapprove much that the psalmists say in their prayers and yet approve the piety to which they were ultimately committed. He regarded the piety which lay behind the psalms as due and proper and, in all essential respects, compatible with his own. In the end it was no doubt precisely because he was so certain he recognized and approved their piety that he could so confidently fault them for their lapses, shortcomings and excesses, while identifying personally with their faith and their failings. I shall take the psalms as Calvin himself read them, and ask how he proceeded from that point to an understanding of their piety. Citations of the biblical text, for example, will follow his translation and stand for the most part without comment. It goes without saying that his judgments about text, translation, authorship and historical setting do not always conform to those of contemporary biblical scholarship, but it serves my purpose best to allow him his own perspective on these matters. His understanding of the piety of the prayer psalms does not hinge upon matters of this sort, and I suspect he would have held to this understanding even if he had known of, and accepted, the latest historical-critical judgments about them. That there are well-known scholars trained in the historical-critical method who espouse a similar understanding today shows well enough that it can be done.

---

3. On Bucer's prolix but widely read commentary, see Hobbs 1984. Calvin refers to the commentaries of Bucer and Musculus in the preface to his 1557 commentary on the Psalms; Bucer's was published under his own name in 1554 (the first edition, under the pseudonym Aretius Felinus, in 1529), Musculus' in 1551; see Parker 1965: 11, 387 nn. 2, 3. By 1557 many such works had been published; the list of books on the Psalter provided by Hobbs (1990: 223-25) includes Latin works by nineteen authors published 1508–46.

4. For example, 'All this may be plausible, and, in its own place, useful, but [it] proceeds upon a complete misapprehension of the meaning of the passage' (*Com. Ps.* 58.1). Citations from the commentary, including Calvin's translations of the biblical text, are taken from Anderson (1845–49) unless otherwise noted.

2. *Discerning a Savor of Intemperance*

a. *Calvin's Disquiet with David*

Calvin is speaking of prayer in his *The Institutes of the Christian Religion* when he writes that 'No one has ever carried this out with the uprightness that was due; for, not to mention the rank and file, how many complaints of David savor of intemperance!' (*Inst.* 3.20.16).[5] With these words he introduces an assessment of the psalms which tells us a great deal about his own understanding of their piety. To be sure, the premise that not even the prayers of biblical saints are wholly satisfactory follows from his basic theological stance. He uses David to clinch the argument precisely because he greatly admires 'that most illustrious prince and prophet' and ranks him above all other psalmists. But there is a certain sense of amazement here that this 'savor of intemperance' should be so prevalent and so obvious, and an implication that the reader must surely have felt this too.

'Not that he would either deliberately expostulate with God or clamor against his judgments', he continues, 'but that, fainting with weakness, he finds no other solace better than to cast his own sorrows into the bosom of God'. He means to put the emphasis here upon David's good intention and the mitigating circumstances; in such cases God is forgiving, and this is the point he has been aiming at all along: 'God tolerates even our stammering and pardons our ignorance whenever something inadvertently escapes us; as indeed without this mercy there would be no freedom to pray'.

At the same time Calvin's own disquiet comes through clearly enough. He must feel David did sometimes 'expostulate with God' and 'clamor against his judgments' or he would not think it an adequate defense to say David would not do either 'deliberately'. The sentence which follows has the same double edge: 'But although David intended to submit completely to God's will, and prayed with no less patience than zeal to obtain his request, yet there come forth—sometimes, rather, boil up—turbulent emotions, quite out of harmony with the first rule we laid down'.

1. *A Work in Revision.* As Calvin writes this he is nearing fifty and his health is deteriorating. Perhaps sensing that his time is short—he would die before he reached fifty-five—he has set himself to produce a new and final edition of his major work, adding here one of several wholly new sections to the chapter on prayer. He had been only twenty-six, and had not yet laid eyes on Geneva, when the first, much smaller edition was published as 'an almost complete summary of piety' (so the 1536 title page).[6] At that time prayer was already the topic of one of the book's six chapters, so he has been thinking and writing about this for half his life.

The chapter had been revised and expanded soon after for the second edition of the *Institutes*, published in 1539, but it had hardly been touched since.[7] He is now

---

5.   All quotations are from McNeill (Calvin 1960).
6.   See Battles' translation of the 1536 edition (Calvin 1975).
7.   The 1559 edition of the chapter comprises some 2500 lines of text in the critical edition of

thoroughly reworking it; by the time it is published in 1559 much of the text will be revised and more than a third will be entirely new.[8] What is surprising—and intriguing—is that the new text will triple the number of references to the Psalter.[9] It will also introduce general observations on the book, most of the references to David by name, and all of the critical remarks about the prayers of the psalmists.

One reason for this must certainly be that he had just recently published (in July, 1557) a commentary on the book of Psalms, the fruit of some five years study and teaching,[10] all of it undertaken since the last major revision of the *Institutes*. In fact, the Friday afternoon *Congrégation*, a study group conducted in French which the Genevan pastors were required to attend and to which others came also, had been working through the book under Calvin's direction for several years and would continue to do so until August 1559, the very month the final edition of the *Institutes* was published.[11] Evidently the book of Psalms had come to play an increasingly prominent part in his thinking about prayer, perhaps precisely because of the problems it posed for him.

Barth and Niesel (Calvin 1926–70: IV, 298-368). Of these, some 1200 lines have been carried over without change from the 1539 edition, including some 680 lines unchanged from the 1536 edition, much of it exposition of the Lord's Prayer as one would expect (*Inst.* 3.20.34-49+50). Some 285 lines are 1536/39 text now re-edited for 1559. There is little text from later editions: some 100 lines added in 1543 (including the whole of section 32, on church singing) and a mere half-dozen in the major edition of 1550. A relatively small part of the earlier text was not carried over into the 1559 edition, mainly in sections 12-15.

8. Of the approximately 2500 lines in the *Opera Selecta*, some 900 (36%) are entirely new text; some 285 lines (an additional 11%) are older text re-edited.

9. Fifty-four references to thirty-six psalms were marked in the printed text of 1559. Six derive from the 1536 edition, and ten from the 1539 edition—together a total of sixteen references to twelve psalms. There are none in the brief sections of text from 1543 and 1550. When earlier text was not carried over in 1559 no references were lost. On this reckoning the 1559 edition added thirty-eight references (70% of the total) and drew upon twenty-four additional psalms (67% of the total). If we added two references marked in earlier editions, two marked in the 1561 printing, one marked in the French editions 1541sqq, and three more identified by Barth and Niesel in footnotes, the count would be sixty-two references to forty-two psalms. On this reckoning forty-one references were added in the 1559 edition (66% of the total), drawing upon twenty-seven additional psalms (64% of the total). On either reckoning there are more than four references per hundred lines in newly composed 1559 text, compared to just over one per hundred in text carried over from earlier editions. Granted that there are always uncertainties in determining what is a 'reference', the pattern of distribution is so striking this hardly matters. While there are additional references to other biblical books also, none is really comparable; the largest additions are six each to Isaiah (to make nineteen), Jeremiah (to make eleven), the Synoptics (to make twenty-one), and James (to make twelve).

10. 'I expounded the Book of Psalms in this small school of mine three years ago' (preface to the commentary, cited in Parker (1965: 15). Parker concludes that this must refer to the lectures, conducted in Latin, which he gave sometime between 1552 and 1555 or 1556. Calvin had worked with the psalms before; at least as early as 1545 he was preaching on them occasionally on Sunday afternoons. For details see Parker 1965: 5-6; 1986: 30.

11. On the *Congrégation*, see Parker 1986: 14-15. The group had begun its study of the book of Psalms in 1555.

Inspired Speech

2. *The Rules for Framing Proper Prayer*. When he writes that David's complaints are 'quite out of harmony with the first rule we laid down', he is referring to the rules 'for framing prayer duly and properly' which he has just finished setting out in the first part of the chapter. To call them 'rules' is perhaps a bit misleading; as François Wendel (1963: 254) remarks, 'it is a question of the general attitude required of the faithful rather than of precise and clearly-distinguishable rules'. Nevertheless, Calvin clearly means them to be taken seriously, and his presentation takes the form of a rather stern lecture on proper attitudes in prayer.

In the course of two decades they have grown from two rules to four, and here in the final edition he takes eleven sections to present them (more than sixteen pages in the McNeill-Battles translation), so they are not easily summarized. Calvin is brilliant, well-educated, eloquent and thorough, but he lacks Luther's gift for the pithy phrase. Of necessity I offer them here in capsule form, but I shall use his own words as much as I can.

'Now...let this be the first rule: that we be disposed in mind and heart as befits those who enter conversation with God.' The metaphor of conversation with divine majesty suggests two proprieties we must observe: to give God our undivided attention and to keep ourselves from shameful desires. Thus, 'we are to rid ourselves of all alien and outside cares, by which the mind, itself a wanderer', is so easily distracted (*Inst.* 3.20.4). The newly added text puts this categorically: 'Let us therefore realize that the only persons who duly and properly gird themselves to pray are those who are so moved by God's majesty that they come to it freed from earthly cares and affections' (3.20.5). The same consideration requires that there 'enter our hearts no desire and no wish at all of which we should be ashamed to make him a witness' (3.20.3). Instead, we must 'rise to a purity worthy of God' (3.20.4).

The first rule has a complement which is almost an additional rule: 'not to ask any more than God allows' (3.20.5), but rather to 'submit completely to God's will' (3.20.16). And we have not been left to wonder what God wills for us; it is what God has promised in the Scriptures. It follows that 'where no certain promise shows itself, we must ask of God conditionally' (3.20.15), which is to say, we must add 'if it be thy will' or 'nevertheless, thy will be done'.

'Let this be the second rule: that in our petitions we ever sense our own insufficiency, and earnestly pondering how [much] we need all we seek, join with this prayer an earnest—nay, burning—desire to attain it' (3.20.6).

The third rule is to repent, and in a sense this comes first. 'Lawful prayer... demands repentance... Let each one, therefore, as he prepares to pray be displeased with his own evil deeds, and (something that cannot happen without repentance) let him take the person and disposition of a beggar' (3.20.7). 'The beginning, and even the preparation, of proper prayer is the plea for pardon with a humble and sincere confession of guilt', for God cannot 'chance to be propitious to any but those whom he has pardoned' (3.20.9).

'The fourth rule is that, thus cast down and overcome by true humility, we should be nonetheless encouraged to pray by a sure hope that our prayer will be answered' (3.20.11). Indeed, 'only that prayer is acceptable to God which is born, if I may so express it, out of such presumption of faith, and is grounded in unshaken assurance of hope' (3.20.12). It is Christ himself who 'calls this principle to the attention of all of us with this saying, "I say unto you, whatever you seek...believe that you will receive it, and it will come to you"' (Mk 11.24). Prayers which lack this are irritating: 'It is amazing how much our lack of trust provokes God if we request of him a boon that we do not expect' (*Inst.* 3.20.11).

Even before he has finished the first rule, Calvin warns this will not be easy. 'Because our abilities are far from able to match such perfection, we must seek a remedy to help us'. It is for this reason 'God gives us the Spirit as our teacher in prayer, to tell us what is right and temper our emotions'. (The 'tempering of the emotions' is a prominent theme in Calvin's piety, and we shall return to it.) But we must not presume upon this divine aid. 'These things are not said in order that we, favoring our own slothfulness, may give over the function of prayer to the Spirit of God, and vegetate in that carelessness to which we are all too prone', for in this matter 'God's will is to test how effectually faith moves in our hearts' (3.20.5).

3. *Bringing the Rules to the Psalms*. These are the four rules Calvin has in mind as he reflects on David and the Psalter. They require reverence, submission to the will of God, earnest desire, humble penitence and unwavering faith. Even though he places his own distinctive construction on several of these elements, as we shall see, the essential piety they describe has already had a long history and is certainly not his own invention.

When he proceeds to judge the psalms by these rules he faces something of a problem. He is too able a biblical scholar to suppose they describe the way the psalmists actually frame their prayers, and yet he cannot imagine that the psalmists were indifferent to them or that the Holy Spirit was nodding. This is a particularly important matter, for his whole understanding of psalm piety is fundamentally shaped by the way he resolves this tension: *it appears self-evident to him that the psalmists intended to follow the rules he has set forth, but often failed to do so for very human reasons we must not approve but can readily understand.*

Seen in this light, the psalms serve to confirm the judgment which prompts him to promulgate rules in the first place. Rules are needed because it does not come to us naturally and spontaneously to frame our prayers aright; on the contrary, due and proper prayer is a 'goal not immediately attainable' toward which we must continually and earnestly strive. On this understanding he is able to turn even David's shortcomings and excesses to advantage; they reinforce his own theology of prayer rather than subvert it. The 'savor of intemperance' in his complaints assures us that God will graciously tolerate and pardon our own ignorance and stammering, and at the same time warns us against carelessly, much less deliberately, praying the same way ourselves.

This inevitably shapes his understanding of the psalms as Holy Scripture. Even though the book of Psalms is inspired by the Holy Spirit, we are not to regard all it contains as exemplary prayer. The book is a record of the long-standing struggle to frame prayers rightly, not a sample-book of unblemished prayers which we can safely imitate. Many psalms represent the way believers do pray, rather than the way they ought to pray. And this is what the Holy Spirit intended in providing such forms of prayer for our instruction. Rather than copying them, we must learn from them not to be too quickly satisfied with our own efforts, or too quickly disheartened when we fall short of the goal ourselves.

The correlate is that the rules for proper prayer are not, indeed cannot be, derived from the book of Psalms itself, since the book exhibits them only imperfectly. They must be discovered elsewhere and then applied to the psalms, just as Calvin is doing. This may, of course, involve us in judging the psalmists by a standard they did not intend to follow and would not even have recognized.

A straightforward comparative study, looking only for similarities and differences and not intending to make judgments about what is proper and what is not, might choose to bracket the issue entirely. It could bring together any collection of prayer texts (the Psalter, or a prayer book perhaps) and any protocol of prayer (even from a non-Judeo-Christian tradition) and ask to what extent they correlate. But even here one would certainly want to ask whether a different protocol is implicit in the text, if only to guard against possible misunderstandings.

Calvin has no such limited objective in mind. The piety he has tried to summarize in a few helpful rules is not one of many equally legitimate ways to frame prayer; it is the form of prayer which God both invites and commands us to use, authorized by Scripture and to be observed throughout the Church, and so he cannot avoid making judgments about the propriety of prayers in the Psalter and their implicit piety.

At the same time, he cannot simply bracket the question of the psalmists' own sense of propriety either, for he brings a self-consciously historical interest to the psalms, even if that is not his sole concern. As a scholar exercised in the New Learning, he wants to understand the psalms on their own terms, as ancient prayers occasioned by real circumstances in the lives of real people. But the intuition which allows him to bring theological conviction and historical interest together so easily—namely, that the psalmists share his own sense of what is right and are trying as best they can to follow it—succeeds rather too well, for it effectively silences the psalms as witnesses to their own intention. If it should happen that this intuition is wrong and the psalms have quite a different sense of what is proper in prayer, he has made it virtually impossible for them to tell him so. Whatever they say or do, he will have little difficulty accounting for it on his own terms.

4. *Measuring the Psalms Against the Rules*. It is in the new text Calvin is composing for the 1559 edition, and especially in three wholly new sections he is adding to his account of the four rules, that he reflects on the negative correlation between his rules and the psalms. In the first (section 9), he is expanding on the third rule, to repent, which he has just introduced in the preceding section. Having said that 'the plea for pardon with a humble and sincere confession of guilt' is 'the beginning, and even the preparation, of proper prayer', he turns to the Psalter to demonstrate this. 'Accordingly, it is no wonder if believers open for themselves the door to prayer with this key, as we learn from numerous passages of the Psalms', and he cites Psalms 25 and 51 as examples.

He has noticed that penitential statements of this sort are often lacking in biblical prayers, and he mentions this, but as a matter of no real consequence. 'But even though the saints do not always beg forgiveness of sins in so many words, if we diligently ponder their prayers that Scripture relates' we will readily see 'that they have received their intention to pray from God's mercy alone, and thus always have begun with appeasing him' (*Inst.* 3.20.9). Here he seems to lean over backwards to reconcile the psalms with a rule, not by chance the rule he regards as indispensable. It is doubtful he would be as generous with non-biblical prayers which did not 'beg forgiveness in so many words' and whose penitential intent could be discovered only by diligent pondering.

The two other new sections (15 and 16) come after he has finished setting out the rules, and reflect on them as a set. The first begins 'Here more than one question is raised: for Scripture relates that God has granted fulfillment of certain prayers' even though they were 'not framed to the rule of the Word'. He then discusses a number of biblical examples. One in particular shows how far he is willing to carry his critical assessment of the psalms: 'And one psalm clearly teaches that prayers which do not reach heaven by faith still are not without effect', for it 'lumps together those prayers which, out of natural feeling, necessity wrings from unbelievers just as much as from believers, yet from the outcome it proves that God is gracious toward them' (Ps. 107). Such divine gentleness does not, however, attest that God finds such prayers acceptable. 'Nay, it is by this circumstance to emphasize or illumine his mercy whenever the prayers of unbelievers are not denied to them; and again to incite his true worshippers to pray the more, when they see that even ungodly wailings sometimes do some good' (3.20.15).

The same note of cautious encouragement opens the new section which immediately follows: 'This also is worth noting: what I have set forth on the four rules of right praying is not so rigorously required that God will reject those prayers in which he finds neither perfect faith nor repentance, together with a warmth of zeal and petitions rightly conceived'. He then proceeds to measure the prayers of the saints against each of the rules in turn, drawing the lessons appropriate to proper piety.

With respect to the first rule, he begins as we have already noted: in many of David's complaints there are intemperate and turbulent emotions 'quite out of harmony with the first rule that we laid down'. As a particularly striking example he offers the way David ends the thirty-ninth psalm. '"Let me alone", he says, "before I depart, and be no more". One might say that this desperate man seeks nothing except to rot in his evils, with God's hand withdrawn.' It is obvious that 'this holy man' is so carried away by violent sorrow that 'he cannot control himself'. But this is not an uncommon failing. 'In those trials also there are often uttered petitions not sufficiently consonant with the rule of God's Word, and in which the saints do not sufficiently weigh what is lawful and expedient'. Whatever the extenuating circumstances, however, 'all prayers marred by these defects deserve to be repudiated'. And there is only one remedy: 'provided the saints bemoan their sins, chastise themselves, and immediately return to themselves, God pardons them' (*Inst.* 3.20.16).

He finds they 'likewise sin with regard to the second rule [keenly to sense our great need]; for they must repeatedly wrestle with their own coldness, and their need and misery do not sharply enough urge them to pray earnestly'. As a result, 'it often happens that their minds slip away and well-nigh vanish; accordingly, in this respect there is also need for pardon, lest our languid or mutilated, or interrupted and vague, prayers suffer a refusal' (*Inst.* 3.20.16).

Since he has already satisfied himself (in section 9) that biblical prayers always begin by appeasing God even though they 'do not always beg forgiveness of sins in so many words', he does not fault the psalms with respect to the third rule (to repent). Instead, he cites David as a worthy example. 'Although no believers neglect this topic'—for him this is a matter of definition, for they would not be believers if they did—'yet those truly versed in prayers know that they do not offer a tenth part of that sacrifice of which David speaks: "The sacrifice acceptable to God is a broken spirit..."' (*Inst.* 3.20.16, citing Ps. 51.17).

He is speaking of the fourth rule (that we pray in the unshakable faith that our prayer will be granted) when he writes: 'Most of all it is weakness or imperfection of faith that vitiates believers' prayers, unless God's mercy succor them'. He adds, 'but no wonder God pardons this defect, since he often tests his own with sharp trials, as if he deliberately willed to snuff out their faith'. To be 'compelled to cry out, "How long wilt thou be angry with the prayer of thy servant?" as if prayers themselves annoyed God', as Ps. 80.4 does, is the hardest trial of all. 'Innumerable examples of this kind occur in Scripture, from which it is clear the faith of the saints was often so mixed and troubled with doubts that in believing and hoping they yet betrayed some want of faith'. But once again he ends with admonition: 'I do not recount these matters in order that believers may confidently pardon themselves for anything but that by severely chastising themselves they may strive to overcome these obstacles'. They should feel the depths of evil, 'seeing that there is no prayer which in justice God would not loathe if he did not overlook the spots with which all are sprinkled'. And yet in spite of Satan's efforts 'they should nonetheless break through, surely persuaded that, although not freed of all hindrances, their efforts still please God and their petitions are approved, provided they endeavor and strive toward a goal not immediately attainable' (*Inst.* 3.20.16).

b. *Calvin's Approach to Psalm Piety*

Before we leave Calvin's chapter on prayer, there are four interrelated matters to which we should give particular attention: the locus of his concern, the theological stance he is bringing to his reading, the manner in which he accounts for the psalmists' lapses and excesses, and the emphasis he lays upon prayer as an introspective discipline.

1. *The Locus of Concern*. Precisely because he has presented the excesses and shortcomings of biblical prayer in his customary thorough way, it is worth noting that he has not even mentioned a topic some would put high on the list, namely, the attitude the psalmists take toward their enemies.[12] In fact he will not refer to it anywhere in this chapter.

---

12. Even Claus Westermann, who has written so much in appreciation of the biblical lament tradition and proposed reintroducing it in the Church, has reservations at this point: 'For side by

When he comes, later in the chapter, to the first two petitions of the Lord's Prayer (*Inst.* 3.20.41-42) he will speak of vengeance and the desire for the destruction of the wicked, but he will do so without mentioning the psalms. However much this aspect of the Psalter may trouble others, he does not consider it to be one of the psalmists' failings. (How he dealt with it will appear shortly, when we come to consider his commentary on the Psalms.)

It is something else that arouses his interest and concern, namely, the attitude the psalmists seem to take toward themselves and toward God. This is where they appear to depart most dramatically from the theology and piety with which he himself identifies and which he urges upon his readers. If we are to understand his approach to psalm piety, we must consider at least briefly the theological stance, by now well worked out and widely published, which his rules for right prayer presuppose.

2. *The Theological Stance Brought to the Psalms.* Earlier in the same book of the *Institutes* Calvin devotes an entire chapter to self-denial, which he calls the sum of the Christian life. This is at the heart of his appeals to submit totally to whatever God wills, and it leaves no room at all for complaints against God. Those who duly deny themselves will not 'break forth into impatience and expostulate with God' even when they are ill and in terrible pain, because they know it to be ordained of God (*Inst.* 3.7.10). It is no surprise, then, that he prefers to believe that David did not reprove God deliberately.

He also rationalizes the common biblical idiom which speaks of God in human terms. This is not a new interpretive strategy by any means, but it is particularly important to him—few things frighten him more than the thought that human beings might underestimate the gulf between themselves and Almighty God. The idiom is the way God 'accommodates himself to the ordinary way of speaking on account of our ignorance, and sometimes, if I may be allowed the expression, stammers' (*Com. Jn* 3.12).[13] As a result, we must not be misled by biblical representations of God's moods or mental activities: '…God, in punishing, has (according to our notion) the *appearance* of one in wrath. It signifies…*no such emotion in God*, but only has a reference to the perception and feeling of the sinner who is punished' (*Com. Rom* 1.18 [emphasis added]). The same is true of God's repenting of a decision, or God's grief (Dowey 1952: 243). The position is developed with great care and subtlety, but there is no mistaking its essential thrust.[14] It cannot help but shape his reading of the psalms, where such language is common coin.

side with some of the psalms, which are among the most beautiful and profound in the Psalter and which we can use in our own prayers, as if they had been written with us in view, there are others of which we are forced to ask whether as Christians we really can recite and pray them, because of the imprecations against the psalmist's enemies' (1989: 65).

13.   Cited by Dowey 1952: 243. Cf. *Inst.* 1.13.1 (text from 1539), 'The Anthropomorphites… are easily refuted. For who even of slight intelligence does not understand that, as nurses commonly do with infants, God is wont in a measure to "lisp" in speaking to us? Thus such forms of speaking do not so much express clearly what God is like as accommodate the knowledge of him to our slight capacity. To do this he must descend far beneath his loftiness.'

14.   Dowey (1952: 243-44) offers a more careful statement than I am able to present here,

But if we must never object or complain, and God's decisions are always for the best and cannot be changed, what can be the purpose of petitioning God in prayer? Is it even appropriate to do so? In good rhetorical fashion he readily acknowledges the problem, and puts the question to himself early in the chapter on prayer: 'But, someone will say, does God not know, even without being reminded, both in what respect we are troubled and what is expedient for us, so that it may seem in a sense superfluous that he should be stirred up by our prayers...?' (*Inst.* 3.20.3). His answer is that people who reason this way do not observe the purpose God had in mind: 'He ordained it not so much for his own sake as for ours'. In fact it is 'for God's sake' only in one respect: God commands that we pray. 'He wills—as is right—that his due be rendered to him'. But prayers do not move God, or change God's attitude, or alter in any way what God has decreed from all eternity. It is we who are changed by the discipline of prayer, by which the Holy Spirit schools us in proper attitudes 'in mind and heart' (3.20.4).[15]

All three of these concerns come together here. Prayer itself is a form of divine accommodation, and the discipline of prayer leads to self-denial. But it is the last point—that prayer is meant to have its effect upon us rather than upon God—which particularly shapes his reading of the Psalms. If he is more articulate and categorical about this than many have been, he at least puts the issue clearly and does not shy from what is, after all, one of the really profound theological puzzles: how to reconcile the practice of prayer with the doctrine that God is omnipotent, omniscient, omnipresent, impassible, and unchanging.

3. *Accounting for the Psalmists' Lapses*. Calvin takes it for granted that in at least all these essentials there is no contradiction between the psalmists' perception of God and his own. That is why it appears self-evident to him that they intend to follow the rules he sets forth, even if they do not always succeed. But these departures are by no means rare, as he recognizes; in psalms of petition they occur more often than not. How is this to be explained? Ultimately by human depravity, to be sure, but if that is all there is to it the psalmists have more claim to our sympathy than to our respect.

As we have seen, Calvin's view is that David's complaints savor of intemperance because he was 'fainting with weakness', he utters petitions 'not sufficiently consonant with the rule of God's Word' because he is desperate, carried away by violent sorrow, and cannot control himself. And this is not uncommon; the saints

distinguishing the ways Calvin treats three different levels of metaphorical language about God. It is worth noting that when Calvin writes about prayer and the Psalms, he is by and large content to employ the biblical idiom himself (there is of course a long tradition for this). But we realize that he has not forgotten it is God's accommodation to us as soon as he begins to explain the purpose of prayer and offer his four rules.

15. Cf. the list of six benefits of prayer in *Inst.* 3.20.3: through prayer we learn to seek God with a burning desire, become accustomed to flee to God in every need, bridle our emotions and purify our desires, prepare ourselves to receive God's gifts with gratitude, embrace what we receive with greater delight, meditate more ardently on God's kindness, and finally confirm God's providence.

often fall into this error when they are similarly tried. When their faith is often 'so mixed and troubled with doubts' that even in their believing and hoping they betray 'some want of faith', this is also a result of the sharp trials they have been made to suffer.

In short, Calvin ascribes these defects in large part to the extremity of the psalmists' situation. David would not have prayed like this if he had been in his right mind. He must be beside himself, overwhelmed by misery and trouble, in such desperate straits that he can no longer give thought to the proprieties of prayer which he would otherwise have been careful to observe.

When the psalmists describe their situation to God, they tend to speak in the direst terms. They present themselves as miserable, bereft of friends, surrounded by gloating and malicious enemies, falsely accused and persecuted, close to death and very nearly despairing. No one, not even God, is coming to their aid. The strategy is pervasive and the language highly conventional, and one might well suspect it is heightened speech calculated to draw God's attention and pity, but we would not expect Calvin to allow for this, and he does not. He pictures their situation precisely as they describe it, and he understandably feels that anyone committed, as he is and as they must surely be, to reverent, restrained, submissive and undoubting prayer would find it difficult to keep to such a form in these overwhelming circumstances.

He finds the argument so persuasive he can even turn it around, and infer the extremity of the psalmists' circumstances from the fact that their prayers depart from the proper form:

> Now, as a man, who is distinguished by courage, does not cry out and complain, and as we know that David did not shrink in bearing his afflictions, we may gather from this, that his sufferings were severe and painful in the extreme, inasmuch as he not only wept bitterly, but was also forced to cry out and complain. (*Com. Ps.* 38.8)

At this point I wish only to observe that, whatever one decides about the psalmists' actual circumstances, it is rather bold to suggest that they pray as they do only because they have been driven to it.[16] Granted that desperate people may utter unseemly prayers, heedless of their own avowed piety, it is still difficult to imagine that any religious community would survive very long if this became the general practice, or that it would develop a conventional form for such prayers, as the psalmists have done. It is equally hard to imagine that a religious community would

16. A supposition often made by modern scholars to account for plaint psalms which make accusations against God follows the same line of reasoning and is open to the same objection. Namely, that these psalms can only be a response to a profound 'crisis of faith' and therefore probably derive from a period of great national calamity (most often proposed: the sixth century BCE following the conquest of Jerusalem and the deportations to Babylon). The same may be said of Westermann's attempt to account for 'what is said concerning the enemy' in the plaint psalms of the individual: 'What can be seen reflected in them...is the phenomenon of the gradual disintegration and decline of the community in which antagonisms (which we are no longer able to discern in detail) become simply overpowering' (1981: 194). It is often the case that biblical scholars appeal to the social context to account for aspects of biblical culture they do not approve; they are less likely to do so for aspects which have their endorsement.

cherish and preserve such prayers, let alone gather more psalms of this genre than any other into its sacred book of collected psalms. But now I am raising questions it would never have occurred to Calvin to ask, and anticipating a discussion to follow later in the study. For the moment it is sufficient to point out that by 'defending' the psalmists in this way he is effectively securing a place for his own piety.

4. *Prayer as an Introspective Discipline*

If the only excuse for the way the psalmists sometimes pray is that they have been driven to it by desperate circumstances, it follows that others must not venture to do the same unless they find themselves in a similar situation. Calvin, as we would expect, draws just this conclusion. As he says of Ps. 25.6, 'This form of prayer cannot be used with propriety, unless when God is hiding his face from us, and seems to take no interest at all in us' (*Com. Ps.*).

He is less concerned to make the point that grave misfortunes may sometimes account for extraordinary biblical prayers, however, than to urge that they should always move us to pray: 'for the saints the occasion that best stimulates them to call upon God is when, distressed by their own need, they are troubled by the greatest unrest, and are almost driven out of their senses, until faith opportunely comes to their relief' (*Inst.* 3.20.11). Indeed, God may send troubles for this very reason: 'On account of these things, our most merciful Father...very often gives the impression of one sleeping or idling in order that he may train us, otherwise idle and lazy, to seek, ask, and entreat him to our great good' (3.20.3). In fact, 'the more harshly troubles, discomforts, fears, and trials of other sorts press us, the freer is our access to him, as if God were summoning us to himself' (3.20.7).

All this serves to direct our attention inwardly, away from the troubles we suffer and toward the way we are responding to them. The gravest misfortune would be no obstacle if there were sufficient faith, and God may allow it precisely as a trial of faith. The real conflict takes place within us, and it has its roots in our carnal and fallen nature. The rules themselves reflect this by giving such close attention to the inner state of the one who is praying: 'As we must turn keenness of mind toward God, so affection of heart has to follow' (3.20.5).

But this inner striving has two aspects, well illustrated in the same paragraph by the dual role of the Holy Spirit, who 'arouses in us assurance, desires, and sighs, to conceive which our natural powers would scarcely suffice', and who is at the same time 'our teacher in prayer, to tell us what is right [in prayer] and temper our emotions' (3.20.5). Behind the Spirit's double role lies the conviction that there are two 'temptations' in particular against which all believers must constantly struggle 'when they groan with weariness under the weight of present ills, and also are troubled and tormented by the fear of greater ones' (3.20.11). One is to feel so despondent they come to be discouraged and lose their confidence, hope, ardor and incentive. The other is to feel so frantic and overwrought they come to be carried away by their emotions and lose their patience, humility, reverence and self-control. The 'goal not immediately attainable' is to bring these extremes under control by faith, self-discipline and moderation.

This is, after all, what the rules are framed to promote, and the central place they give to right attitudes requires that those who pray be constantly monitoring their inmost thoughts, feelings, desires and motivations for any deviation from what is due and proper. This is a decidedly controlled and introspective mode of prayer, self-reflective, self-yielding, self-denying, self-accusing and self-correcting. It is intensely inward-looking even if it is not self-induced or self-empowered, but wholly owing, as Calvin insists, to the grace of God and the working of the Holy Spirit.

Calvin is certainly neither the first nor the last to espouse this mode of prayer or to bring it to his reading of the psalms. I do not doubt that it has its own warrant as a form of piety, but whether assuming it for the psalms allows the voice of the psalmists themselves to be heard is another matter altogether.

3. *Unfolding the Inmost Feelings of David*

a. *The Commentary on the Book of Psalms*

The massive commentary on the Psalms, which Calvin brought to print in July 1557, helps to account for the remarkable increase in psalm references in the chapter on prayer in the final (1559) edition of *The Institutes of the Christian Religion*. It appears that the commentary had a similar impact upon the 1559 *Institutes* as a whole, for there is a striking increase in psalm references in each of the four books.[17]

Few of the new 1559 references outside *Inst.* 3.20 are concerned with the piety of David and the psalmists, and those which are add nothing to what Calvin says in the chapter on prayer. If anyone should doubt, however, that he has carefully considered the stance he takes toward psalm piety in this chapter, these few passages scattered through the other books offer some measure of assurance on the point.

But it is the commentary itself which is decisive. Here Calvin has more space to develop his ideas, and the commentary format itself requires him to deal with each psalm in turn. As we now proceed to examine it, our interest is to discover whether the approach Calvin takes to the piety of David and the other psalmists anticipates the one he will take in the *Institutes*, and to see how he elaborates it.

1. *The Genesis of the Work.* It is worth noting at the outset that we have uncommonly direct access to Calvin's exegesis of the psalms, for he wrote the manuscript for the commentary himself. Among all his Old Testament commentaries, this was the first of only three to be produced this way—'the three commentaries proper', as T.H.L. Parker terms them.[18] The majority were transcripts of his lectures, taken down by others, and prepared for publication under his general supervision. 'His oversight of the material was in no way a revision. He left in the many involutions, repetitions, and asides which a revision would have excised' (Parker 1986: 28).

---

17. By a rough calculation, new and edited text adds something on the order of 240 to 270 psalm references to make a total of 510 or so; that is, about half were evidently introduced in 1559.

18. The others are the Mosaic, published in 1563, and Joshua, published the following year (Parker 1986: 29-33).

In this case he had refused to permit the publication of transcripts, even though others had begun early in the course to record the lectures for this purpose.[19] He had resolved, he says, 'not to publish more extensively what I had uttered familiarly to those of my own household' (Parker 1965: 15). Martin Bucer's 'singular learning...had at least wrought this effect, that there was the less necessity for my work', and soon after, the commentaries of Wolfgang Musculus were before the public also. When he comes to explain why he had at last allowed himself to be prevailed upon, he reports that he had 'one reason for obeying them...and that was, lest at any time what had been taken down from my discourses, should be brought out without my consent or knowledge'; he had been 'driven by this fear, rather than led by my own free will to weave this web' (Parker 1965: 15).

Why had he been so reluctant? According to Parker (1986: 30), 'quite simply they [the lecture transcripts] were below the standards he set himself'. But in this case I suspect there was an additional factor, an uneasiness about reconciling the psalms with his own sense of proper prayer. The way he describes his experience suggests that it was not sub-standard transcripts, but an uncertainty about finding the right words, which was holding him back; the turning point came when 'suddenly, contrary to my purpose (I know not by what impulse), I made a trial of a Latin exposition in one Psalm'. Encouraged that his success, 'while it answered my wishes, far surpassed my hopes', he 'began to attempt the same in some few others', and 'as the work proceeded, I began more distinctly to perceive how far from superfluous this labour would be' (Parker 1965: 15-16). If the task of reconciling the psalms with his own piety had given him trouble before, the problem was now resolved.

2. *The Commentary and the Chapter on Prayer.* Our first question is readily answered. The stance he takes toward psalm piety in this earlier work is essentially the same as in the chapter on prayer in the *Institutes*. Some points stand out because they are so often repeated, and a number are discussed in much greater detail. Prayers for vengeance, which were passed over in the chapter on prayer, receive a good deal of attention here. We will return to these and other matters shortly; the first task is to set out the essential similarity.

The rules for right prayer are implicit throughout, everywhere guiding his reading. He does not offer them as a set, as he does in the chapter on prayer, but when he alludes to them he employs virtually the same language. For example: 'We are to hold this as a general rule in seeking to conciliate God, that we must pray for the pardon of our sins' (*Com. Ps.* 143.2). Or again:

---

19. The earlier commentaries on Isaiah (1551) and Genesis (1554) had been produced from transcripts taken by his secretary, Nicholas des Gallars. The commentary on Hosea, published the same year as the commentary on the Psalms (1557), had been transcribed by three secretaries from notes they had taken. In a letter dated 16 June 1555, des Gallars had offered to send Calvin 'what I took down from your lectures on the Psalms of David...if they can be of any use to you or lighten your task at all'. See Parker 1986: 24-31.

And this is the rule which ought to be observed by us in our prayers; we should in every thing conform our requests to the divine will, as John also instructs us, (1 John v. 14.) And, indeed, we can never pray in faith unless we attend, in the first place, to what God commands, that our minds may not rashly and at random start aside in desiring more than we are permitted to desire and pray for. (*Com. Ps*. 7.6)

He has no doubt that the psalmists are deeply concerned about right attitudes and carefully monitoring them, just as the rules urge all the faithful to be. By saying, 'My God! My God!', David 'keeps all his thoughts and feelings under restraint, that they may not break beyond due bounds' (*Com. Ps*. 22.1). Commenting on the verse 'Make me to know thy ways', he writes that he has 'no hesitation in referring the prayer' to the circumstance that David is 'afraid of yielding to the feeling of impatience, or the desire of revenge, or some extravagant and unlawful impulse' (*Com. Ps*. 25.4). We noted earlier his warning on the opening of Psalm 102: 'No person could utter these words with the mouth without profaning the name of God, unless he were, at the same time, actuated by a sincere and earnest affection of heart' (*Com. Ps*. 102.1-2).

As the last citation already indicates, he finds passages which alarm him. His response to the cry in Psalm 25, 'Remember, O Jehovah! thy tender mercies', is to say 'From this it appears…that David…had lost all sense of God's mercy; for he calls upon God to remember for him his favour, in such a manner as if he had already forgotten it' (*Com. Ps*. 25.6). In Psalm 39 he notes 'a kind of irony' in the petition 'O Jehovah! cause me to know my end'; it is 'not without anger and resentment that David speaks in this manner', and 'seeing he finds fault with God', he exceeds what is proper (*Com. Ps*. 39.4). The reference in Psalm 88 to 'the slain who lie in the grave, whom thou rememberest no more' he ascribes to a psalmist who 'spoke less advisedly than he ought to have done' and allowed 'unadvised words to escape from his lips' (*Com. Ps*. 88.5).

Just as he does in the chapter on prayer, however, he pleads extenuating circumstances:

> …the complaints of the people of God ought not to be judged of according to a perfect rule, because they proceed not from a settled and an undisturbed state of mind, but have always some excess arising from the impetuosity or vehemence of the affections at work in their minds. (*Com. Ps*. 89.47)

To return to the examples above, it appears to him from Ps. 25.6 'that David was grievously afflicted and tried', and from Ps. 39.4-6 'that David was transported by an improper and sinful excess of passion' and 'spoke under the influence of a distempered and troubled state of mind'. As for Ps. 88.5, he is sure the psalmist knew well enough 'that the dead are under the divine protection', but being 'as it were, so stunned and stupefied when sorrow overmastered him', he spoke unadvisedly 'in the first paroxysm of his grief'.

It is important to Calvin that the psalmists are quick to correct such faults themselves: 'There will occasionally escape from the lips of a saint, when he prays, some complaining exclamations which cannot be altogether justified, but he soon recalls himself to the exercise of believing supplication' (*Com. Ps*. 55.9). Thus while the psalmist who calls upon God to 'arise' and 'forget not the poor' in Ps. 10.12 has fallen into the very error he has just condemned in others, 'he proceeds at once to correct it, and resolutely struggles with himself, and restrains his mind from forming such conceptions of God, as would reflect dishonor upon his righteousness and glory' (*Com. Ps.* 10.12; he finds the correction in v. 14, 'Thou hast seen it; for thou considerest mischief...'). In Psalm 30, by crying 'Hear, O Jehovah! and have mercy upon me' (v. 10), David 'softens and corrects his former complaint; for it would have been absurd to expostulate with God like one who despaired of safety [as the psalmist had done in v. 9], and to leave off in this fretful temper' (*Com. Ps.* 30.10).

We may judge how keenly he feels the need for this self-correction by his eagerness to find examples of it. Having criticized David for finding fault with God in Ps. 39.4-6, he takes comfort that David implores God's mercy 'a little after, having corrected himself; for he does not continue to indulge in rash and inconsiderate lamentations, but lifting up his soul in the exercise of faith, he attains heavenly consolation' (*Com. Ps.* 39.6). By his own account, however, the last verse of the psalm 'indicates the feeling almost of despair' (*Com. Ps.* 39.13). In the course of his exposition of Psalm 89 he remarks that 'we shall afterwards see that the prophet, when he blesses God at the close of the psalm, affords a proof of tranquil submission, by which he corrects or qualifies his complaints' (*Com. Ps.* 89.38). But it takes a good deal of imagination to read 'tranquil submission' into v. 52, even if one were to accept that it is the last verse of the psalm rather than one of the conventional blessings which bring books 1 through 4 of the Psalter to a close. Calvin insists it is not a concluding blessing, but his counter-argument—'as if the language of praise and thanksgiving to God were not as suitable at the close of a psalm as at the opening of it'—misses the point entirely.[20]

b. *Four Matters of Particular Interest*
I turn now to several matters which receive particular attention in the commentary. All of them have to do with the means and ends of prayer. For convenience of presentation I have grouped them under four headings: praying for pardon, praying to motivate God, praying to motivate oneself, and praying for vengeance. Taken together they will serve to give a fully rounded view of Calvin's understanding of the prayer psalms. In many respects they will again show continuity with the 1559 revision of the chapter on prayer in *Institutes*. But they will also indicate that he had recognized features of prayer in the Psalter which he did not choose to mention in this chapter or recommend to his readers in his 1557 preface to the commentary.

1. *Praying for Pardon.* It comes as no surprise that Calvin is as emphatic about the need for repentance as he is in the chapter on prayer, and he puts it in almost identical language:

   20.   Although he does not regard any of these verses (Pss. 41.13 [Heb. 14], 72.19 [Heb. 20], 89.52 [Heb. 53], 106.48) as blessings which conclude a book, he acknowledges that 'some interpreters' say this of Ps. 89.52, and (in this case only) 'readily' grants it is true of the last words of the verse ('Amen and amen').

> It is indeed true, in general, that men pray in a wrong way, and in vain, unless they begin by seeking the forgiveness of their sins... The right and proper order of prayer therefore is, as I have said, to ask, at the very outset, that God would pardon our sins. (*Com. Ps.* 25.7)

And he is no less certain that the psalmists observed this order. Of David he asserts categorically that 'in his sickness, as in all his other adversities, David views the hand of God lifted up to punish him for his sins' (*Com. Ps.* 38.2).

At the same time he sees no reason to go out of his way to make a case for this. He is content to claim any allusion to guilt as support (e.g. Ps. 25.7), and, when he encounters a declaration of innocence (e.g. Ps. 7.8), to deny there is any contradiction: the psalmist is only comparing himself with his enemies, and maintaining 'not without cause, that, in respect of them, he was righteous' (*Com. Ps.* 7.8).[21] But if he finds no reference to guilt or innocence he is not likely to raise the subject at all. As a result, he passes without comment over the majority of the prayer psalms, never explaining why they make no issue of guilt or pardon at all.

But if he feels no need to justify his claim that the biblical saints 'always have begun with appeasing' God and that we will readily see this 'if we diligently ponder their prayers' (*Inst.* 3.20.9), he amply illustrates what he has in mind by the phrase 'diligently ponder'. Following what are no doubt well-established paths, he often finds a 'plea for the forgiveness of sins' implied where none is stated. Any reference to God's anger 'imports a tacit confession of sin', even in such phrases as 'Cast not away thy servant in thy wrath' (*Com. Ps.* 27.9) or 'Why hast thou cast us off forever? Why doth thy anger smoke against the flock of thy pastures?' (*Com. Ps.* 74.1; see also *Com. Ps.* 79.5; 102.10). In any reference to sackcloth 'we may perceive that in their mourning they were exercised to repentance', even in such phrases as 'thou hast loosed my sackcloth' (*Com. Ps.* 30.11) or 'when they were sick, my clothing was sackcloth' (*Com. Ps.* 35.13).

Even phrases such as 'Thou hast made us to turn back from the enemy' are taken to be acknowledgments 'that the fear by which they are now actuated was inflicted upon them as a punishment by God' (*Com. Ps.* 44.10). In one case, finding no sign of penitence at all, he argues (on the basis of the title and the phrase 'I have cried to the Lord' in v. 4) that a separate penitential prayer must have preceded the present psalm; on this assumption he can say, 'having acknowledged his sin before, he now takes into consideration only the merits of the present cause' (*Com. Ps.* 3.3).

A penitential reading of this sort seriously misconstrues the piety of the prayer psalms. Of the fifty or so examples of this genre represented in the Psalter, few even mention the psalmist's sin or guilt or plead for forgiveness, and there is only one (Ps. 51) in which this could be said to be the dominant theme.[22]

---

21. He had given the same, doubtless traditional, answer in *Inst.* 3.20.10 in a passage written for the 1539 edition. The psalmists are 'comparing themselves with their enemies', so 'it is no wonder if in this comparison they put forward their own righteousness and simplicity of heart in order that, from the equity of the cause itself, they might the more move the Lord to provide them with assistance'.

22. The count includes *Klagelieder* and two closely associated genres, *Danklieder* ('thank songs') and *Vertrauenspsalmen* ('psalms of confidence'). Apart from Ps. 51, pleas for forgiveness are joined with appeals of other kinds.

2. *Praying to Motivate God.* While he finds it to be no problem that 'the saints do not always beg forgiveness of sins in so many words' (*Inst.* 3.20.9), there are aspects of the psalms which do exercise him, and these will occupy us somewhat longer. The passages which elicit the most interesting and complex responses are those which suggest something 'we must not imagine' of God, namely, 'that he acts contrary to his real character, or that he has changed his purpose' (*Com. Ps.* 25.6). They suggest this by seeking in many different ways to move God to act or, occasionally, to withdraw.

Calvin understands all talk of moving God to be language of accommodation, and on this understanding he employs it himself. When he does so, he often introduces a parenthetical remark to alert the reader: 'The reason why God seems to take no notice of our afflictions is, because he would have us to awaken him by means of our prayers; for when he hears our requests (as if he began but then to be mindful of us), he stretches forth his powerful hand to help us' (*Com. Ps.* 9.18). But he does not always do this: 'The Holy Spirit, in dictating to the faithful this form of prayer, meant to testify that God is moved by such revilings to succor his people'; indeed, 'the more insolent our enemies are against us, the more is God incited to gird himself to aid us' (*Com. Ps.* 102.8); 'he is moved by the sight of our miseries to be merciful to us' (*Com. Ps.* 102.25).

It is easier to find passages like these, where Calvin speaks of God being moved by our troubles, than it is to find ones where he speaks of God being moved by our prayers. He appears to do so once in *Inst.* 3.20 (the chapter on prayer), when he writes, 'they put forward their own righteousness and simplicity of heart in order that, from the equity of the cause itself, they might the more move the Lord to provide them with assistance' (*Inst.* 3.20.10). But he uses variations on this language throughout the commentary also to describe what the psalmists are seeking to do, without implying that they actually effect it.

His reticence is understandable. In truth God cannot be motivated to change, for God is immutable and impassible. This is fundamental to his theological stance and his piety. If it were not so, prayer itself would be impossible, as he argues in the chapter on prayer: 'If [God] were not forever like himself, from his benefits a sufficiently firm reckoning could not be adduced to trust him and call upon him' (*Inst.* 3.20.26). In spite of his great sympathy for the psalmists, he is bound to see in all such attempts both a resistance to God's will, because they seek to move God, and a wavering faith, because they suppose God needs to be moved. They are therefore in conflict with his first and fourth rules for right prayer, to 'submit completely to God's will' and to pray in the 'sure hope that our prayer will be answered'.

Under the circumstances, we might have expected him to draw as little attention to this feature as possible, a strategy not uncommon among devout commentators.[23] Instead, he very often points the reader to it and explains what the psalmists are hoping to achieve by it. He describes them as adducing arguments, putting forth reasons, motives, and circumstances, complaining and expostulating, and employing

---

23.   Among recent commentators Weiser (1962) is an example, although few modern commentaries have much to say about this.

other means as well.[24] Their purpose, put most simply, is to obtain or elicit something from God.[25] More often he uses verbs which indicate how they expect to affect God: to win God over, rouse, change, influence, induce, incline, move, or hasten God.[26] And he frequently adds adverbs, to indicate they expect by these means to move God the more, the more readily, the more easily, the more quickly.[27]

Furthermore, he takes a quite remarkable interest in the various means the psalmists employ. Of some psalms he is content to say, as he does of Psalm 55, that they urge 'every consideration which could be supposed' (*Com. Ps.* 55 preface). But by the end of the commentary he has identified a large number of different means and devices, having given more attention to the psalmists' rhetoric of persuasion than most modern commentators. This is not the place to present a full account, so I shall be content with a summary overview.

One large set comprises the complaints against the psalmists' opponents, their malice and cruelty, their derision, that they act without cause, threaten extermination, and take encouragement from the psalmists' weakness, and the like. He recognizes that these are not simply cries of hurt. They have a rhetorical thrust: the point is 'to render them more hateful [or more odious] in the sight of God' (*Com. Ps.* 35.26 [and 5.9]). And he notices that the psalmists heighten the effect by making use of rhetorical devices such as repetition (*Com. Ps.* 5.9), metaphor (*Com. Ps.* 7.2) and question (*Com. Ps.* 10.13).

Another set comprises what could be termed self-referential complaints, for example, the greatness of the psalmists' misery, grief and distress, their poverty and need, that they are forsaken and have no one to help. These are not simply cries of hurt; the psalmists have a motive for dwelling upon such matters: they enhance the likelihood of a favorable hearing.

If one begins to read the psalms with an eye for their persuasive thrust, passages of this sort stand out immediately. Calvin goes on to identify many other types which are less often acknowledged. Among them are self-referential appeals which are not complaints but the opposite, something more like boasts. It is 'for no other reason but to induce God to continue his goodness towards him' that David calls God's attention to his own previous thankfulness (*Com. Ps.* 40.9). 'As a plea to induce God the more readily to have pity upon him' he proffers his own patience (as well as his humility and dejection; *Com. Ps.* 38.13, also v. 6). In another psalm he adduces two other reasons: 'his own gentleness towards his neighbors, and the

24. The terms Calvin employs are *argumentum, ratio, causa, circumstantia, querimonia* and *expostulatio*.

25. The verbs Calvin employs in this connection are *impetrare* (cf. Pss. 5 introduction; 5.11; 38.5; 40.16; 80 introduction; 83 introduction; 86.1); *invenire* (cf. Ps. 38.19); *elicere* (cf. Ps. 40.11).

26. The verbs Calvin employs are *conciliare* (cf. Pss. 5.4; 7.3; 9.1; 17.9; 27.7; 44.22; 59.4; 64.1; 69.20; 71.10; 74.1, 21; 79.9; 80.17; 86.2, 16; 89.51; 102.8; 140.1); *provocare* (cf. Pss. 5.9; 22.6, 11; 38.11; 40.9; 41.5; 44.1; 79.4; 83.4; 89.5); *flectere* (cf. Pss. 25.2; 27.9; 31.9; 38 introduction; 38.6; 74.20; 89.47); *inducere* (cf. Pss. 9.19; 27.9; 31.3); *inclinare* (cf. Pss. 38.13; 57.4; 64 introduction; 102.14); *movere* (cf. Pss. 55 introduction; 102.8); *permovere* (cf. Ps. 39.5; *Inst.* 3.20.10); *accelerare* (cf. Ps. 142.5).

27. The adverbs Calvin employs are *magis, plus, propensior, facilius, citius*.

trust which he reposed in God' (*Com. Ps.* 86.2). In Psalm 143 'as elsewhere' his plea is 'for in thee have I hoped', 'this being something by which, in a sense, we lay God under obligation to us' (*Com. Ps.* 143.8). In short, Calvin includes among the psalmists' persuasive rhetorical devices even their assertions of thankfulness, patience, trust and hope.

An argument of another sort David 'often adduces' is that others will benefit from his deliverance and be glad for it (*Com. Ps.* 40.16; cf. 5.11; 69.32). David phrases the same argument as a negative petition: 'let not them that wait for thee be ashamed in me' (*Com. Ps.* 69.6). He protests his innocence 'to induce God to show him favor', and 'to give his protestation greater weight, he uses a [self-]impreca-tion' (*Com. Ps.* 7.3). And he calls to mind God's former favors and contrasts them with the present (*Com. Ps.* 27.9), a line of argument employed elsewhere (*Com. Ps.* 44.1; 74.2; 80.8, 17; 83.9).

'As a plea for obtaining greater favour' David puts forward 'the long line of his ancestors, and the continual course of God's grace' (*Com. Ps.* 86.16). And 'although God stands in no need of our praises' (*Com. Ps.* 40.9), David opens one psalm with praise in order to conciliate God (*Com. Ps.* 9.1), in another calls attention to praises he had previously offered 'in order to elicit new favors' (*Com. Ps.* 40.11), and in another, 'to obtain a longer life', he 'draws an argument from praise', namely, that this is the purpose for which we are born and nourished (*Com. Ps.* 30.9).

Indeed the very vehemence of the psalmists' cries is meant to motivate God (*Com. Ps.* 27.7). 'O God of our salvation!' is one of many forms of address they employ 'to induce God to show them favour' (*Com. Ps.* 79.9). 'The object in view' in presenting God's liberality before him 'is, that he should not leave unfinished the work of his hands' (*Com. Ps.* 80.8). They appeal to the brevity of human life 'in order to excite God so much the more to pity' (*Com. Ps.* 39.5). 'The more effec-tually to induce God to listen to his prayer', one psalmist calls upon all the godly to join in the request for Zion's welfare (*Com. Ps.* 102.14).

I find the range and detail of these observations quite remarkable, and I have given only a sample. Whether we accept them all or not, it must be granted that he is attentive to an aspect of the prayer psalms which too often receives only cursory treatment. He is of course writing for an audience which shares his interest. Rheto-ric had a central place in the sixteenth-century world of letters, as historians of the period have emphasized.[28] It is nevertheless striking that he employs this kind of analysis so extensively, given his unyielding conviction that it is neither necessary nor possible to persuade God at all.

As he comments on these passages he does feel obliged, to be sure, to pause now and then to remind the reader of this. In response to the question 'Why do the wicked despise God?' he remarks, 'It is, indeed, superfluous to bring arguments

---

28.   Cf. Selinger 1984: 154: '...in the sixteenth century, rhetoric existed in a context that makes it intriguing as well as interesting to a historian. It existed in a world as conscious and self-con-scious about language as, I think, only the last decade of the twentieth century has been; it was a world of discourse about the significance of discourse, one in which attention to discourse was a conceptual lingua franca'. See also her comments on 'the fundamental significance of rhetoric in Renaissance humanism' (1984: 5-6).

before God, for the purpose of persuading him to grant us what we ask' (*Com. Ps.* 10.13). He assures us that 'God, indeed, does not need to receive information and incitement from us' (*Com. Ps.* 17.9), in response to the psalmist's complaint about 'the ungodly, who go about to destroy me'. And in reference to Ps. 54.3, 'for strangers are risen up against me, and the terrible ones have sought after my soul', he says sharply, 'There was no necessity for his informing God of a fact which was already known to him' (*Com. Ps.* 54.2).

When David, 'to move God to succour him...magnifies the greatness of his misery and grief by the number of his complaints', Calvin again reminds the reader that it is 'not that God needs arguments to persuade him' (*Com. Ps.* 31.9). When David invokes the argument that others will benefit, he cautions, 'not that it is necessary to allege reasons to persuade God' (*Com. Ps.* 40.16), and when David lays before God the danger that the faithful would otherwise be 'exceedingly discouraged', he adds, 'not that God has ever need of being put in mind of anything' (*Com. Ps.* 69.6).

Have the psalmists forgotten these self-evident truths? If they have, it is only for the moment; they know better. When the psalmist cries 'Forsake me not, O Lord my God, and be not far from me', Calvin assures us that 'David was, indeed, persuaded that God is always near to his servants, and that he delays not a single moment longer than is necessary' (*Com. Ps.* 38.21). Of another cry, 'Awake to hasten for my help, and behold', he says, 'Though David may use language of this description, suited to the infirmity of sense, we must not suppose him to have doubted before this time that his afflictions, his innocence, and his wrongs, were known to God' (*Com. Ps.* 59.4).

We may well ask how he knows this, but there is no doubt he thinks it important to offer this assurance to the reader. The assurance is often coupled with lines of argument I have mentioned before: the psalmists are distraught and acting under the pressure of the moment, the extreme trials they are experiencing are extenuating circumstances, and there are passages in which they admit their error and correct themselves.

It can hardly surprise us that this is the stance he takes. The sum of it is that prayers which take the form of God-persuading speech do not reflect the psalmists' strengths but their weaknesses, which we share. Far from admiring the psalmists for their boldness in seeking to motivate God, we ought to pity them that they are in this regard so much like ourselves.

If we are to admire them at all, it is because they hold nothing back: 'They are not ashamed to confess their infirmity, nor is it proper to conceal the doubts which arise in their minds' (*Com. Ps.* 38.21). It is not proper because, as 'we pour out our hearts before him', we must hold nothing back. Full self-disclosure in prayer is at the same time God's gracious invitation and an obligation God lays upon us; anything short of it is hypocrisy.

It is not, however, an end in itself, and there is only one right outcome: to keep our feelings under control and to submit to the divine will. 'If we are anxiously desirous of obtaining his assistance, we must subdue our passion, restrain our impatience, and keep our sorrows within due bounds, waiting until our afflictions call forth the exercise of his compassion, and excite him to manifest his grace in succouring us' (*Com. Ps.* 10.18).

The legitimate role of speech to persuade God exists within the bounds of the subtle and complex dynamics of prayer in an introspective mode. Our prayers may work a change in us while we are mistakenly seeking to effect a change in God. Having said that God still permits us to make use of arguments, even though they are superfluous, Calvin adds,

> It should always be observed, that the use of praying is, that God may be the witness of all our affections; not that they would otherwise be hidden from him, but when we pour out our hearts before him, our cares are hereby greatly lightened, and our confidence of obtaining our requests increases. (*Com. Ps.* 10.13)

God-persuading speech is of course full of anthropomorphic imagery, and he cautions his readers about it. Speaking of the line 'Why standest thou afar off, O Jehovah?' he remarks, 'It is in an improper sense, and by anthropathy, that the Psalmist speaks of God as standing far off'. He continues:

> Nothing can be hid from his eyes; but as God permits us to speak to him as we do to one another, these forms of expression do not contain any thing absurd, provided we understand them as applied to God, not in a strict sense, but only figuratively, according to the judgment which mere sense forms from the present appearance of things. (*Com. Ps.* 10.1)

Does he mean to say that the psalmists themselves understood they were speaking 'not in a strict sense, but only figuratively'? This is not entirely clear, although the passage I will cite next suggests this is what he has in mind. What is clear is that they employ this language to express thoughts which represent human infirmity rather than faith, 'the judgment which mere sense forms from the present appearance of things'. Here at least one might have supposed a charge of impropriety would stick, but Calvin evidently does not think so. He writes,

> Whenever the faithful put the question, 'How long wilt thou forget me, O Lord?' 'Awake, why sleepest thou, O Lord?' (Pss. xiii.1; xliv.23; lxxix.5,) they assuredly are not to be understood as attributing forgetfulness or sleep to him: they only lay before him the temptations which flesh and blood suggest to them in order to induce him speedily to succour them under the infirmity with which they are distressed. (*Com. Ps.* 89.39)

This puts a remarkably subtle spin on the psalmists' questions. They are not the assertive rhetorical challenges they appear to be; instead, they represent what the psalmists are *tempted* to think when they yield to the suggestions of 'flesh and blood'. They voice them only to 'lay before him the temptations' which troubled them so sorely. It is still the case that they do this to induce God to act speedily; the questions do not cease to be God-persuading speech. But a question laid before God as a 'temptation' is quite different from a question put to God directly and rhetorically.

At this point Calvin sees what he expects to see, what he wishes to see. The psalmists' straightforward questions have been so overlaid with supposition they are no longer recognizable. Persuasive speech in the psalms has lost its bite, and taken on a markedly indirect, submissive, and introspective character; it has become part of the 'unburdening' process that Calvin regards as one of the chief functions of prayer. Of Ps. 38.21, for example, he says, 'it is not at all wonderful that the saints, when they unburden themselves of their cares and sorrows into the bosom of God, should make their requests in language according to the feeling of the flesh' (*Com. Ps.* 38.21).

3. *Praying to Motivate Oneself.* The declaration 'My shield is in God, who saves the upright in heart' (Ps. 7.10) is not phrased as direct address to God. It is possible, therefore, to read it as an aside in which the psalmist addresses himself. Calvin has declarations of this sort in mind when he writes in the chapter on prayer, 'Indeed, we may note this in the Psalms: that if the thread of prayer were broken, transition is sometimes made to God's power, sometimes to his goodness, sometimes to the faithfulness of his promises'. He feels these sometimes abrupt transitions interrupt the flow of prayer, but believes they are necessary for our sakes: 'It might seem that David, by inserting these statements inopportunely, mutilates his prayers, but believers know by use and experience that ardor burns low unless they supply new fuel' (*Inst.* 3.20.13).

Psalm 7.10 and other passages like it are not necessarily self-address just because they are not formally addressed to God; they may be spoken aloud (and in prayer) for God's benefit rather than the psalmist's. Instead of supposing that they spring from a feeling 'that ardor burns low', we could, for example, read them as forthright and self-assured declarations of confidence, advanced precisely as a claim upon God's reputation and patronage. That would astound Calvin, for he expects prayer to be a faith-struggle with the carnal and depraved self; it is only with great difficulty that believers rise to ardor and confidence.

As he reads the passage, therefore, Calvin does not question that the psalmist is speaking the words self-reflectively, and intends them to be self-assuring. He tells his readers to expect this frequently in the psalms. 'It is not wonderful', he writes, 'that David often mingles meditations with his prayers, thereby to inspire himself with true confidence'. And he spells out what David is doing here: 'David, therefore, in order to continue in prayer with the same ardour of devotion and affection with which he commenced, brings to his recollection some of the most common truths of religion, and by this means fosters and invigorates his faith' (*Com. Ps.* 7.10). He finds these meditations in an extraordinary variety of passages, many of them in fact addressed directly to God and so quite different in form from a passage like Ps. 7.10. The question put in Ps. 10.1, 'Why standest thou afar off, O Jehovah? and winkest at seasonable times in trouble?', is a particularly helpful example because it is so like passages which he identifies as God-motivating speech. He first assures us that David is speaking 'through the infirmity of sense'; God is never 'afar off'. But his next point comes as something of a surprise: he 'speaks thus not so much in the way of complaining, as to encourage himself in the confidence of obtaining what he desired' (*Com. Ps.* 10.1).

How can such a question raise the level of the psalmist's confidence? The process he has in mind is not well described in his exposition of Ps. 10.1, but he elaborates it in many other passages. The assumption is that they are putting the questions to themselves, not to God, and providing their own answers. By dividing a verse rather awkwardly into a question and an answer, thus translating 'O Lord! [Q.] where are thy former mercies? [A.] thou hast sworn to David in thy truth', he is able to find one passage where they occur together. Here 'the prophet encourages himself, by calling to remembrance God's former benefits, as if his reasoning were that God can never be unlike himself, and that therefore the goodness which he manifested in old time to the fathers cannot come to an end' (*Com. Ps.* 89.49).

For the most part, however, Calvin must deal with passages in which only the questions appear. The answers he must supply himself, on the psalmists' behalf, and he does not hesitate to do so. When the question is put, 'Shall the throne of iniquities have fellowship with thee, framing molestation for law?', he spells out the psalmist's reasoning for us: he 'again derives an argument for confidence from the nature of God, it being impossible that he should show favour to the wicked, or sanction their evil devices' (*Com. Ps.* 94.20). He finds the same line of reasoning behind the question 'Why do the wicked despise God? He saith in his heart, Thou wilt not require it'; as he explains, 'Thus David, in the present passage, by setting before himself how unreasonable and intolerable it would be for the wicked to be allowed to despise God according to their pleasure, thinking he will never bring them to account, was led to cherish the hope of deliverance from his calamities' (*Com. Ps.* 10.13).

I have already mentioned a psalm passage which Calvin reads as God-persuading speech and self-persuading speech at the same time. The last citation is another example. The question 'Why do the wicked despise God? He saith in his heart, Thou wilt not require it' is also identified as an argument to motivate God; in fact it elicits the comment that God 'permits us to make use of them', as we have noted. Many other passages serve double-duty, so to speak, in this same way, among them the extended complaints about 'my enemies' in Pss. 41.5-9 and 71.10-11 (*Com. Ps.* 41.5; 71.10); the self-complaint 'But I am a worm, and not a man' (*Com. Ps.* 22.6); the petitions to be kept 'from the face of the ungodly' (*Com. Ps.* 17.9) and to 'remember thy congregation which thou hast possessed of old' (*Com. Ps.* 74.2); the titles 'God of vengeance' and 'Judge of the earth' (*Com. Ps.* 94.1); and the declarations 'I will tell of thy marvelous works' (*Com. Ps.* 9.1), 'For thou art not a God that hath pleasure in wickedness' (*Com. Ps.* 5.4), 'thou hast been my strength' (*Com. Ps.* 27.9) and 'For thy name's sake thou wilt lead and guide me' (*Com. Ps.* 31.3).

It is easy enough to see how these categories overlap in his mind. He understands both to be implicit arguments, and any motive or argument which could be supposed to move God must surely suffice to assure the psalmist also. Commenting on the phrase 'thou hast been my strength', he remarks, 'by recalling to mind God's former favours, he encourages himself to hope for more, and by this argument he moves God to continue his help, and not to leave his work imperfect' (*Com. Ps.* 27.9). He writes similarly of the phrase 'remember thy congregation': 'These benefits which they had received from God they set before themselves as an encouragement to their trusting in him, and they recount them before him, the benefactor who bestowed them, as an argument with him not to forsake the work of his own hands' (*Com. Ps.* 74.2).

4. *Praying for Vengeance*. I turn now to the passages which Calvin does not mention at all in his chapter on prayer in the *Institutes*, the petitions for the death and destruction of the enemy, for example, 'Let death seize upon them, let them descend alive into the grave: for wickedness is in their dwelling, and in the midst of them' (*Com. Ps.* 55.15). In this case there is a hint that he would prefer to say as little as possible. Relatively early in the commentary he writes, 'Here again occurs the difficult question about praying for vengeance, which, however, I shall dispatch in few words, as I have discussed it elsewhere' (*Com. Ps.* 28.4).[29] But he keeps coming back to it, and he involves himself in an extended exposition whenever such a petition appears.

'David's example...must not be alleged by those who are driven by their own intemperate passion to seek vengeance' (*Com. Ps.* 28.4). This is the point he makes repeatedly, and it seems to be the central focus of his concern: 'We have already frequently spoken of the feelings with which David uttered these imprecations, and it is necessary here again to refresh our memories on the subject, lest any man, when giving loose reins to his passions, should allege the example of David in palliation or excuse' (*Com. Ps.* 40.14). He 'affords no precedent to such as resent private injuries by vending curses on those who have inflicted them' (*Com. Ps.* 59.5). He emphasizes this because he regards it as

> unquestionable, that if the flesh move us to seek revenge, the desire is wicked in the sight of God. He not only forbids us to imprecate evil upon our enemies in revenge for private injuries, but it cannot be otherwise than that all those desires which spring from hatred must be disordered. (*Com. Ps.* 28.4)

The effect of this is to make the decisive issue once again how well mind and will succeed in subduing involuntary thoughts and feelings. Prayers for vengeance are licit only if motives and feelings are entirely pure:

> Before a man can, therefore, denounce vengeance against the wicked, he must first shake himself free from all improper feelings in his own mind. In the second place, prudence must be exercised, that the heinousness of the evils which offend us drive us not to intemperate zeal, which happened even to Christ's disciples, when they desired that fire might be brought from heaven to consume those who refused to entertain their Master (Luke ix.54). (*Com. Ps.* 28.4)

The critical locus is the inner self, as it was in the case of self-motivating and God-motivating speech. What we would expect him to say next is that just as the

---

29. I have not found a prior reference in the commentary to *praying* for vengeance, although he does speak several times of the *taking* of vengeance (cf. the extended passage at *Com. Ps.* 18.47 which distinguishes licit from illicit vengeance). The latter is discussed at length in *Inst.* 4.20.17-19 (almost entirely text composed for the 1539 edition).

psalmists are not exempt from human infirmity in any other respect, so they are not here. Their prayers for vengeance are a complex mixture of faith and doubt, holy zeal and personal revenge, partly founded in a proper and commendable trust in God's promise of justice, but partly motivated as well by the unruly passions to which all flesh is heir.

In fact he says no such thing. He tells us instead that 'David, being free from every evil passion, and likewise endued with the spirit of discretion and judgment, pleads here not so much his own cause as the cause of God' (*Com. Ps.* 28.4), that he

> pleads not simply his own cause, nor utters rashly the dictates of passion, nor with unadvised zeal desires the destruction of his enemies; but under the guidance of the Holy Spirit he entertains and expresses against the reprobate such desires as were characterized by great moderation, and which were far removed from the spirit of those who are impelled either by desire of revenge or hatred, or some other inordinate emotion of the flesh. (*Com. Ps.* 35.4)

'Being free from every evil passion', David may even pray, 'raise me up, and I will recompense them'. But in this case an additional

> two things are to be taken into account: First, David was not as one of the common people, but a king appointed by God, and invested with authority; and, secondly, it is not from an impulse of the flesh, but in virtue of the nature of his office, that he is led to denounce against his enemies the punishment which they had merited. (*Com. Ps.* 41.10)

Few are in that position, and it is not given to many to pray so rightly:

> I acknowledge, indeed, that not a few, while they pretend a similar confidence and hope, nevertheless, recklessly rush beyond the bounds of temperance and moderation. But that which David beheld by the unclouded eye of faith, he also uttered with a zeal becoming a sound mind; for having devoted himself to the cultivation of piety, and being protected by the hand of God, he was aware that the day was approaching when his enemies would meet with merited punishment. (*Com. Ps.* 109.20)

For the most part, 'Even those who are naturally inclined to gentleness and humanity, who desire to do good to all men, and wish to hurt nobody, whenever they are provoked, burst forth into a revengeful mood, carried away by a blind impetuosity' and 'begin to howl with the wolves' (*Com. Ps.* 17.4). Therefore,

> it becomes us to bear in mind what I have previously stated, that the man who would offer up such a prayer as this in a right manner, must be under the influence of zeal for the public welfare; so that, by the wrongs done to himself personally, he may not suffer his carnal affections to be excited... (*Com. Ps.* 79.6)

The claims for David, however, are made without qualification, and seem even to heighten as the commentary progresses. Speaking of the petition I cited at the beginning of this section, he writes, 'In imprecating this curse he was not influenced by *any* bad feeling towards them, and must be understood as speaking not in his own cause but in that of God, and under the immediate guidance of his Spirit'

(*Com. Ps.* 55.15 [emphasis added]). He finds in Psalm 109 a 'David, who, free of *all* inordinate passion, breathed forth his prayers under the influence of the Holy Spirit' (*Com. Ps.* 109.6 [emphasis added]); 'in this instance God elevated his spirit above *all* earthly considerations, stript him of *all* malice, and delivered him from the influence of turbulent passions, so that he might, with holy calmness and spiritual wisdom, doom the reprobate and castaway to destruction' (*Com. Ps.* 109.19 [emphasis added]).

I find this an extraordinary departure from his usual approach to the psalms.[30] David has taken on the role of Christ the Vindicator, and this not as a type of the Divine King to come, but in his own historical office as king of Israel. It is no wonder he wants to safeguard this, 'that no one may rashly take for an example what David here spoke by the special influence of the Holy Spirit' (*Com. Ps.* 109.19). But is it possible that others, also 'appointed by God, and invested with authority', and acting 'not from an impulse of the flesh, but in virtue of the nature of [their] office', may likewise be 'led to denounce against [their] enemies the punishment which they had merited'? I should like to keep this question in mind when we turn in the third part of this study to the preface he wrote for the commentary in July 1557.

c. *From the Commentary to the Chapter on Prayer*

By the time Calvin had completed the manuscript for the commentary, if not before, he had worked out the stance toward the prayer psalms he would assume as he revised the chapter on prayer. The rules by which the psalms are explicitly judged in the chapter are already implicit in the commentary. The same lines of defense are mounted on the psalmists' behalf. The same assumption is made about their unfailingly penitential attitude. And the readers' attention is directed primarily to their inner life and internal struggles.

There are nevertheless differences, although they are primarily matters of emphasis. Coming to the commentary from the chapter on prayer, one is surprised by the attention given to the psalmists' persuasive rhetoric. If one read only the chapter on prayer one would never know how much this interested him. There he seems to emphasize his disapproval by the very terms he uses to describe it, preferring 'expostulate with God' and the like to the relatively mild '(seek) to move God' (the latter appears only once in the chapter, *Inst.* 3.20.10).

Proceeding the other way, from the commentary to the chapter on prayer, one is surprised by the sharpness of his criticism. If one read only the commentary one would not feel the full force of his unease.[31] On the whole he handles the psalmists more gently and graciously there, explaining their failures and excesses rather than rebuking them, at times extending the argument to shield them from criticism. In

---

30. Brevard Childs is generally approving of Calvin's handling of the imprecatory psalms, but remarks, 'However, would it not have been more theologically consistent for him to have recognized also the elements of personal anger and frustration...rather than to have pictured David, the psalmist, as an Old Testament saint with zeal only for God's kingdom?' (1989: 263).

31. Compare, for example, his comments on Ps. 39.13 in *Inst.* 3.20.16 with those in the commentary.

the chapter on prayer the disquiet lies nearer the surface; although he still does not allow that they did so willfully, he makes it clear they often went too far and stood in need of forgiveness.

The two works are quite different in genre, and this no doubt accounts for much of the difference in emphasis. But it may also be the case that after 1557 some of his earlier misgivings had begun to reassert themselves; it was never as easy for him to approve David as he wished it to be.

4. *Appropriating Psalter Piety*

As I have already suggested, Calvin's appropriation of the piety of David and the psalms is no less revealing than his exposition of it. The form this appropriation takes is set out with unusual clarity in the letter he wrote in July 1557, as a preface to his commentary on the book of Psalms.

a. *The Letter to his Readers*

It is particularly this preface, 'John Calvin to the godly readers sends greeting', which shows how personally he had come to be involved with the psalms. It contains one of the few autobiographical passages in all his theological writings, and it turns out to be an interweaving of his life story with the psalms and experiences of David. He has come to feel that his own life experience has made him a particularly sensitive interpreter. The readers will find, 'if I mistake not, that when I unfold the inmost feelings of David and others, I discourse on them no otherwise than as on things well known to me'. His own struggles and conflicts have been 'no small help to me in understanding the Psalms, with the result that I did not journey as it were in an unknown region' (Parker 1965: 23).

We therefore need no special warrant for relating Calvin's response to the Psalter to his own life experience. He has given thought to the connection himself, and even called his readers' attention to it. If I now supplement what he himself reports, it is to note that he is writing the preface itself at a particularly interesting moment in his life—a time when, at the age of forty-eight and after years of struggle, conflict and uncertainty, his position and that of his partisans in Geneva seemed at last to be secure.

Several events had combined to bring this about. Four years earlier a convicted Spanish heretic had entered Geneva in disguise and had been arrested, tried, and burned at the stake. The affair had been painful for Calvin, who had wanted him beheaded instead, but it had turned the elections decidedly in his favor. A year and a half after this, a fairly harmless civil disturbance had been used as a pretext by Calvin's supporters to drive members of the opposition out of the city; one did not escape in time, and was beheaded. Meanwhile, a flood of French Protestant refugees had been pouring into Geneva, severely taxing its space and resources, but adding substantially to the number of Calvin's supporters. The Calvin party moved quickly to consolidate its position by obtaining admission to citizenship for a larger and larger number of these refugees, thereby providing itself with a secure majority.

By the time Calvin gave his lectures on the book of Psalms he was assured that his supporters would win the general elections and be in the majority in the city councils. His long controversy with the magistrates over the Church's right to excommunicate had finally been resolved in his favor. While persons in such a position are likely to find a certain satisfaction in what they have achieved, they are also likely to find themselves reflecting on the checkered path which led to it, gathering the disparate moments of their past into the kind of self-portrait they can both believe and accept, and perhaps even trust to the world.

As Calvin pictures himself in the preface he falls far short of David's virtues. At the same time he sees himself very much like David, given to outbursts and often overwhelmed by strong emotions. And also like David he has been harassed and frustrated by enemies, who suffered at his hands only because they were impossibly stubborn and intractable. The tone is hardly conciliatory; the pain of their enmity still rankles. But he finds in David a model and a comfort, his own nearest counterpart in the Bible.

b. *Two Modes of Appropriation*

When we turn to the preface to see what effective use he makes of the psalms, we find him developing not one but two trajectories, relating the psalms to himself and his own experience in two quite different ways. The first cannot be missed, for he refers to it explicitly, describes it in detail and urges his readers to share it. The second is more easily overlooked, for he simply models it and applies it to himself.

One certainly reflects the way he sees himself as a person, that is, as one who shares all the common human frailties. The other seems to reflect his perception of himself as a public figure, divinely appointed to a task he had not sought and would never have chosen. They are strikingly different in tone, but to a remarkable degree both center in the affective aspect of life and how it must be managed, an indication once again that this is one of the central issues the psalms raise for him.

1. *As a Mirror of the Soul*. When Calvin says he is 'wont to call this book, not without cause, "The Anatomy of all the parts of the soul"', he is speaking of the use which is accessible to everyone, 'for not an affection will a man find in himself, an image of which is not reflected in this glass' (Parker 1965: 16). The passage is often cited, the image portrayed in charming and delightful colors. What Calvin has in mind is considerably more somber, for he continues,

> Nay, all the griefs, sorrows, fears, misgivings, hopes, cares, anxieties, in short, all the troublesome emotions with which the minds of men are wont to be agitated, the Holy Spirit has here pictured to the life. The other scriptures contain the commands which God enjoined His servants to bear to us. But here are prophets themselves talking with God, because they lay bare all their inmost thoughts, invite or hale every one of us to examine himself in particular, lest aught of the many infirmities to which we are liable, or of the many vices with which we are beset should remain hidden. (Parker 1965: 16)

To be sure, the picture he gives of the book of Psalms is not wholly negative; he finds 'faith, patience, fervor, zeal and uprightness' represented there as well. But as this passage shows, and as we have come now to expect, what makes the Psalter such a 'rare and surpassing benefit' for us is its capacity to reflect back to us the thoughts and feelings which vex and trouble us, and even beset us as infirmities and vices. By showing us our inner selves and helping us to recognize what is there, the psalms invite us to self-examination and cleanse us 'from hypocrisy, that most noisome pest'. Even though it sometimes happens that the psalmists' faith is 'not so active as were to be wished' (Parker 1965: 17), they at least 'lay bare all their inmost thoughts' when they talk to God (Parker 1965: 16). Whatever their failings, they speak with astonishing honesty and candor, and do not hide their inmost feelings as (he implies) he and his readers are likely to do.

This essentially purgative use of the psalms provides a counterbalance to Calvin's first rule of right prayer, which would seem to forbid any such outpouring of troublesome thoughts and feelings out of regard for God's holiness and awesome majesty.[32] Pent-up emotions and vexatious thoughts can find an outlet in prayer, and the psalms provide both a warrant and a vehicle for their release. They show us that we are not alone; the prophets and saints were troubled as we are. If even David was caught up in turbulent emotions, we must not be surprised to find that we are also. But above all, as the metaphor of the mirror suggests, the psalms help us to see and recognize ourselves. They stand apart from us, and so they provide the distancing which self-recognition requires.

Self-awareness is not an end in itself, however, nor is it enough to be sincere and open about whatever it is we think and feel, even if this may sometimes be as far as the psalms can take us. Sincerity of this sort rises above hypocrisy, but it still falls well short of what is pleasing and acceptable to God. It would be loathsome to be satisfied with ourselves as we are. Self-recognition should show us how much we need God's grace, prompt us to self-examination and repentance, move us to hearken to 'the other scriptures' which bear to us the commands of God, and make us receptive to the teachings of the Spirit, sent by God 'to tell us what is right and temper our emotions'.

2. *As a Model and Warrant for Dealing with the Enemy*. A quite different use appears when Calvin's self-identification with David leads him to associate his own enemies with David's, and his response to them with the cries against the enemy in the Psalms. Here he thinks of himself as agitated by troublesome people rather than troublesome thoughts and feelings, and as striving against external enemies rather than internal infirmities and vices. The ethos is no longer one of self-examination and humble repentance but of complaint, conflict and combat. Readers who benefit by his commentary should be assured, he says,

> that by the ordinary experience of conflicts with which the Lord has exercised me,
> I have been in no ordinary degree assisted, not only in adapting to my immediate
> use whatever of doctrine I was permitted to draw from hence, but also in that it

---

32.   That the first rule does not forbid this Calvin makes clear as he sets out the rule: 'Now I do not here require the mind to be so detached as never to be pricked or gnawed by vexations, since, on the contrary, great anxiety should kindle in us the desire to pray' (*Inst.* 3.20.4).

opened to me a more ready way towards understanding the purpose of each of the writers of the Psalms. And as David holds the chief place among them, it was no small help to me in obtaining a fuller understanding of the complaints he makes of the inward mischiefs of the church, that I had suffered the same things which he deplores, or similar to them, from enemies of the church who were of her own household. (Parker 1965: 18)

Indeed he feels that David's experience is offered to him as a model: '...so that I knew the more assuredly that whatsoever that most illustrious prince and prophet endured, was held out to me for an ensample' (Parker 1965: 18).

As he proceeds his account begins to take on the sharp invective of the plaint psalms. He describes himself as 'racked by the malignity of those who ceased not to assail myself and my ministry with venomous slanders' (Parker 1965: 21). He speaks scathingly of those who opposed him:

> For five whole years I had to fight without ceasing to preserve order, since forward men were furnished with overgrown influence, and some too of the common people, seduced by the enticements they held out to them, sought to obtain the power of doing what they pleased without control... Many, too, through poverty and hunger, or insatiable ambition, or a vile lust of gain, became so mad, that by throwing everything into confusion, they would rather destroy themselves and us, than continue in a state of order. (Parker 1965: 21)

And he justifies the violent outcome: 'Nor, to such a pass had they come, was there any other way of putting a stop to their wicked machinations, than in the shameful slaughter of them', though this was "indeed a mournful sight". He would rather they had listened to "wholesome counsels"' (Parker 1965: 21).

c. *Putting the Two Together*
This is the person who believes that even those racked with terrible pain ought to submit humbly and without complaining to what God has ordained. The disparity is sharpened by his well-known reluctance to share with others this prerogative for complaining, well illustrated by an incident in January 1546, when a certain Pierre Ameaux, a member of the highest of the city councils, complained to a private gathering in his home that Calvin was nothing but a wicked man, a Picard[33] who preached false doctrine. As François Wendel recounts the episode,

> The Magistrates offered to make the culprit beg Calvin's pardon on bended knees before the Council of the Two Hundred, but Calvin found this an insufficient reparation, and declared that he would not go up into a pulpit again until they had given him satisfaction. The case was then heard over again, and on April 8th Ameaux was sentenced to walk all round the town, dressed only in his shirt, bareheaded and carrying a lighted torch in his hand, and after that to present himself before the tribunal and cry to God for mercy... A pastor of the countryside dared to criticize Calvin's attitude in this affair: he was immediately unfrocked. (Wendel 1963: 86)

---

33. Calvin was born in Noyon, a cathedral town in Picardy (a province north of Paris), but the term 'Picard' had insulting connotations of the sort regional designations often acquire.

Calvin was understandably sensitive to Ameaux's charge that he preached false doctrine, for it challenged the very basis of his authority in Geneva, which rested less on his formal status (he held no civic office) than on his reputation as a biblical scholar and theologian. Even so, his response seems spiteful, a vindictive demand for personal satisfaction.

Would he have conceded this himself? Two passages we have already cited from the commentary suggest he may have been ready to do so now, looking back on the incident after some eleven years. He finds it to be 'unquestionable' that, 'if the flesh move us to seek revenge, the desire is wicked in the sight of God', and God expressly forbids it (*Com. Ps.* 28.4). At the same time he knows that

> even those who are naturally inclined to gentleness and humanity, who desire to do good to all men, and wish to hurt nobody, whenever they are provoked, burst forth into a revengeful mood, carried away by a blind impetuosity; especially when we see all right and equity overthrown, the confusion so blinds us, that we begin to howl with the wolves. (*Com. Ps.* 17.4)

The shift to 'we' suggests he is speaking here of his own experience, and the passage sounds almost like an apology for the way he had handled incidents just like this one. In fact many of his expositions on vengeance in the commentary have this almost-autobiographical and apologetic cast.

Whatever regret he may have come to feel about this affair, however, he does not appear to be at all inhibited by self-doubt when he denounces his opponents in the preface to the commentary. It is troubling to recall that in this one regard he finds no self-doubt in David either, or any reason for it, for there is no fault at all to be found in him. When David hurls invectives at his enemies and prays that they may be humiliated or worse, he is acting out of righteous indignation and holy zeal, not out of personal rancor or enmity. He is defending not himself but his office as prince and prophet, and it is necessary and proper that he should do so. His opponents have set themselves against God's sovereign will and the authority God has bestowed upon him, so they are not his personal enemies but the enemies of God.

If he finds this distinction important for a proper understanding of David's motives, he may well think it relevant to his own. The preface itself suggests that he is in fact thinking along these lines. He wants it clearly understood that his present position in Geneva owes nothing to personal ambition; he is there only because others had prevailed upon him. Having first come to Geneva quite by accident he had not wanted to remain there, and after the city council had banished and forcibly expelled him he had not wished to return. This insistent separation of office and person, duty and personal preference, also gives him leave to threaten to withdraw his services if his demands are not met, just as he refused to preach until the magistrates agreed to take harsher action against Ameaux.

If this prerogative, and the particular appropriation of psalm piety which accompanies it, attaches to the office rather than the person, we can understand why he does not propose it for general use. The plaint psalms provide no general warrant for persons to complain about each other, and no license at all to complain about those whom God has set in authority over them. A special warrant is involved, which has its analog in the divine realm. Just as God may bring complaints against us, but we must learn not to complain against God even in our hearts, so Calvin may assail his opponents, but they may not speak against him even in their homes. The same principle applies to the determination of need. As God does not ask us what we need, knowing better than we do what is good for us, so kings, pastors and magistrates are required to care wisely for the poor, but they are not obliged to listen patiently to all their grievances.

The warrant is, however, balanced by an obligation which also has its analog in the divine realm, in this case Calvin's understanding of God's 'wrath'. Just as God, in punishing us, appears to us to be enraged, but there 'is no such emotion in God', the anger existing solely in 'the perception and feeling of the sinner who is punished', so those who by virtue of their divinely appointed office judge, censure and rebuke others must rise above all such passions as hurt, anger and resentment.

In this respect the two rather different uses he makes of psalm piety may be viewed as complementary. The first provides a means for overcoming the vexing and involuntary thoughts and emotions which beset us. The second provides a model for the legitimate exercise of authority in times of conflict, a circumstance in which these personal feelings must be overcome. If they are not equally applicable to everyone, it is because not all persons are responsible to exercise authority.

In another respect, however, the two uses diverge rather than engage. One recognizes turbulent emotions in David and the other psalmists, which they and all believers must identify in themselves and continually strive to overcome. The other takes as its model prayers of David for which it is claimed that all such improper personal feelings have in fact been overcome.

Why does he go to such remarkable lengths to justify David's prayers for vengeance? As we have seen, he makes the extraordinary claim in his exposition of Psalm 109 that 'God elevated his spirit above all earthly considerations, stript him of all malice, and delivered him from the influence of turbulent passion, so that he might, with holy calmness and spiritual wisdom, doom the reprobate and castaway to destruction' (*Com. Ps*. 109.19). Is this wholly because he sees in David a type of Christ, or is he hinting something of the same for himself and others who oppose the enemies of God and his Church?

Although he would certainly not claim for himself all that he claims for David, he may well consider the difference between himself and David to be one of degree rather than kind. He is, after all, somehow able to recognize in this divinely enabled prince and prophet 'free from every evil passion' the same David who is 'affected by disquietude and trouble' and 'not altogether exempted from human infirmity' (*Com. Ps*. 38.10). We are left with the impression that the thoughts and emotions which troubled David as a person did not intrude when he was empowered by the Spirit to act against the enemies of God and in defense of his office, and if we allow that his claims for himself would be far less categorical, it is at least possible to read the account he gives of himself in the preface in very much the same way.

Would the diagnostic use of the psalms as an 'anatomy of the soul' at least serve as a counterbalance and restraint to this? I think it possible, but the 'anatomy' can be employed in so many ways this is not a foregone conclusion. We could imagine it leading him to recognize the role personal feelings played even in his dealings with the 'enemies of God', at least tempering the rather frightening self-confidence he brings to the task. But we could also imagine it having the opposite effect, leading him to feel that any self-doubts and anxieties he may have about these dealings were themselves the 'vexing and troublesome emotions' he must struggle to overcome.

5. *Recognizing the Piety of the Prayer Psalms*

The basic hermeneutical move which allowed Calvin to bring together so easily his theological conviction and his historical interest succeeded rather too well, for it effectively silenced the prayer psalms as witnesses to their own intention. It is not that the psalms offered no resistance; we have noted on more than one occasion that he was obliged to reach rather far to make his exposition appear reasonable.[34] To this point, however, I have not provided a summary overview of their own implicit self-understanding because I have wanted to present Calvin's view as clearly and faithfully as possible. I must now sketch this self-understanding at least briefly to illustrate how very different their piety is from Calvin's representation of it.

My account will differ considerably from what one would find in those works which have come to be regarded as more or less standard treatments of the subject; in my judgment they share too many of Calvin's preconceptions to be entirely reliable guides.[35] It will differ as well from the views of a number of scholars whose

34. As one would expect, when modern scholars find the psalms resisting their own sense of what psalm piety ought to be they do much the same. Kraus (1986: 137), sharing Calvin's reluctance to accept that the psalmists ever willfully reproached God, could only bring himself to say that the 'pressing questions, "Why?", "How long?"...*often border on being* reproaches and complaints against God' (emphasis added). Ringgren (1963: 27) wrote that 'The main concern in the Psalms is not the welfare of the psalmist, but the glory of God'—a position much like Calvin's—and justified it by the following line of reasoning: 'An important feature of the religion of the Psalms is its theocentric or God-centered character. It is God and not man who is the focus of the psalmist's interest. This does not mean that human concerns are ignored, but they are, for the most part, subordinated to divine purposes. The theocentric attitude is not at all points consistently affirmed. Sometimes it must assert itself in competition with an anthropocentric or man-centered attitude. But a strong theocentric tendency is nonetheless present, *even if at times it can only be detected by reading between the lines*' (emphasis added). It would be easy to multiply examples, but all too often the psalms' resistance is simply ignored: Kraus (1986: 127) simply asserts that 'in the prayers of the national community' the 'question of the "why" of the historical catastrophe is answered in the assumption of the divine judgment' when in fact a penitential stance is not at all typical of these psalms.

35. A representative sampling can be found in the work of three prominent scholars: Artur Weiser (1962), Claus Westermann (1981, 1982 [esp. Part V, 'The Response'], 1989), and Hans-Joachim Kraus (1986, 1988, 1989). While there are significant differences among them, the audiences they address are expected to identify readily with the essential dynamics of psalm piety, even it if they find biblical Israel's cultic practices and this-worldly orientation foreign to their own experience. Issues of piety are Weiser's central concern; in the course of his exposition the psalms are appropriated for and sometimes corrected by a Christian piety in the tradition of the reformers. Kraus, for all his frequent references to Luther and Calvin, has much less to say about psalmic

work has been moving in somewhat the same direction as my own.[36] I do not represent it, therefore, as the consensus of biblical scholarship at the present time—there is none—and I will not attempt here to provide detailed support from the biblical text. I am content to reserve that for a future study, building upon the groundwork I am now laying down. Before I begin, however, it may be useful to explain what I have in mind by the word piety when I am representing my own approach to the Psalter rather than Calvin's.

When I speak of a piety I refer to shared perceptions of, attitudes toward, and responses to the divine. I say shared, because it is piety as a social-religious phenomenon I have in mind. In the Psalter we are dealing with a shared piety; the conventional language of the psalms assures us of that. I regard perceptions, attitudes and responses as focal concerns because they are essential to the dynamics of a living piety, and I link them together because they interact. This interaction is well represented in prayer, so we should be able to discern it in the Psalter.

Prayer is only one manifestation of a piety, to be sure, but it can be particularly revealing. When those who share a particular piety engage in prayer, they do so with a common understanding, often quite comprehensive, about what they may and indeed ought to say in prayer and what they must not say. They share a sense of how they may expect God to deal with them, and how they may in turn expect to deal with God. Implicit understandings of this sort are best discerned in the prayers themselves; they give us more direct access to the functioning dynamics of a living piety than anything people may say about prayer to themselves or to others.[37]

---

prayer and the dynamics of psalm piety; he gives his attention primarily to other matters, although he clearly stands in the same tradition. When he comes to write of the meaning of the psalms for the Church, however, he often finds the plaint psalms addressing the Church's social conscience, as does Westermann. Indeed Westermann writes as an advocate of the biblical lament tradition on the ground that it gives suffering a legitimate voice, and he mourns its loss in the Church. Nevertheless his position is not as much a departure as some have made it out to be; within his larger scheme lament is structurally subordinated to praise. To effect this he follows a path taken also by Weiser and Kraus (and many others), invoking the surety of divine compassion, the notion that biblical Israelites valued praise of God above life itself, and the transformation within the psalmist which certain plaint-psalm motifs (the so-called 'confession of trust', 'certainty of a hearing', and 'sudden change of mood') are said to exhibit. In one very important respect, however, all three differ from Calvin: none has given remotely comparable attention to the suasive rhetoric of the plaint psalms.

36. I refer in particular to Greenberg 1983; Brueggemann 1984; 1985; Miller 1986; 1993; 1994; Broyles 1988; and Balentine 1993. Of these the best account of biblical prayer as suasion is certainly Miller's 1993 article, although it omits to mention the vow, which is one of the most obvious means of suasion. Greenberg intentionally leaves the Psalms out of consideration on the ground that they are learned compositions which cannot be trusted to reflect lay piety. Balentine also focuses primarily on prayers outside the Psalter, but for other reasons: the Psalms provide no narrative context, and they have already been thoroughly studied by form critics. In my view, the Psalms and the prose prayers are remarkably similar in the essential dynamics of their implicit piety, whatever one may say about differences in their mode of composition, and there are still important questions to put to the Psalms which form criticism has not addressed. This is the stance taken by Miller (1994), where the working corpus includes the Psalms together with prayers in prose and prophetic material.

37. The means of suasion are particularly helpful, as Greenberg (1983: 12-13) has noted: 'The

Thus far I have spoken of Psalter piety in the singular for the simple reason that Calvin did not distinguish more than one. I shall continue to do so for simplicity's sake, although I do not wish to foreclose the possibility that several rather different pieties may be discerned in the book of Psalms. There is certainly more than one represented in the biblical corpus as a whole. What I think I can claim to be describing is the predominant piety to be found in the Psalter, the one represented by the majority, at least, of the plaint psalms, thank songs and hymns, which together make up the bulk of the book.

a. *Recognizing the Dissonance*

While Calvin, to his credit, recognized that the book of Psalms does not always follow his rules for framing prayer duly and properly, he found a way, as we have seen, to turn even those aspects which most distress him into a support for his own piety. In fact he accomplished this almost effortlessly. He simply took it for granted that the psalmists intended to follow the rules, but often failed to do so because they were so very like ourselves; and he did not doubt that they were as distressed by their failings as he would be and as anxious to overcome them by earnest striving.

It is this presumption which led him to value the psalms above all for their introspective capacity, the psalmists' willingness to 'lay bare all their innermost thoughts' in prayer and the encouragement they give all believers to do the same. They may not always be models of proper prayer, but they are at least open, forthright, honest, candid and sincere.[38] Since this is the way they are often valued from the pulpit and lectern today, and a use to which they are often put in pastoral counseling, we are dealing here with one of the more lasting and important consequences of the approach to the Psalter Calvin represents.

Quite apart from the fact that there is simply no way to judge such a thing from the wording of a psalm—imagine someone claiming to prove from their liturgies that Presbyterians are more sincere than Methodists or Baptists, or Christians than Jews!—the very notion is a distraction. If the psalms say and do things we would not put into prayer ourselves, we should not suppose it is because they have been more honest; it is rather that they have a different understanding of what one ought to say in prayer, in short, a different sense of piety.

In my judgment, we will not begin to understand the piety of the psalms until we recognize this. Their sense of what is appropriate in prayer has remarkably little in common with the one set forth in Calvin's rules. They revel in spirited engagement with God rather than devout resignation. Their complaints are typically very direct,

---

motivating sentence of a petitionary prayer is revealing for the pray-er's conception of God, since one is persuaded to do what is shown to be most consonant with one's attributes and interests'.

38.   This is, of course, not uniquely a Christian perspective. Greenberg (1983: 49), for example, elaborates upon the phrase 'to pour out one's soul [*nepeš*] before God' much as Calvin might have done. It means 'to expose one's innermost being, revealing its secret concerns without reservation, without withholding anything—to speak all that is in one's mind with utter sincerity and candor'. But once we have recognized that petitonary biblical prayer is suasive speech, as Greenberg himself has so aptly illustrated, how can we continue to ascribe to it such utterly ingenuous, defenseless and innocent self-abandon?

even feisty.[39] They often speak as though God were part of the problem, as Psalm 39 does when it asks God to 'look away'—Calvin's parade example of unlawful petition. When they do so, they can be indignant, reproachful and even bitingly ironic. On the other hand, they do not regard it as improper to be ingratiating and proffer inducements. They can represent themselves as helpless and pitiful, or put forward a claim of unshakable confidence and trust, and often do both together. They know what it is to beg forgiveness, but they do not do so every time they find themselves in trouble. They present themselves to God more often as victims than as sinners. And when they cry to be delivered from their troubles and those who trouble them, they look for deliverance and nothing less; they do not pray for patience and fortitude to bear it, or concede the outcome in advance by deferring to God's sovereign will or superior judgment.

If we start where Calvin starts, this is bound to seem gratuitously and outrageously impertinent, irreverent and impious. To the psalmists, however, Calvin's attitude (and that of much traditional Christian piety, I suspect) would surely seem unaccountably and irresponsibly obsequious, groveling, and servile. The difference, not surprisingly, is both religious and cultural. In biblical Israel the injured party is expected to complain, and to present the grievance as persuasively as possible.[40] In the process there is even room for *chutzpah*, just as there is in biblical Israelite culture generally, so there is nothing remarkable that it should appear in the prayer psalms.[41] The psalmists could easily imagine God replying in kind, as the prophets, not to mention the divine speech 'out of the whirlwind' in the book of Job (chs. 38–41), plainly demonstrate.

If the psalmists speak this way, it is because it seems self-evident to them that psalmody works its effect upon God, not upon themselves, and everything about it—including its poetic form—is designed to enhance this and bring it about. In this way psalmody gives human beings a voice in those matters which most vitally affect their lives, either offering the encouraging praise and thanks which God delights in, or rousing God to action in a crisis by making the most effective plaints and appeals they can manage.[42] They do not feel they must submit humbly and penitently to whatever God ordains. There is always the possibility that God can be persuaded—or provoked, if it comes to that—to change course and act on their behalf. The future may still be open, the final decision not yet made.

Thus the psalmists petition, not to seek out a discrete and sympathetic heavenly confidant to whom they may pour out their troubles, hoping to find inner peace and

39. The prayer psalms observe a less formal protocol in addressing God than people in the books of Samuel observe in addressing David; for the latter, see Jung 1979.

40. In fact, suasive speech is employed for inter-human petitions and requests generally. As Gerstenberger (1980: 17-63) and Greenberg (1983: 19-37) have shown, the forms used for inter-human petition provide the social analogy for petitionary prayer.

41. Cf. Petuchowski 1972: 4-5: 'Prayer, if we think about it carefully, is actually a supreme manifestation of impertinence, of *chutzpah*. But such is the unique Jewish stance towards God that, according to one view in the Talmud, "*Chutzpah*, even against God, is of avail".' The reference is to *b. Sanh.* 105a.

42. As Roberts (1975) has shown, the difference between biblical Israel and its neighbors in this regard has often been greatly exaggerated.

consolation by submitting to a sovereign and unfailingly benevolent divine will, but to seek redress by mounting an appeal to heaven itself where the ultimate power to effect change resides.[43] The point of their prayers is not to express themselves to God, but to impress their situation upon God in the hope that God will take action to correct it. They do not suppose this will be easy, or the persuasive appeals they put forward would not be so elaborate or crafted with such care; moreover, they know from experience that God may not listen even to fervent and repeated pleas, for they frequently testify of this themselves.

b. *Allowing for Cultural and Historical Distance*

The piety of the prayer psalms as I have just described it differs from Calvin's representation in all the aspects I have enumerated above: in the responses to God it regards as appropriate, necessary and productive; in the attitudes toward God it holds to be acceptable, responsible, and justified; and in its very perception of God as one whose thoughts, feelings, motives and actions correspond to a significant degree with what humans expect and experience in each other and themselves.

The remarkable thing is that Calvin saw much of this himself, as we have often noted above. He recognized that the psalms did in fact 'expostulate' with God, challenge God's judgments, and make extensive use of rhetoric to persuade God to act favorably upon their appeals. He could not conceive, however, that the psalmists would do such things deliberately. Since he could not entertain that even as a possibility, he was not in a position to recognize the deep gulf between their piety and his own.

More to the point, it would never have occurred to him to look for such a gulf in the first place. He was expecting to find his own time and situation addressed more or less immediately in the Bible, and he was of course not alone in this. In the sixteenth century, scholars trained in the New Learning were suddenly alive to the importance of studying the ancient documents in their original languages and from the oldest available manuscripts, but they had not yet had time to develop a real sense of historical and cultural distance.

They were, to be sure, doing enough to alarm scholars of the Old Learning, who felt they had all they needed in the received tradition which gave them their license and warrant, and saw nothing to be gained—and much to be lost—by allowing a younger generation of scholars to test it. But the conflicts between them did not focus on the problem of historical distance; they approached the sources in much the same way, expecting biblical and classical writings to correlate quite directly with the life and thought of the sixteenth century.

Two matters above all stand out in this connection, and they involve the two aspects of the psalms which most particularly drew Calvin's interest and concern:

43.   Broyles (1988) has quite properly emphasized that complaint psalms function as appeals. His study of psalms which complain directly against God is an important contribution to our understanding of psalm piety. I think he is wrong, however, to accept the widely held notion that the psalmists experienced a crisis of faith whenever they perceived God to be acting contrary to divine promises. The complaint psalms show well enough that they had developed a conventional way to deal with this situation, and if they had, they cannot have been taken unawares.

their perception of themselves and their perception of God. In each case, lacking a more developed sense of historical distance, there was a very significant dissonance he was not able to hear.

1. *Dissonance in Perceptions of Self.* Calvin took it for granted that the psalmists were caught up in internal conflicts and the complex life of the psyche, and were therefore profoundly introspective. The decisive issue for prayer and faith is how well the intellective and immortal soul succeeds in subduing involuntary thoughts and feelings 'according to the flesh'. If one were to try to make a case for this—Calvin simply assumes it—one would surely appeal first to Psalm 42–43,[44] where an address to the *nepeš* (for the sake of economy usually but inadequately translated 'soul' or 'self') appears three times as a refrain. As we listen to the address, which begins 'Why are you cast down, O my soul?', we cannot miss the inner struggle in which the psalmist is engaged. In his commentary Calvin made as much of it as he could, but in fact it is far different from the kind of introspection he was assuming for the Psalter.

Even if the refrain is an aside, God is surely meant to overhear it.[45] By including it the psalmist effectively calls two things to God's attention. The first, an obvious appeal for pity, is that the psalmist has to deal with a *nepeš* which has an affective life of its own and is even more distressed by persistent misfortune than the psalmist is.[46] But God should also know that the psalmist has not given up, and is even now encouraging the despondent *nepeš* with the one means available, namely, with the assurance that God will indeed grant the petition the psalmist is at this very moment putting to God ('Hope in God, for I shall again praise him…'). Each of these points is of course meant to move God to show favor; when God takes note of them both can help be far away?

The problem here does not lie in a faulty or blameworthy *nepeš*, and reforming or redeeming the *nepeš* is not the solution the psalmist is seeking. The problem is the psalmist's situation, vividly portrayed in the prayer. Under the circumstances, the reaction of the *nepeš* is neither unreasonable nor unexpected; anyone's *nepeš* would feel much the same and need encouragement rather than censure. The second point is that the solution will not come until God responds to the prayer and changes the situation, and the *nepeš* (and the psalmist) are relieved of their troubles. Should this fail to happen, the psalmist will have nothing to show for having labored so hard to persevere, and the already disquieted *nepeš* may very well say 'I told you so'.

44.   Scholars commonly regard Psalms 42 and 43 as a single psalm.

45.   I regard it as an integral part of the prayer, addressed to God indirectly. There is no reason I can see for supposing the address to the *nepeš* interrupts the prayer, or that the psalmist introduces it to gather courage before continuing to pray. The psalmists' manner throughout the Psalter does not at all suggest they were overwhelmed by the divine majesty or reluctant to press their appeals in prayer, and if we should choose to regard Pss. 42–43 as an exception to this general rule it would be hard to explain why the psalm repeats the refrain once again at the close, after the prayer has ended.

46.   Note that the 'I' who speaks represents itself as fully and firmly confident, unlike the *nepeš* it addresses. Ps. 131 takes a similar stance but presents it as a report instead of an inner conversation; the psalmist comes to God having already 'calmed and quieted' his or her own *nepeš* as a mother does a weaned child.

Psalm 42–43 suffices to show that the psalmists could certainly speak of their inner state, and that they even had a conventional form for articulating it. Since the psalm is exceptional and the convention seldom employed, however, it appears they did not often find occasion to do so. In fact while no one would suggest for a moment that they are reticent to express their thoughts and feelings—they speak freely and often at length about their joys and sorrows, hopes and frustrations, loyalties and hatreds—they are not much given to introspection. As they choose to represent it in prayer, at least, their inner life is not in conflict, rarely torn by ambivalent or contrary thoughts and feelings. There is nothing in the Psalter, for example, comparable to the cry of the distraught father in Mk 9.24, 'I believe; help my unbelief!'

In their prayers the psalmists do not engage in deeply probing introspection in order to discover what they truly think or how they really feel; they speak as though they have no doubt about it, and declare it simply and directly. Neither do they engage in critical self-examination. They do not search their inner selves for hidden motivations or repressed feelings, just as they do not wonder whether their enemies may have some good in them after all. It is instructive in this regard that the psalmists do not petition for inward graces such as faith, trust, patience, hope, and perseverance, and rarely admit to a deficiency in such matters. Quite the opposite, when they speak of such graces they regularly talk as though they already possess them, and put them forward as one of their claims upon God's attention and favor.[47]

In all this it is impossible to know how much they are withholding; this may be a stance they assume as a part of their strategy of persuasion, and not their actual experience. But even if this is so, Calvin's portrait of the psalmists is no longer recognizable. Either their self-perception is far less conflicted than he represented it, or they do not often feel it necessary or appropriate to pour out their innermost feelings in prayer. Why did he suppose otherwise? There are at least two factors which may help to account for it: on the one hand he accepted without question the Church's traditional anthropology, on the other he was anticipating a more complex understanding of the self, and he was reading both into the psalms.

The anthropology has been characterized by the Swiss theologian Karl Barth, himself a distinguished exponent of the Calvin tradition, as an 'abstractly dualistic conception' of soul and body which has its roots in the Greek philosophical tradition 'but which unfortunately must also be described as the traditional Christian view' (1960a: 3, 380). Barth (1960a: 3, 384) noted that it had been challenged in Calvin's lifetime in a work published (in 1516) by an Italian philosopher, and regretted that Reformation theology did not at least take this occasion to gird itself for a new understanding; instead Calvin identified himself with the categorical Roman Catholic rejection of the thesis (*Inst.* 1.5.6). 'Is it not clear', Barth asked, 'that in these circumstances soul and body neither have nor can have anything in common, but can only be in conflict and finally part from one another?' (1960a: 3,

---

47. An essential point missed by Kim (1985) in his otherwise helpful study, as it has been by many others. As a result the role of trust in the piety of the prayer psalms is misconstrued; the psalmists do not struggle to achieve it—they set out to capitalize on it.

380). But if this was formative for Calvin, it was not an issue for the psalmists; they would not even have understood the presumption of duality which gives rise to it.

The second factor is at least equally important. Calvin, like Luther, was personally acquainted with intense and deeply probing introspection, and it has been said of them both that they sensed so fully the complexity of psychic life that they anticipated the discovery of the unconscious and many of the specific mechanisms of Freudian psychology (Selinger 1984: 46-47). Calvin's distinctive personal response to this, in many respects quite different from Luther's, seems to have made him unusually well-fitted to address the deepest concerns and longings of the middle third of the sixteenth century, and it is doubtless one of the reasons his writings continue to speak to many in the present. By applying his insight so brilliantly to the psalms, he provided the Church with a mode of appropriation which has been of lasting significance. It was, however, an anachronism to read it into the psalms and to take it for granted that self-knowledge, and more precisely the knowledge of sin, was as central a problem for the psalmists as it was for Luther and himself.

For the most part the resistance the psalmists were seeking so earnestly to overcome by prayer they did not perceive in themselves, but in God. They aimed to improve their situation, not by reforming their attitude toward God, but by cultivating a more favorable disposition on God's part toward themselves.

2. *Dissonance in Perceptions of God.* It is not only the psalmists' approaches and responses to God which are different from Calvin's, however. The root of the matter lies deeper. There are marked differences in their perceptions of God as well, and therefore in the attitudes they take toward God and toward what God does to them and for them. As others have noted, this is a critical issue which even modern biblical scholars have been slow to recognize.[48]

In my view, if we are to understand *what* the Hebrew Bible thinks about God, we must first understand *how* it thinks about God. And this is not a great mystery: it thinks with precisely those anthropomorphic and sociomorphic images Calvin was at such pains to rationalize. It does not think in the abstract categorical terms which have long been traditional in Western theology. As a result, the very perception of God among ancient Israelites was fundamentally different from Calvin's. That is why they did not shy as he did from imagining God in many respects like themselves, or from acting upon this in approaching God in prayer. Not least among these likenesses were the affective aspects of experience, and they took it for granted these were as important to God as they were to themselves.

48. Cf. Fretheim 1984: 17: 'As one surveys the landscape of Old Testament scholarship on the understanding of God, the portrait of God which normally emerges bears a striking resemblance to the quite traditional Jewish or Christian understanding of God regnant in synagogue or church. Save for matters relating to historical development...one can read back and forth between church dogmatics textbooks and most God-talk in Old Testament studies without missing a beat.' I think this is apt, although I am inclined to think that Judaism has preserved more of the biblical perception than the Church has. However that may be, Fretheim's book is a very good start. He goes beyond biblical thought, however, when he represents this as God's self-imposed limitation.

If Calvin found grounds for confidence in the vast gulf which separates heaven and earth—it serves, for one thing, to insulate the divine realm from all human contingencies and infirmities—it was the likeness and sympathy between them which more often encouraged and comforted the psalmists. When it occurred to them, as it sometimes did, that at some points there may be no common ground, they found the thought alarming and did what they could to bring the matter to God's attention. A God in whose sight 'a thousand years...are like yesterday when it is passed' (Ps. 90.4, cf. vv. 1-2), for example, may not entirely understand what it is like to have the very limited life expectancy of a mortal (Ps. 90.3, 5-6, 11-12); as a result, God may not fully realize how devastating the punishing divine wrath actually is (Ps. 90.7-10). The petition which follows is appropriate to this appeal: God is asked to restore some semblance of balance by showing compassion and favor to them now (Ps. 90.13-17; note especially v. 15). A prayer of this sort was incomprehensible to Calvin, except as an example of human frailty; in its own context it was fully in keeping with accepted piety.

In his later years Karl Barth, reflecting self-critically upon his own earlier preoccupation with God as the 'Wholly Other', expressed the wish that Calvin had given more attention to the humanity of God: 'His Geneva would then not have become such a gloomy affair. His letters would then not have contained so much bitterness' (Barth 1960b: 49). My attention was drawn to the passage by W. Fred Graham, who cites it in his book *The Constructive Revolutionary* (1971: 182). Barth (1960b: 49) appealed to the Incarnation as the corrective: 'It is when we look at Jesus Christ that we know decisively that God's deity does not exclude, but includes His *humanity*'. 'My own reflection', Graham writes, 'is that Calvin was true to Chalcedon, that he followed scholastic theology, and that the difficulty lies with the impossible task which Chalcedon presents to the biblical theologian' (1971: 183). In a footnote he adds,

> Perhaps if this were a study of theology proper we would need to ask if the idea of God held by the bishops of the fifth century admits of a solution which can be correlated with the New Testament witness to the God of Israel and the Father of Jesus Christ. Can God—the unchangeable, immutable, impassible—relate seriously to time-fettered humanity or bring any new thing to pass? Is the God of Chalcedon and Calvin recognizable in the Bible? (Graham 1971: 239 n. 16)

By implication Graham reaches behind the christological declarations of Chalcedon in the fifth century to the underlying perception of God the councils were presupposing. That is where the issue lies for those who wish to understand the Psalms, and indeed the Hebrew Bible.

6. *In Conclusion*

In the end, the issue is not whether Calvin was justified in taking the approach to the prayer psalms he did, but whether it is any longer defensible. As I study his exposition of their piety I find much that I recognize in the work of my colleagues in biblical studies at the present time. He has helped me to understand the approach they have taken, and why it is so different from my own. He has not, however, persuaded me that it is a convincing reading of these psalms on their own terms, or helped me to understand why my colleagues go as far as they do to perpetuate it.[49] No doubt there are some things in every age which cannot be seen because they must not be seen—the cost would be too great to bear. But the loss also exacts its own price, and perhaps this is one of the tragedies of human existence. If so, it is one we can hardly expect to escape ourselves. But that gives us no license to continue to ignore what others could not see.

Calvin was an extraordinarily able and convincing interpreter of the Psalter in his own setting; in that sense his reading of the book was undeniably true. Furthermore, he was not deaf to the dissonance between the prayer psalms and his own convictions about due and proper prayer; that is what makes him such an interesting figure to study. At the same time the ethos and imperatives of his time and situation made it virtually impossible for him to recognize that the prayer psalms represented a piety in so many respects alien to his own.

Since he could hear, but not listen to, the quite different voice of the psalmists, he proceeded to harmonize it with his own, and he accomplished this by transposing the prayer psalms into another, more familiar and congenial mode. As a result, whatever he might have learned from these psalms they were unable to teach him. They could not make themselves understood in their own voice, but merely echo his own. When this happens there is always a price to be paid. There is much to be learned from the biblical tradition if it is allowed to speak for itself, and is not simply used as a vehicle to proclaim what its readers have already decided it must say.

The legacy Calvin left to future generations was unquestionably rich, but this is one of its weaknesses. Because it was a historical orientation with only the most limited sense of social and cultural distance, typical of the sixteenth-century, it tended to confirm and perpetuate the belief that the piety of the Psalter, indeed of the Bible—its perceptions, concerns, attitudes and responses—was in every essential way a mirror of Western Christian, and especially Reformed, piety. This is patently an ahistorical view even if it presents itself in historical guise.

This is by no means to suggest that all the problems faced by Church and Synagogue would be solved if they were simply to be more biblical. The humanity of God is an important theological issue; the Psalms and other biblical books raise it, they can help us think about it, but they cannot resolve it for us by themselves. Calvin himself models the risks we run when we try to abstract elements from someone else's piety and appropriate them for ourselves. There are Christian poets

---

49. Part of the motivation has been the complaint that 'modern critical study is so pledged to an ideal of objectivity and neutrality with respect to the text, and so occupied with a notion of past history as the strange and alien' that it is 'boring' (Mays 1990: 203). If it is, the problem lies not in the method itself but in the tendency of modern critical scholars to ignore (or shy from?) the study of biblical piety, which is anything but boring. Reading the psalms in one's own mirror, as Calvin did, is defensible as long as one does it admittedly and intentionally (this is what Mays has in mind), but closing the 'hermeneutical circle' in this way also exacts the price Calvin paid: it is far more difficult for the psalms to speak for themselves.

in the Third World, Ernesto Cardinal[50] among them, who seem to be able to respond more immediately and fully to many aspects of the piety of the Psalter than we have been able to manage in American and European churches. There is no doubt something we can learn from them. But if we do no more than to recognize that our own piety is not simply interchangeable with biblical piety, and that there are other pieties appropriately and responsibly different from our own, it may at least be a beginning. It ought to make us more patient with each other, and a little less arrogant about ourselves.

BIBLIOGRAPHY

Balentine, Samuel E.
1993   *Prayer in the Hebrew Bible: The Drama of Divine–Human Dialogue* (Minneapolis: Fortress Press).
Barth, Karl
1960a   *Church Dogmatics* (Edinburgh: T. &. T. Clark).
1960b   *The Humanity of God* (Richmond, VA: John Knox Press).
Broyles, Craig C.
1988   *The Conflict of Faith and Experience in the Psalms: A Form-Critical and Theological Study* (JSOTSup, 52; Sheffield: JSOT Press).
Brueggemann, Walter
1984   *The Message of the Psalms: A Theological Commentary* (Augsburg Old Testament Studies; Minneapolis: Augsburg).
1985   'A Shape for Old Testament Theology', *CBQ* 47 (1985): 28-46, 395-415.
Calvin, John
1845–49   *Commentary on the Book of Psalms* (ed. J. Anderson; 5 vols.; Edinburgh: The Calvin Translation Society).
1926–70   *Joannis Calvini, Opera Selecta* (ed. P. Barth and W. Niesel; 5 vols.; Munich: Chr. Kaiser Verlag).
1960   *Institution of the Christian Religion* (ed. J.T. McNeill; trans. Ford Lewis Battles; 2 vols.; Philadelphia: Westminster Press).
1975   *Institutes of the Christian Religion* (trans. F. Lewis Battles; Atlanta: John Knox Press).
Cardinal, Ernesto
1969   *Salmos* (Buenos Aires: Ediciones Carlos Lohle).
Childs, Brevard
1989   'The Struggle for God's Righteousness in the Psalter', in Trevor A. Hart and Daniel P. Thimell (eds.), *Christ in Our Place: The Humanity of God in Christ for the Reconciliation of the World* (Exeter: Paternoster; Allison Park, PA: Pickwick Publications): 255-64.
Dowey, J. Edward A., Jr
1952   *The Knowledge of God in Calvin's Theology* (New York: Columbia University Press).

50.   The poems in Ernesto Cardinal's *Salmos* (1969) are modeled on biblical psalms. Cardinal was a novice under Thomas Merton in the Monastery of Our Lady of Gethsemane, was subsequently ordained a priest in Nicaragua, and served as Minister of Culture there.

Fretheim, Terence
1984   *The Suffering of God: An Old Testament Perspective* (Philadelphia: Fortress
            Press).
Gerstenberger, E.S.
1980   *Der bittende Mensch* (WMANT, 51; Neukirchen–Vluyn: Neukirchener
            Verlag).
Graham, W. Fred
1971   *The Constructive Revolutionary: John Calvin and His Socio-Economic
            Impact* (Richmond, VA: John Knox Press).
Greenberg, Moshe
1983   *Biblical Prose Prayer as a Window to the Popular Religion of Ancient Israel*
            (The Taubman Lectures in Jewish Studies: Sixth Series; Berkeley: Univer-
            sity of California Press).
Hobbs, R. Gerald
1984   'How Firm a Foundation: Martin Bucer's Historical Exegesis of the Psalms',
            Church History 53: 477-91.
1990   '*Hebraica Veritas* and *Traditio Apostolica*: Saint Paul and the Interpretation
            of the Psalms in the Sixteenth Century', in David C. Steinmetz (ed.), *The
            Bible in the Sixteenth Century* (Durham, NC: Duke University Press): 83-99.
Jung, Kyu Nam
1979   'Court Etiquette in the Old Testament' (unpublished PhD dissertation, Drew
            University).
Kim, Ee Kon
1985   *The Rapid Change of Mood in the Lament Psalms: A Matrix for the Estab-
            lishment of a Psalm Theology* (Seoul: Korea Theological Study Institute).
Kraus, Hans-Joachim
1986   *Theology of the Psalms* (Minneapolis: Augsburg).
1988   *Psalms 1–59: A Commentary* (Minneapolis: Augsburg).
1989   *Psalms 60–150: A Commentary* (Minneapolis: Augsburg).
Mays, James Luther
1990   'Calvin's Commentary on the Psalms: The Preface as Introduction', in
            Timothy George (ed.), *John Calvin and the Church: A Prism of Reform*
            (Louisville, KY: Westminster/John Knox Press).
Miller, Patrick D.
1986   *Interpreting the Psalms* (Philadelphia: Fortress Press).
1993   'Prayer as Persuasion: The Rhetoric and Intention of Prayer', *Word & World*
            13/4: 356-62.
1994   *They Cried to the Lord: The Form and Theology of Biblical Prayer* (Minnea-
            polis: Fortress Press).
Parker, T.H.L.
1965   *A Commentary on the Psalms by John Calvin*, I (London: James Clarke).
1986   *Calvin's Old Testament Commentaries* (Edinburgh: T. & T. Clark).
Petuchowski, Jacob J.
1972   *Understanding Jewish Prayer* (New York: Ktav).
Ringgren, Helmer
1963   *The Faith of the Psalmists* (Philadelphia: Fortress Press).

Roberts, J.J.M.
  1975   'Divine Freedom and Cultic Manipulation in Israel and Mesopotamia', in
              H. Goedicke and J.J.M. Roberts (eds.), *Unity and Diversity: Essays in the
              History, Literature, and Religion of the Ancient Near East* (Baltimore: The
              Johns Hopkins University Press): 181-90.
Selinger, Suzanne
  1984   *Calvin against Himself: An Inquiry in Intellectual History* (Hamden, CT:
              Archon Books).
Weiser, Artur
  1962   *The Psalms: A Commentary* (Philadelphia: Westminster Press).
Wendel, François
  1963   *Calvin: The Origins and Development of His Religious Thought* (London:
              Collins; New York: Harper & Row).
Westermann, Claus
  1981   *Praise and Lament in the Psalms* (trans. Keith R. Krim and Richard N.
              Soulen; Atlanta: John Knox Press, rev. edn).
  1982   *The Elements of Old Testament Theology* (trans. Douglas W. Scott; Atlanta:
              John Knox Press).
  1989   *The Living Psalms* (trans. J.R. Potter; Grand Rapids: Eerdmans).

HERBERT BARDWELL HUFFMON:
A BIBLIOGRAPHY

1959   'The Covenant Lawsuit in the Prophets', *JBL* 78: 285-95.

1965a   *Amorite Personal Names in the Mari Texts: A Structural and Lexical Study* (Baltimore: The Johns Hopkins University Press).

1965b   'The Exodus, Sinai and the Credo', *CBQ* 27: 101-13.

1966b   'The Treaty Background of Hebrew Yada'', *Bulletin of the American Schools of Oriental Research* 181: 31-37.

1966b   [with Simon B. Parker] 'A Further Note on the Treaty Background of Hebrew Yada'', *Bulletin of the American Schools of Oriental Research* 184: 36-38.

1968   'Prophecy in the Mari Letters', *BA* 31:101-24.

1969   'The Israel of God', *Int* 23: 66-77.

1970a   [with Paul A. Riemann] 'Pointing the Way: Some Suggestions for Old Testament Study', *Drew Gateway* 40.3: 135-42.

1970b   'Prophecy in the Mari Letters', in D.N. Freedman and E.F. Campbell, Jr (eds.), *Biblical Archaeologist Reader* (Garden City, NY: Doubleday): III, 199-224. (Revised version of above article by same title.)

1971   'Yahweh and Mari', in H. Goedicke (ed.), *Near Eastern Studies in Honor of William Foxwell Albright* (Baltimore: The Johns Hopkins University Press): 283-89.

1974a   'Exodus 23.4-5: A Comparative Study', in H.N. Bream *et al.* (eds.), *A Light Unto My Path: Old Testament Studies in Honor of Jacob M. Myers* (Philadelphia: Temple University Press): 271-78.

1974b   'Prophetic Oracles in the Ancient Near East: Reflection on Their Use in Form-Critical Study of the Hebrew Bible', in *Society of Biblical Literature Seminar Papers* 1: 101-104.

1976a   'Amorites' (20-21); 'Benjamin, Benjaminites' (95-96); 'Names, Religious Significance of' (619-21); and 'Prophecy in the Ancient Near East' (697-700), in *IDBSup*.

1976b   'The Origins of Prophecy', in F.M. Cross *et al.* (eds.), *Magnalia Dei, The Mighty Acts of God: Essays on the Bible and Archaeology in Memory of G. Ernest Wright* (Garden City, NY: Doubleday): 171-86.

1977   'Eden, Garden of', in *Encyclopedia International* (New York: Grolier).

1983a   'Babel und Bibel: The Encounter Between Babylon and the Bible', in D.N. Freedman and M. O'Connor (eds.), *The Bible and Its Traditions* (special issue of the *Michigan Quarterly Review* 22.3): 309-20.

1983b   'Priestly Divination of Israel', in C.L. Meyers and M. O'Connor (eds.), *The Word of the Lord Shall Go Forth: Essays in Honor of David Noel Freedman in Celebration of His Sixtieth Birthday* (Philadelphia: American Schools of Oriental Research): 355-59.

1983c   *The Quest for the Kingdom of God: Essays in Honor of George Emery Mendenhall* (eds. H.B. Huffmon, F.A. Spina and A.R.W. Green; Winona Lake, IN: Eisenbrauns) (with 'An Appreciation' by the editor).

1983d   'The Social Role of Amos' Message', in H.B. Huffmon, F.A. Spina and A.R.W. Green (eds.), *The Quest for the Kingdom of God: Essays in Honor of George Emery Mendenhall* (Winona Lake, IN: Eisenbrauns): 109-16.

1983e   'On Trusting Your Own Experience', *Drew Gateway* 53.2: 1-5.

1985a   'Akhenaton'; 'Amarna, Tell el-'; 'Amorites'; 'Avaris'; 'Candace'; 'Egypt'; 'Egypt, Brook of'; 'Hophni'; 'Memphis'; 'Merneptah'; 'Mummification'; 'Neco'; 'Nile'; 'Obelisk'; 'Pashhur'; 'Pithom'; 'Potiphar'; 'Potiphera'; 'Pyramid Texts, the'; and 'Reuel', in P.J. Achtemeier *et al.* (eds.), *Harper's Bible Dictionary* (San Francisco: Harper & Row): *ad loc.*

1985b   'Cain, the Arrogant Sufferer', in A. Kort and S. Morschauser (eds.), *Biblical and Related Studies Presented to Samuel Iwry* (Winona Lake, IN: Eisenbrauns): 109-13.

1985c   'Robert William Rogers: Professor of Hebrew Exegesis, Drew University, 1893–1929; Interpreter of the Ancient Orient', *Drew Gateway* 56.2: 48-61.

1987   'Babel und Bibel: The Encounter between Babylon and the Bible', in M.P. O'Connor and D.N. Freedman (eds.), *Backgrounds for the Bible* (Winona Lake, IN: Eisenbrauns: 125-36. (Expanded form of 1983 article.)

1992   'Lex Talionis' (IV: 321-22), 'Prophecy, Ancient Near Eastern' (V: 477-82), in *ABD*.

1995a   'Brother' (cols. 338-42); 'Father' (cols. 616-19); 'Name (as hypostasis; Old Testament)' (cols. 1148-51); 'Shalem (Old Testament)' (cols. 1428-31), in K. van der Toorn, B. Becking and P.W. van der Horst (eds.), *Dictionary of Deities and Demons in the Bible* (Leiden: E.J. Brill).

1995b   'The Expansion of Prophecy in the Mari Archives: New Texts, New Readings, New Information', in *World Christian Foundation: Global Civilization Curriculum. Module 1, Section 54 B* (Pasadena: Institute of International Studies): 1-6.

1995c   'The Fundamental Code Illustrated: The Third Commandment', in David P. Wright, David Noel Freedman and Avi Hurvitz (eds.), *Pomegranates and Golden Bells: Studies in Biblical, Jewish, and Near Eastern Ritual, Law, and Literature in Honor of Jacob Milgrom* (Winona Lake, IN: Eisenbrauns): 361-69.

1996   'Egypt', in Paul J. Achtemeier *et al.* (eds.), *HarperCollins Bible Dictionary*, (San Francisco: HarperCollins, rev. edn): 271-74. (Revised and expanded version of the 1985 article.)

1997   'The Expansion of Prophecy in the Mari Archives: New Texts, New Readings, New Information', in Yehoshua Gitay (ed.), *Prophecy and Prophets: The Diversity of Contemporary Issues in Scholarship* (SBLSS; Atlanta: Scholars Press): 7-22. (Enlarged edition of above article with the same title.)

1999a   'Babel und Bibel' (92); 'Delitzsch, Friedrich (1850–1922)' (267); 'Jensen, Peter 1861–1935)' (563-64); 'Jeremias, Alfred (1864–1935)' (575-76); and 'Winckler, Hugo (1863–1913)' (647-48), in J.H. Hayes *et al.* (eds.) *Dictionary of Biblical Interpretation* (Nashville: Abingdon Press).

1999b   'A Company of Prophets: Mari, Assyria, Israel', in Martti Nissinen (ed.), *Prophecy in Its Ancient Near Eastern Context: Mesopotamian, Biblical, and Arabian Perspectives* (SBLSymS, 13. Atlanta: SBL): 47-70.

1999c   'Hebrew Bible: Prophets and Judges', in Serinity Young (ed.), *Encyclopedia of Women and World Religion* (New York: Macmillan).

1999d   'The Impossible: God's Words of Assurance in Jeremiah 31.35-37', in Stephen L. Cook and Sara C. Winter (eds.), *On the Way to Nineveh: Studies in Honor of George M. Landes* (Atlanta: Scholars Press): 172-86.

1999e   'Jeremiah of Anathoth: A Prophet for All Israel', in R. Chanan, W.W. Hallo and L.H. Schiffman (eds.), *Ki Baruch Hu: Ancient Near Eastern, Biblical, and Judaic Studies in Honor of Baruch A. Levine* (Winona Lake, IN: Eisenbrauns): 261-71.

2002   'Gender Subversion in the Book of Jeremiah', in S. Parpola and R.M. Whiting (eds.), *Proceedings of the Rencontre Assyriologique International, Helsinki, 2001* (Helsinki: Neo-Assyrian Text Corpus Project): 245-53.

2003   'The One and the Many: Prophets and Deities in the Ancient Near East', in M. Koeckert and M. Nissinen (eds.), *Propheten in Mari, Assyrien und Israel* (FRLANT, 201; Göttingen: Vandenhoeck & Ruprecht, 2003): 116-31

2004   'The *assinnum* as Prophet: Shamans at Mari?', in D. Charpin *et al.* (eds.), *Amurru 3: Proceedings of the Rencontre Assyriologique Internationale, Paris, 2000* (Paris: Éditions Recherche sur les civilizations): 251-55.

2006   'Jezebel: The Corrosive Queen', in J. Rilett-Woods *et al.* (eds.), *Essays on Biblical History and Literature in Honour of Brian Peckham* (JSOTSup, 455; London/New York: T&T Clark International): 273-84. (For a corrected version, see www.users.drew.edu/hhuffmon/)

2007   'The Oracular Process: Greece and the Near East,' *VT* 57: 449-60.

forthcoming   'A Tale of the Prophet and the Courtier: A Responsive Reading of the Nathan Texts', in S. Dolansky (ed.), *Studies in Honor of Richard Elliot Friedman* (Winona Lake. IN: Eisenbrauns).

This bibliography was compiled with the help of The Reverend Margie Huffmon. The editors wish to thank her for the assistance and advice she provided throughout the course of this project.

PH.D. THESIS GRADUATES,
AS DIRECTOR OR 2ND READER—DREW UNIVERSITY
(WITH THESIS DIRECTOR; 2ND READER; 3RD READER)

1977
Joan Chamberlain Engelsman (deceased)
'The Feminine Dimension of the Divine'
  (published by Westminster Press)
  (Thompson, Huffmon, Bakan [Toronto])

Nathaniel Yung-Tse Yen
'Prophet, Sage and Wise Man: A Comparative Study of Intellectual Tradition in Ancient China and Israel'
  M.A., Andrew University
  (Huffmon, Greenblatt, Riemann)

1979
Kyu-Nam Jung
'Court Etiquette in the Old Testament'
  Th.M., Westminster Seminary, 1975
  (Huffmon, Riemann, B. Levine [NYU])

Barry Lowell Ross
'The Individual in the Community: Personal Identification in Ancient Israel'
  Th.M., Asbury, 1965; M.A., University of Michigan, 1967
  (Huffmon, Riemann)

1981
Young-Ihl Kim
'The Vocabulary of Oppression in the Old Testament: 'SHQ, YNH, LHTS and Congeners'
  S.T.M., Boston, 1972; Th.M., Princeton, 1977
  (Huffmon, Riemann)

1982
Louis Stulman
'The Prose Sermons of the Book of Jeremiah: A Redescription of the Correspondences with Deuteronomistic Literature in the Light of Recent Text-Critical Research'
  (published in SBL Dissertation Series)
  (Riemann, Huffmon, Tov [UPenn])

1983

Lyn Bechtel Huber (Lyn Bechtel)
'The Biblical Experience of Shame/Shaming: The Social Experience of Shame/Shaming in Biblical Israel in Relation to Its Use as Religious Metaphor'
    M.Div., McCormick, 1977
    (Riemann, Huffmon, Levine [NYU], Thayer)

Cherie Joyce Lenzen
'The Byzantine/Islamic Occupation at Caesarea Maritima as Evidenced Through the Pottery'
    M.Div., McCormick, 1974; M.A., Johns Hopkins, 1976
    (Bull, Huffmon, Riemann)

1984

Joseph Jung-Min Kuo
'Priestly and Levitical Names in the Hebrew Bible: A Semantic and Distributional Analysis'
    (Huffmon, Riemann)

Alexander Varughese
'The Hebrew Text Underlying the Old Greek Translation of Jeremiah 10–20'
    M.Div., Nazarene, 1975
    (Huffmon, Riemann, Dey)

1985

Terry Lee Brensinger
'Lions, Wind and Fire: A Study of Prophetic Similes'
    (published by Edwin Mellen Press); M.A., 1985
    (Huffmon, Hillers [Johns Hopkins], Riemann)

Rodney Hain Shearer
'A Contextual Analysis of the Phrase *ʿal-tira* as it Occurs in the Hebrew Bible and in Selected Related Literature'
    (Huffmon, Riemann)

1986

James Morris Kennedy
'A Structural Semantic Analysis of Selected Biblical Hebrew Words for Punishment/Discipline'
    (Huffmon, Riemann, Chapman)

1987

Randall Charles Bailey
'Images of the Prophets: An Analysis of the Metaphors and Epithets Used in the Old Testament to Describe Prophets and Prophetic Activity'
    M.A., Alabama Christian, 1974; M.Th., Alabama Christian, 1979
    (Riemann, Huffmon)

Gordon Paul Brubacher
'The Canaanite God of Death in the Myth of Baal and Mot'
    M.A., Wilfrid Laurier, 1982
    (Pope [Yale], Huffmon, Riemann)

Kenneth Hugh Cuffey
'The Coherence of Micah: A Review of the Proposals and a New Interpretation'
    (Huffmon, Riemann)

Daniel Guy Pugerude
'Preaching from the Old Testament: A Study in Exegesis and Hermeneutics of the Free Methodist Church of North America'
    Th.M., Duke, 1978
    (Huffmon, Riemann)

1988
Paul Dean Duerksen
'Canaan as a Land of Milk and Honey: A Study of the Evaluative Descriptions of Israel's Land'
    (Huffmon, Riemann)

Jesse Ceymour Long, Jr
'Sedentary Adaptations at the End of the Third Millennium B.C.: Khirbet Iskander and the Excavated Settlement Sites of Early Bronze IV in Palestine-Transjordan'
    M.A., Alabama Christian, 1978
    (Richard, Huffmon, Riemann)

Michael S. Moore
'The Balaam Traditions: Their Character and Development'
    (published in the SBL Dissertation series)
    M.A., Harding, 1979; Th.M., Princeton, 1983
    (Huffmon, Riemann, Levine [NYU])

Nathaniel Samuel Murrell
'A Critical Appraisal of the Significance of James Barr's Critique of Biblical Theology'
    M.A., Wheaton, 1980
    (Huffmon, Riemann)

1989
Robert Michael Braman
'The Role of Magic in Ancient Israel: A Century of Studies'
    M.A., Oral Roberts, 1977
    (Huffmon, Riemann)

Timothy John Mills
'The Gog Pericope and the Book of Ezekiel'
    Th.M., Luther, 1983
(Riemann, Huffmon)

Jack Wilson
'A Comparative Study of the Diction of the Oracles and Announcements of Salvation in Second Isaiah and the Diction of the Psalter'
    (Riemann, Huffmon)

1990
John Irving Lawlor
'The Esbous North Church in Its Stratigraphic and Historical Context'
    Th.M., Grace, 1969
    (Bull, Huffmon, Riemann)

Mark Ronnie Sneed
'The Social Location of Qoheleth's Thought: Anomie and Alienation in Ptolemaic Jerusalem'
 M.A., Harding, 1986
 (Huffmon, Riemann, Gottwald [NYTS])

Sheldon Weltman (deceased)
'The Biblical Polemic Against the Foreign Divine Images'
 M.H.L., Jewish Theological Seminary, 1960
 (Huffmon, Riemann)

1991
Se-Young Roh
'Creation and Redemption in Priestly Theology'
 (Huffmon, Riemann)

1992
Stephen John Lennox
'Biblical Interpretation in the American Holiness Movement, 1875–1920'
 (Huffmon, Rowe, Handy [Union NY])

1993
John Kaltner
'The Use of Arabic in Biblical Hebrew Lexicography'
 (published in the Catholic Biblical Quarterly Monograph Series)
 (Huffmon, Krotkoff [Johns Hopkins], Riemann)

Mary-Louise Mussell (deceased)
'An Archaeological Evaluation of the Social Revolution Model of the Israelite Settlement in Canaan'
 (Huffmon, Riemann, Gottwald [NYTS])

Jongsoo Park
'Priestly Divination in Ancient Israel: Its Characteristics and Roles'
 (published in Korea)
 (Huffmon, Riemann, Peek)

1994
David A. Leiter
'The Unattainable Ideal: Impractical and/or Unenforceable Rules in the Ancient Israelite Legal Collections'
 (Huffmon, Long, Riemann)

Raymond Roosevelt Neilly
'Human Achievement in the Wisdom Literature of Ancient Israel: The Gift of God'
 M.A., Drew
 (Huffmon, Riemann)

1995
Carlton Alexander Dennis
'Proverbs and the People: A Comparative Study of Afro-Caribbean and Biblical Proverbs'
 (Huffmon, Peek, Riemann)

Geevarughese Mathews
'The Role of the Epilogue in the Book of Job'
    Th.M., Princeton
    (Huffmon, Riemann)

1996
Cheryl L. Hetherington Iverson
'Restoration: A Semantic Domain Study of Restoration and Recovery as it Relates to Persons in the Ancient Israelite Community'
    (Huffmon, Riemann, Chapman)

1997
Mindawati Perangin-Angin
'The Interrelationships of Humankind, Animals, and Plants as Presented in the Old Testament'
    (Huffmon, Riemann, Richard)

1998
Milton Eng
'The Days of Our Years: A Lexical Semantic Study of the Life Cycle in Biblical Israel'
    Th.M., Westminster
    (Huffmon, Riemann, Chapman)

1999
LeAnn Snow Flesher
'The Rhetorical Use of the Negative Petition in the Lament Psalms'
    (Riemann, Huffmon)

2002
Debra Moody Bass
'God Comforts Israel: The Audience and the Message of Isaiah 40–55'
(published by University Press of America)
    (Huffmon, Stroker, Richard)

Frank Gipson
    'Lineage Structure and Local Authority in Ancient Israel'
    Th.M., Calvin Seminary
    (Huffmon, Berlinerblau [Hofstra], Carter [Seton Hall])

Eric A. Seibert
'Propaganda and Subversion in the Solomonic Narrative'
    (Huffmon, Berlinerblau [Hofstra], Knoppers [Penn State])

John Seo
'Creation and Conflict in the Beginning: A Study of the Ancient Near Eastern Background, Historical Context, and Theological Role of the "God's Battle with Chaos" Model of Creation in Isaiah 40–55'
    (Huffmon, Carter [Seton Hall])

2003
Jae Jang
'Persuasion in the Book of Amos'
    (Huffmon, Carter [Seton Hall], Fewell)

2004

Thomas M. Chacko

'Official and Popular Religion in the Northern Kingdom from Omri to Joash (ca. 885–786 B.C.E.)'
    Th.M., Princeton
    (Huffmon, Berlinerblau [Hofstra], Carter [Seton Hall])

2006

Mitchel W. Modine

'"Everything Written in This Book": The Perceptions of the Exile in the Book of Jeremiah'
    (Huffmon, Stulman [Findlay], Carter [Seton Hall])

2007

Jeremiah W. Cataldo

'A Theocratic Yehud? Issues of Government in a Persian Province'
    (Carter [Seton Hall], Huffmon, Berquist [Chalice Press])

Kenneth M. Diable

'Persuading God: A Study in the Individual Lament Psalms'
    (Huffmon, Carter [Seton Hall], Berezov [Morris Township, NJ])

Warren Calhoun Robertson

'Drought, Famine, Plague and Pestilence: Ancient Israel's Understandings of and Responses to Natural Catastrophes'
    (Huffmon, Berlinerblau [Georgetown], Carter [Seton Hall])

Carl E. Savage

'Et-Tell (Bethsaida): A Study of the First Century CE in the Galilee'
    (Huffmon, Freund [Hartford], Greene [Michigan State])

INDEX OF REFERENCES

INDEX OF AUTHORS